THE OFFICIAL PRICE GUIDE TO

Pottery & Porcelain

BY
HOUSE OF COLLECTIBLES, INC.

We have compiled the information contained herein through a *patented computerized process* which relies primarily on a nationwide sampling of information provided by noteworthy collectible experts, auction houses and specialized dealers. This unique retrieval system enables us to provide the reader with the most current and accurate information available.

EDITOR
THOMAS E. HUDGEONS, III

SECOND EDITION

THE HOUSE OF COLLECTIBLES, ORLANDO, FL. 32809

PHOTOGRAPHIC RECOGINITION

Cover and Color Section Photographs: Photographer — Bernie Markell, Orlando, FL 32806; Location — Courtesy Hardee Hudson, 1202 Park Avenue North, Winter Park, FL 32789.
Color Separations: Modern Litho, Grand Rapids, MI 45903.

NOTE: *This publication is in no way associated with Lenox, Inc. or its subsidiary, Lenox China, Inc., and any opinions expressed herein are those of the authors. Prices listed are for those items being sold on the secondary market, and have no relationship to current retail pricing structures. Furthermore, neither Lenox, Inc., nor Lenox China, Inc., has confirmed any of the specific price or volume figures quoted in this book.*

Every effort has been made to minimize clerical and/or printing errors, and we regret any inconvenience such errors might cause. We have tried to be as precise as possible regarding sizes and shape numbers, and the addition of so very many facts and figures increases the possibility of errors.

Published by The House of Collectibles, Inc.
        Orlando Central Park
        1900 Premier Row
        Orlando, FL 32809
        Phone: (305) 857-9095

Printed in the United States of America

Library of Congress Catalog Card Number: 81-81797

ISBN: 0-87637-188-8

TABLE OF CONTENTS

IDENTIFYING TRAITS OF POTTERY AND PORCELAIN

There are many different kinds of ceramics, each with its own distinguishing characteristics. All ceramics have in common *clay* as the major component. Beyond this, there are numerous differences not only in the components, but also in the manufacturing processes, and in the appearance of the finished product. If you are a beginning collector, you need not feel intimidated by the complexities of this subject. You can enjoy the hobby without becoming an expert on the technical aspects. However, you will probably want to know something about them, even if only out of curiosity.

Even if you are completely unfamiliar with pottery making techniques, it is easy to see that some pieces are different than others. Some are glossy while others have a dull surface. Some are smooth as glass while others exhibit a certain porosity. On some the painted decorations appear to be lying directly at the surface, while in others they seem fused to the material. And if you pick them up, some pieces are heavier than others of corresponding size. The many kinds of pottery that exist have come about largely through an evolutional process: crudeness in early workings with clay, periodic advances in techniques and technology. To fully appreciate all of this, you really need to know a bit about the history of pottery making throughout the world. The story of pottery making can be divided into two periods, the non-competitive and the competitive. In the non-competitive period, which began in ancient times and extended up to the European Middle Ages, nearly all pottery was functional: to carry water or oil, to store wine, etc. The makers of non-competitive wares were mainly individual artisans and their customers were the local community. There was no real competition between them, because all were producing the same kind of pottery in more or less the same shapes and forms to serve the same functions. In the *competitive* period, beginning around 1500 A.D., the decorative aspects of European pottery became a selling point, and various changes occurred in the industry. Instead of craftsmen, most of the work was done in factories. Some of these were enormous sizes, and they not only sold locally but exported their products as well. Soon, a rivalry began among them to improve the product's quality, to lower its price, and in general to draw customers away from the wares of other manufacturers. By the 1700's, a good deal of advertising gimmickry had crept into the trade, and it became even more pronounced the following century. The manufacturers continually experimented with new ingredients, new firing and decorating methods in efforts to catch the public's attention. In the era of popularity for ceramic wares from about 1740 to the early 1800's, every new potter's product that was sold in the shops became a subject of lively discussion. The public tried it just as today they might try a new type of soft drink. If one maker could say that he arrived at the *ultimate* ceramic product by including ground-up ox bones in the formula, he would win much attention and sales, at least for a while.

The competitive era was ushered in by the influence of imported Oriental wares. Chinese potters had been making porcelain long before it was made in Europe. In fact, long before any regular trade existed between East and West. By the 1400's, Chinese pottery was arriving in Europe in large numbers and taking the attention away from the local trade, making the European product seem very drab by comparison. For thousands of years, the basic type of European pottery had been terra cotta or earthenware. It was made from local clays, usually red or orange-red. At first it was shaped by hand, then "thrown on the wheel" after development of the potter's wheel. It was a good serviceable ware, quite rugged. It was fired at a low temperature in stone furnaces and had a non-vitrified surface. The surface was rather porous. Pottery of this type did not totally die out in modern times. The earliest pottery makers of colonial America whose objective was mainly to get utilitarian ware on the market produced earthenware. Earthenware could be, and frequently was, painted. In Italy, where the influx of Chinese ceramics was the heaviest, efforts were made to improve the traditional pottery or earthenware. This led to the production of majolica (sometimes spelled maiolica,) which served for several hundred years as Europe's answer to the hardpaste porcelain of China. Though differing considerably from porcelain in its technical aspects, the physical appearance of majolica is surprisingly close to that of porcelain. Many of the early customers believed it to be porcelain, and even many of those who realized the difference were apparently satisfied with it anyway. Majolica has a lead glaze primed with tin ashes. This gives the glaze an opaqueness and a whitish cast, and this is the whitish cast which suggests hardpaste porcelain. From Italy, the art of making majolica spread to the rest of Europe, notably into Holland, where it was called delftware.

The clays used in making majolica were the same as those in earlier pottery. It differed only in the finishing work on its surface. For generations the best scientific minds of the continent believed China's fine porcelain to be nothing more than earthenware with some kind of magic finish. They were unaware that one of its ingredients was kaolin, a special sort of clay, and feldspar, a crystalline mineral, had to be added to the kaolin along with other substances.

Porcelain has a high translucence and a vitrified or glass-like surface. ("Vitrium" was the ancient Romans' word for glass.) It is fine-grained and non-porous. The ingredients yield a smooth formula free of air pockets. Upon firing, the clay is fused with the glaze.

Hardpaste porcelain always contains kaolin and petuntse, "china stone." It is fired at an extremely high temperature, from 1300 to 1400 degrees Centigrade. True porcelain is extremely hard. However, it is fragile in terms of vulnerability to breakage. Cracks in hardpaste porcelain are clean, not jagged or powdery. When chipped, the chipped area is shaped like a shell, and therefore called conchoidal chips. So-called "softpaste" porcelain is similar to hardpaste ware in most respects, but there are differences in the basic ingredients. Soft-paste porcelain is often called the artificial porcelain, because it doesn't contain the required china stone.

Traditionally, the Chinese considered the "ring" of porcelain to be its chief identifying characteristic. In the marketplaces of old China, merchants "rang" their porcelain to insure customers of the quality. The sound was believed to resemble a musical note with a high pitch and vibration. In Europe and later in America, the ringing quality of porcelain did not receive quite so much attention. Nevertheless, any authentic hardpaste ware, regardless of its point of origin, will have this characteristic. The ring of porcelain is most noticeable on plates and least noticeable on figureware.

Similar to porcelain is stoneware, first made in central Europe from as early as the 15th century. Some stoneware contains kaolin, some does not. Many of the German, French and English porcelain factories made stoneware along with the more popular porcelain. It usually retailed for slightly less than porcelain. Stoneware contains silica and flint in addition to the basic clay. The name "stoneware" was used because the Europeans thought it was made primarily from a stone substance. Today, this substance is called feldspar, which is a mineral, and was generally not used in the European stoneware. Stoneware was fired at a temperature comparable to that of porcelain, and generally received a salt glaze. Much stoneware is fired without a glaze and the surface is non-porous.

The word "china," often encountered in reference to ceramics, means the same as porcelain and is used interchangeably. However, many of the American factories which advertised "chinaware" in the 19th century were really selling softpaste porcelain.

The following chart will serve as a summary of the basic differences in pottery and porcelain in six different aspects: most common ingredients, translucency, firing temperature, vitrification, density and porousness.

	MOST COMMOM INGREDIENTS	TRANSL.	FIRING TEMP.	VITRIF.	DENS.	POROUS
PORCELAIN—	Kaolin, feldspar china stone, flint	yes	high	yes	fine	no
POTTERY—	clay (potter's earth)	no	low	no	coarse	yes
EARTHENWARE—	clay (potter's earth)	no	low	no	coarse	lightly
STONEWARE—	clay, silica, flint	no	high	yes	coarse	no

HISTORY OF AMERICAN POTTERY

The history of pottery making in America spans more than 300 years and stretches across the continent. Rubble-heaps now eagerly dug by treasure-hunters mark the spots where many early potteries stood. They dotted the land, spilling from one community to the next, being carried westward by brave adventurous pioneers. Some were lost in the mists of history, leaving scarcely a trace; others grew into industrial empires, spawning thriving communities. Like a vast family tree, links bound many — if not most — of the companies together. A part-owner of one would strike off on his own and from *that* factory others developed. Or a simple workman, who had saved his pennies, decided to stake everything on a fling for independence. Our ancestors were gutsy and, as antique American pottery clearly documents, well provided with raw talent. In reviewing the history of American pottery making, however, you will find that the survival rate for factories both large and small was low. Many lasted a few years or less. The factory which survived as long as a decade was something of a rarity. Why? Obviously not because the product was bad. One cause was the fierce competition, with one company devouring another. Also, and perhaps more significantly, the potters' success was governed to a large extent by the overall economic success of their communities. New towns that sprang up on virgin land, far removed from rail lines or other access, had to battle out their existence. If the crops went bad, or if half the population packed into wagons and followed its dream elsewhere, local manufacturing received an irreversible death sentence. Life was a gamble in many parts of the country in the 19th century. Getting into business was even more of a gamble. Then of course there was the handicap of limited — or non-existent — distribution systems. A maker in Ohio who wanted to sell his pottery in New York and Boston had to send a special representative to each of the retail outlets, who was frequently turned away. Few dealers on the east coast wanted to do business with these "westerners" when they could stock up with imported pottery at about the same price or less. That was what most customers in the socially-conscious big cities wanted anyway. They were convinced that style was made abroad, and that a foreign mark denoted quality. This is precisely why the centers of American pottery making developed in small towns and far-flung places, rather than the towns of huge population and so-called cultured taste. By the late 19th century, this state of affairs had changed, but it was too late to save many small factories and enterprising businessmen who deserved a better fate.

Fascinating as the subject is, its scope is simply too enormous to be compiled in anything more than summary fashion in a book of this nature. Certainly the specialist collector who confines his hobby to the products of a given factory will want to thoroughly know its history. Exhaustive research has been done by the tireless historians of pottery, resulting in many informative books on the subject. Some of these are now out of print, but a selection — at the least — ought to be on hand at most public libraries.

The beginnings of pottery making on these shores were feeble at best, and a very long time elapsed before anything properly called an industry appeared. Our earliest colonial settlers were an industrious people, but they were more concerned — out of sheer necessity — with meeting the needs of daily survival rather than with business ventures. Vessels for use in cooking and serving food were among the bare necessities that every household needed, but chiefly the earliest settlers (following arrival of the Mayflower in 1620) obtained their "plates" from the pewterers. Others used accessories brought over in their baggage. We know that pottery was made at Jamestown and Massachusetts, but this was probably at least at first, so-called "backyard production" by amateurs. Anyone who owned a potter's wheel and could get his hands on some clay was a valued member of the neighborhood, especially where pewter was in short supply. Customers could not have cared very much if the bowls were lopsided and the serving dishes did not measure up to the artistic standards of France and Germany. This was a beginning, and it foreshadowed the direction that pottery making would take for the next hundred years. Until well into the 18th century, the trade remained within the hands of individual, independent craftsmen. Just as the village smithy did the community's ironwork, the local potter kept his neighbors supplied with whatever utility items they required. The thought of expanding into a factory operation probably never entered the minds of these hard-toiling people, most of whom would have been baffled by contracts, paperwork, and the other unavoidable details of a large-scale business. They were artisans in the true sense of the word, almost like Europe's Old Master painters of a few hundred years earlier — men who could put heaven and earth on canvas but who could not, in most cases, sign their own names.

Another obstacle in the way of factory production was our political situation. The American colonies were just *colonies,* the puppet possessions of a government 3,000 miles away which heaped taxes, licenses and redtape upon the colonials. No real tangible progress in the road to a domestic pottery *industry* was made until after independence was won, though a number of gallant efforts occurred in colonial times. Potters, in fact, became renowned for their poverty, and "potter" developed as a synonym for "pauper." Graveyards for the poor were called "potters' fields." In Biblical times, the poor were buried in "fullers' fields." Since "fullers" were workers in clay, the fate of the potter had not improved a great deal in 2,000 years.

One of the longest-surviving potteries of the colonial era was started by the Remmey family of New York. Among the first stoneware producers in this country, it was established in the 1730's (the precise date is lost) in what later became the city's financial quarter. New York's large Dutch population gave it a good climate for pottery, since the Dutch were habitually more inclined toward earthenwares than were the English. Of course, we can well imagine that slews of imported fresh-from-Holland crockery were peddled in New York, but this did not totally extinguish the local trade. The Remmey works was started by John Remmey, a German whose name was really Johannes. Later, he went into partnership and the business of Remmey and Crolius was born. (Absolutely nothing is known about Crolius — the name may be Dutch.) This factory lasted past the year 1800, a very remarkable accomplishment considering the times.

New York City was not as significant in early pottery making as the regions surrounding it. Potteries emerged to the north of the city in Westchester County and on up the Hudson River into Albany, which also boasted a good smattering of Dutch blood. Beginning in the early 1700's, the Dutch started leaving New York City in droves, dissastified with England's takeover of the city. They scurried along the main water routes, laying farms, buying up land parcels, and plying the same trades they had plied in the big town. Their intention was chiefly to ship their produce and handiworks to Manhattan and build an empire out of supplying the city's needs. At the same time, another network of "suppliers" was putting down roots in New Jersey — a colony with only small cities and superb land for farming and manufacturing. Gradually, its resources were developed and full advantage was taken of its strategic location. Situated along side of Pennsylvania and New York, New Jersey could supply two giant cities — New York and Philadelphia — instead of just one. During most of the 18th century and well into the 19th, nearly all farm products sold in Philadelphia markets came from New Jersey. It was also New Jersey's location that led to its dominance in pottery. With so much trade going back and forth between New Jersey and its neighbors, the opportunities to sell manufactured goods seemed very ripe. So, along with the pumpkins and pears that arrived from New Jersey in Philadelphia and New York came ceramic cups, saucers, dishes, jugs, and a full line of other utility wares. By the mid 19th century, pottery had mushroomed into one of the state's biggest industries. And "Jersey ware" had garnered for itself a reputation that spread across the Potomac and up into New England.

For obvious reasons, Trenton, a stone's toss from the City of Brotherly Love, became the center of New Jersey's pottery operations. It was, however, not the only town in the state to make pottery. One of the most influential Jersey potteries responsible for encouraging a number of the Trenton citizens to try the pottery trade was David Henderson's Jersey City Pottery Company. Jersey City is much closer to New York than to Philadelphia, so there is little doubt about where it intended to do most of its selling. The company is believed to have gotten into operation around 1829 and flourished for many years. The old smoke-belching buildings of the Jersey City Pottery Company were a landmark of the town and a memorial to its industrial achievements. They were finally torn down in 1892, having reached total dilapidation. The Jersey City Pottery Company made glazed wares of various kinds, many of them extremely decorative. Its motifs included patriotic themes (now highly collectible) and themes adapted from the then-current European imports. There was imagination at Jersey City and in ample doses: its designers scoured the pages of print-books and transformed anything likely-looking into pottery. John Ridgway was among the English artists whose works were immortalized in Jersey City pottery. This company was responsible in large part for Jersey City's emergence as the state's commerce center.

Jersey City did not, however, succeed in becoming the state's capitol for pottery. Its geographical location just failed to compare with Trenton's and that was the deciding factor. For reasons yet to be explained — perhaps because of the manufacturing in the Albany region — New Yorkers did not buy Jersey pottery with nearly as much appetite as did Philadelphians. So the town nearest Philadelphia was assured a lock on the market.

Trenton was a relative latecomer into the pottery market, but it made up for lost time with meteoric advances in the mid 19th century. Even the Civil War, which drained manpower from northern industries and threatened to bring war itself to the north, failed to bring Trenton potteries to a shutdown. Following the war, their numbers multiplied, and in the years from 1870 to 1890, or even somewhat later, Trenton was unquestionably the pottery mecca of America. Though its grasp on the industry later slipped away, it was not lost to any single town. No American city, of any size, has ever held a reputation comparable to Trenton's for pottery.

The first major pottery works in Trenton was set up by William Young in 1853. At the time of its founding it gave no identification of ever being more than a small local business, but William Young and his son (William Jr.) turned it into a giant. Their first products were porcelain pitchers with decorations very classical in design which undoubtedly went straight to the carriage trade of Philadelphia. Production was limited for a while, but when the labors of this ambitious father and son team bore fruits they quickly opened up a second factory in 1857. It was called the Excelsior Pottery Works. For about two decades, or slightly more, the Excelsior Pottery Works reigned as one of the most prestigeous in the country. Its works were bought even by those who preferred English pottery, and that was no accident. In a sense, the Excelsior products *were* English pottery. William Young the Elder was an Englishman who had been trained at the famous Ridway pottery in Hanley. Thus the Excelsior products, while adapted to domestic tastes, strongly reflected British traditions and ideals. This was precisely what culture-conscious buyers wanted. Excelsior was still thriving in 1876, after William the Elder had retired, and mounted an exhibition for the Centennial Fair in Philadelphia. It received a bronze metal (third place finish.)

During most of the glory years of Excelsior, it specialized in ironstone porcelain. Its ultra-British mark consisted of a lion and unicorn, along with a crowned shield and the letters *W Y S*, for William Young and Son. Collectors who want to concentrate on the pottery of this firm will find it available, but not inexpensive. It had a reputation in its day and the passage of 100-plus years has both increased that reputation and decimated the surviving examples of Excelsior pottery.

Excelsior failed to survive more than three years following the Centennial; strong local competition and a temporary downturn in the demand for British-oriented wares were probably at fault. In 1879, the Willets Manufacturing Company bought out Excelsior and started an expansion program, building new wings on the existing factories. Willets carried on the British flavor of Excelsior's pottery and changed the trademark only slightly. It did, though, introduce other lines, including Irish Belleek porcelain, graniteware, and even old-fashioned (but very handsome) majolica, which the Italians had been making 200 years before porcelain became a reality in Europe. In fact, Willets' quest for diversity knew no bounds. Its tableware and figurines were supplemented by a line of porcelain doorknobs, bathroom fixtures, and other products for customers who truly wanted to surround themselves with porcelain.

Trenton boasted a number of other memorable potteries, most of them active simultaneously. The City Pottery, run by Rhodes and Yates, began in 1859 in a factory that had been known as Hattersley Pottery and was briefly occupied by William Young and Son. It specialized in white granite wares, which enjoyed a peak of popularity at that time both in Europe and on this side of the Atlantic. The Victorians liked white graniteware because it resembled marble, and marble suggested the world of Greeks and Romans. At the Civi War's conclusion, the company name became Yates and Titus, then in 1871 changed to Yates, Bennett and Allan. This was a period of growth for the company and it continued flourishing up to (at least) the Centennial year, when it placed a small exhibition of its typical products in Philadelphia. It is believed that the City Pottery disbanded around 1880, though the exact date is uncertain. In its 21 (approximately) years, it was quite prolific, especially through the early 1870's, and the hobbyist should have no great trouble finding specimens of its work in the shops. Its mark of a striped and starred shield is unmistakable.

A highly successful and diversified Trenton pottery was Greenwood, founded by Stephens and Tams in 1861. Undoubtedly, this firm's organization was inspired by the success of William Young and Son. The Greenwood approach to business was very much the same as Young's, as it concentrated on English style wares for the American market. Rising labor costs in Britain and the increasing expense of shipping had brought about an opportunity for domestic makers to undercut the British product. Of course, this would be meaningless if American manufacturers fell short on quality. The Young pottery was comparable to the best British pottery, and that of Greenwood had about the same quality as Young's. The year 1861 was anything but encouraging for establishing a business of pottery or any other kind, because it marked the opening of the Civil War. Citizens of Trenton convinced themselves that it was nothing really to worry about, and pushed ahead. And even while the cannons rolled and the sabres clashed, Greenwood got off to a fast start. This factory was very strongly influenced by the creations of Royal Worcester, another famous British pottery. Not only its products, but even its trademark was styled closely to that of Royal Worcester. In the earlier years, it turned out impressive lines of finely crafted porcelain dinnerware along with ironstone. Later it adapted itself to shifting tastes and concentrated mostly upon porcelain artware, as it was then called (we would now say "art pottery.") In the 1880's, Greenwood entered into a contract with a large retailer of Brooklyn, New York to manufacture pottery especially for its shop trade. Greenwood's wares were well-respected which built a large following. It can often be found by the antique browser.

A Trenton firm whose fame greatly overshadowed its production was Millington and Astbury, later called Millington, Astbury and Poulson. This factory seized the public's fancy with a single spectacular production, the *Ellsworth Vase,* a large exhibition-style pitcher with a scene of Colonel

Ellsworth's heroic death in the Civil War. Works of this general type had long been popular in Europe where they occupied places of honor in splendid homes. The English potters regularly turned out enormous vases with a panorama of Hercules and his Labors, the Defeat of Napoleon, or other such themes. Though Americans admired them, they rarely bought them, figuring they would be out of place in the smaller American halls and parlors. Consequently, it was rare for a domestic potter to attempt anything of the kind. Millington and Astbury's Ellsworth Vase became the talk of the trade when it made its appearance in 1861. Some were sold in-the-white, with the design standing out in high bas-relief. In other specimens, identical in all other respects, the raised design was carefully enameled. The Ellsworth Pitcher became so popular that the name of its enameler was recorded for posterity: Edward Lycett of New York, who probably received a handsome commission to lend his talents in the porcelain field. Specimens of the Ellsworth Pitcher have acquired the greatest degree of collector interest through the years, especially since it began with a collector status from its inception. The value has grown steadily and is now well past the point where most hobbyists could buy. They are now forced to bow out and just admire specimens they might discover in a museum. Though the uncolored and colored versions are both highly prized, extra interest is (understandably) attached to the ones in colored glazes which makes a rousing display. The Ellsworth Pitcher is perhaps the single most noteworthy example of the American potter's art of the 19th century. Aside from this, however, the firm of Millington and Astbury (or Millington, Astbury, and Poulson) was not of special importance. The company was smaller than several of its immediate rivals, and on the whole its wares lacked the overall imagination and drive with which Trenton pottery came to be associated.

Interestingly enough, the year 1861 (in which the Ellsworth Pitcher made its debut) witnessed a further reorganization of this company. Poulson, the last of the named partners, died in that year and his shares were acquired by a gentleman named Coughley, whose first name is not recorded. There was no immediate change in factory policy and in general the 1860's were not extremely eventful years for Millington, Astbury and Coughley. Towards the close of this decade, Coughley died and Millington, who had steered the organization through fair and lean times, went off on his own to set up the Eagle Pottery Company. At this point, Thomas Maddock bought up what was left of Millington, Astbury, Coughley. For some years, the company carried the name Astbury and Maddock, but then when Astbury dropped out (whether from death or another cause is unknown,) it became known as Thomas Maddock and Sons. Chiefly the firm dealt in dinnerware of which it produced many different patterns. Some of its wares were on view at the Centennial exhibition in 1876. The year in which this company went out of business is not known, but considering its early beginnings, its active run was longer than that of most 19th century potteries. Quite likely, it was terminated in 1893, or slightly before, because that was the year Thomas Maddock launched a new enterprise: the Lamberton Works, also in Trenton. In this, he was joined by several new associates. The name Lamberton was selected because of its similarity to Lambeth (a British factory.) In this venture, the objective was to turn out British style wares in fine porcelain, including tableware, bottles for perfumes and lotions, and miscellaneous items designed for the luxury trade. The letters *M* and *L*, for Maddock and Lamberton, were incorporated into the trademark.

However, this was not the last to be heard of the Maddocks in Trenton pottery. A year after the foundation of the Lamberton Works, one of Thomas Maddocks' Sons, John, went into the pottery business independently. He had formerly been associated with his father and apparently was included in the new Lamberton partnership, but chose to relinquish his ties with that company. Following in the footsteps of his father, he styled his business John Maddock and Sons, for he now had adult children of his own. The factory was called Coalport, named after the celebrated British pottery works. His aim was not to compete against Lamberton, but to specialize, essentially, in decorative bathroom fixtures, door handles, knobs, light switches, and things of a more or less industrial nature. With the many apartments and houses being built in New York and elsewhere in the 1890's, there was overwhelming demand for these types of items from contractors and the business seems to have done very well. John Maddock's ware was officially known as "vitreous glaze," and the remnants of it can still be found in many New York City buildings that were built in the 1890's. Much of it has, of course, perished forever, since it was not generally salvaged when some of the buildings in which it was installed were taken down. As collectors' items, the American Coalport fixtures and miscellaneous wares are original and intriguing, and certainly a refreshing change of pace for those who have collected the more common items like dinnerware.

Another of the great historic potteries of Trenton has roots dating to the year 1863, when the North and the South were embroiled in a death struggle. In terms of collector prestige, the Glasgow Pottery is unsurpassed by any of the other Trenton companies, and by few, if any, American potteries of any location. Its history and development is a classic success story of a type not really uncommon in the 19th century. Glasgow Pottery went into an already crowded battleground, against companies with long-established reputations and clientele, and in less than two decades rose to the top of the pack. Glasgow's wares were certainly not inferior in quality, but largely the smashing success of this operations was due to wise management. Glasgow had a superb gift for promotion and self-advertisement, and saw the need for setting up an impeccable chain of distribution and agents (as some of its competitors failed to do.) Glasgow wares were promoted in the press more than any other Trenton potteries, and they ended up in more shops and more of the *best* shops. Whenever an exhibition of crafts was to be staged anywhere in the country, Glasgow was there. It never overlooked the chance for publicity. This showman-like gusto brought results that were nearly magical. And even today — though few hobbyists are thoroughly informed on Glasgow's history — its wares still hold their magnetic intrigue.

The brains behind Glasgow Pottery was John Moses, whose name sometimes appears in the trademark, but at other times only as initials. The figure of an eagle is the usual mark, when one is used. When the company went into business in 1863, its initial motive was apparently to supply luncheon and dinnerware, astrays and similar items to railroads and steamship companies and also to hotels. These were of white graniteware and creamware. They were marked with the name of the client (the rail line, steampship, etc.) and human nature having changed little in the intervening 130 years, a large proportion disappeared as souvenirs. This created extra business for Glasgow in replacing those with which tourists and travelers had absconded. Of course, there were further plusses in this kind of distribution: literally thousands of people were exposed to the Glasgow products, and many subsequently headed for shops to buy them. With the passing years, Glasgow introduced more and more variety into its lines, especially stepping up the production of colorful pictorial wares with patriotic themes. These gained much popularity at the 1876 Centennial and continued to sell brisky for years thereafter. In conjunction with the Centennial, many mini-celebrations were staged in cities throughout the country, and Glasgow supplied specially designed tea sets for these functions. These were a source of excellent revenue as well as a fortune's worth of free advertising. Stoneware and majolica were also put on display by Glasgow at the Centennial to show the factory's depth and versatility.

An important government commission (very rare in the pottery industry) came to Glasgow in 1899, when Washington contracted the manufacturer for tableware to be used in the National Home for Disabled Volunteer Soldiers. The disabled volunteers were those who had served in the Civil War and were, by 1899, approaching advanced age. A special mark was applied to these wares, which are basically simple in design, showing a pair of soldiers in the field flanked by unfurled flags and various military symbols. They naturally have great collector appeal, not only because of the Civil War connection and the appealing trademark, but the fact that none were originally released to the open market. Any that are now in circulation have come direct from the home itself and, as can be imagined, represent a small fraction of the total produced.

Government satisfaction with this order led to others on a much larger scale, including tableware for the training quarters of the U.S. Marine Corps. Even if Glasgow transacted no other business, the profits from these lucrative commissions would have kept the company on sound footing. But Glasgow turned out many other lines as well, including hospital supplies. Glasgow entered into agreements with agents in many locations in the country, many of whom paid extra fees to have their own names placed on the wares. There is hardly any imaginable kind of pottery which Glasgow did not manufacture at some point along the way. It was the most diverse of all the American potteries.

Ott and Brewer, another name interlaced with glamor and legend, also originated in 1863. Wares from this company are highly collectible in the pottery hobby, so much so that the wares of Lenox and other makers are sometimes found with a counterfeited Ott and Brewer trademark. The ratio in value of two identical or nearly identical pieces, one marked Ott and Brewer and the other Lenox, is approximately 2-to-1, which is a fairly strong incentive for a forger. Originally, Ott and Brewer was known as Etruria Pottery, the name being derived from a Greek colony of ancient times. The first owners were Bloor, Ott and Booth. Brewer did not become involved until 1865, the year of the Civil War's termination, and at that stage, the name officially changed to Ott and Brewer. Though it was not a one-track-mind organization, the thrust of this firm was chiefly in the direction of British style wares, both English and Irish, including good facsimiles of the Irish Belleek wares. As the success of this kind of ware increased, Ott and Brewer went to the Erin Isle and brought several Irish Belleek potters back to America with them. Ott and Brewer was not only the first American manufacturer of Irish Belleek, but the most successful, though there were a number of imitators. The creations in this ceramic medium were varied, including sculptured cameowork and paintings done in pure white enamel on tinted grounds, giving the effect of a reverse or ghost silhouette. The public found them irresistible and no respectable shop in the country was without its stock of Ott and Brewer Belleek during the 1880's. At the same time, other wares were being simultaneously produced, including classical vases and portrait busts in parianware (unglazed white ceramic.) At virtually the height of its success, Ott and Brewer was bought out and the company name was changed to Cook Pottery.

Much of the success of Ott and Brewer was derived from the talents of Isaac Broome, who had been the head modeler of non-Belleek wares. Modelers for American potteries never reached the kind of stardom achieved by their British counterparts, who sometimes ended up in the lap of high society. Broome, however, got much further than most: he emerged as a talent in his own right, and — apparently recognizing this himself — had a brief fling as a potter. Works produced by Broome on his own — also in Trenton — carried marks that have become highly sought collectors' items. There are very few examples. An "original Broome" is among the anticipations of collectors who search among old pottery, but the expectation of finding one is seldom fulfilled. It is said that Broome made nothing but vases on his own, and that the total production counting all specimens, numbered only around 100. Considering breakage over the years, and examples that have drifted into museums, not many are left for hobbyists.

The commercial climate in Trenton encouraged many other companies to get into pottery making. Charles Coxon, whose firm was known as Coxon and Company, had worked in Baltimore before invading the crowded Trenton scene in 1863 (which, for some reason, was a banner year for new potteries starting up.) Coxon manufactured fine quality creamware and white graniteware. Mercer Pottery was started by James Moses, the brother of John Moses of Glasgow Pottery, in 1868. Mercer produced English-style wares in what it referred to as semi-porcelain. Its output was heavy and it flourished throughout the 1870's, being succeeded by the International Pottery Company in 1879. A year after Mercer Pottery went into business, the New Jersey Pottery Company was founded. It was later called Union Pottery Company. Like Coxon, its stock-and-trade was creamware and white graniteware. The New Jersey Pottery Company is remembered primarily for a series of colorful plates, issued in 1880, picturing the Presidential candidates of that year's election. These are treasured collectors' items today, not just with pottery enthusiasts, but also with historians of political memorabilia, and they command heavy prices.

Another company known as International Pottery, also of Trenton but unrelated to the above, started up in 1860. Its director was Henry Speeler. This International Pottery Company had a varied line of population, including works with Chinese and Japanese influence (which probably prompted use of the name "International.") Oriental ceramics were quite popular in America during the Victorian era, not only in the style-conscious East, but likewise in California which had a large Chinese population. Yet very few firms produced Oriental wares or even wares which suggested the far-east styles. About the closest that most companies came was the use of blue printed motifs on white dinnerware, which was the traditional approach for dinnerware in China. Mostly the patterns themselves were nondescript and not inspired by Oriental work.

This International Pottery Company was bought out by a partnership, James Carr and Edward Clark, which in 1879 changed the name to Lincoln

Pottery Company. Later this organization was known as Burgess and Campbell, after another team of partners eventually acquired it. Though its year by year sales volume was probably not equal to some of the competitors, it survived longer than most of them, lasting into the 20th century. The so-called "Wilton china," popular with collectors for many years, was a trade name of Burgess and Campbell. It was one of many they used, others included "Royal China," and "Royal Blue." The company's Japanese-slanted wares went under the names of "Lotus" and "Japonica."

The 1870's was a very active decade for Trenton potters. America's Centennial of 1876 was an inspiration for many new companies to get under way, since it provides an ideal showcase for manufactured goods of every description. Anything exhibited at the fair was guaranteed to be seen by millions of people, and likely to be written about in the newspapers. Also, the fair generated extra business by encouraging the public to buy any Centennial-related items or goods with patriotic motifs. Since the fair was held right on Trenton's doorstep (in Philadelphia,) The Trenton potters viewed its approach with even more enthusiasm than those in other parts of the nation. Today, of course, collecting Centennial-related pottery has become a special branch of the ceramics hobby. A great deal of it exists, in terms of variety. Yet most specimens are rather scarce, in themselves, because they tended to produced just one or two years and terminated when the fair had ended.

The American Crockery Company, which exhibited at the Centennial, specialized in white graniteware or ironstone. This was a thriving organization which appears to have prospered very well throughout the 1880's and continued in business in the following decade. As the name implies it centered its attention on tableware. A major company in the field of art pottery was Burroughs and Mountford, which began three years after the fair in 1879. While Burroughs and Mountford dealt in tableware and general household accessories, it is known to collectors today largely for its high-grade ornamental wares. These were showpieces of superb design and execution, inspired by the best decorative porcelain of Europe and the Far East. Vases, urns, large water pitchers, and other display pieces were included in the line and were retailed by all the fashionable East Coast shops. The hand enameling on Burroughs and Mountford art pottery is unquestionably among the finest seen on America ware. An artist imported to Trenton from Japan is said to have been responsible for much of it. Unfortunately, his name is not recorded. Understandably, the quantity produced of each piece was small and the original list prices stiff. Over the years, they have gained and even wider following and sell today for substantial amounts when they can be found. Burroughs and Mountford Pottery was bought by many American tycoons of the late 1800's who wanted to turn their estates into private museums. It can be seen today in quite a few homes of that era which are now operated as public attractions from Rhode Island to Virginia.

Unfortunately for the modern collector who would like to see more Burroughs and Mountford in the shops, the company did not remain in business too long. Though its products were elegant, it could not survive the various changes in public taste during the 1880's and 1890's. It shut down prior to the turn of the century.

Other potteries of Trenton which can be mentioned in passing are Prospect Hill, which specialized in British-style graniteware; Delware, a short-lived firm that made tobacco humidors, druggists' jars and similar items;

Crescent, which had a mixed line including parianware; and Enterprise, which was active during the 1880's and into the 1890's.

It may seem amazing to the reader that so many potteries could have been established within one single city, all roughly at the same time — especially since Trenton is not a very large city. Actually, we have not even mentioned all of the Trenton potteries — there were more — and when their numbers are added together, you may wonder how the town could possibly have held them. While Trenton was unique among American cities in its quantity of potteries, this same state of affairs was repeated in Europe again and again. Some European towns smaller than Trenton, extremely small in fact, sprouted clusters of potteries — mainly because of the local availability of good clay. This was particularly true of towns located on waterways, giving an access to transportation. It was much cheaper and more convenient for manufacturers to go where the clay was and ship out the finished products, than to have the clay brought to them. In the case of Trenton, it was inevitable that the town would become a capitol of pottery making. After the first few factories became successful, Trenton was then a magnet for investors, enterpreneurs, artists, agents and pottery-laborers. In a short time, the point was reached where many of its citizens were engaged in the pottery industry in one way or other. Anyone going into the pottery business was assured of finding plenty of labor and skilled artists in the town. As far as the extreme competition was concerned, it probably did much more good than harm for all involved. All of the factories, large and small, kept showrooms of their wares for visitors passing through. Just about everyone with an interest in pottery made the trip to Trenton for the prospect of buying wholesale. Wagons piled with pottery would travel each day from Trenton to Philadelphia and New York and elsewhere. In this fashion, by keeping up the reputation of their town as the valhalla for pottery lovers. Trenton's potters added greatly to the attraction the city held for travellers. Otherwise, probably only a few would have bothered coming to visit just a couple of factories.

Several other Trenton makers deserve to be noted, even though the list will still be incomplete. A company called simply Trenton Potteries was one of the more prominent of the town during the 1890's. It was formed as a conglomerate of five already existing companies, including the Empire, Delaware, and Crescent. No central office was established. Trenton Potteries simply used the five already operating factories. Like coins, its wares carry a sort of "mint mark;" they bear the stamp of the factory which produced them. So it is possible, though not very probable, for a collector to own five duplicate specimens of a Trenton Potteries creation, bearing different marks on each. It is not positively established whether all five factories collaborated on specific projects. The likelihood is that they did not, since one of them, the Delaware, was noted chiefly for making pharmaceutical containers.

One company that should not be overlooked, of course, is the Ceramic Art Company of Trenton (C.A.C.,) the organization which evolved into Lenox China. It was founded in 1889 by Jonathan Coxon, who employed Walter Lenox as treasurer and secretary. Determined to capture the art pottery market or a major proportion of it, Ceramic Art Company made a bold entry into the field with many good-quality, original, aesthetically appealing wares. It had a line of Belleek wares in which it was not the pioneer among American factories, having been preceded by a number of years by Glasgow Pottery. Nevertheless, during the 1890's, its Belleek was the best selling in the market. C.A.C. also turned out numerous other wares, including dinner sets,

Jonathan Coxon

vases, candelabra, figurines, bowls, and other items in a good grade of porcelain. Usually its art pieces were retailed in two distinct states: as finished porcelain with applied enameling (hand painted at the factory,) and as biscuit or whiteware, carrying no decoration or coloring. These were seized upon by amateur painters and art students as perfect subjects for the brush, not to mention the fact that many dealers painted these specimens (or hired people to paint them) before placing them on sale. Therefore, any C.A.C. or Lenox figurine is apt to exist in many different styles of coloring. In the factory-colored specimens, there will of course be a fired overglaze. This is not always present in the non-factory jobs, since many of the artists did no have kilns available or simply were satisfied just to leave the piece as they were— unglazed. However, some do-it yourselfers did indeed fire their specimens after painting them, so the presence of an overglaze is not an absolute guarantee of factory work. The company referred to its unpainted wares as "Indian China" and marked the earliest specimens with an Indian's head. What connection it might have had with the American Indian is yet to be discovered.

Walter Lenox eventually took over as president of the company, and the name Ceramic Art Company was dropped in favor of Lenox or "Lenox China." Lenox entered the 20th century in full throttle, having witnessed through the 1890's the downfall of many of the older Trenton companies, and the way was cleared for its domination of the Eastern trade. It continued manufactur-

Walter Scott Lenox

ing art pottery in the 20th century, but gradually its attentions turned more heavily in the direction of tableware. Lenox survived the depression of the 1930's and entered into a new era with the postwar boom of 1946 to 1950 which saw table china sold in huge quantities. By that time, it had become as it remains today, the leading name among American tableware manufacturers. Its products are sold not only in the United States, but also internationally. In a sense, Lenox carries on the noble heritage of Trenton pottery, though the wares made for today's consumers bear very little relationship to those of Trenton's glory years.

For many years, Lenox Pottery was on the whole in a marginal category with collectors and antique dealers. Its fine early art pottery was sought, but most of its tableware was considered too recent and too commercial to rank as collectors' items. In the past decade, this view has undergone a decided change. Many new Lenox hobbyists are entering the field and quite a sizable proportion of them are interested in the firm's tableware of the 1920's, 1930's and 1940's. Prices have been advancing, but are not yet in the prohibitive class. The vast bulk of Lenox's products can still bought inexpensively, and, as a further plus, it continues to turn up at flea markets, estate auctions and at other sources where bargain sales are the order of the day.

Just as Trenton, and New Jersey were a pocket of pottery-making activity, other regions also began to develop their resources and soon emerged as areas famous for much ceramic production. The number of Ohio potters in the 19th and early 20th centuries was comparable to those established at New Jersey, the difference being that Trenton claimed nearly all the state's factories while in Ohio they were distributed among various towns. Ohio's emergence as a force in the pottery industry began gradually in the 1840's and gathered momentum in the succeeding decades, reading its zenith as the century was drawing to its close. It may seem paradoxical, to a beginning reader, that the fortunes of the Ohio potters closely mirrored those of Trenton's: many false starts and short-lived businesses, a heavy crowding of the field in the 1870's and 1880's, and an almost systematic extinction of the smaller companies prior to the turn of the century. This was a natural result of economic condition and trends in public taste. What happened in Trenton was sure to be duplicated or closely paralleled in Ohio and everywhere that pottery was made. Success for one meant success for the other, even though they served different geographical markets. A change of trend in one area was sure, sooner or later, to spread to the other.

Ohio pottery is a vast panoramic story in itself. In the collectors' market it has legions of devoted fans, some of whom specialize by maker, some of whom buy the Ohio art pottery and ignore dinnerware and standard utensils. However the topic is approached, there will be something for everyone, as literally millions of pieces were turned out of all conceivable descriptions. Early generations of hobbyists went to Ohio to hunt "at the source." This is hardly necessary any longer. Ohio pottery of the 19th and early 20th centuries has traveled so extensively through the antique market that it is, today, pretty evenly distributed over the whole country. Collecting interest in the local ware is so strong in Ohio that prices tend to average from 10% to 40% higher than in other parts of the nation. In fact, some small dealers automatically ship newly acquired Ohio pottery to associates in that state, rather than offering it to their clients. On the other hand, the Ohio dealers have a broader selection, and this is likely to be important to a serious advanced collector. But anyone who hesitates to pay the current market prices, fearing that a new "find" will bring down values, is not being very realistic. Finds have been occurring for the past 50 or more years, sometimes substantial ones — probably more substantial than anything we will witness. None of them have had a negative influence on collector values. Also, as a sidenote to the subject of "finds," it should be pointed out that the locations of virtually all 19th century Ohio pottery factories have been pinpointed and the majority of them dug by fortune hunters within recent years. If any great hordes of specimens are yet to be found, they are more likely to be at old town dumps than at the factory sites.

If New Jersey seems an unlikely place for pottery empires, Ohio seems perhaps even less likely — until we examine the circumstances. The Jersey potters, as we have already mentioned, thrived chiefly on sales in Philadelphia and New York, and, to a lesser extent, in the other large coast towns: Boston, Washington, Baltimore. In the mid 19th century, Pennsylvania was the dividing line between "east" and "west." In fact, Pennsylvania itself had a dividing line; eastern Pennsylvania was business and society oriented and very actively involved in cultural activities, while the western portion of the state was engaged mainly in farming. Once out of Pennsylvania and into Ohio, the mid 19th century traveler entered a world of rural communities and slow-paced life. Aside from Chicago there were no large cities, anywhere in the midwest (St. Louis was considered the "south.") Yet population was increasing and rapidly. The market for manufactured goods, when judged in terms of the entire midwest complex, was almost as lucrative as Philadelphia and New York. Since the Trenton potters were directing their products locally and virtually ignoring the area of Philadelphia, a golden opportunity was presented to cater to the midwestern public.

This midwestern public of 1840 to 1860 would be easy for us to underestimate, in the 1980's. We might instinctively picture them as tillers of the soil, unread, uneducated, unaware of anything happening outside their own few acres of land. This was not the case. The eastern portion of Ohio (where, incidentally, most pottery activity occurred) had been settled since the 1700's and the residents were neither pioneers or refugees. Nor were they all cast from the same mold; they consisted of many ethnic and cultural backgrounds, as well as various religious persuasions. But they did seem to have one thing in common: a strong artistic tendency. Ohio was unsurpassed in its production of folk art of every description during the 18th and 19th centuries. Cut off from the eastern supply sources, Ohioans crafted what New Yorkers and Philadelphians bought off store shelves. They made clothing, furniture, toys, dolls. A heritage developed for arts and crafts, as well as an appreciation for fine handmade objects — long after such things ceased to be valued or even noticed in the big metropolitan areas. The Shakers, who never bought anything if they could make it themselves, were partly responsible for Ohio's mastery in folk art.

Unfortunately, we cannot mention all the Ohio potteries, or trace their development in more than elementary detail. It is significant to note, as a general point of information, that the majority were strictly native organizations, not formed by Trentoners striking out for greener pastures. This was unusual even compared to the situation in Europe, where many pottery centers inherited most of their factories from *other* pottery centers. The result of course was that Ohio pottery maintained an individualism which is appealing to collectors. It was not merely New Jersey pottery made somewhere else.

Quite a bit of pottery activity had already occurred in Ohio before the Civil War. At this time, Cincinnati was the state's largest town, and the potters sold many of their wares there. They also shipped consignments outside the state, notably to Chicago, and this increased as the century drew on. The works of all the early Ohio firms, whether prominent at the time or not, are very avidly collected. In fact, there is special interest in the products of short-lived and low-output factories, simply because they have an additional rarity factor. There were several dozens of these, sprinkled throughout the middle and third quarter of the 19th century.

Of the larger Ohio potteries, one of the longest-surviving was William Brunt Pottery of East Liperpool. Very strongly British in its line, Brunt used — for a while — the lion and unicorn mark favored by many American manufacturers of British-style wares. It made ironstone and decorative porcelain, chiefly table wares. Originally, the firm was titled William Brunt and Son (or William Brunt, Son and Company) and went into operation around 1850. It was not very well known in its early years, but expanded steadily in the 1860's and thereafter. In 1894, when nearly half a century old, it was incorporated as

William Brunt Pottery Company. The marks of this firm could make a study in themselves, including "Chicago," "Alpine China," "Chester," "Rocket," "Alliance" and others. Its wares with the "Chicago" marking were not necessarily intended to be retailed exclusively in that city, but designed to reflect the taste which prevailed there.

A neighbor of Brunt at East Liverpool was the Knowles, Taylor and Knowles organization. This was a gigantic operation begun in 1854 but not reaching its height of popularity until the later 1880's and 1890's. During the years immediately preceding the century's turn, Knowles, Taylor and Knowles was believed to be the largest pottery factory in America, in terms of annual gross sales. However, this is a matter which can only be estimated, since actual records are lacking. Its lines were extremely diversified, including tableware of all types and price ranges, as well as fine art porcelain in the European and Oriental styles. Added to these were accessories for hotels, steamships and railroad cars, and numerous miscellaneous lines. Knowles, Taylor and Knowles attempted to cover the West with its pottery and was largely successful, because sales were registered clear across the Rocky Mountains and into areas where, undoubtedly, no Ohio pottery has previously been sold. The study of its products could be both challenging and rewarding for the hobbyist; there are well over a dozen marks to contend with. The majority of marks bear trade names. One of the most distinctive marks is a charging buffalo.

There were various other potteries in East Liverpool, which in its own way was the Trenton of Ohio. They included D.E. McNicol, also referred to as Novelty Pottery Works, C. C. Thompson Pottery Company, which exhibited at the 1876 Philadelphia Centennial, Homer Laughlin China Company, a very successful long-surviving company whose *early* products are in great demand (it was founded 1874,) Cartwright Brothers, and Globe Pottery Company. Among the later makers of fine art pottery in East Liverpool, one of the leading names was Taylor, Smith and Taylor. This firm started in 1899 and within less than a year had captured wide attention. There is very strong collecting interest in its products today, most of which were in semi-vitreous porcelain.

One of the late-comers on the scene, in 1900, was a company whose name could never be forgotten by any porcelain connoisseur, the Sevres China Company. It was of course named for the celebrated Sevres pottery works of France, which in the 18th century was among the most prestigeous of the world. (It was owned by the King of France, which gave it a little added glamor.) The East Liverpool version was not perhaps the equal of old Sevres, but it turned out some highly distinctive and eminently collectible wares. It used as its mark the fleur-de-lis, the French royal symbol.

Though East Liverpool was home to a myriad of small factories and several of impressive proportions, most of the really large and prosperous Ohio potteries were in Cincinnati. This might give the suggestion that Cincinnati's commerce was founded mainly on pottery. Such was not the case. The town had well-varied industries all throughout the 19th century, pottery counting for only one of them. But in distant states, Cincinnati was certainly known as much for its pottery as for anything else. The fame of its makers spread far and wide, penetrating the though New York and Philadelphia markets and extending even to the West Coast. Of these of course the foremost was Rookwood, which we have dealt with at length in the listings portion of this book. Rookwood was the never-seriously-challenged king of art potteries for many years, and its position with today's collectors is just as formidable as with the public of 100 years ago. Rookwood was innovative, daring, and, perhaps most of all, very attentive to the comparisons made between its works and European art pottery. It maintained a level of artistic creativity fully in line with the best European pottery. Rookwood was founded in 1879. It was taken to the top of its field by William Taylor, its proprietor for many years, who became a legendary figure in America pottery making. The characteristic Rookwood porcelain used a ground of delicately balanced color tints, on which colors were hand painted and then glazed and fired. The results were nothing less than dazzling, and the late Victorian public found itself unable to resist. Those who could not afford genuine Rookwood bought the lower priced imitations of other firms, and an industry in itself sprang up for pseudo-Rookwood.

Rookwood's fascination for the collector extends beyond its reputation and obvious visual lure. It's the stuff that amateur historians' dreams are made of! Because Rookwood used an extremely intricate system of marking its wares, more can be learned about them than those of any other 19th century American ceramics factory. On nearly all Rookwood pieces one finds a company mark (trademark,) a body or mold mark, a size mark (to distinguish between identical objects made in more than one size,) a process mark or marks, and an artist's mark. So, the whole story of the piece is an open book to be read and researched. All decorators employed by Rookwood have been identified. Some were in the company's service so long that their mark changed over the years but these, too, are a matter or record. In fact, in terms of record keeping, Rookwood was a model for other potteries to follow. It seemed to know that its wares would be the idols of collectors generations hence and established a groundwork of information for posterity. The superstardom attained by Rookwood naturally means high prices in the current market. Its wares are not necessarily scarce, but the level of competition is stronger than for art pottery in general.

The storm of imitators and those who wished to reap their share of the Rookwood boom brought at least one important firm to the scene. The Roseville Pottery of Zanesville started out producing artware by its own special formula intended to speed production, cut costs and still yield a desirable product. Its wares reached the shops with lower pricetags than those of Rookwood and found a large receptive audience. Though they might have been considered (at the time) somewhat inferior to those of Rookwood, this opinion has all but disappeared through the years, as collectors have developed a strong attraction to Roseville. Zanesville was selected as the factory site because the local soil contained rich clays. The basic shortcut in Roseville's production process was to cast all its pottery in molds rather than hand-shaping. Before firing, the uncolored ware was given a surface color by spraying rather than brush-painting. This was often done by spraying various colors on a piece, then using a powerful airbrush to move the color about and form them into artistic patterns before the paints had a chance to dry. This was followed by brush-painted decoration over this multi-colored ground, achieving a striking effect with a minimum of time and labor.

There was no real challenge to Rookwood's supremecy in Cincinnati among the potters active there. But Rookwood was not the first potter in that city. It had already achieved a reputation before Rookwood's coming in 1879.

In 1862, the Brockmann Pottery was established by a partnership known as Tempest/Brockmann, for the purpose of making ironstone and creamware. These were English-style lines with English-like markings, intended (as always in the case of such markings, generally that of a lion and unicorn flanking a crowned shield) to suggest a foreign origin. One of Brockmann's advertising claims was that its wares were "warranted best ironstone china." Best in what respect was not stated — perhaps the most resistent to breakage.

In the same year that Rookwood set up in Cincinnati, a competitor also making art pottery settled there, the Cincinnati Art Pottery Company. Its director was Frank Huntington. This ambitious company tried to capture the public fancy with many innovative devices, such as a line called "ivory-colored faience." It made both tableware and assorted decorations for the home. Though the Cincinnati Art Pottery's products were not of a uniformly high quality, it was responsible for some spectacular pieces that now enrich museums and private collections. It was not of long duration. The company closed down in 1891 after twelve years of operation. Hence its works are not common on the market; all are a minimum of nearly 100 years old.

Another Cincinnati pottery was run by Matt Morgan, who had been a magazine illustrator in Great Britain. He came to America with the intent of pursuing that career, but settled into the pottery trade instead. The story of the Matt Morgan Art Pottery is one of the real tragedies of the 19th century American trade. With a recognized artist at its head — the only American pottery to claim such a distinction — it might have soared to lofty heights. Morgan set out to produce the finest possible artistic pottery and was well on his way to accomplishing this — perhaps even challenging Rookwood. He went into business in 1883 and hired the best available talent for every department, then laid down strict rules to insure high quality at each step in the manufacturing and decorating process. The beginnings of this company were very promising. It brought out sophisticated wares in the French and Spanish (Moorish) styles, quite different than any of its competitors and virtually on a level with antique European porcelains of the 16th century. Matt Morgan Art Pottery manufactured both highly glazed and matte finish wares. Each piece was painstakingly decorated, at a labor cost which necessitated a high retail selling price. Connoisseurs did not object to the prices. They reacted very favorably to the Morgan products, eagerly buying up the small allotments shipped to various dealers and agents. Everything looked promising for the future, when, almost in an instant, the company was wrecked. Backers who had invested in the venture objected to Mr. Morgan's course of action, protesting that he was ignoring the mass public with his esoteric wares and high prices. They advanced an ultimatum that the company must compete against general potters or they would withdraw their investments. This was refused by Matt Morgan, who, left without financial support and finding no one willing to take the place of his original investors, left the business. He personally disposed of most of the company's equipment, including its fine molds, rather than let them fall into the hands of unappreciative persons. The rise and fall of Matt Morgan Art Pottery occurred all within the space of about one year.

The McLaughlin Pottery of Cincinnati was the only Ohio factory of the 19th century operated by a woman, Louise McLaughlin. Its wares were of high quality and produced in limited numbers to attract the connoisseurs of the time. Miss McLaughlin oversaw all production personally and is believed to have originated most of the designs herself, at least in the company's earlier days.

Outside of Cincinnati and East Liverpool the pottery making activities of Ohio were not nearly as extensive, however a number of other towns did host factories. There was one of fairly substantial size in Steubenville, the Steubenville Pottery Company. It went into the business in 1879 and produced many fine wares, notably a line of "Canton China" with semi-vitreous opaque body. The term referred to the city of Canton in China, which was known for centuries for its superb porcelains. Various other trade names were likewise used in marketing the wares of this maker, including "Florence," "Clio," "Belle," etc. They should not prove too difficult to find in the collector shops. The Steubenville Pottery Company attained the height of its success during the 1890's.

The factories outside Cincinnati and East Liverpool had some advantage in that the local market was not overcrowded, but there was also sometimes the drawback that skilled labor was not easy to find in towns away from the chief centers of pottery making. Some of these scattered factories were quite small, such as that of Baum in Wellsville. Baum used a distinctive trademark of an artist's palette. This factory is believed to have started up around 1890 and failed to last out the century. Also in Wellsville was the United States Pottery Company, which began in 1899. As the date of its inception closely coincided with that of Baum's failure, there might have been a connection between these factories. The United States Pottery Company specialized in semi-vitreous wares. Another pottery located at Steubenville was the Lonhuda. This Oriental-sounding name was coined from the names of this factory's partners, LONg, HUnter, and DAy.

Next to Cincinnati and East Liverpool, the most significant pottery making town of Ohio was Zanesville, not just because of Roseville but a number of other manufacturers who were active toward the 19th century's close. From a collector's standpoint, Zanesville pottery is especially important, more so than it was to the market originally, because it contains a great deal of fine "art pottery." S. A. Weller was among the Zanesville makers, a very prestigeous organization which produced the popular "Aurelian," "Louwelsa," "Auroral," and other wares. Sicardo-Weller ware, a handsome mettalic-lustre pottery, was originated at the Weller Pottery Company in 1901. It was named for the company's founder and for J. Sicard, a French pottery master who developed it after coming to this country. Also at Zanesville were several manufacturers of ceramic titles, including the American Encaustic Tiling Company and the Mosaic Tile Company.

Sebring, Ohio was home of the French China Company and Sebring Pottery Company, both active in the 1880's and 1890's. The French China Company was a moderately large organization which turned out dinnerware in European-inspired styles which were retailed under various trade names. Other Ohio factories were located in East Palestine, Crooksville, Toronto, Cambridge, Niles, Akron and elsewhere. Cleveland, which became the state's largest city in the 20th century had no pottery factories before 1900.

While New Jersey and Ohio were the leading pottery producing states, they did not hold a monopoly on the industry. It should be no surprise that Pennsylvania, lying between the two giants of pottery making, also had a hand in the trade. During the earlier part of the 19th century, before Trenton emerged in the field, the Philadelphia market was principally supplied by the products of Pennsylvania makers. In fact, the fortunes of Pennsylvania as a pottery-making state would have probably soared between 1850 to 1900 when demand grew, if not for the competition of Trenton. The Trenton potters virtually extinguished the industry in their neighboring state. But before this occurred, pottery making had reached noble heights in Pennsylvania, leaving behind many treasures for collectors. Pennsylvania was the center for manufacturing of that distinctive pottery known as "Pennsylvania Dutch," a misnomer, since the communities which made and used it were German rather than Dutch. This ware is generally regarded as folk art, but this is a questionable designation since it was, mainly, produced in factories which operated no differently than other pottery factories. Its reputation as folk art is probably derived from its painted designs, which are very characteristic of the local artwork and have a quaint amateurish quality. They closely correspond with design motifs found on other Pennsylvania Dutch craft items of the era, such as furniture, writing boards, samplers, etc. Some of this ware was almost certainly sold undecorated and later painted by the consumers, but the majority, we can be sure, was factory-decorated. The beginnings of Pennsylvania Dutch pottery are placed at around 1730, but it was not until much later that the trade became organized and large output attained. The earliest specimens are extremely scarce and are hardly ever found on the market, but quite a few have fortunately been preserved in museums, mostly locally in Pennsylvania. There is little doubt that throughout the 18th century as a whole, Pennsylvania turned out more pottery than any other region of the country. The number of factories greatly increased toward the 18th century's close and many more were added in the early 19th century. In Philadelphia itself, the legendary American China Manufactory was operated by William E. Tucker. This company was in business by around 1825 and reigned, for a while, as the foremost pottery in the United States. Of course, its volume of production was small compared to the major factories of 1880 or 1890, because of the much smaller demand. William Tucker was generally believed to be the first manufacturer of true porcelain in this country. He made tableware and various utensils that were very well designed and ornamented. The decoration is rather plain compared to most European porcelains of that era, but tasteful and finely executed. Tucker's constant battle was not against domestic competition, since this was negligible, but against foreign imports. Foreign wares had the reputation and it was difficult for an American maker, even one of obvious skill and taste, to get a foothold on the market. Tucker campaigned vigorously for the government to raise tax duties on imported porcelain, and even sent samples of his wares to President Andrew Jackson to back up his arguments. Tucker envisioned America as a potential giant in the porcelain industry, with employment for thousands and thousands of workers, if only it could be freed from the onslaught of European imports. Several decades later it became the giant he had forecasted — even with foreign imports increasing. Tucker died after only about seven years in the business, but his factory was carried on several years thereafter, up to about 1836. Its products are all top collectors' items. All to due the credit of Tucker, he never attempted — as did many other manufacturers — to mislead buyers into believing his wares came from Europe. His mark clearly carried his place of residence.

Another early Philadelphia manufacturer of porcelain was Smith and Fife, active at the same time as Tucker. Their products tended to carry more lavish ornament, with gilded embellishments and therefore more closely imitated the traditional porcelain wares of the European continent. Another similarity between the Smith and Fife porcelain and European ware was the cream-colored finish on most of its pieces. Tucker's factory had purposely avoided cream coloring, favoring a pale blue tint instead, which gave the Tucker wares a suggestion of "Orientalness." Studies have also revealed that the Smith and Fife fabrique (the material itself) contained more ground animal bone than did Tucker's, which made it questionable for classification as true porcelain. The public reaction to the products of Smith and Fife was disappointing and the firm lasted only briefly. The wares are scarce and, of course, prized by collectors.

New England was involved in pottery making from the very earliest years of colonial settlement. It failed, however, to achieve anything approaching the prominence of the New Jersey or Ohio areas, and the average Boston shop of the 19th century reflected this. The stock consisted mostly of imported wares with smatterings of Trenton and only a minor proportion of locally made New England pottery. Most successful companies of New England were small by the standards of Trenton and Cincinnati and not clustered in any centralized region but well distributed. Massachusetts had the most potteries in the years before 1900. These included the Low Art Tile Company in Chelsea, a manufacturer of decorative ceramic wall and floor titles, the Merrimac Ceramic Company of Newburyport, which chiefly made flower pots, and the somewhat more prestigeous Grueby Faience Company of Boston. Grueby, founded in 1897, competed in the field of art pottery with attractive satin-finished wares decorated by a team of skilled painters. There is a considerable local collecting interest for Grueby in Massachusetts, since the antique shops of that state are the prime hunting ground for it. At first Grueby concentrated its attention on Egyptian-style wares, which were in vogue for a while: designs were adapted from archaelogical specimens and the colors were uniformly green to present a convincing sense of authenticity. The hobbyist who specializes in Grueby will have a most distinctive collection, and, thanks to the prevailing market situation, will save some money along the way.

The important industrial state of Connecticut had only one pottery factory before 1900 — its resources were thrown largely into clock and watch production and in making mechanical equipment of various kinds. This single factory was the New Milford Pottery Company, located close to New Haven. It opened in 1886. New Hampshire had the Hampshire Pottery in Keene, begun in 1871, whose wares went into the neighboring tourist shops. There was also a factory in Burlington, Vermont, and another — as every collector well knows — in Bennington. Without any doubt, the Bennington establishment, officially known as Norton's and then Fenton's, made New England's major contribution to the development of American pottery. It enjoyed an extremely long history and built and reputation which in time was recognized in all parts of the country. Bennington was one of the very few American potteries whose early works were collected by hobbyists while the firm still young, and the collecting fervor for Bennington continues even to the present time. This factory founded in 1793 turned out tableware of all descriptions as well as full lines of decorative figureware. It made figural bottles in flint glass and also Toby jugs (drinking mugs) that were not at all inferior to the English-made specimens of the 19th century. So much was produced at Bennington that the collector can settle on specializing in one line or another rather than attempting to collect it all. In the second half of the 19th century, the factory's name became United States Pottery Company. Bennington wares had a wide distribution and therefore surface in many regions today as well as in New England. There is hardly a good antique shop anywhere which does not stock a few of its pieces, and they can be found in the historical societies and art museums as well. One may speculate about why the success of Bennington did not draw more pottery activity to New England. Very likely the uniqueness of Bennington's wares discouraged competition.

Pottery making flourished all along the Atlantic coast working down gradually into the mid-south and deep-south states. This area had a larger share of the national population in the 19th century than it does today, and was important in many phases of manufacturing and industry. In pottery making, it did not rival New Jersey or Ohio, but if all the works of southern potters are tabulated they amount to a very impressive array. The geographical territory covered by southern potteries is enormous, and much of the wares produced showed a distinct creative imagination which became unique to its locality. So, there are ripe opportunities here for study and collecting. And since the overall competition is not quite as heavy as for New Jersey and Ohio pottery, many of the prices could truthfully be said to present bargains.

Baltimore was considered a southern city in the 19th century (as was Washington, D.C.,) and therefore Baltimore's pottery was are classified as "southern." Baltimore's pottery could be considered southern even by those who object to the city itself being so designated. The fact is that most Baltimore pottery was not intended for local sale and was shipped south into Virginia, the Carolinas, and down into Georgia were it supplied the deep-south markets. Comparatively few wares drifted northward into Philadelphia and New York, since those areas already had closer sources of supply. The major Baltimore pottery was owned by Edwin Bennett. It began as an off-shoot of an Ohio factory formed by Edwin's brother, James Bennett, in 1839. From Ohio, the Bennetts (there were additional brothers as well) took the business into Pittsburgh, and at that point Edwin left the partnership and settled on his own company in Baltimore. The Edwin Bennett Pottery Company was founded in 1846, beginning on a very small scale. Later, one of his brothers who had stayed in Pittsburgh came to assist him, and bit by bit the operation expanded. The firm chiefly dealt in stoneware and majolica. It flourished throughout the 19th century, enjoying great success in the latter decades of the century, especially in the 1890's. Some very large and spectacular display wares were made by Bennett, along with full lines of tableware and general ceramics. More and more trade names were added to the factory's wares in the closing years of the 1800's to denote each individual line. In its importance in the industry, and in the overall quality of its products, this Baltimore factory stood on a level with any pottery manufacturer of its time. Ironically its wares are not quite so zealously collected today as those of some of its rivals. This is almost certainly because of its location. To some collectors of the present day, New Jersey and Ohio pottery has a charm which Baltimore lacks, just because of the place of origin. The Bennett wares undeniably merit more attention.

In terms of originality and collectability, it would be hard to name any domestic pottery to rival that of a deep-south maker named George Ohr. Even to the present day, his works are known to a relatively small circle of devoted specialists who consider them (probably rightly) the supreme achievements in 19th century American art pottery. George Ohr, of Biloxi, Mississippi, was the William Morris of pottery. Morris, and Englishman who loved books, went into the business of handmaking books and did all his own type designing, casting, printing, ink making, and so on. Ohr likewise planned out and handled each phase of his pottery operation, working entirely alone without employees. He was the designer, the clay-gatherer (he used local clays,) the shaper, the kiln-stoker, and finally the salesman for his wares. This in itself would have been noteworthy enough, but Ohr manufactured no commonplace pottery. His ideals of what pottery ought to be differed sharply from the mode of the times. Ohr approaches pottery like a sculptor. He was concerned with shape rather than surface ornament. Each piece was hand-shaped and Ohr was not delicate about it. He pinched and squeezed and literally beat the designs into his wares, achieving styles diametrically opposite to those of regular commercial potters. In his concepts of the marriage of art and pottery, he was at least 50 years ahead of his time. Even today, few potters have matched his accomplishments. His small factory was in operation in the early years of the 20th century. Like other craftsmen who refused to fall into the accepted modes of working, his efforts brought only small financial reward.

The spread of pottery making into America's west was an outgrowth of the success of the many Ohio factories. Their prosperity was a signal for potteries to be established at Chicago, Detroit, and further west, reaching all the way to California. One must understand that the word "west," in the mid 19th century, meant any territory west of Ohio. There was no "midwest." The west began at Illinois, and everything past the Rocky Mountains was "far west." There was boundless potential for the industry throughout this huge portion of the nation. However this was not fully realized for a variety of reasons. In Illinois and Michigan, there was certainly enough population to support a large ceramics industry, but the Ohio potters were channeling their products into these states and drowned out most of the local efforts. In areas where the Ohio pottery was not reaching — such as California — or reaching to only a limited extent, the population was widely scattered and distribution networks were hard to set up. Just before the 19th century's close, in 1899, an art pottery was opened in San Francisco by Mrs. Linna Irelan. There were several potteries in Colorado around this time, most of whose wares were sold in California.

This story of the development of the ceramic industry in the United States is in highly condensed form. Many firms have been omitted, as have full descriptions of the wares produced by each of the firms mentioned. The listings in this book will help in providing further information, and hopefully the reader's interest in American pottery and porcelain will lead to his own investigations into this rewarding study.

TYPES OF DECORATION

Decoration can be either be applied by hand or transferred, and sometimes two will be combined on a single item. The decoration can also be applied either before or after the item is glazed. The glaze firing is the hottest of all the firings, so any color put on underneath the glaze must be able to withstand those high temperatures. The "hard fire" colors are blue, brown, green and yellow, and these colors will predominate in underglaze work. Do not make the mistake, however, of automatically assuming that these colors are always underglaze just because they can be underglaze.

Overglaze decoration allows for a wider variety of decoration, and most of the items being collected today are of the overglaze type. Part of this was due to the decorating styles of the day, and part of it was due to economic reasons. Any time an item is fired, there is the risk that it will not come out of the kiln in satisfactory condition. The two chief firings are the *bisque* firing and the *glost* (glaze) firing. The glost firing is particularly tricky, since minor variations in temperature can cause the glaze to become very runny. If there happens to be artwork already on an item when this happens, the artwork will move when the glaze starts to run. The many long hours spent on the artwork are then a total loss. Overglaze work, on the other hand, is fired at a much lower temperature and accidents of this type are less likely to happen.

Transfer decoration can be applied in any number of ways, and some of the designs used were very clever and innovative. Potteries frequently used transfer decoration which was then touched up by hand. The end results can be quite pleasing, and such items are to be preferred to badly done totally hand-painted ones. Depending on the type of transfer work done, a magnifying glass will sometimes show the design as being made up of series of tiny dots and lines.

Gold trim is of three main types: (1) Flat gold, which is merely applied by brush. (2) Etched gold, which is applied by coating the sections not to be etched with a protective substance and then giving the item a bath in hydrofluoric acid. The unprotected sections are then etched by the acid. The gold is applied over the area, and the final result is some type of design in the gold. (3) Raised gold paste work, which is accomplished by applying a paste-like substance called sizing in the desired design. The gold goes on the sizing, and the result is a raised-up gold design. Different shadings of gold can be used on the same piece to give very striking effects. All of the different types of gold work must be fired.

Applied decorations must be molded and fired and then affixed to the main item and fired again. Samples of this type of work would be the Willets basket with applied flowers on the rim and the Ott & Brewer ewer with turtles climbing up it, both of which are shown in the color section. Applied work must be distinguished from decorations which are molded in as an original part of the casting process, and there is usually no trouble telling them apart since the molded-in designs can never be as finely done as the applied ones.

Molded-in designs are usually referred to as embossed designs, and although some of them are quite original and lovely, this type of work really cannot be called "decoration."

Pate-sur-pate work is extremely rare in ceramics and since most of the collectors have never seen a piece of true pate-sur-pate they tend to corrupt the term and use it for embossed designs. Real pate-sur-pate is done by painstakingly building up a design with slip (liquid porcelain) until the desired effect is achieved.

Although all of the above may or may not have been interesting to you, the real breakdown of decoration of ceramics (as determined by the people who have been collecting it) is into three categories: undecorated, factory-decorated, and nonfactory-decorated. As it usually works, factory-decorated is the best to have, with undecorated and nonfactory-decorated less desirable. Although this can vary somewhat depending on the type of item, factory-decorated is always at the top and this is not likely to change.

Factory-decorated quite literally means any item decorated at the factory and this could include all the different types of decorating. The term as it is commonly used, however, applies to items which were *hand-painted* at the factory. Some of these items will be artist-signed and some will not. Non-factory-decorated means any item decorated away from the factory, by artists ranging from unskilled amateurs to talented professionals who decorated china for a living.

If we loosely group art work into three categories, excellent, mediocre, and bad, the factory artwork invariably falls into the first two categories. Non-factory, however, can include all three and this is where the problems begin for the novice collector. With this in mind, we will go into a brief discussion of good art work vs. bad. Although we cannot turn the novice into an art critic overnight, we can offer a few hints concerning ceramic art work.

Subject Matter: The subject matter should be in keeping with the piece of china, i.e., a formal shape vase should be painted in a formal style. The design should fit on the china nicely, being neither too large nor too small. This is something the professional artist seemed to do almost automatically, whereas the amateur would often make their central design too large for the item.

Use of Color: The professional artist by instinct and by training knows which color to use in combination with the others on his item. We will use as our example a vase with large pink roses on it. The professional artist knows in advance that using a particular shade of green for a leaf will make the pink rose look washed out, something an amateur never seems to grasp. (To better see what we mean, paint 10 squares of the same color pink on a piece of paper. Next to each square of pink place 10 different shades of green. The pink will appear to change color from block to block depending on the shade of green next to it.)

On the leaves of our example vase, the amateur used only shades of green. The professional, on the other hand, frequently would use different colors to enhance a leaf, such as Marsh's use of turquoise to highlight each leaf. The casual observer may never even see that there is blue in the leaf, yet the presence of these colors makes a vast difference in the overall effect.

Use of Gold: The amateur artist apparently viewed gold as something to use when he or she didn't know what else to do. The amateurs also tended to use cheaper commercial grades of gold decoration. The overall effect is usually rather garish, and can be the first clue that a piece is badly done for those of you who will never learn to otherwise tell good from bad artwork. Gold frequently covered bases, lids, handles and anything else that didn't move.

Lenox and other fine china companies employed gilders whose only function was to take an item and apply the gold as an enhancement rather than a cover-up. The factory gilders, instead of doing a whole handle gold, would sometimes use a filigree design, or perhaps a speckled effect. On an item such as a Lenox whisky jug, the factory-decorated items will have only the inside of the spout done in gold, whereas the home-decorated items will have inside and outside of the spout done as well as the handle.

NON-FACTORY ARTISTS

The art of china painting flourished throughout America (and the world, for that matter) during the latter part of the 19th century and on into the first quarter of the 20th century. So extensive was this pastime that the collector will find a wealth of items to select from this category, as opposed to the relative scarcity of factory-done items.

This leads to a distrust among collectors of the value in collecting non-factory wares, which is somewhat unfortunate since there are many beautiful pieces which were done by non-factory decorators.

It is our hope that the following discussion of the nonfactory artists will serve today's collector and dealer in realizing that there are several fine points in determining value for this category. To a large extent some of the best bargains are available in the non-factory field. Unfortunately, this category is also prone to some of the worst examples of overpricing, due in part to the fact that the value is in the artistic content as much as in the piece of porcelain itself. Often the evaluation of that artistic merit is at best a guess based on subjective feelings.

In an effort to broaden the scope of knowledge needed by today's collector and to allow the home-decorated market to take on a more cohesive form, we have divided non-factory artwork into three categories:

(1) Amateur
(2) Studio
(3) Professional

AMATEUR ARTISTS

This category encompasses the majority of non-factory items seen today, perhaps as much as 50 to 75 percent. The amateur artist viewed ceramic decorating as an interesting hobby and perhaps never did more than a few items. Many of them failed miserably in their artistic endeavors, but others produced items which, if not exactly fine art, are at least not objectionable. (These items are known in the trade as "Dear Aunt Martha's Niceties.")

STUDIO ARTISTS

The term "studio artist" would include all those ceramic decorators with some degree of talent and training who were capable of producing accomplished and sometimes innovative works of art. (In all probability, he or she had a studio in which to work, hence the choice of the word to describe the category.)

Some of these amateur studio artists were as talented as the professionals mentioned later, but their credentials are usually less well publicized. Many of these artists were quite prominent in their own time, and either taught ceramic art or belonged to various ceramic clubs around the country. Following are a few of the better-known studio artists from the first quarter of this century.

Henrietta Barclay Paist — Mrs. Paist began decorating china in 1889 and continued until after World War I. She was best known in the Midwest and West as a teacher of ceramic art. In 1896 she received the first place medal in a national exhibition in Chicago (best of 108 entries), and an honorable mention in the 1900 Paris Exhibition. She was president of the Twin City Keramic Club and founder of the ceramic department for the St. Paul Institute of Art. She also worked in pottery, leather, wood block printing, and oil and water colors.

Mrs. Dorothea Warren O'Hara — Mrs. O'Hara was a Kansas City resident who had studied at the Royal College of Art in London. She learned ceramic decorating under Bischoff, Fry, and Robineau. After moving to New York, she was awarded life membership in the National Arts Club of New York as well as a gold medal in the Panama Pacific Exposition. Two of her vases were in the National Museum in Tokyo. She was president of the Keramic Society of Greater New York.

Miss Maud M. Mason — Miss Mason was president of the Association of Women Painters & Sculptors, and received a gold medal at the Panama Pacific Exposition for some of her work. She taught at the Fawcett School of Industrial Art in Newark, NJ.

Mrs. Kathryn E. Cherry — Mrs. Cherry studied under Robineau and Fry, and was a gold medal recipient in St. Louis in 1904. She was a Master Craftsman of the Boston Society of Arts & Crafts, and received honorable mention for the Armour prize at the 1917 exhibition by the Art Institute of Chicago.

Mrs. Vernie Lockwood Williams — Mrs. Williams had studied at the Pratt Institute in Brooklyn, and was an instructor of porcelain decoration at the University of Pittsburgh, as well as an officer of the Duquesne Ceramic Club.

Many of the studio artists founded or were members of the various ceramics clubs. The purpose of these clubs was to bring together talented artists with the idea of improving the state of the art. Many of these clubs came and went quickly while others lasted for a long time and were the forerunners of art leagues still in existence. Information on most of them is sketchy or unavailable, but we can supply the following:

Twin City Keramic Club — This club was based in the Minneapolis-St. Paul area, and was apparently academically oriented. It is known that the Atlar Prize for ceramic art was awarded to this club on at least three occasions. Members included Mrs. Henrietta Paist, Miss Florence Huntington, Etta Beede, Mrs. Arch Coleman, Mrs. Laval, and Mrs. Reed.

Kansas City Ceramic Club — The Kansas City club was a rather large and prosperous one. Club members included: Mrs. J. W. Smith, Mrs. Gibbons, Mrs. M. Barker, Miss Bartholdt, Miss Barker, Miss Halbert, Miss Bayha, Mrs. E. E. Smith, Miss Smith, Miss Borch, Mrs. Alys M. Binney, Mrs. Burney, Mrs. J. H. Daly, Mrs. W. T. Timlin, Mrs. Moore, Mrs. Lynval Davidson, Mrs. G. H. Bilheiner, Mrs. J. E. McFadden, Mrs. Pauline James, Mrs. Maude E. Nutter, Mrs. Estelle McDougal, Mrs. Twyman, Robert D. Haire, Mrs. Kate Ward, Mrs. A. E. Findley, Mrs. Hannah Cuthbertson, Mrs. Gleason, Miss Vic Harris.

Duquesne Ceramic Club — Membership was primarily within a 50 mile radius of Pittsburgh. Instruction for this group was provided by Professor Herbert Kniffin of the University of Pittsburgh. Regular members included: Mrs. V. L. Williams, Miss Anne McIntyre, Mrs. Ray E. Motz, Albert J. Rott, Mrs. L. S. Price, Miss Maud Chapin, Mary C. Walters, Mrs. Anna McIntyre, Ella Faber, Edith Sillaman, Sadie Kier, Mrs. Kolgel, Nettie Davis, Jeannette Negley, Alice McQuade, Leda Harrison, Mrs. D. Horton Lutz, and Mrs. Byron Mitchell.

Keramic Society of Greater New York — Two of the principal members of this club were Marshall Fry, Jr., and Dorothea Warren O'Hara. Other members included Lillian C. Smith, Miss Dalmore, Mrs. Nina Hatfield, Esther A. Coster, Georgia Pierce Unger, Cornelia P. Nelson, Anna E. Fitch, Alice M. Hurd, Marguerite Cameron, Mary E. Harrison, Sarah A. C. Draegert, Annie S. Tardy, Alma P. Kraft, and Frances White Wilcox. This club is known to have been a driving force in spreading the latest of decorative motifs to the home ceramics market. Their styles were always the latest and mlst stunning available, and their work is highly collectible in its own right.

Chicago Ceramic Art Association — The Chicago group began sponsoring ceramic exhibits as early as 1892, and was in the forefront with the New York club when it came to promoting the art of ceramic decoration. The A. H. Abbott prize was offered for best collection of pieces by one decorator; the Burley & Co. prize went for the best design on tableware; and the Hasburg Gold prize was conferred for the best use of gold in decoration. Members included: Mrs. Anne T. Brown, Mary E. Hipple, Mrs. Isabelle C. Kissinger, Miss Ione Wheeler, Mrs. George E. Emmons, Miss Marie B. Bohmann, Miss Grace E. Minister, Mrs. Rena O. Patterson, Mrs. Grace Bush, Miss Amanda E. Edwards, Mrs. Valla Ramey, and Mrs. Marie Sparks.

PROFESSIONAL ARTISTS

Professional artists would be those who were able to earn most or all of their income from decorating china, and as one might imagine this took a great deal of talent. The work of many of them should be considered equal to that of the factory artists.

Marshall Fry, Jr. — decorator from New York City, also instructor in china painting.

Mrs. Adelaide Alsop Robineau — Mrs. Robineau was born in Middletown, CT in 1865. She was married to Samuel E. Robineau, and they lived in Syracuse, NY where she died in 1929. The Robineaus published a magazine called *Keramic Studio* which in addition to giving instructions in various painting techniques also served as source for news about the various clubs and organizations.

Mary F. Overbeck — Ms. Overbeck was one of the founders of Overbeck Pottery of Cambridge City, IN and was a frequent contributor to national magazines devoted to china painting. She introduced various designs and decorating techniques in her articles and was well-known in pottery and porcelain circles.

Lycett — Edwin Lycett was known as "the father of American china painting", and his son, William, opened a decorating shop in Atlanta, GA. Pieces are usually marked with "Lycett, Atlanta, Ga." in a powder blue diamond on the base.

Mary Nourse — Ms. Nourse was at one time an artist at Rookwood Pottery, and her name has been noted on some C.A.C. lavender palette mark items.

Bischoff — a leading American decorator of the day.

Joseph Yeschek — Pickard artist

Schindler — decorated for D'Arcy Studios.

Curtis Marker — Pickard artist

Mr. Messino — Pickard artist

As must be obvious from this section, most of the nonfactory artists were women while most of the factory ones were men. This breakdown by sex had little to do with talent but rather reflects the spirit of the times. For the most part, the men started painting as professionals (even apprentices were paid), while the women made the slow progression from rank amateur to studio to professional.

BUILDING A COLLECTION

If you are a beginning collector of American pottery, you should first try to familiarize yourself with the available selections in antique shops and other such places on the market. This will help you decide what specific type of wares appeal most to you, and which would best suit your available display space and budget. At the same time, it is important to learn the basic techniques of shopping, looking, and buying. You need not be an expert to buy well. Some knowledge is, however, essential in order to make intelligent buys that will not later be a source of regret. This book should provide even the raw beginner with enough information to go out into the marketplace and start building up a collection. It is certainly advisable that the knowledge contained between these covers be supplemented by reading hobbyist magazines, getting involved in club activities if this suits you, and visiting local museums and studying any pottery that might be exhibited. Nothing takes the place of actual experience in handling and viewing the specimens themselves. There are quite a few antique dealers who never "read up" on the items they deal in; yet handling it continuously, day in and day out, has brought their knowledge to the expert level. They can tell a reproduction or a repaired item at a glance, 9 times out of 10. Anyone can achieve this kind of expertise.

One of the purposes of this chapter is to help you avoid a false start and begin with a sense of direction that will carry through many years of enjoyment in the hobby. As a beginner, the hobby and its mechanics are sure to look different to you than they will after a year or so. The average beginner is sometimes a little over-awed by the massive market. You may find hundreds of examples of American pottery in most antique shops along your route and perhaps you are impressed by the extent of the array. Looking in the shops, attending antique shows, and picking out the most intriguing specimens to buy for your collection is nothing less than thrilling. In this whirlwind of excitement, you, as the beginner, will buy what you like most: what catches your eye. You may tend to think in terms of decorative qualities above all else. By purchasing in this manner, you will build a collection which displays very well, and with which most of your neighbors (who know very little about pottery collecting) are duly impressed. There are great advantages with an "it-appeals-to-me" collection. Chances are, however, that you will not remain satisfied with this type of collection. Gradually, the novice collector acquires dashes of sophistication and looks more critically not only at what he buys, but what he already owns. While never losing your enthusiasm for shopping the antique stores, browsing and buying may become less rewarding; and you may turn most of your attention toward the direction being taken by your collection. This becomes, eventually your source of pleasure. There is quite a wide gulf between buying — which anybody with a little cash can do — and serious collecting. A serious collector wants to do more than buy. Now, you want more than the fun of a Saturday afternoon spent browsing through the town's antique shops. You want more than to hear friends compliment your collection. As long as you are convinced of the value of your collection, nothing else counts. A collector, to be a good one, has to develop a bit of an ego. You must be confident of your judgment and knowledge. You must be able to say to yourself "I'm a specialist and a connoisseur. I know more about pottery than those who don't collect. And I value my opinions and my taste more than theirs." The average non-collector many times connot tell the difference between a valuable, historically important group of pottery and a box of odds-and-ends from a charity bazaar.

If you have a miscellaneous collection, you will find that if may have a remarkable tendency to change direction on its own. As more and more specimens are accumulated, a few of them — perhaps by nothing more than pure coincidence — will be related to each other. Thus, they form a kind of collection-within-a-collection. You now have pieces which compliment each other. So, on your next expedition to the antique shops, you begin to look for more of them. You now may devote all your collecting energies to this one particular type of specimen, ignoring everything else. You become a specialist without ever having resolved to do so. The tide simply carried you along over the falls. You are now infinitely more pleased with your collection, even though it probably does not grow as rapidly. When you go out pottery shopping, you know what you want — and what you definitely do not want. If you find a gorgeous specimen of something which does not fit your collection, the temptation to which you may have succumbed six months earlier is stifled.

The lament of the beginner is, often, that his knowledge of pottery is not so well developed to settle on a pet specialty. Of course it isn't. No one is a born collector. But buying is not the way to build knowledge and get on the right path. You would do much better to visit the antique shops without buying — and if this seems like tempting fate, you can leave your cash and checkbook at home. As you visit more and more antique shops, you will inevitably be exposed to a greater variety of American pottery and porcelain. Things you might have bought at the first shop — if you were buying — may seem overshadowed by those in the second shop, or the third. Each has its individual stock and no two are alike. There will be a preponderance of art pottery in one and possibly Pennsylvania Dutch in another and pharmacy wares in a third. It is vital to see as much as you possibly can, before you do any buying. You may very well discover an attachment for a certain line of pottery which you did not think was appealing to you. This is a very personal thing. This is why no one can tell you what is the best or most worthy kind of pottery to collect. Cash value can be pretty closely established, as we have done in the listings in this book. But very few hobbyists collect with cash value uppermost in their motives. Their chosen group of pottery must strike a responsive chord in their sentiments, in their zest for history, or in their enjoyment of visual beauty. What does this for one individual will not necessarily for another. There are collectors — knowledgeable people well-versed in the study of pottery — to whom the most exquisite art pottery is not attractive. To them, the supreme pottery collectibles might be simple tableware of the late 18th century. Who can say, beyond monetary value, that one group is really more worthy of collecting attention than another? Some groups are certainly more popular than others, Roseville and Rookwood as examples. If a census could be taken, it might show that the specialist collectors for Roseville and Rookwood outnumber all other collectors of American art pottery and probably by a vast margin. Does this mean — if your interest is art pottery — you should automatically settle on one of these two groups? Not at all. There are undeniable advantages of "going with a winner." If you collect Roseville or Rookwood, you will find more dealers offering it for sale, and there is probably a somewhat greater chance of monetary appreciation in the future. But these considerations in themselves should not deter anyone from collecting the kind of pottery that most appeals to them, regardless of its popularity standing. Popularity alone is not a guarantee of quality, not is it a guarantee that your collection will earn greater respect. Some marvelous collections have been made in out-of-the-way types of pottery, going all the way out in left field to such things as tobacco humidors, ashtrays from steamships, and even decorative ceramic flooring tiles. These collections have uniqueness on their side. The more popular a subject is, the more competition there will be.

This means higher prices and it may be less likely that your collection will be complete or even close to complete. With a group of pottery which is not heavily collected, you are apt to get very favorable buys from dealers. And it is quite likely your collection may go on to become one of the best on its subject.

The listings in this book should give you some suggestions on what is available for collecting. You will see what exists in fair-sized quantities and what is fairly scarce. The more valuable pieces are not necessarily the hardest to find: they just cost more when you DO find them, generally because of competition. Whether they deserve to cost more on grounds of beauty, historical significance, or other factors is a debatable point. But since few pieces of pottery ever bring prices they deserve, this is really a question not even worth asking! Generally speaking, the earlier wares are the more difficult to find, even if this is not reflected in their prices. Pottery dating from 1850 to 1900 is less plentiful in the antique shops than wares made after 1900. By the same token, specimens going back to before 1850 are less plentiful than those of 1850 to 1900. Specimens dating before 1800 are very seldom found in antique shops, though they do come up for sale in auction galleries from time to time. Despite their vast age, they can sometimes be purchased for no more than an in-demand specimen of 1900's art pottery. There are just not as many competitors for them. Even if something is one-of-a-kind, "unique" as collectors like to say, it is not going to command a big price unless it has credentials behind it. If very few people know or care about it, it could sell for next to nothing. Rarity counts much more in hobbies like coins and stamps than in pottery — probably because with most specimens of pottery, it is a matter of doubt just how rare they truly are.

Assuming you have chosen to become a specialist collector, there are basically two ways to specialize; but within these two are hundreds of approaches, so there is certainly ample space for using your own imagination and ingenuity:

(1) Specializing by manufacturer.
(2) Specializing by type of article.

You could settle on a manufacturer — say Glasgow of Trenton — and try to collect a specimen of everything made by Glasgow. Even if you were not especially enthralled by teacups, you would buy any teacup marked Glasgow, along with anything else you found bearing the mark of this company. But if you chose to specialize only in teacups, you would not just buy those from the Glasgow firm but of other manufacturers as well.

This sounds very simple, but in practice it is not quite that simple — and this is where the personality, motivation and tastes of the hobbyist get into the picture. Assuming you were going to collect teacups, you would probably not want to randomly buy every teacup you find. There are thousands and thousands of teacups in the world! So very likely you would want to restrict yourself somewhat, by collecting only teacups from Trenton or East Liverpool, or setting up some kind of criteria that would narrow down the target. In this way, your collection would be more cohesive and appealing, since the specimens in it would relate more directly to each other. There is really very little in common between a teacup made in Philadelphia in 1830 and one sold at Woolworth's in the Art Deco era. By the same line of reasoning, if you collect by manufacturer and the manufacturer has a 100-year history, you will not necessarily want his current products. The smaller your scope of specialty, the less likely that you will want every specimen to come along. This would probably be the case if you collect the products of mid 19th century manufacturers who were in business for only 10 or 15 years. You will not find an overwhelming number of their products on the market, just enough to keep you collection moving forward if you buy it all. That is certainly a point worth considering before you do any buying. Do you want a specialty which allows you — or encourages you — to pick and choose, or would you be happier going after harder-to-locate material? Most beginners understandably want to see their collections build up fast. It is rather discouraging to start out in a hobby and look at a partially bare shelf for month after month. This is what inspires many stamp collectors to buy a worldwide album and take any stamps of any countries that come along. Keep in mind, though, that the fast-growing collection poses a danger of getting out of hand: overflowing the available space and possibly placing too big a drain on the owner's finances.

Generally speaking, the more advanced collectors — those to whom pottery collecting becomes almost a way of life — tend to specialize by manufacturer, and they often prefer the obscure manufacturers over the "biggies." This is not only because of the lower prices, but the very intriguing research potential. Not as much investigation has been done into the histories of most of the smaller factories. Anyone who assembles a good collection of the works of a small manufacturer has the basis for a volume or two of original research. That is exactly how some of the most useful books on pottery collecting get into print: they start out with someone's private collection, and in time that person has accumulated tons of information and theories which he cannot resist sharing with the world.

Another way of specializing, over and beyond the two listed above, is by era. You could, for example, confine yourself to works of the Late Victorian era, or the Edwardian, or the Art Deco period. You might find the available selection a bit overwhelming unless you narrow it down somewhat. Late Victorian, though it sounds like a well-defined target, would include the works of dozens of Trenton potteries and dozens more from Ohio, not to mention miscellaneous ones in other regions of the country. You might want to combine era collecting with teritorial collecting: Late Victorian pottery of the southeast, for instance; or possibly with type collection, such as Late Victorian dinner plates. Give this some thought. This is why we advise browsing in the shops before coming to any final conclusion. The topic in which you choose to specialize must be something that offers a fair degree of availability, yet will not totally snow you under. The most rewarding specialty is one in which you can nearly always buy an item that fits your collection, when it turns up, rather than having to skip it for lack of finances. A few weeks of buying nothing, because nothing is available, gives you a chance to save up for that really good "find" in the future. When you buy regularly, there is seldom a chance to go beyond your weekly budget allotment for an item of great interest. So it is advantageous to be collecting in an area where the availability is limited and the big "finds" occur only occasionally. As a matter of fact, there are hobbyists with very average means who collect pottery which 99 in 100 people would say is beyond their reach. They are content to go for months without buying, or, when occasion demands, swap two or three of their pieces for a new acquistion. Their collections never grow very large, but this is not a cause of concern to them. They receive as much enjoyment from their collections as if they numbered hundreds and hundreds of specimens. Once again, it's a matter of personality. What suits one collector is not going to suit everyone.

There are some highly esoteric ways of specializing, if the ordinary ways of collecting seem mundane to you. One of the classic approaches — followed much more in Europe by the collectors of foreign pottery than by their American counterparts — is to collect by artists' marks. Most of the pottery artists who signed their works have been identified. Not too much is known about the majority of them, beyond their names and the companies who employed them, but their skills and styles are there to speak for them. If you have a favorite artist or designer among the Rookwood team, you could specialize exclusively in the wares decorated by that artist. This would probably be a rather small collection, but there are some Rookwood artists and designers whose handiwork comes on the market pretty frequently and would offer the opportunity for a really substantial collection. There are collectors for the works of Japanese artists who were employed by American factories. These men on the whole had high reputations and their works cost more than those of most house artists. There are even collectors specializing in the works of unidentified artists whose initials have yet to be traced; many of the Roseville artists are in that class. Quite likely, some of these collectors have an eye toward investment, figuring (and probably correctly) that if the artists are ever identified, this will bring about an immediate increase in values. You can generally buy the works of unidentified artists a little cheaper than those whose names are known. The real superstars among pottery artists are few, but when their works are encountered, the prices are obviously in the premium category.

Specializing regionally is yet another approach, which has its share of devoted followers. If you interest is pottery of the 19th century, and more particularly of the years prior to 1880, regional collecting has possibilities to offer. It is obviously not very suitable to specialize in the pottery of a region so bounteous in pottery as New Jersey or Ohio, since this would lead into the same predicament mentioned above: over-repletion, too much to buy, too much money to spend, not enough space to show your acquisitions. A good potential subject for a regional collection would be Chiago or Detroit, or Hudson River Valley (upper New York State), or one of the New England states. Here the available selection would not be overwhelming; chances are you could buy many of the pieces that come along, and get a really interesting collection going. If you specialized in New Jersey or Ohio wares, you would be able to acquire only a tiny fraction of the pieces passing through the market.

After settling on a specialty, the next consideration is how to buy: that is, how to get the most for your dollar and avoid all purchases which are questionable. If you have any collectors among your friends, you undoubtedly marvel at the skills they have developed in making selections and getting their money's worth. This is not because of any sixth sense. It reverts to the old adage that experience makes the best teacher. As you gain some experience, the questions of WHERE to buy, WHAT to look for, WHAT to be careful of, HOW MUCH to spend will virtually answer themselves. The specimens in antique shops are not standardized in their quality or value, and certainly not in their prices. You can survive the life of a pottery buyer, and probably make some excellent buys along the way. We will give some specific advice here, but *use common sense.* Don't let your enthusiasm get the better of you. Approach each potential purchase carefully and critically. Put the object on the defensive and force it to prove that it deserves to be bought. As a beginner, do not trust your first impressions. First impressions are meaningful to an experienced buyer, who can often tell you everything there is to know about an item after looking at it for five seconds. A beginner has to proceed at a slow pace and be prepared to ask himself questions. Is this what it appears to be? Is it repaired or repainted? Is the price reasonable? Do I really want or need it for my collection, or am I settling for it because I've wasted two hours of the dealer's time? Some people feel guilty when they walk out of an antique shop without buying anything. The dealer was so nice putting up with them browsing around all that time. They felt they just had to show their appreciation by dropping $20 or $30 before leaving. The fact is that browsing (with care, of course) is very common in antique shops and wherever collectors' items are sold. Everyone who comes into an antique shop is there to browse — not to buy things from a grocery list. The dealers expect you to browse. You are not being a nuisance unless you make unreasonable requests, such as having the dealer climb up and down a ladder a dozen times to get things off a high shelf. As long as you show courtesy, you will be welcome in the antique shops, whether or not you buy anything. Keep in mind, though, that the stocks in antique shops do not change too fast. If you gave the shop a thorough going-over on Monday, there's very little to be gained by heading back for the same purpose on Thursday. Put at least two weeks between your visits, preferably three, and you might notice a little movement.

So take it slow and take it easy. Pretend that you were a dealer and someone was offering you a particular piece of pottery. To buy it, you had to convince yourself that a profit could be made on it. Would it be worth your investment? Dealers do not buy emotionally. Whatever the item happens to be, regardless of its rarity or social significance, they think only in terms of whether the specimen is worth THEIR money. And so should you. Is the item worth your money? Is it going to be worthy of your collection, or will it tend to downgrade items already in your collection? It's often hard to say "no" when a specimen really appeals to you because of some minor flaw or doubt. But this is what you may need to do.

As you become an old hand at shopping in the antique stores, the "no" button in your brain will turn on much more easily. You will bypass things that a beginner might jump at, and you will do it with the sort of ease and nonchalance that you would not have dreamed possible when you were a beginner. The more you browse, the more you become hardened to the visual impact of each specimen. You become more and more difficult to impress.

Every antique shop is different, so it's difficult to make rules or give suggestions for browsing. In some, the stock is very well laid out and displayed, and you can inspect just about anything without going to the least trouble. It has always seemed a crime to have dim lighting in antique shops, but this is precisely what you will discover in many of them. There may be really a twofold reason for poor lighting, in the antique shops where this situation exists. The first reason is that dim "mood" lighting tends to give a suggestion of romance and adds to the appeal of the merchandise. The second, the scratches or other surface defects of antiques, especially furniture, are not as noticeable in dim lighting.

In smaller shops, you will often find that pottery and other breakables are displayed on wall shelves. When there isn't much room to move about in a shop without knocking into something, pottery and glass aren't too safe on anything but wall shelves. This is fine as long as the shelves are accessible, but all too often the ceiling is high and the items nearest the ceiling are just not clearly visible. When items are displayed in a locked glass cabinet, you are well within your rights to request that the case be opened to view something which especially interests you. Try, however, to make as good an inspection as you can, before asking for anything to be shown to you. It is usually possible, even with the obstruction of other merchandise around an item, or a dusty pane of glass, to determine if the item is top quality or not. If it does not look exactly right behind the glass or high up on the wall, it will probably look WORSE when you get it up close. On the other hand, something which appears absolutely perfect at a distance or behind a partial obstruction could prove less than perfect upon close examination. It might have its best side forward with an ugly crack, gash or peeling on the other side. There might be a chip on the base. This is why you have to look more closely. But be careful in asking to examine things that you cannot reach for yourself, that you do not reveal any great interest in them. Your manner should be casual at all times, as if you were truly doing nothing more browsing. Any sign of interest on your part could provoke a hard-line on price by the dealer, who knows very well that an eager customer is probably not thinking about the price at all. He wants the item at any price.

The primary questions to answer about any item encountered in an antique shop are:

• Does it suit the nature of my collection?
• Would it be satisfying for me to own?
• What is the condition?
• Is there any chance of it being a fake or reproduction?
• Is the price reasonable?

Let's briefly review these considerations in the order we presented them:

(1) Does it suit the nature of my collection? A specialist may occasionally go a bit outside the normal scope of his collecting for a really fine or unusual piece, as long as it bears SOME relation to the objects in his collection. If you collect art pottery, you would not want to "stretch" to the point of buying an 1825 water pitcher, since that bears no relation to your collection at all. But if you collect saucers made by a certain manufacturer, there would be nothing amiss in getting a few cups from that manufacturer, too — in fact it would be a big help for display purposes. As a general rule it is better to stay within the guidelines you've established for yourself no matter what sort of fabulous opportunities present themselves. However, just because something DOES suit your collection is not, in itself, a recommendation that you should buy it. Which takes us to point #2:

(2) Would it be satisfying for me to own? Depending on the type of pottery in which you specialize, you may encounter a great deal of specimens which would fit into the collection, yet are not of any particular interest to you. A hobbyist should not feel obligated to buy something just because it falls into his line. He's steering the direction of his collection, and he has to "call the shots" about what should go into it and what should stay out. This is what helps to give a collection its individuality. Two people with the exact same specialty will — or should — build different collections, because their tastes will not run in absolutely identical directions. Buying what suits your collection without stopping to think if it suits YOU is "museum philosophy." This is the way museums buy — adding one item on another in striving toward a specific goal. But museum buying is motivated differently than collector buying, so you should not apply the practices of museums or historical societies to your own buying activity. The museums have the public to please but you have only yourself to please.

(3) What is the condition? This is always an important consideration. Quite a bit of old pottery has been broken and repaired or otherwise restored. The item may look satisfactory, but if any repair work is present, its value is considerably less than an undamaged specimen. Most collectors are not interested in repaired pieces even when available at a big savings. The quality of a collection is judged to a large extent on its condition. The presence of even a few repaired items in a collection tends to dampen the whole collection, raising doubts about how many of the other items might be repaired, and just how careful the owner was in buying. It is definitely a sign of lack of discrimination to have repaired items in a collection. The only good excuse for repaired pieces is when the items are very old, very rare, or would be well beyond your financial range in good condition. Even then, it is unwise to overload a collection with repaired pieces. Such a collection is likely to become difficult to sell if you ever want to cash it in.

Repairs are sometimes obvious and sometimes difficult to detect. There may be traces of glue or the design may be muddled at the point of repair. The best advice that can be given is: if you suspect a repair, trust your instincts and do not buy the piece. Carry a magnifying glass along and do not feel embarrassed to use it. One with a lighting attachment will be even more helpful. These are not too expensive; they can be found in most hobby shops.

(4) Is there any chance of it being a fake or reproduction? The section on FAKES AND REPRODUCTIONS will delve more deeply into this aspect of buying.

(5) Is the price reasonable? "Reasonable" is not always easy to define. The item may not be listed in this book and possibly there is no published information on it — at least none which can claim to be current. If you do not personally have any knowledge of its value, it will probably be difficult for you to judge whether the price is fair. This is another one of the plusses of becoming a specialist collector and studying up as much as possible on the subject of your specialty. The more restricted your collecting gets, the greater your knowledge becomes as it zeros in on a smaller and smaller target. Even if you have never seen that particular piece offered for sale and know nothing about it, your knowledge of similar pieces will give you a clue about the value. You will know for example that the works of certain makers invariably sell higher than the works of other makers. Even if you are not sure of the price range into which an item should fall, you should be able to recognize a price which is considerably too high. If the price looks to be within the realm of reason, it is then YOUR choice about whether or not to take the chance of possibly paying 10% or 20% more than the item is really worth. If it's something needed for your collection and which may de difficult to find elsewhere, you will probably not object to paying more than the average market price. Even when a collector KNOWS what an item is selling for throughout the market (as reflected in this book), he will sometimes willingly pay more out of simple frustration. He's tried for ages to find a specimen without success, and figures — probably correctly — that inflation will being up the price even higher the next time around. All these points are to be considered. You want to get the most for your money. It's natural for antiques to sell for more in some places than in others. If you take the position of never paying more than the book value for anything, no matter what, you really place a handicap on yourself. Prices rise almost continually, and they rise because dealers often charge more than book values — and their customers pay more than book values.

Prices in antique shops are not necessarily above negotiation. Sometimes the prices are intentionally set high to allow a margin for "discussion." If you see that this is a pattern in any given shop with nearly every piece tagged for more than the book value, you can assume the prices are really just "asking prices" and that actual sales are made for somewhat less. Obtaining a discount in an antique shop is a matter of making a diplomatic approach, as well as giving the impression that you will become a steady customer (if you aren't already.) The dealers are much more willing to give special considerations to customers who will be back for more.

If you become a regular customer of a dealer who gives discounts, you will get them automatically without having to open the issue each time. He may simply add up your purchases and discount 10% or so of the cost. It isn't too common to receive a larger discount than 10%. This is all a matter of reading the dealer's habits and trying to get an insight on the way he does business. The more you buy at one time, the greater your discount may be. Therefore, if there are a dozen items in a shop that you know you definitely want, make this fact known and try to negotiate a price on the purchase as a whole. It may amount to saving more than piece by piece.

Except as an absolute last resort, do not place deposits on anything. If you do not have the cash to buy it outright on the spot and the dealer will not accept a check or credit card, do not make the purchase. You can try to start over and come back tomorrow for it, but do not leave a deposit. If you change your mind, you may not be able to get the deposit back. There have been some unpleasant experiences involving collectors who have left deposits.

There are various other possible sources for collectible pottery in addition to the antique shops. These include the auction sales, antique shows or fairs, garage sales, flea markets, charity bazaars and the classified section of your local newspaper (in which there may be ads from collectors disposing of their holdings.) The past year has brought a tremendous amount of collectible pottery on the market from all corners. Undoubtedly, the country's economic woes had something to do with this. Many people who really did not wish to sell their collections were forced to do so, because of unemployment. Whether there is mass selling, the result is always that collections are scattered far and wide; some dealers get overstocked and decline more purchases, so the sellers go elsewhere to find a willing buyer. As odd as it may sound, there are quite a few pawnshops in this country where you can find collectible ceramics. How it got there is anybody's guess, but it's there — and the prices tend to be a touch lower than in the mainstream of the antiques trade. In some cases, I think these pieces came out of the pawnbroker's attic and he just wants to move them along.

A word or two should be said on the subjects of bargains, which the average beginner thinks about quite a bit. Not only does he think in terms of bargains, but, sometimes, of making a fabulous find that would qualify for the newspapers headline: A Rare Old $1,000 Vase For 65¢. This is because beginners are slightly out of touch with the reality of the situation. Everyone who actively collects will strike a mild bargain now and then, even without looking for one. These fortunate buys will usually be counterbalanced by overpaying (intentionally) for pieces that you really want, and are willing to stretch a bit for. There are no collections built entirely on bargain buys — in fact no large collections in which more than 10% of the acquisitions could truly be said to be bargains. The great majority of pieces in any collection of American pottery were bought at or near the prevailing market values. Bargain-hunters are foiled because bargains and serious collecting are not compatible. The serious collector has to do most of his shopping at the antique stores, and in nearly all antique stores, the merchandise is priced right around its market value — give or take a little either way. The sources for bargains are the out-of-the-way outlets away from the antique trade, such as flea markets. And there you encounter the problem of hardly ever finding anything suitable for your collection. You run into good bargains, but it's invariably on types of pottery that you simply cannot use. Faced with the option of forming a good collection and paying the market prices or assembling a miscellaneous "bargain" collection, most hobbyists naturally choose to pay for what they get. As far as the fabulous finds are concerned, these are rare and becoming rarer! With so many collectors' items changing hands in this country every day, it's inevitable that once in a while something valuable will be sold for next to nothing. But that happens maybe once in a million sales or in ten million.

SELLING YOUR POTTERY

Fine American pottery and porcelain is always salable. If a collection has been assembled skillfully, avoiding damaged or other doubtful pieces, there will be no problem finding a buyer. Most dealers will be anxious to purchase pieces or the entire collection. They must buy in order to stay in business, and they much prefer buying from a private party than from an antique wholesaler. Additionally, there are other potential methods of selling, such as by auction sale, consignment, or a sale to a fellow collector. If you have the time and a little business flair, lists can be printed up and advertisements inserted in hobbyist magazines. These ads, even when very small, always draw response. Unfortunately, the careful thought and planning that goes into building up a collection are quite often missing when a hobbyist sells. Sales tend to be made haphazardly with the inevitable result that the price obtained is disappointing. Selling is an art, just as much as buying, and possibly even more so. The average person is perhaps somewhat handicapped in selling compared to a dealer, since he does not have the dealer's facilities and business connections. Generally, you may not be able to obtain the full current retail prices for the objects in your collection. Even so, it may still be possible to realize a profit on the collection, if the market has advanced steadily. This will be governed by your approach to selling, your knowledge of the pieces in your collection and of the pottery and porcelain market in general, and your faith in the quality of your collection. Determination is a vital ingredient in being a good seller. Just as you need to learn the word "no" in buying, when the circumstances are not quite favorable, so too does "no" come in handy for the seller. The first offer is not necessarily the best offer; it may be just a fraction of what could be obtained for the collection with a bit more effort. Yet, so many sellers automatically accept the first offer, especially if it happens to be made by a dealer.

The conditions under which a sale is made will always influence the price. If you need money in a hurry and decide to sell your pottery collection to raise it, this will almost certainly result in a loss. This is known as a "forced sale" and is usually carried out without doing any paperwork or getting comparative offers. Since it must be made in a hurry, this rules out the possibility of an auction sale or a sale to another collector. In the typical forced sale, the owner desperately wants to convert his collection into cash right away. This usually means a poorly done packing job with newspapers and grocery cartons, and a trip to the nearest antique dealer. The price obtained may be only half of what was put into the collection or even less. On many such occasions, the owner is not even aware of the extent of loss. He has kept no records of his cost and has not even bothered to make an estimate. He will generally, if he makes a rough guess at all, estimate his investment to be less than it actually was. This is especially true of collections which are large but contain mainly medium-value specimens. Those $10 and $20 purchases do not make much of a mental impression, but they add up. A hundred pieces at $20 each is a $2,000 collection, just the same as ten pieces at $200 each.

Many people making "forced sales" are still actively collecting and do not wish to part with their collection. Their collection is the last thing they want to sell, but they have no other liquid assets, nothing that will yield a sufficient amount of cash at a moment's notice. This is a bad spot to be in. It can generally be avoided if the collector does some planning. Enthusiasm in collecting is fine, but too much enthusiasm may mean that every spare dollar gets spent in furthering a collection. If all your money is in your collection, the collection becomes vulnerable to any emergency that might arise. So, anyone intending to become a serious collector — or who already is one — may want to diversify their holdings somewhat, and always have "something to fall back on." Your collection might grow a bit more slowly this way, but you will be providing valuable protection for it.

In addition to the "forced sale" problem, there is another problem standing in the way of many sellers realizing the maximum return. There is a common belief among so many collectors — and the public in general — that you must take a loss when you sell. There is some truth in this. If you buy a piece of Rookwood pottery today at the top of the market and pay $200, a sale to an antique dealer TOMORROW would result in a loss. He would probably pay you no more than $100, though this could vary depending on the specific circumstances. When you sell fast, you inevitably take a loss. (Unless, of course, you're a dealer — because then you've bought at the wholesale level and a fast sale is precisely what you want.) As time passes, however, the pendulum gradually swings in YOUR favor. If you hold that $200 purchase for a year, you no longer have a $200 item but one which is worth possibly $250, if the market has advanced that far. Five years from now it might be a $500 item, and so on. Therefore, when a dealer buys it from you, he will be basing his offer on the price he can charge for it NOW — not the price you paid at some point in the past. If it has increased in value into a $500 item, he will probably pay you at least $250 for it. In actuality this would not represent a profit for you, because national inflation would have eroded the spending power of money in the meantime. It would, though, bring you fairly close to the break-even point. And if the market advances at a stronger pace, so that (for example) your $200 purchase gets into the $500 category within three years, you almost certainly WILL make some kind of profit on it. There is no reason to believe that you must inevitably take a loss. Nonsense! Whether you profit or lose will depend on the quality of your material, the prices at which it was bought, the length of time held in your possession, and the skill with which you sell.

If building up a collection for 20 years, some of the pieces were bought rather recently, but the collection includes purchases made as long ago as the mid 1960's. At that time, the pottery and porcelain market was a mere shadow of its present self. Everything sold was an eye-popping bargain compared to prices of the 1980's! Chances are, most of the pieces you acquired in your first few years as a collector have risen 10 times in market value — or even more. When this kind of collection is offered for sale, it would need a very bad set of circumstances to FAIL to realize a profit. The longer your collection has been in the process of building, the better chance you stand of realizing a profit on it. Values on American pottery and porcelain do not move upward at an absolutely predictable pace. Some years they do better than others. Nevertheless, over the long pull (10 years, 20, 30), they have invariably multiplied many times over. This is because more and more collectors have become interested in American ceramics. Ten years ago there might have been 100 specimens of a piece, and 200 buyers for it; today there are probably no more than 80 specimens of it due to breakage, and 500 buyers. So if your collection has been building for quite some time, you will do well if you decide to sell it.

One of the standard adjuncts of collecting should be record-keeping. Not too many hobbyists keep records — then they reach a point when they wish they had! Records come in handy for your own personal use and for tax purposes, if you need to claim a capital loss on a sale. They need not be complicated or confusing. If you get a receipt for everything bought (and you should), you need only fill in the item's description on the receipt — or, even better, snap a picture of it and attach the picture to the receipt. Keep the receipts in a filing box, arranged by date. If you wish, you can also keep a running tabulation of the total sum spent on your collection. Just don't get frightened as the sum adds up! If you're buying wisely, you have just as sound an investment with American pottery and porcelain as with almost anything you could be buying.

Assuming you are not making a forced sale, you will want to review your collection and decide on the best selling procedure. The first question to answer is whether the collection should be sold intact, as it stands, or be broken up. In most cases, it proves wiser — not only in terms of convenience but from the financial viewpoint — to sell a private collection intact. There are exceptions, however. If a collection contains highly specialized material in two or more areas, it may be more profitable to split it up and sell each group as a collection in itself to a specialist dealer. For example, if you have a fantastic collection of shaving mugs and decorative porcelain eggs, it would be unlikely that any single dealer will have clients for both types of objects. A non-specialist dealer who buys such a collection will be buying with the idea of selling to ANOTHER dealer — and that naturally means two margins of profit tacked on instead of one. If you can find the right specialist dealer yourself, you will eliminate the middleman and the price received will certainly be higher. Chances are, if you have built up a highly specialized collection, you already know the locations of some dealers. If not, you could try checking the advertisement pages in the monthly hobbyist periodicals, available at your local public library. Many pottery and porcelain dealers run ads in these magazines, and all are willing to transact business by mail or freight.

Another reason for breaking up a collection would be to "weed out" pieces of very low value or anything of a questionable status which might be a reproduction. Don't feel too bad if your collection contains some of these; nearly all collections do. Even the great J. Pierpont Morgan, who owned sixty million dollars worth of art and antiques had some items in his collection which were — shall we say — embarrassing. If sold in the average neighborhood antique shop, the presence of such items should not hurt the sale. But if sold in a posh shop of the Madison Avenue or Beverly Hills variety, you would be well advised to make some deletions if necessary. The swank dealers want to maintain a high level of quality in everything they buy. When a collection contains doubtful or very inexpensive, common specimens, they may decline to buy it just for that reason.

The presence of any damaged or obviously repaired items is very detrimental to the sale of a collection. It gives the impression that the owner did not have very high standards in putting the collection together, and it takes some of the glamor away from the attracting items. Hold back your damaged or repaired items unless they date before 1800 or happen to be very famous pieces of high value. These may prove to be "collection polluters." Throw them out if necessary!

Prior to actually offering your collection for sale, it should be thoroughly cleaned up if necessary. Pottery and porcelain gathers dust rapidly, and dusty specimens do not make quite as favorable as impression as bright gleaming ones. Also, they plant the notion (in the buyer's mind) that you owned them for ages and ages, and probably have very little cash investment in them. Bright shiny specimens look like they were bought very recently at the top of the market. This is one of the little details of selling that falls under the heading of "psychology." The dealers use plenty of psychology in selling — why shouldn't a collector? See the section on CARE AND STORAGE for specific recommendations.

It should be mentioned that presentation — not just in terms of cleanliness — is important in selling a collection, especially if the collection is brought to an antique dealer for a cash offer. You will notice that dealers try to make effective presentations of their merchandise — by putting their most eye-catching things in the shop window or close to a good light. They make an arrangement in the shop — even if it's woefully overcrowded — which intrigues the beholder. Yet so many collectors, when selling, totally ignore presentation and just "cart it over." If your specimens arrive in the dealer's shop jumbled together in boxes, he is surely going to assume they mean very little to you. If you valued them highly, wouldn't you carefully pack them up to make sure no harm came to them? By the same token, poor presentation gives the impression that you're prepared to sell for any amount, that you were planning just a one-way trip with no intention of taking the material back home. Paper wrapping is acceptable if you use thick wads of newspaper and SEAL each bundle with tape. The packing should be done almost as carefully as if the items were intended for shipment.

Another thing you will definitely want to do before selling is to calculate the current retail market values of everything you own. As mentioned earlier, this is going to be different — perhaps vastly different — than the amount paid for them. So you should have two sets of figures: one of your cost prices and another of the values as they stand today. Both of these tabulations will be useful to you. Knowing your cost for the collection as a whole will tell you if you're making a profit on the sale; and, if not, just how far short you're falling. Knowing the current market values will tell you if the dealer is being reasonable in his offer. It's possible that an offer could represent a profit for you, and still fall into the "unreasonable" category. You might be entitled to a much larger profit. Without knowing your cost (or investment) and the current market situation, you're literally flying blind. This book should assist you in calculating the current retail value of your collection. It may be difficult or impossible to arrive at a precise figure, but even if you end up with a range — say $3,000 to $3,500 — this certainly beats taking a wild guess. There are few precise values for any collectors' items, which is why we've presented ranges throughout the listing section of this book.

When you figure up current retail values, be objective! If a specimen is listed at $60 to $80 in fine condition but yours is less than fine, don't calculate it at $60 to $80! This will give you a false impression of the value, and just about ANY offer made by a dealer will seem unfairly low. This also applies if you have incomplete or mismatched sets. Whenever anything deviates from the norm, its sales value is reduced. You may need to examine your pieces a bit more closely than you've ever examined them in the past to judge their actual retail value.

Now you have another question to answer. Armed with the knowledge of your collection's current market value, what would constitute a fair offer on the part of a dealer? Possibly an offer that would be fair and honest from a dealer would still not be satisfactory to you if it represents a loss on your investment. In that case, you will want to explore the possibility of selling in some other way, which of course is always an option available to you.

The offers made by dealers do vary. If you took your collection to ten different dealers, you would probably get ten different offers — and perhaps you would encounter one or two dealers who were just not buying right now. The reason for differences in offers many times has nothing to do with the knowledge or honesty of the dealer. Some dealers can buy slightly higher than others because they do a faster turnover. Also, a dealer who makes a specialty of the exact type of pottery or porcelain you own is certain to offer a higher price than a nonspecialist. Then, too, there are some dealers who get shaky about putting money into rarities and esoteric pieces. They recognize and appreciate the value of these items, but the big question mark is whether their customers will buy. There are antique dealers who stock only items under $100 apiece — and there are some who stock practically nothing under $100. This is all a matter of the dealer's location, reputation, and the class of clientele that does business in his shop. Some dealers tell you — and probably very truthfully — that they could not sell the Hope Diamond for $200, because nobody with $200 to spend ever comes in their shop. The overall size of your collection will be a factor, too. If you have a really huge collection, a dealer with limited floor space will probably make a low offer, figuring he'll have to place part of the collection in storage for a while or resell it to another dealer. Sometimes when a dealer with a crowded shop buys a large collection, he sends off a portion to an auctioneer. Naturally, this means a lower price for you, since he will leave himself a wide margin of leeway to compensate for a disappointing auction result.

If we totaled up all the American pottery and porcelain of all types being sold to dealers, either separately or in collections, the average price would be around 50% of retail. Buying offers higher than 50% of retail do occur. These are usually the result of an exceptionally fine piece or collection which the dealer is confident of reselling without any trouble. When a dealer has a waiting customer or customers for certain pieces within a collection, this naturally influences his offer. He may pay 60% of the market value for these pieces or even more. If the dealer has advertised certain pieces in the newspaper and sold them out quickly, he will be looking to replenish his stock — and will usually pay a premium to do so. Any of these circumstances could be responsible for a buying offer which exceeds 50% of the established market average. Some may be apparent to you, before approaching the dealer, but others (such as whether that dealer has a waiting customer for some of your specimens) are beyond your capability to know. Thus you may fail to approach the one dealer in town who would give a really satisfactory price — just because you are not already acquainted with him.

Buying offers of less than 50% of the current market value also occur, ranging down to about 40% and sometimes even less. These also have various causes behind them: the dealer is not enthusiastic about pottery and porcelain; has limited space; feels the collection has a number of slow-moving pieces in it; and so on. If you receive offers of less than 50% of market value from several dealers, it's time to start wondering if you have correctly tabulated the value.

Fifty percent in itself seems unfairly low to many sellers, who are not acquainted with the antique business. They feel that if a dealer is honest he should be paying much closer to the retail value. Paying 70% would still leave him a healthy margin of profit, they conclude, as it would amount to $30 on an item salable for $100, and $150 on a $500 item. This sounds good but in practice it just doesn't work that way. The simple fact of the matter is that the difference between the dealer's buying and selling prices is NOT his margin of profit! Before he reaches the point of making a profit on anything he sells, he must not only gain back the investment but, also, meet his expenses: his utility bills, phone, shop rent, employee salaries and other costs. In the average antique business, these expenses total up nearly as high as the cost of buying stock. So when the dealer buys from you at 50% of the current market value, his actual profit when selling the item (or collection) may only amount to around 10% or less. Since these miscellaneous expenses of doing business continually go up, dealers' buying offers naturally come down. The only other alternative is for the dealer to charge more when he sells. That would be fine, if he could count on his customers paying a slight increase over the retail market values. But the antique business is competitive, too, so the dealer who habitually charges more is apt to lose customers to his rival down the road.

When selling to a dealer, prepare yourself for the typical reception that sellers receive. Dealers are showmen to an extent. There are knacks to buying just like selling, and the dealers know them all. They will not appear really interested or enthusiastic about anything you show them (which is a good rule for you to follow, when you buy in their shops.) This is a part of the normal routine. It's designed to soften the blow of a low offer. If the dealer appeared to really like your merchandise, you would wonder why he was offering so little. The tone of voice matches the expression. The dealer adopts the attitude of "well I guess I can take it off your hands." Don't be fooled by this. He probably knows to the dollar how much every piece is worth. He can recognize quality. If his offer is low, it is not because he's out of touch with the current standing of the market. It's simply because he's not a collector! He looks at the merchandise offered to him in terms of what it can do for him today in his shop. He would do the same with a Rembrandt canvas.

Just as the dealer plays his part in this mini-drama, you must also play your part. Your part is that of a fully-informed owner who would gladly pack up his valuables and go elsewhere, if the price is not satisfactory. Don't seem anxious. Play it cool and calm. Show that you know the values by talking with the dealer and mentioning the strong points of each piece as he examines it.

Make it like a club meet where everybody is casual. And if the offered price is not to your liking, and you have reason to believe another might offer more, by all means do not accept!

If the dealer attempts to pick and choose, rather than making an offer for the collection as a whole, a polite "no, thank you" is usually in order. The "pick and choose" dealers try to purchase the three or four most salable items from a collection — the things they know they can turn over in a hurry. Even if the offered price for these pieces is in the 60% or 65% of retail area, you would be well advised not to sell, but wait until you can find a buyer for the whole collection. With its best attractions gone, the collection will not be as appealing to ANY potential buyer, and you might have a difficult time selling it for a fair sum.

The question is often asked by prospective sellers: Is it better — or worse — to sell to a dealer from whom you've been buying? Most people would probably assume that a dealer who hasn't already seen and handled the merchandise would be a better prospect — that it will just seem like "old hat" to a dealer from whom you bought some of the pieces. Actually, all other things being equal, a dealer with whom you're acquainted and from whom you've done some buying is apt to offer a better price. The merchandise you bought from him is like an old friend to him. He's already checked it out and knows its condition. And since he was successful in selling it once, he will be more confident of successfully selling it this time around. A dealer who has not handled any of your pieces might not have ever handled ANY pieces similar to them — and be wondering just how well they would do in his shop. The greater the margin of doubt, the lower his offering price will be! The only possible drawback in selling to a dealer you know is that he's aware of your cost prices on some of the material. He is, that is, if his memory stretches back that far. If you bought some of the pieces from him ten years ago, he knows that you paid a small fraction of their current values. But he also knows, by the same token, that you're a serious long-standing collector, and that the quality of your holdings should be as good as anything he'll ever encounter. If you sell to a dealer with whom you've been a steady customer, don't lead him to believe that he won't be seeing you any longer. If he believes you're going to continue buying from him in the future, he might be inspired to make the price somewhat better to keep you thoroughly satisfied. This won't be a lie either. Most hobbyists who sell their collections soon begin another one, whether they have any plans of doing so or not — either on the same theme or something else. So when you comment that you'll "never give up collecting," the odds are very good that this will prove correct.

Instead of selling TO a dealer, you can sell THROUGH a dealer. This is known as consignment selling. You don't get fast cash this way, but in the long run you stand a chance to do better than by selling outright. In selling on consignment, you place your collection (or even just a single item, if it's worthwhile) with the dealer, and you and he agree on prices for each specimen. The material is exhibited in the shop, along with the dealer's regular stock. Customers are not aware that YOU own it — or even that it's being shown on consignment. They just assume it to be part of the dealer's ordinary line. As sales are made, the dealer makes a record of them. At the end of the consignment period, which is always a minimum of one month and can go much longer, you receive payment for the items sold and you also get back the unsold pieces. There are sure to be some of both! Some dealers do not enter into consignment selling but the majority of them do — in fact the number of active consignment sellers is increasing steadily. This really represents an ideal way for most dealers to do business, since they need not make any investment in stock. They pay for their stock only after selling it, which is the sort of arrangement that few merchants can resist whatever their line of business. The advantage for you as the owner is that you can price most consigned items above the usual 50% of retail that you would receive in an outright sale. Some can be priced at 60% and others possibly at 65%. Of course, this is simply your share of the proceeds. The dealer (without any suggestions from you) decides on the actual price to appear on each piece. If, for example, he agrees to take a consigned article at $100, he would place it out on sale at perhaps $175 or $185. When it sells, you would receive $100 and he would get the difference between $100 and the actual selling price. The dealer will require you to name a price for each item before accepting it on consignment. If you simply say, "Just do your best in selling it," he will not accept it. Also, the dealer has the option of turning away any items he feels you have priced too high. Before doing this he will give you an opportunity to lower your prices. If your prices are too close to the current retail market, say 80% or 90%, this does not leave him enough margin. He does not need to work with as large a margin on consigned merchandise since he is taking no risk on it but he wants a margin better than 20%. So if you figure in the neighborhood of 60% to 65% you should be right on target, both for yourself and for the dealer. Of course, you have no way of knowing how much the sale is actually made for, unless you're personally acquainted with the customer! A dealer could conceivably agree to sell an item for you for $50, then get $300 for it. This is not very likely to happen, however, if you're informed of the current values.

Once the 30-day consignment period has expired, the dealer may request that you leave the merchandise with him for another month. He may in fact offer a little inducement for you to do so, such as a 5% bonus or something along those lines. If the dealer does not have much stock of his own, he will not be anxious to part with consigned pieces. In this situation, it's all up to you. If he's been fairly successful in making sales during that initial 30-day period, you would probably be doing the right thing thing by "signing up" for another month. On the other hand, if he's sold only 3 or 4 pieces out of 50, he may only sell a few during the following month. If you decide to take your unsold pieces back, he may at that point offer to buy them at a 10% or 15% discount from the consignment prices.

When leaving items on consignment, obtain a receipt on which each item is listed, along with the price you're to receive in the event of a sale. The receipt should be signed by both parties.

If you do not live near a dealer who specializes in pottery and porcelain, you may want to investigate the possibility of selling to a dealer in another state. This is especially true if you have a highly specialized collection, which may not be quite right for any of the local dealers but ideal for one in another part of the country. Such transactions can be handled by mail with the initial contact made by a phone inquiry. Of course, in these situations it pays to have a list of your items prepared, so you can send it to the dealer or read it over the phone. He will want to know the overall size of your collection; its highlights in terms of the most valuable pieces; and, even if only roughly at the beginning, the price you expect to receive. A collection of pottery presents more of a challenge to ship than some other types of collectors' items, but with care and the use of sturdy packing materials this can be done safely. There should be a prior agreement about who will pay the shipping charges. A dealer who asks to see your collection for possible purchase ought to be willing to reimburse your shipping expenses, whether he buys the collection or not.

Another possible method of sale is by the auction sale route. Billions of dollars worth of collectors' items are auctioned in the U.S. every year at sales ranging from black-tie affairs to small rural gatherings. Just about any auctioneer who handles collectors' items will accept a collection of pottery and porcelain, provided he does not have a restrictive line of specialization. Some auctioneers deal only in stamps, others in coins, and others just in printed material. But most of them gladly take anything that comes along, if it has some sale potential.

Most collectors like to buy at auction, but the thought of selling at auction chills their spine. It seems like nothing more than a gamble — and in many cases, that's precisely what it is! Unless the auctioneer agrees to let you place "reserves" on your material, that is, minimum selling prices, there is nothing to prevent a really disappointing sale at which prices are 30% or 40% of the market averages. And you won't even get that 30% or 40%, since the auctioneer's commission has to be taken out first! But, like any gamble, there is also the chance of doing much better than you possibly could be selling outright to a dealer. At many auctions of collectors' items, SOME of the lots sell for more than dealers are charging, just because of heavy competition between bidders. If an item with a "book" value of $100 goes up to $150 at auction, you will receive more than the full retail value for it — even after the house skims off its commission. This would be impossible in selling to a dealer, or in selling on consignment. You stand the chance of doing very well, moderately well, or taking a beating!

Can anything be done to make the gamble less of a gamble, other than using reserve selling prices (which most auctioneers will not allow)?

In a way, yes. You can choose your auctioneer carefully. Some auctioneers consistently obtain better prices at their sales than others. This is not a matter of luck. They run a more polished operation with good catalogues and extensive promotion. Before placing any items with an auctioneer, check the results of his recent sales (if possible.) If necessary, buy a few of his priced sale catalogues — which should not run more than $10 or $15. These provide an education in themselves. See whether that auctioneer has sold items similar to yours within recent months — and, if so, how much they brought in relation to dealer prices. If the auctioneer has not sold any pottery or porcelain in a long time (longer than six months,) you can pretty safely assume that his clients include few buyers of this material. Therefore, this would not be a favorable place for selling your collection. You may not be able to locate a house that specializes in pottery and porcelain, but there should be no trouble finding one that sells it regularly along with other collectors' items. Of course, if you have a large valuable collection, the major international houses such as Sotheby, Christie, and Phillips, all of whom have U.S. offices, would be the logical choice. To be acceptable for auction by one of these major companies, your collection would need to consist of many pieces worth $200 and more, and a minimum of items valued under $100. There is sometimes a "minimum commission" charged by these large houses which makes the sale of lots for under $100 unprofitable. Commission rates vary but do not be deceived on this point. The houses charging the lowest commissions usually have the lowest overhead, which means unillustrated catalogues, very little in the way of advertising, and LOW sale realizations.

When a collection is handed over to an auctioneer for sale, you have no control on what happens to it from that point onward. You cannot decide to withdraw it from sale, once the contract has been signed. And you can't tell the auctioneer how to set up the sale either. If he wants to make ten lots out of 100 items, ten to a lot, this is entirely his privilege. Unless all the items in your collection are fairly valuable, and in excellent condition, chances are good that the auctioneer will do some bulk lotting. Even at the smaller local sales, there is no desire to have lots sell very cheaply. Selling everything individually prolongs the sale and half the bidders leave before it's over. Remember, the auctioneer is a businessman. He may not know antiques as well as you do but he knows the best approaches to selling them. Since you're both sharing in the proceeds, the better he can do for himself means automatically that you'll do better. So don't be too disturbed if you see 7 or 8 of your prized teacups grouped together in a single lot.

Some auctioneers give cash advances before the sale. Most of them don't. They consider it very risky to give a cash advance because auctions are so uncertain. When an advance is given, it will represent a small fraction of the appraised value, in the vicinity of 20%. This way the merchandise can sell for half of its market value and the auctioneer is still within his "safe" range, if he's working with a 15% or 20% commission. For example:

Collection's market value	$1,000
20% cash advance (of the value)	200
Collection selling price	500
20% dealer commission (of the selling price)	− 100
	400
The 20% that was already advanced to you	− 200
The amount still to be paid to you	200

Payment is made by the auctioneers within 30 to 60 days following the sale. This seems like a long waiting period, but the auctioneers argue that their clients take a long while to pay THEM.

Along with the payment, you will receive a list of the lots you owned and prices for each of them individually. You would do well to add this up and make sure there has been no errors in the auctioneer's arithmetic.

Timing is also a consideration in selling by auction. If you're selling when the national economy and the market for your particular prices is really strong, you will probably do better via the auction route. During these periods, more investors than normal come into the market and pump up the competition at collectors' auctions. Also, there are more dealers buying at auction when the market is hot, as they're anxious to replenish their stocks. The competitive bidding between collectors, investors and dealers can result in some surprisingly high figures. On the other hand, when the economy and the market for pottery and porcelain is sluggish, auction selling is probably less favorable than selling outright to a dealer or in some other fashion.

There is also another point to be considered concerning timing. Sales made at certain times of the year tend to be more successful than at others. In the northern and eastern parts of the country, sales made from the late fall to late winter are usually the most profitable, from about the end of

November to the beginning of March. In areas which have a great deal of summer tourist traffic, the summer months are just as attractive for selling as the winter — and maybe even more so. Remember that in consigning your collection for sale by auction, there is usually quite a long waiting period before it gets sold. It has to be catalogued and advertised, and the catalogues must be distributed well in advance of the auction. There could be a three or four month gap between the contract signing and the sale, though usually the interval is not quite this long. Therefore, to hit the peak season (if you're aiming for late fall to late winter,) get your material into the auctioneer's hands right at the beginning of the fall season. September is the best month to sign an auction contract!

Yet another possibility is selling to a private collector. This can be very lucrative, if you find a willing buyer. Since a private collector need not think about "profit margin," he can pay you more than a dealer. However, in selling to a private individual, you should not ask the full retail value, but offer a discount in the region of 10% or 15% to stimulate interest. If a collector was prepared to give full retail, he could just as well buy from a dealer! The hobbyists who buy from other collectors expect to get some kind of break in the price. You will still do very well this way, because the difference between a "dealer" price and a "collector" price is considerable. Finding the right buyer may not be easy though. The usual approach is to run classified ads in your local newspaper. If a local purchaser can be found, it eliminates the headache of packing and shipping. But there may be one in your area who would be willing to buy a collection of pottery and porcelain. The larger the collection is, the more difficult it will be to find a private buyer. On the other hand, if you have just a few choice pieces to dispose of, you may make the sale as soon as the newspaper hits the stands.

While you're considering all of the above selling possibilities, also think about whether you really want to sell NOW or wait a while longer. If there is no pressing need to sell, you are almost certain to do better financially by waiting. The value of American pottery and porcelain normally rises in value faster than the rate of national inflation. After converting your collection into cash, you have something which goes DOWN in value each year instead of going up.

CARE AND REPAIR

While it is true that pottery is fragile in terms of vulnerability to breakage, it is more durable in other respects than many other collectors' items. If handled with reasonable care, porcelain and pottery can be used enjoyed throughout the owner's lifetime. The material does not deteriorate with age. Nor in fact does its surface decoration. The fading seen on old pottery is not the result of "old age" but of rough handling, harsh cleaning, or long exposure to direct sunlight or excessive heat. If these dangers are avoided, there is no reason for pottery not to retain its original condition for an indefinite length of time.

Although this article is titled Care and Repair, a good deal more stress needs to be placed on caring for ceramic items. Repairing is difficult to do successfully. A broken piece can usually be repaired, but its value as a collectors item can seldom be reattained. Many hobbyists are not interested in repaired specimens and will not buy them at any price. A repair can improve *appearance,* and it may salvage a bit of sales value. But this is about all that can be accomplished by repair. This means that the hobbyist must safeguard his specimens against breakage and also take care to avoid buying repaired pieces. There are no bargains in repaired pottery. An item is either damaged or not damaged. If damaged, its value is fractionally compared to that of a sound example, and unless very old or very scarce, it may not be desired in a collection. You will have little difficulty in recognizing most types of repair work. On figurines, smaller detailing calls for special examination to see that fingers or portions of costuming have not been replaced.

As far as tableware and utility items are concerned, applied handles are in a class of their own. Since these were not an integral part of the product, but merely glued on or attached with slip before firing, it is often acceptible if they come off and need to be glued back on. If this is skillfully done, there is no reason why anyone would even know the difference. Successful reattachment of applied handles means perfect alignment and — very important — the use of an extra-strong bonding cement. Traditionally, model-maker's or Duco cement was recommended for this purpose, but even stronger glues are now available. There is an art to making this kind of repair. If too much glue is applied, the excess will be noticeable on the surface. Do not sand the pieces before gluing, because this will interfere with the fit. The replaced handle must of course be held in place until the glue dries. This can be done manually if a quick-drying glue is used. Otherwise it will be necessary to use rubberbands as a clamp, and you may need someone to help you in applying them. Do not make the mistake of underestimating drying time. If the tube states 10 minutes, allow 15 or 20 minutes and add more time if the weather or indoor atmosphere is humid. (Dry air helps promote the drying of glue.)

Much of the porcelain and pottery, even good art pottery, passing through the hands of antique dealers and other sources needs cleaning. Dealers often clean pieces themselves, which is the logical thing do do since it adds to the sales appeal. However, some dealers have little time or are short of labor, and sell things exactly as they arrive. At flea markets, garage sales, and other secondary sources outside of the usual antique trade, the percentage of specimens needing cleaning is much higher. Much of the merchandise has come straight from attics or other storage areas, where it has been untouched for 10, 20 or more years. The majority of sellers have not even bothered to pass a dry cloth over them. There is no reason to avoid buying pieces which need cleaning, if the price is attractive. Sometimes you may get a good buy this way. Of course, you will want to determine whether the surface dirt and grime is possibly hiding evidence of repair work or of fading. When specimen is very heavily solied, it may be difficult to judge its real condition until after cleaning. In these cases, it may be wise to think twice about the purchase. Such buys represent a gamble.

Porcelain cleans up a bit easier than most other ceramics, because the surface is harder and less porous and therefore more resistent to dirt and grime. In dealing with unglazed wares whose decoration might be water-soluble, dry wiping with a cloth, which will remove dust, may have to suffice. This sort of pottery is far in the minority, fortunately. Most pottery can be washed, and washing will produce a far better result than any other cleaning technique.

Some hobbyists make a routine practice of cleaning every ceramic object they acquire, whether it appears to need it or not. Their philosophy is that full brilliance can be brought only by scrupulous cleanliness, and it is obviously quite true that very few specimens are immaculately clean when purchased. Even if the seller has done some kind of cleaning, it might have been very elementary just to remove the obvious dark spots or streaks. And if the object has been on the dealer's shelf six months after being cleaned, it has already begun building up a fresh layer of dust. Some cleaning may be too harsh for delicate objects. So use the following outline for proper cleaning procedures.

This procedure is designed for ceramics with hard, non-porous surfaces. It may need to be modified slightly to suit special pieces.

We will presume that the piece to be cleaned is rather heavily soiled. It may leave soil marks on the fingers when picked up. And if you're new to pottery-cleaning, you may have doubts that it can be really effectively cleaned. Usually on such an item, several types of soiling are involved. Next to the surface itself is grime resulting from handling by former owners, possibly in the far distant past. This base grime may be intermingled with grease which has attracted dust.

First, the specimen must be cleaned as much as possible before washing it. If washed in this condition the process may be complicated and prolonged, and the item may not get quite as brilliantly clean as it has the potential to be. Much care must be taken when washing ceramic items. Scrubbing is not the way to clean fine ceramics. What can be achieved by cleaning depends on the piece. If the object carries a great deal of gold gilding, especially gold tracery which is thin, wispy and fragile, it must be cleaned with exceptional care for those areas. Any sort of rubbing during the cleaning procedure could scratch some of its gilding. Judge each piece individually and be content, when necessary, with the progress made by a dry cleaning. In dry cleaning, you will remove most of the surface dirt without taking any risk of damage. Wet cleaning means more thorough cleaning but, for some specimens, poses a certain danger and maybe better if not done.

Assuming the piece is to be washed, you can start by feather-dusting the loose surface particles. Having dusted on all sides, the next step is to go in with a smaller soft-bristled brush which can be maneuvered more delicately. Ideal for this purpose is an artist's camel-hair brush, a really necessary piece of equipment for all ceramic hobbyists. Such brushes are not inexpensive, but they last virtually a lifetime. Buy one with the brush at least half an inch wide, or preferably three-quarters of an inch. If made of genuine camel hair it may cost anywhere from $10 to $15. Synthetic brushes are not recommended. The hairs are stiffer and they have a tendency to shed. Virtually all adhering surface particles can be removed with an artist's brush. When this is finished, the item should already look much cleaner. This is followed (when practical) by washing. There are differences of opinion on the best approach to wet cleaning, and the collector is at liberty to choose whichever is best for his specimens. Under no circumstances, however, should bleach or other potent cleaning agents be used. Nor should boiling water, and of course collectible tableware (or other pottery) should not be placed in an automatic dishwasher. Hot water can be used up to a temperature of about 160 degrees.

The first step in washing should be to soak the object in plain warm or moderately hot water for a few minutes without soap. This serves to loosen the inevitable coating of oils and grease which are locking in grime. These oils may become quite hard and fixed, and can cause smearing if not broken down at this stage of the operation. Dunk the item a few times in a basin of hot sudsy water. You should notice the surface becoming much cleaner and brighter. This is the point when rubbing can be done, very gently, if the occasion seems to call for it. Use a cloth rag dipped in the washing water. If some dirt remains, it's better to start over (rinse, then wash again) rather than continuing to scrub. The final step is to rinse several times in warm water. Do not hold the item under running tap water — it could slip out of your hand.

Ceramic items which have been washed can be towel-dried, but be careful not to use a linty towel. Leave the item to air out for a few hours before replacing it in your collection. You should be aware that water can be trapped inside figurines and cause deterioration to unglazed surfaces inside if the water is left in contact with it for a period of time. If you rinse and drain the figurines thoroughly, there should be no problem. Some older figurines may have large vent holes which allow for sufficient draining, but other pieces sometimes have solid bases with small vent holes placed in inconspicuous locations. These holes may be small enough to allow water in, but, of course, they might be too small to allow the water to get out or to let it evaporate. You might want to plug these holes during the washing process to prevent this from occurring.

In displaying your collection, always consider preservation first and foremost, well above the desire to make a spectacular display (which is inherent in all collectors.) Hanging plates on a wall create an attractive display, but be sure the hooks in the wall are secure and the hanging fixtures properly installed. Check the hanger itself and avoid those with sharp or rough edges which could cause abrasion to the gold trim on your plates. Safe hangers are available but not every giftshop has them, you may need to search a bit to get them. Figurines and ceramics in general (including plates) can be kept on wall shelves or in cabinets, depending on your circumstances and preference. Cabinets eliminate the possible danger of a shelf collapsing, and if the cabinet has glass doors it will accomplish yet another purpose: keeping out most dust particles. Your pottery will stay cleaner much longer behind glass. It can be viewed to its maximum advantage by installing a lighting fixture inside the cabinet, an easy task for anyone with do-it-yourself skills. A flouresent light is best, since it spreads the light better and does not generate much heat. About 25 watts is sufficient, even for a large cabinet.

CONDITION STANDARDS

The condition of an item is of great importance in determining its value. To be considered in mint condition, the following must apply:

(1) No worn or missing spots on gold trim;
(2) Decoration not faded or discolored;
(3) No chips, cracks, or repairs;
(4) No noticeable scratching of surfaces.

Damage is more acceptable on some types of items than others. For example, an eggshell-thin Belleek bowl with a ruffled rim is almost expected to have a few rough spots on the rim, and such flecks really do not affect the value to a substantial degree. On ironstone, however, less than perfect condition is not acceptable, for there is an ample supply of perfect samples.

Crazing (the appearance of tiny lines covering the surface of items) is considered normal for many types of lower-level wares. Lenox and the other better porcelains usually are not crazed, and the rare item that shows up with this type of flaw should be examined for possible repairs. Crazing is caused by unequal expansion of bisque and glaze, and the companies spent a great deal of time and money developing formulas that would expand at the same rate. When an item is repaired, the repairer has no idea of the precise formula a company used and the result can be crazing.

Firing cracks do not affect the value as much as other cracks. Certain types of items, figurines in particular, suffer from firing cracks to a great extent.

Whether to repair a damaged item or not is a very individual decision, since in some cases the cost of the repair can exceed the value of the item (especially in the $100 and down range.) Items which have been heavily damaged can almost never be restored to original condition. In addition, if the repair is easy to spot, the value of the item will be down in the range of an unrestored piece. Repairs on undecorated Belleek-type items tend to be particularly easy to spot, since the repairer can never match the color of the china exactly.

The best items to have repaired are ones which are covered with hand-painting, since the person doing the repair work can cover over the repair with paint. These repairs are hard to see and such items are frequently sold as perfect. (Sometimes the fingers can feel what the eye can't see, so always run your hands over an item to feel for subtle differences in thickness of the china or in the texture of the glaze. Look for differences from one part of an item to another—for example, see if both hands on a figurine are the same color, texture, and degree of fineness.)

FAKES AND REPRODUCTIONS

Whenever collectors' items are discussed, the question of fakes naturally arises. They occur in every sphere of "collectibles," Since the opportunity to produce them is, to some individuals, irresistable. Fortunately, the field of American porcelain and pottery is not beset with fakes to nearly the extent of many other collecting areas. The simple fact is that pottery is not easy to reproduce, if we talk in terms of reproductions that would mislead an informed buyer. By the same token, it does not offer quite as much financial inducement for the faker, compared to the profits on (say) a single gold coin rarity. Nevertheless, it would be a mistake for the collector to let down his guard, because faked and doctored pieces *will* turn up from time to item. Their existence should not discourage anyone from enjoying this appealing hobby. Any thinking collector can swing the odds strongly in his favor against ever buying a piece which later proves to be "bad." Knowledgeable dealers are the front line of defense. They act as a filter between the collector and the vast array of pottery traveling through the market. Though criticisms are often pointed toward them, and sometimes justly, the specialist dealers *do* make an effort to protect their reputations, and at the same time they protect their customers. In addition to habitually buying from recognized dealers, a hobbyist can increase his chance of avoiding fakes by beefing up his own personal knowledge of pottery. The human eye and brain are still, in this age of electronic gadgetry, the most effective tools of detection. An ability to spot fakes and items which are potentially questionable is an acquired skill, which anyone can acquire. In fact, as an active collector you will probably acquire it, whether you want to or not. Just in the normal course of examining pieces, studying them, comparing them in the shop or the museum, and becoming familiar with the items in your collection, your knowledge will quickly reach the expert level. No one is born with knowledge of collectibles, and there is no innate talent attached to it. All experts are merely people who have carefully looked, studied, thought, and listened.

In pottery, there are several types of fakes to be wary of. The beginner tends automatically to think of a fake as a specimen made from scratch to imitate a genuine piece. Objects of this sort are produced, but are less plentiful (and usually less convincing) than doctored fakes. A doctored fake is a genuine object which the faker changes by applying a false mark, decoration or design. Doctored fakes are easier to make, and are somewhat more convincing because the piece is professionally made and (in most cases) genuinely old. Unlike total fakes, a doctored piece may have some slight value, but usually far less than asking price.

Fakes of different kinds of ceramics are still being produced, but there is apparently no organized trade in them, unlike the situation that prevails with ancient artifacts, Japanese arms and armor. There is no centralized point of manufacture and no underworld network channeling them through the market. It is simply piecemeal work, much of it very poor, and a good deal almost certainly the work of innocent persons who have no intent of defrauding anyone. Someone who is not a serious collector may, for example, repaint or regild an item just to improve its appearance — this could be done as a hobby in itself. But when the piece has gone back to the market, there is danger of confusion. An uninformed antique shopper does not take all the possibilities into account. He sees an object at its face value and presumes that everything *old* is *original* — just the way it left the manufacturer's factory.

The present generation of collectors is far more attuned to pitfalls in buying, than their predecessors of 20, 30 or 50 years ago. In the past, a cavalier attitude prevailed. Few people knew, or really wanted to know, the origin and history of the antiques they bought. This was true not only of pottery but Old Master oil paintings for which thousands of dollars were paid. Though it may come as something of a shock, the old-time dealers were partially responsible for building up the population of fakes. In the antique trade of the 1920's and 1930's, especially in rural areas, it was a common practice for dealers to "improve" the merchandise passing through their hands. This encompassed not only repair and restoration, but, for example, adding engraved inscriptions on silver plate and dates on country furniture. A good deal of American ceramics was tampered with by the trade, in those Alice-in-Wonderland days. It was not considered deception, but simply "keeping the customer satisfied." Of course these objects are mostly still in existence, and the antique dealers of today are not at all happy about them.

Since a good deal of American porcelain and pottery from the late 19th century is similar or even identical in design, opportunities for fakery are presented by unmarked pieces. The faker needs only to apply a mark of a scarce, highly collectible manufacturer, and has boosted the sales potential considerably. This sort of deception is usually successful only when the buyer is not familiar with the mark in question. A comparison of the faked mark with one on a genuine piece will nearly always reveal some telling difference. Generally, the faked mark is hand drawn and may be too small, too large, unsymmetrical, or recognizable in some other way. It may simply have a fresh, new appearance about it — and it could even wash off with soap and hot water. While far in the minority, some faked marks are quite well done.

Besides placing a mark on an unmarked piece, the faker will sometimes remove an existing mark. This, of course, is also done to make a relatively common piece appear to be a more prestigeous collectible. Once the existing mark has been removed, a faked one is applied. The danger of detection (even by an inexperienced collector) is much greater. Removal of the existing mark leaves a rough spot, a depression, or at least a discoloration. The faker can attempt to fill this in, or paint over it with nail polish, but he is not apt to totally hide the evidence. A small magnifying glass is a useful tool to have handy when shopping for pottery and all related collectors' items. What does not reveal itself to the naked eye will usually not escape a 10X or even 5X lens, if used in a good light. Even the slightest trace of roughness around the mark or surface coloration which differs from that of the surrounding area is cause for suspicion. On an authentic piece with an authentic mark, there is no reason for the mark to have anything doutbful about it. When a mark has been ground out, the area will probably have been filled in with white modeling clay into which a little glue has been added. This makes it level with the surrounding surface but the texture is wrong. To avoid this obvious contrast in texture, the faker may choose not to fill in the ground-out area. If he follows that route, the new (faked) mark will be situated in the recess or depression, and that in itself ought to be a warning signal. There are really no perfect fakes of this kind. Some are better than others, but they can all be detected.

Faked marks may be accompanied by faked decoration. Normally, though, faked decoration is a problem independent of any other, and turns up on pieces with genuine marking. There are several varieties and degress of faked decoration. Heading the list, and unquestionably the easiest to spot under normal conditions, are pieces whose decoration is completely faked. Mostly these are objects which left the factory as undecorated "blanks." If the enameling and gilding are very old, old enough to be considered contemporary with manufacture, the piece would not be referred to as a fake. It was a quite common practice — for better or worse — for purchasers in great-grandma's day to take their brush and paints and fix up undecorated ceramics. Some people made a hobby of this. Such specimens are not in danger of being mistaken for factory work since the designs are original. Fakes are redecorations done at a much later time, using factory patterns, subjects, and color schemes as the guide. While they may present a reasonable facsimile of the original, they are usually not correct in every detail, and this becomes ovbious when comparing a fake with a genuine specimen. Some coloration fakes (as collectors call them) can be instantly recognized by the lack of glaze. These are the more amateurish kind which cannot have seriously been designed to fool anyone. A determined faker will, of course, fire his pieces after painting them, to duplicate the factory process. Therefore, the presence of glaze on an enameled specimen is still not an assurance of authenticity. However, if the painting and glaze looks to have a much more recent origin than the object, it is wise to be suspicious. One method of detecting such work is to examine the surface for scratches or minor abrasions. Almost all ceramic wares dating from the 19th or early 20th century has received slight injuries in its long lifetime. This is especially true of tableware. When no evidence of scratching can be found, the possibility of repainting has to be considered.

"Touching up" falls into the same class as repainting. This usually consists of painting over existing decoration which has faded or become excessively scratched, particularly the gold banding around edges. The nature of gold paint, or "gold varnish" as our ancestors called it, causes it to flake more easily than paint. An antique piece may entirely retain its enamel, but lack most, or all, of the original gold banding. Replaced gold paint will look bolder and somewhat darker than the original. Also, it will be far too "intact," without scratches or flaking, whereas original piping on a 100-year-old item is certain to be marred in some way. If the gold band is quite thick, and appears to have a double outline, it is almost positively an addition to the original piece. It usually happens, when regilding an item, that the area covered by the gold ends up larger than it was before. The faker (or restorer, or whatever we wish to call him) wants to hide all traces of the old gilding, and this results in smothering it with the new. If, for example, a band was $\frac{1}{16}$" wide originally, the new gilding projects a bit at each side and the band swells to $\frac{1}{8}$" or thereabout. If the gilding has been only partially redone, this will be easier to detect, since a contrast will be presented between the old and new. This is quite often the case, because individuals attempt only to deal with the areas of banding which need refurbishing and leave the rest alone. The result may be more visually appealing than it was previously, but the piece has been tampered with — and its sales value is unalterably hurt. This is the crux of the modern collecting philosophy as it applies not only to ceramics but also to most other collectors' items. Buyers much prefer an item in its original state, without alterations or improvements of any kind, *even if the condition "as found" represents a deterioration from the original condition."* A piece with some deterioration is not worth as much as one in its original condition, but its value is greater than an "altered" piece.

Fakes of *artists' signatures or marks* have apparently been on the increase in recent years, thanks to the greater specialization in this hobby and the premium prices given for works of favorite designers. A faked artist mark may be accompanied by faked decoration, or may exist on a piece whose decoration is authentic. By the same token it may or may not be accompanied by a faked manufacturers' mark. The presence of what appears to be a genuine manufacturers' mark is no reason to accept the artist's mark without question. Sometimes this kind of deception is exposed by careless research on the faker's part — using a maker's mark which had become obsolete before the artist in question started working at that factory. If the maker's mark on a piece does not agree with the time-period of the artist's mark, fakery has to be presumed.

Then, of course, there is the question of whether all components in a piece are original. If a pot is accompanied by a lid, the lid may be a later addition from a different piece of approximately the same size and style. But it may possibly be the work of a different manufacturer. Check the fit, the appearance of the enameling, and glaze, and see whether both pieces have a comparable look of age. If one is darker than the other, in terms of glaze, this may very well indicate a "marriage" of components that were not issued as a unit.

In the final analysis, the impression given by a specimen at the very first glance — even though further inspection is definitely recommended — is the vital clue to its authenticity. A doctored or faked item strikes the trained eye as being "wrong." It simply looks out of balance, even if the cause is not immediately apparent. Most dealers will confirm that they get a first-glance reaction to any piece offered to them, and their accuracy in judging authenticity by just giving something a "once over" is remarkable. A beginning collector cannot expect to have quite such acute senses at first, but they will be developed with time and training.

THE CURRENT MARKET

The 1970's were a period of frenzied buying (and selling) activity for all types of collectors' items. American pottery and porcelain benefitted greatly from the increased numbers of investors coming into the market, and the higher prices willingly paid by private collectors. Now that the "soaring seventies" have lapsed into history, what is the current condition of the market and its outlook for the future?

Art pottery continues to lead the pack. When you compare the prices being paid today for Rookwood (the most valuable and prestigeous American art pottery) with those of ten years ago, the increases are very impressive. Even in the recession years of 1981 and 1982, most rare Rookwood pieces were sold at sums equal to — or even higher than — those recorded in 1979. This is significant, since not as many investors are buying these days. Sustained high prices for the best pieces means that private collectors are taking up the slack. More collectors are obviously entering the market and are not objecting to paying the kind of prices established through the competition with investors in 1979.

Is the market truly healthy today? There are some negative and questionable aspects to be sure. But on the whole the market is in remarkably good shape. It has weathered the "selling storm" of pieces thrown *back on the market* by investors seeking either to take their profits or selling in a panic fearing market collapse. By the end of 1979, a large proportion of American art pottery, especially the very expensive wares, was in the hands of investors. This kind of situation is always considered dangerous in any field of collectibles. Collectors tend to hold their purchases regardless of market fluctuations, but investors generally buy *en masse* and sell the same way.

When the numbers of pieces being *sold* by investors exceed being *bought,* one of two things can happen:

1. Prices plummet because of a glut in the market; dealers faced with overstocked shelves and few prospective buyers lower their buying prices.

2. Collectors react to the upswing in supply and go into the market to take bargains, thereby stabilizing the prices.

The years 1981 and 1982 proved conclusively that art pottery is not dependent on investors for its sales strength. Many collectors were convinced, and probably rightly, that the next surge of investment buying would see prices of Rookwood and other fine wares doubling and tripling. Instead of waiting for a return to the low price levels of 1974-77, collectors went out and bought. And they're continuing to buy.

Medium priced wares have been hurt somewhat by the economic slowdown. Investors bought these wares also in 1979 and the early months of 1980. But collectors have not been quite as eager to take up the slack on medium priced items, probably feeling that the opportunity to buy at reasonable sums will prevail throughout 1983. The best prediction of market analysts is that it won't last — that the bargains on medium priced wares seen in 1981 and 1982 will all but vanish as 1983 draws to a close. The economy has already begun turning around and this will mean that collectors will have more money to spend. Competition is sure to increase on the medium priced wares, since the number of potential buyers for them far exceeds those for high priced art pottery.

You must remember that the overwhelming popularity of art pottery dates back only about a decade. It was "discovered" around 1972, having long been considered esoteric and offbeat — a specialty item for the antique dealers. The next several years witnessed a mad rush to the antique marts of New Jersey and Ohio to find art pottery "at the source." Today, collectors have become more sophisticated. They not only know the names of the factories, but they know the artists and designers. They appreciate quality and especially innovation. In this respect, the collectors of art pottery have shown tastes similar to buyers of modern art, and unlike buyers of traditional antiques. Current popularity for the ingenious work of George Ohr of Biloxi, Mississippi is a good example. Ohr worked in the early part of his century, a craftsman who conceived each design and executed each piece by himself. For two generations, his wares were considered intriguing but rather bizarre. Today, his genius is fully recognized, and the prices for Ohr pottery are rapidly increasing.

Regional influences remain very important in the art pottery market. Prices for the most popular Ohio and New Jersey wares tend to be highest when sold in those states. There are more collectors in Ohio and New Jersey and the competition is therefore is great, even though the supply is also great. However, just the reverse holds true for art pottery of less value. Within the past several years, much more of the Ohio and New Jersey wares have turned up in the southwest and west. California has fallen behind the East Coast sales activity on art pottery throughout most of the 1970's. The local California wares were being purchased but very little of anything else. This situation has now thoroughly changed. A lot of art pottery is not only being sold in California but it brings good prices. Also Texas has become a popular source of art pottery activity within the past two years.

In the New England states, art pottery has had a much slower influence, but sales have slowly increased there and are continuing to increase. The traditionally popular pottery in New England is earthenware, with heavy collecting activity for Bennington. The best "buys" on early Bennington can no longer be purchased from roadside antique shops in Vermont and New Hampshire. But the supply of both high and medium priced pieces is still greatest in New England.

"Collecting" began in the later 1700's and very early 1800's, when our first museum (notably the New York Historical Society) included colonial pottery in their displays. Its value then was much more sentimental than monetary, but this situation didn't remain. Antique American pottery is not as glamorous as art pottery and in recent years has not been receiving comparable public interest. It is a quieter market, without big surges and fads; but occasionally it does make news. The most important development within recent years has been growing enthusiasm for the works of obscure potteries of the mid 19th century. Most of this material is quite rare, but its rarity has not traditionally been reflected in the prices. Hobbyists are settling upon collecting items from one factory or another. This is a challenging and rewarding way to collect. Despite the tons of published articles and books on the subject, there is still ample room for research and original investigation. Most published research has centered upon the major early potters, with comparatively little written about the small factories and individual craftsmen.

The Bicentennial of 1976 naturally brought an added flurry of activity into the market for antique American pottery. As prices advanced during that period, critics were quick to doubt that the levels would be maintained — basing their observation on the fact that many Civil War collectibles declined in price after the Civil War Centennial of 1961-65. Not only did this prove untrue, but values climbed steadily to the decade's close, and have mainly been holding firm in the succeeding years.

GLOSSARY

APPLIED MOLDING

Molded decoration which is not formed by pinching from the body itself, but added after shaping the body from separate lengths of clay. This is often done with an applicator which trails lengths of clay from a nozzle.

ARCHAEOLOGICAL POTTERY

Any pottery which has been buried underground for a substantial length of time is called "archaeological pottery." The prime examples of course are wares of Greece, Rome, Egypt, etc., but archeological pottery is also found in the United States.

ART DECO

A term (of rather recent origin) referring to a movement in design which occurred during the 1920's and 1930's. The basic characteristic of Art Deco is the rendering of human forms in geometrical shapes, highly stylized. The Art Deco style extended into virtually every kind of manufactured object as well as drawing, sculpture, etc.

ARTIST'S MARK

Marks of factory painters who applied coloring to pottery are sometimes present on American wares. They are more prevalent on art pottery and occur extensively on the products of Rookwood. An artist's mark customarily consists of his or her initials, but there are occasional variations — such as a spelled-out first name without a last name or initial. The mark may be in block letters or script; when in script it sometimes presents confusion.

ART NOUVEAU

A style of art popular in the 1890's until about 1920. It emphasized decoration rather than form, expressing this often in a whiplash curve lines of floral and leaf-like designs.

ART POTTERY

Pottery of all types (glazed and unglazed, but chiefly glazed) created as display pieces rather than for utilitarian use. Technically all figureware and ornaments would fall under this heading, but collectors use it more restrictively to refer to products of America's art pottery movement (beginning in the late 19th century.) Rookwood and Roseville are examples of art pottery. There are numerous others. Some firms dealt exclusively in art pottery while others manufactured it in conjunction with other wares.

BACKSTAMP

A printed or incised symbol or logo usually found on the underside of an object, which gives one or all of the object's information of origin, like the name of producer, sponsor, artist, the title, issued date, number of sequence and artist's signature.

BANDING

A term used to describe applying metals by hand, such as gold and silver, to the rim of an item.

BAROQUE

A French word meaning an irregular shape. It was used to describe a style of art popular in the 17th and 18th centuries. Baroque art was characteristically displayed by massive forms, as well as florid colors.

BASALT

A dense fine-grained black volcanic stone. Wedgewood introduced black basaltes for ornamental and useful wares.

BAS-RELIEF

A method of decoration on an object where the design is raised above a background. This is produced be either pouring a liquid mixture into a mold or by applying to a backround an already formed design.

BELLEEK

A type of porcelain first popularized in Ireland with thin walls and a satiny finish, resembling the inner side of an oyster shell. It was made in America by a number of firms, notably by the Glasgow Pottery Company of Trenton, New Jersey.

BISQUE or BISCUIT

A name which applies to any pottery item which has been fired in a kiln once but has not been glazed.

BISQUE FIRING

The initial firing for any ceramic object to harden the clay.

BODY

The clay or mixture of substances combined to make any pottery ware.

BONE ASH

The powder produced when animal bones, usually oxen, are crushed and ground. It is an ingredient in bone china that makes it appear whiter and more transluscent.

BONE CHINA or BONE PORCELAIN

Ceramic wares which are pure white due to added bone ash. It is softer than hard paste porcelain, but more durable than soft paste porcelain.

CAMEO

A carving in relief which has a contrasting color with its background.

CERAMIC

Any ware or work of a potter or any object made from baked clay.

CHINA

A term originally used for all wares produced in China. It is now used in reference to any hard, vitreous, or glassy, ceramic consisting of kaolin, ball clay, china stone, feldspar and flint.

CLAY

The chief ingredient in the making of all pottery. Various types and grades of clay are used, but not all types are suitable for all kinds of pottery. Kaolin is the clay used in hard-paste porcelain.

COBALT

A steel-gray metallic element used as a pigment in glazes and tin-enamels. The most common use is in cobalt blue glaze.

CONSERVATOR

An individual employed in repairing, repainting and restoring pottery objects.

CRAZING

A mesh of cracks in the glaze on a piece of pottery; also called CRACKLE if found in Chinese porcelains.

CREAMWARE

Pottery whose base color is an ivory white with a slight suggestion (sometimes) of yellow. The painting, if any, may have any design or color, without altering the fact that the object is still called creamware.

DAMP ROOM

The room in which pottery is stored during the shaping process, if the work cannot be completed in a single session, to assure that the clay remains fully pliable.

DECALCOMANIA or DECAL

A method of decorating pottery by applying a design printed on specially prepared paper; the paper adheres to the pottery and (if the job is well done) gives the appearance of having been printed directly on the object. Decals were widely used in various industries in the earlier part of this century, and in fact became a fad for home decorating — sets of decals were sold in variety stores with one's walls could be embellished.

DECORATION KILN

A kiln in which pottery is fired after being painted to set or fix the colors. Decorating kilns use lower temperatures than the normal firing kilns in which pottery is hardened.

DECORATOR

An alternate term for painter or enameler in a pottery factory.

DELFTWARE

Tin-glazed earthenware that was originally developed in Delft, Holland.

DRESDEN

A term often used synonymously with Meissen porcelain. Dresden and Meissen were two cities in East Germany who produced porcelain. The first porcelain produced outside of China was discovered by Johann Friedrich Bottger in the Dresden factory in 1709.

EARTHENWARE

Any pottery that is not vitrified. It is the largest kind of pottery including delfware, faience and majolica.

EDITION

The total number produced of one design in a series by a producer. An edition may be *limited,* meaning that production ceases when a certain quantity or time-deadline has been reached. Or it may be unlimited, continuing sporadically to meet sales reaction. Nevertheless, an unlimited edition could be — and sometimes is — a smaller size, and scarcer, than a limited.

EGYPTIAN WARE

Various American manufacturers produced "Egyptian ware" in the later 19th century. This was a loose catch-all term meaning pottery whose motifs and/or modes of decoration were inspired by art forms of ancient Egypt. In most cases, great liberties were taken with the authentic Egyptian designs, and often one wonders if any actual model was used. Egyptian-style objects of all kinds, not only pottery, flourished as a fad in this country from the 1870's into the 1890's, mainly because of the widespread publicity given to archaeological "finds" in Egypt.

EMBOSSING

A method of decoration with raised designs produced either in a mold or with a stamp.

ENAMEL

A glassy substance with mineral oxides fused to a surface for decoration. In traditional collector terminology, all types of painting applied to pottery are collectively referred to as "enameling," even if the substance used in painting was not true enamel.

ENGRAVING

A method of decoration produced by cutting into a surface with tools or acids.

FABRIQUE

A word borrowed from the French ceramics industry, now used internationally in referring to the composition of any pottery object (as opposed to its shape, manner of decorating, etc.).

FAIENCE

A type of earthenware covered in a tin glaze. Faience is increasingly being used to mean the same as delftware and majolica. The difference is that the Delft faience uses a more refined clay. The name comes from an Italian town called Faenza.

FELDSPAR

A kind of crystalline rock from which kaolin, one of the main components of porcelain and china, is formed when the rock is decomposed.

FIGUREWARE

Statuettes. This term is over 200 years old. The word "statuette" sounded inglorious to 18th century ears, so the porcelain makers settled on "figureware" instead.

FINISHING

Painting or printing applied to the surface of a pottery object. Factory areas where this was done were called *finishing rooms*.

FIRE

The process of heating a piece of clay to high temperatures transforming it into porcelain or pottery.

FLOW BLUE

The name given to pottery blue underglaze designs because of the slight fuzziness resulting from galzing over the color blue.

GILDING

Decoration to pottery (usually porcelain) applied in liquid gold, painted with a fine brush. Though gilding is very attractive, it wears off quicker than ordinary paint.

GLAZE

A liquid compound which when fired on a ceramic piece becomes a glasslike surface. It is used to seal the surface so it is non-absorbent and resistant to wear.

GLOST FIRE

A process of firing in a kiln to fuse the glaze.

HARD PASTE PORCELAIN

A vitreous ceramic made primarily of kaolin, or china clay, and petuntse, which is china stone. It is somewhat transluscent and when tapped should ring. When chipped, it will have a shell-like or conchoidal shape to the chip.

IMPRESSED MARK

A mark which is recessed in the ware like a cattle brand. These marks were applied "blind" without coloring. Impressed marks are not as common as stamped marks.

INCISING

A method of cutting into the surface of an object for decoration.

INLAID

A kind of decoration produced by etching into a surface and then filling the etched-out areas with another substance, usually silver or gold.

IRIDESCENCE

The intermingling of colors like in a rainbow or as seen in mother of pearl. This may be produced by alkaline glazes on ceramic wares.

JASPER WARE

A hard unglazed stoneware produced by Wedgwood originally in 1775. Color is added to a naturally white body by mixing in metallic oxides. Pale blue is the most common.

KAOLIN

A fine white clay, also called china clay, used to produce china and porcelain.

KLIN

An oven in which ceramic pieces are fired.

LACQUER GLAZE

Glaze which has been brushed on a pottery object after firing, without refiring. It is not difficult to detect because it gives the appearance of sitting directly at the surface rather than radiating out from the body as does a true glaze.

LIMITED EDITION

A term used to describe an item which is produced for a period of time or in a particular amount previously decide upon by the manufacturer.

LOGO

Any company trademark is technically a logo, but the word is often applied only to decorative marks comprising a special, distinctive symbol. Marks of this type were uncommon on American pottery until the final quarter of the 19th century. Many earlier makers, wishing to give the impression that their wares came from Britain, used a lion and unicorn mark like that on much British pottery. Others used no illustrative symbol but merely signed their name with or without their place of residence.

LUSTER

A film covering an item made of silver, copper, gold or platinum pigment reduced from an oxide for decoration.

MAJOLICA

Any tin-glazed earthenware from Italy. Majolica has very early origins and was the accepted substitute for porcelain in the 16th and 17th centuries before Europeans discovered the "secret" of true porcelain.

MARK

Unless preceded by some qualifying reference, such as "artist's mark," this always refers to the manufacturer's mark. Not all pottery (past or recent) carries a manufacturer's mark. When one is present, it will invariably be on the underside of the base, either printed, hand-drawn, or blind-stamped (incised) into the surface. Variously called "factory mark," "potter's mark," "maker's mark."

MODEL

This term several meanings:
(1) To form clay into an object in the wet state is more correctly called *shaping,* but is sometimes referred to as modeling.
(2) A model may be an object (in any medium) which serves as the inspiration for a work in pottery.
(3) In British usage, a model is any pottery object, but especially a figurine or decorative piece. This application of the term is seldom made in America.

MOLD

The form which shapes ceramic pieces of art. The object is formed by either pressing clay into the mold or by pouring a liquid clay formula into the mold and the excess water is absorbed to leave a hardened shape.

MOLD NUMBERS

Mold numers appear on a minority of American pottery. Usually, they were used only when a given design was being produced in several different sizes to eliminate any possible confusion on the part of distributors and retailers.

MONOCHROME

A monochrome design is one in black and white, rather than colors. It may be painted or printed, but usually printed.

NEO

New, used in the sense of a revival (of an artistic style.) The Victorian revival of Renaissance styles was called neo-Renaissance.

OVERGLAZE

An enameled design painted on top of a fired glaze and then fired again at a lower temperature for permanence.

PARIAN

A hard paste porcelain named after parian marble. It is a vitrified china that could be fired at a lower temperature which allowed for a greater variety of possible colors for designs.

PENTUNTSE

A fusible component of hard paste porcelain.

PORCELAIN

A fine, hard, white, vitrified material which is generally fired at about 1400 degrees Celsius. Its chief components are kaolin and petuntse, and when they are fired produce a translucent material that will ring when tapped. The Chinese were manufacturing porcelain for several hundred years before Europeans. Even today, Chinese procelains of the T'ang and early Ming dynasties are regarded as the finest ever produced — possibly because the Chinese clays were exceptionally pure or a now-forgotten method of firing was used.

POTTERY

A general name given to all ceramic wares. In the present market, it sometimes refers only to earthenware, not including porcelain or any ceramic with a vitrified surface.

POUNCING

Applying outlines for paintings with wax stencils. Powder is sprinkled on the stencils and serves as a guide for the company artists.

PRINTED WARE

An object whose designs are applied by printing rather than hand painting. There are various techniques, but in all cases, the design is first printed on transfer paper (which does not absorb the ink) and then pressed on the item. The design may be either in color or balck and white.

QUEEN'S WARE

An earthenware developed by Wedgwood for Queen Charlotte of England in 1765. It is cream in color and is also called white ware.

RECONSTRUCTION

This term is used to describe a specimen which at some time in the past was broken into a number of pieces, then restored. There are two types:

(1) The object exists exactly as it did before breakage, except for evidence of repair work.

(2) Some pieces were lost in breakage and have been replaced by building up these missing areas with clay and painting them to match the surrounding portion.

RELIEF DECORATION

A design that is raised above a background. This is produced by either pouring a liquid clay mixture into a mold or by applying an already formed design to an object.

SALT GLAZE

A traditional form of ceramic glaze developed in England in which table salt is sprinkled in the kiln during the firing process. It rather closely imitates the glaze of early Chinese ceramics, which at one time were thought to have been salt glazed (but probably weren't.)

SECOND

A specimen flawed in one way or another, which the factory (if it detects it) either descards or places in a special batch to be sold at a discount.

SEVRES

This is the name of the leading French porcelain manufacturer in the 18th century. It is of interest to collectors of American wares because its designs were (at a later time) widely copied in this country.

SLIP TRAILING

Applying decoration in the form of liquid slip, pressed from a cone-shaped bag through a nozzle just the way a cake is decorated with icing. It gives the impression of molded decoration. Slip trailing is used on both uncolored and colored wares. Though fairly solid if properly applied and fired, it is naturally more liable to break or fall than components which are intergral with the body.

SOFT PASTE PORCELAIN

A porcelain made of white firing clay and silicate, a ground up mass of glass, sand or broken china. This very transluscent material is also called artificial porcelain and is generally fired at about 1100 degrees Celsius.

STONEWARE

A name that applies to all vitrified and non-porous pottery, except porcelain.

STOVE ROOM

A drying-out room for shaped clay, where it is stored before being taken to the firing kiln. The object is to remove as much moisture as possible to speed up the firing process and prevent cracking.

STRIATIONS

Streaks or veins running through the body, colored design or glaze (but most often the color,) purposely applied for visual appeal. The word is borrowed from minerology, where it denotes streaks of one mineral running within another mineral.

TERRA COTTA

The name used for clay fired without glaze. This type of is more often formed by a potter than by a sculptor who produces earthenware.

TIN GLAZE

A dense lead glaze which is colored white and made opaque by adding ashes of tin. It may also be colored by adding metallic oxides.

TOBY JUG

Drinking mug modeled in the likeness of a human face or full-length figure. The name is derived from the fact that one of the perennial sujects is Toby Weller, a character from the novels of Charles Dickens. "Jug," which we take to mean a bottle with a handle, was the old-fashioned British word for a drinking cup.

TRANSLUCENCE

A property of some ceramics. It is where light can be seen through an object without it being it being transparent.

UNDERGLAZE

Painting colors on a ceramic bisque before it is dipped in glaze and fired a second time.

VICTORIAN

A period in art roughly paralleling the reign of Britain's Queen Victoria (1837-1901). Most Victorian styles and influences in arts and crafts were based on revivals of earlier styles.

VITREOUS or VITRIFICATION

The condition of a ceramic object when fired which results in a glassy and impermeable surface.

TYPES OF BACKSTAMPS

Applied Molded Marks: A separate piece of china is applied to an item. The maker's mark is impressed into the added section. The only known version of this type of mark in Trenton ceramics is the so-called chewing gum mark used on Belleek-type baskets by Willets and possibly other companies. Some marks which might look like applied molded marks are in fact cast in as part of the original molding process.

Impressed Marks: The mark is stamped onto items by means of a metal die before the item is fired or decorated. Many of the Trenton ironstone companies used this type of mark, and it is also seen many times on bisque or parian items.

Incised Marks: Incised marks are similar to impressed ones, except that they are written in by hand rather than being stamped in. As was also the case with impressed marks, this must be done before the item is fired. Isaac Broome marks are usually incised.

Painted Marks: Painted marks are just that—marks which are painted on either underglaze or overglaze.

Printed Marks: These are by far the most common marks seen on china, and can be applied by engraved copper plate, rubber stamp, or other such processes.

As a rule, the impressed and incised marks are the hardest to fake, indeed practically impossible.

BACKSTAMPS REFERENCE GUIDE

American Art China Works-Mark A,
page 85

AMERICAN CHINA

A.C. Co.

American Crockery Company, *page 86*

BELLEEK

American Art China Works-Mark B

ANCHOR POTTERY

J. E.N.

Anchor Pottery - Mark A,
page 87

Anchor Pottery-Mark B

Broome-Mark A,
page 93

Broome-Mark B

BROOME

Broome-Mark C

B–M

Burroughs & Mountford Co.-Mark A,
page 129

$$\frac{B \& M}{CHINA}$$

Burroughs & Mountford Co. Mark B

B-M

**Burroughs & Mountford Co.
Mark C**

HONITON
B.& M. Co.

Burroughs & Mountford Co.-Mark D

C. P. Co.

City Pottery-Mark A, *page 130*

N. J.

Mark A

COLUMBIAN
TRENTON
N. J.
ART POTTERY

Mark B

Columbian Art Pottery
page 131

Mark A

Mark B
Cook Pottery Co., *page 133*

Mark C

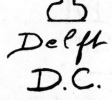

Cook Pottery Company
Mark D

Cook Pottery Company·
Mark E

Coxon & Company,
page 135

Delaware Pottery, *page 139*

Enterprise
Pottery Co

Enterprise Pottery Co.,
page 143

**IRONSTONE CHINA
J M. & CO**

Mark A

Glasgow Pottery
page 154

Mark B

U.S.M.C. Q.M.D.

Mark C **Glasgow Pottery** Mark D

**Glasgow Pottery-
Mark E**

**TRILBY
J.M.&S.CO.
TRENTON, N.J.**

Glasgow Pottery-Mark F

SAPPHO
J.M.&S.CO.

Glasgow Pottery-Mark G

**GLASGOW CHINA
VITRIFIED
TRENTON, N.J.**

Glasgow Pottery-Mark H

Glasgow Pottery-Mark I

Glasgow Pottery-Mark J

**Greenwood Pottery-
Mark A**, *page 157*

GREENWOOD CHINA
TRENTON, N. J.

Greenwood Pottery-Mark B

G.P.
Co.

**Greenwood Pottery-
Mark C**

Loubat
N.O.LA.
GREENWOOD

Greenwood Pottery-Mark D

GREENWOOD CHINA
— l l —
M. GOLDBERG
CONEY ISLAND
N. Y.

Greenwood Pottery-Mark E

Greenwood Pottery-Mark F

GREENWOOD

CHINA

I

Greenwood Pottery-Mark G

GREENWOOD CHINA

TRENTON, N. J.

Greenwood Pottery-Mark H

PATENTED
OCT. 27-25
Greenwood
WM AKERS JR. Co.
PHILA. PA.
china
PATAPPLIED FOR

Greenwood Pottery-Mark I

GREENWOOD CHINA
COOK'S
HOTEL & RESTAURANT
SUPPLY CO
NEW YORK

Greenwood Pottery-Mark J

Greenwood Pottery-Mark K

International Pottery-Mark B

International Pottery-Mark D

B-C

WILTON

International Pottery-Mark A, *page 172*

International Pottery-Mark C

John Maddock & Sons,
Inc., *page 174*

Lenox-Mark A, *page 181*

Lenox-Mark B
page 183

Lenox-Mark C
page 184

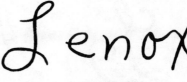

Lenox-Mark D
page 185

Lenox-Mark E
page 185

Lenox-Mark F
page 185

Lenox-Mark G
page 187

Lenox-Mark H
page 188

BELLEEK

Lenox-Mark I
page 189

LENOX

Lenox-Mark J
page 190

Lenox-Mark K
page 191

Lenox-Mark L, *page 191*

M
CHINA
L

Maddock Pottery, *page 418*

LENOX

Lenox-Mark M
page 191

Mercer Pottery-Mark A,. *page 419*

Mercer Pottery-Mark B

Mercer Pottery-Mark C

Mercer Pottery-Mark D

MERCER POTTERY
TRENTON, N.J.

Mercer Pottery-Mark E

Mercer Pottery-Mark F

Millington, Astbury & Poulson-Mark A, *page 420*

Millington, Astbury & Poulson-Mark B

Ott & Brewer-Mark A,
page 427

O. – B.
CHINA

Ott & Brewer-Mark B

Ott & Brewer-Mark C

Ott & Brewer-Mark D

O.&B.

Ott & Brewer-Mark E

MANUFACTURED BY
OTT&BREWER
TRENTON, N.J. USA

Ott & Brewer-Mark F

Ott & Brewer-Mark G

Ott & Brewer-Mark H

Ott & Brewer-Mark I

Ott & Brewer-Mark J

Ott & Brewer-Mark K

Ott & Brewer-Mark L

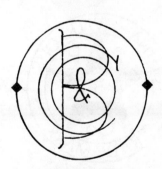

Ott & Brewer-Mark M

Star Porcelain Company, *page 503*

Thomas Maddock & Sons, *page 505*

TRENTON CHINA CO.

TRENTON, N.J.

Trenton China Company, *page 506*

THE TRENTON POTTERIES CO

HOTEL CHINA

Trenton Potteries-Mark A, *page 507*

TRENTON POTTERIES CO

TRENTON, NEW JERSEY

U S A

Trenton Potteries-Mark B

Trenton Potteries-Mark C

Trenton Potteries-Mark D

Trenton Potteries-Mark E

Trenton Potteries-Mark F

Trenton Potteries-Mark G

Trenton Potteries-Mark H

Trenton Potteries-Mark I

T. P. Co.

CHINA

Trenton Pottery, *page 509*

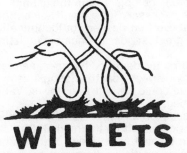

Willets-Mark A, *page 523*

Willets-Mark B

Willets-Mark C

Willets-Mark D

WILLETS

CHINA

Willets-Mark E

HOW TO USE THIS BOOK

The Official 1983 Price Guide to American Pottery and Porcelain has been arranged for maximun convenience in use. Listings are grouped by manufacturer, and the manufacturers are listed alphabetically throughout the book. Within each manufacturer's section, the listings are arranged alphabetically by type of object or by pattern name. In cases where items carried item or shape numbers, as most of the Lenox products do, these pieces are listed sequentially by number (305, 306, 307, etc.) The objective in the listings has been provide as much information as is necessary for a positive identification. Additional information, over and above that needed for identification, has been kept to a minimum so that the greatest possible number of listings could be included.

In using this book, be sure you have correctly identified the specimen to be evaluated. If your specimen differs in any respect from the listing, it is most likely a different specimen and the value could be higher or lower. Values shown are for the specific items described.

Values are given in the form of a range, such as $60 to $80. Ranges allow for the inevitable variations in price that occur within the market. But, still, sales can (and do) occur both above and below the extremes of the ranges. The ranges simply present the average or median values that have been obtained. In all cases they are retail values, or values to collectors — not prices that a dealer pays when buying.

ACME SANITARY POTTERY COMPANY

Acme was founded in 1901 by James A. Dorety, John Meagher, and S. P. Deasy. They produced sanitary wares.

Marks: *Not known*
Prices: We have never seen any of Acme's product sold on the open market and it is possible they never made anything but sanitary wares. A miniature three-piece bathroom set by them would be valued at a minimum of $65.

ALPAUGH & MAGOWAN

See Coxon & Company.

AMERICAN ART CHINA WORKS

In December of 1891, Rittenhouse and Evans formed the American Art China Works for the production of a Belleek-type ware which was sold both decorated and undecorated. The company was located in what had previously been the Washington Pottery. Their china tends to have a slightly whiter appearance than many of the other Trenton wares. The company was not in business long and items by them are rare. Few people know the company by its proper rame and it is generally called Rittenhouse & Evans.

Marks: Mark A is the most common one, and appears primarily (but not always) on factory-decorated items. Mark B can also appear on both factory and home-decorated items. Marks A and B are usually printed in blue. Variations of the marks occur.

Mark A  Mark B

		Price Range	
☐ **Bon-bon dish,** *5" round, ruffled top, pearlized pink interior, gold trim on rim, factory decorated, Mark B*		150.00	175.00
☐ **Pin tray,** *4" x 3", scalloped rim, home-decorated with flowers and gold trim, Mark B*		90.00	110.00
☐ **Salt dip,** *2-1/2" diameter round, ruffled top, pearlized lavender interior, sponged gold on exterior, Mark A*		80.00	95.00

Price Range

☐ **Shell,** 6" diameter, raised on two small almond-shaped feet,
  gold paste trim, Mark B 365.00   435.00
☐ **Vase,** 13" high, handles, gold paste and hand-painting, Mark A   400.00   470.00

AMERICAN CHINA COMPANY

American China Company produced stone china, and may have been a part of the American Crockery Company. The company should not be confused with a company of the same name in Toronto, Canada.

Marks: *Not Known*

AMERICAN CHINA
A . C . Co.

Prices: We have never seen any products from this company. If you come across a quality porcelain or Belleek-type item by them, it can be compared to a comparable Willets item.

☐ **Bowls** 15.00   25.00
☐ **Cups and saucers** 8.00   13.00
☐ **Dessert plates** 3.00   6.00
☐ **Dinner plates** 10.00   25.00
☐ **Mugs** 10.00   30.00
☐ **Platters** 15.00   40.00
☐ **Soup bowls** 5.00   8.00

AMERICAN CROCKERY COMPANY

Although the founding date of this company is uncertain, it is known that they exhibited at the 1876 Centennial Exposition in Philadelphia. They manufactured white granite and bisque items, frequently decorated with American historical scenes.

Marks: American Crockery marks include the British coat of arms with IRON STONE CHINA above and A.C.Co. underneath, and an American eagle on top of the initials ACCO, which are intertwined. A third mark is shown below. All three marks were printed in black.
Prices: We are totally unfamiliar with this company's products, so the following prices are estimates:
  Bisque items — if interesting, compare against comparable Lenox items; if boring, divide Lenox prices in half.
  Centennial items — a minimum of $50 for any backstamped sample Granite-ware or stoneware.

☐ **Bowls** 15.00   25.00
☐ **Cups and saucers** 8.00   13.00
☐ **Dessert plates** 3.00   6.00

	Price Range	
☐ Dinner plates	10.00	25.00
☐ Mugs	10.00	30.00
☐ Platters	15.00	40.00
☐ Soup bowls	5.00	8.00

AMERICAN PORCELAIN WORKS

This company was founded in 1895 by N. W. Boch. No other information available.

Marks: *Not Known*
Prices: Not only are we unfamiliar with American Porcelain Works' products, we're not even sure what they made. If something respectable turns up, compare against comparable Lenox items. Lower-level wares can be rated against a company like Greenwood.

AMISON POTTERIES

No information available.

Marks: *Not known*
Prices: Without knowing what Amison made we cannot list any prices. Compare against comparable items from known companies.

ANCHOR POTTERY

Anchor was established in 1894 by James E. Norris. Fulper Pottery took over the plant at a later date.

Marks: A British coat of arms with the words IRONSTONE CHINA and the word WARRANTED underneath was the first mark. The initials AP were inside the shield. Other company marks include the ones shown and numerous other variations.

ANCHOR POTTERY
J. E. N.

Prices: Vase, 15″ high, two handles, orange lustre finish, transfer decoration of pink roses which are touched up by hand, gold trim on handles, very possible the ugliest piece of china to ever come out of Trenton, $20.

The above prices is fairly representative for Anchor products of this type.

	Price Range	
☐ Bowls	15.00	25.00
☐ Cups and saucers	8.00	13.00
☐ Dessert plates	3.00	6.00
☐ Dinner plates	10.00	25.00
☐ Mugs	10.00	30.00
☐ Platters	15.00	40.00
☐ Soup bowls	5.00	8.00

ARSENAL POTTERY

This relatively obscure Trenton company supposedly made fine Toby jugs, majolica and decorated porcelain. It was part of the Mayer Pottery Manufacturing Company, which is equally obscure. The proprietor was Joseph Mayer.

Marks: *Not known*
Prices: We have never seen any of their "fine Toby jugs, majolica and decorated procelain," and will have to take it on faith that they do indeed exist somewhere. Since they are obviously rare, we would estimate a minimum of $100 on one of their Toby jugs. The decorated porcelain and the majolica would be anyone's guess.

ARTISTIC PORCELAIN COMPANY

Artistic was founded in 1893 by N. W. Boch.

Marks: *Not known*
Prices: Artistic is even more obscure than Arsenal (if that is possible,) and we will offer the advice to compare their items against comparable items by other companies.

ARTON STUDIOS

Original name of Cordey, q.v.

ASTBURY & MADDOCK

See Thomas Maddock & Sons.

ASTBURY & MILLINGTON

See Millington Astbury & Poulson

BAY RIDGE SPECIALITIES

This still-existing company was founded in Brooklyn, New York, c. 1907 by a Mr. Tscheuden. The company moved to Stokes Avenue in Trenton c. 1910. Their output included bath accesories, beer mugs, and decorative items sometimes embellished with applied flowers. When the Fairfacts Company went out of business, Bay Ridge bought their machines and designs.

Marks: Many items unmarked, others marked with company name in one fashion or another.

Prices: Since this company is still functioning, prices for their wares will probably be a little lower than for those have closed their doors forever. Their items will, of course, still have interest for those trying to complete a one-from-each company collection.

	Price Range	
☐ **Beer mugs,** *undecorated*	4.00	8.00
☐ **Beer mugs,** *decorated*	40.00	60.00
☐ **Items with applied flowers,** *a minimum of*	10.00	16.00

BELLMARK POTTERY COMPANY

Bellmark was founded in 1893 by Sidney, Robert and Hughes Oliphant. They manufactured plumber's and druggists' items.

Marks: A bell with the words VITREOUS CHINA.

Prices: We can only conjecture about what their plumbers' and druggists' items were, but if their line included something like a mortar and pestle, we would estimate $65 for such a set. (Keep in mind that "druggists' supplies" in those days did not necessarily mean a piece of porcelain or pottery. Some of the concoctions sold by druggists in those days were made up of the ingredients which go into ceramics, and many of the companies sold these compounds to druggists.)

BENNINGTON

Bennington ranks in a special class among American pottery. It was the first U.S. factory to gain an international reputation, and the first on this soil to produce truly creative artistic works. The popularity of Bennington among collectors stretches back before the beginning of the America's antique trade. By as early as 1890, the wares had become solidly established as collectors' items, and some of the pieces were already on the verge of rarity.

Since the factory's operations were shut down in 1858, all of its products have for many years been ranked as antiques.

The period of *true Bennington* was brief, extending only from 1842 to 1858, but this may be deceiving since the output during those 16 years was heavy. For the actual beginnings of Bennington, we must delve back into the 18th century. In 1793, John Norton established a pottery works of rather humble proportions in the town of Bennington, Vermont. Its products were red earthenware and mason's bricks. Sometimes around the War of 1812, Norton installed a stoneware kiln and began making English-style wares. Brown glazed wares were also produced. The earlier Bennington wares were all sold locally without any effort apparently to invade the more lucrative market of the mid-Atlantic states. From all available information, it seems that production during these years was modest. Things took a dramatic change in the winter of 1842 to 1843, when Julius Norton (a grandson of the founder) went into partnership with Christopher Fenton. The aim of this new alliance was to diversify the Bennington line and bring it fully up to par with the imported English stonewares. With the kind of ambition that characterized few American potters of that era, Norton and Fenton set out to duplicate the much admired bold surface finished of Rockingham wares. This they fully accomplished and, many collectors would argue, even surpassed Rockingham in their best specimens.

The Bennington products were marvels of free-spirited designing. Among the best known are its stoneware figures with mottled, deep-brown color. The same type of unique coloration also appears on water pitchers and various other items, including conventional tableware. In 1849, the company filed for a patent on colored glazes, the first of its kind in the United States. The secret of the Bennington process was to take the fired wares and coat them with metallic oxides. They were afterwards dipped in flint enamel — the glaze was *not* brush-painted. The myth of brush-painted glaze on Bennington stoneware was probably inspired by the presence of what appear to be brush markings. These, however, were the result of natural texturing as the liquid glaze gradually solidified. If the glaze was thick on some areas of a piece, which was almost inevitable from the dipping process, it gathered into the crevices before drying. Much to the credit of Bennington, it never strove to achieve a smooth ware, free of mottling. The company was quite proud of the individuality of its product, and public response confirmed this confidence. In its time, however, the popularity of Bennington was small compared to heights reached later on the antique market.

The company underwent several name changes. From the original name of "Norton and Fenton," it became "Fenton's Works," then "Lyman, Fenton and Co." Finally, the name was changed to "United States Pottery" in 1850 which was in use at the time of the company's collapse in 1858.

In addition to the instantly recognizable wares mentioned above, Bennington also produced parianware. This was a minor phase of its operations.

Marks: The earliest mark upon the association of Norton and Fenton in 1842, was a circle composed of the wording *NORTON & FENTON, BENNINGTON, Vt.* Block lettering was used without any symbol. When the company name was changed, after Norton left in 1847, the mark became *FENTON'S WORKS; BENNINGTON, VERMONT* enclosed in a rectangular decorative border. This distinctive mark was set in two styles of lettering with *FENTON'S WORKS* in slanting characters resembling italics. The address was set in standard vertical lettering. The next mark, that of Lyman, Fenton and Co., was contained within a plain oval frame and read *LYMAN FENTON & CO., FENTON'S ENAMEL, PATENTED 1849, BENNINGTON, Vt.* This ushered in the era of colored glazes. Within this mark, the year (1849) is very prominently displayed. When the name became United States Pottery Co., two different marks were introduced, both reading *UNITED STATES POTTERY Co., BENNINGTON, Vt.* One carries the wording within an oval frame and contains two small ornamental flourishes; the other is a modified diamond-shape composed of decorative printer's type, but without further ornamentation.

	Price Range	
☐ **Basin,** *12", mottled brown Rockingham glaze*	70.00	80.00
☐ **Bed pan,** *mottled brown Rockingham glaze*	70.00	80.00
☐ **Bowl,** *6", Rockingham glaze, bell-shaped*	90.00	100.00
☐ **Bowl,** *7½", mottled brown glaze*	90.00	100.00
☐ **Bowl,** *9", mottled brown Rockingham glaze*	70.00	80.00
☐ **Bowl,** *10" oval, mottled brown Rockingham glaze*	70.00	80.00
☐ **Box, covered,** *5¾" oval, all white, parian, shell-molded base and lid with sell finial*	80.00	95.00
☐ **Box,** *5¾", square, all white parian, shell finial*	95.00	105.00
☐ **Box,** *4⅜", square, parian, top with figure, Lion of Lucerne*	115.00	125.00
☐ **Candlesticks,** *11", mottled brown glaze, pair*	200.00	250.00
☐ **Churn,** *mottled brown glaze, wooden lid and dasher*	220.00	270.00
☐ **Compote,** *on low footed base, molded design on body*	115.00	125.00
☐ **Creamer,** *cow, mottled brown glaze*	175.00	200.00
☐ **Cream pot,** *1 qt., cobalt floral, covered, J. & E. Norton*	140.00	160.00
☐ **Crock,** *4 gal., yellow-brown with "4" impressed with cobalt blue*	300.00	350.00
☐ **Cuspidor,** *8½", mottled brown glaze, shell pattern*	125.00	150.00
☐ **Egg cup,** *molded lily pad feet, all white, set of 6*	125.00	150.00
☐ **Flower pot,** *6", Rockingham glaze, eagles in relief on sides* . . .	30.00	40.00
☐ **Inkwell,** *5"x2½", mottled brown Rockingham glaze*	115.00	140.00
☐ **Inkwell,** *4 quill holes, usual color, design in relief*	200.00	250.00
☐ **Inkwell,** *cylindrical, Rockingham glaze*	100.00	125.00
☐ **Jar,** *1 gal., gray stoneware, cobalt blue, butterfly and floral decor, impressed "E. & L. Norton, Bennington, Vt."*	110.00	125.00
☐ **Jug,** *1½ gal., 9½", mottled brown glaze*	140.00	170.00
☐ **Jug,** *2 gal., gray stoneware with cobalt blue scrolling feather design, impressed "E. & L.P. Norton, Bennington, Vt."*	125.00	175.00
☐ **Jug,** *2 gal., blue and green, flint enamel*	95.00	115.00
☐ **Jug,** *3 gal., 16", gray stoneware with cobalt blue floral decor, impressed "E. & L.P., Bennington, Vt.," 1861-81*	125.00	175.00
☐ **Jug,** *3 gal., ovoid, gray stoneware with cobalt blue floral decor, impressed "Norton & Fenton, Bennington, Vt."*	140.00	170.00
☐ **Mug,** *6", Rockingham glaze*	100.00	125.00
☐ **Pie plate,** *10½", mottled brown Rockingham glaze*	110.00	140.00
☐ **Pitcher,** *7", hunting scene with dogs and hunters on horseback in relief, mottle brown Rockingham glaze*	95.00	105.00
☐ **Pitcher,** *7½", parian, relief-molded white palm trees and exotic flowers designed for syrup cover, marked "U.S.P." on base* . . .	95.00	105.00
☐ **Pitcher,** *8¼", tulip and heart, flint enamel*	150.00	175.00
☐ **Pitcher,** *8½", parian, blue and white, molded grape cluster leaves*	110.00	125.00
☐ **Pitcher,** *8¾", Rockingham glaze, castle scene*	350.00	400.00
☐ **Pitcher,** *11", hexagonal, brown birds and flowers*	275.00	325.00

	Price	Range
☐ **Snuff jar,** *3⅞", flint enamel, flat bottom*	750.00	850.00
☐ **Teapot,** *7¾", "Rebecca at the Well"*	70.00	80.00
☐ **Teapot,** *2 qt., mottled brown glaze*	120.00	140.00
☐ **Tobacco jar,** *11", mottled brown glaze, covered*	200.00	250.00
☐ **Toby creamer,** *6⅛", mottled brown Rockingham glaze, seated Toby*	325.00	375.00
☐ **Vase,** *7¼", mottled brown glaze, ear of corn shape*	95.00	115.00
☐ **Vase,** *7½", all white, parian*	50.00	60.00
☐ **Vase,** *7½, flint enamel, tulip in relief*	250.00	300.00

BOEHM

Edward Marshall Boehm founded a studio pottery in Trenton in 1949. His first workshop was on Stokes Avenue, and he later moved to Fairfacts Avenue. Following Mr. Boehm's death, his wife Helen took over the company. Studios have now been opened in England as well as in Trenton, so the Trentoniana collector might go to special pains to select an item which was made in Trenton rather than in England.

Both authors have to confess to a lack of knowledge about Boehm porcelains, and all of the information here, including the prices listed below, is secondhand material gleaned from trade journals and Boehm advertising material. Their items are beautifully made and show a great deal of time and attention to detail. Considering the amount of work that must go into them, the current prices seem fair.

Prices: Following are selected auction results for items which are no longer being made. Because they are all pre-1971 items, it is assumed they were made in Trenton although we are not certain of this.

☐ **Blue Grosbeak**	875.00	1075.00
☐ **Bobolink**	950.00	1150.00
☐ **Boxer,** *large size*	1000.00	1200.00
☐ **Carolina Wrens**	5000.00	5750.00
☐ **Catbird**	1675.00	1975.00
☐ **Crested Flycatcher**	2150.00	2550.00
☐ **Downy Woodpecker**	1350.00	1550.00
☐ **Fledgling Blue Jay**	140.00	160.00
☐ **Fledgling Canada Warbler**	1450.00	1650.00
☐ **Fledgling Goldfinch**	175.00	220.00
☐ **Fledgling Magpie**	680.00	800.00
☐ **Fledgling Red Poll**	160.00	190.00
☐ **Green Jays**	4425.00	4925.00
☐ **Lazuli Bunting Paperweight**	120.00	140.00
☐ **Mourning Doves**	4625.00	5125.00
☐ **Nuthatch**	235.00	285.00
☐ **Oven–Bird**	1350.00	1550.00
☐ **Parula Warbler**	2350.00	2850.00
☐ **Polo Player**	3750.00	4300.00
☐ **Prothonotary Warblers**	400.00	470.00
☐ **Road Runner**	4300.00	4800.00

	Price Range	
☐ **Rufous Hummingbirds**	1800.00	2100.00
☐ **Scottish Terrier**	460.00	550.00
☐ **Standing Poodle,** *apricot-colored*	1450.00	1650.00
☐ **Thoroughbred and Exercise Boy,** *decorated*	6800.00	8000.00
☐ **Towhee**	1850.00	2150.00
☐ **Tufted Titmice**	1075.00	1275.00
☐ **Varied Buntings**	4625.00	5125.00
☐ **Whippets**	3250.00	4000.00

Note: Current items range all the way from an $18 cup and saucer to a $35,000 Prince Rudolph's Blue Bird of Paradise.

BRIAN POTTERY COMPANY

Brian was founded in 1898 by Richard, James and George Brian. They manufactured sanitary items.

Marks: *Not known*
Prices: A miniature three-piece bathroom set by this company would be valued at a minimum of $65.00.

BROOME

Isaac Broome, who is perhaps best known for his work at the Ott & Brewer pottery, at one point went out on his own for a brief time c. 1880. The items made while on his own were primarily small vases.

Marks: Mark A is the one used on the items he made on his own. Marks B and C are more likely to appear on items he did for other companies. All three marks are incised. A European modeller named Tebo used a mark similar to Mark A, and the two should not be confused.

Prices: No known recent sales for items made by Broome while on his own. Our estimate would be a minimum of $1250 for any perfect, signed specimen.
Note: See the other companies where Broome worked for additional listings on Broome items.

BRUSH — McCOY

This 20th century company is noted both for its artware and general lines of tableware, as well as decorative pieces and utilitarian pottery of many kinds. The majority of its fine artware, now so avidly sought, was produced in its earlier years of operation prior to 1930. As was the case with a number of other firms, a cutback on artware production became necessary during the Depression of the 1930's, because only essential merchandise was sought by the public. Brush-McCoy's lines of popular-priced wares fared extremely well in stores throughout the nation. They were continued and expanded in the 1940's and 1950's with many sales registered by mail order via the major catalogue houses. Today the available variety of Brush-McCoy wares for the collector is overwhelming, offering something for just about all tastes and budgets. There are even many pieces of very recent vintage, going back to the 1960's.

The Brush-McCoy Pottery was first established as the J.W. McCoy Pottery Company, located in Roseville, Ohio — the heart of Ohio "clay country." From all available evidence, it seems that the company got off to an ambitious start when it was incorporated in 1899. J.W. McCoy reportedly had $15,000 capital at the outset, then two years later had multiplied this investment to $100,000. A large factory was built and an engraving of the building with a smoke-belching furnace room was placed on the firm's letterheads. The intention at first was to produce general tablewares, glazed majolica novelties and restaurant fixtures, and two lines of artware. One of these artware lines was called Mt. Pelee; the other apparently did not receive a name. Both remained in production very briefly and are rare. The cause of discontinuing was due in part to a serious fire which occurred in the spring of 1903. All stock on hand was destroyed and after making repairs and getting the factory back into production, it was decided to take new directions. Almost immediately thereafter, the company began selling its ROSEWOOD line of artware, which became its first big success on the market. The name Rosewood was coined from RookWOOD and ROSEville, and has sometimes proved a little confusing to hobbyists. Some mail-order buyers have ordered Rosewood, thinking they were ordering Rookwood or Roseville!

In 1909, George Brush joined the organization after a pottery works he had been operating was ruined by fire. It was not however until two years thereafter in 1911 that the name became Brush-McCoy. During the earlier stages of the Art Deco movement, Brush-McCoy's artware attracted considerable attention. Much of it was based on classical themes, but it was rendered in a manner that blended well with contemporary settings. The large vases of this era, some of them featuring very dramatic paintings, acquired a particulary strong connoisseur following. At the very same time, the factory was also producing popular-priced lines, and thereby laying the groundwork for what would become its chief trade in later years.

In terms of current appeal, Brush-McCoy's "King Tut" line of artware, introduced in 1923, ranks foremost. In the previous year, a pair of young British archaeologists, Howard Carter and Lord Carnarvan, had discovered King Tut's tomb. The news of this historic discovery made interntional headlines and ushered in — almost immediately — a public fad for Egyptian styles. While the fad itself has long since faded, things relating to King Tut, especially those made at the time of the great discovery, have been building in collector popularity. While the source of designs for Brush-McCoy's "King

Tut" ware is not known, it is considerably more authentic-looking than those on most "Egyptian ware" of the period.

Marks: Many different marks were used by this company for its various lines. In its earlier days and up to the Depression, it rarely marked any of its art pottery, and therefore identifiction must be made on the basis of style. Later, its artware was customarily marked. This firm, though its name officially was Brush-McCoy, habitually used only the name of Brush in its markings. The more commonly found mark (used on later wares) is the name *BRUSH* in block capitals with flourishing serifs on the first and last letters. This is above the initials *USA*. There are several varieties of this mark. The variations are not of great help in dating as they were often used simultaneously. Several of the marks of this organization, both early and late, made a play on the word "Brush," picturing artists' brushes. These would sometimes be accompanied by an inkwell or a palette. Beginning in the late 1930's, it was customary for the object's mold number to appear in the mark. The collector of Brush-McCoy is certain to learn far more from studying the works themselves, than from studying the marks.

AGEAN *(Introduction during World War I)*

A deep green ware in basic classical shapes and decorative elements, intending to suggest pottery of the ancient Agean sea region of Greece.

Price Range

☐ **Jardiniere,** *10", white, with decoration, pot form, recessed sections along neck formed by band of Greek key ornament* 68.00   80.00

AMARYLLIS *(Introduced 1920's)*

Mold-formed patterns of flowers with six petals, set into arrangements of palm fronds which form rows of vertical panels.

☐ **Bowl,** *pastel ware amaryllis, 2", camel brown with highlights of pink, squat form, wide mouth, 1926* 11.00   14.00

☐ **Candleholder,** *majolica amaryllis, 3", deep rust brown with highlighting in camel brown and vivid deep green, nightstick form, without handle, domed base, sloping drip-pan, pair* 23.00   27.00

☐ **Jardiniere,** *Egyptian amaryllis, 5¼", solid slate blue, modified bulbous form with pinched collar and slightly flaring lip, wide mouth, curved architectural vaulting along rim, horizontal beadwork within panels, 1923* 17.00   21.00

☐ **Jardiniere,** *majolica amaryllis, 8", shape #252, lavender blue with washes of burnt orange at the molded panels, rich glazing, pot form with modestly pinched neck, flaring lip, wide mouth* 24.00   29.00

☐ **Vase,** *majolica amaryllis, 6½", deep orange rust at lower body shading to intense jungle green, dark salmon at lip, swelled shoulder, narrow mouth* 19.00   23.00

☐ **Vase,** *majolica amaryllis, 4¼", green and yellow with touches of dark pink on the molded floral ornaments, bottle form with long thick neck, wide mouth* 12.00   15.00

ART VELLUM *(Introduction date undetermined, sold in mid 1920's)*

A smooth-surface, matt-finish ware, made in various colors. Apparently the name related to its smoothness of texture — certainly not to the colors, since vellum (parchment) is always white.

Price Range

☐ **Vase,** *robin's-egg blue, 8", shape #069, bulb form, tapering neck, flaring lip, broad base, undecorated, value as pair* 26.00   31.00
☐ **Same as above,** *but single vase* 11.00   14.00

ATHENIAN *(Introduced about 1928)*

Grecian-style wares, stressing fluted architectural molding, some very heroic-size pieces were produced for this line as garden ornaments.

☐ **Jardiniere,** *with pedestal, jardiniere 13", pedestal 26", caramel-brown with gray-brown toning, pot form with architectural fluting on the body and molded flowers and leaves, terminating in an octagonal foot, the pedestal is a squat column with fluting and a similar base, matching colors* 220.00   250.00
☐ **Sand Jar,** *18", caramel-brown, bulbous form with fluted panels at body and a ring of molded flowers and leaves at the neck with removable pan* 115.00   135.00

AUTUMN OAK LEAF *(Introduction during World War I)*

The Autumn Oak Leaf line had richly textured surfaces, designed in the form of a blanket of autumn leaves strewn upon the ground. The leaves are fully modeled with textured veins, and the brown body surface representing the ground can be seen between them.

☐ **Jardiniere,** *10½", shape #29, yellow, beige and mahogany with touches of rust-red, pot form, decorated with textured leaves filling the entire body* 95.00   110.00

BASKETWARE *(Introduction date undetermined; sold during World War I)*

Basketware creations featured molded bodies in basketweave patterns, usually straw-colored but sometimes a pale gray. Though the style was novel and not unappealing, it was suited to only a limited range of objects.

☐ **Jardiniere,** *7½", gray body, slate brown at shoulder with apple-green enameling, pot form with vaulting vertical shoulder, decorated along the shoulder with molded berries, leaves and twigs* 28.00   34.00

BONTON *(Introduction date undetermined; sold during World War I)*

A white ware with high-gloss glaze, featuring small molded ornament with touches of colored enamel. Bonton could not have been intended to represent marble sculpture, because the glaze was much too strong. More likely it was inspired by Chinese porcelains of the early Ming dynasty, even though the shapes are decidedly not Chinese.

Price Range

☐ **Jardiniere,** *7″, ivory white with touches of blue, squat bulbous form, flaring outward toward base and resting upon an inverted pedestal foot, molded decoration of bunches of grapes at sides, highlighted with strokes of lavender blue* 26.00   31.00

CAMEO *(Made during the 1930's)*

Non-standard coloration but usually a marble white with molded decoration in green. The only uniform characteristic throughout this line was the use of a cameo-like ornament or ornaments, which of course gave the ware a distinctly European touch.

☐ **Jardiniere,** *6″, shape #273, marble white body, sea green at base and neck, bulbous form, with molded spiral decoration at the base and neck, molded cameos on pink background and pink and blue floral garlands encircling the body* 23.00   27.00

CATTAIL *(Introduced 1923)*

Dusky cream-white with a printed illustration of one or more cattails. This line gave the appearance of English stoneware of the 19th century.

☐ **Pitcher,** *6½″, dusky cream-white with stenciled illustration in greenish-blue, stunted form with tall handle, cattail on either side, supplemented by double horizontal banding on the base and single horizontal banding at the rim* 37.00   44.00

CLEO *(Introduced 1915)*

Chiefly a creamware with bold patterns based upon natural history subjects, executed in a rather parochial style. This line was not extensively produced, possibly because of the hectic conditions of World War I.

☐ **Vase,** *11″, cream body decoration in yellow and pale gray, cylindrical form widening slightly at the shoulder, narrow mouth, decorated with stylized figures of trees and flowers in sweeping brushwork* 75.00   90.00

COLONIAL MAT *(Manufactured in the late 1920's)*

A slate-black ware, the designs based on ancient Roman models, and having a matt finish.

☐ **Jardiniere,** *6½″, pot form, wide neck decorated with molded lion's heads and floral garlands, tapering body with a pair of bands in graduated sizes, resting on ball feet* 22.00   26.00

CORN *(Introduced 1910)*

Cornware is made to resemble ears of corn with textured kernels. The colors are yellow and green.

☐ **Pitcher,** *6″, shape #44, cylindrical form with short spout, loop handle* 23.00   27.00

DANDYLINE *(Introduced about 1916)*

Dandyline was a dandelion color (actually a bit darker,) and was a "dandy line." This is a high gloss ware with simple banded ornament. It gives the impression of being more modern than it is — like something from the post-World War II battle against occupied Japan imports.

Price Range

☐ **Bowl,** 7" wide, saffron yellow, inverted cap form with rounded lip, decorated with triple banding of white 7.00   10.00

DRIP GLAZE *(Introduced probably in 1931)*

This is a type of ware sold by this factory during the depression years. Raw clay body with enamel glaze upon portions only, literally poured or dripped on and allowed to assume random formations.

☐ **Umbrella stand,** 25", slate gray unglazed with blue enamel glaze at the top only, nearly cylindrical form, swelling at the shoulder, the glazed portion occupies about a fourth of the body, covering the whole collar and running unevenly down the sides, terminating in blotches 50.00   65.00

DUTCH KIDS *(Introduced about 1922)*

The only distinguishing characteristic of this line was the figure, or figures, of Dutch-costumed children molded on the ware. Decoration of this nature was first used by Brush-McCoy in its "Amsterdam" line during World War I. The "Dutch Kids" pieces were made after Amsterdam had been discontinued.

☐ **Pitcher,** 7", with nuglaze finish, olive green shading into very deep jungle green, mug style with small pointed spout, T-square handle, impressed with a figure of a Dutch boy and girl kissing, also with floral banding 32.00   37.00

FLORA *(Introduced about 1914)*

Black painted flowers against a white marble-like ground.

☐ **Pedestal,** 17½", cream white with pale beige foot and rim, column form, flaring out at the shoulder and pinched at head and base, decorated with black floral motifs 90.00   115.00

FLORASTONE *(Introduced 1924)*

Similar to the Jewel pattern which preceded it in 1923. Florastone was apparently inspired by archaeological pottery of the Central and South American Indians. Colores are somber grays and browns, suggesting rugged old leather, shapes are virtually freeform, decoration consists mainly of molded leaves in fleur-de-lys style surmounted by small flowers. Beadworks decoration, both raised and painted is also used.

☐ **Jug,** 10", an almost uniform dark leathery brown, tall tapered neck with squat body, narrow handle, dome-type cap, decorated around the body with raised leafwork emblems and flowers 90.00   115.00

Price Range

☐ **Vase,** 6", shape #077, light maroon base, shading to a grayish brown and finally a dark dull brown at the mouth, bulbous form with octagonal sides, molded decoration in the upper portions of panels, raised black beadwork along mouth 45.00   57.00

GRAPE (Date of introduction undetermined)

Marble-white with molded unpainted decorations of grape bunches, and accessory decorations of leaves.

☐ **Casserole,** shape #110, marble-white, ovoid squat form with a lid and flattened closed handles 52.00   65.00

IVOTINT (Introduced 1929)

Ivotint meant "tinted ivory," and this fairly well describes the line. This is whiteware brushed with rust brown and burnt orange, to give the effect of aged ivory. Motifs were loosely based upon Asian themes.

☐ **Bookends,** 5½"x5", ivory white set against a slate brown ground, square plaque-type bearing a molded profile portrait of an Indian, pair 56.00   64.00
☐ **Oil Lamp,** 8"x4", ivory white base with touches of yellow, white body highlighted in rust brown and lake green, bowl form with curved wick-holder, cap shaped as mosque dome, stunted handle, decorated with molded figures of lions 120.00   140.00

JETWOOD (Introduced 1923)

A gray to purple-gray toned ware, decorated in cream white with varying intensities of brown. The bodycolor is allowed to intermingle with the surface coloration, producing subtle effects.

☐ **Bowl,** 7½"x2½", shape #01, cream white shading to light beige, then to deep beige at top, squat shape, decorated with a mountainous landscape 37.00   43.00
☐ **Candlestick,** 7", shape #030, grayish-purple at base and neck, brown stem, glossy black slip decoration of a landscape with tree at the foreground, valued as pair 70.00   85.00
☐ **Candlestick,** 10¼", shape #032, grayish purple base shading to browns along the stem and terminating in cream white at the collar, the drip-pan is grayish purple, tapering cylindrical form with wide base, glossy black slip decoration of a landscape with several prominent trees, value as pair 75.00   95.00
☐ **Vase,** 10½", cream heightened with reddish beige, cylindrical form with modest narrowing at top and bottom, glossy black slip decoration of a mountainous landscape with tree in the foreground 100.00   120.00
☐ **Vase,** 12", bright cream base shading to hues of reddish brown at center, terminating in grayish purple, flared base with pinched shoulder, widening out slightly at mouth, decorated with a landscape at sunset 52.00   65.00

JEWELL *(Introduced 1923)*

A basically Indian-inspired pattern in its shapes and decoration. The chief color is beige-tinted cream, with darker browns used for highlighting. Some pieces were in an overall dark brown. Lozenge motifs are used in the decoration, often with circular ornaments at the centers — a style originated by the ancient Egyptians.

	Price Range	
☐ **Bowl,** *2½", shape #055, buff cream with hints of purple at the rim, vertical sides with broad mouth, no neck, decorated in pink, green and black, with a double banding of black and white beadwork ornament at the mouth*	33.00	38.00
☐ **Vase,** *3", dark brown, squat bulbous form with narrow mouth, no neck, decorated with a network of lozenges circling the body, broken at the centers to form smaller lozenges, surrounded by white beadwork*	47.00	56.00

KEG NOVELTIES *(Introduced 1932)*

Each item in this line is in the shape of a wooden beer keg, with banding to suggest iron straps. The coloring was walnut brown with a woodgrain finish.

☐ **Mug,** *4", walnut brown with reddish overtones, beerkeg form, with double bands to suggest iron barrel straps*	3.25	4.50

KING TUT *(Introduced 1923)*

This line was inspired by the discovery of the tomb of the Pharaoh Tutankhamen (Tut) in Egypt's Valley of Kings. Brush-McCoy's King Tut ware is a little puzzling. The line began with real effort to reproduce Egyptian styles and motifs then generated into a somewhat non-descript ware.

☐ **Candlesticks,** *10", shape #032, stone gray, tapering outward to a twin pedestaled base, decorated with a stem-painting of Egyptian figures carrying staffs, and small emblems intended to suggest hieroglyphic writing, on a vellum-cream ground, the figures being in solid white and mahogany brown*	130.00	150.00
☐ **Vase,** *7", parchment-cream ground, bulbous ovoid form with wide shoulders, narrow mouth, decorated with a landscape and seascape painting in which sailboats are shown on a lake, simple narrow banding*	140.00	170.00
☐ **Vase,** *12", deep mud-gray with tones of green, ovoid form with pinched neck, flaring lip, decorated with a tall painting on rust ground, showing Egyptian figures carrying staffs and other implements, bordered by wide bands of oxblood ground, containing pale violet rectangular ornaments*	275.00	335.00

KRAKLE-KRAFT *(Introduced 1924)*

Judging from the shapes of Krakle-Kraft, it almost seems as though Brush-McCoy took some of its King Tut creations and gave them a different finish. This is an ivory whiteware with a crackle finish. Bluish-violet highlights run through the crackling.

Price Range

☐ **Vase,** *8", ivory white with bluish-violet crackling, modified bulb
form* 38.00   46.00
☐ **Vase,** *10", ivory white with bluish-violet crackling, cylindrical
form widening at the shoulder, narrow mouth, decorated with
the figure of a dragon, composed of deep and highly color
crackling* 77.00   90.00

LOY-NEL-ART *(Introduced about 1900)*

Among the most prestigeous lines of this company's art pottery. Deep,
rich brown bodies, exhibiting the play of various brown tones and shades,
with hand-painted decoration. High-gloss glaze. Loy-Nel-Art was adapted
from the Rookwood wares.

☐ **Jardiniere,** *11", shape #205, dark brown with various subtle
shadings, pot form, rimless, decorated with a painting of
yellow and orange flower buds and long green leaves* 90.00   115.00
☐ **Pedestal,** *17½", dark brown with various subtle shadings, column form widening out toward base, flared lip, recessed foot,
decorated with a painting of a flower in tones of orange and
yellow* 80.00   95.00
☐ **Umbrella stand,** *17½", dark brown with various subtle
shadings, cylindrical form, molded Greek key pattern at head
and foot, vaulting moldwork on body, decorated with a painting of yellow and burnt-orange flowers, accompanied by
leaves and black berries* 160.00   185.00
☐ **Vase,** *18", shape #16, dark brown with various subtle shadings,
cylindrical form, tapering inward toward neck, decorated with
a painting of ferns and leaves in tones of amber, moss green,
and yellow* 70.00   85.00

LUCILE *(Date of introduction undetermined)*

A highly glazed marble-white ware, with shallow molded ornament. This
line was used for serviceable objects in the low to medium price range.

☐ **Soap dish,** *lidded, marble-white, in circular shape, squat
bulbous form, with an overhanging lid surmounted by an
applied handle* 27.00   33.00

MATT-GLAZE *(Introduced about 1920)*

Various colors, semi-solid or solid, with matt-finish glaze. It does not seem
to have been a popular line — possibly because of its close similarity to
several other Brush-McCoy lines, and to dozens of those of other potters.

☐ **Bookends,** *5"x5½", greenish beige with rust highlighting, in
the form of the base of a fluter architectural pillar, fronted by a
molded vine with leaves and berries, pair* 17.00   22.00

MIRROR BLACK *(Introduced about 1925)*

A highly glazed, smooth-surfaced, unpainted ware. At a distance it gives
the appearance of jet blackness, but on closer inspection tones of red and
purple can be seen.

Price Range

☐ **Teapot,** 4", black with faint traces of red and purple, most
noticeable at the lip and along the lid's edge, globular form
with shovel handle 7.00   10.00

MODERNE KOLORKRAFT (Introduced about 1928)

An Art Deco line with spacy shapes and highly stylistic modeling. Colors
vary. Brush-McCoy spelled "modern" with a second "E" (MODERNE) to give
it a European flair.

☐ **Jardiniere,** 10", blue, pot form with octagonal sides, each
panel bisected diagonally and containing, in one of the compartments, the impressed figure of a flower and its stem 27.00   32.00
☐ **Vase,** 12", red and pink streaked with white, modified bulbous
form, surmounted by a series of four platforms, set with
enclosed handles at either side, narrow mouth, pair 38.00   46.00

MOUNT PELEE (Introduced 1902)

This ware can occur in jet black or moss green, and probably other colors. The
coloring is very rich and the surface smooth. The effect is of chiseled lava.

☐ **Bowl, Console,** 12"x3½", in moss and sea green with subdued
glaze, representing a sea-nymph tossed about in waves 320.00   370.00
☐ **Tray,** 7"x2", with twin bowls and handle, jet black with heavy
luminous glaze 135.00   160.00

NAVARRE (Introduced 1912)

One of the more purely artistic of Brush-McCoy's lines.

☐ **Vase,** 9", wrought iron black, in impressionist freeform style
with wide squat body, sharply tapering shoulders, and twin
sets of handles — large handles rising from the bowl to the
nect, and small handles at the neck. Decorated in white with a
bust-length figure of a maiden, her head turned backward, long
hair billowing as if buffeted by wind 210.00   240.00

NUROCK (Introduced 1916)

Nurock was a smooth, unpainted, high-gloss ware, with deep mottled surface colors of (usually) brown and yellow. In the darker pieces — which were
in the majority — this gave the effect of a conch shell, and the high-gloss
finish added to that impression. (Occasionally spelled NU-ROCK.)

☐ **Bowl,** 2", smoky cream yellow richly mottled with very dark
mahogany brown, inverted dome form 7.00   10.00
☐ **Butter pat,** shape #3, cream yellow richly mottled with rust
brown, traditional flattened form 3.00   4.50
☐ **Cup, custard,** 2½", shape #556, cream yellow richly mottled
with rust brown 7.00   10.00
☐ **Cuspidor,** 5", smoky cream yellow richly mottled with very dark
mahogany brown, squat bowl form with wide flared lip, probably dates to 1916 or 1917 .... 33.00   39.00

Price Range

☐ **Jug,** 7", *smoky cream yellow richly mottled with very dark mahogany brown, cylindrical pitcher form with primitive-style handle* 42.00   48.00

☐ **Pitcher,** 5", *smoky cream yellow richly mottled with very dark mahogany brown, squat mug form, loop handle, rim base* 40.00   48.00

☐ **Pitcher, cream,** 4½", *cream yellow richly mottled with rust brown, cylindrical form with long pinched spout, ovoid handle, with molded decoration of a series of shaped panels around the body* 24.00   29.00

OLD MILL *(Introduced about 1916)*

Very pale lavender with dusky white, and molded designs in deep violet. The chief design element is a windmill.

☐ **Box, hanging salt,** 6¼"x4¼", *white, with a wooden hinged lid, rectangular shape with pierced hanger, also set with feet for optional standing, decorated with a stenciled figure of a windmill in bluish violet, at the lower right of the front panel, with the word "SALT" printed in black script characters* 37.00   43.00

☐ **Pitcher,** 7", *very pale lavender with dusky white, cylindrical form with a broader base, molded tulips along the base and extending partially up the sides, molded decoration of a windmill, colored in deep violet* 54.00   65.00

ONYX *(Introduced 1910)*

One of the best selling of Brush-McCoy's lines. There was no basic or characteristc color scheme; the ware was intended to give the impression of onyx stone, and more emphasis was placed upon the highlighting and play of colors than the colors themselves. During the Art Deco period — to which most Onyxware belongs — decorative objects carved from onyx became very popular. Brush-McCoy's Onyxware represented an effort to combine the beauty of onyx and porcelain. And, since actual carving was not necessary, the prices were lower than for real onyx.

☐ **Bottle,** 10½", *dark lavender blue with cloud-like highlighting in lighter tones of the same color, circular form with flattened sides, cork stopper with pointed dome-type cap* 38.00   45.00

☐ **Same as above,** *but without stopper* 23.00   28.00

☐ **Bottle,** 10", *sea green with brown and black mottling, freeform bulbous shape, handle, dome-type cap, the cap has rich accents of cedar-brown mottling* 37.00   43.00

☐ **Bowl,** 5"x2¼", *shape #055, forest green with highlights of yellow, giving the impression of sunlight filtering through dense trees, cylindrical pot form, wide mouth, narrow molded lip* 11.00   14.00

☐ **Bowl,** 6"x2", *midnight and lavender blue mingled with jet black, squat form with broad shoulder* 13.00   17.00

☐ **Candlestick,** 7", *shape #030, lavender blue intermingled with very dark blue and washes of jet black, ovoid form stem, column head with widely flaring drip-pan, molded shellwork decoration along base, pair* 30.00   35.00

Price Range

☐ **Candlestick,** *10½", marbelized blending of cream and ivory whites, green, black and rust-red, column form flaring out toward base, pair* 30.00   36.00

☐ **Clock,** *7", cedar brown with mottling in dark brown, traces of reddish highlights, in the form of a bulbous jug with flattened sides and looped handle, clock set into side, known as JUGTIME CLOCK and bearing the following legends: JUGTIME NOVELTY ART CLOCK, MADE IN U.S.A., PATENTED OCT. 21, 1924, BRUSH-McCOY POTTERY CO., in working order* 60.00   80.00

☐ **Same as above,** *non-working but intact* 28.00   34.00

☐ **Same as above,** *body only, no clock* 10.00   14.00

☐ **Jardiniere,** *6", burnt rust with black streaking, pot form with widened shoulder, wide mouth, molded vine and leafwork texturing encircling body* 23.00   27.00

☐ **Jardiniere,** *9", slate brown with blue-gray, bulbous pot form in extra large size, sloping sides composed of a series of elongated oval, panels, wide mouth* 33.00   39.00

☐ **Urn,** *6", mahogany brown shading to various tones of gray and light brown with streaks of lavender, pot form with a pair of scrolling handles, narrow mouth* 23.00   27.00

☐ **Urn, footed,** *9", black and deep green mottled with seablue, some goldwork, bulbous form with rising lip, a pair of squared handles, resting upon a pedestaled foot, blue highlights encircling the body give the appearance of greater width than this piece actually possesses* 28.00   34.00

☐ **Vase,** *4", black with mottling in beige and red, some hints of green, cylindrical form widening out toward top, then sloping inward to a narrow mouth, value as pair* 19.00   24.00

☐ **Same as above,** *but single vase* 8.00   11.00

☐ **Vase,** *5½", shape #058, wheat brown with dark brown highlighting, bulbous form severely foreshortened toward base, wide shoulder, pinched neck, wide mouth, value as pair* 22.00   26.00

☐ **Same as above,** *but single vase* 10.00   12.00

☐ **Vase,** *8", shape #064, dark brown and burnt orange, bulb form with flaring base, tapering sides and moderately flared lip, narrow mouth* 16.00   20.00

☐ **Same as above,** *pair* 35.00   42.00

☐ **Vase,** *9", shape #22, rust brown at base with mottled effects in pastel brown and mahogany across most of the body, bulbous form with stylistically shaped twin handles, value as pair* 36.00   43.00

☐ **Same as above,** *but single vase* 17.00   22.00

☐ **Vase,** *10", shape #041, forest green with mottled overtones of various colors, chiefly variations of yellow, columnar form widening out slightly at the top, narrow base* 16.00   20.00

Note: The green is dark and from a distance this appear to be a black vase. On closer examination, the green color not only shows itself but fine mesh-like networks of highlighting can be seen.

ORIENTAL *(Introduced before 1914)*

Brush-McCoy's Oriental line was neither Oriental in shapes or painting; its only suggestion of "Orientalness" was in molded ornament of a very incidental nature, usually at the base. It does not appear that this line survived World War I.

	Price Range	
☐ **Jardiniere,** 9", shape #221, cream white and red with some yellow shading, pot form, resting upon a molded foot with irregular edge, molded fanlike decoration along the bowl, with a painting of Grecian-style ruins in a landscape with trees	140.00	170.00
☐ **Same as above,** but with matching pedestal	290.00	330.00
☐ **Umbrella stand,** 23", pale sea-green at base, blending into various tones of brown, pink and sky-blue, ovoid form, resting on a squared base without foot, irregular lip (wavy,) decorated with large-scale paintings of a landscape with walled garden, trees, and mountains at the background	280.00	330.00

POMPEY (Date of introduction undetermined, probably 1918 or 1919)

A severe ware styled to represent fragments of ancient masons' blocks, into which scenes or figures had been carved. The color was always the reddish-brown of old bricks, and sometimes lines were molded into the ware, to suggest the joining of one brick with another. The inspiration for Pompey was the discovery of numerous wall-carvings at the ancient city of that name.

☐ **Window box,** 13"x5", rust brown with tones of gray and green, rectangular shape, molded to suggest a chisel-carved relief scene of a seated harpist, who serenades a pair of maidens one of whom holds an object which appears to be a water jug .	57.00	68.00

PASTEL KITCHENWARE (Introduced 1931)

Pale green or gray-green, with large molded and painted figures of flowers. One of many lines introduced by the factory in an effort to meet the depression-inspired demand for low priced tableware.

☐ **Pitcher,** 5", pot form with vertical ribbing encircling the bowl, decorated with a molded and painted rose with large green leaves	22.00	27.00

RAINBOW (Introduced about 1931)

Solid colors, quite deep, with medium-gloss finish. Another of the many Brush-McCoy lines introduced at the beginning of America's financial depression, intended to provide appealing dinnerware at lower prices than those of the 1920's.

☐ **Bowl,** 9" wide, dark blue, bell form with tall pedestal base, the base and upper rim decorated with molded banding, no other decoration	8.00	11.00

ROMAN (Date of introduction undetermined; sold during the 1920's)

The only characteristic in common, among the pieces of this line, was their classical Roman themes. Glazed and matt-finish wares are included.

☐ **Jardiniere,** 9", slate gray with hints of blue, pot form with wide-brimmed collar, decorated at the collar with molded lion's heads and floral garlands, decorated along the body with a set of creamwork bands in graduated thicknesses	31.00	36.00

STONECRAFT *(Date of introduction undetermined; probably 1921 or 1922)*

A basic white body similar to English and domestic stoneware of the 19th century, usually with ribbed paneling and small decorative touches in various tones of enamel.

Price Range

☐ **Jardiniere,** *6", shape #241, pale beige and white with colored ornamentation, pot form, molded along the upper body in architectural vaulting, decorated with stylized roses formed of square blocks, supplemented by leaves, enameled in pink and green* 19.00 23.00

☐ **Jardiniere,** *7", marble white with touches of beige and ornamented in purple and pale sea-green, pot form, the bowl molded with vertical ribbed panels, and with further molding to suggest the presence of a holder in which the bowl rests, decorated with large stylized flowers having purple petals and pale sea-green leaves* 23.00 27.00

SYLVAN *(Date of introduction undetermined; sold during World War I)*

The concept of Sylvan is intriguing: each piece is decorated with molded woodland scenes, always with trees at the foreground. The thick upper portions of the trees, molded in very high relief, meld together at the top of the object to form a continuous rim or lip. The colors vary from dark to pale brown and from dark to pale green.

☐ **Vase,** *7¼", cream white with orange base, highlights of beige and various shades of green on the molded body, pot form with irregular lip, designed to represent a series of treetops, molded petalwork ornament at the base* 32.00 37.00

☐ **Vase,** *10", shape #08, jade green at base and neck, lighter green body, with various tonal effects running throughout, cylindrical form with swelling neck, representing the tops of trees and textured to suggest leaves* 24.00 29.00

SYLVAN II *(Date of introduction undetermined; sold during the 1930's)*

In the depression, Brush-McCoy altered its well-known Sylvan line. Sylvan II eliminated the woodland scenes. The trees were still present, but in a stylized form, each of them more or less identical and arranged in a symmetrical grouping. In Sylvan II, the treetops terminated beneath the lip or collar of the object and played no special role.

☐ **Jardiniere,** *4½", shape #280, gray and rose-pink, pot form with irregular (wavy) rim, gray base, molded trees colored chiefly in gray, rose-pink ground* 6.00 9.00

☐ **Same as above,** *brown and gray, 3½"* 5.00 7.00

☐ **Same as above,** *brown and gray, 4½"* 6.00 9.00

☐ **Same as above,** *bone white, 4½"* 5.00 8.00

☐ **Same as above,** *brown and gray, 5¼"* 11.00 14.00

☐ **Same as above,** *bone white, 5½"* 10.00 13.00

VOGUE, *(Introduced 1916)*

Classical-inspired ware intended to suggest the marble sculpture of ancient Greece. Bodies are marble-white, with molded and painted decoration utilizing standard themes such as Greek Key, fluting, etc. Not a great deal of Vogue seems to have been produced, possibly because of World War I. Some experimental pieces exist with coloring in green and/or gold. These will invariably bring higher prices.

	Price Range	
☐ **Candlestick,** *12", marble-white, columnar form with fluted stem resting on wide pediment base, triple cups to accommodate three candles, Greek key decoration at sides of drip-pan and at base, pair*	100.00	125.00
☐ **Same as above,** *but single candlestick*	48.00	58.00
☐ **Jardiniere,** *7", marble-white, pot form with widely flaring shoulder, pinched sides decorated with a row of molded fluting, shellwork molding at base*	38.00	44.00
☐ **Vase,** *10", marble-white, cylindrical form with a very slightly flaring lip, glossy black slipwork decoration of Greek key motifs at the shoulder and small lozenges in panels at the foot*	26.00	31.00

WATER LILY, *(Introduced about 1931)*

Aquamarine with molded water lillies and texturing representing waves in a sea.

☐ **Pitcher,** *5½", shape #30, aquamarine with very subtle green tonal highlighting, swelled cylindrical form*	13.00	17.00

WILLOW WARE, *(Introduced about 1916)*

Pale lavender, marble-white and touches of pastel beige. Molded in the form of basket weaving.

☐ **Jar,** *pale lavender, marble-white and pastel beige with tinges of yellow, pot form, with a molded banner bearing the message "PUT YOUR FIST IN," 5¼"*	68.00	79.00
☐ **Jar, cracker,** *lavender, marble-white and pastel beige, pot form with a molded banner reading "CRACKERS" in Old English lettering, with a lavender lid with button handle, with lid*	70.00	85.00
☐ **Same as above,** *but without lid*	55.00	67.00
☐ **Jar, nutmeg,** *pale lavender, marble-white, pot form with a molded banner reading "NUTMEG" 3"*	33.00	38.00

ZUNIART, *(Introduced 1923)*

Most of Brush-McCoy's Zuniart has a rich cream body but the intensity varies and so do tonal effects; some pieces are more distinctly grayish than cream, and hints of browns and reds will be found. Apparently this line was modeled after American Indian pottery and other creations, but it was less faithful to Indian patterns than some of the factory's other work. Presence of the most consistent design element in Zuniart — the swaskita — can be explained by the date. In 1923, Adolf Hitler had not yet come to power and the swaskita was merely an ages old decorative motif without political overtones.

Price Range

☐ **Bowl,** *7"x2", cream-ivory white, of flattened form with sharply pinched base, decorated with a series of black and red-brown narrow bands along the gridle, and near the month with swaskitas and lozenges* 34.00   39.00

☐ **Candlestick,** *10", shape #032, pale grayish cream, stem widens into a twin-platformed base. Decorated with narrow bands of black and with red zig-zagging, a pink lozenge with glossy black slip decoration is placed midway up the stem, pair* 72.00   88.00

☐ **Same as above,** *but single candlestick* 31.00   37.00

☐ **Jardiniere,** *9", shape #240, dusky vellum creamware with lighter tones intermingled mainly at mouth, pot form with narrowing toward base, wide mouth, decorated with black swaskitas and pink lozenges* 82.00   97.00

☐ **Plaque,** *11½", varying shades of brown highlighted with cream and red, representing a profile portrait of an American Indian male wearing feathered headdress, set against a textured background composed of horizontal incised lines. The frame is circular and slightly raised, and decorated with glossy black slipwork ornament* 275.00   320.00

☐ **Shoe,** *Indian moccasin, cream exterior with pearl white interior, decorated with stars, crosses and beadwork, to suggest sewn-on ornaments* 140.00   165.00

☐ **Vase,** *10", vellum-ivory creamware, cylindrical form tapering inward toward base, pinched at shoulder, narrow mouth, decorated with glossy black slipwork swaskitas and pink lozenge emblems, and additionally with painted bands of black and red, triple purple banding near base* 80.00   100.00

MISCELLANOUS

☐ **Ashtray, frogs,** *6½", mud brown, green and marble-white, a pair of frogs, seated at either side of a shallow bowl tray, their heads turned upward and moutns open (the open mouths designed as rests for cigars or cigarettes), the frogs have alternate stripes of brown and pale green on their legs* 6.00   8.00

☐ **Ashtray, turtle,** *5", ivory-white and various reddish hues mixed with brown, the form of a standing turtle* 4.00   6.00

☐ **Bank, frog,** *3½", forest green and yellow, a bullfrog seated on a circular platform with ribbed edge, both are green, with yellow highlights* 22.00   26.00

☐ **Birdbath Ornament, frog,** *8", beige and slate purple with gray, a frog seated on a tree stump, slate purple with hints of gray, his chest a pale cream-beige, the tree stump is a somewhat deeper beige with slate purple streaking to suggest wood texture* 25.00   30.00

☐ **Birdbath Ornament, frog,** *7½", marble-white, a pair of frogs, one standing with legs crossed, the other seated with hand on knee* 24.00   28.00

☐ **Bookends, "Wise Bird,"** *7", burnt orange, lavender and yellow, an owl wearing spectacles, holding an open book and reading, he perches upon a stump and faces a lectern which forms the support of each bookend, pair* 70.00   85.00

☐ **Same as above,** *but single bookend* 28.00   33.00

Note: Since single specimens could easily be mistaken for figurines, the value is somewhat higher than for most single bookends.

Price Range

☐ **Bowl,** 8", bright canary yellow, modified pot form with molded banding, giving the appearance of graduated sections joined together, small handles 7.00 10.00

☐ **Bowl,** 2½", shape #133, cream white, pink and rose red, inverted dome form, decorated with narrow ribbing vertically encircling the body 5.00 7.00

☐ **Bowl,** shape #195, ivory white streaked with jade green, to appear like carved ivory, inverted cap form, with molded decoration beneath the rim 6.00 8.00

☐ **Bowl,** 10" wide, slate white, inverted dome form, with flared lip, decorated with a wide central black band, blocked at either side by a similar but narrower band 7.00 10.00

☐ **Box, hanging salt,** 4½", cream white with a wooden hinged lid, cylindrical form flattened at the back (to fit flush with a wall), decorated with vertical molded fluting, at the front a cartouche with the word "SALT" 23.00 27.00

☐ **Box, hanging salt,** 4½", marble-white and blue, with a wooden hinged lid, half-cylindrical form (flattened at the back to fit flush against a wall), with pierced hanger, decorated with a triple horizontal blue band, with the word "SALT" printed in black script characters 43.00 49.00

☐ **Box, hanging salt,** 6¼"x4¼", marble-white and blue, with a wooden hinged lid, rectangular shape with pierced hanger, also set with feet for optionally standing, decorated with stenciled motifs in the upper left and lower right corners of the front panel, in blue, with the word "SALT" printed in black script characters 38.00 44.00

☐ **Box, hanging salt,** 6½"x4¼", marble-white and blue, with a wooden hinged lid, rectangular shape with pierced hanger, also set with feet for optionally standing, decorated with a modified Greek key emblem at top and bottom of front panel in blue, with the word "SALT" printed in black script characters 41.00 47.00

☐ **Cookie jar, antique auto,** steel gray, bone white and yellow, form of a touring car of World War I vintage, with convertible top, the body is steel gray and the top white, wheel spokes are yellow, the lid is formed by the convertible top 18.00 23.00

☐ **Cookie jar, "Balloon Boy,"** cream white with yellow, green and other colors, representing a boy dressed like a child of the 1920's holding two balloons in his left hand. He wears a moss-green jacket, blue knickers, yellow shoes and a yellow boater hat. The balloons are magenta and pastel blue. The jar's lid is formed by his head and upper shoulders, including the balloons 14.00 17.00

☐ **Cookie jar, carousel horse,** (also known as Circus Horse), cream white, brown, a few touches of grayish green. A performing horse with a small dog on its back. The mane and tail are chiefly grayish green, black hooves, the jar's lid is formed by an ornamental saddle worn by the horse, with the dog serving as a handle, c. 1952 .... 23.00 27.00

☐ **Cookie jar, "Chick And Nest,"** primarily cream white with grayish green base, some pastel yellow highlighting. Bird modeled in caricature, wearing a hat, seated on a nest. Remains of a cracked egg, out of which the bird has emerged,

	Price Range	

are modeled near the base. The hat, bird's beak and egg fragments are pastel yellow. The lid is formed by the bird's head ..   13.00   16.00

☐ **Cookie jar, "Cinderella Pumpkin,"** *burnt orange with gray and pink, and touches of other colors. In the form of the "pumpkin coach" from the fairy tale "Cinderella," surmounted by a pair of gray mice. The coach has molded windows and dark pink molded wheels. The mice are actually the lid handle* 14.00   17.00

☐ **Cookie jar, clown,** *marble white with magenta, dark red, black and blue, the head of a clown, wearing black boater hat with white band, magenta-colored mop-like hair, blue eyes, red bulbous nose, dark red exaggerated lips, black collar, the lid is formed by the hat* 15.00   18.00

☐ **Cookie jar, "Covered Wagon,"** *light cream beige with brown and black, model of a covered wagon with a terrier-type dog seated on top. The wagon is chiefly light cream beige with black spokework at the wheels. The dog is cream beige and charcoal gray. The jar's lid is formed by the upper portion of the wagon, with the dog serving as a handle* 19.00   23.00

☐ **Cookie jar, "Cow And Cat,"** *marble white with purple shading, and touches of various colors. Representing a satirical model of a cow with smiling face, wearing blue cowbell, a cream-yellow cat perched on her back. The cow is chiefly white with washes of purple, brown hooves, cream yellow horns. The lid is formed by the cow's back, with the cat serving as its handle* ..   14.00   17.00

☐ **Cookie jar, "Davy Crockett,"** *caramel brown with other shades of light and deep brown, white and yellow, highly glazed. A half-length figure of the celebrated plainsman and Indian fighter, shown as a youth, wearing coonskin cap and leather jacket, hands clasped together at chest. Blonde hair, with a narrow streak of red at the mouth. The lid is formed by his head and upper shoulders* 19.00   23.00

☐ **Cookie jar, dog and basket,** *cream white touched with yellow, beige and black. Figure of a thicky-furred poodle-type dog, seated on its hind legs. Between its legs is a basket, on which it rests its front paws. The dog wears a beret and a defiant facial expression. The jar's lid is formed by the upper part of the dog, and by the basket lid; the bowl consists of the dog's lower portion and the basket, which are molded together to form a continuous object* 14.00   17.00

☐ **Cookie jar, elephant,** *bone white with magenta and blue, caricature figure of a seated elephant with blonde hair and a blue bonnet, wearing a blue shirt and magenta bowtie. The elephant is smiling and holding its forelegs across its chest. The jar's lid is formed by the elephant's head, c. 1952* 23.00   27.00

☐ **Cookie jar, fish,** *marble white with blue and blue-green, in the form of a blowfish resting upon its stomach, the lid formed by its back, black eyes and a black line drawn across the mouth* .   14.00   17.00

☐ **Cookie jar, "Formal Pig,"** *bone white, black, blue and other colors, in the form of a rotund seated pig, wearing a black tuxedo jacket, blue vest, yellow cravat, and black tophat, he has a moustache. The lid is composed of the pig's head, which lifts off the body at the collar-line* 19.00   24.00

Price Range

☐ Cookie jar, "Granny," *dusky white with salmon, yellow and gray, a stout rosy-cheeked woman holding a rolling pin, dressed in a polka-dotted gown and salmon-colored apron, grey hair. The jar's lid is formed by the upper portion of her body, the dividing line occurring at the shoulders* 14.00 17.00

☐ Cookie jar, "Hen on Basket," *marble white with no coloring other than touches of deep oxblood red and yellow at the hen's head, representing a hen seated on a basket. The lid formed by the hen (the basket is the jar's bowl,) molded wickerwork pattern on basket* 11.00 14.00

☐ Cookie jar, "Hippopotamus," *gray and brown seated hippo wearing overalls and a derby hat, one hand to his face, the other resting on his stomach, black hands, black feet, and the hat is black, both his face and the costuming are gray. The lid is formed by the upper portion of the hippo's body, with the dividing line occuring slightly below the shoulders* 11.00 14.00

☐ Cookie jar, "Hobby Horse," *cream white with beige, black and yellow. The body is molded to suggest wooden planks, and the neck and head give the appearance of being sawn from a flat board. With saddle which serves as the jar's lid* 14.00 17.00

☐ Cookie jar, house, *dusky white with pale green, a shack with wooden slat sides and a sloping shingled roof. The sides are white, the roof pale green, surmounted by a red chimney. The lid is formed by the upper part of the roof, with the chimney serving as its handle* 12.00 15.00

☐ Cookie jar, "Humpty Dumpty," *white with touches of brown, blue and dark pink, representing Humpty Dumpty seated, hands on knees, wearing a cone-shaped mountaineer's hat. The jar lid is the upper portion of his head, and the hat forms its handle* 20.00 25.00

☐ Cookie jar, "Laughing Hippo," *purple, dark magenta brown, rust brown and ochre, a standing hippopotamus with a broad grin on its face, tongue extended to side as if relishing food. On its back is a monkey seated on a rug. The monkey is brown with a yellow-brown face, the hippo is chiefly purple with tones of magenta. The jar's lid is composed of the monkey and rug* . 17.00 21.00

☐ Cookie jar, "Little Angel," *cream white with blue and yellow, a child-angel wearing a billowing skirt, which forms a bulbous bowl. She has blonde hair, red lips, blue wings. She wears an apron with the message, "FOR LITTLE ANGELS ONLY." The lid is formed by the upper part of her body* 13.00 16.00

☐ Cookie jar, "Little Boy Blue," *bone white with blue and carrot, a model of the character, wearing a blue outfit with a farmer's straw hat slung over his shoulder, and reddish brown shoes. He has carrot colored hair and dark red lips. The jar's lid is formed by the upper portion of his body, the dividing line falling slightly below the shoulders* 18.00 22.00

☐ Cookie jar, "Little Girl," *dusky white with blue, yellow and dark rust-red, a young girl wearing a widely billowing floor-length dress, which forms the jar's bowl. She lifts a yellow cookie to her mouth. Her dress has patches of various colors. The jar's lid is formed by the upper portions of the girl's body, the dividing line occurring at the waist* 14.00 17.00

Price Range

☐ **Cookie jar, "Little Red Riding Hood,"** *reddish violet with yellow and pastel robin's-egg blue. Little Red Riding Hood is shown standing, holding a basketweave basket, hands together, wearing blue mittens, blue shoes, and a reddish violet coat with cape and hood. She has blonde hair. The lid is formed by her head and upper shoulders, the coat's cape being the dividing line* 19.00   23.00

☐ **Cookie jar, "Old Woman Who Lived in a Shoe,"** *pastel beige, pale blue, medium brown, in the form of a laced boot topped by an arched roof and chimney, inspired by the fairy tale "The Old Woman Who Lived in a Shoe." The jar lid is the roof, and the chimney its handle* 19.00   23.00

☐ **Cookie jar, "Old Clock,"** *brown, white and blue, shelf clock with molded and painted numbers, molded and painted, hands, blue, with eyes and mouth to give the appearance of a human face, with lid* 13.00   17.00

☐ **Cookie jar, "Peter Pan,"** *reddish brown with black and yellow, representing the storybook character seated, elbows on knees, hands to sides of face, head cocked to one side, impishly smiling. He wears a cone-shaped black cap. The lid is formed by his head and shoulders* 17.00   21.00

☐ **Cookie jar, pumpkin,** *squash orange with white, yellow, black, in the form of a pumpkin with a hasp and lock on the body, and a child gazing out from an opening in the pumpkin, an elf seated on top. The lid is formed by the top of the pumpkin, the elf serving as its handle. High-gloss glaze, c. 1960* 14.00   17.00

☐ **Cookie jar, "Puppy Police,"** *cream white and maroon with black, a seated white dog, wearing policeman's cap and short maroon jacket, white belt. The dog's head serves as the lid* . . . 13.00   16.00

☐ **Cookie jar, Siamese cat,** *buff white and yellow-brown, an impressionistic modeling of a Siamese cat, with tubular body, short chunky legs, pipestem tail, caricature face. The cat's back serves as the lid* 10.00   13.00

☐ **Cookie jar, standing clown,** *light cream beige with white and assorted colors. Figure of a standing circus clown, with humorous bulging pantaloons, an oversized speckled bowtie, and a tiny cone-shaped blue hat surmounted by a yellow rose. His hands are draped at the chest. He has a red nose and smiling facial expression. The lid is formed by the upper part of the clown's body. Made in the mid 1960's* 19.00   23.00

☐ **Cookie jar, "Teddy Bear,"** *sometimes referred to as "Seated Teddy Bear," cream white, brown and grayish green. A chubby seated teddy bear, grinning facial expression, wearing a grayish green bib or apron as if in anticipation of food. The lid is formed by the bear's head* 24.00   29.00

☐ **Cookie jar, "Treasure Chest,"** *beige and walnut brown with other brown tonal effects, and areas of cream white. A pirate's wooden strongbox with molded features including a padlock and staple, iron banding, carrying handles at the sides, and "treasure" (strings of pearls) oozing out. Surmounted by a shell ornament. The lid is composed of the chest's top, with the ornament serving as a handle* 14.00   17.00

Price Range

☐ **Cruet, vinegar,** *9", bone-white, of square form, sloping shoulders surmounted by a squared neck, nipple-shaped cap, T-square handle. With small recesses cut into the base at all sides, giving the suggestion of feet, decorated with stenciled ornament, in blue, and with the word "VINEGAR" printed in black script characters* 34.00   39.00

☐ **Cuspidor,** *5½", black with suggestions of dark brown, pot form with severely pinched neck, widely flaring lip, carving molded decoration of frogs at either side, perched upon the bowl with their backs supporting the neck* 42.00   48.00

☐ **Cuspidor,** *bone-white and lavender blue, squat bowl form with long neck and wide flaring lip, decorated with mottled lavender blue pattern of closely set leaves, along the lower bowl and neck, banded at top of bowl with lavender blue (wide band,) c. 1910* 26.00   32.00

☐ **Cuspidor,** *ivory white and cobalt blue with high-gloss glaze, inverted hat form, deeply pinched at collar, wide flaring lip, decorated with a series of large, bold drawer-handle devices in deep cobalt blue. Believed to date form around 1900* 42.00   48.00

☐ **Cuspidor,** *5½", shape #13, ivory white with black painted decoration, of pot form with severely pinched neck, widely flaring lip, decorated with a series of wreaths enclosing small symbols, and with circular black banding* 23.00   27.00
Note: Retailed around 1918. In the 1950's, antique dealers were selling these as soup tureens.

☐ **Decanter, "Wise Bird,"** *8", iron gray with various other colors, an owl perched on a stump, the decanter cap resting on his head. The owl is chiefly burnt orange with tones of canary yellow, and has a blue-lavender chest. The stump is iron gray* . 38.00   44.00
Note: Name "Wise Bird Decanter" was used by the factory when distributing this work in 1927.

☐ **Figurine, Frog,** *10", cream white with light grayish-green and mahogany brown, stylized likeness of a rotund bullfrog, reclining with chin resting on hand, other hand on kneecap. The frog's upper lip is outlined in brown; the bodycolor is chiefly green, with a white chest* 8.00   10.00

☐ **Figurine, Frog,** *4½", dusky white and mahogany, in a naturalistic pose, poised on all fours with upturned eyes* 3.25   4.50

☐ **Figurine, Frog,** *7", ivory-white with various tones of green and brown, touches of yellow, in a stylized pose, seated, with knees drawn up to neck and hands clasped, pensive facial expression* 6.00   9.00

☐ **Figurine, Frog,** *11½", pale beige shading to white, tones of mahogany and lighter brown, in naturalistic pose on all fours, with mouth open* 27.00   33.00

☐ **Same as above,** *but with slight mold and color differences* 7.00   10.00

☐ **Figurine, hand-painted cat,** *bone white with painting in varied colors, naturalistic figure of a seated cat, entirely white, with colored flowers and leaves painted on its head and body, World War II era* 5.00   7.00

☐ **Figurine, Rooster,** *pastel beige with rust orange and red, realistically modeled standing rooster with body texturing to represent feathers, rust orange legs and feet, standing on small circular base of pastel beige* 13.00   16.00

Price Range

☐ **Figurine, Squirrel,** *10", gray with touches of blue and purple over dusky white, reclining gray squirrel with forelegs tucked beneath him, tail curled and set above the body, very short ears* 24.00   29.00

☐ **Figurine, Turtle,** *6½", marble-white with greens, browns and reds, highly naturalistic model of a sea turtle, with finely sculptured shell, its head extended and turned upward* 11.00   14.00

☐ **Figurine, "Wise Bird,"** *8¾", iron gray, brown, lavender and yellow, owl perched on a log, which rests at an angle upon a stump. The stump is iron gray and has molded foliage at the front, the owl is chiefly brown and yellow with various tonal highlighting* 25.00   29.00

☐ **Garden ornament, Turtle,** *15½", mud-brown with gray and strokes of orange. A device (of the type popular many years ago) used to conceal a garden hose. The hose was inserted in the turtle's body and water spirted out at its mouth* 140.00   170.00
Note: Not too many of these were manufactured. The timing was wrong: they were introduced in the late twenties, and soon thereafter the depression put an end to the demand for "novelty luxuries."

☐ **Jar, "Hillbilly Frog,"** *various tones of green with white and beige, in the form of a seated frog wearing a pointed mountaineer's cap, the upper portion of the frog's head lifts off to reveal the jar* 26.00   31.00

☐ **Jar, "Nite Owl,"** *ivory white with gray and touches of yellow, in the form of a standing owl whose head lifts off to reveal the jar, with black feet* 17.00   21.00

☐ **Lamp base, " Wise Bird,"** *9", charcoal gray with grayish lavender, brown and cream yellow, in the form of an owl perched on a log, which rests upon a rock or boulder, socket fitted into head, in operating condition* 39.00   45.00
☐ **Same as above,** *if non-operating but intact* 24.00   29.00
☐ **Same as above,** *but with lighting attachment missing* 16.00   20.00
NOTE: The above was also made in an 8" size, with values as follows:
☐ **Same as above,** *but in operating condition* 34.00   40.00
☐ **Same as above,** *if non-operating but intact* 19.00   24.00
☐ **Same as above,** *but with lighting attachment missing* 12.00   15.00

☐ **Match Holder,** *6", pale green with darker green texturing. A hanging match holder, in vertical rectangular form, bowed out at the bottom to serve as dispenser, ribbed decoration running vertically at the front and horizontally at the sides, with a curved banner at the front reading "MATCHES" in block lettering, pierced for hanging* 23.00   28.00

☐ **Mug,** *6", shape #327, forest green, cylindrical shape with slightly swelled platform base, tall handle with vertical grip, decorated with a molded scene of peasant revelers, and additionally with ropework banding* 8.00   11.00

☐ **Patriotic Bee,** *a ceramic lapel pin in the form of a bumblebee with spread wings, red stripes on its body and stars on its wings, to suggest the American flag* 33.00   39.00
Note: It would be natural to call this some kind of political campaign novelty. More likely, however, it was issued to take

Price Range

advantage of the patriotic fervor which accompanied the end of World War I (1918.)

☐ **Pitcher,** 6", deep rich violet and brown with high-gloss glaze, tankard form with loop handle 8.00   11.00

☐ **Pitcher,** 6½", shape #33, pale rust orange, globular form, with molded banding at the lower bowl and neck, tall curved handle, vaulting bird's-wing spout, high gloss glaze 7.00   10.00

☐ **Pitcher, "Wise Bird,"** 10", iron gray base with body of rust brown and white, an owl perched on a stump, a handle at its back, the owl's head and upper portion of its back form the pitcher's mouth 42.00   49.00

☐ **Planter, bird and rose,** shape #246, yellow, dark brown and pink, with other colors, representing a canary with dark brown highlighting on wing and tail edges, alongside an oversize rose with open petals, mid to late 1950's 5.00   7.00

☐ **Planter, black bull,** very dark brown shading to black, several tan patches, standing bull with thick legs, in a striding pose, World War II era 4.00   6.00

☐ **Planter, camel,** ivory white with faint touches of brown, standing camel in striding pose, realistically modeled, back hollowed out to serve as a planter, sold in the 1950's 3.50   5.00

☐ **Planter, cat,** ivory yellow, realistically modeled figure of a long-haired cat with a bushy tail, head turned to the side, back hollowed out to form the planter, early 1950's 8.00   11.00

☐ **Planter, cat with bucket,** cream white, very pale pink and black, caricature figure of a cat with haughty facial expression alongside a pail or bucket, which forms the planter, 1950's 6.00   8.00

☐ **Planter, cub on log,** steel gray with brown and marble white, representing a bear cub with brown body and white face, standing on the top of a horizontal log (which forms the planter.) The log is textured to represent tree bark, and colored at the ends to suggest freshly sawn wood. Mid 1950's 6.00   8.00

Note: In addition to the above, there were a number of variations: Skunk on Log, Chipmunk on Log, Rabbit on Long, etc. Without exception the values all fall into the same range.

☐ **Planter, deer,** bone white with faint pastel brown, reclining deer with its forelegs tucked beneath its body, head turned around to look behind, back hollowed out to serve as a planter, made in the late 1930's 5.00   7.00

☐ **Planter, dolphins,** bone white, classically-inspired shape representing a pair of dolphins at either side of an urn or vase, with molded decoration of sea-foliage, the planter is the vase, before 1940 . . . .   5.00   7.00

☐ **Planter, elephant,** dusky white with red, a stylized elephant in caricature, standing, with stumpy legs, its trunk reaches the ground and turns upward. Back hollowed out to serve as a planter, pre-1940 . . . .   12.00   16.00

☐ **Planter, elephant,** gray and bluish-gray with bone white, standing elephant with upraised trunk, black hollowed out to serve as a planter, made in the late 1930's 5.00   7.00

☐ **Planter, frog,** 3", pale blue and white, the frog rests upon all fours, its face turned upward, its back is hollowed out to form the planter 10.00   13.00

Price Range

☐ **Planter, frog,** *pale sea green, seated bullfrog with upturned head, open mouth, body textured with lumps to represent warts, back hollowed out to serve as a planter* 4.00   6.00
Note: This early model dates to the 1930's. It originally carried a gold and black label at the base — not too many specimens still have it.

☐ **Planter, frog,** *slate green and gray, a frog on all fours, low-slung, with subdued molded decoration along the mouth of the planter at the frog's back, probably 1950's* 3.00   5.00

☐ **Planter, girl with hobby horse,** *cream white, black, red and other colors, representing a young girl seated casually beside a hobby horse or wooden rocking horse. The girl has blonde hair and wears a red hat, the horse is white with patches of black, and is mounted on a black stand, the horse's back is hollowed out to serve as a planter, made in the 1950's* 4.50   6.00

☐ **Planter, goat,** *ivory white with hints of yellow, standing goat with head turned to the side and looking upward, textured body to suggest fur, back hollowed out to serve as a planter, sold in the early 1950's* 3.50   5.00

☐ **Planter, hobby horse,** *pale salmon, green and burnt orange, a child's hobby horse with eyelashes, stump tail, back hollowed out to serve as a planter* 4.00   6.00

☐ **Planter, kitten and shoe,** *blue and cream white with pale brown shading, a blue shoe from which the head of a kitten protrudes, the kitten's face is chiefly white with pale brown touches at the sides, black eyes, the mouth is indicted by thin red brush strokes, late 1950's* 4.50   6.00

☐ **Planter, lamb and corral,** *slate blue with white, yellow and other colors, a lamb standing alongside the slatted sides of a corral fence, which forms the planter, mid to late 1950's* 5.00   7.00

☐ **Planter, ostrich,** *cream beige shading to almost white, with bright orange-brown, in the form of a reclining ostrich, realistically modeled, finely textured wings, the back hollowed out to serve as a planter, sold in the 1950's* 8.00   11.00

☐ **Planter, parakeet and rose,** *deep rose red, black, gray and yellow, representing a parakeet with yellow body and black wings perched on the edge of an oversized rose with open petals which serves as the planter, sold in the 1950's* 5.00   7.00

☐ **Planter, pig,** *gray and henna brown with mud green along the base, stout pig, realistically modeled, with head turned upward, back hollowed out to serve as a planter* 4.50   6.00

☐ **Planter, pink elephant,** *pale cream pink, stylized elephant with upturned trunk, ears flat, red eyes, back hollowed out to serve as a planter, pre-1940* 3.00   5.00

☐ **Planter, polar bear,** *bone with red and black, seated polar bear, open mouth, claws indicated by streaks of black paint, interior of ears and mouth colored red, red nose, black eyes, back hollowed out to serve as planter, sold in 1941* 3.50   5.00

☐ **Planter, puppy,** *black, dark brown and blue, a terrier-type dog alongside a bowl, grasping it with his forepaws, mainly black with touches of dark brown and a white face* 5.00   7.00

☐ **Planter, puppy,** *bone white and pale beige, a reclining puppy dog with forelegs tucked beneath body, pale beige coloring on*

Price Range

top of head and somewhat darker on hindquarters, back hollowed out to serve as a planter 5.00   7.00

☐ **Planter, rooster,** bluish gray and white, a low-slung rooster with back hollowed out as planter with textured tail feathers .. 4.50   6.00

☐ **Planter, skunk with cart,** blue, black, dark brown and other colors, a skunk seated next to a wheelcart, primarily black and white, the planter is the cart, late 1950's 4.50   6.00

☐ **Planter, stylized horse,** bone white with iron gray and charcoal gray, a horse in modified Art Deco style, the front portion of its body (neck to forelegs) modeled as symmetrical curve, head turned downward, back hollowed out to serve as a planter, made before 1940 .... 7.00   9.00

☐ **Planter, "Trojan Horse,"** walnut brown with touches of yellow, modeled figure of the Trojan Horse shown in Art Deco style, with very tall legs, curved neck (head rests on front of neck) .. 4.00   6.00

☐ **Planter, turtle,** 7", dusky white with rust brown and light washes of pastel green, the underside of the turtle's body is dusky white 4.00   6.00

☐ **Planter, turtle,** shape #205, pale lavender and beige, a standing turtle, wearing a long-sleeve sweater with ribbed collar and knitted cap, the planter is formed by the turtle's shell, World War II era 3.00   5.00

☐ **Planter, "Twin Swans,"** bone white with black and pink, a pair of swans, face to face, their heads touching in such a manner that their necks create a heart-shaped outline, back of each hollowed out as a planter, manufactured in early 1940's 7.00   9.00

☐ **Radio receiver,** 9½" x 3", a ceramic bug (a beetle) which contained a radio receiver, contained a crystal receiver, value as stated is for a specimen without the receiver 95.00   112.00

☐ **Rolling pin,** marble-white and black, with turned wooden holders, cylindrical form with foliage designs stenciled at either end 130.00   150.00

☐ **Spoon rack,** standing, cream-white and green, in form of a standing fish with the head of a woman emerging from the center of a flower, attached to a shaped copper wire which forms the rack 14.00   18.00

☐ **Tankard,** 10", salmon, traditional tankard body with long pointed spout, decorated with a molded scene of peasant revelers in a field based upon Dutch "tavern art" of the 17th century 28.00   34.00

☐ **Vase, "Wise Bird,"** 8", deep mahogany brown with yellow and touches of green, an owl, perched on a stump, next to a hollow tree trunk (which forms the vase,) the owl is dark brown with some black coloring to highlight the texturing of its feathers, both the stump and the lower part of the tree trunk are yellow with tones of pale and deep green 23.00   27.00

☐ **Vase, hangin,** 8", white, cream-white and brown, in the form of a cone, at the front of which is a figure of a perched owl, the cone is brown and has molded leaves at the sides, intended to give the appearance of a tree trunk, the owl is chiefly white with touches of brown and yellow 24.00   29.00

☐ **Wall ornament, jewelry caddy, mermaid,** yellow, pale blue and rust brown, vertical rectangular plaque with a sculptured mer-

	Price Range	

maid, tail upturned, holding a shell which serves as a rest for jewelry 13.00 16.00

☐ **Wall ornament, boxer dog,** *caramel brown with violet-brown, touches of yellowish beige, extremely realistic modeling of a standing boxer dog, set against a textured background, with storage compartment* 14.00 17.00

☐ **Wall ornament, "Bucking Bronco,"** *cream white and brown with black, white stallion wearing a brown saddle, bucking with all four hooves off the ground, next to a fence or rodeo gate, with storage compartment* 14.00 17.00

☐ **Wall ornament, doghouse,** *bone white, brown, black and very pale yellow, a doghouse with sides sloping inward, at the entrance sits a doberman-type dog. The dog is white with large black spots, with storage compartment* 13.00 16.00

☐ **Wall ornament, horse,** *shape #545, dark brown, white and black, horse in profile with head downward as if about to nibble grass, set against a textured background, high gloss glaze, sold in 1956, with storage compartment* 13.00 16.00

☐ **Wall plaques, African masks,** *10", black, brown, cream yellow and blue, with steaks of cream white, a pair of decorations in the form of African tribal ceremonial masks, in ovoid shape with pointed tops, large bulging blue eyes, one has the eyes set near the top of the mask, the other near the bottom, pair* .. 16.00 20.00

☐ **Same as above,** *but single plaque* 7.00 9.00

BUFFALO POTTERY

Buffalo Pottery's wares probably include more colorful and sprightly works than those of any other domestic manufacturer. Though the greatest variety is found in its early products, even those of later vintage include a high proportion of artistic creations — such as the famous Christmas plates. This firm is still operating, now approaching its 100th anniversary and has customers in every part of the world.

Buffalo Pottery had beginnings that were quite unique. The company grew out of a business which had nothing to do with pottery making and was conceived as a regular commercial firm. Buffalo Pottery's parent was the Larkin Company of Buffalo, New York, one of the great industrial giants of the 19th century. Larkin manufactured soaps and household cleansers of various kinds. With meager beginnings in the 1870's, the Larkin Company rapidly expanded, establishing factories and branch offices in most of the larger U.S. cities. Its annual gross sales were among the highest of any American manufacturer. Partially responsible for its huge success was an innovative, hard-driving merchandising program in which consumers were given premiums with their purchases of the Larkin goods. At first, this was done on a small scale with items such as handkerchiefs enclosed in cartons of soap bars. Gradually, the program was expanded and placed on the coupon system: customers saved up coupons and turned them in for merchandise. Larkin published special catalogue of its merchandise premiums. These included everything from small trinkets to rooms of furniture. It was said that the Larkin catalogues went into more than 1,000,000 homes at a time when the population of the United States was about one-fourth its present size.

Among the most frequently requested premiums were ceramics of all kinds, especially tableware and decorative display items. After contracting for these with suppliers for several years, Larkin concluded that it would be more convenient to open up a pottery factory and manufacture its own. The company was called Buffalo Pottery and went into operation in 1903. Since the number of experienced pottery workers in Buffalo was few, recruits came in from Trenton and elsewhere, and very soon an able staff had been assembled. The premium program went along in high gear for several years thereafter. Eventually, it seemed apparent that there was a willing market for Buffalo Pottery outside the sphere of Larkin customers and coupon-savers. Not everyone was willing to save up the coupons — but they would buy the pottery if offered for a price. So on an experimental basis, some consignments were freighted around the country to selected retail outlets. The response was tremendous. So the output of Buffalo Pottery was soon being sold more and more into ordinary retail shops and distributed less by premium catalogues. By around 1908, it had become one of the largest selling lines of pottery in the entire country. It was in 1908 that Buffalo began manufacturing its celebrated Deldare ware, the favorite of so many present day collectors. The firm received a further — and wholly unexpected — boost in World War I, when the government decided to equip all branches of the Armed Services with Buffalo ware.

Marks: Marks used by Buffalo Pottery Company are mostly very ornamental and distinctive. A figure of a buffalo is usually incorporated in the mark, but there are also special marks for lines with trade names (such as a feathered cap for Buffalo's "Robin Hood" ware.) The buffalo, when pictured, is shown facing left and looking directly forward. In one version of the mark, the term *SEMI-VITREOUS* is position in an arch above the buffalo, with the name *BUFFALO POTTERY* beneath. In another, the buffalo is pictured as an ornament surmounting a hanging shop-sign, reading *MADE AT YE BUFFALO POTTERY.* This was the trademark for Deldare and was intended to give a flavor of old-time England. In yet another variation, the buffalo is enclosed within a circular frame in which *BUFFALO POTTERY, SEMI-VITREOUS* appears. There was a patriotic version of the mark in which the buffalo (enclosed in a circular frame) was surmounted by an eagle and standard. This carried the word *WARRANTED* along with the usual wording. The collector should recognize that the system of markings on Buffalo Pottery did not always follow an established order. The principal lines usually received their prescribed marks but other lines frequently did not. Pieces will often be found in which the mark is nothing more than a hand-inked inscription. These differences, while they might arouse curiosity, seem to have no influence on value.

ABINO WARE *(Introduced 1911)*

Each item in this line carries one of several scenes in wispy detail decorated by one of three artists. Ralph Stuart, Charles Harris and W. E. Simpson each signed every piece they hand-decorated on semi-vitreous Deldare blanks. The themes include seascapes, sailing ships, windmills, lighthouses and a few with pastoral scenes. The name Abino comes from a small peninsula on the north Canadian shore of Lake Erie, a few miles from Buffalo. The Abino Point was the vacation spot for Buffalo sailors and canoeists who liked the protective harbor that was created by the point.

Many of the scenes on these wares show rough waters, because the area outside the harbor was known to be dangerous during a storm. Some ships and barges hit the reefs and sank during the storms or while in dense fog. The lighthouse sometimes used on the wares was a symbol of the much-needed lighthouse erected on Point Abino by the Canadian government in 1917.

Price Range

☐ **Basket,** *13″, sailing boats, fan-shaped with handle, signed "C. Harris," 1912* 1050.00   1250.00

☐ **Bread and butter plate,** *6½″, windmill scene, with recessed center ring, signed "C. Harris," 1912.* 210.00   260.00

☐ **Candlestick,** *9″, sailing boat, signed "W. E. Simpson," 1913* .. 665.00   785.00

☐ **Cup and saucer,** *sailing ships* 235.00   285.00

☐ **Hair receiver,** *highlights of blue, round, sailing scene, signed "W. E. Simpson," 1913* 325.00   400.00

☐ **Match box holder and ash tray combination,** *3¾″, 1912* 425.00   500.00

☐ **Mug,** *3½″, sailing scene* 300.00   360.00

☐ **Pitcher,** *6¾″, sailing ships* 425.00   500.00

☐ **Pitcher,** *7″, Portland Head Light, Portland, Me., eight-sided with decorative handle, signed "R. Stuart," 1912* 565.00   665.00

☐ **Plaque,** *12″, nautical scene, with one boat near and others in the distance, signed "C. Harris," 1911* 700.00   825.00

☐ **Plaque,** *12¼″, sailing ships, on rough seas, signed "R. Stuart," 1911* 700.00   825.00

☐ **Plaque,** *13½″, In The Pastures, with recessed center ring, signed "R. Stuart," 1912* 1200.00   1600.00

☐ **Plaque,** *13½″, The Waning Day* 1200.00   1600.00

☐ **Plate,** *8½″, Portland Head Light, Portland, Me., signed "C. Harris," 1912* 340.00   410.00

☐ **Plate,** *10″, windmill scene, recessed center ring, signed "C. Harris," 1912* 425.00   500.0

☐ **Salt and pepper shakers,** *pair* 425.00   500.00

☐ **Sugar bowl,** *with cover, sailing ships on rough seas, signed "C. Harris," 1912* 365.00   435.00

☐ **Tankard,** *7″, cylindrical with decorative handle, signed "C. Harris," 1912* 650.00   775.00

☐ **Teapot,** *with cover, sailing ships on rough seas, signed "C. Harris," 1912* 365.00   435.00

☐ **Tea Tile,** *6″, nautical scene, round, signed "C. Harris," 1913* .. 425.00   500.00

☐ **Tray,** *9″x12″, windmill scene, and lake, signed "C. Harris," 1912* 850.00   1000.00

☐ **Tray,** *9¾″x12″, mountain lake scene, signed "R. Stuart," 1911,* 1050.00   1250.00

☐ **Tray, dresser,** *13¾″x10½″, highlights of blue, farming scene, rectangular, signed "W.E. Simpson," 1913* 1050.00   1250.00

☐ **Vase,** *6¾″, windmill scene, signed "C. Harris," 1912* 550.00   650.00

BLUE WILLOW *(Introduced 1905)*

"Once upon a time there was a rich old Mandarin who had an only daughter named Li-Chi. She and her father lived in a beautiful home...." This is the beginning of a legend that has accompanied the Blue Willow pattern for many years. The story of two lovers who are destined to be together, even if they must become turtle doves, is beautifully told on these wares with ornate border designs and oriental flavor. The blue underglaze decoration is traditional for European willow on porcelain, but on Buffalo Blue Willow, the design is applied to semiporcelain. This differs from porcelain in that it is opaque and has a finish like that of earthenware. Besides the traditional blue willow, other colors were used to create the same design, and these wares were called Gaudy Willow. The other colors used were rust, green, brown and gold. Gaudy Willow pieces are very rare and hold a higher collector value.

	Price	Range
☐ **Baker,** *3", oblong*	5.00	8.00
☐ **Baker,** *4", oblong*	5.00	8.00
☐ **Baker,** *5", oblong*	7.50	10.00
☐ **Baker,** *6", oblong*	7.50	10.00
☐ **Baker,** *7", oblong*	10.00	13.00
☐ **Baker,** *8", oblong*	12.00	15.00
☐ **Baker,** *9", oblong*	14.00	18.00
☐ **Bouillon,** *with two handles*	10.00	12.50
☐ **Bowl,** *2 pints, 1 ounce, without decorative border*	14.00	18.00
☐ **Bowl,** *1 pint, 7½ ounces, without decorative border*	12.00	15.00
☐ **Bowl,** *14 ounces, without decorative border*	12.00	15.00
☐ **Butter dish,** *7¾", with cover, and handle*	70.00	85.00
☐ **Butter dish,** *individual, round*	5.00	8.00
☐ **Cake plate,** *10¹⁄₁₆", round, with two handles*	42.50	40.00
☐ **Cake cover,** *6³⁄₈", round*	30.00	35.00
☐ **Casserole,** *8³⁄₁₆", round, with two handles, and lid with handle*	60.00	75.00
☐ **Coaster,** *3½", round*	12.00	15.00
☐ **Coffee cup,** *10 ounces, flaired rim, with handle*	12.00	15.00
☐ **Coffee cup,** *10 ounces, with handle*	12.00	15.00
☐ **Coffee cup,** *3 ounces, cylindrical, with handle*	12.00	15.00
☐ **Chop dish,** *11¹⁄₈", round, thick decorative border*	30.00	35.00
☐ **Chop dish,** *13", round, thick decorative border*	32.50	40.00
☐ **Coupe,** *7¹⁰⁄₁₆", round*	12.00	15.00
☐ **Coupe,** *8¾", round*	12.00	15.00
☐ **Creamer,** *1 pint, 2 ounces, bulbous, with handle*	25.00	30.00
☐ **Creamer,** *15 ounces, four-sided, with decorative handle and spout*	20.00	25.00
☐ **Creamer,** *8½ ounces, bulbous with handle*	12.00	15.00
☐ **Creamer,** *7¾ ounces, spherical, with handle*	12.00	15.00
☐ **Cup and saucer,** *1 pint, 5½ ounces, flaired rim, with handle*	40.00	45.00
☐ **Custard,** *7 ounces, with handle, on small pedestal base*	12.00	15.00
☐ **Dish,** *7³⁄₁₆", oblong*	16.00	20.00
☐ **Dish,** *8¹¹⁄₁₆", oblong*	16.00	20.00
☐ **Dish,** *9¹¹⁄₁₆", oblong*	25.00	30.00
☐ **Dish,** *10¹¹⁄₁₆", oblong*	25.00	30.00
☐ **Dish,** *11¹⁵⁄₁₆", oblong*	30.00	35.00
☐ **Dish,** *14", oblong*	30.00	35.00
☐ **Dish,** *16", oblong*	35.00	40.00
☐ **Dish,** *18", oblong*	40.00	45.00
☐ **Dish,** *7½"x9½", square, with lid, flaired rim*	60.00	75.00
☐ **Dish,** *8¾x11¹⁄₈", square, with lid, flaired rim*	70.00	85.00
☐ **Egg cup,** *7 ounces, Boston, on small pedestal base*	16.00	20.00
☐ **Egg cup,** *5½ ounces, double, on small pedestal base*	16.00	20.00
☐ **Egg cup,** *1¼ ounces, single, on small pedestal base*	16.00	20.00
☐ **Fruit dish,** *4⁷⁄₈", round, shallow*	12.00	15.00
☐ **Fruit dish,** *5¾", round, shallow*	12.00	15.00
☐ **Jug,** *3 pints, 5½ ounces, cylindrical, with handle*	130.00	150.00
☐ **Jug,** *2 pints, 4 ounces, cylindrical, with handle*	105.00	125.00
☐ **Jug,** *1 pint, 7 ounces, cylindrical, with handle*	100.00	115.00

	Price Range	
☐ **Jug,** 1 pint, cylindrical, with handle	85.00	100.00
☐ **Jug,** 3 pints, 14 ounces, bulbous, with handle	120.00	140.00
☐ **Jug,** 2 pints, 14 ounces, bulbous, with handle	100.00	125.00
☐ **Jug,** 2 pints, bulbous, with handle	100.00	115.00
☐ **Jug,** 1 pint, 4½ ounces, bulbous, with handle	85.00	100.00
☐ **Jug,** 11½ ounces	75.00	90.00
☐ **Jug,** 3 pints, 6½ ounces, hall boy, cylindrical, with handle	130.00	150.00
☐ **Mug,** 11 ounces, with handle, cylindrical, flaired base, without decorative border	12.00	15.00
☐ **Mustard jar,** 5½ ounces, with lid	40.00	45.00
☐ **Nappy,** 7⁹⁄₁₆", round, shallow, flat extended rim	15.00	20.00
☐ **Nappy,** 8½", round, shallow, flat extended rim	16.00	20.00
☐ **Nappy,** 9⅜", round, shallow, flat extended rim	16.00	20.00
☐ **Oyster tureen,** 9¾", with two handles, covered lid with handle	70.00	85.00
☐ **Oatmeal dish,** 6⁵⁄₁₆", round, shallow, flat extended rim	7.50	10.00
☐ **Plate,** 5¼", round	5.00	7.50
☐ **Plate,** 6¼", round	5.00	8.00
☐ **Plate,** 7⁷⁄₁₆", round	7.50	10.00
☐ **Plate,** 8¼", round	10.00	12.00
☐ **Plate,** 9¼", round	12.00	15.00
☐ **Plate,** 10¼", round	12.00	15.00
☐ **Plate,** 10½", round	16.00	20.00
☐ **Ramekin,** 3½ ounces, with flaired rim	7.50	10.00
☐ **Salad bowl,** 9¹⁄₁₆"x9⁵⁄₁₆", square, decorative border in lining	25.00	30.00
☐ **Sauceboat,** 14½ ounces, square, with decorative handled and spout	25.00	30.00
☐ **Sauceboat,** double handle, with saucer	30.00	35.00
☐ **Sauce tureen,** with notched cover and two handles	55.00	70.00
☐ **Sauce tureen stand,** 8½"x6⅛", square shallow	12.00	15.00
☐ **Sugar,** 25½ ounces, square with notched lid, and two handles	25.00	30.00
☐ **Sugar,** 24½ ounces, round, with two handles and lid	25.00	30.00
☐ **Sugar,** 12 ounces, round with lid and two pinch handles	16.00	20.00
☐ **Sugar,** 12 ounces, bulbous, decorative stand, handles and lid .	16.00	20.00
☐ **Teapot,** 2 pints, 5¼ ounces, square, with decorative handles, lid and spout	70.00	85.00
☐ **Teapot,** 3 pints, 3 ounces, round, with lid and handle	70.00	85.00
☐ **Teapot,** 14 ounces, cylindrical, with lid and handle	30.00	35.00
☐ **Teapot,** 1 pint, bulbous, with decorative lid handle and spout ..	30.00	35.00
☐ **Tea cup,** 7 ounces, round, with, flaired rim and handle	12.00	15.00
☐ **Tea cup,** 7 ounces, round, with handle	12.00	15.00

DELDARE WARE (Introduced 1905))

Deldare wares are distinctly noted for their unusual colors on very busy and decorative scenes on an olive green background. The name, however, does not specifically apply to the designs, but to the basic body formula that was created by William Rea, a ceramic engineer, and George Wood, the superintendent of Buffalo's clay shop. The color of the clay is consistent throughout the fired object, so if it was broken, olive green would be seen clear through.

The designs are the distinguishing factor in Deldare ware. Scenes outlined in black cover each item almost completely. One of the most famous scenes are the "Fallowfield Hunt." These scenes tell in sequence a story of an English fox hunt. They were reproduced from drawings by Cecil Charles

Aldin. Wares with these hunting scenes were produced in 1908 and 1909.
Another set of English designs came from books, such as *The Vicar of Wakefield*. These wares, also produced in 1908 and 1909, depict English life in scenes called "Ye Olden Days." After discountinuing Deldare in 1911, production was again started and "Ye Olden Days" was again reproduced in 1923 to 1925.

Another design that was produced on these wares was also taken from sayings found in *The Vicar of Wakefield*. These designs, which are possibly original illustrations from the artists at Buffalo, tell a story about the phrases. Some that were used are "To Spare an Old Broken Soldier," "To Advise Me in A Whisper" and "All You Have to do is Teach the Dutchman English."

The next set of designs depicted occurrences in English taverns. "Ye Lion Inn" was produced in 1908, 1909, and in 1923 to 1925. And the last type of designs were taken from paintings by Thomas Rowlandson and explained in verses by William Combe. "Dr. Syntax" specimens were frivolous illustrations and rhyming verses that were produced on mostly Emerald Deldare in 1911. The Emerald Deldare was distinguished by its Art Nouveau decorative borders. Some wares, even without the Dr. Syntax verses, were entirely Art Nouveau decoration.

	Price Range	
☐ **Basket,** *13", Art Nouveau, dragon flies and butterflies on geometric borders, 1911*	850.00	1150.00
☐ **Bowl,** *5", The Fallowfield Hunt, Breakfast at the Three Pigeons, 1909*	575.00	675.00
☐ **Bowl,** *9", The Fallowfield Hunt, The Death, signed "W. Foster," 1909*	435.00	505.00
☐ **Bowl, cereal,** *6¼", The Fallowfield Hunt, The Start*	235.00	285.00
☐ **Bowl, cereal,** *6½", Ye Olden Days, signed "H.B.," 1908*	235.00	285.00
☐ **Bowl, fruit,** *9", Dr. Syntax Reading His Tour, signed "M. Broel,"*	665.00	785.00
☐ **Bowl, fruit,** *9"x3¾", Ye Village Tavern, signed "H. Ford," 1908*	385.00	455.00
☐ **Bowl, fruit,** *5", Peacocks, 1911*	1100.00	1300.00
☐ **Bowl, nut,** *3¼", Ye Lion Inn, 1909*	425.00	500.00
☐ **Bowl, punch,** *9¼", Fallowfield Hunt Scenes, signed "W. Foster," 1909*	4500.00	5000.00
☐ **Bread and butter plate,** *6¼", At Ye Lion Inn, signed "E. Broel," 1924*	85.00	100.00
☐ **Bullion cup and saucer,** *Untitled Village Scenes*	210.00	260.00
☐ **Candle holder and match holder combination,** *5½", Untitled Village Scenes, signed "B. Wilton," 1909*	320.00	380.00
☐ **Candlestick, shield back,** *7", Untitled Village Scenes, signed "G. R.," 1909*	575.00	675.00
☐ **Candlesticks,** *9", Bayberry, signed "Sauter," pair*	600.00	700.00
☐ **Candlesticks,** *9", owls, pair*	625.00	725.00
☐ **Candlesticks,** *9½", Untitled Village Scenes, signed "W. F.," and "E.B.," 1909, 1925, pair*	425.00	500.00
☐ **Creamer,** *Dr. Syntax With the Dairy Maid, 1911*	260.00	320.00
☐ **Creamer,** *Scenes of Village Life in Ye Olden Days, signed "G.H.S.," 1924*	150.00	175.00
☐ **Cup and saucer,** *Dr. Syntax at Liverpool, Dr. Syntax and The Bookseller, signed "M. Ramlin"*	225.00	275.00
☐ **Cup and saucer,** *The Fallowfield Hunt, signed "Ed. J. Mars," 1909*	170.00	200.00

Price Range

☐ **Cup and saucer,** Ye Olden Days, signed "J. Nekolk," "G. H.
Jone," 1909 .... 160.00 190.00

☐ **Dish, fern,** 3¼", Butterflies and Flowers 500.00 600.00

☐ **Dish, relish,** 12"x6½", The Fallowfield Hunt, The Dash, signed
"A. Lang," 1909 .... 260.00 320.00

☐ **Dish, sauce,** Breaking Cover, signed "R. Windsor," 1909 ..... 130.00 150.00

☐ **Hair receiver,** Ye Village Street, with lid, 1909 .... 250.00 300.00

☐ **Humidor,** 4½", octagon shaped, Ye Lion Inn 425.00 500.00

☐ **Humidor,** 7", Ye Lion Inn, eight-sided, signed "E.B.," 1909 .... 625.00 725.00

☐ **Humidor,** 8", There Was an Old Sailor, signed "C.B.," 1909 ... 635.00 745.00

☐ **Inkwell set,** with covers, 1911 .... 3100.00 3600.00

☐ **Jar, powder,** Ye Village Street, with lid, signed "J. Gerhardt,"
1909 .... 240.00 290.00

☐ **Jardiniere,** 6", Ye Village Street, signed "P. Hall," 1909 .... 425.00 500.00

☐ **Jardiniere,** 9", Butterflies and Flowers, 1910 .... 1200.00 1600.00

☐ **Match box holder and ashtray combination,** Scenes of Village
Life in Ye Olden Days, signed "E.B.," 1925 .... 320.00 380.00

☐ **Mug,** 2¼", I Give The Law to That Are Owing, signed "A.
Roth," 1911 .... 300.00 350.00

☐ **Mug,** 2½", The Fallowfield Hunt, signed "F. Mac," 1909 ...... 220.00 270.00

☐ **Mug,** 2½", Scenes of Village Life in Ye Olden Days 210.00 260.00

☐ **Mug,** 3½", Breaking Cover, signed "R. Caird," 1909 .... 195.00 235.00

☐ **Mug,** 3½", Ye Lion Inn, signed "E. Dowman," 1908 .... 200.00 240.00

☐ **Mug,** 4¼", At The Three Pigeons, signed "E. Ditmars," 1908 .. 220.00 270.00

☐ **Mug,** 4¼", Dr. Syntax Again Filled Up His Glass, signed "L.
Newman," 1911 .... 300.00 350.00

☐ **Mug,** 4¼", Dr. Syntax Made Free of The Cellar, 1911 .... 300.00 350.00

☐ **Mug,** 4¼", Indian scene, signed "R. Stuart," 1908 .... 400.00 470.00

☐ **Mug,** 4¼", Ye Lion Inn, signed "M. Gerhardt," 1908 .... 210.00 260.00

☐ **Mug,** 4½", Fallowfield Hunt, signed "M. Gerhardt" 210.00 260.00

☐ **Pitcher,** 6", Dr. Syntax Stopped by Highwaymen, signed " H.
Robin" 425.00 500.00

☐ **Pitcher,** 6", Their Manner of Telling Stories, Which He Returned
With a Curtsey, eight-sided, signed "G.H.S.," 1923 .... 340.00 400.00

☐ **Pitcher,** 7", To Spare an Old Broken Solder, To Advise Me in a
Whisper, eight-sided, 1923 .... 385.00 450.00

☐ **Pitcher,** 8", Dr. Syntax Bound to A Tree by Highwaymen, eight-
sided 565.00 665.00

☐ **Pitcher,** 8", The Fallowfield Hunt, The Return, eight-sided,
signed "P. Hall," 1909 .... 425.00 500.00

☐ **Pitcher,** 8", To Demand My Annual Rent, Welcome Me with The
Most Cordial Hospitality 400.00 470.00

☐ **Pitcher,** 8¾", Dr. Syntax Setting Out to The Lakes, signed"R.
Stuart" 635.00 745.00

☐ **Pitcher,** 9", With A Cane Superior Air, This Amazed Me, signed
"P. Hall," 1908 .... 450.00 525.00

☐ **Pitcher,** 10", A Noble Hunting Party, signed "R. Stuart," 1911 . 750.00 900.00

☐ **Pitcher,** 10", The Fallowfield Hunt, Breaking Cover, eight-
sided, 1909 .... 500.00 600.00

☐ **Pitcher,** 10", Ye Old English Village, eight-sided, signed "H.
Steiner," 1909 .... 425.00 500.00

☐ **Pitcher,** 10½", tankard shaped, Dr. Syntax Entertained At College, signed "W. Foster," 1911 .... 750.00 900.00

	Price Range	
☐ **Pitcher**, *12", tankard shaped, To Becky's Hand He Gave a Squeeze, signed "Newman"*	750.00	900.00
☐ **Pitcher**, *12½", tankard shaped, All You Have To Do Is Teach The Dutchman English, The Great Controversy, signed "M. Broel," 1908*	635.00	745.00
☐ **Pitcher**, *12½", tankard shaped, Fallowfield Hunt, signed "M. Caird"*	635.00	745.00
☐ **Plaque**, *12", Doves and Peacocks, signed "M. Gerhardt," 1911*	850.00	1050.00
☐ **Plaque**, *12", Dr. Syntax Sketching The Lake, signed "J. Gerhardt"*	750.00	900.00
☐ **Plaque**, *12", Friday, signed "M. Gerhardt," set*	1000.00	1200.00
☐ **Plaque**, *12", Thursday, signed "J. Gerhardt," 1914*	1000.00	1200.00
☐ **Plaque**, *13½", Lost, signed "R. Stuart," 1911*	1200.00	1600.0
☐ **Plaque**, *13½", Penn's Treaty With The Indians, signed "R. Stuart," 1911*	1200.00	1600.00
☐ **Plaque**, *16½", The Garden Trio, signed "J. Wigley" 1911*	3000.00	3500.00
☐ **Plate**, *6½", The Fallowfield Hunt, signed "M. Bron," 1909*	95.00	115.00
☐ **Plate**, *7¼", Dr. Syntax Soliloquising, signed "J. Gerhardt"*	340.00	400.00
☐ **Plate**, *7¼", Ye Village Street, signed "O. Sauter," 1908*	105.00	120.00
☐ **Plate**, *8¼", John Alden and Priscilla, signed "J. Gerhardt," 1911*	740.00	860.00
☐ **Plate**, *8¼", Ye Town Crier, signed "E.B.," 1908*	120.00	150.00
☐ **Plate**, *8½", The Fallowfield Hunt, The Death, signed "L. Streissel," 1909*	110.00	125.00
☐ **Plate**, *8½", Misfortune At Tulip Hall, signed "E. Miessel," 1911*	385.00	455.00
☐ **Plate**, *8½", Spanish Galleons, marked "Buffalo Pottery"*	290.00	350.00
☐ **Plate, soup**, *9", The Fallowfield Hunt, Breaking Cover, signed "E. Dowman," 1909*	235.00	285.00
☐ **Plate**, *9¼", The Fallowfield Hunt, The Start, signed "M. H. F.," 1908*	160.00	190.00
☐ **Plate**, *9¼", Syntax Star Gazing, signed "M. Ramlin," 1911*	400.00	470.0
☐ **Plate**, *9½", Daughter Of The American Revolution, signed "B. Wilton," 1909*	740.00	860.00
☐ **Plate**, *9½", Ye Olden Times, signed "R. Wade," 1908*	135.00	155.00
☐ **Plate**, *10", Dr. Syntax Making a Discovery, signed "M. Broel," 1911*	500.00	600.00
☐ **Plate**, *10", The Fallowfield Hunt, Breaking cover, signed "H. Biddle," 1909*	170.00	200.00
☐ **Plate**, *10", Yankee Doodle, signed "M. Broel," 1908*	750.00	900.00
☐ **Plate, cake**, *10", Ye Village Gossips, with two handles, signed "M. Snediker" 1908*	260.00	320.00
☐ **Plate**, *12", The Coming Storm*	850.00	1050.00
☐ **Plate, chop**, *13½", Dr. Syntax Sells Grizzle, signed "A. Sauter"*	740.00	860.00
☐ **Plate chop**, *14", An Evening At Ye Lion Inn, pierced rim, signed "M. Sned," 1909*	460.00	550.00
☐ **Plate, chop**, *14", The Fallowfield Hunt, The Start, signed "J. Gerhardt," 1908*	460.00	550.00
☐ **Salt and pepper shakers**, *Art Nouveau, geometric and floral designs, signed "M.G.," 1915*	300.00	360.00
☐ **Sugar bowl**, *covered, Dr. Syntax In The Wrong Lodging House, 1911*	300.00	360.00
☐ **Sugar bowl**, *3½", Fallowfield Hunt, six-sided, 1908*	210.00	260.00
☐ **Sugar bowl**, *Scenes of Village Life In Ye Olden Days, signed "G.H.S.," 1925*	160.00	190.00

Price Range

☐ **Tankard,** 6¾", *English Street Scene, white lining, signed "R. Stuart," 1911* 575.00 675.00

☐ **Tankard,** 6¾", *Ye Lion Inn, Ye Old English Village, white lining, signed "W.F.," 1924* 650.00 750.00

☐ **Teapot,** *covered, Dr. Syntax Disputing His Bill* 340.00 410.00

☐ **Teapot,** 3¾", *Scenes of Village Life In Ye Olden Days, signed "C.D.," 1909* 210.00 260.00

☐ **Teapot,** 5¾", *Scenes of Village Life In Ye Olden Days, signed "G.H.S.," 1924* 300.00 360.00

☐ **Tea tile,** *Dr. Syntax Taking Possession of His Living, 6", signed "H. Robin," 1911* 425.00 500.00

☐ **Tea tile,** 6", *Traveling In Ye Olden Days* 235.00 285.00

☐ **Toothpick holder,** 2¼", *Art Nouveau, flower and leaf design, signed "M.G.B."* 260.00 320.00

☐ **Tray, calling card,** 7", *Dr. Syntax Robbed of His Property, signed "A. Roth"* 440.00 510.00

☐ **Tray, calling card,** 7", *Mr. Pickwick Addresses The Club, signed "L. Anna," 1908* 440.00 510.00

☐ **Tray, calling card,** 7¾", *The Fallowfield Hunt, signed "O. Sauter," 1908* 235.00 285.00

☐ **Tray, calling card,** 7¾", *Ye Lion Inn, signed "L. Newman," 1909* 235.00 285.00

☐ **Tray, dresser,** 9"x12", *Dr. Syntax, Rural Sports* 700.00 820.00

☐ **Tray, pin,** 6¼"x3½", *Ye Old Olden Days, signed "E.B." 1909* .. 160.00 190.00

☐ **Tray, relish,** 12"x6", *Ye Olden Days, signed "W. Foster," 1908* . 275.00 335.00

☐ **Tray, tea,** 12"x10", *heirlooms, signed "W. Foster," 1908* 500.00 600.00

☐ **Tray, tea,** 13¾"x10¾", *Dr. Syntax Mistakes A Gentleman's House For An Inn, signed "R. Stuart," 1911* 750.00 875.00

☐ **Vase,** 8", *kingfisher, dragonflies, iris and waterlilies, 1911* 725.00 850.00

☐ **Vase,** 8", *untitled, decorated with fashionable men and women, signed "B.S."* 600.00 700.00

☐ **Vase,** 8½", *Ye Village Parson, Ye Village Schoolmaster, 1909* . 600.00 700.00

☐ **Vase,** 9", *untitled village scenes, 1909* 260.00 320.00

☐ **Vase,** 13½", *American beauty, signed "M. Gerhardt," 1911* ... 750.00 900.00

☐ **Vase,** 22½", *ducks, pheasant and crane, marked "Buffalo Pottery," 1914* 3000.00 3500.00

☐ **Vegetable server,** 8½"x6½", *Ye Olden Times, signed "H. Ford," 1909* 320.00 380.00

☐ **Wall plaque,** 12", *The Fallowfield Hunt, Breakfast At The Three Pigeons* 425.00 500.00

☐ **Wall plaque,** 12", *Ye Lion Inn* 425.00 500.00

MISCELLANEOUS

ADVERTISING PLATES

☐ **Advance,** 7½" 50.00 65.00

☐ **Bing and Nathan,** 7½", *Buffalo, N.Y.* 50.00 65.00

☐ **Crane,** 7½" 70.00 85.00

☐ **Independence Hall,** 7½" 50.00 65.00

☐ **Jack Knife Bridge,** 7½", *Buffalo, N.Y.* 100.00 125.00

☐ **The Locks,** 7½", *Lockport, N.Y.* 100.00 125.00

☐ **Main St.,** 7½", *Buffalo, N.Y.* 70.00 85.00

Price Range

ANIMALS PLATES
Deer

☐ **Caribou,** *9"* 45.00   55.00
☐ **Eastern White Tail Deer,** *9"* 45.00   55.00
☐ **Elk,** *9"* 45.00   55.00
☐ **Fallow Deer,** *9"* 45.00   55.00
☐ **Moose,** *9"* 45.00   55.00
☐ **Sika Deer,** *9"* 45.00   55.00
☐ **White Tail Deer,** *15" x 11"* 100.00   125.00

Fish

☐ **Atlantic Salmon,** *9"* 45.00   55.00
☐ **Cut Throat Trout,** *9"* 45.00   55.00
☐ **Great Northern Pike,** *9"* 45.00   55.00
☐ **Land Locked Salmon,** *9"* 45.00   55.00
☐ **Rainbow Trout,** *9"* 45.00   55.00
☐ **Small Mount Black Bass,** *15" x 11", signed "R.K. Beck"* 100.00   125.00
☐ **Striped Bass,** *9"* 45.00   55.00

Fowl

☐ **American Herring Gull,** *9", dated 1907* 48.00   60.00
☐ **American Woodcock,** *9", dated 1907* 48.00   60.00
☐ **Bird in Forest,** *9", hand painted underglazed decoration, dated 1916* 150.00   175.00
☐ **Crane,** *9", hand painted underglazed decoration* 48.00   60.00
☐ **Dusky Grouse,** *9", dated 1908* 48.00   60.00
☐ **Mallard Duck,** *9", dated 1908* 48.00   60.00
☐ **Peacock and Vines,** *9", hand painted underglaze decoration* .. 55.00   70.00
☐ **Quail,** *8½", hand painted overglaze, dated 1915* 95.00   110.00
☐ **Ring-Necked Pheasant,** *10½", hand painted underglaze decoration* 95.00   110.00
☐ **Wild Ducks,** *9", dated 1908* 45.00   60.00
☐ **Wild Turkey,** *9", dated 1907* 48.00   60.00

COMMEMORATIVE PLATES

☐ **Buffalo, N.Y.,** *8", dark blue underglaze decoration, dated 1905-15* 85.00   100.00
☐ **Buffalo, N.Y.,** *7½", dark blue green, underglaze decoration, dated 1905-15* 85.00   100.00
☐ **Erie Tribe,** *7½", Improved Order of Red Men* 60.00   75.00
☐ **Faneuil Hall,** *7½", Boston, Mass., blue green, c. 1906* 55.00   70.00
☐ **Gates Circle,** *7½", Buffalo, N.Y., blue green* 75.00   90.00
☐ **George Washington,** *7½", blue green, with reproduction of signature* 150.00   175.00
☐ **Hudson Terminal Buildings,** *7½", blue green underglazed decoration* 70.00   80.00
☐ **Improved order of Red Men,** *7½", sixth anniversary, 1902-1908 on front* 65.00   80.00
☐ **Martha Washington,** *7½", blue green, with reproduction of signature* 150.00   175.00
☐ **Modern Woodmen of America,** *7½", blue green underglaze decoration, dated 1911* 70.00   85.00
☐ **New Bedford, Mass.** *10½", blue underglaze decoration, dated 1908* 85.00   100.00

	Price Range	
☐ **Odd Fellows Hall**, *Cambridge, Mass., 7½″, blue green, 1884-1910 on front*	70.00	85.00
☐ **Protective Order of Elks**, *7½″, blue green underglaze decoration*	50.00	65.00
☐ **St. Mary Magdelen Church, Bufffalo, N.Y.**, *7½″, blue green* ...	55.00	70.00
☐ **Theodore Roosevelt**, *8″, blue underglaze decoration, gold accents, dated 1905*	175.00	200.00
☐ **Trinity Church, N.Y. City**, *7½″, blue green underglaze decoration*	60.00	75.00
☐ **United Daughters of The Confederacy**, *10½″, blue underglaze*	85.00	100.00
☐ **Washington's Home At Mt. Vernon**, *7½″, hand decorated*	50.00	65.00
☐ **W.C.T.U.**, *9″, blue underglaze decoration, for the Woman's Christian Temperance Union*	125.00	150.00
☐ **White House, Washington, D.C.**, *7½″, back reads "erected 1792"*	55.00	70.00

HISTORICAL PLATES

☐ **Faneuil Hall, Boston**, *10″*	40.00	50.00
☐ **Independence Hall, Philadelphia, Pa.**, *10″*	40.00	50.00
☐ **Niagara Falls**, *10″*	40.00	50.00
☐ **The U.S. Capital, Washington, D.C.**, *10″*	40.00	50.00
☐ **The White House, Washington, D.C.**, *10″*	40.00	50.00
☐ **Washington's Home in Mt. Vernon**, *10″*	40.00	50.00

BURGESS & CAMPBELL

See International Pottery.

BURROUGHS & MOUNTFORD COMPANY

Burroughs & Mountford is somewhat more interesting than many of the other Trenton companies making similar wares, for B&M apparently paid a little more attention to the fine details of manufacturing and decorating.

The company was founded in 1879 in what had formerly been the Eagle Pottery. Wares included the usual assortment of granite and cream-colored wares, and they also made a limited amount of porcelain, little of which is seen today. They employed a Japanese artist who did gold paste work for them. Tiles with both printed and embossed designs were also produced at B&M.

Marks: All of the marks shown were used on various types of decorated cream-colored and granite ware items. It is not known which of these marks was used on their porcelain and tiles.

☐ **Pitcher**, *6¼″ to top of spout, transfer decoration with hand-coloring and sponged gold, Mark B, see photo*	85.00	100.00
☐ **Pot, chocolate**, *10″ high, decoration similar to above, Mark C* .	85.00	100.00
Note: Nearly all B&M items suffer from crazing of the glaze, and this is generally not held against them where price is concerned.		

Lower-level Burroughs & Mountford items can be estimated as follows:

B – M

B-M

	Price Range	
☐ **Bowls,** *dessert or soup*	6.50	13.00
☐ **Bowls,** *serving size*	13.00	25.00
☐ **Cups and Saucers**	6.50	13.00
☐ **Dinner Plates**	6.50	13.00
☐ **Mugs**	6.50	30.00
☐ **Platters,** *depending on size*	15.00	45.00
☐ **Smaller Plates**	3.00	6.00

Pitcher, *hand-colored, 6-1/2"*

C. B. WALTON COMPANY

This company was founded in 1900 by C. B. Walton for the manufacture of sanitary items.

Marks: *Not Known*
Prices: A three-piece miniature bathroom set would be estimated at a minimum of $65. If this company made any other wares, compare them against comparable products from other companies.

CERAMIC ART COMPANY

See Lenox.

CITY POTTERY

The City Pottery was formed by Rhodes & Yates in 1859 in the old Hattersley Pottery. Although they were primarily concerned with making cream-colored wares and white granite, they were known to have also made some parian and to have done some applied flower work. The name City Pottery did not appear until 1875 and prior to that time the company was known first as Rhodes & Yates, then as Yates & Titus, and finally as Yates, Bennett & Allan. They went out of business c. 1880.

Marks: As shown.

Prices: We have no known sales for City Pottery items, but considering its early founding date and closing date, anything by them should have a premium on it. Compare their cream-colored and other lower-type wares to similar Ott & Brewer products. Their parian and applied flower pieces would probably rate a little lower than Ott & Brewer's. If they made anything for the Centennial, it is probably worth a minimum of $100.

CLARK & CARR

See International Pottery.

COALPORT WORKS

See John Maddock & Sons.

COCHRAN-DRUGAN SANITARY MANUFACTURING COMPANY

This company was founded in 1907 by E.C. Hutchinson, Andrew Cochran, and Samual Drugan. They manufactured sanitary iems.

Marks: *Not Known*
Prices: A three-piece miniature bathroom set would be worth a minimum of $75. Compare anything else they made against similar items listed under other companies. Since this company came along rather late, there should be no premium on any of their products.

COLUMBIAN ART POTTERY

Columbian Art Pottery was founded late in 1892 by Morris and Willmore, and was so named for the Chicago World's Columbian Exposition at that time. Although they did make some opaque wares, they are best known for their very fine Belleek-type items. The company is usually referred to as Morris & Willmore rather than as Columbian Art Pottery.

Perhaps their most famous items is the Belleek Liberty Bell shown on the next page. Other items include a nice assortment of transfer-decorated mugs and tankards which are touched up by hand and which have hand-painted shaded backgrounds.

Marks: Mark A appears usually on Belleek-type items regardless of type of decoration. Mark B is usually found on opaque type items regardless of type of decoration. Exceptions occur.

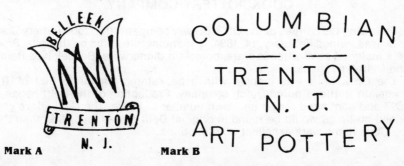

Mark A **Mark B**

Liberty Bell

Mug

	Price Range	
☐ **Creamer,** *gold paste trim, Mark A*	180.00	220.00
☐ **Liberty Bell,** *transfer cobalt decoration, Mark A*	275.00	335.00

Note: The lettering on Liberty Bell varies considerably, and the $225 price is for one with clear lettering. An unreadable one would be worth about $25 less.

☐ **Mug,** *5½" high, transfer decoration of Napoleon, Mark A*	85.00	100.00
☐ **Plate,** *opaque, transfer decorated with red cross-hatching, Mark B*	4.00	8.00

Note: Their opaque items are usually unattractive and are primarily purchased for the backstamp rather than for the item. Most of the Columbian items of this type can be compared against Table X.

COOK & HANCOCK

See Crescent Pottery.

COOK POTTERY COMPANY

Following the demise of the Ott & Brewer company, the Cook Pottery Company was formed February, 14, 1894, to manufacture china on that site. Products included semi-vitreous ware, porcelain dinnerware, Belleek-type items, and Delft-type items.

The Cook Delft was marked with a backstamp similar to that of The Porcelain Bottle, a noted Dutch company. Production of the Delft began c. 1897 and continued for an unknown number of years. The Cook glaze contained no tin as would be found in original Delft glazes, but other than this the Cook items were excellent reproductions.

Cook Belleek is extremely rare, and production of it probably did not last for very long. It is possible that Cook inherited O&B molds as well as the building.

Perhaps the best known Cook item is their Admiral Dewey pitcher, which commemorated Dewey's victory at Manila in 1899.

Marks: Marks include variations on the British coat of arms, with the words Mellor & Co. underneath. The name of Mellor, who was vice-president of Cook, was used to avoid confusion with Cook & Hancock items. A four-leaf clover mark, again with the name Mellor & Co., was used on semi-vitreous wares. All of the marks shown here were used on porcelain or Belleek-type products. Marks A and B were used on porcelain dinnerwares. Marks A and C were used on Belleek items. Mark D, a copy of the mark of The Porcelain Bottle, was used on Delft items. Mark E is found on the Admiral Dewey pitcher. Variations of all the marks are seen, and frequently the Mellor & Co. will be replaced by "C.H.C." and the word Belleek.

Mark A

Mark B

Mark C

Mark D

Mark E

		Price Range	
☐ **Admiral Dewey pitcher,** *earthenware, Mark E*		175.00	225.00
☐ **Bottle, Belleek ware,** *probably had a stopper, when it started out, Mark A with C.H.C. variation*		400.00	475.00

CORDEY

Cordey is frequently (and erroneously) referred to as "early Cybis". The company was in existence before Cybis came to Trenton and is still very much alive in the same location. The company was founded in the 1930's as Arton Studio by Harry Greenberg of Philadelphia, and is located in a building which may very well be the old Enterprise Pottery.

Greenberg met Cybis at the New York World's Fair, where Cybis was working in the Polish Pavillion. Cybis came to Trenton to work at Cordey, where he designed many of the items being collected today.

The company is now officially Schiller/Cordey, Inc., and is a part of Instrument Systems Corporation, which is a division of Litron Corporation. They are primarily engaged in making table lamps.

Marks: The word Cordey, either impressed or written in gold.

Bust of woman

	Price Range	
☐ **Bust of woman,** *16" high, see photo*	150.00	175.00
☐ **Figurine of woman,** *8" high*	30.00	35.00
☐ **Figurine of lamb,** *14" high*	150.00	175.00
☐ **Figurines, man and woman,** *11" high, pair*	75.00	85.00
☐ **Figurines, man and woman,** *8" high, pair*	75.00	85.00
☐ **Figurines, man and woman,** *14" high, pair*	175.00	225.00
☐ **Wall plaque,** *12", woman in center*	55.00	63.00

COXON & COMPANY

Coxon & Company was founded in 1863 as Coxon & Thompson, and they produced cream-colored and granite wares. The founders were Charles Coxon and J. F. Thompson. At some point Coxon acquired Thompson's interest in the company and re-named it Coxon & Co. After Charles Coxon died in 1868, the company was run by his wife and sons. S. M. Alpaugh and J. G. Forman helped the Coxon family run the pottery, and in 1884 Alpaugh & Magowan acquired the company, which was merged into the Trenton Pottery Company.

Marks: The one shown is the only known mark for Coxon & Company, although there must have been at least one other mark when the company was Coxon & Thompson.

Items by Coxon & Company are very rare, and they are also vital to a collection of Trenton items. Expect to pay a minimum of $35 for any item by them.

	Price Range	
☐ **Centennial cup and saucer,** *transfer decoration of the U.S. exhibition, rivals the Anchor Pottery vase as being the ugliest piece of Trenton china, very heavy and unattractive*	110.00	125.00

COXON & THOMPSON

See Coxon & Company.

CRESCENT POTTERY

The Crescent Pottery manufactured cream-colored wares and sanitary specialties. The company was established in 1881 by Charles Howell Cook and William S. Hancock. In 1892, they were consolidated with four other companies into the Trenton Potteries Company.

Marks: At least 13 different marks were used by Crescent, most of which incorporated either the word Crescent or the names of the founders, Cook & Hancock.

Prices: The following prices are estimates:

	Price Range	
☐ **Bowls,** *serving*	15.00	25.00
☐ **Bowls,** *soup or dessert*	5.00	8.00
☐ **Cups and saucers**	8.00	13.00
☐ **Dinner plates**	8.00	13.00
☐ **Mugs**	10.00	35.00
☐ **Platters,** *depending on size*	15.00	40.00
☐ **Smaller plates**	3.00	6.00
☐ **Three-piece minature bathroom set**	60.00	70.00

CROOKSVILLE

Crooksville has been gaining in popularity as a chinaware for the collector of average means, especially suitable for those who enjoy building sets from random "finds." The mainstay of this company for the half-century of its operations was its dinnerware sets, retailed in several price ranges. It also made breakfast sets, youth sets, waffle sets, etc. Additionally, there is, of course, the well-known Crooksville artware, which has had a reputation with collectors for generations.

The Crooksville China Company was established at Crooksville, Ohio in 1902. The great age of Ohio's dominance in pottery was then beginning to wane, but the region still offered potential to new factories with good capital backing. As originally organized, the firm name was Crooksville Art Pottery Company, and the chief executive was J.L. Bennett. There were a number of stockholders and other officers. Manufacturing began late in 1902 and the first products reached circulation in the early part of the following year.

The business grew throughout the next two decades and reached record highs in the 1920's, spurned on by the economic boom following World War I. The lines were expanded at this time with the introduction of many new patterns. In addition to its nationwide distribution system, Crooksville also maintained a retail outlet of its own within easy reach of the factory. This was called "Yel-O-Gren Cottage," after one of the company's lines. It had a lawn sign outside reading "Beautiful American Dinnerware Sold Here." The shop was indeed a cottage, having been converted from a 19th century private residence, and its quaintness probably attracted many visitors.

The Depression years, beginning in 1930, obliged Crooksville (along with most other potteries) to reorganize its operations and concentrate more heavily on low and medium priced lines. In terms of output, there appears to have been little, if any, decline from the 1920's to the 1930's. The 1940's brought an all-too-brief resurgence of good fortune, reaching its peak in the years from about 1946 to 1949. A good deal of Crooksville found on the collectibles market are products from these years. During the 1950's, Crooksville gradually began developing symptoms of the disease which claimed so many old established potteries in that decade: declining sales due to imported and cheaply made dinnerwares flooding the trade. After months of rumor and discussion on the company's future, an announcement was made in 1959 that the factory would terminate operations.

Marks: In the earlier years, the standard mark for Crooksville China was a pigeon or dove, shown flying with a banner unfurled from his beak. On this banner appears the wording *CROOKSVILLE CHINA.* This elegant though unassuming mark had a definite European flavor. Later markings abandoned the dove. The name Crooksville usually appears in bold block letters, styled in such a way that a long bar extends from the "C" to the "K," and another bar from the "K" to the end of the word; thus the whole name is underlined. The name may be accompanied by the words *MADE IN U.S.A.*, or merely *U.S.A.* Sometimes the name is found as *CROOKSVILLE CHINA CO.* Special lines are apt to have special markings, such as *PANTRY BAK-IN WARE,* baking dishes that were advertised to withstand high oven temperatures. The Crooksville Bak-In Ware was introduced in the 1930's and did well in the Depression economy, because it saved families the cost of buying separate baking utensils.

CROWN PORCELAIN WORKS

In 1890 partners by the names of Barlow and Marsh started the Crown Porcelain Works to make faience.

Marks: *Not known*
Prices: We are not familiar with this company's products. Compare their wares to other similar items in this book.

CYBIS PORCELAIN

Cybis was started by Polish-born Boleslaw Cybis and his wife Marja after he left Cordey. They specialize in a wide range of sculptures. The company is too new to be covered in depth here.

DALE & DAVIS

See Prospect Hill Pottery for first partnership by this name. In 1892 James J. Dale and Thomas Davis manufactured sanitary wares under the Dale & Davis name.

Prices: A three-piece minature bathroom set by this company would be worth $50 or more. All other wares they might have made should be rated against comparable items elsewhere.

DEDHAM

Dedham, one of the aristocrats of art pottery, was manufactured neither in Ohio or New Jersey — but in Massachusetts. Cut out from the direct influences of the trade's mainstream and using mainly regional talent, this company produced extremely distinctive wares that were unmistakably of its own special style. Production per item was invariably low, especially in the earlier years. Dedham tried not only to capture some of the "foreign market" (Americans who were buying imported wares, in the belief they were of better quality), but to truly deserve their attention by bringing out wares fully equal to the best European imports. The unique glaze achieved by Dedham — instantly recognizable by all collectors — was a carefully protected factory secret, the exact nature of which was unknown even to most of the company's ranking officers. So justifiably proud was J. Milton Robertson (Dedham's last owner) of this glaze that he refused to divulge the formula even after the factory closed down in 1943. The secret could never be wrested from him; when he died in 1966 all hope of obtaining the formula came to an end.

Origins of the Dedham Pottery Company can be traced into the middle 19th century, before even Trenton itself has emerged as a dominant power in ceramics. In 1866, Alexander Robertson opened up his Chelsea Keramic Art Works at Chelsea, Massachusetts. This was a town ideally suited — if only in name — as the site of a pottery factory, since one of the world's foremost porcelain manufacturers was located in Chelsea, England. The spelling of "ceramic" as "keramic" was unusual in America but rather common abroad. Robertson was interested in the rapidly expanding market for museum-type wares for the home. His work were excellent quality reproductions of antique Chinese procelains and other high-priced ceramics, which in the original specimens sold at very high prices. In 1891, the business was officially incorporated and the name changed to Chelsea Pottery, U.S., in an effort to distinguish it from the Chelsea of England. Since 1891 was the year in which a law was passed requiring all imported goods to show their place of origin, this might have played some part in the name change. Several years later, the headquarters was shifted to Dedham, Massachusetts, and the name Dedham Pottery was adopted.

Among the memorable achievements of Dedham was its "Chinese red" glaze called *Sang de Boeuf* (blood of the ox), and its "Volanic" glaze in which two glazes were intermingled to give the appearance of flowing lava. The Dedham Volcanic Ware has proved more popular with collectors than it did with the contemporary public. The marvelous Dedham vases are characteristic of what this factory could accomplish when doing its best work. Dedham remained in the hands of the Robertson family through the entire period of its operations. Unlike most other potteries, which already had lines of low-priced dinnerware on the market, it could not adapt well to conditions of the Depression and suffered throughout the 1930's. The business was closed down in 1943.

Marks: In the era of Chelsea Keramic Art Works, there are two varieties of the trademark. One consisted simply of the letters *C K A W,* arranged to form a kind of lozenge. The other spelled out the company name and also carried the wording *ROBERTSON & SONS.* Neither of these marks bore ornaments or symbols. When the firm operated briefly as Chelsea Pottery U.S., the mark was a four-leaf clover, with the initials *C P U S* placed on the leaves. This was followed in the Dedham era by the adoption of a rabbit as the company symbol for its trademarks, which appeared either in a plain mark without lettering or in square mark reading *DEDHAM POTTERY* along the top. It served as the company's mark from 1896 until the dissolution in 1943, with only a slight alteration in design occurring in 1929. Dedham is one of relatively few American artware manufacturers whose marks do not lead the collector into a web of confusion. In this respect, they well echoed the foreign wares they sought to emulate.

DELAWARE POTTERY

A group consisting of Mr. Oliphant, his three sons, Mr. Charles Fay, and Mr. Thomas Connelly (formerly of the Irish Belleek Company got together in 1884 and formed Oliphant & Company for the purpose of operating the Delaware Pottery.

The company expiremented with a Belleek-type formula around 1886 and supposedly produced and exceptionally high-quality china. The ware was never manufactured on anything than an experimental basis, however, and we have not seen any samples. Other products included sanitary items and druggists' supplies. Delaware was merged into the Trenton Potteries Company in 1892.

Marks: The mark shown here can be either impressed or printed. Variations of the mark occur.

Prices: Belleek-type items (you should be so lucky as to ever fine one!) — compare to Ott & Brewer prices.

All other wares — compare to similar items elsewhere.

DOWNS POTTERY

We have no first-hand information about this pottery but have been informed that they operated during the 1930's. The one sample at hand is a 6" vase, very attractive in form, and decorated with a lovely blue glaze. Right now things by Downs are still inexpensive, but considering how rare they are and how attractive, we would expect to see sharp increases in value shortly.

Marks: "Downs Pottery" incised in the bottom.

	Price Range	
☐ **Vase,** *as described above.*	23.00	28.00

DUGAN'S POTTERY

Dugan is possibly a misspelling of Drugan (see Cochran-Drugan), and the only information we have about "Dugan" is that the building burned to the ground, was re-built, and then burned again.

Marks: *Not known*
Prices: Since we don't know what they made, we really can be of much help with prices.

EAGLE POTTERY

Eagle was founded in 1876 by Richard Millington, and at a later date, the pottery's officers included: John B.. Riley, President; J. W. Foster, Secretary/Treasurer; and Elijah Mountford, General Manager. The pottery eventually had four biscuit kilns and four glost kilns and employed 250 people. First Burroughs & Mountford in 1879 and eventually Cook Pottery took over the building.

Marks: *Not known*
Prices: Their products are unknown to us; compare against similar items appearing elsewhere in this book.

EAST TRENTON POTTERY COMPANY

East Trenton Pottery produced white granite ware, and was founded in 1888. Their most interesting items had the pictures of Presidential candidates printed on them.

Marks: Presidential campaign items were marked with the New Jersey state seal and the initials "E.T.P.Co." White granite was marked with the British coat of arms with the company's initials underneath. Variations occur.
Price: The following prices are estimates.

	Price Range	
☐ **Bowls,** *serving*	15.00	30.00
☐ **Bowls,** *soup or dessert*	7.00	8.00
☐ **Cups and saucers**	7.00	14.00
☐ **Dinner plates**	7.00	14.00
☐ **Mugs**	10.00	30.00
☐ **Platters,** *depending on size*	15.00	40.00
☐ **Presidential campaign items,** *a minimum of*	45.00	60.00
☐ **Smaller plates**	3.00	7.00

ECONOMY POTTERY COMPANY

Economy was founded in 1900 by Williamm H. Bradbury for the production of sanitary wares.

Marks: *Not known*
Prices: A three-piece miniature bathroom set by this company can be valued at a minimum of $65. All other items they might have made can be rated against comparable items appearing elsewhere.

EDWIN M. KNOWLES

Edwin M. Knowles was chiefly a manufacturer of dinnerware, though it produced general kitchenware items at various times in its lengthy history (including some very attractive cookie jars.) Its wares were marketed under numerous trade names and therefore present the hobbyist with an opportunity to buy them collectively, or to specialize in the patterns which appeal most to him. Floral and fruit patterns predominate, but there are also solid-color wares.

The Edwin M. Knowles Pottery Co. was located in Chester, West Virginia, very close to the bustling center of Ohio pottery making when it was initially established. In 1900, it resettled in Newell, West Virginia, and this remained its headquarters for many years. The most successful years of the firm were in the 1920's, which was an extremely lucrative decade for the market as a whole (thanks in large part to the booming mail-order business,) and the postwar era from about 1946 into the 1950's. The earlier wares are somewhat more appealing for collectors because of their softer, richer coloring and satiny glazes.

Marks: The Edwin M. Knowles mark exists in a number of versions, some of them highly ornamental. Probably the best known is a figure of a sailing ship with twin masts, a wooden hull and a flag standard at the front. This is surrounded by the wording *THE EDWIN M. KNOWLES CHINA CO.* Another mark has the figure of a bulbous vase with two handles and a textured surface which reads *VITREOUS.* Beneath this is the wording *EDWIN M. KNOWLES CHINA CO.* Some pieces are simply marked *KNOWLES UTILITY WARE.* This mark is not accompanied by any kind of symbol or decoration.

EGYPTIAN POTTERY

Egyptian was founded in 1891 by Charles H. Baker and Cornelius Turford for the production of sanitary items.

Marks: *Not known*
Prices: A three-piece miniature bathroom set by this company can be estimated at no less than $65. Any other items can be compared to similar items appearing elsewhere in this book.

ELI POTTERY

No information available, unless Eli is a shortened version of Elite, q.v.

Marks: *Not known*
Prices: If a pottery by this name did indeed exist, compare their items to similar ones elsewhere in this book.

ELITE POTTERY

Elite was founded in 1901 by G. W. Page, Samuel Bedson, and Louis J. Deihl for the production of sanitary wares.

Marks: *Not known*
Prices: A three-piece miniature bathroom set by this company is worth no less than $65. All other wares they might have produced can be compared to similar items elsewhere in this book.

EMPIRE POTTERY

When the Coxon family gave up the Coxon & Co. pottery, it was taken over by Alpaugh & Magowan, who renamed it as the Empire Pottery. Later the company ownership passed to Wood & Barlow and eventually it became part of the Trenton Potteries Company. Wares included granite ware, sanitary items, and (supposedly) a very fine grade of porcelain.

Marks: The first mark was the British coat of arms with the words Empire Pottery above and the initials A&M below. During the Wood & Barlow period the term "Imperial China" was used, and the last mark was a wreath with the word "Empire" above, "Trenton, N.J." below, and the initials TPCO intertwined inside a wreath.
Prices: The following prices are estimates.

	Price Range	
☐ **Miniature bathroom set,** *three pieces*	45.00	60.00

Granite ware can be estimated as follows:

☐ **Bowls,** *serving*	15.00	30.00
☐ **Bowls,** *soup or dessert size*	7.00	10.00
☐ **Cups and saucers**	7.00	14.00
☐ **Dinner plates**	7.00	14.00
☐ **Mugs**	10.00	30.00
☐ **Platters,** *depending on size*	15.00	40.00
☐ **Smaller plates**	3.00	6.00

ENTERPRISE POTTERY COMPANY

Enterprise was founded c. 1879 by W. H. Umpleby, John Brian, and Charles H. Skirm. General Oliphant was also connected to the company. The company made sanitary items and later became part of the Trenton Potteries Company.

Mark: *Only one known mark*

Enterprise
Pottery Co

Prices: A three-piece miniature bathroom set is worth no less than $50. Anything else they might have made can be compared to similar items appearing elsewhere in this book.

EQUITABLE POTTERY COMPANY

Equitable was founded in 1888 by Andrew Cochran, John Leukel, and Jonathan Coxon. They made sanitary wares and later became part of the Trenton Potteries Company.

Marks: *Not known*
Prices: A three-piece miniature bathroom set by Equitable is worth no less than $50. All other items should be rated against similar items elsewhere in this book.

ETRURIA POTTERY

See Ott & Brewer and Cook Pottery.

EXCELSIOR POTTERY COMPANY

Excelsior was founded in 1905 by G.W. Page and William Cook. They made sanitary wares.

Marks: *Not known*
Prices: A three-piece miniature bathroom set by Excelsior should be worth no less than $50. All other items can be compared to similar items elsewhere in this book.

EXCELSIOR POTTERY WORKS

See William Young & Sons.

FAIRFACTS COMPANY

Fairfacts manufactured bath accessories. After they went out of business By Ridge bought their machines and designs and Star bought the building.

Marks: *Not known*
Prices: A soap dish or similar item should probably be worth no less than $6.50.

FELL & THROPP COMPANY

Samuel E. Thropp and J. Hart Brewer were co-owners of the Fell & Thropp Company c. 1889-1892. The company, which was located in the old Taylor & Speeler pottery, manufactured white granite and cream-colored wares. They made sanitary wares 1892-1894 when the company was under Robert Gruessner.

Marks: Marks include both the New Jersey and the British coats of arms as well as a circular mark with a cougar's head inside of it. All three marks have the initials "F&T" with them.
Prices: White granite items are estimated as follows:

	Price Range	
☐ **Bowls,** *serving*	15.00	30.00
☐ **Bowls,** *soup or dessert*	7.00	10.00
☐ **Cups and saucers**	7.00	14.00
☐ **Dinner plates**	7.00	14.00
☐ **Mugs**	10.00	30.00
☐ **Platters,** *depending on size*	15.00	40.00
☐ **Smaller plates**	3.00	6.00

FIDELITY POTTERY COMPANY

Charles H. Baker and J. Harris Cogill founded Fidelity in 1902 to manufacture sanitary items.

Marks: *Not known*
Prices: $50 for a miniature bathroom set. Since the company came along rather late, anything else they might have made would be of minimal value, less than comparable earlier items.

FORTUNE COMPANY

Manufacturers of bath accessories.

Marks: *Not known*
Prices: $3 and up for any item by this company.

FRANKOMA

In 1927, a young man of 23 moved from Chicago to Norman, Oklahoma, to become an instructor of art and ceramics at the University of Oklahoma. Because of his involvement in studies and geological surveys of the Oklahoma clays, John Frank set a goal to open the first pottery there to produce wares made only from Oklahoma clays. He founded the Frankoma Pottery in 1933, and with one kiln, a butter churn to mix the clay and fruit jars of glaze, he began making pottery for everyday uses. A clay from Ada was originally used, but upon discovering a red-burning clay in Sapula, Frank chose this clay to be the substance from which all Frankoma pottery is made.

Frank and his wife, Grace Lee, struggled through some hard times trying to make their pottery a success. They had grown into a small factory by 1938 when they moved to Sapula to further their studies on clays. The next years were hard and with their seven employees, the Franks developed a once-fired process, where the clay and glaze are fired at the same time at the maturing point of the clay. The rugged, everyday earthenware was durable and beautiful with its bright colored glazes, but the Frank family decided to try something new.

In 1965, Frank designed a decorative plate that became the first Christmas plate annually produced in America. Inspired by the Christmas story, Frank chose "Good Will Toward Men" as the title of this first in a series that still continues today. A Dell Robbia white glaze has a unique affect on each Christmas theme shown in bas-relief. Another series titled *Teen-agers of the Bible* was started in 1973, and a *Madonnas Series* was designed by Grace Lee. Each issue for each series is produced for one year and then the mold is destroyed on Christmas Eve.

Since Frank's death in 1973, his daughter, Joneice, has continued designing the two series originally designed by her father. The Frankoma Pottery today produces about 375 pieces of earthenware pottery, artware and sculptures. It continues to fill the public's need for the colorful and durable earthenware pottery.

The last 5 to 10 years have seen a rise of collector interest in Frankoma. Most of its older table wares can still be bought in odd pieces at extremely low prices. The determined collector may be able to assemble a set in this way at a fraction of the normal set price. He will probably want to specialize in one type of ware or another, since the whole range of Frankoma would be a little too overwhelming for most hobbyists.

Marks: The earliest Frankoma mark read either *FRANK POTTERY* or *FRANK POTTERIES* and was sometimes incised into the ware, sometimes printed. In 1934, the name *FRANKOMA* was introduced in the mark, in block letters, without symbol or decoration. The first — and only — decorative symbol in this factory's markings appeared in 1936. This was the familiar leopard-and-pot in which the animal is striding across a banner reading *FRANKOMA*. It was discontinued in 1938. In the 1940's, Frankoma began using a pair of gold labels for its markings, which remain in use to the present day. One is circular with irregular or wavy edge, and reads *ORIGINAL CREATION BY FRANKOMA*. The other is a narrow rectangle reading *THIS IS GUARANTEED OVEN PROOF.* Another gold lable marking, which made its appearance somewhat later and is also used currently, reads *SAFE IN DISHWASHER, OVEN AND MICRO-WAVE.* Initial markings are also found on many pieces. The earliest Frankoma initial mark introduced in the 1960's, consists of an F set above a P. A later version of this mark combines the letters J and F, superimposed to give the appearance of a curved tail on the F.

LAZYBONES *(Introduced 1953)*

A popular functional ware with some interesting styling touches. The Lazybones line is unprinted and unpainted; its decoration takes the form of creative shaping. In the creamer, for example, the handle is a part of the bowl, squeezed into a projection at the back. The factory number for this line is 4; the Lazybones products all carry the number as a prefix.

	Price Range	
☐ **Bowl, divided,** *11″, peach glow, item #4qd*	6.00	8.00
☐ **Creamer and sugar,** *8 ounces, peach glow, lidded, item #4a and 4b*	8.00	10.00
☐ **Cup,** *clay blue, item #4c*	4.00	5.50
☐ **Dish, butter,** *peach glow, lidded, item #4k*	7.00	10.00
☐ **Pitcher,** *two quart, clay blue, item #4d*	9.00	12.00
☐ **Platter, serving,** *12-7/8″, clay blue, item #4p*	11.00	14.00
☐ **Plate, dinner,** *10″, peach glow, item #4f*	5.00	6.00
☐ **Saucer,** *5-1/4″, clay blue, item #4e*	1.75	2.00

MAYAN-AZTEC *(Introduced about 1936)*

Earlier, a number of pottery companies had experimented with wares utilizing the traditional pottery designs and symbols of the Central and South American Indians. Frankoma's "Mayan-Aztec" ware became the most extensive series of such products. Included among the design elements are birds, grotesque heads, and pictograph writing symbols — all of which will be instantly familiar to any fan of pre-Columbian Indian culture.

☐ **Bowl, salad,** *20 ounces, woodland moss, item #7x1*	6.00	8.00
☐ **Bowl, sugar,** *prairie green, unlidded, item #7b*	9.00	12.00
☐ **Bowl, vegetable,** *one quart, woodland moss, item #7n*	7.00	9.00
☐ **Creamer and sugar,** *woodland moss, lidded, items #7a and 7b, C-shape handles, the sugar bowl's lid with a plug-type handle, the creamer featuring a vaulted pouring spout.*	13.00	16.00
☐ **Cup,** *woodland moss, item #7c, sculptured handle.*	4.00	5.00
☐ **Dish, fruit,** *8 ounces, woodland moss, item #7xo*	4.00	5.50
☐ **Dish, sauce,** *10 ounces, desert gold, lidded, item #7s*	2.50	3.25
☐ **Mug,** *woodland moss, item #7cl, modified loop handle.*	3.00	4.00
☐ **Pitcher,** *woodland moss, item #7d, pot form with tall loop handle.*	10.00	14.00

	Price Range	
☐ **Plate, dinner,** 9", *woodland moss, item #7f*	4.00	5.50
☐ **Saucer,** 5", *woodland moss, item #7e*	2.75	3.75

PLAINSMAN *(Introduced 1948)*

Rustic shapes with gilt borders, characterized by random notches and imperfections that give the suggestion of objects roughly carved from raw wood. This has been an extremely popular line for Frankoma.

☐ **Bowl, salad,** *two quart, onyx black, item #5ns*	6.00	8.00
☐ **Mug,** *16 ounces, onyx black, item #5m*	4.00	5.50
☐ **Plate, dinner,** 10", *clay blue, item #5f*	4.00	5.00
☐ **Platter,** 16", *red bud, item #5p*	13.00	16.00

WAGON WHEEL *(Introduced 1948)*

In this highly creative line, each object was patterned after the wooden wheels of western stage coaches or "covered wagons." Thus, plates had an axle tip at the center and wheel spokes radiating outward to the plate's rim. Upright items had this design molded into both sides. The Wagon Wheel line is designated by the factory as its series "94" and all items have the 94 prefix to their article number.

☐ **Ashtray candleholder,** 6", *saddle brown, item #454*	34.00	40.00
☐ **Bowl, soup,** *16 ounces, red bud, item #94x*	5.00	7.00
☐ **Cream and sugar,** *10 ounces, prairie green, unlidded, items #94a and 94b*	5.00	7.00
☐ **Plate, dinner,** 10", *onyx black, item #94fl*	6.00	8.00
☐ **Teapot,** *6-cups, prairie green, item #94t*	7.00	9.00
Note: The value in Desert Gold is about the same. However, this item in Red Bud (one of the more desirable colors for the Wagon Wheel line), sells in the 10-13 range.		
☐ **Water tumbler,** *onyx black, item #941.*	4.00	5.00

WESTWIND *(Introduced 1962)*

The last of Frankoma's lines (up to this point), Westwind has the charm of early American earthenware coupled with modernized, sleeker shapes. For example the salt and pepper shakers (not listed here) are neither cylindrical or bowl-shaped, but a sort of modified teardrop shape. Most pieces have a band of dark coloration around the rim. There is no printing or painting.

☐ **Bowl, fruit,** *10 ounces, peach glow, item #6xs*	2.00	2.50
☐ **Bowl, gravy,** *woodland moss, item #6s*	6.00	8.00
☐ **Bowl, soup,** *14 ounces, woodland moss, item #6x*	3.00	4.00
☐ **Teapot,** *6 cups, peach glow, item #6t*	9.00	12.00
☐ **Tureen, soup,** *2-1/2 quarts, woodland moss, item #6vt*	13.00	16.00

BOTTLE VASE

This is a special line of limited editions to which a new addition is made annually. It was begun in 1969. The number produced has ranged from as few as 3,000 to as many as 10,000. The molds are destroyed after production to insure that further specimens cannot be made at any time in the future. Now that the series is well into its second decade, a complete set of the Frankoma Bottle Vases has become the collecting target of many pottery hobbyists. Those who bought at the original issue prices have seen their investments grow handsomely; but even by buying on today's secondary market, the collector may well find that these pieces bring a satisfactory return. The demand is certainly increasing, and there seems to be a noticeable drain of specimens from the market.

	Price Range	
☐ **1969,** *15", green, black platform base, item #V-1, modified cylindrical form with a tall narrow neck, simply designed, apparently inspired by the traditional soda bottle shape though with a narrower and somewhat longer neck, limit 4,000.*	95.00	115.00
☐ **1970,** *12", turquoise exterior with white interior, item #V-2, elongated flask form with a pinched neck, decorated at the sides with foliage and berry molding, limit 10,000.*	47.00	58.00
☐ **1971,** *12", red exterior with white interior, resting on a black base, item #V-3, cone form with very light horizontal ribbed molding, decorated with a knoblike ornament beneath the neck, formed by deep-cut horizontal lines, limit 7,500.*	47.00	58.00
☐ **1972,** *12", terra cotta, black gloss highlighting, item #V-4, modified ovoid body with a slightly flared neck, dome-type cap, the sides decorated with molded lobing, the lobes appear to be in higher relief than they actually are, because black gloss is spread between them and gives the impression of deep recesses, resting on a flat stand base, limit 5,000.*	70.00	85.00
☐ **1973,** *12-7/8", red exterior, white interior, black base, item #V-5, twisted freeform shape roughly resembling a cornucopia shell, pointed top, dome-style base, limit 5,000.*	47.00	58.00
☐ **1974,** *13", grayish green ("Chinese celadon"), item #V-6, freeform cone shape with a turned neck, sliced diagonally to create a wide exaggerated mouth, limit 4,000.*	38.00	46.00
☐ **1975,** *12-3/4", desert gold with dark brown lid and base, item #V-7, elongated ovoid form with tall neck, resting upon a high footed base, decorated with colored speckling along the bowl, limit 3,500.*	33.00	39.00
☐ **1976,** *13", red and cream white, item #V-8, of bottle form with tall neck, dome-type lid, decorated at the bowl with a series of horizontal ribs, resting upon a white dome-type base, limited to 3,500.*	33.00	39.00
☐ **1977,** *13", black and cream white, item #V-9, narrow bottle form with tapering neck, resting upon a stand-type base, limit 3,000.*	23.00	28.00
☐ **1978,** *11-1/4", morning glory blue exterior, white interior, or brown and white interior, item #V-10, ewer form with a bulbous bowl surmounted by tall cylindrical neck, set with a tall vertical handle rising from the bowl and connecting to the neck, limit 3,000.*	19.00	23.00
☐ **1979,** *11-1/4", morning glory blue exterior, white interior, or brown and white interior, item #V-11, squat bulbous bowl with tall cylindrical neck, wide mouth, set with a pair of vertical handles, limit 3,000.*	19.00	23.00

FULPER POTTERY

This long-surviving factory was one of few American potters whose history spanned more than 100 years. Its earliest products, reaching back to the first years of the 19th century, are rare and highly desirable. They bear, however, little relation to the wares for which the company is best known among today's collectors: the fine figurewear, lamp bases, jugs, jars, mugs and decorative pieces made in later years. Fulper became a pioneer among domestic potteries by heavily producing figurewear and figural pieces that had a utilitarian use. Such items had long been commonplace in Europe, but considered too daring for an American maker to risk his capital upon. The "best" period of old Fulper wear was immediately following the Civil War. The economic revival that followed the war ushered in innovative ideas in home decoration and other styles. Fulper gave the public unique lines of water and milk pitchers, bear mugs, butter churns, and even jars for pickling fruits and vegetables. In addition, it produced purely ornamental items to add splashes of color to a parlor and dining room. The modeling on most of these, as well as the painting and glazing, are of a superb quality; and the subjects themselves are primarily of original design, not copied from imports as was often the case with other makers.

Fulper Pottery was a family business operated by the Fulper brothers. According to available information, the company began in 1805, at Flemington, New Jersey. The antiquity of its beginnings can be better comprehended when one considers that George Washington had died only six years before. The area was rich in clays suitable for stoneware. There were probably no grandiose plans at the outset. Other pioneer factories sought mainly to supply the local community with utilitarian pottery, and this was indoubtedly Fulper's aim. We do know, however, that industrial and farmware were among the company's first projects. It manufactured tile bricks from which drainpipes could be built. Brick drainpipes were considered superior to those of iron, as they were quieter and did not corrode. Also in the line were drinking troughs for chickens, and we are probably safe in guessing similar items. It might not have been a glamorous debut, but this business got the company on good financial footing.

In its later years, the Fulper Pottery Co. was under direction of J.M. Stangl, who had started with the firm as engineer in 1910. He gained control around the time of World War I and his innovative genius in designing helped to propel Fulper, once more, to the forefront of sales. Business became so brisk that a subsidiary factory was opened at Trenton, previously used by Anchor Pottery. When the Flemington factory was destroyed by fire in 1929, all operations were switched to Trenton and the company name was changed to Stangl Pottery (see the entry in this book).

Fulper had been in business 124 years in the same town. Some local families had five or six generations of its members on the company staff.

Marks: The Fulper marks are all very simple, reflecting a strong desire NOT to imitate European marking approaches. The name is usually given simply as *FULPER* without any further wording, arranged vertically within a rectangular or oval shield. There are various marks for the trade-named lines of Fulper products. These, likewise, are simple in design, though slight ornamentation is provided by a ribbon, banner, or scroll-like device.

Price Range

☐ **Bowl,** *blue and cat's eye brown, 2" x 6", shallow, with curved base and rim, ink stamp* 50.00 60.00

☐ **Bowl,** *green and turquoise, 3" x 10-1/2", shallow, with curved base and rim, impressed letters* 90.00 100.00

☐ **Chamberstick,** *shield back with handle, green, 7", flat base and shield, curved handle, ink stamp* 120.00 150.00

☐ **Tumbler,** *rose and cream, 4-1/2", cylindrical, with flaired rim, ink stamp* 40.00 50.00

☐ **Urn,** *blue, with ring handles, 7", Greek classic shape, with flaired rim on a pedestal base, impressed block letters,* 115.00 140.00

☐ **Vase,** *light blue drizzle over dark blue, 4-1/2", bulbous base, with cylindrical rim, ink stamp* 50.00 60.00

☐ **Vase,** *blue, with embossed geometric design, 5-1/2", four-sided, on small round base, ink stamp* 90.00 100.00

☐ **Vase,** *pink, beige and blue, 12", ovoid shape, with flaired neck and trim, paper label* 300.00 400.00

☐ **Vase,** *blue and green, 15-1/4", bulbous base, with flaired rim, impressed letters* 450.00 550.00

☐ **Vase,** *blue and rose, 15-1/2", urn shape, narrowing at the neck, flat rim, raised letters* 450.00 550.00

☐ **Vase,** *light green, with two handles, 17-1/2", barrel shape, no mark.* 350.00 450.00

GENERAL PORCELAIN

This company is located on Pennsylvania Avenue in Trenton, and was founded in 1939 by Stephen J. Judnak and Joseph Przechacki. Products include porcelain forms for the rubber industry and lamp bases. Their Just-Rite subsidiary makes bathroom accessories.

Marks: *Not known*
Prices: $5 and up.

GEORGE OHR

George Ohr became one of the most successful pottery makers of his time — thanks to his belief in his abilities. Not only did he believe in his abilities, he never missed a chance to tell the world that George Ohr was the supreme genius of pottery making. He was a colorful man who wore a foot-long mustache and liked to make funny faces when having his picture taken. Some of his pottery was fairly different, too. Some were just a bit TOO unconventional for the tastes of the times. Today, however, collectors are reaching the conclusion that Ohr was indeed the genius he claimed to be.

The George Ohr pottery holds a unique position among all American pottery wares. Ohr, of Biloxi, Mississippi designed and manufactured all his products himself. He was totally unconcerned about what would appeal to the public. Rather than letting the public dictate taste to him, he dictated to the public — something which even the giant potteries would not dare to do. He took a totally casual attitude about whether or not anyone wanted to buy it. If there were no customers for one line of his products, he did not stop producing it. Instead, he made more and more, stockpiling it away, feeling certain that someday its real worth would be recognized. It is said he planned to sell his warehouse filled with pottery to the Smithsonian Institute in Washington D.C., so that it could have the greatest collection of pottery in existence.

The Ohr pottery is almost totally freehand work, like doodles done in clay, but some striking results were achieved. Ohr's boundless confidence in himself shows through in every piece. No matter how offbeat the idea or design, each item was created with masterful skill.

Ohr ran away from home when he was a young boy and worked as a ship chandler's assistant, among various other odd jobs. He entered the pottery business in the early 1880's and continued producing items until 1906. Then he simply retired, without passing on any of his trade secrets.

Today, among collectors, the Ohr pottery is loved by some and detested by others — which is about the same response it received when it was being produced. Except that today the prices are quite a bit higher. Some collectors are prejudiced against these products, believing that a potter of Ohr's background and character could not possibly have produced respectable work. The foolishness of this line of thinking can easily be seen, if one examines other lives and personalities of the world's artists — great painters and sculptors.

Marks: Just like the wares themselves, George Ohr's markings followed no special pattern. He seems to have experimented with marks just as much as with designs and working procedures. Most pieces are marked *G.E. OHR, BILOXI* but this can be a small or large mark, in block or script lettering, by itself or in conjunction with numbers and legends of various kinds. Some of Ohr's pieces are dated — not only with the year, but the month and day on which the mold was ready for casting or on which the piece was fired. Ohr sometimes numbered his works like limited editions. But he had no real plan in that direction, either, and would begin numbering after many pieces had already left the kiln.

	Price Range	
☐ **Bowl,** 3½ ", beige, of squat form with cylindrical sides flaring out into a wide base, crimped along the lip and decorated with small ornaments along the base rim. Marked G.E. OHR, BILOXI, MISS. Believed to date from the late 19th or early 20th centuries.	120.00	145.00
☐ **Bowl,** 2½ ", brown, of freeform design giving the appearance of an ashtray with shaped rim, marked G.E. OHR, BILOXI, MISS. Believed to date from the 19th or early 20 centuries.	220.00	270.00
☐ **Bowl,** 2½ ", brown-green, of freeform design giving the appearance of an ashtray, caved-in sides, high-gloss glaze. Marked G.E. OHR, BILOXI. Believed to date from the late 19th or early 20th centuries.	600.00	750.00
☐ **Bowl,** 4", green and mud-brown flecked with very dark brown, circular. Marked G.E. OHR, BILOXI. Believed to date from the late 19th or early 20th centuries.	300.00	375.00
☐ **Bowl,** 3¼ ", green and mud-brown, of squat freeform design with openwork along the sides of the bowl. Marked G.E. OHR, BILOXI, MISS. Believed to date from the late 19th or early 20th centuries.	230.00	290.00

Price Range

☐ **Bowl,** 7″, various shades of brown, diameter, of V-form with severely crimped sides. Marked GEO. E. OHR, BILOXI, MISS. Believed to date from the late 19th or early 20th centuries. 310.00   380.00

☐ **Ink stand,** 6¼″, green streak-glaze, in the form of a semi-rectangular artist's palette with thumb-hole and molded brush, the inkwell resting to one corner. The entire palette encircled by small beadwork at the rim. Marked G.E. OHR, BILOXI. Believed to date from the late 19th or early 20th centuries. 320.00   370.00

☐ **Pitcher,** 5″, brown with green mottling, of freeform design resembling a fish in which the tal is pierced and serves as the handle. Marked G.E. OHR. Believed to date from the late 19th or early 20th centuries. 600.00   730.00

☐ **Teapot,** 3⅞″, brown and green spatter glaze, ovoid bulbous form with thumbprint designing, ropework handle, disc-type lid. Marked GEO. E. OHR, BILOXI, MISS. Believed to date from the late 19th or early 20th centuries. 700.00   850.00

☐ **Vase,** 7″, blue, of modified cylindrical form with a bulging shoulder and tall neck, molded designwork along the lip. Marked G.E. OHR. Believed to date from the late 19th or early 20th centuries. 600.00   750.00

☐ **Vase,** 10″, blue, of basically cylindrical form widening out slightly at the bottom, very glossy glaze. Marked G.E. OHR BILOXI, MISS. Believed to date from the late 19th or early 20th centuries. 480.00   570.00

☐ **Vase,** 3¼″, brown, bulbous shaped form with pinched and dented sides. Marked G.E. OHR, BILOXI, MISS. Believed to date from the late 19th or early 20th centuries. 210.00   240.00

☐ **Vase,** 3½″, brown smear glaze, of bulbous form with crimped neck. Marked G.E. OHR. Believed to date from the late 19th or early 20th centuries. 410.00   520.00

☐ **Vase,** 5¼″, burnt orange and green glaze, in cologne-bottle form with dome-shaped bowl, pinched neck and funnel-type neck and mouth. Marked GEO. E. OHR, BILOXI. Believed to date from the late 19th or early 20th centuries. 190.00   235.00

☐ **Vase,** 5¼″, burnt orange and olive glaze with rust brown, of hurricane lamp form with a bulbous bowl and inverted dome neck, wide mouth. Decorated with the applied likeness of a caterpillar. Marked G.E. OHR. Believed to date from the late 19th or early 20th centuries. 500.00   615.00

☐ **Vase,** 3½″, cream white and blue with black mottled glaze, highlighted in red, of squat bulbous form with pinched neck and flaring rim, swirled molded decoration at the base of the neck. Marked G.E. OHR, BILOXI, MISS. Believed to date from the late 19th or early 20th centuries. 220.00   270.00

☐ **Vase,** 5¾″, dark brown highlighted with green, of spittoon form with bulbous body and flaring cylindrical neck, neck crimped. Marked G.E. OHR. Believed to date from the late 19th or early 20th centuries. 600.00   735.00
The neck actually forms into a squared shape.

☐ **Vase,** 4½″, dark brown with gunmetal mottling, cylindrical form with pinching at the neck and bowl. Marked G.E. OHR, BILOXI, MISS. Believed to date from the late 19th or early 20th centuries. 400.00   500.00

Price Range

☐ **Vase,** 5″, green and burnt orange glaze with traces of brown, worked up to a tortoise-shell mottling, the lower portion of pot form, the upper portion of inverted cone shape. Marked G.E. OHR, BILOXI. Believed to date from the late 19th or early 20th centuries. 400.00 485.00

☐ **Vase,** 6¼″, green and mud-brown, metallic mottling, of pot form with a crimped neck and lip, wide mouth. Marked G.E. OHR, BILOXI, MISS. Believed to date from the late 19th or early 20th centuries. 800.00 950.00

☐ **Vase,** 3¾″, green and pinkish glaze, of cylindrical form with a sectioned body, the upper portion in bulb form with a flaring lip and wide mouth. Marked G.E. OHR, BILOXI. Believed to date from the late 19th or early 20th centuries. 240.00 285.00

☐ **Vase, miniature,** green with gun-metal glaze, ovoid form. Marked G.E. OHR, Believed to date from the late 19th or early 20th centuries. 80.00 100.00

Note:There hasn't been a real rush as yet for the George Ohr miniatures, which (given the usual practices of collectors) is a bit surprising. Despite the vast differences in design from one piece to the next, much of the Ohr pottery is still valued according to its size with the larger items bringing the best sums.

☐ **Vase,** 4¼″, gunmetal finish, of pot form with flaring lip. Marked BILOXI (without Ohr's name). Believed to date from the late 19th or early 20th centuries. 230.00 280.00

☐ **Vase,** 6½″, gunmetal glaze, of cologne-bottle form with severely pinched neck, inverted dome top. Marked OHR. Believed to date from the late 19th or early 20th centuries. 400.00 475.00

Note: George Ohr loved to experiment. Here he borrowed a traditional shape from the world of glassmaking, one which had a reputation for glamor, and gave it a deliberately unglamorous finish.

☐ **Vase,** 5″, gunmetal glaze, of spherical form with a crinkled neck and lip. Marked G.E. OHR. Believed to date from the late 19th or early 20th centuries. 240.00 295.00

☐ **Vase,** 2⅞″, gunmetal glaze, of squat cylindrical form with a sculptured freeform neck and rim, resting on a narrow pedestal base. Marked G.E. OHR, BILOXI, MISS. Believed to date from the late 19th or early 20th centuries. 300.00 370.00

☐ **Vase,** 8½″, olive glaze highlighted in gunmetal, the bowl of bulbous form with a cylindrical double-tiered neck, one section wider than the other. C-shape cup handles at either side of the upper neck, and verticle supports reaching from them to the midpoint of the bowl. Resting on a pedestal base. Marked G.E. OHR, BILOXI, MISS. 3100.00 3700.00

Note: One of Ohr's more bizarre productions; this looks like a spitoon with a drinking mug resting upside-down on it ... except that the mug has two handles instead of one.

☐ **Vase,** 4″, olive green and mud-brown with mottling in gunmetal, of squat cylindrical form surmounted with a sculptured neck and rim in a scalloped pattern. Marked G.E. OHR, BILOXI, MISS. Believed to date from the late 19th or early 20th centuries. 300.00 360.00

Price Range

Note: Usually — not always — when Ohr added "Miss." to his marking, it indicated he was especially proud of the item.

☐ **Vase,** *2½", olive green with mud-brown, some gunmetal mottling, of squat freeform design giving the appearance of an ashtry with the neck collapsed on two sides (vaulting on the other two), marked G.E. OHR, BILOXI, MISS. Believed to date from the late 19th or early 20th centuries.* 310.00   360.00

☐ **Vase,** *2", olive and mud-brown glaze, of flattened bulbous form giving the appearance of an ashtray, with double projections in freeform artistic style at the top. Marked G.E. OHR, BILOXI. Believed to date from the late 19th or early 20th centuries.* 320.00   365.00

Note: George Ohr was one of few potters whose vases sometimes ended up wider than they were tall.

☐ **Vase,** *3½", rust brown speckled in yellow and black, crimped body and neck. Marked G.E. OHR, 06. Believed to date from the late 19th or early 20th centuries.* 500.00   625.00

☐ **Vase,** *olive green with mud-brown speckled glaze, bulb form with flaring rim and molded decoration along the upper body. Marked G.E. OHR, BILOXI, MISS. Believed to date from the late 19th or early 20th centuries.* 220.00   270.00

☐ **Vase,** *5", violet glaze with sea-green streak-mottling, of pot form with a pinched neck, flaring lip, and lightly molded decoration at the neck. Marked G.E. OHR. Believed to date from the late 19th or early 20th centuries.* 230.00   275.00

GLASGOW POTTERY

The Glasgow Pottery was founded in 1863 by Mr. John Moses and the company engaged in the manufacture of white granite, semi-porcelain, opaque wares, ironstone and cream-colored items. Other names for the pottery included John Moses & Company and John Moses & Sons Company.

Marks: Numerous marks, including those shown.

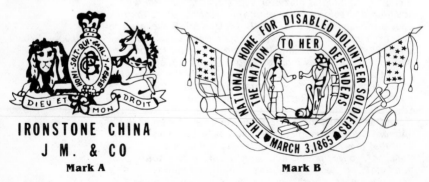

IRONSTONE CHINA
J M. & CO
Mark A

Mark B

U.S.M.C. Q.M.D.

Mark C   **Mark D**

Mark E

TRILBY
J.M.&S.CO.
TRENTON, N.J.

Mark F

SAPPHO
J.M.&S. CO.

Mark G

GLASGOW CHINA
VITRIFIED
TRENTON, N.J.
Mark H

Mark I

GLASGOW POTTERY
— CO. —
TRENTON
N. J.

Mark J

Prices: The only actual sale we have for a Glasgow item is $20 for a berry dish decorated with the inscription "Martha Washington Tea Party, Millville, N.J., Feb. 22, 1874". In the center of the bowl is a circle with "1776-Centennial-1876". Although there is no backstamp, Glasgow is known to have created this set of china. The little dish is quite the worse for wear since both the lettering and the gold trim on the rim are worn.

Since Glasgow was a very early company, prices for most of their wares will be higher than for other similar wares. Following are estimeates:

	Price Range	
☐ **Bowls,** *dessert or soup*	20.00	30.00
☐ **Bowls,** *serving*	30.00	50.00
☐ **Cups and saucers**	25.00	35.00
☐ **Dinner plates**	15.00	20.00
☐ **Mugs**	7.00	20.00
☐ **Platters,** *depending on size*	65.00	85.00
☐ **Smaller plates**	7.00	13.00

GLOBE

Manufacturers of bath accessories.

Marks: *Not known*

GREENWOOD ART POTTERY COMPANY

See Greenwood Pottery Company.

GREENWOOD POTTERY COMPANY

In 1861, James Tams and James P. Stephens organized Stephens, Tams, & Co. In 1868, the company was incorporated under the name of Greenwood Pottery Company, with Tams as its president and Stephens as secretary/treasurer. The company made white granite ware, stone china, vitrified and translucent china, and a wide assortment of electrical and hardware items.

Greenwood also made a fine porcelain art line, typically decorated in the Royal Worcester style, which is very rare today. The names of those who developed this line and the artists who decorated them are not known.

Marks: In addition to the marks shown there are countless others, usually incorporating the name or initials of the company in one fashion or another.

Mark A

GREENWOOD CHINA
TRENTON, N. J.

Mark B

G.P.
Co.

Mark C

Mark D

GREENWOOD CHINA
—| |—
M. GOLDBERG
CONEY ISLAND
N. Y.

Mark E

Mark F

GREENWOOD
CHINA
I
Mark G

GREENWOOD CHINA
TRENTON, N. J.
Mark H

PATENTED
OCT . 27-25
Greenwood
WM AKERS JR. CO.
PHILA. PA.
china
PAT APPLIED FOR

Mark I

Mark J

GREENWOOD CHINA
COOK'S
HOTEL & RESTAURANT
SUPPLY CO
NEW YORK

Mark K

1862
GREENWOOD CHINA
TRENTON, N.J.
1876
REG. U.S. PAT. OFF.

BELLEEK AND PORCELAIN ITEMS

Any of their finer wares can be rated at a hint less than the comparable Ott & Brewer items. Although these items are very rare, the demand for them is not quite as great as for the Ott & Brewer.

IRONSTONE AND OTHER LOWER LOWER-LEVEL WARES

Jar, *women's head handles, cobalt blue trim*

	Price	Range
☐ **Bowl,** *round, 9" diameter, plain white*	17.50	22.50
☐ **Bowl,** *round, 10" diameter, green banding*	17.50	22.50
☐ **Bowl,** *round, 6" diameter, cereal size, hotel insignia*	5.00	7.00
☐ **Bowl,** *round, 6" diameter, cereal size, undecorated*	3.00	5.00
☐ **Bowl,** *round, 6" diameter, cereal size, gold trim*	3.00	5.00
☐ **Bowl,** *round, 5" diameter, military insignia*	4.00	6.00
☐ **Bowl,** *round, 4" diameter, undecorated*	3.00	5.00
☐ **Butter par,** *uncorated*	2.00	3.00
☐ **Cup and saucer,** *undecorated*	5.00	7.00
☐ **Cup and saucer,** *cobalt blue banding on both pieces*	5.00	7.00
☐ **Cup and saucer,** *hotel insignia*	6.00	10.00
☐ **Cup and saucer,** *after size, undecorated, very cute shape*	10.00	14.00
☐ **Cup and saucer,** *full size, undecorated*	5.00	8.00
☐ **Cup and saucer,** *West Point Military Academy insignia*	23.00	28.00
☐ **Cup and saucer,** *Blue Onion trim*	10.00	15.00
☐ **Jar,** *women's head handles, cobalt blue trim, mark C*	40.00	47.50
☐ **Jar,** *identical to above but undecorated and unmarked*	3.00	5.00
☐ **Plate,** *10" diameter, undecorated*	3.00	5.00
☐ **Plate,** *10" diameter, cobalt blue bands on border*	4.00	6.00
☐ **Plate,** *10" diameter, Blue Onion pattern*	10.00	15.00
☐ **Plate,** *10" diameter, hotel insignia on rim*	8.00	12.00
☐ **Plate,** *9" diameter, undecorated*	3.00	5.00
☐ **Plate,** *9" diameter, maroon trim*	3.00	5.00
☐ **Plate,** *8" square, cobalt decoration, mark D variation*	85.00	100.00
☐ **Plate,** *8" diameter, hotel crest*	3.00	5.00

	Price	Range
☐ **Plate,** *8" diameter, undecorated*	1.50	3.00
☐ **Plate,** *6" diameter, hotel insignia*	2.00	3.00
☐ **Plate,** *6" diameter, gold trim*	1.50	3.00
☐ **Plate,** *6" diameter, green gadroon trim*	1.50	3.00
☐ **Plate,** *5" diameter, blue floral design on rim*	1.50	3.00
☐ **Platter,** *10" oval, undecorated*	17.50	22.50
☐ **Platter,** *10" oval, maroon border*	23.00	28.00
☐ **Platter,** *12" oval, undecorated*	30.00	35.00
☐ **Platter,** *13" oval, undecorated*	30.00	35.00
☐ **Platter,** *13" oval, hotel insignia*	38.00	43.00
☐ **Platter,** *14" oval, hotel insignia*	30.00	35.00
☐ **Platter,** *14" oval, green and black trim, hotel insignia in center,*		
marks A and B	40.00	47.50
☐ **Pot,** *mustard, 3¼" high, undecorated, very cute*	17.50	22.50
☐ **Shell dishes,** *undecorated, mark A, pair*	30.00	35.00

GRUEBY

This very prestigeous art pottery manufacturer was in business rather briefly, a total of 16 years. In that time, it rose to the top of its market, was considered one of the foremost trend-setters, and established an enviable reputation for creativity and quality. Its years of operation were from 1891 to 1907. They coincided exactly with the glory years of art pottery when it not only made a resounding public splash but influenced other crafts and arts. The Grueby ware was expensive and was intended for a limited audience. Its buyers were the socially prominent citizens of the time, who wanted to be fully in step with the latest tastes for interior decoration. Current scarcity and high prices for Grueby are simply a reflection of a long-standing tradition: even when new, this pottery could be found only in the more elite shops in large metropolitan areas.

Grueby had as diverse a line as any art pottery manufacturer. Its products included vases, ornamental wares of various kinds including statuettes, and decorative tiles.

Though always referred to simply as "Grueby," the company's name was Grueby Faience and Tile Co. It was founded in June of 1891 by William H. Grueby in Boston. There was no doubt, even at the outset, that the intention was to cater to affluent citizens of Boston and the other large East Coast cities. But for the first two years, the company went almost unnoticed. Its climb to prominence began in 1893, inspired (it is said) by the Columbian Exposition and the displays of foreign porcelain which delighted tourists. Grueby decided against making true porcelain but turned his attentions to semiporcelain or faience (softpaste ware). He gave this a non-vitreous glaze which produced a warm, satin-like finish. It was not so much the glaze, however, as the brilliant colorings and imaginative shaping which won throngs of admirers for Grueby.

When the next great exposition came along — in St. Louis in 1903 — Grueby displayed many of its creations. They dazzled visitors even more than had the foreign wares at the Columbian, 11 years earlier. Already enjoying huge success, this was the boost that brought Grueby squarely to the front rank in art pottery. It was thereafter the acknowledged leader in the field.

Customers as well as press critics respected the painstaking approaches made to Grueby pottery and the constant cavalade of fresh ideas, shapes, and color motifs. Like snowflakes, there were really no two alike.

Grueby did so well that, in a sense, it put itself out of business. The Tiffany Co. of New York, which had been selling fine jewelry and decorative glassware for many years, decided to add art pottery to its inventory. Rather than selling the products of another manufacturer, Tiffany would consider nothing less than manufacturing its own pottery. Since Grueby had the outstanding reputation in the industry, Tiffany approached the company with offers of purchase. The purchase plan was completed in 1907 and thereafter all Grueby pottery was manufactured and sold under the name of Tiffany.

Marks: The majority of Grueby ware carries not only a factory stamp but an artist's marking as well. There are several variations of the company mark, which fall into two basic categories: straight-line and circular. The straight-line mark will sometimes read *GRUEBY POTTERY* and, directly beneath this in lettering of a slightly smaller size *BOSTON, U.S.A.* A variation of this mark reads *GRUEBY* at the top line and *BOSTON MASS.* below. Of the circular marks, the chief difference is that some read *GRUEBY POTTERY* and others *GRUEBY FAIENCE, but both of these versions are accompanied by the same style of address: BOSTON, U.S.A.* A small ornament is placed in the circle's center. These marks are without frames or borders of any sort.

	Price Range	
☐ **Bowl,** 4½", greenish brown glaze (mottled), pressed bulbous form, bearing an impressed factory mark.	160.00	190.00
☐ **Tile,** 6¼" square, blue, decorated with a painting of green flowers, bearing an impressed factory mark and an artist's initials. Probably early 1900's.	300.00	375.00

Note: It should be mentioned that when such items occur for sale in groups, such as half a dozen of the same design, the priced per tile is higher than for a single specimen. This is because their decorative uses are greater, when one has a number of them.

☐ **Tile, horse,** 6¼" square, pastel blue, decorated with a painting of a white horse, bearing an impressed factory mark and an artist's initials. Probably early 1900's.	275.00	335.00
☐ **Tile, landscape,** 4" square, chiefly green and beige, bearing an impressed factory mark and hand-inked artist's initials P.S. Late 19th to early 20th centuries.	120.00	145.00

Note: While Rookwood was selling its huge tile murals (more than a yard square), Grueby was doing a good business with these small individual tiles. Naturally, each pattern was turned out in the thousands, since it would take hundreds just to cover a single wall. Nevertheless, they aren't common — because when the houses they decorated came down, they went with them.

☐ **Vase,** 5¾", brown glaze (speckled), of flattened spherical form with short neck, bearing an impressed factory mark. c. 1900 . .	300.00	375.00
☐ **Vase,** 10", green, decorated by Ruth Erickson, bearing an impressed factory mark and artist's initials. c. 1900.	1200.00	1600.00
☐ **Vase,** 6¼", green glaze, bulbous bowl with a tall squared cylindrical neck, bearing an impressed factory mark and artist's initials. Late 19th century to early 20th century.	425.00	525.00

Price Range

☐ **Vase,** 7", green, of modified ovoid form with molded panels encircling the body, bearing an impressed factory mark and artist's initials. Late 19th century to early 20th century. 470.00   560.00

☐ **Vase,** 7½", green, ovoid flask-style form with pinched neck, decorated by Lillian Newman, bearing an impressed factory mark. c. 1898/1901. . . . .   530.00   615.00

HALL CHINA COMPANY

This giant of the dinnerware industry was noteworthy not only for the volume of its sales and variety of its patterns, but because it produced the first leadless glaze in the trade. This resulted in strong hardpaste wares with non-porous surfaces which required only a single trip through the firing kiln. Not only were labor costs reduced, but the sales impact was enormous. Hall could claim — very authentically — that it was manufacturing chinaware by the same process used in China centuries earlier, because the ancient Oriental potters fired their wares only once.

Because of the Hall's huge production and long career in the trade (the business is still thriving), speculation traditionally was voiced about its collectability. Today, the earlier Hall patterns are about 70 years old, some reaching back even further, and there is no longer any doubting their appeal to hobbyists. Those who specialize in Hall pottery seek out these early specimens and pay ever-increasing sums for them. Even the more recent creations have their collector following on a smaller scale; and quite likely the current Hall line of production will, in time, get into the realm of collectors' pieces, too. The abundance is, in itself, an incentive for many potential hobbyists, because the Hall wares turn up virtually everywhere china is sold.

This was an Ohio company, founded in East Liverpool in 1903 by Robert Hall. At its outset and for several years thereafter the firm was small compared to many of its Ohio rivals. Dinnerware was not even among the earliest products; Hall turned its attentions to sanitary wares and related lines. Robert Hall died in the year following the company's inauguration and the business was taken over by his son, Robert T. Hall. It was to Robert T. Hall that credit belongs for developing the method of "Chinese firing," which the company called "bisque firing." This historic advance was made in 1911. It could not have occurred at a more opportune time. When World War I began a few years later, American potters, freed from the competition of mounting imports, saw their sales double and triple. Hall was naturally at the forefront since it had the most talked-about product of the day. Even after the war ended, the Hall business continued growing. Nor was it seriously hurt by the financial depression of the 1930's.

Hall's best known dinnerwares were in white or cream usually with a gilt border and decorated with soft pastel flowers. This was the standard line which found new customers in each succeeding generation. In addition, it manufactured numerous other styles in creative patterns, including solid-color wares with richly painted decoration. There were even some classical motifs that were inspired by the artwork of ancient Greece. Whatever the consumer wanted, Hall usually had it somewhere in its highly diverse line — and now the collector can enjoy these pieces too. Quite a bit of Art Deco flavor will be found in the Hall products from the 1920's and 1930's. There are hobbyists who collect Hall strictly for its Art Deco creations.

Marks: There are numerous marks and variations of them, sometimes accompanied by trade names applying to the different lines. The earlier markings were very simple compared to those of later eras, usually consisting of nothing more than the words *HALL'S CHINA* arranged in a plain circular frame, containing a mold or pattern number at the center. This was sometimes accompanied by *MADE IN U.S.A.* directly beneath the stamp. Later, the name Hall was placed in a rectangular frame with wider border, with a small R in a circle beneath it (signifying registration as a trademark). A more eleborate marking reads *HALL'S SUPERIOR QUALITY KITCHENWARE* in a rectangular frame with bars above and beneath. There are also many retailers' marks to be encountered on the Hall products.

HAMILTON DECORATING COMPANY

This very obscure Trenton decorating company did very competent work that equalled that done at the Lenox Company. The one sample we have at hand is a bouillon cup and saucer tastefully decorated with a banding of lime green and hand-painted pink roses. The gold trim is restrained and well done. Although we have no hard information about this company, if we had to take a guess, it would be that a former Lenox dinnerware decorator set up shop on his/her own.

Marks: "Decorated by Hamilton Decorating Co., Trenton, NJ" in reddish-brown.
Prices: The above-mentioned cup and saucer was priced at about $15 which is probably a little low for such a scarce item.

HARKER

The historic Harker Pottery played an important role in the rise of Ohio's prominence in the industry. Benjamin Harker got into the business more or less by lucky circumstance. He had been a self-employed roofer in England. After saving up some money, he embarked for America and found his way to East Liverpool, Ohio in 1840. There he bought a farm for $3,500 and apparently settled down to live the life of a gentleman farmer. The area was well suited to farming, but it proved to be even better suited to another kind of business. Harker discovered rich clay deposits on the property. Having no use for clay himself, he began selling it to a neighbor, James Bennett, who went into the pottery business. Gradually, it began occurring to Harker that an opportunity was being missed. So he began making pottery himself and kept all the clay on his farm for his own use. Before the year 1840 ended, Benjamin Harker was in the pottery trade along with his sons, Benjamin Jr. and George.

The earliest products of the Harker Pottery Co. were yellowware table articles, which Harker packed in barrels and shipped by boat to the larger towns to be retailed. It was not long before the East Liverpool area was swarming with potteries, mostly inspired by Harker's success. Some were larger and better financed. Because Harker had built up a reputation and had good business connections, the company experienced no trouble in withstanding the increasing competition. The older Harker died not long after the company was established, and so it passed to the hands of his sons who ran it for many years. Following the Civil War, a period of renewed prosperity ensued, culminating in the debut of Harker's whiteware pottery in 1879. A serious flood threatened to cripple the factory in 1884, but it made a fast recovery. Sales increased as the 19th century drew to a close, and the 20th century saw further growth.

In the early part of the Depression, the Harker operations moved from East Liverpool to Chester, West Virginia, where there was less threat of flood and also a better tax situation. Harker was purchased by the Jeanette Glass Company after World War II and continued in operation until 1972. Its 132 years in the business was one of the longest careers for an American pottery maker. Harker was more than a little proud of its long heritage and often used the slogan "Oldest Pottery in America."

The Harker wares, though aimed at the middleclass market, are mainly high quality, especially in the originality of designs and their detailed application. Most motifs are subdued and feature an interplay of many different subtle shadings which seems to render them more lifelike and appealing. Floral patterns were the perennial favorite of this company, but the approach was changed often enough to avoid monotony. Harker made salt and pepper sets, coffee scoops, and even rolling pins — just about everything from the kitchen. A visit to almost any antique shop will introduce the collector to these products.

Marks: The most familiar mark of the Harker Co. is a scroll, reading *HARKER, THE OLDEST POTTERY IN AMERICA,* and portraying a house in the form of a vase with a tree beside it. This mark will also carry the wording *HOT OVEN CHINAWARE* or *HOT OVEN COOKINGWARE.* The words "hot oven" are run together to appear as "hotoven." Many pieces with this type of marking also carry the Good Housekeeping seal. This is a late mark found on pieces of the 20th century. In its earlier days, the Harker Co. used a variety of much more delicate markings. Several of these incorporated a figure of a bow and arrow, the arrow pointed upward and bisecting the words *STONE CHINA.* A similar mark has the wording *SEMI PORCELAIN.* While these are 19th century markings, they are obviously later than 1879. Another old mark is a letter *H* in which the letter loops out on the side to form a *P.*

HARRIS MANUFACTURING COMPANY

See Trent Tile.

HART BREWER POTTERY COMPANY

In 1895, John Hart Brewer and Henry D. Phillips took over the Fell & Thropp operation. The company manufactured sanitary specialties.

Marks: *Not known*
Prices: Since John Hart Brewer was associated with this company, their items would have perhaps a greater interest than other similar wares. A three-piece miniature bathroom set by this company would perhaps be valued at around $100 instead of the usual $50.

HATTERSLEY POTTERY

The name Hattersley Pottery probably refers to a building rather than a company, and it is doubtful that a company by that name existed. Charls Hattersley erected the building in 1852 and possibly ran a company by that name for a short while. William Young & Sons were tenants in the building, as were the City Pottery and Maddock and Company. The building was located on Perry Street.

HOMER LAUGHLIN

One of the best known and most successful of the pottery companies, Homer Laughlin rides just as high today with hobbyists as it did for many years with the consumer who bought tableware. Homer Laughlin is best known for its Fiesta ware, a collecting specialty which has attracted tens of thousands of active hobbyists. Fiesta began to be actively collected as long ago as the 1960's and a big surge of popularity followed in the next decade. Prices on the secondhand market zoomed from an average of 25¢ and 35¢ to the $5 to $10 range. This seemed unbelievable, because everyone knew Fiesta ware was very common — it had been one of the most widely manufactured tablewares of the 20th century. Nevertheless, buyer demand was strong, and with this kind of demand ANYTHING can happen to retail prices.

However, other Homer Laughlin lines have not been ignored by the collecting enthusiasts. Everything made by the firm up to around 1950 ranks in the "collectible" realm. No other single line has as many active competitors as Fiesta. Yet, because the rarity of some other groups is much greater, their retail market values are average more than those on Fiesta. Since the company is still in business and has been extremely productive right up to the present time, beginning collectors may have a little trouble distinguishing the fairly recent pieces from those of collectible standing. We hope the following listings will be of some assistance. Some of the more recent Laughlin wares are marked with the date of production.

This historic factory began in 1871. It was originally a two-man operation on a very small scale, the family business of Homer Laughlin and his brother Shakespeare. The Laughlins chose East Liverpool, Ohio as their headquarters, and the Homer Laughlin Pottery Co. became the most consistently successful of all the many factories in that town. However, things got off to a slow start. Shakespeare Laughlin left the business in 1879. For the next 17 years, Homer ran the company himself; growth was slow and steady. His goal was to turn out good-quality tableware that the average American family could afford. After the firm attracted some attention at the 1876 Centennial, distributors from other parts of the country became interested in the products. But it was many years later before Laughlin set up the intricate network of mass distribution which marked its operations in the 20th century.

The enormous growth of Homer Laughlin Pottery Co. saw the establishment of five factories in nearby West Virginia. As each was opened, the company's executives staunchly believed that it could handle the production for the next 20 or 30 years. But within just a few years — sometimes less — the business volume increased so much that another factory had to be added. Each factory had its assigned task of turning out certain tableware lines. The years following World War II, which were very lucrative for the pottery and porcelain industry in general, were the most profitable in Laughlin's history. Millions of homes used its table services. They were advertised everywhere, and sold by the major mail-order suppliers.

During the 1970's, production reached an average of *50,000,000 pieces* of tableware annually — by far a record for any American pottery.

Marks: The marks will vary depending on the item's trade name. Laughlin's traditional trademark from its earliest years is one of the most interesting in the industry. It shows a lion being mauled by an eagle. This mark was intended to represent the American eagle triumphing over the British lion. Of course, the implication was that Homer Laughlin pottery surpassed the imported British wares. This mark sometimes carries the name *LAUGHLIN* written out in fine script characters, while in other versions there is a printed text reading *PREMIUM STONE CHINA HOMER LAUGHLIN.* The earliest lines introduced by the firm were "Colonial," "Golden Gate," and "American Beauty." The marks for each of these depict the eagle and lion with a circular frame superimposed over them, reading *LAUGHLIN SEMI-VITREOUS CHINA* or *HOMER LAUGHLIN SEMI-VITREOUS CHINA.* The trade name appears at the foot of the mark. Whenever these marks are encountered, the finder can be assured that he has an early item. Another mark used by the company in its earlier years consists of a horseshoe pierced by a pair of dueling swords. Within the horseshoe is the wording *LAUGHLIN CHINA.*

FIESTA WARE *(Introduced 1935)*

Fiesta wares are very simple designs produced on very bright colors. The design is a series of rings which graduate in size, with the smallest ring at the center and the greatest width between rings also at the center. This design is mostly used on the rims and at the center of items such as plates, bowls, etc. It is also used on pieces with small pedestal bases and on lids. The colors used for these wares are Fiesta red, rose, dark green, medium green, light green, chartreuse, yellow, old ivory, gray, turquoise and dark blue. Each piece, except a very few, is marked with the Fiesta trademark, either in the mold or an ink handstamped mark.

Price Range

☐ **Ashtray,** *experimental, basketweave, flowers in relief*	40.00	50.00
☐ **Ashtray,** *yellow, with three impressions, c. 1936*	15.00	20.00
☐ **Bowl, dessert,** *6", blue, c. 1959*	7.50	10.00
☐ **Bowl, dessert,** *medium green, 1959*	20.00	25.00
☐ **Bowl, fruit,** *4-3/4", with flaired rim*	5.00	7.50
☐ **Bowl, fruit,** *medium green, with flaired rim*	20.00	25.00
☐ **Bowl, fruit,** *5-1/2", with flaired rim*	5.00	7.50
☐ **Bowl, fruit,** *11-3/4", with pronounced rim*	50.00	58.00
☐ **Bowl, nested,** *5", numbered "1" on the bottom*	17.50	22.50
☐ **Bowl, nested,** *6", numbered "2" on the bottom*	10.00	15.00
☐ **Bowl, nested,** *7", numbered "3" on the bottom*	15.00	20.00
☐ **Bowl, nested,** *8", numbered "4" on the bottom*	20.00	25.00
☐ **Bowl, nested,** *9", numbered "5" on the bottom*	20.00	25.00
☐ **Bowl, nested,** *10", numbered "6" on the bottom*	25.00	30.00
☐ **Bowl, nested,** *11", numbered "7" on the bottom*	30.00	35.00
☐ **Bowl, salad,** *7-5/8"*	20.00	25.00
☐ **Bowl, salad,** *9-1/2", yellow, with pronounced rim*	25.00	30.00
☐ **Bowl, salad,** *footed*	65.00	80.00
☐ **Bowl, salad,** *footed, with decal*	65.00	80.00
☐ **Bread box**	25.00	30.00
☐ **Bud vase,** *tubular shape, on small pedestal base*	20.00	25.00
☐ **Candleholders,** *blue, pair, spherical body on square base, c.* *1936*	60.00	70.00
☐ **Candleholders,** *yellow, pair, tripod*	30.00	35.00
☐ **Canister set**	25.00	30.00
☐ **Carafe,** *three-pint, old ivory, cork seal top, c. 1941*	28.00	32.00
☐ **Casserole,** *covered, with two curved pinch handles*	28.00	32.00
☐ **Casserole, French,** *yellow, with notched lid and plug handle* ..	65.00	80.00
☐ **Coffeepot,** *with notched lid and plug handle*	30.00	35.00
☐ **Coffeepot,** *red, with notched lid and handle, c. 1936*	50.00	60.00
☐ **Comport,** *10" x 2-1/2", with extended rim, on pedestal base,* *rare*	65.00	80.00
☐ **Comport,** *12", on small pedestal base*	30.00	35.00
☐ **Comport, sweets**	15.00	20.00
☐ **Creamer,** *with ring handle, on small pedestal base*	5.00	7.00
☐ **Creamer,** *with plug handle, on small pedestal base*	30.00	35.00
☐ **Creamer,** *in turquoise*	50.00	65.00
☐ **Creamer,** *4", experimental, with ring handle*	20.00	25.00
☐ **Creamer,** *with plug, on small pedestal base*	7.50	10.00
☐ **Cups, coffee,** *with ring handles, on small pedestal base*	12.00	16.00
☐ **Cup, cream soup**	10.00	13.00
☐ **Cups, tea**	10.00	13.00
☐ **Cup and saucer,** *red*	12.00	15.00
☐ **Cup and saucer,** *yellow*	9.00	14.00
☐ **Egg cup**	23.00	28.00
☐ **Egg cups,** *on small pedestal base*	15.00	20.00
☐ **Egg cooker**	30.00	40.00
☐ **Egg cooker,** *electric, with egg cups and tray*	45.00	60.00
☐ **Gravy boat**	7.50	10.00
☐ **Jug,** *2 pint, with ring handle*	15.00	20.00
☐ **Mug,** *turquoise*	20.00	25.00
☐ **Mug,** *yellow*	20.00	25.00
☐ **Napkin holder**	12.00	16.00

	Price Range	
☐ **Nappy,** *8-1/2", with flaired rim*	7.50	10.00
☐ **Nappy,** *9-1/2", with flaired rim*	10.00	13.00
☐ **Pitcher, ice,** *two-quart, red, with handle on small pedestal base*	25.00	30.00
☐ **Pitcher, juice,** *disk shape, 30 ounces, yellow, with handle*	7.50	10.00
☐ **Same as above,** *in red or gray*	30.00	35.00
☐ **Pitcher, syrup,** *twist on top, with slide-back release*	55.00	70.00
☐ **Pitcher, water,** *disk shape, 2 quart, with handle*	20.00	25.00
☐ **Plate, 7"**	1.25	2.25
☐ **Plate, 9"**	1.25	2.25
☐ **Plate, 10"**	1.25	2.25
☐ **Plate, bread and butter,** *7-3/8"*	2.50	3.50
☐ **Plate, cake,** *10"*	45.00	60.00
☐ **Plate, calendar,** *10", 1954*	15.00	20.0
☐ **Plate, calendar,** *10", 1955*	20.00	25.00
☐ **Plate, chop,** *6", yellow*	5.00	7.50
☐ **Plate, chop,** *12-1/4"*	10.00	13.00
☐ **Plate, chop,** *13", with handle*	30.00	35.00
☐ **Plate, chop,** *15"*	12.00	16.00
☐ **Plate, compartment,** *10-1/2", turquoise, three compartments, flaired rim, c. 1941*	7.50	10.00
☐ **Plate, compartment,** *11-5/8", three compartments, flaired rim* .	10.00	13.00
☐ **Plate, deep,** *8", with flaired rim*	10.00	13.00
☐ **Plate, dessert,** *6", yellow*	5.00	7.50
☐ **Plate, dinner,** *10", rose, c. 1936*	4.00	8.00
☐ **Plate, luncheon,** *9-1/2"*	4.00	8.00
☐ **Platter,** *12", turquoise, oval, with extended rim, c. 1939*	7.50	10.00
☐ **Platter,** *12", oval*	10.00	13.00
☐ **Salt and pepper shakers,** *spherical shape on small pedestal base*	6.00	9.00
☐ **Saucers**	1.25	2.25
☐ **Sauces,** *A.D.*	4.00	7.50
☐ **Sauceboat,** *green, with handle, on small pedestal base, c. 1939*	10.00	13.00
☐ **Sugar,** *covered, with lid and curved pinch handles, on small pedestal base*	7.50	10.00
☐ **Sugar and creamer,** *red, c. 1941*	12.00	16.00
☐ **Teapot,** *medium, holds six cups, with semi-circle handle*	20.00	25.00
☐ **Teapot,** *large, red, holds eight cups, with ring handle, c. 1936* .	25.00	30.00
☐ **Teapot,** *with cover, experimental*	85.00	100.00
☐ **Tray,** *turquoise*	50.00	60.00
☐ **Tray,** *yellow*	50.00	60.00
☐ **Tray, relish,** *green base, red center, multi-color inserts*	35.00	40.00
☐ **Tray, relish,** *old ivory, c. 1939*	35.00	40.00
☐ **Tray, utility,** *green, oblong, with extended rim*	10.00	13.00
☐ **Tray, utility,** *yellow, c. 1941*	7.50	10.00
☐ **Tumbler,** *5 ounces, cylindrical, ivory, turquoise, yellow*	10.00	13.00
☐ **Tumbler,** *10 ounces*	15.00	20.00
☐ **Vase,** *8", rippled sides, rim looks like the outline of a flower* ...	75.00	90.00
☐ **Vase,** *10", rippled sides, rim looks like the outline of a flower* ..	100.00	120.00
☐ **Vase,** *12", rippled sides, rim looks like the outline of a flower* ..	120.00	140.00

HARLEQUIN *(Introduced 1938)*

The Harlequin wares are somewhat like Fiesta, having bright colors and simple shapes. They have an Art Deco flair with the same series of rings, but they are not on the rim. Instead, they appear farther into the center after a thin band with no design. The colors that were used on Harlequin are tangerine, salmon, forest green, medium green, light green, chartreuse, Harlequin yellow, gray, turquoise, mauve blue, maroon and spruce green.

	Price Range	
☐ **Ashtray,** *with three impressions*	15.00	20.00
☐ **Ashtray,** *basketweave, with three impressions*	15.00	20.00
☐ **Baker,** *9", oval, with lid and pointed handles*	4.00	7.00
☐ **Bowl, fruit,** *5-1/2", flaired rim*	2.00	4.00
☐ **Bowl, salad,** *7", shallow, no rings*	5.00	7.50
☐ **Butter dish,** *with cover*	25.00	30.00
☐ **Candleholder,** *inkwell shape, with three level base, pair*	30.00	35.00
☐ **Casserole,** *with lid*	17.50	22.50
☐ **Creamer,** *inverted dome shape, with printed handles*	3.00	5.00
☐ **Creamer,** *inverted dome shape, with high lip, with pointed handles*	15.00	20.00
☐ **Cup, coffee,** *with pointed handle*	7.50	10.00
☐ **Cup, cream soup,** *with two pointed handles*	4.00	7.00
☐ **Dish, nut,** *3", basketweave design*	4.00	7.00
☐ **Egg cup,** *on pedestal base*	10.00	13.00
☐ **Egg cup,** *double, on round pedestal base*	4.00	7.00
☐ **Jug,** *22 ounce, cylindrical, with pointed handle*	10.00	13.00
☐ **Jug, water,** *spherical, with handle*	10.00	13.00
☐ **Nappy,** *9", flaired rim*	4.00	7.00
☐ **Pitcher, syrup,** *with twist-on lid, and slide back release*	50.00	60.00
☐ **Plate,** *6", recessed center*	1.00	2.00
☐ **Plate,** *7", recessed center*	1.25	2.25
☐ **Plate,** *9", recessed center*	2.50	3.50
☐ **Plate,** *10", recessed center*	3.50	4.50
☐ **Platter,** *11", oval, recessed center*	4.00	7.00
☐ **Platter,** *13", oval, recessed center*	4.00	7.00
☐ **Salt and pepper shakers,** *inverted dome shape, on small pedestal base*	5.00	7.00
☐ **Sauceboat,** *oblong, squared, with handle*	5.00	7.00
☐ **Saucer,** *with recessed ring for cup*	1.00	1.50
☐ **Sugar bowl,** *inverted dome shape, with lid, with pointed handles*	4.00	7.00
☐ **Tea cup,** *inverted dome shape, with pointed handles*	3.50	5.00
☐ **Teapot,** *inverted dome shape, with pointed handles*	12.00	16.00
☐ **Tumbler, water,** *cylindrical*	10.00	13.00

RIVIERA *(Introduced 1938)*

These wares are basically square in shape with decorative corners. Plates and platters are square or rectangular with a recessed center ring that is either round or oval. Some bowls and nappies are flaired slightly at the rims. These wares were produced in colors such as ivory, yellow, light green, red and blue. Most pieces were not marked, but occasionally a gold stamp will be found on a piece identifying it as a Homer Laughlin specimen.

	Price Range	
☐ **Baker,** *9", flat extended rim, straight sides*	4.00	7.00
☐ **Baker,** *9-1/4", oval, flaired rim, curving sides*	4.00	7.00
☐ **Bowl, fruit,** *5-1/2", flat extended rim*	2.00	4.00
☐ **Butter dish,** *with cover and pinch handles*	30.00	35.00
☐ **Creamer,** *on square pedestal base*	4.00	7.00
☐ **Jug,** *with lid that covers open spout*	30.00	35.00
☐ **Jug, juice,** *disk shape, yellow*	30.00	35.00
☐ **Nappy,** *8-1/4", curving sides*	5.00	7.00
☐ **Plate,** *6", recessed center*	1.25	2.25
☐ **Plate,** *7", recessed center*	1.50	2.50
☐ **Plate,** *9", recessed center*	4.00	6.00
☐ **Plate,** *10", recessed center*	4.00	7.00
☐ **Platter,** *11-1/4", with pinch handles*	5.00	7.50
☐ **Platter,** *11-1/2", oval, recessed center*	5.00	7.50
☐ **Platter,** *12", with pinch handles*	7.50	10.00
☐ **Platter,** *12", with pinch handles*	7.50	10.00
☐ **Salt and pepper shakers,** *spherical*	5.00	7.50
☐ **Sauceboat,** *with handle on square pedestal base*	5.00	7.50
☐ **Saucer**	1.25	2.25
☐ **Sugar,** *with lid, on square pedestal base*	5.00	7.50
☐ **Tea cup**	5.00	7.50
☐ **Teapot,** *on square pedestal base*	20.00	25.00
☐ **Tumblers,** *cylindrical, with pointed handles*	15.00	20.00
☐ **Tumbler, juice,** *cylindrical, pronounced rim*	15.00	20.00

HULL POTTERY COMPANY

The long history of the Hull Pottery Co. produced a diverse range of products. Though the firm did not work exclusively in artware, its production of art pottery rivaled that of its leading competitors. Its jugs, pitchers and vases, sometimes of heroic proportions, are typical examples of the flamboyant Art Pottery era. Prices for these are high. However, many Hull creations can be purchased modestly in fields other than art pottery, such as the containers it made for after-shave lotion in the 1930's. Something in the neighborhood of 11,000,000 of these were produced and retailed across the country for the Shulton Company. The diligent hobbyist will learn to inspect every item for a Hull marking, because the firm made wares of every conceivable description.

Hull started out as the Acme Pottery Co. in Crooksville, Ohio in 1903. After two years of operations under the Acme name, it changed ownership and the name became A.E. Hull Pottery Co. Addis E. Hull was a potter who wanted to make his mark on the industry. This was the era of Art Pottery, but Hull was enjoying satisfactory success with his other lines and did not immediately venture into artware. He was encouraged to do so because of World War I, which limited imports and created more opportunities for domestic manufacturers. The first Hull art pottery entered the market in 1917 and met with enthusiastic response. Hull's artware was somewhat more European-oriented than that of most other American makers. In fact, Hull got so caught up in European wares that the firm set up an agency for the sale of French and

English porcelains beginning in 1921. This was a rare instance of an American potter competing against himself! The stock market crash of 1929 brought this phase of Hull's operations to a close and almost did likewise to Hull's other products too. But the company struggled through the depression and was eventually brought out resoundingly by the work done for Shulton (contracted for in 1937).

Hull gained further momentum with the postwar boom in 1946. Then, amid one of the best sales periods in its history, disaster struck: the factory was destroyed by fire in 1950. After remaining closed for two years, it was reopened in 1952 and is still active to the present day.

Marks: The marking practices of this manufacturer was rather confusing. Most of the artware is stamped with numbers, which give the suggestion of denoting edition sizes: 100, 200, 300 and so on. Actually they have nothing to do with the quantity manufactured, but relate to a coding system in which each color was referred to by an assigned number. Some Hull pottery has a paper label. The usual marking is *HULL ART U.S.,* sometimes *HULL U.S.A.* When the name is spelled without the first letter capitalized, simply as *hull,* this points to a manufacturing date of 1952 or later. This practice was not instituted until after the fire and reorganization.

I. DAVIS

See Prospect Hill Pottery.

IDEAL POTTERY

See Trenton Potteries Company.

IMPERIAL PORCELAIN WORKS

No information available.

INTERNATIONAL POTTERY COMPANY

International was founded in 1860 by Henry Speeler. In 1868 his two sons entejed the firm and the name was changed to Speeler & Sons. The business was purchased by Edward Clark and James Carr, who re-entered the firm and the name was changed to Speeler & Sons. The business was purchased by Edward Clark and James Carr, who re-named it as the Lincoln Pottery Company, or as Carr & Clark. Burgess and Campbell were the next to own the property.

The name International probably refers to the building itself rather than to a company. One of the owners did use the name International as a backstamp, however.

Products included semi-porcelain and white granite ware.

Marks: Backstamps include those shown plus many others. Most of the marks use either the initials "B&C" (for Burgess & Campbell) or "I.P.Co." (for International Pottery Company.)

B-C
WILTON

Mark A

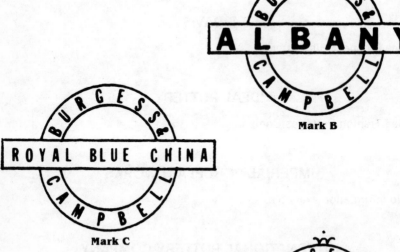

Mark B

Mark C

Mark D

		Price Range	
☐ **Bowl,** *serving*		15.00	25.00
☐ **Bowls,** *soup or dessert*		7.00	10.00
☐ **Cups and saucers**		7.00	15.00
☐ **Dinner plates**		7.00	15.00
☐ **Mugs**		10.00	30.00
☐ **Platters,** *depending on size*		15.00	40.00
☐ **Smaller plates**		3.00	6.00

INTERSTATE POTTERY COMPANY

This sanitary ware company was founded in 1909 by Frank E. Weeden, Benjamin Walton, Jr., and Charles C. Hill.

Marks: *Not known*
Prices: A three-piece miniature bathroom set would be in the area of $65.

JESSE DEAN DECORATING COMPANY

The name of this Trenton decorating company will sometimes appear along with that of the manufacturers of the china.

☐ **Plate,** *9" diameter, transfer decoration of William Jennings Bryant, very poor quality work*	10.00	15.00

Note: Since samples by the Jesse Dean outfit are not that common, this figure is low especially considering it is a Presidential campaign item. The thought occurred to us to tamper with the price but we managed to restrain ourselves. We would estimate its worth at more like $30 to $50.

JOHN MADDOCK & SONS, INC.

John Maddock & Sons was founded in 1894 or 1895 to make earthenware and sanitary specialties. They operated out of the Coalport Works. The company was incorporated in 1905. John Maddock was in charge, aided by his sons (Thomas, A.H., W.B., and H.E. Maddock.)

Marks: Backstamps include the one shown and some variations on it.
Prices: The following prices are estimates.

☐ **Bowls,** *serving*		15.00	25.00
☐ **Bowls,** *soup or dessert*		7.00	10.00
☐ **Cups and saucers**		7.00	15.00
☐ **Dinner plates**		7.00	15.00
☐ **Mugs**		10.00	30.00
☐ **Platters,** *depending on size*		15.00	40.00
☐ **Smaller plates**		3.00	6.00

JOHN MOSES & COMPANY

See Glasgow Pottery.

JOHN MOSES & SONS COMPANY

See Glasgow Pottery.

JUST-RITE

See General Porcelain.

KEYSTONE POTTERY COMPANY

Keystone made vitreous china and sanitary specialties beginning c. 1892. Company officers included James H. Lyons, J. W. Lyons, Joseph Umpleby, and John Brian.

Marks: A keystone within a wreath.

	Price Range	
☐ **Bowls,** *serving*	15.00	25.00
☐ **Bowls,** *soup or dessert*	7.00	10.00
☐ **Cups and saucers**	7.00	15.00
☐ **Dinner plates**	7.00	15.00
☐ **Mugs**	10.00	30.00
☐ **Platters,** *depending on size*	15.00	40.00
☐ **Smaller plates**	3.00	6.00
☐ **Three-piece miniature bathroom set**	50.00	60.00

LAMBERTON WORKS

Site of John Maddock & Sons and later of Scammell China.

LENOX

Lenox China was founded on May 18, 1889 by Jonathan Coxon, Sr. and Walter Scott Lenox, who had met when both were employed by Ott & Brewer. The original name of the new company was the Ceramic Art Company, and Coxon was its president with Lenox as secretary/treasurer and art director.

The partnership did not last long, due both to personality conflicts and to disputes over company management. Most sources tell us that 1894 was the date when the partnership was dissolved, but the *State Gazette* of August 31, 1916, states that Coxon was associated with C.A.C. for seven years, which would make 1896 the date of departure.

The early years were lean ones for the young company, and it was only with great difficulty that the original loan of $4,000 from William Hancock was repaid. We quote from *The Story of Walter Scott Lenox:* "The flame of a zealot glowed in the heart of Lenox. Not so in the hearts of some of his backers, who stipulated that the factory he erected at the corner of Meade and Prince Streets in Trenton should be so constructed as to be converted into a tenement should the pottery fail."

Company activities in the early years included production of both decorated and undecorated wares. By the end of the C.A.C. period, they were producing around 600 different shapes decorated both in standard and original fashion. The emphasis was on giftware instead of dinnerware, and many of the more interesting Lenox collectibles date from this time.

With the formation of Lenox, Inc., in 1906, the company started taking more direction. Dinnerware production was expanded greatly and handpainting, although it would continue for another half-century, became less important than transfer decoration. World War I perhaps gave the company the chance it had been waiting for, since foreign-made china became impossible to obtain. President Wilson's order of Lenox for the White House helped to establish their fine reputation for dinnerware. The Lenox shapes and designs took on a look of their own rather than being copies of European items, and the Lenox Company was among the first to bring a 20th century look to porcelain.

By the time of World War II, the company had produced more than 3,000 different shapes decorated with any of thousands of different designs. During the war, the Lenoxite Division was started to produce steatite as a radioradar ceramic insulating material. The same product was used to make cylinders for the manufacture of penicillin. The standard Lenox porcelain was used to make marine dials for Navy vessels.

Since World War II, the company has added crystal bone china, and ovenproof ware to their list. The china is now made in Pomona, NJ, and new corporate headquarters were recently opened in Lawrenceville, NJ. The Lenox corporate umbrella now covers a diversified group of companies making everything from school rings to candles.

MARKINGS ON LENOX CHINA

The various marks used on Lenox china down through the years can cause considerable confusion for both beginning and advanced collectors. It is possible to garner a wealth of information concerning a particular item by examining the sometimes cryptic little marks on the back or bottom. This information might include any or all of the following:

(l) Approximate date of manufacture (from design and/or color of backstamp);

(2) Shape number (very important if a collector is trying to assemble, perhaps, a set of cups and saucers);

(3) Pattern number (vital to matching old china);

(4) The store that retailed the item (can occasionally be interesting);

(5) Whether an item was decorated at the factory or elsewhere (often the deciding factor in purchasing an item);

(6) The name of any other company that was involved in making an item. (For example, the name of a silver company that did overlay work, or the name of a decorating studio).

As we proceed with this discussion of the marking system, we have made the assumption that the marks do indeed mean something and that each new mark was introduced to indicate either a particular type of item or a change in the company's status. Although this assumption may appear self-evident to some readers, we found it necessary to keep reminding ourselves of it as we delved into the marking system, particularly the backstamps.

Although we will introduce information on markings which to the best of our knowledge cannot be found elsewhere, we will also be adding to the general confusion concerning Lenox because what was previously considered a fairly cut and dried area becomes a tangle of contradictions and inconsistencies.

We will try to be as specific as possible regarding sources for our information, items used as examples, etc., and hope that as more samples come to light that some of the problem areas can be cleared up.

Although the beginning collector may find this section moderately uninteresting, he or she will no doubt profit the most from this information. Since beginners lack the experience to buy wisely based on other considerations, the various markings can be of great importance to them. The advanced collector, on the other hand, really only uses the marks to verify initial impressions of an item.

ITEM NUMBERS, PATTERN NUMBERS AND COLOR CODES

Item numbers (shape numbers) rarely if ever appear on C.A.C. items, perhaps because there was little need for them. The 1891 C.A.C. catalogue lists only 132 items, so it would have been fairly simple to keep them straight without actually putting a number on the bottom of an item. (In the catalogue they are, of course, numbered.) It was with the expansion of the company that it became necessary to begin marking the items with the appropriate number.

Item numbers can be impressed and/or handwritten, and in some cases do not appear on an item at all (even on later Lenox items). Once an item receives a number, it keeps that number throughout the entire time it is in production. When a shape is discontinued, no new item is matched up with that number.

When an item number is handwritten it is generally followed by a slash and then another number (e.g., 1830/P44.) The item number is always the first number, and any numbers appearing after the slash are always decorating (pattern) numbers. The above code would properly be interpreted as a shape 1830 dinner plate decorated with the pattern P44 etched gold banding. Those of you with a keen interest in decoding pattern numbers are referred to the dinnerware section where this information is discussed at greater length. We will mention, however, that those patterns without a letter before them (e.g., 70, 86-1/2, 338, etc.) were originally C.A.C. patterns, even though they might have been in production for many years after the Lenox takeover.

A letter at the end of a shape and pattern designation refers to the color of the rim. For example, 1830/P44C would be the same shape 1830 dinner plate with the same P44 etched gold rim but with cobalt blue trim on the rim.

Body colors (the color actually in the china itself) are achieved by adding dyes to the liquid porcelain early in the production process. The Lenox body color codes are:

X- 9 Goeblin Blue	X-17 Dawn Blue	X-31 Ivory
X-10 Egyptian Blue	X-19 Primrose Yellow	X-34 Gray
X-11 Lenox Green	X-24 Ivory	X-39 Green
X-12 Gazelle	X-26 Ashes of Roses	X-40 Yellow
X-14 Sky Blue	X-27 Malachite Green	(Black came along at
X-15 Coral	X-28 Buff	a much later date as
X-16 Fawn	X-30 Celadon	a china body color.)

Overglaze groundlay colors are done by putting sizing on the area to be covered and then carefully dusting powdered dyes onto the space. When the china is fired the color fuses to the surface. (If a piece of overglaze groundlay is broken, the color will be only on the very edge, while a body color item will have the color throughout.) The groundlay color codes follow, but keep in mind that the codes were adopted by Lenox in 1918, and they only apply to patterns beginning with code letters R to Z, numbers 1 to 299, and on all patterns with numbers higher than 300. Those patterns designed prior to 1918 had individualized color designations. (For example, O-46F is pink, not turquoise gray.)

A. Ivory	J. Salmon	S. Leather Brown
B. Cobalt Blue	K. Brown	T. Night Green
C. Chinese Blue	L. Shading Green	V. Russian Green
D. Yellow	M. Turquoise Blue	W. Red
E. Pink	N. Ecru	X. Dark Green
F. Turquoise Grey	O. Violet	Y. Pearl Grey
G. Lettuce Green	P. Deep Plum	Z. Black
H. Old Rose	R. Maroon	

BACKSTAMPS

Several of the backstamps used by Lenox through the years are shown on the following pages. Many of these marks can be found in more than one color, and there are variations of the shape as well. The table is in no particular order, and we have used letters instead of numbers to designate the marks, since we felt that giving a mark number 1 might establish an undue importance for that mark. These marks have in many cases been given nicknames by collectors, which will be listed below.

Mark A—written-out C.A.C.	Mark G—Indianhead
Mark B—written-out double	Mark H—transition mark
wreath C.A.C.	Mark I—L palette ✕
Mark C—C.A.C. wreath	Mark J—L wreath
Mark D—script Lenox	Mark K—L porcelain
Mark E—metal mark	Mark L—L opaque
Mark F—C.A.C. palette	Mark M—gold wreath

Although there are other Lenox marks, we have listed those most likely to be encountered by the collector or those marks which cause the most confusion. Some of the marks not shown in the table will be mentioned at the end of the backstamp section.

Minor variations of the marks shown do occur, and can include the lettering and/or the squiggles in the wreaths. The palette marks have been seen both with and without the circle extending through the palette.

All of the colors listed in the text can vary from pale to dark, and it can be difficult at times to distinguish light brown from gold, for example, or to tell the pinkish-red from light lavender.

The following table, labeled Table I, lists backstamps by the factory artists whose names have appeared on items with certain marks. Since employment dates for some of the artists is questionable, we cannot use a particular artist's signature as proof positive concerning backstamps, but when taken with all the other available information they can certainly help establish possibilities.

Table II shows the type of decoration which has appeared with the various backstamps, and although it was not a big help in piecing together the backstamp puzzle, we have included it as an aid to the beginner in assembling a collection. By sticking to those marks listed as factory decorated, the collector can be relatively certain of obtaining items which have at least an acceptable level of artistic merit. This, of course, means that they will be passing by some beautiful examples of hand-painting on palette mark items, but it is probably better to be safe than sorry. As a beginner, you can tell that you are no longer a beginner when you are able to walk past a transition mark Morley-signed item with a comment about how it is not the best sample of Morley's work.

Table III is the Robinson/Feeny version of the dating for Lenox backstamps, based on the text which follows and relying heavily on assumptions and theories. Although our version may be no more correct than any of the others, we have tried to give a date and use for each mark. As we stated earlier, it is likely that each mark and the color variations within marks had a meaning at the time it was introduced. In the course of our investigation, we have made genuine pests of ourselves by going into friends' homes and turning over their china or by calling them at inconvenient times to ask which artist signed which item.

In spite of our efforts, we are still somewhat in the dark concerning some of the marks, and particularly about the color variations. For example, we are still unable to explain why some transition mark items have the mark in lavender and other times it will be green. As is possibly the case with all the marks, this may have been an internal factory code of some sort, relating perhaps to inventory or quality control.

It was previously reported in an article about Lenox steins that the color of the backstamp is coordinated with the color of the stein, but we have found this not to be true. Most of the steins are monochromatic brown, green, or blue, and since the backstamps in use at the time were the same colors, by happenstance you will find, many blue steins with a blue backstamp. Identical steins can also be found, however, with other color backstamps, and we suppose the color coordination theory is another assumption.

Double-marked items are always interesting, and from them we can assume that the marks involved were in use at about the same time. They also tend to bear out our feeling that occasionally items were taken from the white ware pile to be decorated at the factory. (Double-marked items always seem to have a premium value on them.)

Palette-mark items with a known factory artist's signature on them do not necessarily prove that things were taken from the white ware pile for factory decoration, since so many of the artists are known to have decorated on their own time and a few actually set up shop as decorators.

Dated items can be a help in that we know what year a piece was decorated, but dates cannot tell us when an item was actually manufactured. Remember that an item could have been on a shelf for a long time before someone actually got around to painting on it, or that a date might be put on an already decorated item when it was presented as a gift. This would be particularly true of the items which have silver on them, since the item would have gone from Lenox to the silver company to a jewelry store to a retail customer, which might have taken some time.

A date does not even necessarily prove the latest date when an item could have been made, for it is possible that an artist pre-dated an item for reasons we will never know.

We look forward to a time when enough early items have been examined for someone to make definitive statements about backstamps, and will not mind at all if we are proven wrong in our assumptions.

TABLE I
Backstamps/Factory Artist Comparison

Baker—Lenox wreath
Boullemier—transition mark
Boullimer/Bullimer—no known signed samples
Campana—transition mark, L palette
Clayton—transition mark
DeLan—C.A.C. wreath, transition, L palette
Fauji—no known signed samples
Fenzel—L wreath
Geyer—transition
Heidrich—C.A.C. wreath
Hicks—uncertain
Kuhn—transition mark
Laurence—C.A.C. wreath
Lenox—no known signed samples
Marsh—transition mark, L palette
Martell—transition
Mayer—no known signed samples
Morley (George)—transition, Lenox wreath, Lenox wreath/U.S.A.
Morley (William)—transition, Lenox wreath, Lenox wreath/U.S.A.
Naylor—no known signed samples
Nosek—transition mark, L wreath, L wreath/U.S.A., gold wreath
Sully—transition mark
Swalk—transition mark
Tekauchi—no known signed samples
Wirkner—transition mark
Witte—transition mark

TABLE II
Backstamps by Type of Decoration

Usually Factory-Decorated
Mark A, written-out wreath in lavender
Mark C, all colors C.A.C. wreath
Mark E, metal mark
Mark F, red C.A.C. palette
Mark H, all colors transition
Mark J, Lenox wreath
Mark K, L porcelain
Mark L, L opaque
Mark M, gold wreath

Always Non-Factory Decorated
None of the marks are exclusively non-factory, but the following come the closest:

Mark A, written-out wreath in green
Mark F, green C.A.C. palette
Mark I, green L palette

Either Factory or Non-Factory
Mark F, C.A.C. palette, in lavender—about evenly divided
Mark F, C.A.C. palette, brown, gold and black—usually non-factory but many exceptions seen

Too Few Samples Seen
Mark B, double wreath written-out
Mark D, script Lenox
Mark G, Indianhead

TABLE III
Backstamps Dates and Uses
(According to Robinson and Feeny)

Mark	Color	Date	Primary Use
Written-out C.A.C. (Mark A)	Lavender	1891-1906	Special orders
	Green	No later than 1906	Uncertain
Written-out C.A.C. double wreath (Mark B)	Probably green	1897	Decorating contest
C.A.C. wreath (Mark C)	Blue, green, brown, lavender	1892-1896	Factory-decorated with original artist designs
Script Lenox (Mark D)	Not applicable	Uncertain	Uncertain
Metal mark (Mark E)	Not appicable	No later than 1906	Items with bronze fittings
C.A.C. palette (Mark F)	Red	1889-1896	Factory-decorated in standard designs
	Lavender	No later than 1906	Both factory decorated and white ware
	Green	No later than 1906	White ware
	Gold	No later than 1906	White ware
	Black	No later than 1906	White ware
Indianhead (Mark G)	Unknown	1889-1895	White ware
Transition (Mark H)	Lavender, green, brown, black, gold	1896 1906	Factory-decorated, all types
L palette (Mark I)	Green & others	1906-1924	White ware
L wreath (Mark J)	Green & others	1906-1930	Factory-decorated items
	"Made in U.S.A."	1930-1952	Factory-decorated items
L porcelain (Mark K)	Black	1930's & 1940's	Lamps
L opaque (Mark L)	Black	1930's & 1940's	Non-porcelain items
Gold wreath (Mark M)	Gold	1906-1930's	Special items
		1952-present	All wares

TABLE IV
Lenox Artists

1889 — Lenox

1890 — Lenox, Fauji, E. Boullimer, Heidrich, Tekauchi, Naylor

1891 — Lenox, Fauji, E. Boullimer, Heidrich, Tekauchi, Naylor, Clayton

1892 — Lenox, Fauji, E. Boullimer, Heidrich, Naylor, Clayton

1893 — Lenox, Fauji, E. Boullimer, Heidrich, Naylor, Clayton, Laurence

1894 — Lenox*, E. Boullimer, Heidrich, Clayton, Laurence

1895 — E. Boullimer, Heidrich, Clayton, Laurence

1896 — E. Boullimer, Heidrich, Clayton, Laurence, Hicks

1897 — Heidrich, Clayton, Laurence, Kuhn, Sully.

1898 — Heidrich, Clayton, Laurence, Kuhn, Swalk

1899 — Heidrich, Clayton, Kuhn, De-Lan, Des, Witte

1900 — Heidrich, Clayton, Kuhn, De-Lan, L. Boullemier, Wirkner, George Morley, William Morley

TABLE IV CONTINUED

1901 — Clayton, DeLan, L. Boullemier, Wirkner, George Morley, William Morley
1902 — Clayton, DeLan, L. Boullemier, Wirkner, George Morley, William Morley
1903 — Clayton, DeLan, L. Boullemier, Wirkner, George Morley, William Morley, Nosek, Marsh
1904 — Clayton, DeLan, L. Boullemier, Wirkner, William Morley, Nosek, Marsh, Mayer, Campana, Martell, Baker, Geyer.
1905 — Clayton, DeLan, L. Boullemier, Wirkner, William Morley, Nosek, Marsh, Baker, Geyer
1906 — Clayton, DeLan, L. Boullemier, Wirkner, William Morley, Nosek, Marsh, Mayer, Baker, Geyer
1907 — Clayton, DeLan, Wirkner, William Morley, Nosek, Marsh, Mayer, Baker
1908 — Clayton, DeLan, Wirkner, William Morley, Nosek, Marsh, Mayer, Baker
1909 — DeLan, Wirkner, William Morley, Marsh
1910 — DeLan, Wirkner, William Morley, Marsh
1911-1915 — DeLan, Wirkner, William Morley
1916-1925 — Wirkner, William Morley
1926-1929 — William Morley
1930-1935 — William Morley, George Morley
1936 — George Morley
1937-1938 — George Morley, Fenzel
1939 — George Morley, Fenzel, Nosek
1940-1946 — Fenzel, Nosek
1947-1954 — Nosek

(All hand-painting was discontinued in 1954) (The 1891 C.A.C. catalogue pictures the art department with eight people. At this late date we have no way of knowing if this has any basis in fact or whether it was some engraver's idea of what an art department should look like, but it does fit in nicely with our list of seven artists and one gilder for the year 1891.)
* We assume Lenox did not continue painting after going blind.

TABLE V

Heads of the Lenox Art Department
Walter Lenox—1889 to 1904
Mayer—1904 to 1908
Clayton—1908 to 1950
Hedt—1950 to 1955

Enamelers
G. Heufel, Germany—1894 to 1906
Mrs. Bradberry—1918 to 1930
Minnie Swan, Mamie Dougherty, Elizabeth Eggert—all 1920's and 1930's
Bertha Walton—1930
Jane Eardley—1941

Gilders
Alfred Powner—1890 to 1891, later returned to Mintons
Pholes (Tholes??) did the gold work on the Wilson china
Otto Barr—dates unknown
Alice van der Griff—1920's
Bertha Walton—1933
George Baker—1940's
Howard Fort, still employed at Lenox
Eleanor Peters—1946
Joan Guy—1952 to 1959
Lillian Kolb—1950's

MARK A—C.A.C. WRITTEN OUT

This mark was possibly one of the earlier ones in use at the Ceramic Art Company. The Mohr article lists a date of 1891 for the lavender version of this mark, and Barber, while he gives us no dates or colors, concurs with Mohr in the use of the mark—for special order items. On page 26 of the 1891 catalogue the company states, "We are also prepared to manufacture special forms of articles for private parties who may desire to control an exclusive and uncommon line." This would indicate a willingness on the company's part to make special order items, and it would seem likely that they might have had a special mark for these items. The catalogue, however, does not tell us what that mark was.

It would be very possible that the Mohr date of 1891 for this mark is correct, for it would be unlikely that a customer would give a special order to a company without having seen their regular line. The company was two years old in 1891, which would have given them enough time to establish production of standard items which could serve as samples of their work. (The same page of the catalogue goes on to tell us that they maintained a show room for display of their wares.)

THE
CERAMIC ART Co
TRENTON, N.J.

POTTERS and DECORATORS

We have seen enough non-catalogue shapes to verify that C.A.C. probably did produce special-order items, and most of the items with Mark A are indeed distinctive. Two of these items, however, create problems for us since they bring up the likelihood that C.A.C. did, on at least a few occasions, decorate on products which were not of their own manufacture. The first item is a cup and saucer, decorated primarily with transfers, and double-stamped with "Limoges, France" and the C.A.C. written-out mark. (Two of these have been seen.) The second item is the clock shown elsewhere in this book which is double-stamped with Mark A and the German letters N.A. inside a wreath. The German mark might be taken to mean that the clockwork was made in Germany and the china part by C.A.C., but the clockwork was American. The china is much heavier than most Lenox of the day, but is the proper creamy color.

A brief examination fo the economic situation in the 1890's shows a depression beginning with the Panic of 1893. Perhaps it was necessary for the company to take such orders to stay afloat. We can place only four artists at C.A.C. in 1895, down from seven in 1893, so perhaps the theory is correct.

Other items with the written-out wreath mark include a loving cup decorated for an Irish-American fraternal organization and dated March 17, 1898, and a mug decorated with a picture of Admiral Dewey. Although the mug is not dated, it is no doubt in honor of his victory at Manila in 1898.

Another mug with Mark A is additionally marked as being made for Theodore Starr, a New York silver company which began operating in 1900. This mug, although not artist-signed, could very well be the work of Walter Marsh who began working at C.A.C. in 1903. It is possible that this mark was in use up until 1906, when all C.A.C. marks were dropped.

Mark A can be either green or lavender, and the items already discussed have been with the lavender mark. Green appears primarily on what appear to be home-decorated items, and unless these items are somehow related to Mark B, we are at a loss to explain them. It is always possible that Mark A in green was used for white ware, but it is unlikely considering how few samples turn up.

This mark is sometimes seen with the words "Potters and Decorators" and sometimes not. Variations in the basic lettering also occur, but we consider this to be meaningless in terms of usage and date. There are simply too few samples of Mark A to draw any definite conclusions.

MARK B—C.A.C. WRITTEN OUT DOUBLE WREATH

Merely by looking at Mark B we are able to determine that it is somehow connected to an art competition held in 1897. What we do not know for sure is if the contest were held by C.A.C. with artists submitting pieces to them or if the C.A.C. artists sent their items to a contest held elsewhere. The first possibility seems more likely and fits in nicely with rumors we have heard concerning just such a contest.

The story has the Lenox Company sponsoring a decorating contest in an effort to find talented artists. The company has no record of this event, unlike the soap carving contest which they can verify—the winning sculpture was eventually produced in porcelain. We have heard of the decorating contest from two widely-separated individuals, both of whom said Walter Lenox had given the items to their families along with the tale that they were the non-winning entries in a decorating contest. Neither of the items had a backstamp, and both were earthenware rather than porcelain. Excluding the possibility that they are the long-missing Indian China, it would seem likely that the contestants used whatever blanks they had at hand. The items, one a large round platter signed Callowhill (a noted ceramics artist) and the other a pitcher signed Boullemier, were both beautifully decorated with hand-painting and gold. It is interesting to note that Boullemier did indeed later come to work at Lenox. (Somehow we can't help but wonder who the winner might have been if Callowhill and Boullemier were the losers.)

We have never actually seen Mark B on an item, but reliable sources tell us they have and we will acknowledge the existence of items so marked. Our sources indicate that it appears mainly on bowls. The Barber book tells us this mark was a special one for decorators used in 1897, and nothing more.

Since the bottom wreath is left empty, we feel perhaps that only the best entries received the mark and the bottom half of it was filled in with "First Place", "Honorable Mention" or some such notation. Non-winning entries would have presumably been marked with only the top half of the mark, and this would account for the green mark pieces mentioned under Mark A. All of this is, of course, only theory until such time as a sample shows up with the bottom wreath filled in.

MARK C—C.A.C. WREATH

The C.A.C. wreath mark is not mentioned by any of our quoted sources, yet several items with this mark appear in our book. The small blue vase shown later in the book, and a similarly decorated one which is not shown both have this mark, although one mark is green and the other blue. There is no artist signature on either to help us date them. The jug with silver overlay by Heidrich, shown later, also has this mark and is engraved on the silver with the date 1896. The Sturgis Laurence vase, also shown later, is dated 1894 and has Mark C in blue. There also exists a tankard by DeLan with this mark in brown, which gives us headaches since we cannot otherwise place DeLan at the factory earlier than 1899.

It is rather obvious that this mark was in use for factory decorated items prior to the introduction of the transition mark, and was probably not used after 1896 despite the DeLan piece. What we do not know is when it was first used, and we will have to guess that it was 1892 or 1893. We know that the red C.A.C. palette mark was in use from 1889 until at least 1894, and it is possible that the C.A.C. wreath replaced the red palette mark during the period 1894-1896 on factory-decorated items. It is equally possible, however, that the two marks co-existed at least for a while, with the red palette mark indicating dinnerware type decoration or patterns and the C.A.C. wreath being used on more individualized items.

Returning once again to the 1891 catalogue we find on page 34 the following statement: "One of the strongest claims that we can possibly make for the originality of our decorations is that, *with the exception of the after-dinner coffees, teas, and plate services,* our decorations are never duplicated. This is effected mainly by the varied schools of art pursued by our artists, who are allowed the fullest latitude in the display of their special talents." (The emphasis is ours, not the catalogue's.)

We can see from this that even at this early date the company was already making a distinction between frequently repeated designs, such as those on dinnerware, and original works of art. It would not seem unlikely that at some point they decided to differentiate between the two types of decoration by giving the artistic creations their very own mark. Since the catalogue shows the palette mark but not the wreath mark, we assume that this differentiation was not made in 1891 but perhaps a few years later. The pieces we have seen thus far seem to bear out our theories concerning both dating and usage.

MARK D—SCRIPT LENOX

Our reason for placing this mark with the earlier ones is based on the fact that the only known sample of the incised version of this mark was on a Kate Sears type item. Since Kate Sears was apparently at C.A.C. only a short while during the earlier years, her work should not appear on a piece so marked. The only explanation we can offer is that this might have been done by Walter Lenox himself, either while at C.A.C. or at one of the other companies where he worked. Since he started out as a sculptor, a Kate Sears type item would not have been too much of a problem for him. The general appearance of the mark is that of a signature rather than a backstamp.

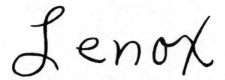

A very similar mark, impressed rather than incised, appears on some very special pieces of Lenox, including the doll shown in the color section.

The mark is altogether too rare to draw any concrete conclusions regarding it.

MARK E—METAL MARK

This mark appears on the metal portions of urns such as the bronze and Lenox one in the color section. When this mark appears on the metal, the china never seems to be marked. All of these items should be considered extremely rare.

MARK F—C.A.C. PALETTE

The Barber book lists this mark in red from 1889, and goes on to inform us that lavender and other colors were used at a later date. The Mohr article gives us the dates 1894-1898 in green or gold on undecorated ware, and 1898-1906 in black for undecorated. The 1891 catalogue shows a palette mark on every page, and from what little text appears in this catalogue we can perhaps ascertain that this mark was certainly used on white ware and probably on factory-decorated items as well. Other Lenox sources indicate this mark was used on decorated ware from 1889-1906. Unfortunately, only Barber mentions which color was being used when for what type of item.

Our personal observations of this mark would indicate the following:

The red is virtually always factory-decorated. The fern pot shown on page 220 bears this mark, and additionally has the Davis Collamore store mark. Many items with this red backstamp are decorated in a fashion similar to the fern pot, leading us to believe that this red palette mark was used on items decorated in a more or less standard fashion. The "red" is more often that not actually a pink, and can be easily confused with the lavender mark.

It is the other colors of C.A.C. palette mark which cause us the most problems, since they are not actually documented anywhere. From our quoted sources and from our own observations, we have this mark in lavender, green, gold, black and brown as well as the above-mentioned red or pinkish-red. This gives us a total of six colors to be fitted in somehow into the 18-year period everyone agrees they covered.

BELLEEK

We can fairly well document the red for factory-decorated items from 1889 to 1894 or 1896, but have a problem deciding what color they were using during that same period for non-factory items. If we look at Table II we see that the three marks available for use would have been the written out one, the red palette one, and the Indianhead mark. Having already established that the red palette and written out marks were not used for the white ware and considering that the Indianhead mark is virtually non-existent, we can possibly surmise that the palette mark in some other color was used for non-factory items.

The lavender palette mark seems about evenly divided between factory and non-factory items. The bouillon cup and saucer shown elsewhere is obviously factory-done, since almost all of this type of gold paste work was factory. The ramekin shown is one of a set of six, five of which have lavender transition mark and one of which has lavender C.A.C. palette mark, yet all are identical. Although samples of fully-decorated items such as vases have been seen which are apparently factory-done, many very poor examples of artwork are also seen with this backstamp. We think it is equally possible that the lavender palette mark was (1) for some amount of time a very definite factory-decorated mark, or (2) primarily for home-decorated items but items were frequently pulled from the white ware pile to fill orders for factory-decorated wares.

The green C.A.C. palette mark seems to be almost always in the province of the amateur artist, and that this mark would appear on a factory-done item only in the instance listed above, where they used items from the white ware inventory in an emergency.

The gold C.A.C. palette mark mentioned by others has not been seen by us, and we can conjecture that it is perhaps a faded version of the brown mark. If it does indeed exist, we have no idea of its age or use. The brown palette mark appears on the inkwell on page 380, which also bears the transition mark in green. We theorize that the brown palettemark was intended for the non-factory artist, but cannot date it accurately. The Hawthorn cup and saucer on which it appears was produced first in 1889 and was made for many years thereafter, so it is no real help to us, except to note that it is eggshell thin and possibly a very early piece. The inkwell on which it appears places the use of the brown mark in the same time frame as the transition mark.

A true black C.A.C. palette mark would be very rare, and we do not recall ever seeing one. Many of these so-called black palette marks are probably either a very dark green or brown. As was the case with the gold one, we cannot help with the dating of the black mark if it indeed does exist.

MARK G—INDIANHEAD

In the marks section of the Barber book he lists this as being for undecorated ware prior to 1895, and in the part of the text written in 1893 he tells us that C.A.C. produced "Belleek and Indian China." The 1891 C.A.C. catalogue also lists Belleek and Indian China, so from these sources it is possible to say that this Indian China was not the Belleek-type china we generally associate with Lenox, and that it was undecorated.

It must be pointed out that to the best of our knowledge this mark simply does not exist. We have never seen it on an actual item, and none of our collector friends have seen it either. If this mark had indeed been used from 1889 to 1895, surely samples would have materialized by now. If we accept the idea that it was not a Belleek-type product, we have the inevitable question: what was it? We can only theorize:

(1) It was a heavier type of china, perhaps of the type known as hotel ware, and it was not marked because the company was not particularly proud of it. It could very well have been the case that in the earlier years this type of ware had to be made in order to meet expenses while they experimented around with the finer ware. This would allow for the possibility that we are all walking right past Indian China items without knowing it.

(2) It was so easily broken that no samples remain. This is unlikely considering the number of years it was supposed to be in production.

(3) The white porcelain that later received the same marks as the creamy was originally designated as Indian China, but the earlier versions were not marked because the company wanted to be known for the Belleek-type ware and not an inferior version of European white porcelains. The idea may have some merit to it, since even in the early years their Belleek ware was the equal of other similar chinas, while this white china suffers from many imperfections as a rule. Even in the early years, imperfect items were a no-no, so

not marking this white china might appear to make sense. Although the 1891 catalogue does not actually so state, it would seem from the use of the Indianhead mark on every page that the items appearing on those pages would have been available in either the Belleek or the Indian China. In this case, the Indian China was probably a porcelain rather than an earthenware or hotel ware, since many of the items shown could really only have been done in porcelain.

(4) After having spent a great deal of time explaining Indian China and the use of the various colors of the palette mark, we now with some hesitation offer the suggestion that Indian China and Belleek were one and the same, with factory-decorated items receiving the red palette mark, special orders receiving the written-out mark, and undecorated ware for the amateur artist receiving no mark. This very nicely solves the problem of which color palette mark was used on undecorated items during the earliest years. As to why undecorated items received no backstamp, we can only suggest that the company wanted no association with home-decorated items. The Indianhead mark itself might very well have been used on advertising literature without ever actually appearing on the items.

Choose whichever explanation you like, for until a marked item turns up no one can say you are wrong. We ourselves are accepting explanation #4 as the most reasonable.

MARK H—TRANSITION

This mark is perhaps the least confusing of all the early marks, since everyone agrees that it was used on factory-decorated items, although there is some disagreement about whether it was first used in 1894 or 1896. It is called by this name because it relates to the transitional period when Lenox was taking over control of the company and Coxon was bowing out, and it is perhaps the confusion over precisely when Coxon left that gives us this minor discrepancy in the beginning date for the mark.

MARK "H"

Ceramic Art Company

LENOX

An additional minor point is the use of three different colors—gold, green and lavender. Gold is very rare, but the green and lavender seem about evenly divided. If we attempt to date the colors by known dates of employment for various artists, we are still somewhat confused since we have signed Morley items (both Morleys 1900 and later) on green transition mark, and yet we have the signed Marsh items primarily on lavender even though he was also after the turn of the century.

We next made what we felt was a logical conclusion—that the two colors were not meant as dating distinctions, but rather to identify different types of items. Once again, we were quickly proven wrong by an examination of several items. Items with silver overlay are about evenly divided between the two color marks, as was also the case with liners for silver holders. Artist-signed vases and other large items also turned up with both colors. Small type items such as salt dips are seen with both.

Perhaps if we could gather together in one place a couple hundred examples of these transition marks we could make more conclusive statements regarding the color variation in the mark, but as it is now we cannot explain why some pieces are green, some are lavender, and a few others marked in gold.

The transition mark has a rather interesting variation which is seen only on rare occasions. The mark itself is the same as other transition marks, but underneath are the words "Glen-Iris." All of the items with this mark apparently were done with floral motifs, and most were signed by Walter Marsh. Although we have no hard facts concerning this mark, we can theorize that Marsh came to Lenox to develop this particular line. For years we had no first name for Marsh, and were very disappointed to finally determine that it was Walter and not Glen as we had hoped, for this would have solved the problem for us. Since an alternate meaning for iris is rainbow, this "Glen-Iris" could have then been loosely translated as "Marsh's Rainbow." Since the words marsh and glen conjure up somewhat the same image, perhaps our little theory still holds true.

Items bearing this mark are done in a tri-color fashion in only two known variations: (1) orange, yellow, and lavender; and (2) green, purplish-red, and yellow. The flowers themselves would seem to be almost secondary to the use of color, unlike other hand-painted items where the flower would be the focusing point. The black and white photograph of the Glen-Iris vase in the artware section, however, brings out the flowers for reasons we can't explain.

A quick examination of the five Glen-Iris pieces which are readily accessible to us shows they all have the lavender transition mark, but we do not exclude the possibility of the green version of the mark showing up.

MARK I—LENOX PALETTE OR L PALETTE

In 1906, the familiar C.A.C. palette mark was changed slightly by the substitution of an L for the C.A.C. inside the palette. This new mark took over the function of the former one, i.e., indicating that an item was not factory-decorated. Most of the examples we have seen of this mark were in the green color, although black and others are not unknown. The Lenox palette mark was in use until 1924, at which time the white ware part of the business was discontinued.

Although we would like to be able to state unequivocally that at this stage the company has finally managed to separate out their white ware and decorated ware, this is unfortunately not the case. We offer at least one item as proof that this Lenox palette mark was occasionally factory decorated, and that item is a small ramekin decorated in a common Lenox pattern, with numbers on the bottom to match the proper decorating codes for that pattern. There is just no way this can be a home-decorated item. A second less-convincing offering would be a lovely DeLan vase, among the best we have seen by him, with this green L palette mark. We cannot prove, however, that he did this vase while employed at the factory.

MARK "I"

BELLEEK

MARK J—LENOX WREATH OR L WREATH

This mark was used on factory-decorated items from 1906 until 1930, usually in green but also occasionally in blue, red, black, and even sometimes gold. (We will delay discussion of this early use of the gold wreath mark until we get to Mark M.) Most of the giftware items from this period will have the green version, but others do turn up. Dinnerware had the full range of wreath mark colors, some of which might appear to correspond to the color of the pattern (i.e., the use of a rose-colored wreath on Lenox Rose), but this was probably coincidence.

MARK "J"

LENOX

Lenox wreath mark is virtually 100 percent factory decorated, and the collector must be wary only of the occasional item which was embellished after leaving the factory.

In 1930 the words "Made in U.S.A." were added to this mark, and the mark continued to be used on factory-decorated and intentionally undecorated items. Green remained the predominant color for this mark.

MARK "K"

PORCELAIN

MARK "L"

OPAQUE

MARK K AND L—L PORCELAIN AND L OPAQUE

These two marks date from the 1930's and 1940's. The L porcelain mark is often found on lamp bases, and on rare occasions on standard giftware. The L opaque mark is a very obscure one sometimes noted on what we will call hotel type ware, for the items are not porcelain.

MARK M—GOLD WREATH

Mark M is actually a continuation of Mark J, the Lenox green wreath, and we originally planned to include it in the discussion of Mark J. Since it is the current mark, however, we decided to give it a letter and discussion of its very own.

MARK "M"

Gold wreath made its appearance as the standard mark for all types of Lenox items in the early 1950's, and it continues to the present day. To the best of our knowledge, there are no plans to change it.

The only problem with this mark is that is sometimes turns up on items done by artists long-since gone from this world. Morley and DeLan fish plates are examples of this discrepancy, and the most plausible explanation for this is that the gold mark was in use much earlier than the 1950's for particular types of items. Since the transition mark can also be gold, it seems reasonable that a gold mark continued to be used on occasional items, or that the gold wreath mark was used to indicate a special order after the written-out C.A.C. mark was dropped. (The other explanation for the use of the gold wreath mark on these items is that items were discovered in some cranny of the warehouse at a much later date and stamped then. We think this is about as likely as the story that the company still has boxes of figurines stashed away somewhere.)

Variations of the gold wreath mark include the addition of the word "Special" under the regular mark. This indicates nothing more than the item was specially done for the sale Lenox holds at regular intervals. Another variation is the substitution of "Trenton, New Jersey" for "Made in U.S.A.," for no apparent reason.

OTHER BACKSTAMPS

Perhaps the chief mark not shown is the impressed LENOX mark, primarily used on bisque Art Deco figures but also seen on other items. It can appear by itself or with other impressed information such as the year of copyright.

This mark is interesting because it is the only one that appears on the visible portion of items, usually on the back, instead of being on the bottom like most backstamps.

Another mark, perhaps a variation of the current gold wreath, has the word Lenox spelled out. From the general appearance of the items and the mark, it would seem this is a fairly recent mark.

Lenox crystal is marked on the bottom with a few different marks, all of which include the word LENOX in block letters. Oxford Bone China is marked with the addition of the letter L in script form. Temperware is marked this way also, plus additional information.

CONFUSING MARKS

(1) Dinnerware bearing the Lenox wreath mark and the added words "The White House" turns up now and then. This should not be confused with Presidential china, because "The White House" was a store in San Francisco. Apparently, someone objected to the use of the White House name, because some items can be found where the words have been rubbed out (but still are readable.)

(2) There were two Ceramic Art Companies in England. The first dates from 1893 to 1903. Godden's book lists them as decorators located on Stoke Road, Hanley, Staffordshire. Their mark is:

THE CERAMIC ART
CO. LTD. HANLEY
STAFFORDSHIRE
ENGLAND

Another Ceramic Art Company in England was in business from 1905 to 1919, and they are listed as manufacturers of earthenware. Their mark is:

CERAMIC ART CO.
LTD. CROWN
POTTERY
STOKE-ON-TRENT
MANUF. OF FAIENCE

(3) Lenox Silver, Inc., New York, is listed in the Rainwater book as manufacturers of sterling silver around 1950. There is no connection between this silver company and the Lenox China Company.

(4) China liners for silver holders sometimes have a mark which very much resembles the Lenox green wreath mark. Instead of having the word Lenox underneath the wreath, however, the word "Excelsior" appears there. In addition, the "L" inside the wreath will have a small "X" through the middle. Items with this mark do bear a resemblance to Lenox, although they are generally heavier, and one of the decorations commonly used is a version of Lenox pattern #86. This mark could possibly have been a mark used by the Excelsior Pottery Works started by William Young and sons in 1857 also in Trenton.

UNMARKED ITEMS

Certain items, because of their shape or intended use, are rarely marked with a Lenox backstamp. Included in this group are pens, thimbles, door knobs, sherbert liners, cane handles, knife handles, etc. Drawings of many of these items can be found on the next three pages. Virtually every other item that left the Lenox factory through legitimate channels will have the Lenox mark on it somewhere.

Unmarked items do appear with some frequency, however, and for the most part these are items that were taken by workmen before the manufacturing process was completed. Many of the unmarked items were rejects that were scheduled for destruction before being given a reprieve, and such items are often referred to as "back door" Lenox.

ADDITIONAL INFORMATION ON MARKS

(1) Professional decorating firms sometimes added their own mark to Lenox blanks they were painting. These companies include Pope and Lee, Poole and Stockton, DeLan and McGill, Tatler, W. C. Hendrickson, Jesse Dean, D'Arcy, Stouffer, and Pickard.

(2) The letter C in a circle, of course, means that the design is copyrighted. We only include this here because we actually heard a dealer telling a would-be customer that this mark indicated the piece was done by Jonathan Coxon.

(3) In addition to shape and pattern numbers written in gold on items, there will sometimes be small numbers somewhere on the bottom. These marks were probably internal Lenox numbers, used to identify decorator or gilder. Since in years past, factory workers might have been paid "by the piece," this seems logical. They could also represent quality control numbers of one type or another. In any event, they give the collector no practical information.

(4) On bisque items where the green wreath mark appears instead of an impressed mark, the wreath mark will frequently have a rather strange appearance, as if someone had dabbed brown shellac over the mark. The appearance of this mark has to do with production problems with putting a mark on a bisque item and having it stay there, and does not mean the item is questionable.

ARTWARE AND GIFTWARE

Although some of the more advanced collectors reading this book may be disturbed to find undecorated giftware mentioned in the same breath with fine samples of hand-painting, we have grouped them together in this section for this reason: Many readers are novice collectors, and we felt it was important to show them how the same undecorated vase valued at $25 can be worth $100 by the addition of some fair art work by an amateur artist, and can also be worth $300 if it is beautifully decorated and signed by a Lenox factory artist.

This section will include the vases, cigarette boxes, candy dishes and the like that Lenox has produced down through the years. Dinnerware items such as plates and cups and saucers will be found in this section only if they are hand-painted in something other than a standard Lenox pattern.

Since age is one of the determining factors, we have included the backstamp which appeared on the items listed. Item numbers (shape numbers) are given in most cases as well to aid in proper identification.

Sets or groupings were broken down into their constituent parts since this is the way they are sometimes found, and we felt it was a no-harm way of helping the novice identify items. Since there is not yet a premium placed on completed sets, separating the items does not affect the pricing scheme.

Names of amateur artists have been omitted since they are not important to the value. Factory artists matter a great deal, however, and we will give the next several pages to some discussion of the Lenox art department.

Table IV lists by year the artist who might have been employed at Lenox at that time. Even allowing for a few unknown artists wandering in and out during a given year, we still arrive at what we consider to be plausible figures. It would appear that except for the founding year there would have been an ample supply of artists on hand to take care of orders, and that the company would not have had to seek outside help in filling them. Additionally, it would seem that the art department did not suffer from overcrowding at any particular time.

If we take the year 1900 as an example, we have eight known artists: Heidrich (portraits), Clayton (monochromes), Kuhn (portraits), DeLan (animals and scenics), L. Boullemier (figures), Wirkner (portraits), and George and William Morley (animals, fruit, flowers.) Even in 1895, where we have only four known artists, there would have been enough diversification of talent to negate stories about pieces being sent outside to be done.

To be sure, our chart suffers from some flaws:

(1) We have taken the liberty of listing Lenox and Mayer as working artists, with nothing more to back us up than the notion that those who could probably did. (For those of you who are wondering who Mayer might be, see Table V.)

(2) Employment dates for some of the artists are questionable, and others are mere guesses on our part. Those artists whose employment dates are completely unknown were placed in a year corresponding to the backstamps seen on their work.)

(3) We simply do not know how many other artists might have been there at one time or another.

In addition to the artist-signed items already discussed, the collector will find many samples of factory-decorated items (as determined by back-stamps) which are not artist signed. The reason for this could be any of the following:

(1) More than one artist worked on some items. We know this to be true in at least one case—an urn signed by both Morley and Boullemier, with one artist (probably Morley) doing the flowers and background and the other (probably Boullemier) doing the figure of a little girl. If this were done with top-of-the-line items such as this, it could have been done on lesser pieces as well.

(2) Such items were parts of sets, only one item of which was signed. For example, a teapot might be signed but not the matching sugar and creamer. If the pieces to the set were separated, there would be no way to ever prove who painted the sugar and creamer.

(3) When they were very busy, the artists didn't bother signing their work.

(4) They were done by apprentice artists who were not allowed to sign their work.

Whatever the reason, these unsigned works of art just do not command the same prices as those which are artist-signed, although in many cases they are at least the equal of the signed items.

ASHTRAYS

	Price Range	
☐ **Ashtray,** *shape #2030, 5" x 1-3/8" high, undecorated, Lenox wreath mark*	9.00	13.00
☐ **Ashtray,** *shape #2030, 5" x 1-3/8" high, Lenox Rose pattern, Lenox wreath mark*	27.50	32.50
☐ **Ashtray,** *shape #2030, 5" x 1-3/8" high, Ming pattern, Lenox wreath mark*	33.00	38.00
☐ **Ashtray,** *shape #2030, 5" x 1-3/8" high, solid green, Lenox wreath mark*	23.00	28.00
☐ **Ashtray,** *shape #2030, 5" x 1-3/8" high, solid green, Lenox wreath mark*	23.00	28.00

Price Range

☐ **Ashtray,** *shape #2030, 5" x 1-3/8" high, solid coral, Lenox wreath mark* 17.50   22.50

☐ **Ashtray,** *shape #2030, 5" x 1-3/8" high, white with gold trim, monogram in center, Lenox wreath mark* 18.50   23.50

☐ **Ashtray,** *shape #2399, 2-1/8" x 3-3/4" x 1-7/8" high, undecorated, Lenox wreath mark* 6.75   7.75

☐ **Ashtray,** *shape #2399, 2-1/8" x 3-3/4" x 1-7/8" high, Lenox Rose pattern, Lenox wreath mark* 17.50   22.50

☐ **Ashtray,** *shape #2399, 2-1/8" x 3-3/4" x 1-7/8" high, pale pink outside, white inside, gold trim on rim, Lenox wreath mark* ... 18.50   23.50

☐ **Ashtray,** *shape #2399, 2-1/8" x 3-3/4" x 1-7/8" high, cobalt, Lenox wreath mark* 11.00   15.00

☐ **Ashtray,** *shape #2427, 2-5/8" x 4-1/4" x 3/4" high, undecorated, Lenox wreath mark* 6.75   7.75

☐ **Ashtray,** *shape #2427, 2-5/8" x 4-1/4" x 3/4" high, green with gold trim, Lenox wreath mark* 9.00   13.00

☐ **Ashtray,** *shape #2427, 2-5/8" x 4-1/4" x 3/4" high, yellow with gold trim, Lenox wreath mark* 15.00   20.00

☐ **Ashtray,** *shape #2427, 2-5/8" x 4-1/4" x 3/4" high, coral, Lenox wreath mark* 8.00   9.50

☐ **Ashtray,** *shape #2997, coral and white apple blossom design, Lenox wreath mark* 18.50   23.50

☐ **Ashtray,** *shape #2997, blue and white apple blossom design, Lenox wreath mark* 18.50   23.50

☐ **Ashtray,** *shape #3003, 5-1/8" x 1-1/2" undecorated, Lenox wreath mark* 13.00   16.00

☐ **Ashtray,** *shape #3003, 5-1/8" x 1-1/2" gold trim, Lenox wreath mark* 18.50   23.50

☐ **Ashtray,** *shape #3008, 5-1/8" x 1" high, undecorated, Lenox wreath mark* 13.00   16.00

☐ **Ashtray,** *shape #3032, 3-3/8" x 1" high, white, Lenox wreath mark* 13.00   16.00

☐ **Ashtray,** *shape #3032, 3-3/8" x 1" high, coral, Lenox wreath mark* 16.50   21.50

☐ **Ashtray,** *shape #3032, 3-3/8" x 1" high, green, Lenox wreath mark* 20.00   25.00

☐ **Ashtray,** *shape #3066, 3-3/8" x 1" high, undecorated, Lenox wreath mark* 13.00   16.00

☐ **Ashtray,** *shape #3066, 3-3/8" x 1" high, blue, Lenox wreath mark* 18.50   23.50

☐ **Ashtray,** *shape number unknown, has knob in center for tapping tobacco out of pipe, white with royal blue knob, raised laurel wreath design on outside, Lenox wreath mark* 40.00   47.50

☐ **Ashtray,** *shape number unknown, approximately 7" diameter, full-color pheasant scene, Lenox wreath mark* 47.50   55.00

☐ **Ashtray,** *shape number unknown, coat of arms shape and decoration, gold trim* 32.00   38.00

☐ **Ashtray,** *shape number unknown, green with gold trim* 18.50   23.50

☐ **Ashtray,** *shape number unknown, pheasant scene, gold trim* .. 27.50   32.50

BONE DISHES

Lenox made one style of bone dishes, shape #263, in a four-inch long size with a vague S-shape to it. Bone dishes were very common items around the turn of the century, and we cannot explain why so few Lenox bone dishes are seen today. A marked sample would be in the $70 range for an undecorated one, up to around $140 for one that is decorated.

BOUILLON CUPS

Price Range

Bouillon cups are two-handled soup cups which come with an underplate and, on rare occasions, with a lid. The underplate can be either a saucer type, with an indentation where the cup rests, or else can resemble a bread and butter plate with no indentation. (We refer to both types as saucers.)

☐ **Bouillon cup and saucer,** *shape #104, dimpled surface, ring handles, cover also has a ring for finial, C.A.C. brown palette mark, raised on ball feet* 47.50   55.00

☐ **Bouillon cup and saucer,** *shape #104, dimpled surface, ring handles, cover missing, C.A.C. green palette mark* 32.00   38.00

☐ **Bouillon cup and saucer,** *shape #175, scalloped rim and fancy handles, undecorated, Lenox palette mark raised on ball feet .* 18.00   23.50

☐ **Bouillon cup and saucer,** *shape #175, scalloped rim and fancy handles, hand-painted tiny roses, C.A.C. lavender palette mark* 68.00   78.00

☐ **Bouillon cup and saucer,** *shape #175, scalloped rim and fancy handles, gold trim on handles and rim, gold monograms, Lenox palette mark* 18.50   23.50

Bouillon cup and saucer, *shape number unknown*

☐ **Bouillon cup and saucer,** *shape #557-1/2, squared-off handles, plain shape, undecorated, Lenox palette mark* 13.00   16.00

☐ **Bouillon cup and saucer,** *shape #557-1/2, square-off handles, single large red rose, Lenox palette mark* 27.50   32.50

☐ **Bouillon cup and saucer,** *shape #628, transfer decorated with vegetables, gold trim, Lenox palette mark* 23.00   28.00

☐ **Bouillon cup and saucer,** *shape #628, undecorated, Lenox wreath mark* 15.00   20.00

☐ **Bouillon cup and saucer,** *shape #633, undecorated, Lenox wreath mark* 13.00   16.00

☐ **Bouillon cup and saucer,** *shape #757, gold trim, Lenox palette mark* 18.50   23.50

☐ **Bouillon cup and saucer,** *shape #839-1/2, undecorated, Lenox wreath mark* 16.50   21.50

Price Range

☐ **Bouillon cup and saucer,** *shape #846-1/2, undecorated, Lenox wreath mark* 13.00   16.00

☐ **Bouillon cup and saucer,** *shape number not known, had lid, raised gold paste work, gold trim on twig type handles and lid finial, C.A.C. lavender palette mark* 80.00   95.00

BOWLS

☐ **Bowl,** *shape #11, 3-1/2", lotus leaf style, very early and thin, undecorated, C.A.C. brown palette mark, some small flecks on ruffles* 170.00   200.00

☐ **Bowl,** *shape #11, 3-1/2", lotus leaf style, top part coral, base white, Lenox wreath mark* 80.00   95.00

☐ **Bowl,** *shape #11, 3-1/2", lotus leaf type, top part white, base blue, Lenox wreath mark* 80.00   95.00

☐ **Bowl,** *shape #11, 3-1/2", pearlized finish with gold trim on rim and base, Lenox palette mark* 150.00   175.00

☐ **Bowl,** *shape #23, 3-3/4" x 6-1/2", ruffled rim, hand-painted small wildflowers, artist signed and dated, C.A.C. lavender palette mark* 90.00   105.00

☐ **Bowl,** *shape #23, 3-3/4" x 6-1/2", ruffled rim, hand-painted with Cupids and hearts, gold trim, several flecks on ruffles, Lenox palette mark* 135.00   155.00

NOTE: Bowl shape #43 is shown in catalogues with a 10" round underplate which was not present with either of the above two samples.

☐ **Bowl,** *shape #37, 6-1/4" high, lotus leaf type, white base with coral top section, Lenox wreath mark* 120.00   140.00

☐ **Bowl,** *shape #37, 6-1/4" high, lotus leaf type white base with yellow top section, Lenox wreath mark* 150.00   175.00

☐ **Bowl,** *shape #37, 6-1/4" high, early and very thin, pearlized lavender finish inside, speckled gold trim on outside and rims, C.A.C. red palette mark, Bailey, Banks & Biddle store mark* ... 215.00   245.00

Note: All of the lotus leaf bowls listed here are commonly referred to as "cabbage leaf" bowls by collectors. The early catalogues, however, list them as lotus leaves.

☐ **Bowl,** *shape #53, 3-1/2", lotus leaf type, top section done in pearlized pink, whole base covered with gold, artist signed and dated, C.A.C. green palette mark* 80.00   95.00

☐ **Bowl,** *shape #53, 3-1/2", lotus leaf type, undecorated, Lenox palette mark* 90.00   105.00

☐ **Bowl,** *shape #54, 6-1/4" high, lotus leaf type, sponged gold trim, C.A.C. lavender palette mark* 150.00   175.00

☐ **Bowl,** *shape #54, 6-1/4" high, lotus leaf type, undecorated, Lenox wreath mark* 105.00   120.00

☐ **Bowl,** *shape #65, 6-1/2" high, lotus leaf type, top part white, base yellow, Lenox wreath mark* 135.00   155.00

☐ **Bowl,** *shape #92, 2-1/2" x 5", ruffled top, hand-painted butterflies, gold trim, blue glaze inside bowl, C.A.C. green palette mark* 52.00   60.00

☐ **Bowl,** *shape #92, 2-1/2" x 5", ruffled top, undecorated, C.A.C. brown palette mark* 47.50   55.00

☐ **Bowl,** *shape #92, 2-1/2" x 5", ruffled top, hand-painted small pink roses, gold trim on rim, part of one ruffle missing, C.A.C. red palette mark* 90.00   105.00

☐ **Bowl,** *shape #92, 2-1/2" x 5", hand-painted with elves and rabbits, gold trim, nicely done, C.A.C. green palette mark* 135.00   155.00

Price Range

Note: Bowl shape #92 originally came with a 6-3/4" underplate and was perhaps intended to be a mush set. None of the bowls we have seen have had the underplate, however.

☐ Bowl, *shape #96, 5-1/2" high, lotus leaf type, very early and thin, no decoration, C.A.C. brown palette mark* 170.00 200.00

☐ Bowl, *shape #512, 10-1/4" diameter, hand-painted chrysan-themums, signed Morley, transition mark* 325.00 375.00

☐ Bowl, *shape #512, 10-1/4" diameter, undecorated, Lenox palette mark* 40.00 47.50

☐ Bowl, *shape #512, 10-1/4" diameter, hand-painted inside and out with badly done red and pink roses, gold trim on rim, artist signed and dated, small fleck on base, C.A.C. green palette mark* 68.00 78.00

☐ Bowl, *shape #512, 10-1/4" diameter, hand-painted fruit on inside, outside covered with gold, artist signed and dated, Lenox palette mark* 60.00 70.00

☐ Bowl, *shape #512, 10-1/4" diameter, hand-painted small pink roses in scatter pattern, gold trim on rim, C.A.C. lavender palette mark* 110.00 125.00

☐ Bowl, *shape #512, 10-1/4" diameter, gold pencil-line trim, Lenox wreath mark* 80.00 95.00

☐ Bowl, *shape #513, 8" x 3-1/2", hand-painted fruit on outside, pearlized orange inside, gold trim, artist's initials and date, C.A.C. green palette mark* 68.00 78.00

☐ Bowl, *shape #513, 8" x 3-1/2", hand-painted fruit on outside, inside plain, gold trim on rim, transition mark, beautifully done* 215.00 245.00

☐ Bowl, *shape #513, 8" x 3-1/2", geometric enamel pattern inside and out, Lenox palette mark* 40.00 47.50

☐ Bowl, *shape #513, 8" x 3-1/2", undecorated, Lenox wreath mark* 55.00 63.00

☐ Bowl, *shape #527, 8-3/4" x 4", hand-painted garlands of flowers outside, gold trim, small chip on rim, transition mark* . 135.00 155.00

☐ Bowl, *shape #527, 8-3/4" x 4", hand-painted pansies on out-side, single large pansy inside on bottom, gold trim, shaded background inside and out, C.A.C. green palette mark* 105.00 120.00

☐ Bowl, *shape #527, 8-3/4" x 4", transfer decorated with medallion portraits in four places, inside pearlized pink, gold trim on rim, Lenox palette mark* 55.00 63.00

☐ Bowl, *shape #553, 6" x 2-1/2", hand-painted berries and leaves on outside, gold trim, artist signed and dated, C.A.C. green palette mark* 80.00 95.00

☐ Bowl, *shape #553, 6" x 2-1/2", undecorated, Lenox palette mark* 18.50 23.50

☐ Bowl, *shape #553, 6 x 2-1/2", hand-painted scattered flowers, set of six, each marked with what are apparently dogs' names, one cracked, occasional chips on others, artist signed and dated, C.A.C. green palette mark (and we thought we had seen everything!), each* 18.50 23.50

☐ Bowl, *shape #575, 5-1/2" diameter, hand-painted bees and flowers, gold trim, Lenox palette mark* 32.00 38.00

☐ Bowl, *shape #575, 5-1/2" diameter, hand-painted flowers inside, pearlized blue exterior, gold trim, artist's initials, Lenox palette mark* 27.50 32.50

☐ Bowl, *shape #586, 10" handle to handle, 3" high, undecorated, Lenox palette mark* 47.50 55.00

☐ Bowl, *shape #586, 10" handle to handle, 3" high, gold trim, Lenox palette mark* 55.00 63.00

Price Range

☐ **Bowl,** *shape #586, 10" handle to handle, 3" high, hand-painted harvest scene, very professisonal looking, Lenox palette mark*   215.00   245.00

☐ **Bowl,** *shape #586, 10" handle to handle, 3" high, all over black with white Art Nouveau florals, outlined in gold, not badly done but a poor choice of design for this type of bowl, Lenox palette mark* 40.00   47.50

☐ **Bowl,** *shape #586, 10" handle to handle, 3" high, gold trim, Lenox wreath mark* 68.00   78.00

☐ **Bowl,** *shape #587, 5-1/2" x 1-1/4", undecorated, Lenox palette mark* 13.00   16.00

☐ **Bowl,** *shape #589, 9" x 2-5/8", hand-painted asters on shaded background, artist signed, Lenox palette mark* 120.00   140.00

☐ **Bowl,** *shape #590, 5-1/8" diameter, undecorated, Lenox palette mark* 9.00   13.00

☐ **Bowl,** *shape #644, (mayonnaise bowl), undecorated, Lenox palette mark* 32.00   38.00

☐ **Bowl,** *shape #644, (mayonnaise bowl), hand-painted single small pink roses, green leaves, raised gold work, Lenox wreath mark* 105.00   120.00

☐ **Bowl,** *shape #690, (listed in catalogue as finger bowl), pencil line gold trim, Lenox wreath mark* 18.50   23.50

☐ **Bowl,** *shape #690, (listed in catalogue as finger bowl), hand-painted daffodils on outside, gold trim, artist signed and dated, not badly done, Lenox palette mark, set of six* 120.00   140.00

☐ **Bowl,** *shape #715, 8-1/2" diameter, hexagon shape, footed, undecorated, Lenox wreath mark* 47.50   55.00

☐ **Bowl,** *shape #715, 8-1/2" diameter, hexagon shape, footed, covered all over with brown glaze as if intended for silver overlay, Lenox palette mark* 68.00   78.00

☐ **Bowl,** *shape #715, 8-1/2" diameter hexagon shape, footed, hand-painted geometric pattern, Lenox palette mark* 55.00   63.00

☐ **Bowl,** *shape #730, 10-1/2" x 3-1/8", undecorated, Lenox palette mark* 32.00   38.00

☐ **Bowl,** *shape #730, 10-1/2" x 3-1/8", hand-painted fruit on outside, lustre finish inside, gold trim, artist signed and dated, Lenox palette mark* 85.00   100.00

☐ **Bowl,** *shape #730, 10-1/2" x 3-1/8", rainbow striped effect outside, pale pink inside, Lenox palette mark* 40.00   47.50

☐ **Bowl,** *shape #730, 10-1/2" x 3-1/8", gold and silver bands alternating with narrow strips of black, unusual looking but neatly done, inside of bowl done entirely in gold, artist's initials and date, Lenox palette mark* 105.00   120.00

☐ **Bowl,** *shape #730, 10-1/2" x 3-1/8", apple green exterior, white inside, pencil line of gold on rim, Lenox wreath mark* 105.00   120.00

☐ **Bowl,** *shape #730, 10-1/2" x 3-1/8", outside glazed in purple, hand-painted lilacs in bottom of bowl, gold trim on rim, artist signed and dated, very nicely done, Lenox palette mark* 150.00   175.00

☐ **Bowl,** *shape #730-1/2, same as above but with salamander handles, plain white with gold trim on rim and on salamanders, Lenox palette mark* 85.00   100.00

☐ **Bowl,** *shape #730-1/2, same as above, transfer decoration with Oriental scenes in bright colors, salamanders done in burnt orange color, same color on rim and base, overall effect very pleasant, Lenox palette mark* 125.00   150.00

Price Range

☐ **Bowl,** *shape #730-1/2, same as above, hand-enameled flowers separated by bands of black, artist's initials and date, Lenox palette mark* 60.00 70.00

☐ **Bowl,** *shape #730-1/2, same as above, overall light green glaze, salamanders darker green with speckles of gold on them, tastefully done, dated on bottom, Lenox palette mark* 135.00 155.00

NOTE: Bowls #730 and 730-1/2 are frequently referred to as console bowls.

☐ **Bowl,** *shape #778, mayonnaise, hand-painted berries on outside, pink lustre inside, gold trim, Lenox palette mark* 47.50 55.00

☐ **Bowl,** *shape #778, mayonnaise, raised gold and blue dot work, home decorated but not bad, Lenox palette mark* 68.00 78.00

☐ **Bowl,** *shape #778, mayonnaise, undecorated, Lenox wreath mark* 40.00 47.50

☐ **Bowl,** *shape #778, mayonnaise, 1/2" gold trim, etched, Lenox wreath mark* 47.50 55.00

☐ **Bowl,** *shape #779, mayonnaise, with underplate, gold trim and gold initial on front and on plate, Lenox palette mark* 40.00 45.00

☐ **Bowl,** *shape #780, small scattered hand-painted violets, gold trim, artist's initials and date on bottom, Lenox palette mark* . . 68.00 78.00

☐ **Bowl,** *shape #781, mayonnaise, cobalt covering bowl, gold trim, Lenox wreath mark* 80.00 95.00

☐ **Bowl,** *shape #781, mayonnaise, undecorated, Lenox palette mark* 18.00 23.50

☐ **Bowl,** *shape #782, mayonnaise, hand-painted small pink roses on rim, gold trim, Lenox palette mark* 47.50 55.00

☐ **Bowl,** *shape #783, mayonnaise, hand-painted lemons and oranges on shade background, gold trim, artist's initials, Lenox palette mark* 60.00 70.00

☐ **Bowl,** *shape #784, mayonnaise, pencil-line gold trim, Lenox wreath mark* 40.00 47.50

☐ **Bowl,** *shape #785, mayonnaise, hand-painted butterflies on shaded background, gold trim, Lenox palette mark* 68.00 78.00

Although many of the bowls listed above had other uses, we are referring to them all as mayonnaise bowls.

☐ **Bowl,** *shape #796, 9" diameter, 4-1/4" high, hand-painted forget-me-nots, gold trim, artist signed and dated, Lenox palette mark* 100.00 120.00

☐ **Bowl,** *shape #811, 2-1/4", hand-painted in rainbow swirls, interior of bowl done in pink, gold trim on rim, artist's initials and date, Lenox palette mark, tiny chip on base of one, set of six* . . 120.00 140.00

☐ **Bowl,** *shape #811, 2-1/4", tiny raised gold teardrops covering exterior, gold trim on rim, Lenox palette mark* 55.00 63.00

☐ **Bowl,** *shape #823, 4" x 10", hand-painted exterior with fruit and vines, gold trim on rim and base, artist signed and dated, nicely done, Lenox palette mark* 110.00 125.00

☐ **Bowl,** *shape #823, 4" x 10", pencil-line gold trim on rim, exterior done in shaded greens, inside plain, Lenox palette mark* . . . 105.00 120.00

☐ **Bowl,** *shape #823, 4" x 10", undecorated, Lenox palette mark* . 40.00 45.00

☐ **Bowl,** *shape #823, 4" x 10", scattered hand-painted tiny flowers inside and out, gold trim, artist's initials, Lenox palette mark* 85.00 100.00

☐ **Bowl,** *shape #824, 5-1/2" diameter, undecorated, Lenox wreath mark* 9.00 13.00

☐ **Bowl,** *shape #824, 5-1/2" diameter, pencil-line gold trim on rim, Lenox wreath mark* 15.00 20. 00

Price Range

☐ **Bowl,** *shape #940, 5-3/8" diameter, fruit saucer type, solid coral, Lenox wreath mark* 13.00   16.00

☐ **Bowl,** *shape #961, 5-1/2" diameter, transfer decorated with baby's picture in bottom, gold trim on rim, Lenox palette mark* 16.50   21.50

☐ **Bowl,** *shape #971, 2-5/8" high, pale pink with raised gold in floral design and gold trim on rim, home-decorated but tastefully done, artist signed and dated, several flea bite flecks on bottom, Lenox palette mark* 23.00   28.00

☐ **Bowl,** *shape #1254, 9-1/2" x 3", scalloped rim, hand-painted small roses on each scallop connected by garlands of blue dot enamel work, possibly intended to be a liner for a sterling holder but quite usable on its own, Lenox wreath mark* 135.00   155.00

☐ **Bowl,** *shape #1376, coral exterior, plain inside, Lenox wreath mark* 47.50   55.00

☐ **Bowl,** *shape #1667, 5-1/2" x 9", hand-painted grapes on exterior, green inside, the same green from the inside comes up over the rim and down the outside shading eventually to a pale ivory, beautifully done, no artist signature, Lenox palette mark* 165.00   215.00

☐ **Bowl,** *shape #1929, double-handled fruit bowl, decorated in shades of pink and coral, gold handles, rather garish, Lenox palette mark* 68.00   78.00

☐ **Bowl,** *shape #1929, two-handled fruit bowl, gold trim on handles and rim, Lenox wreath mark* 75.00   85.00

☐ **Bowl,** *shape #1929-1/2, same shape as 1929 but without handles, hand-painted with holly berries and leaves with Christmas inscription in center of bowl, rather nice overall effect, artist signed, Lenox palette mark, tiny chip on base* ... 80.00   95.00

BRUSHES, COMBS, MIRRORS AND OTHER VANITY ITEMS

All of these items are in the rare category, probably because they were the type of item which would have been picked up frequently and, therefore, were likely to be broken. In addition, the marks can be hidden by the looking glass or brush, making positive identification difficult unless such items are parts of larger sets which have other marked items.

Vanity items

Those vanity items which were factory-decorated tend to be done either with little roses or with violets, both usually in a scatter pattern.

The smaller unmarked pieces have a starting price of $75 undecorated, going up to perhaps $200 for decorated and marked items.

BUTTER PATS

Butter pats are not common Lenox items. Item #178 is perhaps the most available of them. We have included #176 as a butter pat, since it is rather shallow to be a salt or nut dish and it appear sequentially in catalogues with the other butter pats.

Butterpat, *item #178, pink roses*

	Price Range	
☐ **Butter pat,** *item #176, 3", hand-painted little pink roses with gold trim, Lenox wreath mark*	33.00	38.00
☐ **Butter pat,** *item #176, 3", gold trim, C.A.C. lavender palette mark*	18.50	23.50
☐ **Butter pat,** *item #177, 3-1/4" round, scalloped rim similar to that of item #178, undecorated, Lenox palette mark*	13.00	16.00
☐ **Butter pat,** *item #178, 3-1/4", hand-painted with small pink roses, gold trim, transition mark*	33.00	38.00
☐ **Butter pat,** *item #178, 3-1/4", gold trim, Lenox palette mark* . . .	18.50	23.50
☐ **Butter pat,** *item #178, 3-1/4", undecorated and unmarked*	6.75	8.00

CANDLESTICKS

☐ **Candlesticks,** *shape #147, 10-1/2" high, embossing, undecorated, Lenox wreath mark, pair*	105.00	120.00
☐ **Candlesticks,** *shape #147, 10-1/2" high, brushed gold trim, Lenox wreath mark, pair*	110.00	125.00
☐ **Candlesticks,** *shape #147, 10-1/2" high, embossing, undecorated, C.A.C. green palette mark, pair*	135.00	155.00
☐ **Candlesticks,** *shape #147-1/2, same styling as #147 but much shorter, undecorated, Lenox wreath mark, pair*	60.00	70.00
☐ **Candlesticks,** *shape #147-1/2, light blue, Lenox wreath mark, pair*	55.00	63.00

Price Range

☐ **Candlesticks,** *shape #156, 1-3/4" high, attached underplate with ring handle, ruffled rim, undecorated C.A.C. green palette mark* 75.00   85.00

☐ **Candlesticks,** *shape #156, 1-3/4" high, attached underplate with ring handle, ruffled rim, hand-painted tiny pink roses, gold trim, few small flecks on ruffled rim, C.A.C. red palette mark* . .   18.50   23.50

☐ **Candlesticks,** *shape #156, 1-3/4" high, attached underplate with ring handle, ruffled rim, hand-painted flowers on light blue background, gold trim, Lenox palette mark* 110.00   125.00

☐ **Candlesticks,** *shape #220, 8" high, hand-painted green vines on yellow background, gold trim, C.A.C. green palette mark, pair* 110.00   125.00

☐ **Candlesticks,** *shape #220, 8" high, undecorated, Lenox palette mark, one only* 27.50   32.50

☐ **Candlesticks,** *shape #220, 8" high, gold trim, artist signed and dated, C.A.C. lavender palette mark, pair* 80.00   95.00

☐ **Candlesticks,** *shape #250, 5-1/8" high, hand-painted violets on green background, gold trim, artist signed and dated, C.A.C. green palette mark, pair* 135.00   135.00

☐ **Candlesticks,** *shape #250, 5-1/8" high, undecorated, Lenox palette mark, pair* 55.00   63.00

Candlesticks, *shape #2029, holes for electrification*

☐ **Candlesticks,** *shape #250, 5-1/8" high, gold trim, Lenox wreath mark, pair* 75.00   85.00

☐ **Candlesticks,** *shape #300, 6-1/4" high, one side of base comes up high to form shield against drafts, handle, hand-painted blue floral design on rim, blue handle, Lenox palette mark* 68.00   78.00

☐ **Candlesticks,** *shape #300, 6-1/4" high, one side of base comes up high to form shield against drafts, handle, small violets in scatter pattern, gold trim on rims and handle, small chip on base, C.A.C. red palette mark* 200.00   250.00

☐ **Candlesticks,** *shape #353, 6" high, same type as #300 above but with scalloped rim, undecorated, C.A.C. green palette mark*   165.00   215.00

☐ **Candlesticks,** *shape #930, 8-1/4" high, hexagon shape, undecorated, Lenox palette mark, pair* 40.00   47.50

☐ **Candlesticks,** *shape #930, 8-1/4" high, hand-painted roses and blue enamel ribbons, gold trim top and bottom, artist signed and dated, Lenox palette mark, pair* 105.00   120.00

☐ **Candlesticks,** *shape #930, 8-1/4" high, gold pencil-line trim, Lenox wreath mark, pair* 40.00   47.50

☐ **Candlesticks,** *shape #930, 8-1/4" high, hand-painted roses in scatter pattern, Lenox palette mark, one only* 40.00   47.50

Price Range

☐ **Candlesticks,** shape #973, 8-1/2" high, hand-painted in Art Deco style, gold trim, artist signed and dated, Lenox palette mark, pair 40.00   47.50

☐ **Candlesticks,** shape #973, 8-1/2" high, hand-painted with flowering vines, artist's initials on bottom, Lenox palette mark, pair 75.00   85.00

☐ **Candlesticks,** shape #973, 8-1/2" high, undecorated, Lenox palette mark, one only 18.50   23.50

☐ **Candlesticks,** shape #973, 8-1/2" high, wide flat gold trim, Lenox wreath mark, pair 68.00   78.00

☐ **Candlesticks,** shape #974, 8-1/4" high, undecorated, Lenox palette mark, one only 13.00   16.00

☐ **Candlesticks,** shape #974, 8-1/4" high, hand-painted bees and butterflies, gold trim on top and bottom, artist signed and dated, small fleck on base of one, Lenox palette mark, pair ... 135.00   155.00

☐ **Candlesticks,** shape #975, 2" high, attached underplate with handle, gold trim on all rims and handle, Lenox palette mark .. 68.00   78.00

☐ **Candlesticks,** shape #975, 2" high, pencil-line gold trim, Lenox wreath mark 55.00   63.00

☐ **Candlesticks,** shape #1992, tall, undecorated, Lenox wreath mark, pair 47.50   55.00

☐ **Candlesticks,** shape #1992, tall, gold trim, Lenox wreath mark, pair 60.00   70.00

☐ **Candlesticks,** shape #2029, deep greenish-blue, ornate gold trim, factory-drilled holes for electrification, Lenox wreath mark, pair 55.00   63.00

CHOCOLATE POTS

☐ **Chocolate pot,** shape #26, 10" high, mask spout, embossed aquatic figures on bottom half of pot and on lid, shaded from green to lavender to almost white, gold trim high-lighting embossed sections and handle, 1/8" high on spout, C.A.C. wreath mark 300.00   360.00

☐ **Chocolate pot,** shape #26, 10" high, mask spout, embossed aquatic figures on bottom half of pot and lid, undecorated, C.A.C. lavender palette mark 175.00   225.00

☐ **Chocolate pot,** shape #107, 8" high, hand-painted cabbage roses, pink on one side of pot, yellow on other, shaded blue background, gold trim on spout, handle, rims and lid, C.A.C. green palette mark, artist signed and dated 165.00   215.00

☐ **Chocolate pot,** shape #107, 8" high, beautifully done floral design on shaded background, gold trim, signed W. H. Morley, transition mark 400.00   470.00

☐ **Chocolate pot,** shape #107, 8" high, brushed gold trim on handle, spout, and lid, single yellow tea rose on either side, very nice for home decoration, C.A.C. lavender palette mark 165.00   215.00

☐ **Chocolate pot,** shape #107, 8" high, undecorated, Lenox palette mark 90.00   105.00

☐ **Chocolate pot,** shape #842, 11" high, plain design, gold trim on handle, rim and lid finial, gold initials on front, Lenox palette mark 68.00   78.00

☐ **Chocolate pot,** shape #842, 11" high, plain shape, hand-painted scattered violet design, gold trim, although home decorated it is a good copy of the basic factory pattern of violets and was possibly an attempt to replace a missing piece to a set, artist signed on bottom, Lenox palette mark ... 105.00   120.00

	Price Range	
☐ **Chocolate pot,** *shape #842, 11" high, undecorated and unmarked*	27.50	32.50
☐ **Chocolate pot,** *shape #842, 11" high, undecorated, Lenox wreath mark*	60.00	70.00
☐ **Chocolate pot,** *shape #905, 11" high, hexagon shape, hand-painted spring flowers on shaded background, gold trim, really messy looking, Lenox palette mark*	90.00	105.00
☐ **Chocolate pot,** *shape #905, 11" high, hexagon shape, hand-painted Delft-type scene in monochromatic blue, nice work for a home artist, artist signed and dated, Lenox palette mark, small chip on base*	165.00	215.00

CIGAR JARS

☐ **Cigar jar,** *shape #346, 3-1/2" x 3-1/2", gold trim and monogram, Lenox palette mark*	33.00	38.00
☐ **Cigar jar,** *shape #346, 3-1/2" x 3-1/2", hand-painted tiny roses, C.A.C. palette mark*	68.00	78.00

CIGARETTE BOXES

☐ **Cigarette box,** *shape #2424, plain green, Lenox wreath mark*	28.00	33.00
☐ **Cigarette box,** *shape #2424, white with Lenox Rose trim, Lenox wreath mark*	42.00	48.00
☐ **Cigarette box,** *shape #2424, white with Ming trim, Lenox wreath mark*	47.50	55.00
☐ **Cigarette box,** *shape #2996, feather finial, coral and white, Lenox wreath mark*	33.00	38.00
☐ **Cigarette box,** *shape #2996, feather finial, green and white, Lenox wreath mark*	33.00	38.00
☐ **Cigarette box,** *shape #2996, feather finial yellow and white, Lenox wreath mark*	40.00	47.50
☐ **Cigarette box,** *shape #2996, feather finial, green with gold on finial, Lenox wreath mark*	47.50	55.00
☐ **Cigarette box,** *shape #2996, feather finial, white with gold trim, Lenox wreath mark*	33.00	38.00
☐ **Cigarette box,** *shape #3006, relief floral design on top section, plain white, Lenox wreath mark*	30.00	36.00
☐ **Cigarette box,** *shape #3006, relief floral design on top section, plain coral, Lenox wreath mark*	33.00	38.00
☐ **Cigarette box,** *shape #3006, relief floral design on top section, yellow and white, Lenox wreath mark*	55.00	63.00
☐ **Cigarette box,** *shape #3006, relief floral design on top section, Lenox Rose design on bottom section, Lenox wreath mark*	27.50	32.50
☐ **Cigarette box,** *shape #3006, relief floral design on top section, gold tracing on flowers, Lenox wreath mark*	33.00	38.00
☐ **Cigarette box,** *shape #3006, relief floral design on top section, large single rose design on bottom, Lenox wreath mark*	33.00	38.00
☐ **Cigarette box,** *shape #3006, relief floral design on top section, Ming pattern on bottom section, Lenox wreath mark*	40.00	47.50
☐ **Cigarette box,** *shape #3018, rounded corners, ribbing, relief apple blossom design, Lenox wreath mark*	33.00	38.00
☐ **Cigarette box,** *shape #3018, rounded corners, ribbing, relief apple blossom design, green with white flowers, Lenox wreath mark*	47.50	55.00
☐ **Cigarette box,** *shape #3018, rounded corners, ribbing, relief apple blossom design, coral and white, Lenox wreath mark*	47.50	55.00

X

Cigarette box, *shape #3018, apple blossom design*

Price Range

☐ **Cigarette box,** *shape #3018, rounded corners, ribbing, relief apple blossom design, white with gold tracing on flowers and finial, Lenox wreath mark* 40.00 47.50
☐ **Cigarette box,** *shape #3018, rounded corners, ribbing, relief apple blossom design, green with gold trim on handle and flowers, Lenox wreath mark* 55.00 63.00
☐ **Cigarette box,** *shape #3033, rounded corners, Lenox Rose pattern, Lenox wreath mark* 47.50 55.00

Cigarette box, *shape #3033, single rose design*

Price Range

☐ **Cigarette box,** *shape #3033, rounded corners, solid green, Lenox wreath mark* 38.00 43.00

☐ **Cigarette box,** *shape #3033, rounded corners, solid yellow, Lenox wreath mark* 55.00 63.00

☐ **Cigarette box,** *shape #3033, rounded corners, full-color clipper ship motif, Lenox wreath mark* 68.00 78.00

☐ **Cigarette box,** *shape #3033, rounded corners, Blue Ridge pattern, Lenox wreath mark* 40.00 47.50

☐ **Cigarette box,** *shape #3033, rounded corners, Rhodora pattern, Lenox wreath mark* 40.00 47.50

☐ **Cigarette box,** *shape #3033, rounded corners, Fairmount pattern, Lenox wreath mark* 40.00 47.50

Cigarette box, *shape #3033, floral design*

☐ **Cigarette box,** *shape #3033, rounded corners, Caprice pattern, Lenox wreath mark* 40.00 47.50

☐ **Cigarette box,** *shape #3033, rounded corners, laurel wreath in gold around outer rim of top, Lenox wreath mark* 33.00 38.00

☐ **Cigarette box,** *shape #3033, rounded corners, maroon with gold trim and single rose design, Lenox wreath mark* 55.00 63.00

☐ **Cigarette box,** *shape #3033, rounded corners, pale blue with gold floral design on top, Lenox wreath mark* 47.00 47.50

☐ **Cigarette box,** *shape #3165, bird finial, undecorated, Lenox wreath mark* 68.00 78.00

☐ **Cigarette box,** *shape #3165, bird finial, coral and white, Lenox wreath mark* 75.00 85.00

☐ **Cigarette box,** *shape #3165, bird finial, blue and white, Lenox wreath mark* 75.00 85.00

CIGARETTE HOLDERS AND JARS

☐ **Cigarette holder,** *shape #2614, 3" high, white with gold trim, Lenox wreath mark* 13.00 16.00

☐ **Cigarette holder,** *shape #2614, 3" high, coral, Lenox wreath mark* 16.50 21.50

Price Range

☐ Cigarette holder, *shape #2614, 3" high, blue, Lenox wreath mark* 16.50   21.50

☐ Cigarette holder, *shape #2619, 2-7/8" high, gadroon base, coral, Lenox wreath mark* 17.50   22.50

☐ Cigarette holder, *shape #2619, 2-7/8" high, gadroon base, blue, Lenox wreath mark* 18.00   23.50

☐ Cigarette holder, *shape #2619, 2-7/8" high, gadroon base, yellow, Lenox wreath mark* 22.50   27.50

☐ Cigarette holder, *shape #2629, 3" high, fluted base, coral, Lenox wreath mark* 16.50   21.50

☐ Cigarette holder, *shape #2629, 3" high, fluted base, coral and white, Lenox wreath mark* 17.50   22.50

☐ Cigarette holder, *shape #2629, 3" high, fluted base, blue, Lenox wreath mark* 17.50   22.50

☐ Cigarette holder, *shape #2635, 3" high, relief laurel wreath on base, coral, Lenox wreath mark* 18.50   23.50

☐ Cigarette holder, *shape #2635, 3" high, relief laurel wreath on base, blue, Lenox wreath mark* 18.50   23.50

☐ Cigarette holder, *shape #2635, 3" high, relief laurel wreath on base, green, Lenox wreath mark* 18.50   23.50

☐ Cigarette holder, *shape #2635, 3" high, relief laurel wreath on base, white with gold trim, Lenox wreath mark* 16.50   21.50

☐ Cigarette holder, *shape #2643, yellow and white, Lenox wreath mark* 18.50   23.50

☐ Cigarette holder, *shape #2643, undecorated, Lenox wreath mark* 13.00   16.00

☐ Cigarette holder, *shape #2643, gold trim, Lenox wreath mark* . 15.00   20.00

☐ Cigarette holder, *shape #2646, yellow and white, Lenox wreath mark* 22.50   27.50

☐ Cigarette holder, *shape #2646, gold laurel wreath trim, Lenox wreath mark* 15.00   20.00

☐ Cigarette holder, *shape #2646, undecorated, Lenox wreath mark* 9.00   11.00

☐ Cigarette holder, *shape #2656, 2-1/4" high, shape with fluting on base, plain white, Lenox wreath mark* 14.00   18.00

☐ Cigarette holder, *shape #2656, 2-1/4" high, oval shape with fluting on base white with gold trim, Lenox wreath mark* 16.50   21.50

Note: The above-listed cigarette holders are small, urn-shaped items and not something through which to smoke a cigarette.

☐ Cigarette jar, *shape #347, 2-1/2" x 2-1/2", undecorated, Lenox wreath mark* 18.50   23.50

☐ Cigarette jar, *shape #347, 2-1/2" x 2-1/2", blue lustre exterior, gold trim, Lenox palette mark* 16.50   21.50

COFFEEPOTS

☐ **Coffeepot,** *shape #108, 8" high, hand-painted scattered wild flowers, nicely done gold trim, artist signed and dated, C.A.C. lavender palette mark* 125.00   150.00

☐ **Coffeepot,** *shape #108, 8" high, hand-painted yellow daffodils on shaded green background, gold trim all over the place, in addition to being bad artwork it is also very messy, artist's initials, C.A.C. green palette mark* 68.00   78.00

Price Range

☐ **Coffeepot,** shape #108, 8" high, floral design in monochromatic green, speckled gold trim, chip on end of spout, C.A.C. green palette mark 135.00   155.00

☐ **Coffeepot,** shape #108, 8" high, undecorated, C.A.C. lavender palette mark 95.00   110.00

☐ **Coffeepot,** shape #365, 8-1/2" high, Turkish shape demitasse pot, undecorated, Lenox palette mark 90.00   105.00

☐ **Coffeepot,** shape #365, 8-1/2" high, Turkish shape demitasse pot, portrait medallion, remainder of pot decorated in aqua with gold trim, artist signed, C.A.C. green palette mark 200.00   250.00

☐ **Coffeepot,** shape #365, 8-1/2" high, Turkish shape demitasse pot, gold trim over brown glaze, raised gold paste pseudo-Arabic lettering, C.A.C. lavender palette mark, tiny fleck on end of spout 200.00   250.00

☐ **Coffeepot,** shape #371, 10" high, square pedestal base, hand-painted single yellow rose on front, rosebud on back, gold trim on handle, base and top, appears to be a variation of pattern #82, transition mark 18.50   23.50

☐ **Coffeepot,** shape #371, 10" high, square pedestal base, hand-painted floral garlands, on shaded pale turquoise background, elaborate gold trim, finial repaired, C.A.C. lavender palette mark 105.00   120.00

☐ **Coffeepot,** shape #371, 10" high, square pedestal base, undecorated, Lenox palette mark 60.00   70.00

☐ **Coffeepot,** shape #371, 10" high, square pedestal base, transfer portrait surrounded by blue and gold dot work, smaller blue dots covering rest of pot, gold trim on handle and rim, nice for its type, C.A.C. green palette mark 200.00   250.00

☐ **Coffeepot,** shape #371, 10" high, square pedestal base, bunch of violets on front and back, small violets on lid, gold trim, well-done, artist signed, Lenox palette mark 175.00   225.00

☐ **Coffeepot,** shape #521-1/2, 7-3/4" high, hand-painted pink and red cabbage roses on both sides, lots of gold trim, artist signed and dated, C.A.C. green palette mark 135.00   155.00

☐ **Coffeepot,** shape #521-1/2, 7-3/4" high, transfer decorated with Oriental scene in cobalt, coffeepot shades from white around decal to dark cobal on end of spout and on handle and lid, well-executed, Lenox palette mark 115.00   145.00

☐ **Coffeepot,** shape #521-1/2, 7-3/4" high, decorated all over with disc-shaped enamel work in different shades of pink, rather resembles anemic-looking blood cells, gold trim on handle, spout, rim and lid, artist's initials and date, Lenox palette mark 80.00   95.00

☐ **Coffeepot,** shape #542-1/2, 6-1/2" high, angular modernistic shape, gold trim on handle and spout, gold initial on front, Lenox palette mark 47.50   55.00

☐ **Coffeepot,** shape #542-1/2, 6-1/2" high, angular modernistic shape, hand-painted black rose on front, black handle and trim, Lenox palette mark 40.00   47.50

☐ **Coffeepot,** shape #542-1/2, 6-1/2" high, undecorated, Lenox wreath mark 33.00   38.00

☐ **Coffeepot,** shape #579, 6-1/2" high, hand-painted group of roses on pale beige background, gold trim on handle and finial, good for its type, Lenox palette mark 105.00   120.00

Price Range

☐ **Coffeepot,** *shape #579, 6-1/2" high, all cobalt, no trim, Lenox palette mark* 33.00   38.00

☐ **Coffeepot,** *shape #579, 6-1/2" high, pale pink with raised gold work, artist's initials and date, Lenox palette mark* 80.00   95.00

☐ **Coffeepot,** *shape #660, 8" high, hexagon shape, panels of small flowers separated by maroon and raised gold bands, spout is maroon with scattered flowers, handle and lid maroon with gold trim, the pattern would make beautiful drapery material, Lenox palette mark* 135.00   155.00

☐ **Coffeepot,** *shape #660, 8" high, gold trim and monogram, Lenox palette mark* 47.50   55.00

☐ **Coffeepot,** *shape #692, 9" high, decorated with enamel ribbons and hearts, gold trim, artist signed and dated, Lenox palette mark* 115.00   145.00

☐ **Coffeepot,** *shape #692, 9" high, gold geometric design top and bottom, gold handle, Lenox palette mark, small chips on rim opening and bottom of lid* 33.00   38.00

☐ **Coffeepot,** *shape #699, 7" high, undecorated, Lenox wreath mark* 33.00   38.00

☐ **Coffeepot,** *shape #699, 7" high, hand-painted pansies on shaded green background, gold trim, artist's initials and date, Lenox palette mark* 105.00   120.00

☐ **Coffeepot,** *shape #731, 10-5/8" high, hexagon shape, undecorated, Lenox palette mark* 55.00   63.00

☐ **Coffeepot,** *shape #731, 10-5/8" high, beige pearlized finish with gold trim and gold initials on front, Lenox palette mark* 47.50   55.00

☐ **Coffeepot,** *shape #731, 10-5/8" high, hand-painted bunch of wildflowers, gold trim, artist signed, Lenox palette mark* 135.00   155.00

☐ **Coffeepot,** *shape #741, 10" high, hand-painted irises in blue, purple and maroon, green leaves, shaded yellow background, well-done gold trim, artist's initials, Lenox palette mark* 200.00   250.00

☐ **Coffeepot,** *shape #741, 10" high, undecorated, Lenox wreath mark* 55.00   63.00

☐ **Coffeepot,** *shape #741, 10" high, powder blue with transfer gold floral decoration, gold trim on handle and rims, gold finial, crack in handle* 47.50   55.00

☐ **Coffeepot,** *shape #787, 8-7/8" high, hexagon shape, hand-painted lily of the valley on pale green background, gold trim in appropriate places, Lenox palette mark* 85.00   100.00

☐ **Coffeepot,** *shape #887, 10-1/2" high, undecorated, Lenox palette mark* 68.00   78.00

☐ **Coffeepot,** *shape #933, 5-5/8" high, individual size, solid coral, Lenox wreath mark* 33.00   38.00

☐ **Coffeepot,** *shape #933, 5-5/8" high, individual size, gold trim on handle and rims, gold monogram surrounded by tiny blue forget-me-nots, Lenox palette mark* 80.00   95.00

☐ **Coffeepot,** *shape #933, 5-5/8" high, individual size, blue dot enamel work and small hand-painted little pink roses, artist's initials and date on bottom, Lenox palette mark, two small chips on rim and several flecks on bottom* 68.00   78.00

☐ **Coffeepot,** *shape #933, 5-5/8" high, undecorated, Lenox palette mark* 18.50   23.50

Price Range

COMPORTS

☐ **Comport,** *shape #441, 9-3/4", open ornate handles, tall base, undecorated, C.A.C. green palette mark* 120.00 150.00

☐ **Comport,** *shape #441, 9-3/4", open ornate handles, tall base, hand-painted roses, yellow on one side, pink on other, gold trim on rims and handles, artist signed and dated, C.A.C. lavender palette mark* 120.00 145.00

COVERED BOXES *(EXCLUDING CIGARETTE BOXES)*

☐ **Box,** *shape #60, 1" x 3", embossed design, ribbon finial, undecorated, C.A.C. lavender palette mark* 68.00 78.00

☐ **Box,** *shape #128, 2" x 3", gadroon border, hand-painted roses on blue background, artist signed and dated, C.A.C. green palette mark* 75.00 85.00

☐ **Box,** *shape #146, 3-1/4", plain with gold trim, C.A.C. green palette mark* 60.00 70.00

☐ **Box,** *shape #152, 3-1/2" x 2-7/8", hand-painted white doves on lavender background, gold trim, artist signed, C.A.C. green palette mark* 85.00 100.00

☐ **Box,** *shape #169, 4", gentle scalloping on rim, hand-painted violets in scatter pattern, gold trim, C.A.C. pink palette mark* .. 135.00 155.00

☐ **Box,** *shape #170, 3-1/4", embossed design, gentle scalloping to rim, undecorated, C.A.C. brown palette mark* 47.50 55.00

☐ **Box,** *shape #171, 5-3/4", embossed design, gentle scalloping to rim, gold tracings on embossed sections, gold trim on rim, C.A.C. green palette mark* 80.00 95.00

☐ **Box,** *shape #172, 2" x 4", rectangle shape, hand-painted small red roses, gold trim and initial, Lenox palette mark, small chip on underside of rim* 68.00 78.00

☐ **Box,** *shape #194, 4-1/2" x 3-1/8", heart shaped, embossing on lid and base, undecorated C.A.C. brown palette mark* 105.00 120.00

Box, *shape #514, Lenox rose pattern*

Box, *shape number unknown, white finial*

Price Range

☐ **Box,** *shape #275, 5", round, plain shape with finial, hand-painted flowers in ring around middle, gold trim on finial and rims, artist signed, Lenox palette mark* 110.00   125.00

☐ **Box,** *shape #278, 2", for rouge, round, embossing on rims, ornate finial, undecorated, C.A.C. green palette mark, spider crack in bottom* 33.00   38.00

☐ **Box,** *shape #308, 5-1/4", round, embossed design, finial, solid green with gold trim, Lenox wreath mark* 55.00   63.00

☐ **Box,** *shape #514, 3-3/4", round, undecorated, Lenox palette mark* 40.00   47.50

☐ **Box,** *shape #514, 3-3/4", round, Ming pattern, Lenox wreath mark* 110.00   125.00

☐ **Box,** *shape #514, 3-3/4", round, hand-painted flowers and gold trim, artist signed, Lenox palette mark* 105.00   120.00

☐ **Box,** *shape #514, 8" x 3-3/4", round, solid coral, Lenox wreath mark* 68.00   78.00

☐ **Box,** *shape #514, 8" x 3-3/4", round, powder blue with gold trim, Lenox wreath mark* 80.00   95.00

☐ **Box,** *shape #514, 8" x 3-3/4", round, yellow, Lenox wreath mark* 100.00   115.00

☐ **Box,** *shape #514, 8" x 3-3/4", round, plain with gold trim, Lenox palette mark* 47.50   55.00

☐ **Box,** *shape #514, 3-3/4", round, Lenox rose pattern, Lenox wreath mark* 105.00   120.00

☐ **Box,** *shape #819, 5-1/2" x 3", finial, round, medium pink with gold trim, gold finial, Lenox wreath mark* 47.50   55.00

☐ **Box,** *shape number unknown, same as #514 but larger, entire rim covered in etched gold, wide gold banding on bottom section, Lenox wreath mark, looks like a Pickard piece* 135.00   155.00

☐ **Box,** *shape number unknown, approx. 3" x 7", rectangle, gray with silver trim, white finial, Lenox gold wreath mark* 47.50   55.00

CUPS AND SAUCERS—COFFEE, TEA AND CHOCOLATE

☐ **Cup and saucer,** *shape #2, 2-1/4", ribbed design, fancy handle, eggshell thin, undecorated, C.A.C. brown palette mark* 47.50   55.00

☐ **Cup and saucer,** *shape #2, 2-1/4", ribbed design, fancy handle, eggshell thin, beige matte finish with gold trim, C.A.C. red palette mark* 68.00   78.00

Cup and saucer, *Palmer-Cox brownie decoration*

	Price Range	
☐ **Cup and saucer,** *shape #2, 2-1/4", ribbed design, fancy handle, gold trim, Lenox palette mark*	33.00	38.00
☐ **Cup and saucer,** *shape #3, 2-1/4", six panels with fish scale design, fancy handle, undecorated, C.A.C. lavender palette mark*	47.50	55.00
☐ **Cup and saucer,** *shape #3, 2-1/4", six panels with fish scale design, handle trimmed in gold and fish scales outlined in gold, handle repaired, small fleck on rim, transition mark*	68.00	78.00
☐ **Cup and saucer,** *shape #4, 2-1/4", fluted design with fancy handle, decorated with hand-painted forget-me-nots and gold, C.A.C. lavender palette mark*	55.00	63.00
☐ **Cup and saucer,** *shape #4, 2-1/4", fluted design with fancy handle, matte finish with raised gold paste in floral design, C.A.C. pink palette mark*	85.00	100.00
☐ **Cup and saucer,** *shape #5, 2", swirled rib design, undecorated, Lenox palette mark*	27.50	32.50
☐ **Cup and saucer,** *shape #5, 2", swirled rib design, gold trim on handle, sponged gold effect on ribs, transition mark*	68.00	78.00
☐ **Cup and saucer,** *shape #6, 2-1/4", swirled rib design, undecorated, Lenox wreath mark*	27.50	32.50
☐ **Cup and saucer,** *shape #8, 2-1/2", seashell design, eggshell thin, undecorated, C.A.C. lavender palette mark*	68.00	78.00
☐ **Cup and saucer,** *shape #8, 2-1/4", seashell design, eggshell thin, gold trim, C.A.C. green palette mark*	75.00	85.00
☐ **Cup and saucer,** *shape #46, 2", square shape with rounded corners, forked handle, narrow ribbed design on cup and saucer, undecorated, Lenox wreath mark*	47.50	55.00
☐ **Cup and saucer,** *shape #46, 2", square shape with rounded corners, forked handle, narrow ribbed design on cup and saucer, gold trim, C.A.C. brown palette mark*	60.00	70.00
☐ **Cup and saucer,** *shape #98, 2-1/4", fluted design with ring handle, saucer comes up very high and resembles a small bowl rather than a saucer, known as the "engagement cup", Lenox wreath mark*	33.00	38.00

Price Range

☐ **Cup and saucer,** *shape #98, 2" x 2-1/4", fluted design with ring handle, deep saucer, hand-painted small pink roses in a scatter pattern on inside of cup and on top side of saucer, outside of cup and bottom part of saucer completely covered in gold, saucer repaired, C.A.C. red palette mark* 55.00   63.00

☐ **Cup and saucer,** *shape #105, 3-1/4", melon ribbed with dimpled finish, ring handle, raised on ball feet, C.A.C. brown palette mark* 68.00   78.00

☐ **Cup and saucer,** *shape #105, 3-1/4", melon ribbed with dimpled finish, ring handles, raised on ball feet, gold trim on handle and rims, small fleck on bottom edge of saucer, C.A.C. pink palette mark* 75.00   85.00

☐ **Cup and saucer,** *shape #106, 2-1/4", melon ribbed with dimpled finish, ring handle, raised on ball feet, undecorated, C.A.C. green palette mark* 60.00   70.00

☐ **Cup and saucer,** *shape #117, 2-1/8" x 2-7/8", tall thin shape, ribbed design, fancy ring handle, gold trim on handle and rims, C.A.C. green palette mark* 60.00   70.00

☐ **Cup and saucer,** *shape #121, 2" x 2-7/8", fluted design, flared rim, saucer very deep, gold trim, artist's initials on bottom of saucer, Lenox, palette mark* 40.00   47.50

☐ **Cup and saucer,** *shape #162, 1-1/4", double ring handle, wide fluting on cup and saucer, hand-painted with tiny pink roses, sponged gold near rims, gold handle, transition mark* 90.00   110.00

☐ **Cup and saucer,** *shape #162, 1-1/4", double ring handle, wide fluting on cup and saucer, undecorated, Lenox palette mark* .. 27.50   32.50

☐ **Cup and saucer,** *shape #163, 1-1/2", double ring handle, square shape with rounded corners, large red roses hand-painted on front and on saucer, gold trim on handle and rim, Lenox palette mark* 40.00   47.50

☐ **Cup and saucer,** *shape #163, 1-1/2", double ring handle, square shape with rounded corners, small violets in scatter pattern, gold trim on handle and rims, transition mark* 85.00   100.00

☐ **Cup and saucer,** *shape #163, 1-1/2", double ring handle, square shape with rounded corners, small violets in scatter pattern, gold trim on handle and rims, transition mark* 85.00   100.00

☐ **Cup and saucer,** *shape #164, 2", very plain shape and handle, undecorated, C.A.C. green palette mark* 27.50   32.50

☐ **Cup and saucer,** *shape #164, 2", very plain shape and handle, hand-painted with cherries, gold trim, C.A.C. lavender palette mark* 52.00   58.00

☐ **Cup and saucer,** *shape #164, 2", very plain shape and handle, hand-painted with small pink roses in scatter pattern and gold trim, transition mark* 85.00   100.00

☐ **Cup and saucer,** *shape #164, 2", very plain shape and handle, undecorated, C.A.C. green palette mark* 27.50   32.50

☐ **Cup and saucer,** *shape #164, 2", very plain shape and handle, hand-painted with fruit, gold trim, C.A.C. lavender palette mark* 52.00   58.00

☐ **Cup and saucer,** *shape #164, 2", very plain shape and handle, hand-painted with small pink roses and gold trim, transition mark* 85.00   100.00

☐ **Cup and saucer,** *shape #174, 2-1/8", ruffled rim and fancy handle, gold trim, Lenox palette mark* 47.50   55.00

Price Range

☐ **Cup and saucer,** shape #174, 2-1/8", beige matte finish with raised gold paste floral design, gold trim on rims, C.A.C. red palette mark 110.00 125.00

☐ **Cup and saucer,** shape #174, 2-1/8", ruffled rim and fancy handle, gold trim, Lenox palette mark 47.50 55.00

☐ **Cup and saucer,** shape #174, 2-1/8", ruffled rim and fancy handle, beige matte finish with raised gold paste floral pattern, gold trim on handle and rims, C.A.C. red palette mark 110.00 125.00

☐ **Cup and saucer,** shape #179, 2", slight melon ribbed shape with fancy handle, gold trim on handle and rims and gold monogram on front of cup, Lenox palette mark 33.00 38.00

☐ **Cup and saucer,** shape #179, 2", slight melon ribbed shape with fancy handle, beige matte finish, raised gold paste design, centers of flowers tinted a pale coral color, transition mark 100.00 120.00

☐ **Cup and saucer,** shape #180, 2", swirled ribbing, undecorated, C.A.C. green palette mark 27.00 32.00

☐ **Cup and saucer,** shape #180, 2", swirled ribbing, rainbow effect with each rib a different pastel color separated by gold, gold speckling on handle, home decorated but nicely done and an interesting decorating concept, C.A.C. green palette mark 80.00 95.00

☐ **Cup and saucer,** shape #216, 2", flared scalloped rim, fancy handle, undecorated, Lenox palette mark 33.00 38.00

☐ **Cup and saucer,** shape #216, 2", flared scalloped rim, fancy handle, hand-painted with large roses in pink, gold handle, gold trim, on rims, C.A.C. green palette mark 47.50 55.00

☐ **Cup and saucer,** shape #247, 2-1/4", ornate handle, hand-painted poppies (badly done), gold trim on handle and rims, Lenox palette mark 40.00 47.50

☐ **Cup and saucer,** shape #261, Palmer-Cox brownie decoration, gold trim, C.A.C. lavender palette mark 110.00 125.00

☐ **Cup and saucer,** shape #301, 1-7/8", resembles Irish Belleek's "Tridacna" pattern, forked handle, pearl glaze on inside, speckled gold on handle, C.A.C. lavender palette mark 80.00 95.00

☐ **Cup and saucer,** shape #301, 1-7/8", resembles Irish Belleek's "Tridacna" pattern, forked handle, small, hand-painted roses around inside of rim, pearl glaze on outside, very badly done, Lenox palette mark 47.50 55.00

☐ **Cup and saucer,** shape #309, 2-1/2", large ribbed design, reverse "C" handle, hand-painted with different fruit designs, gold trim on handle and rims, Lenox palette mark 47.50 55.00

☐ **Cup and saucer,** shape #309, 2-1/2", large ribbed design, reverse "C" handle, undecorated, C.A.C. lavender palette mark 40.00 47.50

☐ **Cup and saucer,** shape #402, shell-shaped, forked handle, white with gold trim, Lenox palette mark 40.00 47.50

☐ **Cup and saucer,** shape #448, plain with squared-off handle, hand-painted flowers, gold trim on handle and rims, Lenox palette mark 40.00 47.50

☐ **Cup and saucer,** shape #448, plain shape with squared-off handle, hand-painted fruit, gold trim on handle and rims, Lenox palette mark 47.50 55.00

☐ **Cup and saucer,** shape #448, plain shape with square-off handle, gold trim on handle and rims, gold monogram in front of cup, Lenox palette mark 27.00 32.50

Price Range

☐ **Cup and saucer,** *shape #495, square pedestal base, plain shape with squared-off handle, hand-painted overall floral design, gold trim on handle and rims, Lenox palette mark* 47.50   55.00

☐ **Cup and saucer,** *shape #495, square pedestal base, plain shape with squared-off handle, hand-painted garlands of flowers, gold trim on handles and rims, Lenox wreath mark* ... 85.00   100.00

☐ **Cup and saucer,** *shape #551, plain, undecorated, Lenox palette mark* 23.00   28.00

☐ **Cup and saucer,** *shape #551, hand-painted roses, gold trim, Lenox palette mark* 40.00   47.50

☐ **Cup and saucer,** *shape #556, tall and thin, square handle, covered with badly done blue dot enamel work, Lenox palette mark* 33.00   38.00

☐ **Cup and saucer,** *shape #557, hand-painted small pink roses in a scattered design, gold pencil-line on rim and handle, Lenox wreath mark* 68.00   78.00

☐ **Cup and saucer,** *shape #595, 2-1/4", hand-painted with butterflies and flowers, artist signed, Lenox palette mark* 47.50   55.00

☐ **Cup and saucer,** *shape #600, hand-painted with cherub and flowers, gold trim (worn), Lenox palette mark* 68.00   78.00

☐ **Cup and saucer,** *shape #608, solid coral outside, cream color inside, Lenox wreath mark* 18.50   23.50

☐ **Cup and saucer,** *shape #610, hand-painted monochromatic "Blue Willow" type scene, home decorated but nicely done, Lenox palette mark* 80.00   95.00

☐ **Cup and saucer,** *shape #633D, plain white, Lenox wreath mark* 13.00   16.00

☐ **Cup and saucer,** *shape #633D, floral transfer design, pink handle, Lenox palette mark* 37.00   43.00

☐ **Cup and saucer,** *shape #654-1/2, squared-off handle, gold trim and gold flower design, Lenox palette mark* 27.50   32.50

☐ **Cup and saucer,** *shape #664, all cobalt (probably a piece earmarked for silver overlay that never got that far), Lenox wreath mark* 27.50   32.50

☐ **Cup and saucer,** *shape #665, hand-painted with little hearts and flowers, Lenox palette mark* 47.50   55.00

☐ **Cup and saucer,** *shape #668, hand-painted berries, gold trim, Lenox palette mark* 37.00   43.00

☐ **Cup and saucer,** *shape #669, blue dot enamel work with small pink roses, artist signed and dated, Lenox palette mark* 68.00   78.00

☐ **Cup and saucer,** *shape #670, hand-painted fruit, gold trim, signed J. Nosek, Lenox wreath mark* 68.00   78.00

☐ **Cup and saucer,** *shape #714, hexagon shape, hand-painted pink roses on green background, gold trim, Lenox palette mark* 40.00   47.50

☐ **Cup and saucer,** *shape #756, gold trim with gold initial on front, artist initialed and dated on bottom, Lenox palette mark* 18.50   23.50

☐ **Cup and saucer,** *shape #773, floral garlands, gold trim, Lenox palette mark* 40.00   47.50

☐ **Cup and saucer,** *shape #813, hexagon shape, brown glaze, (probably meant for silver overlay), Lenox palette mark* 22.00   26.00

☐ **Cup and saucer,** *shape #814, hexagon shape, gold trim and outlining, dreadful artwork, Lenox palette mark* 17.50   22.50

☐ **Cup and saucer,** *shape #815, hand-painted morning glories on yellow background, Lenox palette mark* 33.00   38.00

Price Range

☐ **Cup and saucer,** *shape #816, hand-painted roses on tan back-ground, Lenox palette mark* 40.00   47.50

☐ **Cup and saucer,** *shape #837, undecorated, Lenox palette mark*   15.00   20.00

☐ **Cup and saucer,** *shape #838, hand-painted with wildflowers and gold trim, Lenox palette mark* 47.50   55.00

☐ **Cup and saucer,** *shape #839, undecorated, Lenox palette mark*   18.50   23.50

☐ **Cup and saucer,** *shape #841, gold trim, Lenox palette mark* ...   18.50   23.50

☐ **Cup and saucer,** *shape #843, hand-painted with small violets in a scatter pattern, Lenox wreath mark* 80.00   95.00

☐ **Cup and saucer,** *shape #845, hand-painted with picture of gray cat, silver trim, rather unusual looking but not badly done, Lenox palette mark* 68.00   78.00

☐ **Cup and saucer,** *shape #846, undecorated, Lenox palette mark*   16.50   21.50

☐ **Cup and saucer,** *shape #847, hand-painted with large pink rose on both sides, pale green background, gold trim, the absolute pits in home decorating, Lenox palette mark* 40.00   47.50

☐ **Cup and saucer,** *shape #852, hand-painted with pastel enam-els in a drippy sort of effect, gold trim, Lenox palette mark* 33.00   38.00

☐ **Cup and saucer,** *shape #852, undecorated, Lenox palette mark*   18.50   23.00

☐ **Cup and saucer,** *shape #854, gold trim on handle and rims, Lenox palette mark* 18.50   23.00

☐ **Cup and saucer,** *shape #866, cup has small knob instead of regular handle, undecorated, Lenox palette mark* 27.50   32.50

☐ **Cup and saucer,** *shape #866, cup has small knob instead of regular handle, gold trim on handle and rim, Lenox palette mark* 27.50   32.50

☐ **Cup and saucer,** *shape #885, hand-painted butterflies on tan background, artist signed and dated, Lenox palette mark* 40.00   47.50

☐ **Cup and saucer,** *shape #886, undecorated, Lenox palette mark*   16.50   21.50

☐ **Cup and saucer,** *shape #895, hand-painted pansies on cream background, nicely done, gold trim, Lenox palette mark* 47.50   55.00

☐ **Cup and saucer,** *shape #943, solid deep blue-green, Lenox wreath mark* 33.00   38.00

☐ **Cup and saucer,** *shape #1006, undecorated, Lenox palette mark* 18.50   23.50

☐ **Cup and saucer,** *shape #1006, transfer decoration of Martha Washington, gold trim, Lenox palette mark* 18.50   23.50

DARNING EGGS

Lenox darning eggs are usually unmarked. They were made in two shapes. Number 217, 6" long, is a full-sized egg, and #287 is a smaller, skinnier one used to repair the fingers on gloves. Both are very rare.

We have no actual selling prices for these two darning eggs, but would estimate their worth from $70 to $140 depending on condition and trim. Although an item this rare would typically be worth more, since they are not marked there is no way to verify they are Lenox.

DESK ITEMS

☐ **Inkwell,** *shape #61, 2-1/2" high, beehive-shaped, undecorated, C.A.C. green palette mark* 68.00   78.00

☐ **Inkwell,** *shape #136, hand-decorated with musical symbols, C.A.C. lavender palette mark, very pretty* 100.00   120.00

Note: The above inkwell came with a ruffled-rim tray originally, but no tray was present with the sample listed.

Three-piece desk set, *item numbers unknown*

	Price Range	
☐ **Inkwell,** *shape #157, underplate 5" diameter, tiny inkwell, hand-painted yellow flower on both parts, gold trim, transition mark*	175.00	225.00
☐ **Inkwell,** *shape #157, underplate missing, small blue flowers, C.A.C. lavender palette mark*	85.00	100.00
☐ **Inkwell,** *shape #239, 2-1/4" high, embossed design, cobalt with gold trim, liner missing, C.A.C. brown palette mark*	120.00	140.00
☐ **Inkwell,** *shape #239, 2-1/4" high, embossed design, undecorated and unmarked, liner present*	68.00	78.00
☐ **Inkwell,** *shape #239, 2-1/4" high, embossed design, gold trim on embossing, Lenox palette mark*	125.00	150.00
☐ **Inkwell,** *shape #313, 4" across base, square shape with round lid, undecorated and unmarked*	33.00	38.00
☐ **Inkwell,** *shape #313, 4" across base, square shape with round lid, hand-painted flowers and gold trim, artist signed and dated, C.A.C. green palette mark*	135.00	155.00
☐ **Inkwell,** *shape #549, 2-1/2", round, gold trim and initial, Lenox palette mark*	100.00	125.00
☐ **Inkwell,** *shape #549, 2-1/2", little pink flowers with gold trim, Lenox palette mark*	120.00	140.00
☐ **Inkwell,** *shape #550, 3-1/4", round, gold quill pen on side and on lid, green all over, artist signed and dated, unmarked*	55.00	63.00
☐ **Three-piece desk set,** *item numbers unknown, unmarked rolling blotters, two-compartment standing letter holder (6" x 8"), and covered inkwell with 5" underplate, monochromatic blue Delft type scene with houses, children, etc., artist's initials, transition mark and Tiffany & Company mark*	640.00	720.00

DOOR KNOBS AND DRAWER PULLS

Most of the knobs which were sold are probably still in place on the purchaser's furniture or doors. They are usually unmarked, and an identifiable knob would have to be priced at $150 or better.

EWERS

☐ **Ewer,** *shape #33, 8-1/4" high, yellow and orange enamel work, gold handle and rims, C.A.C. purple palette mark*	110.00	125.00
☐ **Ewer,** *shape #33, 8-1/4" high, undecorated, C.A.C. brown palette mark*	200.00	250.00
☐ **Ewer,** *shape #33, 8-1/4" high, gold trim on handle and brushed gold effect on rims, Lenox green wreath mark*	135.00	155.00

	Price Range	
☐ **Ewer,** *shape #36, 10" high, undecorated, Lenox palette mark* ..	105.00	120.00
☐ **Ewer,** *shape #36, 10" high, hand-painted roses, gold trim on handle and rims, C.A.C. palette mark, artist signed and dated* .	165.00	195.00
☐ **Ewer,** *shape #36, 10" high, monochromatic green scenic with gold on handle, not factory done but a very interesting look and not badly painted, C.A.C. palette mark*	195.00	235.00
☐ **Ewer,** *shape #36, 10" high, white with coral handle, Lenox green wreath mark*	105.00	120.00
☐ **Ewer,** *shape #39, 9-1/4" high, twig handle, shaded from rust brown to yellow to lavender, roses painted in tri-colors already mentioned, signed Marsh, transition/Glen-Iris mark*	400.00	475.00
☐ **Ewer,** *shape #39, 9-1/4" high, undecorated, Lenox palette mark*	165.00	195.00
☐ **Ewer,** *shape #39, 9-1/4" high, sponged gold work on upper half, handle gold, home-done but beautiful, C.A.C. green palette mark*	330.00	395.00
☐ **Ewer,** *shape #39, 9-1/4" high, beige matte finish, raised gold trim, gold on handle, C.A.C. wreath mark*	400.00	475.00
☐ **Ewer,** *shape #40, 10" high, undecorated, Lenox palette mark* ..	135.00	155.00
☐ **Ewer,** *shape #40, 10" high, nasturtiums on shaded brown to tan background, artist signed and dated, C.A.C. green palette mark*	225.00	275.00
☐ **Ewer,** *shape #40, 10" high, enamel flowers, gold trim on handle and rim, Lenox palette mark*	165.00	195.00
☐ **Ewer,** *shape #41, 9" high, shaded from green to pink to lavender, gold work on handle and rims, small repaired spot on rim, transition mark*	225.00	275.00
☐ **Ewer,** *shape #41, 9" high, yellow floral trim, gold handle and rim, artist signed and dated, C.A.C. lavender palette mark*	195.00	235.00
☐ **Ewer,** *shape #41, 9" high, undecorated, C.A.C. brown palette mark*	225.00	275.00
☐ **Ewer,** *shape #42, 10-1/2" tall, beautifully decorated with pale yellow and brown orchids outlined in gold, beige satin background, speckled gold trim on handle and near rim, no artist signature, transition mark*	435.00	505.00
☐ **Ewer,** *shape #42, 10-1/2" high, plain with gold trim, Lenox wreath mark*	135.00	155.00
☐ **Ewer,** *shape #42, 10-1/2" high, hand-painted spray of small roses, gold handle and rims, nicely done, C.A.C. green palette mark*	195.00	235.00
☐ **Ewer,** *shape #43, 10" high, beige satin background, gold work on handle and rims, gold tracings on detailing of ewer, C.A.C. wreath mark*	330.00	395.00
☐ **Ewer,** *shape #43, 10" high, undecorated, Lenox palette mark* ..	165.00	195.00
☐ **Ewer,** *shape #44, 10-1/2" high, single yellow rose on front and back, gold trim on handle and rims, Lenox palette mark*	170.00	220.00
☐ **Ewer,** *shape #44, 10-1/2" high, gold handle, no other decoration, C.A.C. palette mark*	175.00	220.00
☐ **Ewer,** *shape #45, shaded from green to lavender, raised gold work, factory done but strangely unappealing, transition mark*	225.00	275.00
☐ **Ewer,** *shape #45, 10-1/2" high, hand-painted spray of autumn leaves on front and back, shaded tan background, C.A.C. palette mark*	260.00	320.00

Price Range

☐ **Ewer,** *shape #69, 6-1/4" high, shaped like leaf with curly end to form spout and tendril coming up to form handle, white with gold trim, Lenox wreath mark* 85.00   100.00

☐ **Ewer,** *shape #69, 6-1/4" high, description as above, solid dark green, Lenox wreath mark* 80.00   95.00

☐ **Ewer,** *shape #69, 6-1/4" high, description as above, white with coral tendrils, Lenox wreath mark* 68.00   78.00

☐ **Ewer,** *shape #69, 6-1/4" high, hand-painted violets on front and back, tendrils painted green, although not great art work the overall effect is very nice, C.A.C. palette mark* 195.00   235.00

☐ **Ewer,** *shape #354, 10-1/4" high, portrait of Victorian woman, raised gold paste and blue dot enamel work, gold handle and pedestal base, artist signed and dated, perfectly dreadful, C.A.C. green palette mark* 330.00   395.00

☐ **Ewer,** *shape #354, 10-1/4" high, satin beige background with raised gold floral work, gold handle, gold pencil-line rims, C.A.C. wreath mark* 525.00   625.00

☐ **Ewer,** *shape #443, 14-1/2" high, undecorated, C.A.C. green palette mark* 195.00   235.00

☐ **Ewer,** *shape #443, 14-1/2" high, hand-painted roses, gold handle and rims, C.A.C. lavender palette mark* 330.00   395.00

☐ **Ewer,** *shape #444, 12" high, hand-painted peacock on shaded background, artist signed, C.A.C. palette mark* 195.00   235.00

FERN POTS AND PLANTERS

☐ **Fern pot,** *shape #154, 2-1/2" high, 8-1/2" diameter, has lift-out liner with several holes in bottom to allow for proper drainage, hand-painted maroon, pink and blue flowers and green leaves, gold trim, C.A.C. pink palette mark, Davis Collamore store mark, liner unmarked* 195.00   235.00

Fern pot, *shape #154*

Price Range

☐ **Fern pot,** *shape #173, 3" high, bulbous shape, ruffled rim, catalogue picture looks like it might have had a liner like the one in shape #154 but none present with this example, hand-painted small violets in scatter pattern, C.A.C. lavender palette mark* **135.00** **155.00**

☐ **Fern pot,** *shape #181, 6-1/4", round shape, ruffled rim, speckld gold trim, C.A.C. lavender palette mark, several flecks on rim* . **105.00** **120.00**

☐ **Fern pot,** *shape #182, 6-1/4", same basic shape as #181 but rim is scalloped as well as ruffled, pale lavender exterior, gold trim on rim, C.A.C. pink palette mark* **165.00** **195.00**

☐ **Fern pot,** *shape #299, 10-1/2" x 13", undecorated, embossed neck, round body, C.A.C. green palette mark* **125.00** **145.00**

☐ **Planter,** *shape #2400, white with blue handles, Lenox wreath mark* **68.00** **78.00**

☐ **Planter,** *shape #2441, plain white, Lenox wreath mark* **33.00** **38.00**

Planter, *shape #2616, coral handles*

☐ **Planter,** *shape #2616, white with coral handles, Lenox wreath mark* **85.00** **100.00**

☐ **Planter,** *shape #2616, all white, Lenox wreath mark* **33.00** **38.00**

☐ **Planter,** *shape #2616, yellow with white handles, Lenox wreath mark* **110.00** **125.00**

☐ **Planter,** *shape #2634, similar to #2616, white with pale green handles, Lenox wreath mark* **60.00** **70.00**

☐ **Planter,** *shape #2637, similar to #2616, white with blue handles, Lenox wreath mark* **47.50** **55.00**

☐ **Planter,** *shape #2788, white with gold trim, Lenox wreath mark* **42.00** **48.00**

☐ **Planter,** *shape #3010, undecorated, embossed design, Lenox wreath mark* **40.00** **47.50**

☐ **Planter,** *shape #3011, undecorated, embossed design, Lenox wreath mark* **40.00** **47.50**

☐ **Planter,** *shape #3019, white embossed design on pale peach background, Lenox wreath mark* **85.00** **100.00**

FRAMES

Although they were made in several shapes and sizes during the early days of the Lenox Company, few picture frames have survived to the present day. They would have been prime candidates for breakage considering that they would have been left out in vulnerable spots like dressing tables and desks.

Both of the sales we have listed for last year were for unmarked specimens. The price for a plain frame was $100, and for an ornate one $160.

HONEY POTS

Item #894 is a 4-1/4" beehive-shaped honey pot with applied bees on the sides and lid. The same shape was used much earlier on a 2-1/2" item, but this one is actually an inkwell and is listed in that section.

	Price Range	
☐ **Beehive honey pot,** *undecorated, Lenox palette mark*	40.00	47.50
☐ **Beehive honey pot,** *each bee a different color, red stripe on top and bottom of pot, Lenox palette mark*	60.00	70.00
☐ **Beehive honey pot,** *beige background, multi-colored bees, dark brown banding top and bottom, Lenox wreath mark*	85.00	100.00
☐ **Beehive honey pot,** *gold bees and banding, Lenox wreath mark, top bee glued on*	47.50	55.00
☐ **Beehive honey pot,** *pearlized champagne color, each bee a different color, several wing chips on bees, Lenox palette mark* . .	33.00	38.00

HORNS OF PLENTY

The horn of plenty was done in five different sizes in an upright position and a tiny horizontal one is in current production.

☐ **Horn of plenty,** *shape #70, 4-1/2" high, plain white, Lenox wreath mark*	30.00	35.00
☐ **Horn of plenty,** *shape #70, 4-1/2" high, white with gold trim, Lenox palette mark*	33.00	38.00

Horn of Plenty, *shape #70, hand-painted*

	Price Range	

☐ **Horn of plenty,** *shape #70, 4-1/2" high, solid coral, Lenox wreath mark* 40.00 47.50

☐ **Horn of plenty,** *shape #70, 4-1/2" high, white with blue handle, Lenox wreath mark* 42.00 48.00

☐ **Horn of plenty,** *shape #70, 4-1/2" high, solid green, Lenox wreath mark* 47.50 55.00

☐ **Horn of plenty,** *shape #70, 4-1/2" high, hand-painted roses and raised blue enamel work, gold trim, artist signed, C.A.C. lavender palette mark* 225.00 275.00

☐ **Horn of plenty,** *shape #2442, 10" high, plain white, Lenox wreath mark* 47.50 55.00

☐ **Horn of plenty,** *shape #2442, 10" high, white with gold trim, Lenox wreath mark* 60.00 70.00

☐ **Horn of plenty,** *shape #2442, 10" high, coral and white, Lenox wreath mark* 80.00 95.00

☐ **Horn of plenty,** *shape #2442, 10" high, hand-painted fall flowers, gold trim, signed J. Nosek, Lenox wreath mark* 565.00 665.00

☐ **Horn of plenty,** *shape #2443, 8-1/4" high, plain white, Lenox wreath mark* 55.00 63.00

☐ **Horn of plenty,** *shape #2443, 8-1/4" high, gold trim on white, Lenox wreath mark* 68.00 78.00

☐ **Horn of plenty,** *shape #2443, 8-1/4" high, blue and white, Lenox wreath mark* 68.00 78.00

☐ **Horn of plenty,** *shape #2443, 8-1/4" high, floral transfer design, gold trim, Lenox wreath mark* 85.00 100.00

☐ **Horn of plenty,** *shape #2754, 7" high, plain white, Lenox wreath mark* 50.00 58.00

☐ **Horn of plenty,** *shape #2754, 7" high, solid coral, Lenox wreath mark* 60.00 70.00

☐ **Horn of plenty,** *shape #2754, 7" high, solid green, Lenox wreath mark* 68.00 78.00

☐ **Horn of plenty,** *shape #2754, 7" high, Lenox Rose pattern, Lenox wreath mark* 105.00 120.00

☐ **Horn of plenty,** *shape #2818, 6-1/8" high, plain white, Lenox wreath mark* 42.00 48.00

INVALID FEEDERS

These are relatively scarce Lenox items, and were made in only one shape.

Invalid feeder

Price Range

☐ **Invalid feeder,** *shape number unknown, hand-painted leaves with gold trim, Lenox wreath mark* 125.00   145.00

JUGS

Although we have several listings for whiskey jugs, they should not be considered common items. For the most part they are found only with early marks.

☐ **Jug,** *shape #271, 8" tall, undecorated, Lenox palette mark* 55.00   63.00
☐ **Jug,** *shape #271, 8" tall, badly decorated with wheat stalks on mottled background, artist initialed, Lenox palette mark* 85.00   100.00
☐ **Jug,** *shape #357, 6" tall, gold trim with "Whisky" written across front, C.A.C. palette mark* 105.00   120.00
☐ **Jug,** *shape #357, 6" tall, hand-painted hops and leaves on shaded background, nicely done, C.A.C. palette mark* 170.00   200.00
☐ **Jug,** *shape #357, 6" tall, grapes and blackberries on shaded background, gold handle, Lenox palette mark* 135.00   155.00
☐ **Jug,** *shape #358, 6-1/2" tall, beautifully decorated with spotted hunting dogs, transition mark* 330.00   395.00

Jug, *shape #534*

☐ **Jug,** *shape #358, 6-1/2" tall, hand-painted ears of corn on shaded background, gold handle, Lenox palette mark, artist signed* 160.00   190.00
☐ **Jug,** *shape #358, 6-1/2" tall, monochromatic blue monk scene, transition mark* 260.00   320.00
☐ **Jug,** *shape #359, 6" tall, monochromatic brown monk scene, transition mark* 225.00   275.00
☐ **Jug,** *shape #359, 6" tall, hand-painted berries with gold trim on spout and handle, C.A.C. lavender palette mark* 165.00   195.00
☐ **Jug,** *shape #359, 6" tall, undecorated, Lenox palette mark* 105.00   120.00

Price Range

☐ **Jug,** *shape #360, 6" tall, transfer decorated with drunken Irish-man and appropriate inscription, Lenox palette mark* 135.00 155.00

☐ **Jug,** *shape #360, 6" tall, monochromatic monk scene in green, transition mark* 210.00 255.00

☐ **Jug,** *shape #361, 7-1/4" tall, monochromatic blue monk scene, C.A.C. wreath mark* 330.00 395.00

☐ **Jug,** *shape #361, 7-1/4" tall, hand-painted fruit and berries on shaded background, nicely done, C.A.C. palette mark* 260.00 320.00

☐ **Jug,** *shape #362, 6" tall, trimmed in gold with "Papa" written across front, Lenox palette mark* 105.00 120.00

☐ **Jug,** *shape #362, 6" tall, hand-painted vines in greens and rusts, C.A.C. palette mark* 195.00 235.00

☐ **Jug,** *shape #363, 6-1/4" tall, monochromatic monk scene, transition mark* 195.00 235.00

☐ **Jug,** *shape #363, 6-1/4" tall, hand-painted ears of corn on solid brown background, gold trim on handle and rim, C.A.C. palette mark* 135.00 155.00

☐ **Jug,** *shape #364, 6" tall, monochromatic blue monk scene, transition mark* 165.00 195.00

☐ **Jug,** *shape #364, 6" tall, beautifully decorated with fruit and leaves on shaded background, undoubtedly the work of Morley but unsigned, transition mark* 260.00 320.00

☐ **Jug,** *shape #364, 6" tall, undecorated, Lenox palette mark* 80.00 95.00

☐ **Jug,** *shape #364, 6" tall, blackberries on shaded background and gold trim on spout and handle, artist signed and dated, Lenox palette mark* 135.00 155.00

☐ **Jug,** *shape #364, 6" tall, full-color cavalier drinking a toast, shaded background, C.A.C. palette mark* 135.00 155.00

Note: Shape #364 is the most common of the jugs to be found. For picture of shape, see the jug with silver stopper in metal section.

☐ **Jug,** *shape #407, 8-1/4" tall, undecorated, Lenox palette mark* . 68.00 78.00

☐ **Jug,** *shape #407, 8-1/4" tall, transfer decoration with ear of corn and gold trim, overall effect not bad, C.A.C. palette mark* . 125.00 145.00

☐ **Jug,** *shape #417, 5-3/4" tall, hand-painted berries on shaded background, home decorated but nicely done, Lenox palette mark* 165.00 195.00

☐ **Jug,** *shape #417, 5-3/4" tall, hand-painted purple grapes on green shaded background, dreadful, Lenox palette mark, artist signed and dated* 110.00 125.00

☐ **Jug,** *shape #534, 4" tall, hand-painted grapes and leaves on shaded background, gold inside spout, signed G. Morley, transition mark* 300.00 360.00

LADLE RESTS

The item most commonly referred to as a ladle rest is in fact a holder for sugar cubes. Since there are so few of the matching creamers, we feel it possible that many home decorators bought only the sugar holder intending to use it as a rest.

☐ **Ladle rest/sugar bowl,** *shape #72-1/2, 4-1/2" diameter, undecorated, Lenox wreath mark* 33.00 38.00

Price Range

☐ **Ladle rest/sugar bowl,** *shape #72-1/2, 4-1/2" diameter, gold trim, Lenox palette mark* 47.50   55.00

☐ **Ladle rest/sugar bowl,** *shape #72-1/2, 4-1/2" diameter, tiny pink flowers beneath rim, gold trim, artist signed and dated, C.A.C. green palette mark* 55.00   63.00

LOVING CUPS

We have listed as loving cups any drinking vessels which have more than one handle. Those with one handle are listed later as mugs.

☐ **Loving cup,** *shape #258, three-handled, undecorated, Lenox palette mark* 80.00   95.00

☐ **Loving cup,** *shape #258, three-handled, decorated with fruit on a shaded background, gold handles and rims, C.A.C. lavender palette mark* 80.00   95.00

☐ **Loving cup,** *shape #258, three-handled, monochromatic blue monk scenes, transition mark* 175.00   220.00

☐ **Loving cup,** *shape #259, three-handled, transfer cavaliers on shaded background, gold handles, C.A.C. lavender palette mark* 85.00   100.00

☐ **Loving cup,** *shape #259, multi-colored scenic, transition mark* 260.00   320.00

☐ **Loving cup,** *shape #259, pink roses with blue knotted ribbon bows on cream background, C.A.C. lavender palette mark* 175.00   220.00

☐ **Loving cup,** *shape #260, undecorated, C.A.C. lavender palette mark* 80.00   95.00

☐ **Loving cup,** *shape #260, purple flowers with green leaves and gold trim, dated 1905, very professional artwork, C.A.C. lavender palette mark* 225.00   275.00

☐ **Loving cup,** *shape #260, monochromatic green golfing scene, signed W.H. Clayton, transition mark* 300.00   360.00

Loving cup, *shape #317, monk scene*

Price Range

☐ **Loving cup,** *shape #317, 4-1/4" tall, transfer pictures of horses on hand-painted background, overall effect very nice, Lenox palette mark* 135.00   155.00

☐ **Loving cup,** *shape #317, 4-1/4" tall, plain with gold trim and monogram, Lenox palette mark* 80.00   95.00

☐ **Loving cup,** *shape #317, 5-1/4" tall, monochromatic blue monk scene, C.A.C. wreath mark* 175.00   220.00

☐ **Loving cup,** *shape #331, 3-1/2" tall, cherry blossoms on shaded background, artist initialed and dated, C.A.C. lavender palette mark* 120.00   140.00

☐ **Loving cup,** *shape #331, 3-1/2" tall, raised enamel work with garlands of roses, gold handles, C.A.C. green palette mark* ... 135.00   155.00

☐ **Loving cup,** *shape #341, 8-1/4" tall, pedestal base, gold trim on handles and rims, gold outlining on body of item, Lenox palette mark* 80.00   95.00

Loving cup, *shape number uncertain, golfing scene*

☐ **Loving cup,** *shape #342, 6-3/4" tall, undecorated, C.A.C. green palette mark* 105.00   120.00

☐ **Loving cup,** *shape #342, 6-3/4" tall, hand-painted with hops on shaded background, nicely done, Lenox palette mark* 170.00   220.00

☐ **Loving cup,** *shape #440, 8-1/4" tall, figural handles, hand-painted monks in full color, C.A.C. transition mark, signed Wirkner, magnificent* 525.00   625.00

☐ **Loving cup,** *shape #446, 8" tall, gold trim on figural handles, brushed gold on rims, Lenox palette mark* 195.00   235.00

☐ **Loving cup,** *shape number uncertain, similar to #259 but shorter and fatter, monochromatic green golfing scene, signed W.H. Clayton, transition mark* 225.00   175.00

MATCH HOLDERS AND JARS

	Price Range	
☐ **Match holder,** *shape #2425, undecorated, Lenox wreath mark* .	40.00	47.50
☐ **Match holder,** *shape #2425, undecorated and unmarked*	9.00	13.00
☐ **Match holder,** *shape #2425, gold trim, Lenox wreath mark*	40.00	47.50
☐ **Match holder,** *shape #2426, undecorated, Lenox wreath mark* .	33.00	38.00
☐ **Match holder,** *shape #2426, floral transfer decoration, Lenox wreath mark*	47.00	55.00
☐ **Match holder,** *shape #2426, gold trim, Lenox wreath mark*	33.00	38.00
☐ **Match jar,** *shape #348, 1-3/4" x 1-3/4", undecorated, Lenox wreath mark*	15.00	20.00
☐ **Match jar,** *shape #348, 1-3/4" x 1-3/4", hand-painted small pink roses, C.A.C. palette mark*	60.00	70.00

MENU STANDS

Menu stands are extremely scarce. The catalogue lists the one shape as 6-1/4" x 4-3/4". It has a fancy outer rim, which is glazed, and an unglazed inner section which looks like it is framed by the outer section. It would seem likely that the inner portion was left unglazed so that the surface would be easier to write on. We have no sales for this item to list, but would estimate the value of a decorated, signed specimen at around $200. One unmarked sample reportedly sold recently for $65.

MINIATURES

Most of the Lenox miniatures seen today were probably salesman samples to begin with, but there are a few items which were probably intended just to be cute little collectibles. As a rule, if an item is the same shape as a standard Lenox item only smaller, it was probably a sample. If the shape is unfamiliar, it was probably meant for a doll house. (We seem to recall reading somewhere that to be a true miniature, an item must be 1/12th the size of the original.)

Most of the miniatures are priced in the $75 to $150 range, depending both on shape and type of decoration. Lenox Rose pattern seems to be popular on miniatures, and of course plain gold trim can also be found. Most are undecorated.

The little creamer, less than 1" high, is well-liked because it can be worn as a necklace. (Keep the chain short so the china can't fall forward and hit something.) The creamer is part of a little teaset, complete with teapot, sugar bowl, cups and saucers, and tiny tea plates. The teapot and sugar bowl have removable lids.

MUFFINEERS

☐ **Muffineer,** *shape number unknown, hand-painted flowers, Lenox wreath mark*	65.00	75.00
☐ **Muffineer,** *shape number unknown, undecorated, gold wreath mark*	33.00	38.00

MUGS

☐ **Mug,** *shape #251, 4-7/8" high, undecorated, Lenox palette mark*	18.50	23.00
☐ **Mug,** *shape #251, 4-7/8" high, gold trim on handle and rims, gold monogram on front, Lenox palette mark*	40.00	47.50
☐ **Mug,** *shape #251, 4-7/8" high, blue bands top and bottom and blue on handle, mediocre central scenic section, C.A.C. lavender palette mark*	80.00	95.00

Price Range

☐ **Mug,** *shape #251, 4-7/8" high, Indian brave, full color, shaded background and handle, transition mark* 210.00   255.00

☐ **Mug,** *shape #252, 5" high, undecorated, Lenox palette mark* .. 33.00   38.00

☐ **Mug,** *shape #252, 5" high, hand-painted grapes on shaded background, gold handle, C.A.C. purple palette mark* 68.00   78.00

☐ **Mug,** *shape #252, 5" high, hand-painted pinecones on plain background, C.A.C. green palette mark* 55.00   63.00

☐ **Mug,** *shape #252, 5" high, monochromatic green monk scene, transition mark* 105.00   120.00

☐ **Mug,** *shape #252, 5" high, transfer monk on hand-painted background, C.A.C. green palette mark* 85.00   100.00

☐ **Mug,** *shape #252, 5" high, monk on green background, artist signed and dated 1901, C.A.C. lavender palette mark* 90.00   110.00

☐ **Mug,** *shape #252, 5" high, blackberries and leaves on shaded background, Lenox palette mark* 68.00   78.00

☐ **Mug,** *shape #252, 5" high, beer taster with German saying on reverse side, nicely done, artist initialed, C.A.C. green palette mark* 115.00   130.00

☐ **Mug,** *shape #253, 5" high, full-color portrait of Indian in head-dress, dated 1901, fine artwork, C.A.C. lavender palette mark* . 240.00   290.00

☐ **Mug,** *shape #253, 5" high, hand-painted grapes and leaves, off-white background, C.A.C. green palette mark* 110.00   125.00

☐ **Mug,** *shape #253, 5" high, red berries and branches, gold rims and handle, Lenox palette mark* 105.00   120.00

☐ **Mug,** *shape #253, 5" high, monochromatic monk scene, blue, transition mark* 120.00   140.00

☐ **Mug,** *shape #254, 5-1/2" high, monochromatic browns, monk with wine casket, gold rim and handle, no Lenox mark, artist signed DeLan* 125.00   145.00

☐ **Mug,** *shape #254, 5-1/2" high, monochromatic monk scene, very badly done, Lenox palette mark* 37.00   43.00

☐ **Mug,** *shape #254, 5-1/2" high, portrait of a black boy with straw hat, monochromatic green, transition mark* 165.00   195.00

☐ **Mug,** *shape #254, 5-1/2" high, monochromatic blues, monk making sandwich, transition mark* 105.00   120.00

☐ **Mug,** *shape #254, 5-1/2" high, ears of corn on shaded brown background, artist signed, Lenox palette mark* 80.00   95.00

☐ **Mug,** *shape #255, 5-1/2" high, portrait of old woman done in monochromatic browns, C.A.C. green palette mark* 105.00   120.00

☐ **Mug,** *shape #255, 5-1/2" high, seascape (ocean with light-house), artist signed and dated 1897, C.A.C. lavender palette mark* 110.00   125.00

☐ **Mug,** *shape #255, 5-1/2" high, multi-colored fruit decoration with gold handle and rims, Lenox palette mark* 105.00   120.00

☐ **Mug,** *shape #255, 5-1/2" high, Dutch scenes, full color, nicely done, C.A.C. lavender palette mark* 110.00   125.00

☐ **Mug,** *shape #255, 5-1/2" high, monochromatic browns, monks seated, standing and drinking, transition mark* 160.00   190.00

☐ **Mug,** *shape #255, 5-1/2" high, full-color, trees on light brown background, Lenox palette mark* 60.00   70.00

☐ **Mug,** *shape #256, 5-3/4" high, plain white with gold trim on handle and brushed gold on top rim, gold initials on front, Lenox palette mark* 68.00   78.00

Mug, *shape #604, Dickens type characters*

	Price Range	
☐ **Mug,** *shape #256, 5-3/4" high, monochromatic browns, monk drinking wine, transition mark*	135.00	155.00
☐ **Mug,** *shape #256, 5-3/4" high, multi-colored pinecones on shaded background, nicely done, C.A.C. lavender palette mark*	110.00	125.00
☐ **Mug,** *shape #257, 6" high, undecorated, Lenox palette mark* . .	27.50	32.50
☐ **Mug,** *shape #257, 6" high, monochromatic monk scene in blue, transition mark*	165.00	195.00
☐ **Mug,** *shape #257, 6" high, transfer decorated scene, gold trim, Lenox palette mark*	68.00	78.00
☐ **Mug,** *shape #311, 5" high, monochromatic monk scene in brown, transition mark*	135.00	155.00
☐ **Mug,** *shape #311, 5" high, monochromatic green, three Dickens type characters seated in a pub, transition mark*	225.00	275.00
☐ **Mug,** *shape #311, 5" high, monochromatic blue, standing monk, C.A.C. wreath mark*	195.00	235.00
☐ **Mug,** *shape #311, 5" high, undecorated, Lenox palette mark* . .	40.00	47.50
☐ **Mug,** *shape #312, 5-3/4" high, undecorated, C.A.C. green palette mark*	55.00	63.00
☐ **Mug,** *shape #312, 5-3/4" high, gold trim on handles and rims, Lenox palette mark*	55.00	63.00
☐ **Mug,** *shape #312, 5-3/4" high, full-color automobile scene, nicely done, Lenox palette mark*	165.00	195.00
Note: Shapes #311 and 312 are the same only #312 is taller.		
☐ **Mug,** *shape #500, 7" high, decorated with gold insignia and gold trim on handle and rims, Lenox palette mark*	68.00	78.00
☐ **Mug,** *shape #500, 7" high, monochromatic monk scene, transition mark*	165.00	195.00
☐ **Mug,** *shape #601, 4" high, raised enamel work and floral design, handwritten on bottom "To Baby Eleanor, June 16, 1915", Lenox palette mark*	13.00	16.00
☐ **Mug,** *shape #601, 4" high, undecorated, Lenox palette mark* . .	33.00	38.00
☐ **Mug,** *shape #604, 4-1/2" high, ear of corn on brown background, Lenox palette mark*	60.00	70.00

Price Range

☐ **Mug,** *shape #604, 4-1/2" high, berries on shaded background, artist's initials,Lenox palette mark* 80.00   95.00

☐ **Mug,** *shape #604, 4-1/2" high, monochromatic Dickens type characters, transition mark, pair* 300.00   360.00

☐ **Mug,** *shape #754, no decoration, Lenox wreath mark* 13.00   16.00

☐ **Mug,** *shape #754, transfer decorated with baby chicks, gold trim, Lenox palette mark* 55.00   63.00

☐ **Mug,** *shape #812, 3" high, gold trim, Lenox wreath mark* 40.00   47.50

☐ **Mug,** *shape #812, 3" high, pearlized finish with word "Coffee" written across front, Lenox palette mark* 33.00   38.00

☐ **Mug,** *shape #1313, no decoration, Lenox wreath mark* 15.00   20.00

☐ **Mug,** *shape #1493, no decoration, Lenox wreath mark* 17.50   22.50

☐ **Mug,** *no shape number but similar to #311 and #312, probably a special order, transfer decoration possibly Admiral Dewey framed by laurel wreath, background is off white shading to turquoise, red, white and blue banding at top, written-out C.A.C. lavender mark* 175.00   220.00

PITCHERS

Any pitcher-type item which is not a creamer or a ewer will be found in this section.

☐ **Pitcher,** *shape #24, 5" high, undecorated, C.A.C. brown palette mark* 105.00   120.00

☐ **Pitcher,** *shape #24, 5" high, gold trim on handle and brushed gold near rims, C.A.C. wreath mark, eggshell thin* 18.50   23.50

☐ **Pitcher,** *shape #24, 5" high, green with white handle, Lenox wreath mark* 40.00   47.50

☐ **Pitcher,** *shape #24, 5" high, coral with white handle, Lenox wreath mark* 33.00   38.00

☐ **Pitcher,** *shape #24, 5" high, white with gold trim, Lenox wreath mark* 33.00   38.00

☐ **Pitcher,** *shape #24, 5" high, solid baby pink with gold trim, Lenox wreath mark* 33.00   38.00

Note: The shape #24 pitcher is a fat-bottomed one with beading at mid-section and on handle. It is known as the Colonial pitcher, and is currently being made in a smaller version as a sugar and creamer.

☐ **Pitcher,** *shape #47, 10-1/2" high, bark-type finish on upper portion, rustic handle, covered, undecorated, C.A.C. lavender palette mark* 195.00   235.00

☐ **Pitcher,** *shape #47, 10-1/2" high, bark-type finish on upper portion, rustic handle, cover missing, done in shades of green and lavender, C.A.C. lavender palette mark* 260.00   320.00

☐ **Pitcher,** *shape #64, 7-1/4" high, all-over hammered finish, mask spout, eggshell thin, C.A.C. brown palette mark* 225.00   275.00

☐ **Pitcher,** *shape #64, 7-1/4" high, all-over hammered finish, mask spout, pale pink with pearlized finish, Lenox wreath mark* 105.00   120.00

☐ **Pitcher,** *shape #64, 7-1/4" high, all-over hammered finish, mask spout, medium green outside, white inside, Lenox wreath mark* 110.00   125.00

☐ **Pitcher,** *shape #64, 7-1/4" high, all-over hammered finish, mask spout, white with gold trim, Lenox palette mark* 90.00   110.00

Note: Shape #64 is known as the mask pitcher.

Price Range

☐ **Pitcher,** shape #71, 4" high, undecorated, hand-painted roses, gold trim, Lenox palette mark 47.50   55.00

☐ **Pitcher,** shape #71, 4" high, undecorated, C.A.C. lavender palette mark 40.00   47.50

☐ **Pitcher,** shape #184, 4" high, undecorated, C.A.C. green palette mark 42.00   48.00

☐ **Pitcher,** shape #184, 4" high, hand-painted with small violets and gold trim, C.A.C. lavender palette mark 120.00   140.00

☐ **Pitcher,** shape #184, 4" high, white with gold trim, Lenox palette mark 68.00   78.00

☐ **Pitcher,** shape #185, 4" high, tiny red flowers, gold filigree and scroll work, plain background, C.A.C. lavender palette mark .. 105.00   120.00

☐ **Pitcher,** shape #185, 4" high, undecorated, Lenox palette mark 33.00   38.00

☐ **Pitcher,** shape #270, 12" high, covered, hand-painted apples and leaves on plain background, gold trim, Lenox palette mark 120.00   140.00

☐ **Pitcher,** shape #270, 12" high, covered, overall grape decoration on wine-colored background, C.A.C. green palette mark .. 135.00   155.00

☐ **Pitcher,** shape #270, 12" high, covered, overall pearlized orange color, gold trim, perfectly dreadful, Lenox palette mark 40.00   47.50

☐ **Pitcher,** shape #337, 14" high, monochromatic brown monk scene, transition mark 250.00   300.00

☐ **Pitcher,** shape #337, 14" high, hand-painted red berries and green leaves on cream-colored background, artist signed and dated, C.A.C. green palette mark 220.00   270.00

Pitcher, shape #352, transition mark

☐ **Pitcher,** shape #352, 5-1/4" high, undecorated and unmarked but verifiably Lenox 13.00   16.00

☐ **Pitcher,** shape #352, 5-1/4" high, beautifully decorated with fruit on shaded background, unsigned but possibly the work of Morley, gold trim inside top rim and on handle, transition mark 330.00   395.00

Price Range

☐ **Pitcher,** *shape #352, 5-1/4" high, plain with gold trim, Lenox palette mark* 55.00   63.00

☐ **Pitcher,** *shape #352, 5-1/4" high, hand-painted fruit on brown background, artist signed and dated, C.A.C. green palette mark* 165.00   195.00
Note: The above pitcher is generally called a cider pitcher.

☐ **Pitcher,** *shape #456, 13" high, undecorated, Lenox palette mark* 68.00   78.00

☐ **Pitcher,** *shape #456, 13" high, overall grape design on green shaded background, artist signed, C.A.C. green palette mark* . 165.00   195.00

☐ **Pitcher,** *shape #456, 13" high, bridal portrait in oval medallion, blue dot enamel work, overall effect so-so, artist signed and dated, C.A.C. palette mark* 195.00   235.00

☐ **Pitcher,** *shape #457, 12" high, overall floral design of roses, baby's breath and daisies on pale blue background, Lenox palette mark* 165.00   195.00

☐ **Pitcher,** *shape #457, 13" high, hand-painted blackberries and flowers on shaded background, C.A.C. green palette mark, signed Fuchs (Pickard artist)* 225.00   275.00

☐ **Pitcher,** *shape #467, 8" high, cherries and blossoms on pale green background, gold trim, the worst in home decorating, C.A.C. lavender palette mark* 105.00   120.00

☐ **Pitcher,** *shape #467, 8" high, undecorated, C.A.C. green palette mark* 85.00   100.00

☐ **Pitcher,** *tankard shape, 14" high, undecorated, C.A.C. green palette mark* 68.00   78.00

☐ **Pitcher,** *tankard shape, 14" high, hand-painted green and purple on background which is shaded green to yellow, artist signed and dated, nicely done, C.A.C. green palette mark* 225.00   275.00

☐ **Pitcher,** *tankard shape, 14" high, monochromatic green scene of monk holding pig, C.A.C. wreath mark, signed E.A. DeLan* . . 365.00   435.00

☐ **Pitcher,** *tankard shape, 14" high, hand-painted ears of corn on brown shaded background, artist signed, Lenox palette mark* . 165.00   195.00

☐ **Pitcher,** *tankard shape, 14" high, overall grape and hops motif, lavish gold, professional look, C.A.C. green palette mark* 260.00   320.00

☐ **Pitcher,** *tankard, 14" high, floral sprays of mums on green background, artist signed, Lenox palette mark* 210.00   255.00

☐ **Pitcher,** *tankard, 14" high, monochromatic blue monk scene, excellent artwork, C.A.C. wreath mark* 330.00   395.00

☐ **Pitcher,** *tankard, 14" high, monochromatic browns, monk drawing wine from a cask, signed M. Nourse, C.A.C. lavender palette mark* 330.00   395.00

☐ **Pitcher,** *tankard, 14" high, monochromatic green monk scene, transition mark* 260.00   320.00

☐ **Pitcher,** *tankard, 14" high, purple and red grapes on cream colored background, artist's initials and date, Lenox palette mark* 195.00   235.00
Note: There were two shapes of tankard pitchers, only slightly different. Our catalogue pictures are not good enough to tell one from the other, so we have omitted shape numbers for this category. The two numbers would be #514 and #519.

☐ **Pitcher,** *shape #526, 6" high, gold trim and initials, Lenox palette mark* 55.00   63.00

Price Range

☐ **Pitcher,** *shape #526, 6" high, hand-painted berries and fruit on shaded green background, C.A.C. lavender palette mark* 165.00 195.00

☐ **Pitcher,** *shape #526, 6" high, undecorated and unmarked, verifiably Lenox* 27.50 32.50

☐ **Pitcher,** *shape #555, 11" high, covered hand-painted roses with gold trim, artist signed, Lenox palette mark* 135.00 155.00

☐ **Pitcher,** *shape #555, 11" high, covered, hand-painted grapes on both sides, Lenox palette mark* 120.00 140.00

☐ **Pitcher,** *shape #566, 8-1/4" high, covered, undecorated, Lenox palette mark* 55.00 63.00

☐ **Pitcher,** *shape #566, 8-1/4" high, covered, hand-painted ears of corn, Lenox palette mark* 90.00 110.00

☐ **Pitcher,** *shape #566, 8-1/4" high, covered, transfer decorated with French-type scene, gold trim, Lenox palette mark* 55.00 63.00

☐ **Pitcher,** *shape #567, 7-1/2" high, single orchid on either side, Lenox wreath mark* 195.00 235.00

Pitcher, *tankard, monk scene*

☐ **Pitcher,** *shape #568, 6" high, undecorated, Lenox palette mark* 40.00 47.50

☐ **Pitcher,** *shape #568, 6" high, hand-painted grapes and leaves on tan background, nicely done, artist signed and dated, Lenox palette mark* 120.00 140.00

☐ **Pitcher,** *shape #666, 8-1/2", high, hand-painted with lemons and oranges, gold trim, Lenox palette mark* 135.00 155.00

☐ **Pitcher,** *shape #666, 8-1/2" high, hand-painted with roses and gold trim, Lenox palette mark* 68.00 78.00

☐ **Pitcher,** *shape #667, 8-1/2" high, decorated with stylized tulips in panels down the sides in raised enamel work, Lenox palette mark* 68.00 78.00

☐ **Pitcher,** *shape #667, 8-1/2" high, undecorated, Lenox wreath mark* 40.00 47.50

Pitcher, *shape number unknown, embossed floral design*

Price Range

☐ **Pitcher,** *shape #918, 9-1/2" high, hand-painted fruit on brown background, gold trim, artist signed and dated, Lenox palette mark* 68.00   78.00

☐ **Pitcher,** *shape #918, 9-1/2" high, hand-painted with Dutch type designs in blue, Lenox palette mark* 47.50   55.00

☐ **Pitcher,** *shape number unknown, embossed floral design, all white, Lenox wreath mark* 40.00   47.50

Pitcher, *shape number unknown, modernistic styling*

Pitcher, *shape number unknown, modernistic look*

	Price Range	
☐ **Pitcher,** *shape number unknown, modernistic styling with transfer decoration, Lenox wreath mark*	40.00	47.50
☐ **Pitcher,** *shape number unknown, modernistic look, gold trim on pink, Lenox wreath mark*	40.00	47.50

PLATES

Animals

Farm animals are the subject of one of the more famous series of Morley plates. The first set, done from a photograph (black and white in those days) and a description of the colors, was of a prize-winning horse owned by a Pennsylvania farmer. The second set, ordered by the same man, pictured a champion hog and was also done by Morley from photographs. The farmer was to eventually order 18 sets of plates, all with pictures of his winning livestock.

Birds

Bird plates are scarcer than fish, and a well-done bird plate should be priced at around twice the going rate for a comparable fish plate. The birds most often found are:

Pintail duck	Canada goose	Canvasback duck
Snipe	Woodcock	Pheasant
Prairie chicken	Redhead duck	Quail
Partridge	Oyster catcher	Ptarmigan

The following border trims have been noted: B-312, C-317, C-421, D-343, D-345, D-346, E-25, E-35, E-82, E-325, E-414, J-9, J-28, J-57, J-405, J-406, J-407, L-431, M-382, O-15, P-28, R-17, S-71, T-23, V-38, V-39, W-11, W-12, and X-1. The birds can be shown in winter or summer settings, but the winter settings are somewhat less common.

Perhaps the most famous set of game birds by Lenox is the exotic pheasant set by William Morley done in 1927. The man who ordered the plates,

Colonel Anthony R. Kuser of Bernardsville, New Jersey, financed an expedition to the far corners of the world to photograph and sketch pheasants. They are currently owned by a private collector.

A few slightly less impressive copies of the same plates were also made, although the exact number of copies is uncertain. The Lenox Company owns a set of twelve plates which (judging by backstamps) might be made up of parts of two different sets. The owner of the originals also owns a set of the copies. There is also a single plate in the Lenox showroom which might have been part of another set of copies although it is equally possible that it was a single sample.

Matching platters are very much the exception rather than the rule with Lenox game sets. The company owns two of the platters, both decorated with the pheasant. A platter in good condition should be valued in the $600 range.

Bird plate, *Ptarmigan*

	Price Range	
☐ **Bird plates,** *9" diameter, J-57 etched gold borders, signed W. H. Morley, one has ptarmigan in winter plumage, the other has canvasback duck also in a winter setting, Lenox wreath mark, pair*	500.00	600.00
☐ **Bird plates,** *9" diameter, 1/2" flat gold border with pencil line gold inside (variation of pattern 86-1/2), gold monogram R.A. at top for Robert Adrian, past president of N. J. Senate, pheasants in snow, misty look to pictures, signed W. H. Morley, Lenox wreath mark, pair*	195.00	235.00
☐ **Bird plates,** *10-1/2" diameter, narrow flat gold trim on rims, 12 different game birds, not as detailed as some of the earlier plates, signed J. Nosek, Lenox wreath/Made in U.S.A. mark, set of 12*	800.00	940.00

Bird plate, *Canvasback duck*

Fish

Fish plates for the most part saw very little actual use and are often in prime condition. Although William Morley did the majority of them, samples by other artists are not unknown. The 12 fish appearing most frequently are:

Sun fish	Blue fish	Spanish mackerel
Weak fish	Black bass	Striped bass
Salmon	Pike	Porgy
Brook trout	Common mackerel	Yellow perch

The standard sets will typically have the names of the fish hand-printed on the back (as is also the case with the standard bird sets.)

Fish plate, *K-49 etched border*

Fish plate, *K-49 etched border*

Border trims include: B-312, C-312, C-421, D-343, D-345, D-346, E-25, E-35, E-325, E-82, E-414, J-9, J-38, J-57, J-405, J-406, J-407, K-49, L-431, M-153, M-382, O-15, P-28, R-17, S-71, T-17, T-23, V-38, V-39, W-11, W-12, and X-1.

For reasons we are unable to explain, the sunfish is almost invariably the most attractive in any given set of plates. Since the fish plates were a stock item for many years, anything unusual about a plate increases its value quite a bit.

Price Range

☐ **Fish plate,** *9" diameter, central pastel fish, very fine background work, signed E. A. DeLan, Lenox gold wreath mark*   **105.00   120.00**

Fish plate, *J-57 etched gold border*

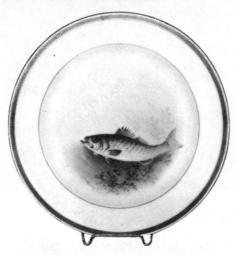

Fish plate, *J-57 etched gold border*

Price Range

☐ **Fish plate,** *9" diameter, fish painted near the borders rather than being centered like most fish plates, good detailing and color, K-49 etched gold borders, Lenox wreath mark, set of six*   **600.00   710.00**

☐ **Fish plate,** *9" diameter, -312 etched gold borders, well-done fish with good background detailing, gold not quite as bright as it might be, s' diameter, B-312 etched gold borders, well-done fish with good background detailing, gold not quite as bright as it might be, signed W. H. Morley, Lenox wreath mark, Ovington's store mark, set of five* **435.00   505.00**

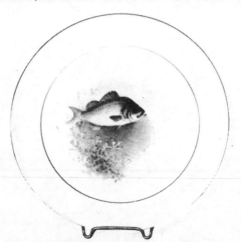

Fish plate, *narrow gold trim*

Fish plate, *narrow gold trim*

Price Range

☐ **Fish plate,** 9" diameter, J-57 etched gold borders, large, well-done fish with good color and background details, signed W. H. Morley, Lenox wreath mark and Ovington's store mark, set of four, see photos 430.00 495.00

☐ **Fish plate,** 9" diameter, large, well-done fish, good detailing, narrow flat gold trim, signed W. H. Morley, Lenox gold wreath mark, set of four 400.00 470.00

☐ **Fish plate,** 9" diameter, fish average as to size and detailing, color fair, 3/4" etched gold border in J-28 pattern, gold very bright and new looking, plates in absolutely mint condition, signed W. H. Morley, Lenox wreath mark and Gilman Collamore & Co. store mark, complete set of 12 .... 1025.00 1225.00

☐ **Fish plate,** 9" diameter, fish done in dull greens and grays with washed-out appearance, gold pencil-line trim, coupe shape plate instead of standard shape, signed W. H. Morley, Lenox wreath mark, set of 12, two had tiny flecks on rim 400.00 470.00

Floral

Perhaps the most spectacular set of flower plates we have seen were by W.H. Morley. Each plate had a different rose, beautifully done, and the entire rim had an etched gold floral design (the same rim which appears on the Nosek portrait plate.)

Similar plates with orchids instead of roses were sold at auction in 1978, and brought in the area of $200 each. They no doubt would have gone higher except that there were 54 of them at the auction, all apparently purchased by the same party.

Less-ornate floral plates seem to fluctuate quite a bit. Recently, a set of 12 Morley floral plates sold at a Trenton auction for $18 each. The problem with this particular set was that it had changed hands a few times too often, and had become "jinxed". The plates first showed up at a Trenton auction about six years ago, and made several appearances in the area. They actually went down in value with each auction, from $50 or so six years ago to the recent $18.

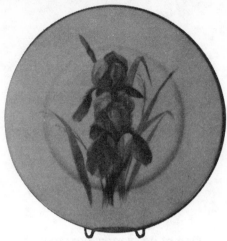

Floral plate, *orchid*

Comparable plates, however, typically sell in the $50 and up range. Nicely done but not ornate orchid plates are probably worth a minimum of $140, more if they have the scalloped rims. Nosek did a decent series of floral plates, and these can bring anywhere from $75 to $200, depending on workmanship and luck.

Transfer-decorated floral plates which were filled in by hand are not yet particularly desirable and might well be considered as dinnerware rather than artware. They can bring up to around $25 for the prettier ones. Rim decorations include O-433, O-434, O-435, O-436, O-438, O-450, O-451, O-452, R-302, R-303, R-334, R-429, and R-449. Plate shapes include #2020, #1881, #2803, and #2249.

Fruit

Hand-painted fruit plates from the Morley period are quite lovely, and are actually fully-detailed still life paintings of the fruit. Frequently, the design did not fill the entire center, but rather took up about a 5" diameter, with the rim color coming down into the well to meet the artwork. Plates such as these should probably be valued at $100 minimum.

Later fruit plates have only the fruit in the center of the plate, with no background at all. The subjects became more standardized, and most sets consisted of the following:

Apples	Grapes	Peaches
Cherries	Raspberries	Gooseberries
Strawberries	Apples	Blackberries
Plums	Grapes	Pears

They were available on more than one shape, and rim decorations included D-341, P-359, P-420, X-5, Y-21, Y-78, and Z-66. These plates, sometimes by Morley and other times by Nosek, are usually priced in the $75 range.

Nautical

Morley is known to have hand-painted at least one set of clipper ship plates, but for the most part the nautical plates were transfers filled in by hand. They are all attractive to see and sell particularly well in the New England area. The transfer-done series included the following clipper ships:

Black Prince; Boston MA; 1856   Young America; NY; 1853
Junenta; Thomaston, ME; 1953   Galatea; Charleston, MA; 1854
Aracle; ME; 1853   Great Republic; Boston, MA; 1853
Sweepstakes; NY; 1853   Northern Light; Boston, MA; 1851
Ringleader; Medford, MA; 1853   Golden West; Boston, MA; 1852
Red Jacket; Rockland, ME; 1853   John Wade; Boston, MA; 1851

Rim decorations included F-355A, F-395A, F-405B, F-406B, L-352A, and O-333B.

The Yacht Defender plates included some combination of the following yachts:

Volunteer	America	Resolute
Defender	Madeleine	Rainbow
Columbia	Ranger	Enterprise
Puritan	Sappho	Mischief
Vigilant		

Rim for the yacht plates included J-410B, J-411, J-413A, J-414B, J-415B, and L-398B.

Both types of plates typically sell in the $75 to $150 each range, with prices being the highest in sailing-oriented parts of the country.

Portraits

Hand-painted Lenox portrait plates are extremely scarce and desirable. Those by Geyer, one of which is shown in the color section, are absolutely divine and very much in that area of Lenox collecting where it is foolish to quibble over prices. The Nosek portraits, although not quite up to the Geyers, should also be considered as prize pieces of Lenox. The owner of the Nosek recently rejected an offer of $300, and we cannot find much fault with his decision.

Portrait plate, *Geyer*

Portrait plate, *Nosek*

Scenics

Perhaps the most famous Lenox scenic plates are known as the European garden set for the scenes they depict or as the Scammell plates for the woman who commissioned them. They were done from black and white photographs of the gardens, with the woman describing to Morley the colors in each photograph. (This is supposedly the only time Morley allowed anyone to look over his shoulder while he was working.) The plates have wide acid-etched gold borders, and are stunning. They are currently owned by a private collector.

Another series of plates had views of 18 bridges built by a Trenton firm, the owner of which commissioned the plates. Although we have not seen these plates, we gather that they were photographic transfers which were filled in by hand. The set is in private hands.

PUNCH BOWLS

C.A.C. made a large punchbowl, 12-1/2" x 16-3/4", with an embossed design. We have heard that at least one does still indeed exist. Undecorated, it would be in the $200 to $275 range. A beautifully decorated one by perhaps one of the better known factory artists would be in the $500 to $1,000 range.

Lenox later made several good-sized bowls which could pass for small punch bowls. Typically, they are about 12" in diameter and 8" high. For the most part, they are under $140 undecorated.

RING TREES

Two types of ring trees were made by Lenox. The tree part of both is pretty much the same, but the earlier one has a ruffled rim around it while the later one has a plain base.

	Price Range	
☐ **Ring tree,** *shape #161 small hand-painted roses with gold trim, C.A.C. lavender palette mark*	150.00	175.00
☐ **Ring tree,** *shape #161, undecorated and unmarked*	18.50	23.50
☐ **Ring tree,** *later shape, undecorated, Lenox wreath mark*	60.00	70.00

Price Range

SALT SHAKERS AND DIPS

☐ **Salt dip,** *shape #103, 1-3/4" across bottom, undecorated, Lenox palette mark* 8.00   9.50

☐ **Salt dip,** *shape #103, 1-3/4" across bottom, covered all over with gold, Lenox palette mark* 9.00   13.00

☐ **Salt dip,** *shape #103, 1-3/4" across bottom, pink roses and gold trim, Lenox palette mark* 13.00   16.00

☐ **Salt dip,** *shape #103, 1-3/4" across bottom, tiny pink roses, gold trim, transition mark* 16.50   21.50

☐ **Salt dip,** *shape #103, 1-3/4" across bottom, brushed gold on rim, transition mark* 14.00   18.00

☐ **Salt dip,** *shape #103, 1-3/4" across bottom, violets with gold trim, C.A.C. wreath mark* 18.00   23.50

☐ **Salt dip,** *shape #236, 2-1/4" across, pale green with gold trim and gold on feet, C.A.C. green palette mark* 15.00   20.00

☐ **Salt dip,** *shape #236, 2-1/4" across, undecorated, Lenox palette mark* 13.00   16.00

☐ **Salt dip,** *shape #236, 2-1/4" across, pink roses with gold trim, transition mark* 33.00   38.00

☐ **Salt dip,** *shape #236, 2-1/4" across, small violets and gold trim, C.A.C. pink palette mark and Bailey, Banks and Biddle store mark* 33.00   38.00

☐ **Salt dip,** *shape #236, 2-1/4" across, covered all over with gold, Lenox palette mark* 15.00   20.00

☐ **Salt dip,** *shape #806, 2-1/2", hexagon shape, gold inside and out, Lenox palette mark* 15.00   20.00

☐ **Salt dip,** *shape #806, 2-1/2", hexagon shape, gold rims, and gold initial, Lenox palette mark* 15.00   20.00

☐ **Salt dip,** *shape #807, 1-5/8", hexagon shape, solid cobalt, apparently meant to have silver overlay, Lenox palette mark* .. 9.00   13.00

☐ **Salt dip,** *shape #807, 1-5/8", hexagon shape, lavender lustre finish outside, gold rim, Lenox palette mark* 13.00   16.00

☐ **Salt shaker,** *shape #215, 2-1/2" high, pink roses and gold trim, no mark* 13.00   16.00

☐ **Salt shaker,** *shape #215, 2-1/2" high, brushed gold trim, no mark* 13.00   16.00

☐ **Salt shaker,** *shape #215, 2-1/2" high, undecorated, no mark* ... 6.75   7.75

Note: Shape #215 shaker is usually not marked because the hole for the cork takes up most of the bottom. It frequently was paired with the #103 salt dip to make a set, or with the smallest swan. In pairs, the #215 was meant to be a salt and pepper shaker set.

☐ **Salt shaker,** *shape #531, 3" high, undecorated, Lenox wreath mark, pair* 18.50   23.50

☐ **Salt shaker,** *shape #531, 3" high, hand-painted with roses and gold trim, Lenox palette mark, pair* 18.50   23.50

☐ **Salt shaker,** *shape #531, 3" high, gold initial and trim, Lenox palette mark, pair* 18.50   23.50

☐ **Salt shaker,** *shape #584, 2-3/8" high, pearlized blue finish with gold trim, Lenox palette mark, pair* 15.00   20.00

☐ **Salt shaker,** *shape #584, 2-3/8" high, hand-painted violets and gold trim, Lenox wreath mark, pair* 37.00   43.00

Price Range

☐ **Salt shaker,** *shape #584, 2-3/8" high, undecorated and unmarked, pair* 9.00   13.00
☐ **Salt shaker,** *shape #585, 3-1/2" high, hand-painted in a gaudy geometric fashion, Lenox palette mark, pair* 15.00   20.00
☐ **Salt shaker,** *shape #585, 3-1/2" high, hand-painted with roses and gold trim, Lenox palette mark, pair* 17.50   22.50
☐ **Salt shaker,** *shape #585, 3-1/2" high, undecorated, Lenox wreath mark, pair* 15.00   20.00
☐ **Salt shaker,** *shape #882, 5" high, undecorated, Lenox wreath mark, pair* 18.50   23.50
☐ **Salt shaker,** *shape #882, 5" high, hand-painted with Art Deco type design in raised enamel effect, Lenox palette mark, pair* . 23.00   28.00

SHAVING MUGS

Lenox shaving mugs are extremely rare, and they were made in only the one shape.

☐ **Shaving mug,** *shape #201, 4" tall, hand-painted violets on shaded background, C.A.C. palette mark* 165.00   195.00
☐ **Shaving mug,** *shape #201, 4" tall, undecorated, C.A.C. palette mark* 135.00   155.00

SHERBET CUPS AND PUNCH CUPS

These two types of cups are listed together because it is difficult, if not impossible, to tell them apart just by appearance. In general, they are footed cups with one or two handles and no underplate. A few of them came with small trays, apparently for cookies. We would suppose that those cups with ruffled rims are sherberts, since drinking out of them would have been tricky. In the price guide, we are just calling them all cups.

☐ **Cup,** *shape #12, two-handled, ruffled rim, undecorated, Lenox palette mark* 40.00   47.50
☐ **Cup,** *shape #12, two-handled, ruffled rim, matte finish with raised gold work, C.A.C. lavender palette mark* 80.00   95.00
☐ **Cup,** *shape #12, two-handled, ruffled rim, small hand-painted roses, gold trim on handles and rims, transition mark* 135.00   155.00
☐ **Cup,** *shape #13, same size and shape as #12 but only has one handle, blue dot enamel work and gold trim, C.A.C. palette mark* 105.00   120.00
☐ **Cup,** *shape #13, undecorated, C.A.C. green palette mark, several flecks on ruffled rim* 33.00   38.00
Note: Cup #13 is shown in catalogues with the shape #14 tray, a small square item with ruffled rim also. None of the listings we have for this cup had the tray with them.
☐ **Cup,** *shape #197, footed, fancy handle, undecorated, C.A.C. green palette mark* 18.50   23.50
☐ **Cup,** *shape #197, footed, fancy handles, decorated with gold trim and monograms, C.A.C. green palette mark* 33.00   38.00
☐ **Cup,** *shape #198, footed, same shape as #197 except base is shorter, undecorated, Lenox palette mark* 18.50   23.50
☐ **Cup,** *shape #198, footed, gold trim and single large pink rose, Lenox palette mark* 47.50   55.00

Price Range

☐ **Cup,** *shape #264, two-handled, plain shape, undecorated, C.A.C. brown palette mark* 40.00 47.50

☐ **Cup,** *shape #264, two-handled, plain shape, all-over fruit decoration, gold handles, Lenox palette mark* 47.50 55.00

☐ **Cup,** *shape #274, two-handled, with underplate, gold trim on handle and rims, C.A.C. brown palette mark* 40.00 47.50

SMALL DISHES

The following items are small dishes meant to be used for candy, olives, nuts, and other type items. Since they were multiple-purpose items, we are grouping them all together under this one heading.

☐ **Dish,** *shape #9, 5" x 7-1/4", free-form shape, ruffled rim, undecorated, C.A.C. palette mark* 40.00 47.50

☐ **Dish,** *shape #9, 5" x 7-1/4", hand-painted butterflies and flowers on blue background, gold trim on ruffled rim, C.A.C. green palette mark, several flecks on rim* 47.50 55.00

☐ **Dish,** *shape #10, 5" x 7-1/4", free form, scalloped rim, pale pink pearlized finish with gold trim, Lenox palette mark* 33.00 38.00

☐ **Dish,** *shape #10, 5" x 7-1/4", free form, scalloped rim, hand-painted tiny violets in bunch, gold trim, C.A.C. green palette mark* 68.00 78.00

☐ **Dish,** *shape #10, 5" x 7-1/4", free form, scalloped rim, undecorated and unmarked* 6.75 7.75

☐ **Dish,** *shape #19, 10-1/2", rolled rim with ruffles in four plates, undecorated, C.A.C. lavender palette mark, several flecks on rim* 30.00 35.00

☐ **Dish,** *shape #51, 3", shell shape on footed base, solid coral, Lenox wreath mark* 33.00 38.00

☐ **Dish,** *shape #51, 3", shell shape on footed base, white with gold trim, Lenox palette mark* 30.00 35.00

☐ **Dish,** *shape #91, 3-1/2" x 6-1/4", leaf shape with erose edges, rolled handle, undecorated, very early and eggshell thin, C.A.C. lavender palette mark* 58.00 68.00

☐ **Dish,** *shape #91, 3-1/2" x 6-1/4", leaf shape with erose edges, rolled handle, plain with gold trim, Lenox wreath mark* 33.00 38.00

☐ **Dish,** *shape #91, 3-1/2" x 6-1/4", pale pink with white handle, Lenox wreath mark* 30.00 35.00

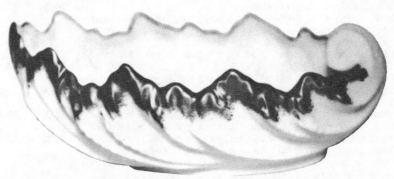

Dish, *shape #91, Lenox wreath mark*

Price Range

☐ **Dish,** *shape #91, 3-1/2" x 6-1/4", green with gold trim, Lenox wreath mark* 37.00 43.00
☐ **Dish,** *shape #91, 3-1/2" x 6-1/4", Lenox Rose design with gold trim, Lenox wreath mark* 42.00 48.00
☐ **Dish,** *shape #91, 3-1/2" x 6-1/4", blue with gold trim, Lenox wreath mark* 33.00 38.00

Dish, *shape #91, pale pink*

☐ **Dish,** *shape #95, 5-1/2" x 9-1/4", leaf shape with erose edges, rolled handle, exceptionally thin with fine detailing, brushed gold trim, on handle and raised sections of leaf, C.A.C. red palette mark* 135.00 155.00
☐ **Dish,** *shape #95, 5-1/2" x 9-1/4", leaf shape with erose edges, rolled handle, solid coral, Lenox wreath mark* 47.50 55.00
☐ **Dish,** *shape #95, 5-1/2" x 9-1/4", leaf shape with erose edges, rolled handle, exceptionally good detailing, solid gold outside, little scattered flowers inside, beautiful, C.A.C. lavender palette mark* 165.00 195.00
☐ **Dish,** *shape #102, 1-1/4" x 4-1/2", swirled ribbing, undecorated, lenox palette mark* 18.50 23.50
☐ **Dish,** *shape #112, 3-1/2" x 6-1/4", (shape #91 with feet), gold trim, C.A.C. brown palette mark* 70.00 80.00
☐ **Dish,** *shape #113, 5-1/2" x 9-1/4", (shape #95 with feet), pale pink pearlized finish inside, gold trim, on outside, C.A.C. green palette mark* 115.00 130.00
☐ **Dish,** *shape #133, 3-1/4" x 3-3/4", shallow, vertical bands of fluting, undecorated, unmarked* 4.00 5.00
☐ **Dish,** *shape #134, 3-1/4" x 3-3/4", cross-hatching and fluting, pale pink, Lenox wreath mark* 23.00 28.00
☐ **Dish,** *shape #135, 3-1/4" x 3-3/4", fluting and embossed design around bottom, white with gold trim, Lenox palette mark* 23.00 28.00
☐ **Dish,** *shape #307, 5-1/2", heart shaped with embossed shell motif at top, gold trim, C.A.C. green palette mark* 70.00 80.00
☐ **Dish,** *shape #307, 5-1/2", heart shaped with embossed shell motif at top, hand-painted large pink rose in center, artist signed, Lenox palette mark* 80.00 95.00

Dish, *shape number uncertain, heart shape*

	Price Range	
☐ **Dish,** *shape #324, 5", heart shaped with embossed shell motif at top, small pink roses in scatter pattern, C.A.C. red palette mark*	125.00	145.00
☐ **Dish,** *shape number uncertain but possibly #977, 5-1/2", heart shape, embossing on rim, hand-painted child with garlands of roses, gold trim on embossed sections shows some wear, artist signed, very well done, C.A.C. green palette mark*	125.00	145.00

SPOONS

Lenox made two spoons, one for demitasse coffee and the other for salt. Both are typically unmarked and are extremely scarce. We have no listings on spoons for this past year, but would estimate their value at around $145.

SUGARS AND CREAMERS *(ALL PRICES ARE FOR THE PAIR)*

☐ **Sugar and creamer,** *shape #38, creamer 4", sugar 4-1/2" diameter, raised gold paste trim, C.A.C. lavender palette mark*	165.00	195.00
☐ **Sugar and creamer,** *shape #38, creamer 4", sugar 4-1/2" diameter, pale blue inside bowl, reversed on creamer so that the blue is on the outside, brushed gold trim on rims, several flecks on ruffled rim of sugar, C.A.C. red palette mark*	155.00	180.00
☐ **Sugar and creamer,** *shape #38, creamer 4", sugar 4-1/2" diameter, undecorated, very thin, C.A.C. brown palette mark* . .	135.00	155.00
☐ **Sugar and creamer,** *shape #72 and 72-1/2, creamer 4-1/", sugar 4-1/4", small blue flowers, gold trim, C.A.C. green palette mark*	105.00	120.00
☐ **Sugar and creamer,** *shaer 4-1/4", sugar 4-1/4", small blue flowers, gold trim, C.A.C. green palette mark*	105.00	120.00
☐ **Sugar and creamer,** *shape #72 and 72-1/2, creamer 4-1/4", sugar 4-1/4", hand-painted work outlining the embossed work in the china, C.A.C. green palette mark*	68.00	78.00

Price Range

☐ **Sugar and creamer,** *shape #89 and 90, sugar bowl 5", creamer 4", ribbed seashell effect, pale pink pearlized finish, speckled gold trim, C.A.C. lavender palette mark* 165.00   195.00

☐ **Sugar and creamer,** *shape #89 and 90, sugar bowl 5", creamer 4", ribbed seashell effect, undecorated, Lenox wreath mark* .. 85.00   100.00

☐ **Sugar and creamer,** *shape #183 and 183-1/2, melon-ribbed, creamer 4", sugar 3-1/2", undecorated, very thin, C.A.C. lavender palette mark* 115.00   130.00

☐ **Sugar and creamer,** *shape #213 and 214, sugar 4-5/8", creamer 3-1/2", hand-painted forsythia, gold trim, C.A.C. palette mark* . 135.00   155.00

☐ **Sugar and creamer,** *shape #213 and 214, sugar 4-5/8", creamer 3-1/2", hand-painted small violets in scatter pattern, gold filigree trim, C.A.C. red palette mark, Bailey, Banks and Biddle store mark* 150.00   175.00

Sugar and creamer, *shape #38, lavendar palette mark*

☐ **Sugar and creamer,** *shape #213 and 214, sugar 4-5/8", creamer 3-1/2", undecorated, Lenox palette mark* 55.00   63.00

☐ **Sugar and creamer,** *shape #366 and 367, Turkish shape, gold trim over brown glaze, raised gold paste pseudo-Arabic lettering, C.A.C. lavender palette mark* 195.00   235.00

☐ **Sugar and creamer,** *shape #366 and 373, square pedestal bases, square handles, orange lustre finish with gold trim and gold monogram, badly done, Lenox palette mark* 33.00   38.00

☐ **Sugar and creamer,** *shape #372 and 373, square pedestal bases and square handles, yellow rose on front of each and rosebud on backs, gold trim on handle, base and top, appears to be a variation of pattern #82, transition mark* 165.00   195.00

☐ **Sugar and creamer,** *shape #372 and 373, square pedestal bases and square handles, gold trim and monogram, Lenox palette mark* 80.00   95.00

Price Range

☐ **Sugar and creamer,** *shape #523 and 524, transfer-decorated with Oriental scene in cobalt, items shade from white around decal to dark cobalt on end of handles and lids, well-executed, Lenox palette mark* 120.00 140.00

☐ **Sugar and creamer,** *shape #523 and 524, hand-painted small pink roses in scatter pattern, gold filigree trim, transition mark* 195.00 235.00

☐ **Sugar and creamer,** *shape #523 and 524, undecorated, Lenox wreath mark* 40.00 47.50

☐ **Sugar and creamer,** *shape #523 and 524, groups of violets, gold trim, unsigned but nicely done, Lenox palette mark, chip on inside rim of sugar* 85.00 100.00

☐ **Sugar and creamer,** *shape #543 and 544, angular modernistic shape, hand-painted black rose on fronts, black handles and trim, Lenox palette mark* 40.00 47.50

☐ **Sugar and creamer,** *shape #543 and 544, angular, modernistic shape, undecorated, Lenox wreath mark* 47.50 55.00

☐ **Sugar and creamer,** *shape #580 and 581, small hand-painted roses, gold trim, Lenox palette mark* 68.00 78.00

☐ **Sugar and creamer,** *shape #598 and 599, undecorated, Lenox palette mark* 33.00 38.00

☐ **Sugar and creamer,** *shape #662 and 663, hexagon shape, gold trim and monogram, Lenox palette mark* 47.50 55.00

☐ **Sugar and creamer,** *shape #662 and 663, deep aquamarine with nicely done gold trim, Lenox palette mark* 80.00 95.00

☐ **Sugar and creamer,** *shape #697 and 698, hand-painted pansies on shaded green background, gold trim, artist's initials and date, Lenox palette mark* 105.00 120.00

☐ **Sugar and creamer,** *shape #733 and 734, hexagon shape, undecorated, Lenox palette mark* 47.50 55.00

☐ **Sugar and creamer,** *shape #733 and 734, hexagon shape, hand-painted mixed flowers, gold trim, Lenox palette mark* 105.00 120.00

☐ **Sugar and creamer,** *shape #733 and 734, hexagon shape, gold trim, Lenox palette mark* 47.50 55.00

☐ **Sugar and creamer,** *shape #743 and 744, gold trim over a pale tan background, overall effect attractive, Lenox palette mark* . 85.00 100.00

☐ **Sugar and creamer,** *shape #788 and 789, hexagon shape, hand-painted flowers (possibly bachelor buttons), gold trim, Lenox palette mark* 68.00 78.00

☐ **Sugar and creamer,** *shape #935 and 936, individual size, solid coral, Lenox wreath mark* 33.00 38.00

☐ **Sugar and creamer,** *shape #935 and 936, individual size, hand-painted floral spray, gold trim, artist signed and dated, Lenox palette mark, very pretty* 110.00 125.00

It is not always easy to tell if a Lenox sugar bowl had a lid or not, and we will solve the problem by listing, from old catalogue pictures, those sugars which did **not** have lids.

#38	#366	#598	#1183	#1948
#72-1/2	#543	#935	#1516	#2101
#183	#580	#1062		

Note: The #1948 sugar bowl, in addition to having no lid, also had no handles.

TEA BALLS

Lenox only made one type of tea ball, and this is unfortunately not always marked. It has a swirled rib effect and holes to let the tea brew. The top one fourth of the ball twists off to allow the tea to go in.

There are no verified examples of this tea ball to the best of our knowledge, and,therefore, there can be no prices. We would estimate the value of one at $75 to $150.

TEAPOTS

	Price Range	
☐ **Teapot**, *shape #88, 5-1/4", ribbed seashell effect, pale pink pearlized finish, speckled gold trim, C.A.C. lavender palette mark*	165.00	195.00
☐ **Teapot**, *shape #88, 5-1/4", ribbed seashell effect, gold trim, Lenox wreath mark*	105.00	120.00
☐ **Teapot**, *shape #88, 5-1/4", ribbed seashell effect, undecorated, Lenox palette mark*	68.00	78.00
☐ **Teapot**, *shape #101, 4-1/4" high, swan shape, very early and thin, undecorated, C.A.C. brown palette mark, lower half of swan's beak has 1/8" chip*	125.00	145.00
☐ **Teapot**, *shape #101, 4-1/4" high, swan shape, very early and thin, gold tracing on feathers and handle, unmarked*	135.00	155.00
☐ **Teapot**, *shape #167, 5" high, hand-painted red roses front and back, finial, handle and spout done in same red with gold highlighting, artist signed and dated, C.A.C. green palette mark*	165.00	195.00
☐ **Teapot**, *shape #167, 5" high, hand-painted bouquet of flowers on shaded brown background, gold trim on handle, spout and finial, C.A.C. lavender palette mark*	105.00	120.00
☐ **Teapot**, *shape #167, 5" high, hand-painted chrysanthemums in several colors, tiny flowers on lid, gold trim on spout, handle and finial, artist's initials and year, C.A.C. green palette mark*	80.00	95.00
☐ **Teapot**, *shape #167, 5" high, gold trim on handle, spout and finial, Lenox palette mark*	68.00	78.00
☐ **Teapot**, *shape #167, 5" high, small hand-painted violets in scatter pattern, brushed gold trim, C.A.C. red palette mark and Davis Collamore store mark, fleck on spout, crack in handle*	135.00	155.00
☐ **Teapot**, *shape #167, 5" high, undecorated, Lenox palette mark*	33.00	38.00
☐ **Teapot**, *shape #476, 7-1/4" spout to handle, square pedestal base, square handle, hand-painted roses and blue dot enamel work, the perfect example of an otherwise beautiful item ruined by messy gilding, artist signed, C.A.C. green palette mark*	165.00	195.00
☐ **Teapot**, *shape #476, 7-1/4" spout to handle, square pedestal base, square handle, hand-painted orchid, delicate gold filigree trim, unsigned but probably the work of W. H. Morley, transition mark*	225.00	275.00
☐ **Teapot**, *shape #476, 7-1/4" spout to handle, square pedestal base, square handle, undecorated, C.A.C. brown palette mark*	85.00	100.00
.☐ **Teapot**, *shape #476, 7-1/4" handle to spout, square peddstal base, squad, C.A.C. brown palette mark*	85.00	100.00

Price Range

☐ **Teapot,** *shape #476, 7-1/4" handle to spout, square pedestal base, square handle, orange lustre finish with gold trim and gold monogram, badly done, Lenox palette mark* 33.00   38.00

☐ **Teapot,** *shape #476, 7-1/4" spout to handle, square pedestal base, square handle, delicate gold filigree work on base, spout, midsection, handle and lid, transition mark* 105.00   120.00

☐ **Teapot,** *shape #522 7-1/2", infuser typen base, spout, midsection, handle and lid, transition mark* 105.00   120.00

☐ **Teapot,** *shape #522, 7-1/2", infuser type, overall brown glaze, Lenox wreath mark* 105.00   120.00

☐ **Teapot,** *shape #522, 7-1/2", infuser type, hand-painted fruit on shaded tan background, gold trim, beautiful artwork, infuser cracked, spider crack in bottom of pot, artist signed and dated, C.A.C. green palette mark* 105.00   120.00

☐ **Teapot,** *shape #522, 7-1/2", infuser type, undecorated, Lenox palette mark* 80.00   95.00

☐ **Teapot,** *shape #522, 7-1/2", infuser type, hand-painted roses, gold trim, infuser missing, Lenox palette mark* 60.00   70.00

☐ **Teapot,** *shape #522, 7-1/2", infuser type, geometric gold work, Lenox palette mark* 105.00   120.00

☐ **Teapot,** *shape #522, 7-1/2", infuser type, hand-painted small pink roses in scatter pattern, gold filigree trim, transition mark* 195.00   235.00

☐ **Teapot,** *shape #522, 7-1/2", infuser type, single yellow rose on front, bud on reverse side, gold trim, neatly done, Lenox palette mark* 135.00   155.00

☐ **Teapot,** *shape #522, 7-1/2", infuser type, hand-painted Oriental dragons in green, gold highlights on dragon, gold trim on handle, spout, and lid, one of the more original designs we have seen, Lenox palette mark* 170.00   200.00

Note: The infuser teapots sell somewhat higher than other types since they are avidly sought by tea drinkers as well as Lenox collectors. If the infuser is missing or unusable, the value drops below that of comparable teapots which are not the infuser type. The lid will not fit properly if the infuser is gone.

☐ **Teapot,** *shape #542, 3-1/4", angular shape, undecorated, Lenox palette mark* 33.00   38.00

☐ **Teapot,** *shape #542, 3-1/4", 3-1/4", angular shape, gold trim, Lenox palette mark* 47.50   55.00

☐ **Teapot,** *shape #579-1/2, 4-1/2", small hand-painted roses, gold trim, Lenox palette mark* 68.00   78.00

☐ **Teapot,** *shape #661, 4-1/2", hexagon shape, three small rosebuds on front, one bud on back, gold handle and trim, Lenox palette mark* 85.00   100.00

☐ **Teapot,** *shape #661, 4-1/2", hexagon shape, undecorated, Lenox wreath mark* 40.00   47.50

☐ **Teapot,** *shape #708, 5-3/8", hexagon shape, raised gold paste dots, artist signed, Lenox palette mark* 47.50   55.00

☐ **Teapot,** *shape #732, 6-1/4", hexagon shape, hand-painted leaves (possibly teagleaves) on both sidark* 47.50   55.00

☐ **Teapot,** *shape #732, 6-1/4" hexagon shape, hand-painted leaves (possibly tea leaves) on both sides, gold trim, rather attractive all things considered, artist signed, Lenox palette mark* 68.00   78.00

Price Range

☐ **Teapot,** *shape #732, 6-1/4", entire outside covered with a crudely done silver lustre effect, Lenox palette mark* 85.00 100.00

☐ **Teapot,** *shape #742, 6-1/8", hand-painted morning glories on ivory background, gold trim, tiny fleck on spout, Lenox palette mark* 105.00 120.00

☐ **Teapot,** *shape #742, 6-1/8", hand-painted pink and yellow roses, gold trim, not artist signed but similar to work done by Marsh, Lenox palette mark* 135.00 155.00

☐ **Teapot,** *shape #742, 6-1/8", hand-painted white roses surrounded by blue dot work, very professional look, gold trim, Lenox palette mark* 195.00 235.00

☐ **Teapot,** *shape #786, 5", tiny floral sprays, gold trim, artist's initials, Lenox palette mark* 85.00 100.00

☐ **Teapot,** *shape #786, 5", undecorated, Lenox palette mark* 18.50 23.50

☐ **Teapot,** *shape #786, 5", pencil-line gold trim and monogram, Lenox wreath mark* 33.00 38.00

☐ **Teapot,** *shape #888, 6-1/2", stylized tulips on black background, red trim, Lenox palette mark* 23.00 28.00

☐ **Teapot,** *shape #888, 6-1/2", transfer-decorated with Oriental scene, gold trim, Lenox palette mark* 47.50 55.00

☐ **Teapot,** *shape #888, 6-1/2", undecorated, Lenox palette mark* . 18.50 23.50

☐ **Teapot,** *shape #934, 4-3/4", individual size, undecorated, Lenox palette mark* 27.50 32.50

☐ **Teapot,** *shape #934, individual size, solid coral Lenox wreath mark* 33.00 38.00

☐ **Teapot,** *shape #934, 4-3/4", individual size, hand-painted small pink roses in scatter pattern, gold trim, Lenox wreath mark* ... 135.00 155.00

☐ **Teapot,** *shape #934, 4-3/4", individual size, hand-painted berries and leaves, artist signed and dated, gold trim, not bad, Lenox palette mark* 105.00 120.00

☐ **Teapot,** *shape #946, 3-3/4", hand-painted pansies on pale yellow shaded background, very pretty, handle and spout shade to a deeper yellow instead of having the usual gloppy gold, Lenox palette mark* 115.00 130.00

☐ **Teapot,** *shape #946, 3-3/4", hand-painted roses, pink on one side, red on the other, gold trim, artist signed, Lenox palette mark* 60.00 70.00

TEA STRAINERS

Tea strainers are very scarce, perhaps due more to excessive breakage than to limited production. The top half is never marked. All that we have seen have had the C.A.C. marks.

☐ **Tea strainer,** *shape #339, hand-painted roses and gold trim, transition mark* 260.00 320.00

☐ **Tea strainer,** *shape #339, hand-painted and signed by George Morley (both halves artist-signed for some reason), transition mark* 365.00 435.00

☐ **Tea strainer,** *shape #339, hand-painted flowers, C.A.C. palette mark* 195.00 235.00

☐ **Tea strainer,** *top half only, hand-painted violets, obviously factory done* 135.00 155.00

Tea strainer

	Price Range	
☐ **Tea strainer,** *bottom half only, hand-painted violets, C.A.C. palette mark*	47.50	55.00

Note: The above two items were never mates—the artwork is very different.

TOBACCO JARS

Lenox made only one true tobacco jar, but biscuit jars can also be considered tobacco jars depending on the style of decoration.

☐ **Tobacco jar,** *shape #328, 7-1/2" high, monochrome green, monk smoking cigarette, signed E.A. DeLan, transition mark* .	225.00	275.00
☐ **Tobacco jar,** *shape #328, 7-1/2" high, hand-painted ears of corn, C.A.C. palette mark, artist signed and dated*	135.00	155.00

Tobacco jar, *Lenox wreath mark*

Price Range

☐ **Tobacco jar,** *shape #328, 7-1/2" high, hand-painted Indian smoking peace pipe, Lenox palette mark* 175.00   220.00

☐ **Tobacco jar,** *no shape number, 5-1/2" high, Canada geese in flight, blue sky, green grass and swamp plants, signed W. H. Morley, Lenox wreath mark* 460.00   550.00

TRAYS

☐ **Tray,** *shape #15, 6-1/2" square, ruffled rim, plain white, Lenox palette mark* 27.50   32.50

☐ **Tray,** *shape #15, 6-1/2" square, ruffled rim, matte finish with raised gold paste decoration, C.A.C. red palette mark* 165.00   195.00

☐ **Tray,** *shape #15, 6-1/2" square, ruffled rim, hand-painted butterflies on blue background, gold trim on rim, Lenox palette mark* 40.00   47.50

☐ **Tray,** *shape #16, 9-3/4" square, ruffled rim, raised on four feet, hand-painted rose in center, gold trim on rim, C.A.C. green palette mark, probably home decorated but nicely done* 135.00   155.00

☐ **Tray,** *shape #16, 9-3/4" square, ruffled rim, raised on four feet, plain with gold trim, C.A.C. palette mark, several flecks on ruffled rim* 80.00   95.00

☐ **Tray,** *shape #17, 10-1/2" round, ruffled rim, plain, white, a few small flecks on rim, Lenox palette mark* 68.00   78.00

☐ **Tray,** *shape #17, 10-1/2" round, ruffled rim, white with gold trim, C.A.C. palette mark* 105.00   120.00

☐ **Tray,** *shape #132, 8" round, swirled ribs on rim, undecorated, C.A.C. palette mark* 105.00   120.00

☐ **Tray,** *shape #132, 8" round, swirled ribs on rim, undecorated, C.A.C. lavender palette mark* 60.00   70.00

☐ **Tray,** *shape #132, 8" round, swirled ribs on rim, gold tracings on scalloping, Lenox palette mark* 80.00   95.00

☐ **Tray,** *shape #137, 5-1/4" x 7-3/4", gourd shaped, ruffled rim, gold trim on rim and gold tracings in center, Lenox palette mark* 135.00   155.00

☐ **Tray,** *shape #148, 3-1/2" x 8-1/2", for pens, ruffled rim, Delft type scene in monochromatic blue, C.A.C. wreath mark* 170.00   220.00

☐ **Tray,** *shape #159, 8-1/4" x 11", ruffled rim, decorated with hand-painted and gold trim, C.A.C. green wreath mark, flecks on ruffles* 135.00   155.00

☐ **Tray,** *shape #159, 8-1/4" x 11", ruffled rim, plain white, flecks on rim, C.A.C. lavender palette mark* 68.00   78.00

☐ **Tray,** *shape #168, 3-1/4" x 5", ruffled rim, hand-painted fruit in center, Lenox green palette mark, artist signed and dated 1908* 90.00   110.00

☐ **Tray,** *shape #323, 7-1/8" x 11-3/8", embossed rim, hand-painted flowers in center and gold trim on rim, gold shows considerable wear, C.A.C. brown palette mark* 130.00   155.00

☐ **Tray,** *shape #323, 7-1/8" x 11-3/8", embossed rim, hand-painted violets, beautifully done, C.A.C. lavender palette mark* 130.00   155.00

☐ **Tray,** *shape #323, 7-1/8" x 11-3/8", embossed rim, small hand-painted roses with gold trim, C.A.C. green palette mark* 260.00   320.00

☐ **Tray,** *shape #616, 6", for pins, plain white, Lenox palette mark* 18.50   23.50

☐ **Tray,** *shape #616, 6", for pins, small bees and flowers on yellow background, Lenox palette mark* 68.00   78.00

Price Range

☐ **Tray,** *shape #616, 6", hand-painted small roses in scatter design, pencil-line gold on rim, Lenox wreath mark* 120.00 140.00

☐ **Tray,** *shape #617, 7-1/2", for pins, white with gold trim on rim and monogram in center, gold shows wear, C.A.C. green palette mark* 33.00 38.00

☐ **Tray,** *shape #617, 7-1/2", small hand-painted violets with gold trim on edge, C.A.C. pink palette mark and Bailey, Banks and Biddle store mark* 120.00 140.00

☐ **Tray,** *shape #617, pins, 7-1/2", plain white, Lenox palette mark* 23.00 28.00

☐ **Tray,** *shape #647, 13-1/4" x 7-3/4", orange poppy design, gold trim on rim, Lenox palette mark, artist's initials and date on bottom* 120.00 140.00

☐ **Tray,** *shape #647, 13-1/4" x 7-3/4", pink roses on green background, nicely done, Lenox palette mark* 135.00 155.00

☐ **Tray,** *shape #648, 5-1/4" square, plain white, C.A.C. lavender palette mark* 27.50 32.50

☐ **Tray,** *shape #648, 5-1/4" square, small hand-painted roses, transition mark* 105.00 120.00

☐ **Tray,** *shape #648, 5-1/4" square, entire rim done in very sloppy gold trim, Lenox palette mark* 33.00 38.00

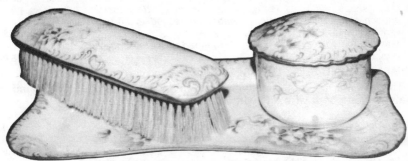

Tray, shape #323, hand-painted violets

☐ **Tray,** *shape #771, 14-1/2" x 6", gold trim on edges, wedding inscription in middle, slight wear on gold, Lenox palette mark .* 80.00 95.00

☐ **Tray,** *shape #898, 9-1/2" hexagon shape with handles, single large daffodil in center, gold trim on rim, Lenox palette mark, artist's initials* 135.00 155.00

☐ **Tray,** *shape #898, 9-1/2" hexagon shape, plain white, Lenox palette mark* 47.50 55.00

☐ **Tray,** *shape #898, 9-1/2" hexagon shape, white with gold trim, Lenox wreath mark* 68.00 78.00

☐ **Tray,** *shape #954, 9", round, handle, plain white, Lenox palette mark* 47.50 55.00

☐ **Tray,** *shape #954, 9" round, handled, hand-painted (nicely) with tulips and butterflies, Lenox palette mark, artist's initials and date on bottom* 165.00 195.00

☐ **Tray,** *shape #954, 9" round, handled, hand-painted in geometric enamels, artist's initials, Lenox palette mark* 85.00 100.00

	Price Range	

☐ **Tray,** *shape #955, 12" round, handled, gold trim, Lenox wreath mark* 68.00 78.00

☐ **Tray,** *shape #955, 12" round, handled, Art Nouveau enamel work, Lenox palette mark, artisst signed and dated* 165.00 195.00

☐ **Tray,** *shape #956, 14" round, handled, Art Nouveau style hand-painting with water lily design and gold trim, Lenox palette mark, artist initialed and dated* 135.00 155.00

☐ **Tray,** *shape #956, 14" round, handled, plain white, Lenox palette mark* 55.00 63.00

☐ **Tray,** *shape #957, 9" round, hand-painted with wildflowers design around rim, gold trim, gold handles, Lenox palette mark* 85.00 100.00

☐ **Tray,** *shape #957, 9" round, gold trim, monogram "C" in center, Lenox palette mark* 68.00 78.00

☐ **Tray,** *shape #958, 12" round, handled, hand-painted butterflies in center, gold trim, artist signed and dated, dreadful art work, Lenox palette mark* 85.00 100.00

☐ **Tray,** *shape #958, 12" round, handled, hand-painted with stylized tulips and gold trim, Lenox palette mark* 80.00 95.00

☐ **Tray,** *shape #959, 14" round, handled, undecorated, Lenox palette mark* 60.00 70.00

☐ **Tray,** *shape #959, 14" round, handled, gold trim, small chip on underside of one handle, Lenox wreath mark* 55.00 63.00

☐ **Tray,** *shape #983, 11-3/8" x 7-1/8", rounded-off corners, undecorated, unmarked, item number impressed in bottom verifies it's Lenox* 27.50 32.50

☐ **Tray,** *shape #983, 11-3/8" x 7-1/8", rounded-off corners, gold trim, Lenox palette mark* 68.00 78.00

TUMBLERS AND SHOT GLASSES

These items are not especially rare, and can occasionally be found in matched sets both with and without pitchers or whiskey jugs.

☐ **Shot glass,** *shape #269, undecorated, Lenox palette mark* 15.00 20.00

☐ **Shot glass,** *shape #269, tiny ears or corn hand-painted on front, gold trim, Lenox palette mark* 27.50 32.50

☐ **Shot glass,** *shape #269, hand-painted plums on green shaded background, C.A.C. green palette mark* 40.00 47.50

☐ **Shot glass,** *shape #269, gold trim, Lenox wreath mark* 15.00 20.00

☐ **Shot glass,** *shape #394, hand-painted berries on plain background, gold trim, artist's initials and date* 23.00 28.00

☐ **Tumbler,** *shape number unknown, 4" high, undecorated, Lenox palette mark* 27.50 32.50

VASES AND URNS

We will not attempt to differentiate between urns and vases here, but instead will refer to all the items as vases. The term urn can be loosely applied to any large, ornamental, usually footed vase.

☐ **Vase,** *item #27, 7-1/2" high, bulbous bottom, undecorated, Lenox wreath mark* 18.50 23.50

☐ **Vase,** *item #27, 7-1/2" high, bulbous bottom, white top with coral bottom, Lenox wreath mark, see photo* 33.00 38.00

Vase, *item #27, bulbous bottom*

	Price Range	
☐ **Vase,** *item #27, 7-1/2" high, bulbous bottom, white bottom with blue top, Lenox wreath mark*	33.00	38.00
☐ **Vase,** *item #27, 7½" high, bulbous, bottom, beige matte finish with raised gold paste work, lavender palette C.A.C. mark*	105.00	120.00
Note: Item #27 is the only item from ihe early catalogues to have survived down to the present day in its original shape and size.		
☐ **Vase,** *item #28, 7-1/2" high, bulbous bottom, one handle, white with gold trim, Lenox palette mark*	40.00	47.50
☐ **Vase,** *item #28, 7-1/2" high, bulbous bottom, one handle, undecorated, Lenox wreath mark*	27.50	32.50
☐ **Vase,** *item #28, 7-1/2" high, bulbous bottom, one handle, brushed gold near rim, gold filigree work on handle, transition mark*	105.00	120.00
☐ **Vase,** *item #29, 7-1/2" high, bulbous bottom, two handles, white bottom with blue top and handles, Lenox wreath mark* . .	40.00	47.50
☐ **Vase,** *item #29, 7-1/2" high, bulbous bottom, two handles, undecorated, Levox wreath mark*	27.50	32.50
☐ **Vase,** *item #29, 7-1/2" high, bulbous bottom, two handles, undecorated, Lenox wreath mark*	27.50	32.50
☐ **Vase,** *item #29, 7-1/2" high, bulbous bottom, two handles, yellow and white floral trim, C.A.C. green palette mark*	55.00	63.00
☐ **Vase,** *item #29, 7-1/2" high, bulbous bottom, two handles, transfer decoration on bottom part, gold trim on handles and neck, really bad, Lenox palette mark*	18.50	23.50
☐ **Vase,** *item #30, 6-3/4" high, long neck, two handles, undecorated C.A.C. green palette mark*	55.00	63.00
☐ **Vase,** *item #30, 6-3/4" high, long neck two handles, beige matte finish with gold trim on handles and inside the rim, C.A.C. lavender palette mark*	135.00	155.00
☐ **Vase,** *item #30, 6-3/4" high, long neck, two handles, Art Nouveau style grapes with gold trim, C.A.C. brown palette mark*	135.00	155.00

Price Range

☐ **Vase,** *item #31, 6-3/4" high, long neck, two handles, yellow and orange hand-painted daisies on pale blue background, Lenox palette mark* 80.00   95.00

☐ **Vase,** *item #31, 6-3/4" high, long neck, two handles, transfer decorated with portrait of a woman, gold trim on handles and inside rim, C.A.C. green palette mark* 80.00   95.00

☐ **Vase,** *item #31, 6-3/4" high, long neck, two handles, pink lustre exterior, gold trim on handles, Lenox palette mark* 33.00   38.00

☐ **Vase,** *item #32, 6-3/4" high, long neck, two handles, not decorated, C.A.C. green palette mark* 40.50   47.50

☐ **Vase,** *item #32, 6-3/4" high, long neck, two handles, gold grapes with black outlining, gold trim on handles, C.A.C. lavender palette mark* 47.50   55.00

☐ **Vase,** *item #34, 9" high, long neck, two handles, geometric enamel trim, gold handles and gold trim top and bottom, Lenox palette mark* 68.00   78.00

☐ **Vase,** *item #34, 9" high, long neck, two handles, undecorated, C.A.C. brown palette mark* 80.00   95.00

☐ **Vase,** *item #34, 9" high, long neck, two handles, rainbow shaded from lavender to yellow, speckled gold over the shading, gold trim on handles and rims, rather strange-looking but nicely done and interesting, C.A.C. lavender palette mark* 195.00   235.00

☐ **Vase,** *item #35, 7-1/2" high, undecorated, C.A.C. green palette mark* 80.00   95.00

☐ **Vase,** *item #35, 7-1/2" high, hand-painted in center, gold trim, artist signed and dated on bottom, C.A.C. green palette mark* . 135.00   155.00

☐ **Vase,** *item #49, 10-1/4" high, bulbous shape with ruffled rim, melon-ribbed effect, white shading to deep turquoise, very nice raised gold paste around middle, transition mark* 300.00   360.00

☐ **Vase,** *item #49, 10-1/4" high, undecorated, Lenox palette mark* 105.00   120.00

☐ **Vase,** *item #52, 10-1/2" high, undecorated, Lenox palette mark* 80.00   95.00

Vase, *item #52, lavendar palette mark*

Price Range

☐ **Vase,** *item #52, 10-1/2" high, beige matte finish, hand-painted pink flowers and green leaves all outlined with gold tracing, gold handles and trim, C.A.C. lavender palette mark* 260.00 320.00

☐ **Vase,** *item #52, 10-1/2" high, red, white and pink hand-painted roses, gold trim, artist signed, Lenox palette mark* 85.00 100.00

☐ **Vase,** *item #81, 6-1/4" high, Lenox Rose trim with gold, Lenox wreath mark* 40.00 47.50

☐ **Vase,** *item #81, 6-1/4" high, undecorated, Lenox palette mark* . 18.50 23.50

☐ **Vase,** *item #81, 6-1/4" high, hand-painted flowers, gold trim, C.A.C. green palette mark* 80.00 95.00

☐ **Vase,** *item #81, 6-1/4" high, undecorated and unmarked* 13.00 16.00

☐ **Vase,** *item #83, 11" high, twisted neck, four side openings and top opening, gold paste trim, C.A.C. lavender palette mark* ... 260.00 320.00

Vase, *item #81, Lenox rose trim*

☐ **Vase,** *item #86, 8-1/2" high, matte finish with brushed gold and tiny blue forget-me-nots on both sides, gold paste leaves, C.A.C. lavender palette mark* 135.00 155.00

☐ **Vase,** *item #86, 8-1/2" high, undecorated, Lenox wreath mark* . 33.00 38.00

☐ **Vase,** *item #86, 8-1/2" high, white with gold trim, Lenox wreath mark* 37.00 43.00

☐ **Vase,** *item #86, 8-1/2" high, coral, Lenox wreath mark* 42.00 48.00

Note: Item #86 is frequently called the "aorta vase" due to its resemblance to a human heart with arteries coming out from it. It is also sometimes referred to as an "onion vase". Lenox catalogues call it simply "four-part flower holder."

☐ **Vase,** *item #109, 7-3/4" high, two handles, narrow tall neck with ruffled rim, hand-painted roses in pink and red, gold trim on handles and rim, C.A.C. green palette mark* 165.00 195.00

☐ **Vase,** *item #109, 7-3/4" high, two handles, narrow tall neck, hand-painted dog on shaded background, gold trim on handles and rim, C.A.C. green palette mark, artist signed and date, not bad* 195.00 235.00

Vase, *item #86*

Price Range

☐ **Vase,** *item #110, 7-3/4" high, same as #109 except handles different, undecorated, Lenox palette mark* 85.00   100.00

☐ **Vase,** *item #110, 7-3/4" high, same as #109 except handles different, hand-painted jonquils on blue background, gold trim on handles and rim, C.A.C. green palette mark* 175.00   225.00

☐ **Vase,** *item #119, 11-1/4" high, hand-painted lilies with gold trim, artist signed and dated, nicely done, C.A.C. green palette mark* 330.00   395.00

☐ **Vase,** *item #120, 7-1/2" high, undecorated, unmarked* 68.00   78.00

☐ **Vase,** *7-1/2" high, hand-painted with morning glories and gold trim, Lenox palette mark* 80.00   95.00

☐ **Vase,** *item #122, 7-3/4" high, same shape as #109 but no handles, hand-painted chrysanthemums on shaded brown background, unsigned but possibly the work of Morley, transition mark* 260.00   320.00

☐ **Vase,** *item #122, 7-3/4" high, hand-painted nasturtium on shaded background, artist signed and dated, C.A.C. green palette mark* 165.00   195.00

☐ **Vase,** *item #126, 7-1/2" high, brushed gold trim near top and bottom, Lenox palette mark* 90.00   110.00

☐ **Vase,** *item #126, 7-1/2" high, hand-painted wildflowers with gold trim, artist signed and dated, C.A.C. green palette mark* . .   110.00   125.00

☐ **Vase,** *item #129, 7-1/2" high, undecorated, Lenox green wreath mark, yellow and white* 80.00   95.00

☐ **Vase,** *item #129, 7-1/2" high, cabbage roses in yellow and pink, gold rims, and handles, C.A.C. palette mark* 105.00   120.00

☐ **Vase,** *item #129, 7-1/2" high, floral spray on cream background, Lenox palette mark* 135.00   155.00

☐ **Vase,** *item #131, 11-1/4" high, undecorated, C.A.C. palette mark* 165.00   195.00

Price Range

☐ **Vase**, *covered, item #145, 11-1/2" high, white and pink roses in garlands from the top, cream background, gold trim on handles and rim, C.A.C. palette mark* 330.00   395.00

☐ **Vase**, *item #199, 8-1/2" high, sponged gold effect on embossed portions of vase, C.A.C. wreath mark* 330.00   395.00

☐ **Vase**, *item #218, 15-1/2" high, trumpet shaped, undecorated, C.A.C. green palette mark* 68.00   78.00

☐ **Vase**, *item #218, 15-1/2" high, trumpet shaped, green vines coming down sides, gold trim top and bottom, Lenox palette mark* 165.00   195.00

☐ **Vase**, *item #224, 12-3/4" high, celadon green with gold trim, Lenox wreath mark* 120.00   140.00

☐ **Vase**, *item #224, 12-3/4" high, yellow roses on pale pink background, gold trim, C.A.C. green Balette mark* 165.00   195.00

☐ **Vase**, *item #265, 7-1/2" high, mottled spongeware type decoration with gold trim, Lenox palette mark* 47.50   55.00

☐ **Vase**, *item #265, 7-1/2" high, red, white and pink roses, gold trim, artist signed, C.A.C. palette mark* 135.00   155.00

☐ **Vase**, *item #272, 12-1/2" high, undecorated, Lenox palette mark* 225.00   275.00

☐ **Vase**, *item #272, 12-1/2" high, Victorian garden scene with man and woman, pastel colors, unmarked, unsigned but looks very much like the work of Heidrich* 400.00   470.00

☐ **Vase**, *item #289, 3-1/4" high, overall chrysanthemum decoration, excellent color and artwork, C.A.C. palette mark* 80.00   95.00

☐ **Vase**, *item #289, 3-1/4" high, gold rim and base, gold birds in flight on black background, Oriental look, Lenox palette mark* 68.00   78.00

☐ **Vase**, *item #289, overall design of small pink roses, C.A.C. red palette mark* 90.00   110.00

☐ **Vase**, *item #296, 11" high, tropical seascape with seagulls, moon, sailboat and palm trees, artist signed and dated, Lenox palette mark* 165.00   195.00

Vase, *item #314, by Sully*

Vase, *item #315, pheasants*

Price Range

☐ **Vase,** *item #296, 11" high, cabbage roses, gold trim on top and bottom, C.A.C. palette mark* 175.00 220.00
☐ **Vase,** *item #297, 8-1/4" high, gold colored vines with black outlining and geometrics, Lenox palette mark* 120.00 140.00
☐ **Vase,** *item #314, 8" high, portrait of young girl standing in a rose garden, gold on rim, signed Sully, transition mark* 300.00 360.00
☐ **Vase,** *item #314, 8" high, outdoor scene of lake and swans, good artwork, artist signed and dated, C.A.C. green palette mark* 300.00 360.00
☐ **Vase,** *item #314, 8" high, overall rose decoration, gold trim on rim, C.A.C. palette mark* 195.00 235.00

Vase, *item #318, springer spaniel*

Price Range

☐ **Vase,** *item #314, 8" high, Art Nouveau florals in red, black and gold, gold trim on rim, Lenox palette mark* 105.00   120.00

☐ **Vase,** *item #315, 5-3/4" high, monochromatic blues, male and female pheasant on ground, C.A.C. wreath mark* 225.00   275.00

☐ **Vase,** *item #315, 5-3/4" high, two finches in flight, monochromatic blue, very similar to above item in general look but not by same artist, C.A.C. wreath mark (decorating style very similar to items done by S. Laurence at Rookwood)* 225.00   275.00

☐ **Vase,** *item #315, 5-3/4" high, undecorated, Lenox wreath mark*   18.50   23.50

☐ **Vase,** *item #315, pink lustre exterior, gold trim on rim, Lenox palette mark* 23.00   28.00

☐ **Vase,** *item #316, 9" high, hand-painted roses, gold trim, Lenox palette mark* 68.00   78.00

☐ **Vase,** *item #316, 9" high, yellow daffodils on blue background, artist signed and dated, C.A.C. green palette mark* 135.00   155.00

☐ **Vase,** *item #318, 8-1/4" high, portrait of springer spaniel on cream background, back of piece marked "Hunter Arms Co. First Prize", signed Baker, Lenox wreath mark* 300.00   360.00

☐ **Vase,** *item #318, 8-1/4" high, hand-painted jonquils on shaded purplish-red and green background, signed "Des", gold trim inside rim, transition mark with Glen-Iris stamp* 300.00   360.00

Vase, *item #318, jonquils*

☐ **Vase,** *item #318, Oriental motif with dragons and geometric design, red, black and gold, artist signed and dated, Lenox palette mark* 165.00   195.00

☐ **Vase,** *item #318, 8-1/4" high, seascape signed by DeLan and bearing both the Lenox and DeLan & McGill marks* 400.00   470.00

☐ **Vase,** *item #319, 9-1/4" high, top part aqua with raised gold work, bottom half creamy color with garlands of blue dot and gold paste work, C.A.C. lavender palette mark* 120.00   140.00

Vase, *item #319, aqua top*

	Price Range	
☐ **Vase,** *item #319, 9-1/4" high, hand-painted purple irises on green background, below-average artwork, C.A.C. green palette mark*	68.00	78.00
☐ **Vase,** *item #319, 9-1/4" high, overall floral decoration, no artist signature, transition mark*	225.00	275.00
☐ **Vase,** *item #320, 10-1/4" high, various shadings of color forming attractive background for raised enamel work in a latticework pattern, C.A.C. lavender palette mark*	165.00	195.00
☐ **Vase,** *item #320, 10-1/4" high, gold iris decoration on white shading to turquoise, gold trim on rim, transition mark*	175.00	220.00

Vase, *item #326, jonquils*

Price Range

☐ **Vase**, item #326, 9" high, jonquils on purplish-red and green background, no artist signature, gold trim on rim, transition mark and Glen-Iris stamp 300.00   360.00

☐ **Vase**, item #326, 9" high, enameled flowers, artist signed and dated, C.A.C. palette mark 47.50   55.00

☐ **Vase**, item #326, 9" high, portrait of Victorian woman artist signed, gold trim, C.A.C. green palette mark 240.00   290.00

☐ **Vase**, item #355, 8-1/2", yellow, L opaque mark 80.00   95.00

☐ **Vase**, item #355, 8-1/2" high, pink, L opaque mark 75.00   85.00

☐ **Vase**, item #355, 8-1/2", hand-painted water lilies, fair artwork, artist signed, C.A.C. green palette mark 170.00   200.00

☐ **Vase**, item #355, 8-1/2", peacock feathers hand-painted to form panels, gold trim, Lenox palette mark 140.00   160.00

☐ **Vase**, item #355, 8-1/2" high, Dutch scene, polychromatic, C.A.C. green palette mark 225.00   275.00

☐ **Vase**, item #355, 8-1/2" high, undecorated, Lenox wreath mark   33.00   38.00

☐ **Vase**, item #355, 8-1/2" high, pink wcth gold trim, Lenox wreath mark 68.00   78.00

☐ **Vase**, item #355, 8-1/2" high, Ming pattern, Lenox wreath mark   150.00   175.00

☐ **Vase**, item #356, 7" high, bittersweet blossom and berry design, gold trim, C.A.C. green palette mark 165.00   195.00

☐ **Vase**, item #356, 7" high, blue and gold Art Nouveau stylized lilies, Lenox palette mark 80.00   95.00

☐ **Vase**, item #368, 9-7/8" high, hand-painted deep red cabbage roses, gold trim on top and bottom, artist signed and dated, C.A.C. lavender palette mark 235.00   285.00

☐ **Vase**, item #368, 9-7/8" high, hand-painted poppies on tan background, C.A.C. green palette mark 195.00   235.00

☐ **Vase**, item #369, 13" high, undecorated, Lenox palette mark .. 55.00   63.00

☐ **Vase**, item #369, 13" high, hand-painted morning glories on tan background, artist's initials, C.A.C. green palette mark 110.00   125.00

☐ **Vase**, item #370, 13" high, yellow crocuses on shaded brown background, gold trim on rim, Lenox palette mark 165.00   195.00

☐ **Vase**, item #381, undecorated, Lenox wreath mark 60.00   70.00

☐ **Vase**, item #409, 8-1/4" high, overall design of small hand-painted violets, gold trim, transition mark 165.00   195.00

☐ **Vase**, item #412, 9" high, ball-shaped with narrow neck, hand-painted chrysanthemums on brown background, signed W. H. Morley, transition mark 400.00   470.00

☐ **Vase**, item #412, 9" high, hand-painted cabbage roses, gold trim, artist signed and dated, C.A.C. green palette mark 165.00   195.00

☐ **Vase**, item #412, 9" high, undecorated, Lenox palette mark .. 55.00   63.00

☐ **Vase**, item #416, 5-3/4" high, hand-painted portrait of girl with roses in her hair, badly done, artist signed, Lenox palette mark   135.00   155.00

☐ **Vase**, item #420, 5" high, hand-painted ivy on off-white background, gold trim, nicely done, artist signed and dated, C.A.C. palette mark 135.00   155.00

☐ **Vase**, item #420, 5" high, hand-painted buttercups on blue background, Lenox palette mark 40.00   47.50

☐ **Vase**, item #425, 12-1/4" high, hand-painted roses, gold trim on handles and on lid finial, artist signed and dated, not bad artwork for type, C.A.C. lavender palette mark 330.00   395.00

Vase, item #426

Price Range

☐ **Vase,** item #426, 11" high, lid missing, monochromatic blue
portrait of man, dated 1894 and signed by Sturgis Laurence,
C.A.C. wreath mark 525.00   625.00
☐ **Vase,** item #427, 11" high, portrait of girl wreathed by raised
gold paste work, maroon over rest of urn with more gold paste,
gold handles and trim on rim, signed Campana, transition
mark, size and type of trim put item into the "pay whatever you
have to" category.

Vase, item #427, portrait of girl

Vase, *item #428, orange poppies*

Price Range

☐ **Vase,** *item #428, 8-1/4" high, orange poppies on shaded green background, gold trim on handles, base and rim, home-decorated but nice, C.A.C. green palette mark* 320.00   380.00

☐ **Vase,** *item #428, 8-1/4" high, pink roses on shaded background, gold handles and rim, C.A.C. green palette mark* .   300.00   360.00

☐ **Vase,** *item #429, 13-1/2" high, undecorated, C.A.C. green palette mark* 105.00   120.00

☐ **Vase,** *item #429, 13-1/2" high, gold trim, C.A.C. lavender palette mark* 135.00   155.00

☐ **Vase,** *item #430, 16" high, monochromatic blue Dutch type scene, transition mark* 370.00   440.00

☐ **Vase,** *item #431, 15" high, hand-painted begonias on tan background, gold trim on handles, foot and rim, Lenox palette mark* 260.00   320.00

☐ **Vase,** *item #433, 15-1/4" high, hand-painted portrait of Victorian woman, blue dot enamel trim, gold on handles and rims, repaired on one handle, C.A.C. green palette mark* 400.00   470.00

☐ **Vase,** *item #435, 16-1/2" high, hand-painted pink roses on one side, yellow roses on other side, shaded background, gold trim, artist signed and dated, C.A.C. lavender palette mark* . . .   400.00   470.00

☐ **Vase,** *item #436, 14" high, hand-painted Grecian temple scene, gold trim, artist signed, home decorated but overall effect rather nice, Lenox, palette mark* 365.00   435.00

☐ **Vase,** *item #437, 12" high, undecorated, unmarked* 105.00   120.00

☐ **Vase,** *item #438, 13" high, hand-painted irises in blue and burgundy on off-white background, gold trim on handles and rim, artist signed, C.A.C. green palette mark* 260.00   320.00

☐ **Vase,** *item #439, 11" high, hand-painted chrysanthemums in orange and yellow on shaded tan background, gold trim on handles, Lenox palette mark* 330.00   395.00

Price Range

☐ **Vase**, *item #442, 17" high, hand-painted cabbage roses on shaded green background, gold trim, Lenox palette mark* 225.00 275.00

☐ **Vase**, *item #445, 16-3/4" high, gold trim, no Lenox mark* 90.00 110.00

☐ **Vase**, *item #451, 10-1/2" high, hand-done with geometric enamel designs, gold trim on rim, artist's initials and date, Lenox palette mark* 80.00 95.00

☐ **Vase**, *item #451 10-1/2" high, hand-painted tulips and daffodils on pink background, 1/4" chip on rim, C.A.C. palette mark* 105.00 120.00

☐ **Vase**, *item #452, 11-1/4" high, hand-painted pink roses with baby's breath on green background, gold trim on rim, Lenox palette mark* 135.00 155.00

☐ **Vase**, *item #452, 11-1/4" high, pink and white peonies on green background, gold trim, Lenox palette mark* 135.00 155.00

☐ **Vase**, *item #452, 11-1/4" high, hand-painted birds on a pine branch, muted effect as if viewed through a mist, artist's initials, C.A.C. palette mark* 305.00 365.00

☐ **Vase**, *item #453, 12" high, hand-painted purple iris on one side and one gold iris on other side, green leaves, neck of vase done in green, gold trim, C.A.C. lavender palette mark, artist signed* 210.00 255.00

☐ **Vase**, *item #454, 9-1/2" high, undecorated, Lenox palette mark* 47.50 55.00

☐ **Vase**, *item #454, 9-1/2" high, hand-painted roses in pink on plain background, gold trim, signed Marsh, transition mark* ... 400.00 470.00

☐ **Vase**, *item #459, 13" high, hand-painted purple and red grapes, shaded yellow and green background, gold trim on inside of rim, transition mark* 400.00 470.00

☐ **Vase**, *item #470, 18-1/2", high, plain with gold trim, Lenox wreath mark* 155.00 185.00

☐ **Vase**, *item #493, 14-3/4" high, hand-painted purple orchid on one side, yellow orchid on other, gold trim on top and bottom, transition mark* 525.00 625.00

☐ **Vase**, *item #501, 6" high, overall small pink rose design, gold trim on top rim, transition mark* 120.00 140.00

☐ **Vase**, *item #501, 6" high, hand-painted orange and pink poppies on tan background, Lenox palette mark* 105.00 120.00

☐ **Vase**, *item #501, 6" high, undecorated, Lenox palette mark, small fleck on rim* 18.50 23.50

☐ **Vase**, *item #502, 6" high, bayberry decoration on white background, silver trim on handles, artist signed, Lenox palette mark* 105.00 120.00

☐ **Vase**, *item #502, 6" high, magnolia blossoms on pale green background, Lenox palette mark* 80.00 95.00

☐ **Vase**, *item #503, 8" tall, Siamese cat on tan background, Lenox palette mark* 195.00 235.00

☐ **Vase**, *item #503, 8" tall, scattered butterflies on blue background, gold trim inside rim, C.A.C. green palette mark* .. 80.00 95.00

☐ **Vase**, *item #504, 10-1/2" high, monochromatic monk scene, transition mark* 400.00 470.00

☐ **Vase**, *item #505, 4-1/2" high, black exterior with pencil-line gold trim on rim, Lenox wreath mark* 260.00 320.00

☐ **Vase**, *item #505, 14-1/2" high, red berries and green leaves on shaded brown background, gold trim on rim, C.A.C. green palette mark* 330.00 395.00

☐ **Vase**, *item #506, 14-3/8" high, undecorated, Lenox wreath mark* 80.00 95.00

Price Range

☐ **Vase,** *item #506, 14-3/8" high, white with gold trim, Lenox palette mark* 85.00   100.00

☐ **Vase,** *item #507, 6-1/4" high, hand-painted flowering vines down sides, Lenox palette mark* 68.00   78.00

☐ **Vase,** *item #508, 12" high, hand-painted Grecian woman with flowing robes in pinkish background, garlands of roses, artist signed, Lenox palette mark* 330.00   395.00

☐ **Vase,** *item #525, 15" high, spray of fall flowers on shaded background, transition mark* 400.00   470.00

☐ **Vase,** *item #525, 15" undecorated, C.A.C. green palette mark* . 105.00   120.00

☐ **Vase,** *item #528, 15-1/2" high, bunch of violets, gold pencil-line on rim, Lenox palette mark* 195.00   235.00

☐ **Vase,** *item #528, 15-1/2" high, polychromatic monk scene all the way around, hairline crack about 2" long, transition mark* . 165.00   195.00

☐ **Vase,** *item #529, 12" high, metallic gold and copper hand-painted design in geometric pattern, Lenox palette mark* 105.00   120.00

☐ **Vase,** *item #530, 15" high, hand-painted background with transfer decoration of military figures, gold trim on rim, Lenox palette mark* 165.00   195.00

☐ **Vase,** *item #559, 3" high, hand-painted scattered rosebud design, gold trim, C.A.C. palette mark* 105.00   120.00

☐ **Vase,** *item #574, 4" high, hand-painted orange berries and brown branches on white background, gold trim on rim, Lenox palette mark* 55.00   63.00

☐ **Vase,** *item #574, 4" high, monochromatic green chrysanthemum design, transition mark* 135.00   155.00

☐ **Vase,** *item #576, 3-1/8" high, enamel panels in different colors separated by gold trim, Lenox palette mark* 18.50   23.50

☐ **Vase,** *item #605, 3-3/4" high, undecorated, Lenox wreath mark* 18.50   23.50

☐ **Vase,** *item #877, 12-1/2" high, gold handles and gold initial on front, Lenox palette mark* 80.00   95.00

☐ **Vase,** *item #877, 12-1/2" high, coral with white handles, Lenox wreath mark* 68.00   78.00

☐ **Vase,** *item #877, 12-1/2" high, undecorated, Lenox palette mark* 60.00   70.00

☐ **Vase,** *item #879, 7" high, hand-painted dog on one side, cat on other, blue background, nicely done, Lenox palette mark* 225.00   275.00

☐ **Vase,** *item #880 7-7/8" high, Art Deco style geometric banding in vibrant colors, Lenox palette mark* 33.00   38.00

☐ **Vase,** *item #897, 12-1/4" high, plain with gold trim on feet and rim, Lenox wreath mark* 55.00   63.00

☐ **Vase,** *item #897, 12-1/4" high, hand-painted daisies on pale orange background, gold trim on rim and feet, Lenox palette mark* 68.00   78.00

☐ **Vase,** *item #897, 12-1/4" high, undecorated, Lenox palette mark* 50.00   58.00

☐ **Vase,** *item #919, blue with white handles, Lenox wreath mark* . 60.00   70.00

☐ **Vase,** *item #919, blue with white handles, Lenox wreath mark* . 60.00   70.00

☐ **Vase,** *item #919, all coral, Lenox wreath mark* 68.00   78.00

☐ **Vase,** *item #922, 10-3/4" high, hand-painted horse head on blue background, artist signed, Lenox palette mark* 165.00   195.00

☐ **Vase,** *item #922, 10-3/4" high, undecorated, Lenox wreath mark* 47.50   55.00

☐ **Vase,** *item #922, 10-3/4" high, light pink, Lenox wreath mark* . . 40.00   47.50

☐ **Vase,** *item #937, 5-7/8" high, turquoise panels alternating with peacock feathers, gold trim, Lenox palette mark* 33.00   38.00

Price Range

☐ **Vase,** *item #937, 5-7/8" high, gold trim and initial on front, artist signed, Lenox palette mark* 18.50   23.50

☐ **Vase,** *item #1025, 8" high, hexagon shape, each panel done in a different enamel color, Lenox palette mark* 23.00   28.00

☐ **Vase,** *item #1025, 8" high, undecorated, Lenox wreath mark* .. 16.50   21.50

☐ **Vase,** *item #1036, 8" high, hand-painted berries and leaves on brown background, artist signed, Lenox palette mark* 33.00   38.00

☐ **Vase,** *item #1036, 8" high, geometric pattern in American Indian style, artist's initials, Lenox palette mark* 40.00   47.50

☐ **Vase,** *item #1053, 15-1/4" high, hand-painted grapes and leaves on pale yellow background, Lenox palette mark* 260.00   320.00

☐ **Vase,** *item #1053, 15-1/4" high, undecorated, Lenox wreath mark* 55.00   63.00

☐ **Vase,** *item #1063, 5-3/4" high, shaded from light to dark green, Lenox wreath mark* 40.00   47.50

☐ **Vase,** *item #1063, 5-3/4" high, Lenox Rose pattern with gold trim* 33.00   38.00

☐ **Vase,** *item #1063, 5-3/4" high, gold covering outside of vase, artist's initials, Lenox palette mark* 18.50   23.50

☐ **Vase,** *item #1099, 7-1/2" high, hand-painted finch on oak leaf branch, shaded tan background, beautifully done, Lenox palette mark* 165.00   195.00

☐ **Vase,** *item #1099, 7-1/2" high, undecorated, Lenox palette mark* 27.50   32.50

☐ **Vase,** *item #1185, 10" high, orange blossoms on off-white to blue background, marriage inscription on bottom, Lenox palette mark* 135.00   155.00

☐ **Vase,** *item #1185, 10" high, celadon green with gold trim on trim, Lenox wreath mark* 68.00   78.00

☐ **Vase,** *item #1308, 7" high, slight fan shape, light blue, Lenox wreath mark* 33.00   38.00

Vase, *item #1308, fan shape*

Price Range

☐ **Vase,** item #1308, 7" high, slight fan shape, dark green with gold trim, Lenox wreath mark 55.00 63.00

☐ **Vase,** item #1308, 7" high, slight fan shape, Lenox Rose pattern with gold trim, Lenox wreath mark 42.00 48.00

☐ **Vase,** item #1308, 7" high, slight fan shape, yellow, Lenox wreath mark 47.50 55.00

☐ **Vase,** item #1308, 7" high, slight fan shape, undecorated, Lenox palette mark 18.50 23.50

☐ **Vase,** item #1309, 4-1/4" high, slight fan shape, undecorated, Lenox palette mark 23.00 28.00

☐ **Vase,** item #1309, 4-1/4" high, slight fan shape, celadon green, Lenox wreath mark 30.00 35.00

☐ **Vase,** item #1309, 4-1/4" high, gold trim, Lenox wreath mark ... 23.00 28.00

☐ **Vase,** item #1310, 2-7/8" high, slight fan shape, gold trim, Lenox wreath mark 18.50 23.50

☐ **Vase,** item #1310, 2-7/8" high, light blue, Lenox wreath mark .. 18.50 23.50

☐ **Vase,** item #1311, 2-7/8" high, coral, Lenox wreath mark 18.50 23.50

☐ **Vase,** item #1311, 2-7/8" high, light pink, Lenox wreath mark .. 15.00 20.00

☐ **Vase,** item #1311, 2-7/8" high, undecorated and unmarked 6.75 7.75

☐ **Vase,** item #1312, 8-3/4" high, hand-painted cabbage roses on multi-colored background, artist signed and dated, Lenox palette mark 150.00 175.00

☐ **Vase,** item #1316, 11-3/4" high, apple green, Lenox wreath mark 105.00 120.00

☐ **Vase,** item #1316, 11-3/4" high, green and brown vines coming down from top, gold trim, Lenox palette mark 110.00 125.00

☐ **Vase,** item #1378, 11-3/4" high, pale blue exterior, plain Lenox inside, Lenox palette mark 105.00 120.00

☐ **Vase,** item #1378, 11-3/4" high, hand-painted grapes and leaves on tan background, nicely done, artist signed, Lenox palette mark 225.00 275.00

☐ **Vase,** item #1479, bulbous, Ming pattern with yellow banding top and bottom, probably a one of a kind item, Lenox wreath mark 195.00 235.00

☐ **Vase,** item #1715, 7-1/4" high, coral, Lenox wreath mark 68.00 78.00

☐ **Vase,** item #1717, 11-1/2" high, cylinder shape, white, Lenox wreath mark 40.00 47.50

☐ **Vase,** item #1717, 11-1/2" high, coral, cylinder shape, Lenox wreath mark 47.50 55.00

☐ **Vase,** item #1717, 11-1/2" high, transfer decorated with seahorses and gold trim on turquoise background, Lenox wreath mark 75.00 85.00

☐ **Vase,** item #1718, 10-1/8" high, powder blue, Lenox wreath mark 47.50 55.00

☐ **Vase,** item #1718, 10-1/8" high, coral, Lenox wreath mark 50.00 58.00

☐ **Vase,** item #1724, 13" high, bulbous bottom bud vase, Art Deco style banding, Lenox palette mark 30.00 35.00

☐ **Vase,** item #1724, 13" high, undecorated, Lenox wreath mark . 27.50 32.50

☐ **Vase,** item #1724, 13" high, white with gold trim, Lenox palette mark 37.00 43.00

☐ **Vase,** item #1725, 10" high, hand-painted tiny roses and gold trim, Lenox palette mark 47.50 55.00

	Price Range	
☐ **Vase,** *item #1725, 10" high, pale blue exterior, gold pencil-line on rim, Lenox wreath mark*	40.00	47.50
☐ **Vase,** *item #1726, 8" high, 1/2" gold band at top, Lenox wreath mark*	27.50	32.50
☐ **Vase,** *item #1726, 8" high, hand-painted berries, gold trim on rim, Lenox palette mark*	55.00	63.00
☐ **Vase,** *item #1726, 8" high, undecorated and unmarked*	4.00	5.00
☐ **Vase,** *item #1727, 6" high, hand-painted laurel wreath in green around bottom on lighter green background, gold trim on top and bottom, Lenox palette mark*	33.00	38.00
☐ **Vase,** *item #1733, 15-3/4" high, undecorated, Lenox palette mark*	47.50	55.00
☐ **Vase,** *item #1733, 15-3/4" high, hand-painted picture of French poodle, pale green background, not artist signed but very nicely done, Lenox palette mark*	260.00	320.00
☐ **Vase,** *item #1734, 12" high, plain white, Lenox wreath mark* ...	55.00	65.00
☐ **Vase,** *item #1734, 12" high, green exterior, gold trim on rim, Lenox wreath mark*	85.00	100.00
☐ **Vase,** *item #1743, 6-7/8" high, hand-painted bees and butterflies, Lenox palette mark*	60.00	70.00
☐ **Vase,** *item #1786, 6" high, hand-painted orchid on both sides, gold trim, band of green near bottom, signed by Morley, Lenox wreath mark*	170.00	200.00

Vase, *item #1786, by G. Morley*

☐ **Vase,** *item #1786, 6" high, hand-painted roses on both sides, gold trim, one signed G. Morley the other identical but unsigned, Lenox wreath mark, pair*	565.00	665.00
☐ **Vase,** *item #1786, 6" high, undecorated, Lenox wreath mark* ..	19.00	24.00
☐ **Vase,** *item #1786, 6" high, Lenox Rose pattern, Lenox wreath mark*	80.00	95.00
☐ **Vase,** *item #1786, 6" high, deep blue, Lenox wreath mark*	80.00	95.00

Price Range

☐ **Vase,** *item #1786, 6" high, gold trim, Lenox wreath mark* 40.00   47.50
☐ **Vase,** *item #1798, undecorated, Lenox wreath mark* 33.00   38.00
☐ **Vase,** *item #2078, undecorated, Lenox wreath mark* 80.00   95.00
☐ **Vase,** *item #2081, 8-1/2" pedestal base, gold trim, Lenox wreath mark* 68.00   78.00
☐ **Vase,** *item #2118, 7-5/8" high, coral with small white handles, Lenox wreath mark* 60.00   70.00
☐ **Vase,** *item #2118, 7-5/8" high, undecorated, Lenox wreath mark* 47.50   55.00
☐ **Vase,** *item #2155, 8-1/8" high, undecorated, Lenox wreath mark* 37.00   43.00
☐ **Vase,** *item #2261, 10" high, Lenox Rose trim, Lenox wreath mark* 85.00   100.00
☐ **Vase,** *item #2261, 10" high, white with gold trim, Lenox wreath mark* 80.00   95.00
☐ **Vase,** *item #2262, 8-1/2" high, swan handles, undecorated, unmarked* 27.50   32.50
☐ **Vase,** *item #2263, 10-3/8" high, swan handles, light green and white, Lenox wreath mark* 105.00   120.00
☐ **Vase,** *item #2263, 10-3/8" high, swan handles, solid coral, Lenox wreath mark* 80.00   95.00
☐ **Vase,** *item #2317, 7" high, pedestal base, two small handles, undecorated, Lenox wreath mark* 37.00   43.00
☐ **Vase,** *item #2317, 7" high, pedestal base, white with blue handles, Lenox wreath mark* 40.00   47.50
☐ **Vase,** *item #2317, 7" high, two small handles trimmed in gold, Lenox Rose pattern in center, Lenox wreath mark* 68.00   78.00
☐ **Vase,** *item #2317, 7" high, pedestal base, green with white handles, Lenox wreath mark* 55.00   63.00
☐ **Vase,** *item #2318, 10" high, Grecian styling, swan handles, oxblood with ornate gold trim, Lenox Rose pattern in center, Lenox wreath mark* 125.00   145.00
☐ **Vase,** *item #2318, 10" high, Grecian styling, swan handles, blue with white, Lenox wreath mark* 80.00   95.00
☐ **Vase,** *item #2318, 10" high, Grecian styling, swan handles, plain white, Lenox wreath mark* 60.00   70.00
☐ **Vase,** *item #2334, 10-1/2" high, Grecian styling, handles, blue with white, Lenox wreath mark* 55.00   63.00
☐ **Vase,** *item #2338, 14" high, Grecian styling, handles shaped like women's heads, plain white, Lenox wreath mark* 80.00   95.00
☐ **Vase,** *item #2338, 14" high, Grecian styling, handles shaped like women's heads, coral and white, Lenox wreath mark* 90.00   110.00
☐ **Vase,** *item #2338, 14" high, Grecian styling, handles shaped like women's heads, Lenox Rose pattern, Lenox wreath mark* . 120.00   140.00
☐ **Vase,** *item #2338-1/4, 10-1/8" high, Grecian styling, handles shaped like women's heads, green and white, Lenox wreath mark* 85.00   100.00
☐ **Vase,** *item #2338-1/4, 10-1/8" high, Grecian styling, handles shaped like women's heads, white with gold trim, Lenox wreath mark* 80.00   95.00
☐ **Vase,** *item #2360, 5-1/2" high, pedestal base, small handles, white with coral, Lenox wreath mark, small chip on one handle* 42.00   48.00
☐ **Vase,** *item #2370, 8" high, Grecian styling, small handles, white with gold trim, Lenox wreath mark* 68.00   78.00

Price Range

☐ **Vase,** *item #2409, 8-1/4" high, pedestal base, small handles, gold and white, Lenox wreath mark* 55.00   63.00

☐ **Vase,** *item #2419, 9-7/8" high, Grecian styling, small handles, undecorated, Lenox wreath mark* 60.00   70.00

☐ **Vase,** *item #2429, 7" high, Grecian styling, small handles, undecorated, Lenox wreath mark* 47.50   55.00

☐ **Vase,** *item #2458-1/2, 9-1/8" high, elaborate drape base, small handles, undecorated, Lenox wreath mark* 105.00   120.00

☐ **Vase,** *item #2459, 11" high, large pedestal base, Grecian styling, small handles, undecorated, Lenox wreath mark* 105.00   120.00

☐ **Vase,** *item #2497-1/2, 10-1/2" high, pedestal base, thin shape, undecorated, Lenox wreath mark* 50.00   58.00

☐ **Vase,** *item #2568, 12" high, Grecian style draping, white and yellow, Lenox wreath mark* 135.00   155.00

☐ **Vase,** *item #2568, 12" high, Grecian style draping, undecorated, Lenox wreath mark* 85.00   100.00

☐ **Vase,** *item #2568-1/2, 10-1/2" high, Grecian style draping, green and white, Lenox wreath mark* 105.00   120.00

☐ **Vase,** *item #2585-1/2, 7-1/2" high, flaring top, undecorated, Lenox wreath mark* 40.00   47.50

☐ **Vase,** *item #2587-1/2, 7-1/8" high, embossed flamingo with reeds, undecorated, Lenox wreath mark* 105.00   120.00

☐ **Vase,** *item #2605, 8-1/4" high, bulbous bottom to narrow top, undecorated, Lenox wreath mark* 18.50   23.50

☐ **Vase,** *item #2606, 6" high, bulbous bottom to narrow top, undecorated, Lenox wreath mark* 15.00   20.00

Vase, *item #2650, undecorated*

☐ **Vase,** *item #2650, 8-5/8" high, square pedestal base, fluting, flared rim, undecorated, Lenox wreath mark* 42.00   48.00

☐ **Vase,** *item #2650, 8-5/8" high, square pedestal base, fluting, flared rim, pink and white, Lenox wreath mark* 55.00   63.00

	Price Range	
☐ **Vase**, *item #2650, 8-5/8" high, square pedestal base, fluting, flared rim, green, Lenox wreath mark*	**47.50**	**55.00**
☐ **Vase**, *item #2650, 8-5/8" high, square pedestal base, fluting, flared rim, green with gold trim, Lenox wreath mark*	**55.00**	**63.00**
☐ **Vase**, *item #2650, 8-5/8" high, square pedestal base, fluting, flared rim, white with gold trim, Lenox wreath mark*	**47.50**	**55.00**

Note: Vase #2650 is known as the Regal vase, and although it is a fairly common shape it remains popular because its shape is perfectly designed to hold a dozen roses or other flowers.

☐ **Vase**, *item #2709-1/2, 7-5/8" high, Chinese styling, handles, round shape, undecorated, Lenox wreath mark*	**80.00**	**95.00**
☐ **Vase**, *item #2710-1/2, 8-1/2" high, Chinese styling, square open-work handles, relief floral design on round body, Lenox wreath mark*	**120.00**	**140.00**
☐ **Vase**, *item #2723, 10-3/8" high, wide flaring rim, undecorated, Lenox wreath mark*	**68.00**	**78.00**
☐ **Vase**, *item #2757-1/2, 9-3/4" high, cylinder shape with slight flare at top and bottom, relief Oriental design (Pagoda pattern), undecorated, Lenox wreath mark*	**85.00**	**100.00**
☐ **Vase**, *item #2763, 10-3/4" high, relief gadroon pattern around mid-section, wide flaring top, undecorated, Lenox wreath mark*	**55.00**	**63.00**
☐ **Vase**, *item #2833, 10-5/8" high, classical styling, small rolled handles, coral and white, Lenox wreath mark*	**55.00**	**63.00**
☐ **Vase**, *item #2833, 10-5/8" high, classical styling, small rolled handles, yellow and white, Lenox wreath mark*	**105.00**	**120.00**
☐ **Vase**, *item #2834-1/2, 10-1/4" high, cylinder shape, relief design, undecorated, Lenox wreath mark*	**60.00**	**70.00**
☐ **Vase**, *item #2842-1/2, 8-1/2" high, rounded bottom to 4-1/2" mouth, swirled wide ribs, undecorated, Lenox wreath mark* . . .	**40.00**	**47.50**
☐ **Vase**, *item #2876, 10" high, pedestal base, no handles, undecorated, Lenox wreath mark*	**50.00**	**58.00**
☐ **Vase**, *item #2898-1/2, 11" high, round body, relief pattern, undecorated, Lenox wreath mark*	**165.00**	**195.00**
☐ **Vase**, *item #2902-1/2, 13" high, floral relief work, undecorated, Lenox wreath mark*	**80.00**	**95.00**
☐ **Vase**, *item #2902-1/2, 13" high, floral relief work, yellow and white, Lenox wreath mark*	**155.00**	**185.00**
☐ **Vase**, *item #2908, 11" high, narrow with slight flare on top and bottom, fluting, small chip on rim, Lenox wreath mark*	**40.00**	**47.50**
☐ **Vase**, *item #2908-1/4, 8" high, narrow with slight flare top and bottom, fluting, undecorated, Lenox wreath mark*	**30.00**	**35.00**
☐ **Vase**, *item #2908-1/2, 9-1/2" high, narrow with slight flare top and bottom, fluting, undecorated, Lenox wreath mark*	**33.00**	**38.00**
☐ **Vase**, *item #2913, 10" high, square pedestal base, swan handles, green and white, Lenox wreath mark*	**80.00**	**95.00**
☐ **Vase**, *item #2913-1/2", 8-1/2" high, square pedestal base, swan handles, all white, Lenox wreath mark*	**47.50**	**55.00**
☐ **Vase**, *item #2914, 10-1/4" high, round pedestal base, slight flare at rim, undecorated, Lenox wreath mark*	**42.00**	**48.00**
☐ **Vase**, *item #2920, high, round pedestal base, undecorated, Lenox wreath mark*	**47.50**	**55.00**
☐ **Vase**, *item #2920-1/2, 8" high, round pedestal base, undecorated, Lenox wreath mark*	**40.00**	**47.50**

	Price Range	

☐ **Vase**, *item #2929, 11-1/4" high, round base, fluting, undecorated, Lenox wreath mark* 37.00 43.00

☐ **Vase**, *item #2930, 12-1/2" high, fluted, slight flare to rim and base, undecorated, Lenox wreath mark* 47.50 55.00

☐ **Vase**, *item #2937, 12" high, square pedestal base, round shape, draping and reeding, undecorated, Lenox wreath mark* . 80.00 95.00

☐ **Vase**, *item #2938, 7-1/8" high, shaped like large egg cup, relief work, undecorated, Lenox wreath mark* 68.00 78.00

☐ **Vase**, *item #2939, 10-3/4" high, square pedestal base, ribbon and garland embossing, undecorated, Lenox wreath mark* 68.00 78.00

☐ **Vase**, *item #2942, 5-1/4" high, urn shape, no handles, white, Lenox wreath mark* 18.50 23.50

☐ **Vase**, *item #2946-1/2, 9-3/4" high, swirled rib design, tall neck, green, Lenox wreath mark* 58.00 68.00

☐ **Vase**, *item #2947-1/2, 10-1/2" high, hexagon shape, embossed floral design, undecorated, Lenox wreath mark* 40.00 47.50

☐ **Vase**, *item #2947-1/2, 10-1/2" high, hexagon shape, relief floral design, white and green, Lenox wreath mark* 68.00 78.00

☐ **Vase**, *item #2954-1/2, 7-1/2" high, overall pattern of small flowers (Hawthorn pattern), undecorated, Lenox wreath mark* 110.00 125.00

☐ **Vase**, *item #2963-1/2, 7-1/2" high, cylinder shape, embossed fruit pattern, undecorated, Lenox wreath mark* 55.00 63.00

☐ **Vase**, *item #3019, 7-3/8" high, embossed flowers alternating with tiny ribs, pale pink and white, Lenox wreath mark* 55.00 63.00

☐ **Vase**, *item number unknown, pink exterior, creamy interior, gold trim on rim, gold wreath mark* 18.50 23.50

☐ **Vase**, *item number unknown, 8" high, square pedestal base, yellow with white swan handles, Lenox wreath mark* 68.00 78.00

☐ **Vase**, *item number unknown, 9" high, portrait of David Teniers (European artist), on shaded green and mahogany background, gold trim inside lip, signed S. Wirkner, transition mark* 400.00 470.00

Vase, *portrait of David Teniers by S. Wirkner*

Vase, *item number unknown, picture of woman*

Price Range

☐ **Vase,** *item number unknown, 10" high, hand-painted poppies on shaded brown background, signed W. H. Morley, transition mark* 525.00   625.00

☐ **Vase,** *item number unknown, 11" high, monochromatic turquoise picture of woman, signed W. H. Clayton, transition mark* 400.00   470.00

☐ **Vase,** *item number unknown, yellow and red cabbage roses on butterscotch background, signed W. H. Morley, transition mark* 660.00   780.00

Vase, *item number unknown, cabbage roses*

Vase, *item number unknown, blue dot*

Price Range

☐ **Vase,** *item number unknown, 11" high, hand-painted pink roses, gold trim on rim, signed W. Marsh, Lenox palette mark* .   400.00   470.00

☐ **Vase,** *item number unknown, 8" high, pinched neck, raised gold paste and blue dot enamel work in banding around middle, pale yellow background, transition mark* 195.00   235.00

☐ **Vase,** *item number unknown, approximate size 8" high, landscape in oval, background maroon, gold trim, signed Nosek, Lenox wreath mark, one vase has repair on rim, pair* 565.00   665.00

Vase, *item number unknown, landscape in oval*

Vase, *item number unknown, white roses*

Price Range

☐ **Vase,** *item number unknown, 12" high, white roses on green background, handles painted silver, artist signed, C.A.C. palette mark* 330.00 395.00

☐ **Vase,** *item # unknown, 13" high, plume handles, tri-color background with roses, gold inside of rim, signed Marsh, transition/Glen/Iris backstamp* 460.00 550.00

WALL VASES *(WALL POCKETS)*

☐ **Wall vase,** *item #2135, bisque finish, gold outlining on embossed details, Lenox wreath mark* 120.00 140.00

Wall vase, *item #2135*

Price Range

☐ **Wall vase,** *item #2135, glazed, undecorated, Lenox wreath mark* 110.00   125.00

☐ **Wall vase,** *item #2193, glazed, undecorated, Lenox wreath mark* 105.00   120.00

WORLD'S FAIR ITEMS

Lenox produced several items in cooperation with the Ovington's store in New York for the New York World's Fair of 1939. Most of the items are simple shapes showing embossed scenes of the fair and bearing the inscription "Officially Approved N.Y.W.F., Inc., Lic., Designed in Honor of New York World's Fair, Ovington's, New York." The Lenox wreath/Made in U.S.A. mark has the dates 1789 and 1939 on either side of it.

Although one or two samples of World's Fair items keep most Lenox collectors happy, there are collectors of just World's Fair items, Lenox and otherwise, who search for these items and who (apparently) are willing to pay more for them than Lenox collectors. We have heard rumors of Lenox World's Fair items bringing as high as $250 among such people, but have never been able to track down these stories. The prices listed below are, therefore, the prices paid by Lenox collectors only.

☐ **Ashtray,** *small, round, coral with white embossing* 37.00   43.00
☐ **Ashtray,** *small, round, royal blue with white embossing* 40.00   47.50
☐ **Ashtray,** *small, round, all white* 33.00   38.00
☐ **Cigarette box,** *covered, all white* 47.50   55.00
☐ **Cigarette box,** *covered, coral and white* 55.00   63.00
☐ **Vase,** *cylinder shape, all white* 47.50   55.00
☐ **Vase,** *cylinder shape, yellow and white* 68.00   78.00
☐ **Vase,** *cylinder shape, coral and white* 60.00   70.00

DINNERWARE

The variety of Lenox patterns is endless—counting all the variations on basic patterns, there are thousands of different patterns. Approximately 300 of the patterns were given names, while the remainder will be known forever only by their number. (Named patterns also had numbers which sometimes appear on the bottom of items along with the names.) Table VI lists those patterns which had names as well as numbers.

It is possible to determine what year a given pattern was first introduced by its number. Table VII lists the year/letter codes, the letter in this case being the first letter of the pattern's code number. For example, Lenox Rose J300 would have been introduced in 1934.

Table VIII lists the more common dinnerware items by shape and/or capacity. These numbers are particularly important when trying to match a particular type of cup and saucer, for example.

Table IX is a listing of those dinnerware pattern numbers which were available only on service plates and not as general production dinnerware patterns.

Lenox dinnerware could fill a book of its very own quite easily, and we regret not being able to list more of the numbered patterns here. As a general rule, any pattern from the past can be compared to current Lenox retail prices. Following is some general information about Lenox dinnerware.

TABLE VI
Pattern Name/Number Codes

A-300	Fountain	~~1934~~ J-33 *1912*	Tuxedo	
A-303	Pasadena	J-300	Lenox Rose	
A-557	Jewel	J-325A	Villa	
A-558	Chalet	J-332	Rhythm	
		J-374A	Chesterfield	
B-300	Blue Tree	J-471B	Rhapsody	
B-343A	Evanston	J-476B	Georgian	
B-344A	Princeton			
B-345A	Madison	K-330	Gadroon Rose	
B-346A	Springfield	K-348B	Orleans	
B-347A	Carolina	K-352	Stradivarius	
B-348A	Hudson	K-366B	Trianon	
B-368A	Bellaire	K-367	Fountainbleu	
B-369A	Lincoln	K-369A	Rock Garden	
B-372A	Palisade	K-392G	Athenia	
B-374A	Belmont	K-395B	Revere	
B-375A	Saratoga			
B-376B	Lexington	L-300A	Normand	
		L-303A	Westbury	
C-300	Monticello	L-304	Vendome	
C-301	Renaissance	L-306A	Chippendale	
		L-315A	Minerva	
D-300	Floralia	L-335	Radiance	
D-304A	Floralia Ivory	L-347	Aurora	
D-514	Chanson	L-355-247	Berkeley	
D-515	Orleans	L-368B	Josephine	
		L-369B	Platina	
E-300	Grenoble	L-371B	Casino	
E-300A	Grenoble Ivory	L-373B	Diana	
E-301	Sheraton	L-383A	Newport	
E-301A	Sheraton Ivory			
E-302	Trellis	M-3	Meadowbrook	
E-302A	Trellis Ivory	M-139	Westchester	
E-500	Rondelle	M-161	Windsor *12 dinner*	
E-501	Romance	M-311B	Etruscan *plates*	
E-536	Symphony	M-319A	Gold Casino	
		M-320	Arden Rose	
F-300	Harwood	M-326	Golden Blossom	
F-308A	Malmaison	M-328A	Troy	
F-529	Majesty	M-356	Antoinette	
		M-440	Corinthian	
G-87	Virginian	M-441B	Olympia	
G-345	Oak Leaf			
G-347B	Lombardy	O-12 *12 soup bowls* Stanford *~ 1916*		
G-386B	Cambridge	O-300	Pembrook	
G-388B	Alden	O-301	Monterey	
G-510	Tableaux	O-302A	Claremont	
G-511	Capri	O-312B	Royal	
		O-313	Golden Wreath	
H-48	Mt. Vernon	O-314B	Marlboro	
H-310A	Chelsea	O-315	Lansdale	
H-502	Maywood	O-316	Cretan	

Hull Pottery (top to bottom), Row #1, **"Cinderella" Cookie Jar**, c. 1943, *extremely rare*, **$125.00:** **"Tokay" Basket**, c. 1958, **$25.00-$35.00:** Row #2, **"Dancing Girl" Planter**, c. mid 1940's, **$12.00-$22.00:** **"Baby" Planter**, *with gold trim*, **$15.00-$20.00:** Row #3, **"Woodland" Flower Pot**, c. 1949, **$18.00-$25.00:** **"Bandana Duck" Planter**, c. 1950, **$14.00-$20.00:** Row #4, **"Serenade" Ewer**, c. 1957, **$18.00-$28.00:** **"Red Riding Hood" Salt And Pepper Shakers**, c. 1943-57, **$20.00-$25.00.**

Hull Pottery *(top to bottom), Row #1,* "Calla Lily" Vase, *c. 1938,* $38.00-$45.00: "Tokay" Vase, *c. 1958,* $20.00-$28.00: "Dogwood" Vase, *c. mid 1940's,* $22.00-$32.00: *Row #2,* "Blossom Flite" Cornucopia Planter, *c. 1955,* $20.00-$28.00: "Bow-Knot" Planter, *c. 1949,* $30.00-$40.00: "Leeds Elephant" Liquor Bottle, *c. mid 1940's,* $15.00-$25.00: *Row #3,* "Corky Pig" Bank, *c. 1957-58,* $20.00-$30.00: "Utility" Pitcher, *c. 1920's,* $20.00-$28.00.

Cowan Pottery, *c. 1913-31 (top to bottom), Row #1,* **Bowl**, *with nude flower frog,* **$250.00-$275.00;** *Row #2,* **Nude 17" Lamp Base, $375.00-$400.00; Pedestal Console Bowl**, *with nude flower frog,* **$165.00-$195.00; Luster Vase, $28.00-$35.00;** *Row #3,* **Luster Console Bowl**, *with candlesticks, set,* **$60.00-$70.00; Matte Blue Vase, $32.00-$40.00; Pedestal Compote, $32.00-$42.00;** *Row #4,* **Duck Ashtray, $32.00-$40.00; Luster Bowl, $28.00-$35.00.**

Owens Pottery, *c. 1896-1906, (top to bottom), Row #1,* **"Majolica" 7"**
Planter, $85.00-$100.00: *Row #2,* **13" Vase, $250.00-$275.00:**
"Utopian" 7½" Vase, $150.00-$175.00: "Utopian" 12½" Bottle
Vase, $190.00-$225.00: *Row #3,* **"Utopian" Left-Hand Mug, $130.00**
-$150.00: 6" Vase, *with squeeze bag decal, rare,* **$200.00-$225.00:**
"Utopian" Mug, $140.00-$150.00: *Row #4,* **"Utopian" Left-Hand**
Mug, $135.00-$150.00: Matte Green Mug, $46.00-$55.00.

Weller Pottery (top to bottom) Row #1, "Hobart" Console Set, with nudes flower frog, c, 1920, **$135.00-$150.00**: Row #2, "Floretta" Vase, c. 1904, **$160.00-$185.00**; "Blueware" Flower Pot, before 1920, **$180.00-$195.00**: Row #3, "Etna" Vase, c. 1906, **$110.00-$125.00**: "La Sa" Vase, c. 1920-25, **$250.00-$275.00**; "Hudson" Vase, c. 1920's-30's, **$110.00-125.00**: Row #4, "Lustre Cloudburst" Vase, **$60.00-$75.00**; "Hudson" Vase, early 1920's, **$80.00-$100.00**.

TABLE VII
Year/Letter Codes

Numbers 1 thru 299	Numbers 300 - 500	Exceptions
A — 1904	A — 1926	W-331 Pine — 1951
B — 1905	B — 1927	W-341 Cattail — 1951
C — 1906	C — 1928	X-302 Starlight — 1952
D — 1907	D — 1929	X-304 Roselyn — 1952
E — 1908	E — 1930	X-303 Olympia — 1952
F — 1909	F — 1931	X-407 West Wind — 1953
G — 1910	G — 1932	X-421 Athenia Coupe — 1953
H — 1911	H — 1933	X-444 Caribbee — 1954
J — 1912	J — 1934	X-445 Kingsley — 1954
K — 1913	K — 1935	X-446 Trio — 1954
L — 1914	L — 1936	X-516 Princess — 1954
M — 1915	M — 1937	X-559 Glendale — 1955
O — 1916	O — 1938	A-500 Wyndcrest — 1956
P — 1917	P — 1939	A-501 Alaris — 1956
R — 1918	R — 1940	A-557 Jewel — 1957
S — 1919	S — 1941	A-558 Chalet — 1957
T — 1920	T — 1942 to 1946*	C-512 Charmaine — 1957
V — 1921	V — 1947	
W — 1922	W — 1948	*Note: The Letters I, N, Q and U were not used.*
X — 1923	X — 1950	
Y — 1924	* war years	
Z — 1925		

TABLE VIII
Lenox Dinnerware Shapes and Sizes

After Dinner Cups and Saucers

No.	Shape	Size
448	— round	2 oz.
610	— round	3 oz.
670	— round	2 oz.
813	— hexagonal	1-1/2 oz.
841	— hexagonal	2 oz.
852	— round	1-1/2 oz.
885	— round	3-1/2 oz.
895	— round	2 oz.
895-1/2	— round	3 oz.
1079	— round	2 oz.
1095	— octagonal	3 oz.
1395	— round	3-1/2 oz.
1569	— round	2 oz.
1615	— round	3 oz.
1742	— round	1-1/2 oz.
2358	— round	4 oz.
2854	— round	4 oz.

Baked Apple Dish

No.		Size
784	—	5-5/8" d. x 2-1/2" h.

Bouillon Cups and Saucers

No.	Shape	Size
557-1/2	— round	5-1/2 oz.
628	— round	7 oz.
757	— hexagonal	6 oz.
839-1/2	— hexagonal	5 oz.
846-1/2	— round	6 oz.
942-1/2	— round	5 oz.
944	— round	7 oz.
1394	— round	7 oz.

Bowls

No.	Description	Size
512	—	10-1/4" d. x 5" h.
513	—	8-1/8" d. x 3" h.
527	—	9" d. x 4" h.
553	—	6" d. x 2-1/2" h.
575	—	5-3/8" d. x 1-7/8" h.
589	—	7-3/8" d. x 2-3/4" h.
624	—	7-5/8" d. x 2-1/4" h.
690	— finger bowl	4-3/4" d. x 2-1/4" h.
715	— berry bowl	7-3/4" x 8-3/4" hexa. x 3-3/4" h.
796	— berry bowl	9-1/2" d. x 4-3/8" h.
799	—	7" d. x 2-1/4" h.
800	—	5-3/4" d. x 2" h.
811	—	5-1/4" d. x 2-1/2" h.
823	—	10-1/4" d. x 4-1/4" h.
970	—	7-3/4" d. x 5" h.
971	—	7-3/8" d. x 2-3/4" h.
1082	—	9-3/8" d. x 4-1/8" h.
1122	—	9-3/8" d. x 4-1/8" h.
1128	—	6-1/4" d. x 3-1/8" h.
1129	—	5-3/8" d. x 2-3/8" h.
1245	— berry bowl	8-5/8" d. x 3" h.
1247	— berry bowl	8-1/2" d. x 3" h.
1254	— berry bowl	9-5/8" d. x 3-1/8" h.
1261	—	5-1/8" d. x 1-7/8" h.
1667	—	9-1/4" d. x 5-1/2" h.
1722	— finger bowl	4-1/2" d. x 1-3/4" h.
1929-1/2	— berry bowl	9-5/8" d. x 4" h.
1972	—	6-3/4" d. x 1-3/4" h.
2073	—	8-3/4" d. x 3-3/4" h.

Breakfast items

No.	Description	Size
584	— salt and pepper	1-3/8" d. x 2-1/2" h.
585	— salt and pepper	1-5/8" d. x 3-1/2" h.
933	— coffeepot	13 oz.
934	— teapot	13 oz.
935	— sugar	3-1/4" d. x 2-3/4" h.
936	— cream	3-1/2" oz.
964	— hot milk	13 oz.
1056	— egg cup	1-7/8" d. x 2-3/8" h.
1060	— coffeepot	16 oz.

1060-1/2	— hot milk	14 oz.
1061	— teapot	18 oz.
1062	— sugar	3-1/4" d. x 2-3/4" h.
1063	— creamer	4-1/2 oz.
1121	— double egg cup	2-1/2" d. x 3-3/4" h.
1125	— covered muffin	plate 7-3/8" d., cover 5-1/4" d.
1126	— covered muffin	plate 8-3/4" d., cover 6-1/4" d.
1126-1/2	— cover for muffin dish	
1337	— combination coffee set	11 oz.
1400	— combination cereal set	5-1/8"
1500	— combination cake set	8-3/4" d.
1518	— covered chop dish	4-3/8" x 6-3/4"
1610	— combination tea set	18 oz.
1628	— egg cup	2-3/4" d. x 3-1/2" h.
1774	— coffeepot	5 oz.
1775	— tray	6" x 9-3/4"
1936	— teapot	10 oz.
1946	— coffeepot	12 oz.
1947	— hot milk	11 oz.
1948	— sugar	2-3/4" d. x 2-1/2" h.
1949	— cream	3-1/2 oz.

Butter Dishes

No.	Shape	Size
932	— hexagonal	3-3/4" x 4-1/4" d. x 1-1/2" h.
1096	—	4-1/2" d. x 2" h.
1125	— covered	plate 7-3/8" d., cover 5-1/4" d.
1126	— covered	plate 8-3/4" d., cover 6-1/4" d.

Casseroles

No.	Shape	Size
640	— no handles	7-1/2" d. x 4-1/8" h.
641	— no handles	8-3/4" d. x 4-1/2" h.
642	— no handles	5-7/8" d. x 3-3/8" h.
643	— no handles	4-1/4" d. x 2-3/8" h.
716	— handled	8-3/4" d. x 4-1/2" h.
717	— handled	7-1/2" d. x 4-1/8" h.
718	— handled	5-7/8" d. x 3-3/8" h.
719	— handled	4-1/4" d. x 2-3/8" h.
2519	— handled	8-3/4" d. x 4-3/8" h.

Celery Trays

No.	Shape	Size
1599	— oval	6-1/4" x 12-3/8"
1971	— oval	5-7/8" x 11-3/4"
2012	— oval	6-1/8" x 12"
2013	— oval	5-1/8" x 10-1/4"

Cheese Dishes

No.	Shape	Size
829	— covered	7" d. x 5" h.
1396	— plate	10-3/4" d., top 5-1/2" d.

Chocolate Cups and Saucers

No.	Shape	Size
556	— round	4 oz.
600	— round	4 oz.
665	— hexagonal	1-3/4" oz.
669	— round	4 oz.
714	— hexagonal	3 oz.
815	— hexagonal	4 oz.
843	— round	4 oz.
1078	— round	4 oz.
1189	— round	4-1/2 oz.
1430	— round	5 oz.

Chocolate Pots

No.	Shape	Size
842	— round	42 oz.
905	— hexagonal	36 oz.
1367	— round	45 oz.
1429	— round	27 oz.
1960-1/2	— round	40 oz.

Cracker Jars

No.	Shape	Size
351	— round	5-3/4" d. x 5-3/4" h.
688	— round	6-1/4" d. x 6" h.
691	— round	6-3/4" d. x 6-5/8" h.
803	— hexagonal	5-3/8" x 6-1/4" d. x 7-1/4" h.
850	— hexagonal	5" x 5-7/8" d. x 7" h.
1623	— round	6-1/8" d. x 6-3/4" h.

Crescent Salad Plates

No.		Size
1314	—	6-1/4" x 9-1/4"
1414-1/2	—	5" x 7-3/4"

Horse Radish Jars

No.	Shape	Size
761	— round	2-3/4" d. x 4-3/8" h.
1288	— round	2-1/2" d. x 4-7/8" h.
1405	— round	2-1/4" d. x 5" h.

Jugs and Pitchers

No.	Shape	Size
566	— round, covered	45 oz.
567	— round, covered	32 oz.
568	— round, covered	16 oz.
666	— hexagonal	54 oz.
794	— hexagonal, covered	12 oz.
1038	— round	16 oz.
1039	— round	30 oz.
1040	— round	42 oz.
1041	— round	60 oz.
1073	— round	45 oz.
1074	— round	32 oz.

1075	— round	16 oz.
1404	— round	64 oz.
1520	— round	50 oz.
1680	— rectangular, covered	16 oz.

Luncheon Plates and Cups

These plates have identations on one side to hold a cup, while the main part of the plate was to be used for cakes or sandwiches. In our text we have referred to these items as tete-a-tete sets to avoid confusion with the standard 9" size luncheon plates which have no place for a cup.

No.	Description	Size
943	— cup	6 oz.
1094	— cup	5 oz.
1305	— cup	6 oz.
1617-1/2	— octagonal plate	7-1/2" x 8-1/4"
1620	— cup	6 oz.
1671	— plate	7-1/2"
1684	— plate	8-3/8" d.
1755	— plate	7-1/4" d.
2069	— plate	8-1/4" d.

Marmalade Jars

No.	Shape	Size
755	— round	4" d. x 4-5/8" h.
760	— round	3-3/4" d. x 5-1/2" h.
763	— round	3-3/4" d. x 5-1/2" h.
766	— round	3-1/4" d. x 5-1/8" h.
767	— round	3-1/4" d. x 5-1/8" h.
774	— round	4-7/8" d. x 3-3/4" h.
775	— round	4-5/8" d. x 4" h.
804	— hexagonal	3-1/4" x 3-3/4" d. x 5-1/4" h.
809	— round	3-1/2" d. x 5-1/4" h.
818	— rectangular	3-1/4" x 3-7/8" d. x 4-1/4" h.
830	— round	3-3/4" d. x 4" h.
831	— round	3-3/4" d. x 4" h.
851	— hexagonal	3-5/8" x 4" d. x 5-3/8" h.
1032	— hexagonal	4-1/4" x 4-3/4" d. x 5" h.
1064	— round	4-1/4" d. x 4-3/4" h.
1274	— rectangular	3-1/4" x 3-7/8" d. x 4-1/4" h.
1289	— round	3-1/2" d. x 5-1/4" h.
2000	— round	5-1/4" d. x 2-3/8" h.

Mayonnaise Bowls

No.	Shape	Size
644	— oval	4-3/4" x 6-1/2" d. x 3-1/2" h.
745	— oval	3-7/8" x 5-1/8" d. x 4" h.
778	—	6-3/8" d. x 4-1/4" h.
779	—	5-1/8" d. x 3-1/8" h.
780	— oval	3-3/4" x 5" d. x 3" h.
781	— oval	5" x 6" d. x 3-1/2" h.
782	—	5-1/4" d. x 3-1/2" h.
783	— oval	4" x 5-1/2" d. x 3-3/8" h.
785	—	6" d. x 3-1/4" h.
795	—	5-3/8" d. x 2-3/4" h.

805	— hexagonal	4-3/8" x 5" d. x 3-1/8" h.
828	—	4-3/8" d. x 3-3/4" h.
1605	— oval	4-1/2" x 6-1/4" d. x 3-3/4" h.
2028	—	5-3/8" d. x 3-3/8" h.
2074	—	5-1/8" d. x 3" h.

Mayonnaise Underplates

No.	Description	Size
1180	— plate	6-3/8" d.
1672	— oval plate	4-1/4" x 6-1/8"

Mugs

No.	Shape	Size
754	—	6 oz.
812	—	8 oz.
1313	—	7 oz.
1493	—	6 oz.

Mustard Jars

No.	Shape	Size
679	— round	2-1/2" d. x 2-7/8" h.
680	— round	1-7/8" d. x. 3-1/4" h.
681	— round	2-1/8" d. x 3-5/8" h.
682	— round	2" d. x 3-1/4" h.
737	— hexagonal	1-3/4" x 2" d. x 3-7/8" h.
762	— round	2-1/2" d. x 3-3/8" h.
765	— round	2-1/2" d. x 3-1/2" h.
790	— hexagonal	1-3/4" x 2" d. x 3-1/2" h.
915	— hexagonal	2-1/8" x 2-3/8" d. x 4" h.
1030	— hexagonal	2" x 2-1/4" d. x 3-3/4" h.

Relish and Pickle Dishes

No.	Shape	Size
792	— oval	4" x 7-1/8" d. x 3" h.
793	— oval	4" x 7" d. x 2-3/4" h.
1106	— oval	6-1/4" x 10-1/4"
1190	— oval	3-1/8" x 6-1/4"
1191	— oval	4" x 6"
1242	— oval	3-3/8" x 4-3/4"
1246	— oval (partitioned)	4-3/8" x 7-3/4"
1366	— round	4-3/8" d.
1419	— oval	3-5/8" x 6-3/4"
1426	— oval	3-7/8" x 6-3/8"
1598	— oval	5-1/4" x 8-5/8"
2312	— compartments	9" d.

Sandwich Trays

No.	Shape	Size
1564	— cut edge, footed	8-7/8" d.
1604	— cut edge, footed	10-5/8" d.

Teacups and Saucers

No.	Shape	Size
551	— round	6 oz.
557	— round	5-1/2 oz.
654-1/2	— round	7 oz.
664	— hexagonal	4 oz.
668	— round	6 oz.
756	— round	6 oz.
773	— round	3-1/2 oz.
814	— hexagonal	4 oz.
816	— hexagonal	7 oz.
837	— hexagonal	6 oz.
838	— hexagonal	8 oz.
839	— hexagonal	5 oz.
845	— round	4-1/2 oz.
846	— round	6-1/2 oz.
853	— round	5-1/2 oz.
886	— round	4 oz.
942	— round	5 oz.
1006	— hexagonal	4 oz.
1019	— round	7 oz.
1080	— round	6 oz.
1094-1/2	— octagonal	5-1/2 oz.
1302	— round	12 oz.
1303	— round	11 oz.
1304	— round	10 oz.
1331	— round	7 oz.
1389	— round	15 oz.
1693	— round	7-1/2 oz.
1705	— round	10 oz.
1837	— round	6 oz.
2040	— round	8-1/2 oz.
2408	— round	6 oz.

Tumblers

No.	Shape	Size
378	— round	8 oz.
539	— round	10 oz.
540	— round	8 oz.
1102-1/2	— round	15 oz.
2097	— round, handled	8 oz.

TABLE IX
Lenox Service Plate Patterns

A-301	A-320-4	A-328-1	A-348-2	B-361	D-395		
A-301-1	A-320-5	A-328-2	A-348-3	B-363	D-405		F-61
A-301-2	A-320-6	A-328-3	A-348-4	B-366	D-412		F-304
A-301-3	A-321	A-328-4	A-348-5	B-379			F-305
A-301-4	A-321-1	A-328-5	A-348-6	B-390		E-51	F-309
A-301-5	A-321-2	A-328-6	A-349	B-400		E-303	F-313
A-301-6	A-321-3	A-329	A-349-1	B-410		E-304	F-315
A-302	A-321-4	A-329-1	A-349-2	B-414		E-305	F-318
A-302-1	A-321-5	A-329-2	A-349-3	C-305		E-307	F-323
A-302-2	A-321-6	A-329-3	A-349-4	C-306		E-309	F-331
A-302-3	A-322	A-329-4	A-349-5	C-316		E-310	F-334
A-302-4	A-322-1	A-329-5	A-349-6	C-318		E-311	F-334
A-302-5	A-322-2	A-329-6	A-353	C-324		E-312	F-339
A-302-6	A-322-3	A-330	A-355	C-332		E-313	F-345
A-303-1	A-322-4	A-330-1	A-358	C-339		E-314	F-347
A-303-2	A-322-5	A-330-2	A-369	C-349		E-315	F-348
A-303-3	A-322-6	A-330-3	A-372	C-350		E-316	F-349
A-303-4	A-323	A-330-4	A-375	C-358		E-317	F-351
A-303-5	A-323-1	A-330-5	A-377	C-366		E-318	F-352
A-304	A-323-2	A-330-6	A-378	C-378		E-319	F-359
A-304-1	A-323-3	A-331	A-380	C-379		E-320	F-361
A-304-2	A-323-5	A-332	A-382	C-380		E-321	F-365
A-304-3	A-323-6	A-335	A-387	C-381		E-323	F-366
A-304-4	A-324	A-344	A-388	C-386		E-329	F-367
A-304-5	A-324-1	A-344-1	A-391	C-389		E-336	F-388
A-304-6	A-324-2	A-344-2	A-394	C-392		E-386	F-389
A-305	A-324-3	A-344-3	A-395	C-395		E-344	
A-305-1	A-324-4	A-344-4	A-396	C-418		E-345	G-32
A-305-2	A-324-5	A-344-5	A-397	C-431		E-346	G-35
A-305-3	A-324-6	A-344-6	A-398	C-432		E-348	G-44
A-305-4	A-325	A-345	A-414	C-433		E-349	G-75
A-305-5	A-325-1	A-345-1	A-415	C-434		E-351	G-88
A-305-6	A-325-2	A-345-2		C-441		E-354	G-89
A-306	A-325-3	A-345-3	B-304	C-443		E-355	G-330
A-306-1	A-325-4	A-345-4	B-306			E-358	G-339
A-306-2	A-325-5	A-345-5	B-307		D-307	E-363	G-352
A-306-3	A-325-6	A-345-6	B-311		D-308	E-364	G-359
A-306-4	A-326	A-346	B-315		D-319	E-367	
A-306-5	A-326-1	A-346-1	B-316		D-321	E-369	H-44
A-306-6	A-326-2	A-346-2	B-317		D-325	E-373	H-46
A-306-7	A-326-3	A-336-3	B-318		D-326	E-374	G-53
A-310	A-326-4	A-346-4	B-332		D-327	E-378	H-341
A-319	A-323-4	A-346-5	B-337		D-330	E-382	H-342
A-319-1	A-326-5	A-347	B-342		D-338	E-388	H-343
A-319-2	A-326-6	A-348	B-349		D-347	E-389	H-344
A-319-3	A-327	A-347-1	B-350		D-348	E-390	H-345
A-319-4	A-327-1	A-347-2	A-392		D-351	E-415	H-346
A-319-5	A-327-2	A-347-3	B-352		D-355	E-420	H-347
A-319-6	A-327-3	A-347-4	B-353	C-416		E-348	H-348
A-320	A-327-4	A-347-5	B-354		D-360	E-440	H-349
A-320-1	A-327-5	A-347-6	B-355		D-366	E-347	H-350
A-320-2	A-327-6	A-348	B-356		D-370	E-441	H-351
A-320-3	A-328	A-348-1	B-357		D-386	E-443	G-47

TABLE IX continued

H-352	J-339	K-325	M-316	O-364	P-388	S-333
H-353	J-340	K-328	M-317	O-365	P-389	
H-354	J-341	K-331	M-321	O-368	P-441	T-5
H-355	J-342	K-332	M-325	O-373	P-442	T-12
H-356	J-343	K-333	M-336	O-374	P-444	T-13
H-357	J-344	K-335	M-337	O-399	P-445	T-19
H-358	J-345	K-336	M-338	O-400	P-446	T-22
H-359	J-346	K-338	M-339	O-401	P-447	T-26
H-362	J-347	K-339	M-342	O-403	P-460	T-27
H-363	J-348	K-340	M-343	O-404	P-472	T-37
H-364	J-349	K-342	M-347	O-406	P-480	
H-365	J-350	K-351	M-350	O-408	P-482	V-1
H-366	J-351	K-353	M-354	O-409	P-483	V-2
H-367	J-352	K-371	M-359	O-412	P-484	V-17
H-368	J-379	K-374	M-372	O-422	P-485	V-22
H-370	J-421	K-387	M-383	O-426	P-487	V-24
H-371	J-342	K-396	M-384	O-427	P-488	V-46
H-372	J-433	K-397	M-392	O-429	P-489	V-51
H-373	J-434		M-404	O-457	P-508	V-58
H-374	J-435		M-406	O-475	P-526	
H-376	J-436	L-10	M-407	O-486	P-527	W-5
H-377	J-437	L-12	M-418	O-492	P-528	W-22
H-389	J-445	L-36		O-493		W-23
H-390	J-446	L-37		O-495	R-2	W-26
H-391	J-447	L-43	O-24	O-496	R-7	W-28
H-395	J-448	L-46	O-39		R-8	W-39
	J-449	L-49	O-40		R-13	W-42
J-5	J-450	L-49A	O-48	P-4	R-14	
J-8	J-453	L-68	O-53	P-7	R-16	X-15-8
J-22	J-454	L-69	O-55	P-9	R-300	X-17-8
J-304	J-455	L-71	O-56	P-10	R-301	X-17-9
J-305	J-456	L-72	O-58	P-12	R-377	X-19-8
J-306	J-457	L-81	O-50	P-13	R-378	X-19-9
J-307	J-458	L-85	O-303	P-24	R-390	X-22
J-308	J-459	L-310	O-304	P-25	R-392	X-23
J-309	J-460	L-311	O-305	P-26	R-414	X-24
J-310	J-461	L-312	O-306	P-29	R-434	X-25-8
J-311	J-469	L-322	O-307	P-33		X-36
J-313	J-480	L-323	O-308	P-38		X-84
J-314	J-481	L-324	O-309	P-48	S-5	X-85
J-315	J-482	L-336	O-310	P-50	S-6	X-87
J-316	J-484	L-339	O-311	P-69	S-9	X-89
J-317	J-499	L-349	O-321	P-75	S-10	X-90
J-318		L-358	O-322	P-81	S-11	X-91
J-319		L-365	O-323	P-323	S-12	X-93
J-320	K-24	L-410	O-324	P-332	S-16	X-93-1
J-321	K-26	L-417	O-325	P-333	S-18	X-93-2
J-322	K-28		O-329	P-344	S-45	X-93-3
J-323	K-29	M-72	O-332	P-375	S-47	X-93-4
J-324	K-31	M-89	O-334	P-380	S-64	X-93-5
J-326	K-37	M-93	O-335	P-382	S-65	X-94
J-328	K-42	M-167	O-347	P-383	S-66	X-94-1
J-329	K-47	M-300	O-348	P-384	S-67	X-94-2
J-337	K-64	M-309	O-361	P-385	S-68	X-94-3
J-338	K-65	M-310	O-362	P-386	S-73	X-94-4
	K-80	M-315	O-363	P-387	S-78	

TABLE IX continued

X-94-5	X-98-5	X-102-3	Y-70	Z-5	Z-61	Z-93
X-94-6	X-98-6	X-102-4	Y-71	Z-6	Z-63	Z-94
X-95	X-99	X-102-5	Y-72	Z-7	Z-74	Z-96
X-97	X-99-1	X-111	Y-73	Z-8	Z-75	Z-97
X-97-1	X-99-2	X-X-114	Y-75	Z-9	Z-76	Z-99
X-97-2	X-99-3	X-115	Y-76	Z-20	Z-78	Z-101
X-97-3	X-99-4	X-118	Y-78	Z-29	Z-79	Z-103
X-97-4	X-99-5	X-120	Y-84	Z-30	Z-80	Z-104
X-97-5	X-99-6	Y-18	Y-85	Z-32	Z-81	Z-106
X-97-6	X-99-7	Y-25	Y-87	Z-33	Z-82	Z-112
X-97-7	X-101	Y-36	Y-89	Z-48	Z-83	Z-114
X-98	X-101-1	Y-40	Y-93	Z-53	Z-84	Z-115
X-98-1	X-101-2	Y-48	Y-94	Z-57	Z-87	Z-118
X-98-2	X-102	Y-56		Z-58	Z-91	Z-119
X-98-3	X-102-1	Y-68		Z-2Z-60	Z-92	Z-122
X-98-4	X-102-2	Y-69				

TYPES OF PATTERNS

Although it is impossible for us to describe here every pattern ever made by Lenox, we will briefly cover the different types of patterns that were made.

Transfer Decorated: Transfer-decorated patterns are the largest single group of Lenox patterns, and this group includes some of the most popular patterns ever made there (Ming, Lenox Rose, etc.). They range from overall designs to those with only a small amount of decoration, and are frequently embellished with hand work (gold trim, enamel work).

Hand-Painted: Many of the early Lenox patterns were entirely hand-painted, and the combination of the hand-painting and the early marks puts them in the highly-collectible category. This is, or course, reflected in their value. Since they were done by hand, there will be considerable variation in both color and placement of design. Much of the information listed under pattern #82 in the price guide applies to the hand-painted grouping as a whole.

Gold-Banded Patterns: Lenox patterns decorated with only gold, silver or platinum bands have always been popular, and one of them (Tuxedo) is the oldest (1912) Lenox pattern still being made today. The bands can be either acid-etched or flat gold. These patterns tend to hold up very well under use, and they have a listing appeal (unlike some of the transfer patterns which can look "dated" twenty years after they were first made). Lenox has always made a wide variety of these patterns, and they range in price from the least expensive patterns (Mansfield) to the most expensive (Westchester).

Gold trim predominated in early years, no doubt in part because the early silver trims needed polishing. The current use of platinum instead of silver has taken care of that problem, and the platinum trims seem very popular. It is interesting to note, however, that on the secondary market gold patterns almost always bring more than the platinum ones.

See following pages for illustrations of the more common gold borders.

Undecorated: Up until a few years ago, all of the various Lenox shapes were available completely undecorated. The ones most frequently encountered are Temple Plain and Coupe Plain, although the others do turn up now and then. One should be careful to differentiate between undecorated Lenox shapes with the wreath mark and those pieces of platte mark Lenox which were sold to be decorated and never were for some reason. Although all different marks can be used to fill in missing pieces, the palette mark items should be considered incomplete, and therefore not worth quite so much. Lenox is not currently making any undecorated dinnerware, and prices for these items should be figured by comparing them to the least expensive pattern in a given shape.

Embossed Dinnerware: The dinnerware discussed in previous sections is a type where decoration was applied as the china was nearing completion. There was another type, where the pattern was actually part of the china, having been molded in as part of the production process. The proper name for this ware is embossed dinnerware, although it is commonly (and incorrectly) referred to as pate-sur-pate or as glazed jasperware.

Embossed dinnerware was available both in plain white and in colors with the white sections standing up in relief against the colored background. It is these colored pieces that gave rise to the misnomers, since from a distance they do hear a passing resemblance to other types of wares with raised designs. Those patterns with color on the rims tend to be rather heavy in appearance and feel.

ETCHED BORDERS

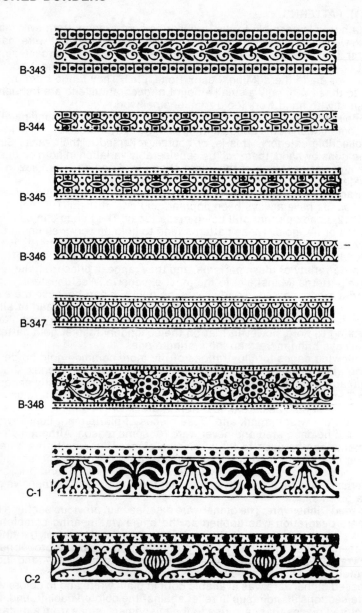

B-343

B-344

B-345

B-346

B-347

B-348

C-1

C-2

ETCHED BORDERS

ETCHED BORDERS

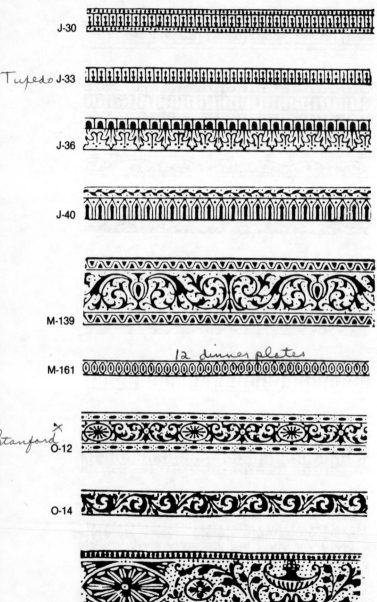

J-30

Tuxedo J-33

J-36

J-40

M-139

12 dinner plates
M-161

Stanford O-12

O-14

P-22

ETCHED BORDERS

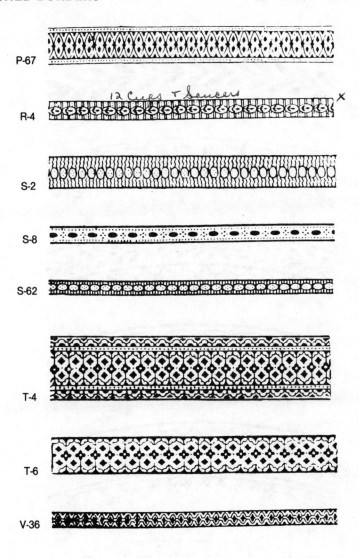

P-67

R-4   12 Cups T Saucers   X

S-2

S-8

S-62

T-4

T-6

V-36

GOLD PRINT BORDERS

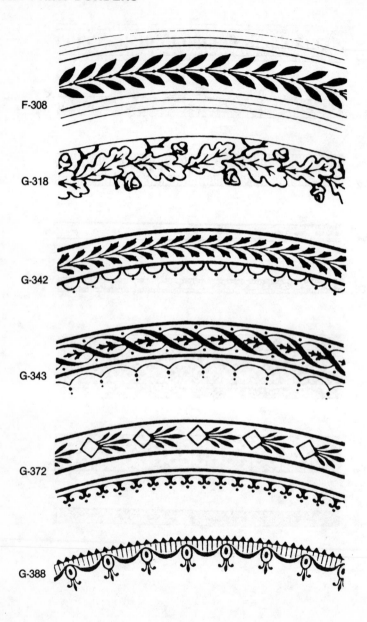

F-308

G-318

G-342

G-343

G-372

G-388

GOLD PRINT BORDERS

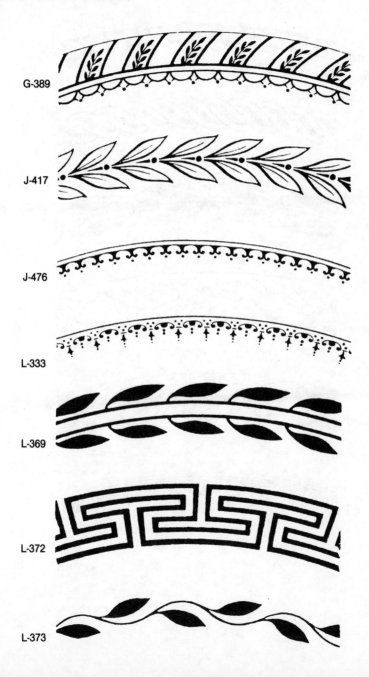

G-389

J-417

J-476

L-333

L-369

L-372

L-373

GOLD PRINT BORDERS

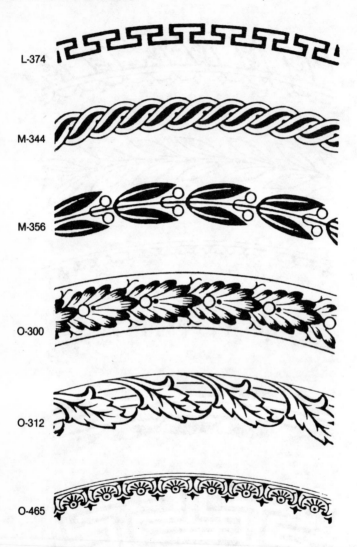

L-374

M-344

M-356

O-300

O-312

O-465

Many of the embossed patterns had a limited assortment of available shapes and sizes, and some of the patterns had no serving pieces. Some of the embossed patterns are frequently seen on gift items, and there could quite possibly do double duty on the dinner table.

Below is a list of embossed dinnerware patterns.

Apple Blossom	Hawthorn	Temple
Beltane	Pagoda	Terrace
Classic	Plymouth	Three-Step
Fontaine	Sheffield	Washington/Wakefield
Gadroon		

Many of the embossed patterns were also available in decorated versions (e.g., Gadroon Rose), but the plain versions are much more common. They have the added attraction of not showing wear, and damage is also very hard to see.

The embossed patterns do have one great disadvantage, and that is that they are very difficult to clean, particularly once food has dried in the crevices. (Try a toothbrush!)

DISCONTINUED PATTERNS

Due to production poblems or declining sales, the Lenox Company occasionally finds it necessary to discontinue a particular pattern. Although this is, of course, distressing to the people who own these patterns, it is not an insurmountable problem. Before the patterns are dropped completely, they are always available on special order for a while.

Many people have the mistaken notion that "open stock" means that a pattern will be made forever, and they become rather upset when their pattern is discontinued. (Open stock simply means that you can buy a piece at a time, as opposed to the idea of having to buy whole or partial sets at one time as is the case, for example, with many cheap sets of china.) Try to keep in mind that if the Lenox Company (or any other fine china company, for that matter) were forced to continue making unprofitable patterns, there would soon be no Lenox Company.

We would like to put to rest, once and for all, the persistent rumor that the Lenox Company will buy back your china should it be discontinued. This is definitely not the case.

If your pattern is still in production, it is a good idea to check in with your local retail outlet once a year or so to verify that the pattern is still available. It is also recommended that you purchase perhaps an extra place setting or so (or at the very least an extra cup, since they are always the first to go.)

If your pattern is one of those that has been discontinued, it is probably a good idea to try to complete your set only if you have at least half of what you will finally want. Looking for discontinued patterns can be frustrating and/or expensive, and it is probably not a worthwhile endeavor if you only have a few place settings of a pattern.

The place to start is with stores in your area that carry Lenox china. If your pattern has been discontinued only recently, there is a good chance you will be able to find what you need at these stores. We find it best to go in person rathern than to call.

The next step is to write to the Lenox Company for a list of dealers who specialize in handling discontinued china. When writing to these dealers, be as precise as possible in your first letter, since this will save everyone a great deal of time and trouble. Give dimensions of pieces you are trying to match, as well as all the information stamped on the back (pattern names and numbers, shape numbers, and the color of the backstamp if that matters to you.) It is also a good idea to enclose a self-addressed, stamped envelope since a few of the dealers will not answer you without one. Since there are waiting lists for some of the more popular patterns, do not expect immediate results. All of these matching services maintain "wants" lists, and they will let you know when they have what you need.

The prices charged by these matching services tend to be high and you will probably find considerable price variations among them, though, so don't be too quick to order from the first one to answer you.

If you decide to place an order, be very specific about what it is you are ordering and whether or not you will accept a partial order. Be sure to include your name and address where the package is to be shipped, since the dealer may not be able to find your original correspondence quickly, or may have more than one customer by that name. Double check your arithemetic and add in any shipping costs or sales tax.

It is important for you to know whether you are buying new or used china, and if it is used, what the condition of it is. To the best of our knowledge, they all allow returns if the customer is not happy, but it is best to check on this in advance to avoid any misunderstandings.

Other sources for old china include flea markets, yard sales, auctions, antique shows, etc. The chief problem in obtaining your china this way is that you may have to buy items you don't want to obtain those you do (i.e., taking a teapot you will never use to get the sugar and creamer that are with it). Prices tend to be lower than those of the matching services, but remember to mentally add in your time and travel expenses, plus the fact that you may never find what you want.

An ad in the "china wanted" section of antiques publications may bring results, and many dealers clip out the wanted ads and save them for future reference.

In general, the chances of finding your pattern are good unless your pattern is particularly obscure or you are being unrealistic about how much you want to spend.

CURRENT LENOX DINNERWARE

The Lenox Company presently has about fifty patterns in active production, ranging from the very formal to the informal. An additional twenty or so patterns are available only on a custom order basis. These current patterns are so marked within the listings. No specific pieces are mentioned because they currently can be purchased at retail cost and therefore carry no range of collector value.

Oxford Bone China is also produced by Lenox, and is currently available in about twenty different patterns. Since the Oxford line is still relatively new, very little of the china has shown up on the used market, and we have not included any prices for the Oxford because of this.

Lenox Temper-Ware is freezer and oven-proof, and can also be used in a microwave oven. It is guaranteed against breakage, chipping cracking and crazing for two years of normal home use. We have not yet seen any Temper-Ware on the secondary market so cannot list prices for it.

Crystal is available in some forty patterns, many of which coordinate with

Lenox dinnerware patterns. Used Lenox crystal does turn up now and then in antiques shops, and as a rule seems to be priced at about half to three-quarters of the going retail rate.

ADDISON

☐ **No recent listings.**

	Price Range	
ADRIENNE		
☐ **Bread and butter plate**	10.00	12.00
☐ **Cup and saucer**	37.00	43.00
☐ **Dinner plate**	23.00	28.00
☐ **Salad, dessert plate**	17.00	22.00
ALARIS		
☐ **Bread and butter plate**	6.75	7.75
☐ **Cigarette lighter and urn**	40.00	47.00
☐ **Cup and saucer**	33.00	38.00
☐ **Dinner plate**	18.00	23.00
☐ **Salad, dessert plate**	15.00	20.00
☐ **Sugar and creamer**	68.00	78.00
☐ **Vegetable bowl,** *large, open, oval*	40.00	47.00
☐ **Vegetable bowl,** *small, open, oval*	33.00	38.00
ALDEN		
☐ **Dinner plate**	23.00	28.00
ANGELINA		
☐ **Cup and saucer**	18.00	23.00
ANTOINETTE		
☐ **Cup and saucer**	40.00	47.00
☐ **Dinner plate**	23.00	28.00

APPLE BLOSSOM

Apple Blossom is most commonly seen in the white and coral combination, although it was also available in other colors as well as plain white. There were no serving pieces in Apple Blossom, and the selection of place

Apple Blossom, *cream soup cup and plate*

setting items was also limited. All of the following prices are for coral and white items. Other colors should be priced about the same, while the plain white should generally be slightly less. Additional listings of Apple Blossom can be found in the giftware section.

	Price	Range
☐ Bread and butter plate	14.00	18.00
☐ Cream soup cup and underplate	18.00	23.00
☐ Cup and saucer	33.00	38.00
☐ Demitasse cup and saucer	78.00	23.00
☐ Dinner plate	23.00	28.00
☐ Salad, dessert plate	15.00	20.00

ARCADIA

☐ Bread and butter plate	14.00	18.00
☐ Salad, dessert plate	15.00	20.00

ARDEN ROSE
☐ No recent listings.

ARISTOCRAT
☐ Current pattern

ARROWHEAD

☐ Bread and butter plate	10.00	14.00
☐ Cup and saucer	33.00	38.00
☐ Dinner plate	17.00	22.00
☐ Gravy boat	47.00	55.00
☐ Salad, dessert plate	14.00	18.00
☐ Vegetable bowl, *large, oval*	47.00	55.00

ATHENIA
☐ No recent listings.

ATHENIA COUPE
☐ No recent listings.

AURORA

☐ Bread and butter plate	9.00	13.00
☐ Cream soup cup and underplate	18.00	23.00
☐ Cup and saucer	33.00	38.00
☐ Salad plate, *square*	15.00	20.00

AUTUMN

Autumn was first introduced in 1919, and remains one of the more popular Lenox patterns. Since it is still being made, prices for the more common items can be found in a current retail list. All of the items listed below are out-of-production items.

☐ Baked apple dish *with underplate*	75.00	85.00
☐ Bouillon cup and saucer	27.00	32.00
☐ Cheese and cracker dish, *two pieces*	68.00	78.00
☐ Chocolate pot	105.00	120.00
☐ Coffee cup and saucer	33.00	38.00
☐ Compote, *3" high, 9" diameter, badly worn*	6.00	7.75
☐ Fruit bowl, *double handled, 9" diameter, not including handle*	105.00	120.00

	Price Range	
☐ Coffee cup and saucer	33.00	38.00
☐ Compote, *3" high, 9" diameter, badly worn*	6.75	7.75
☐ Fruit bowl, *double handled, 9" diameter not including handles*	105.00	120.00
☐ Platter, *16" round*	135.00	155.00
☐ Ramekin, *small chip under rim*	6.75	7.75
☐ Vegetable bowl, *covered, double-handled*	135.00	155.00

AVON

☐ Bread and butter plate	14.00	18.00
☐ Cup and saucer	33.00	38.00
☐ Dinner plate	18.00	23.00
☐ Salad, dessert plate	16.00	21.00

BALLAD

☐ Bread and butter plate	10.00	14.00
☐ Cup and saucer	27.00	32.00
☐ Dinner plate	17.00	22.00
☐ Salad, dessert plate	13.00	16.00

BANCROFT
☐ No recent listings.

BARCLAY
☐ Current pattern.

BARCLAY R-307 *(DISCONTINUED)*
☐ No recent listings.

BEACON HILL

☐ Bread and butter plate	13.00	16.00
☐ Cup and saucer	33.00	38.00
☐ Teapot	60.00	70.00

BELFORD
☐ No recent listings.

BELLAIRE
☐ No recent listings.

BELLEFONTE *(ALSO SEEN SPELLED BELFONT)*

☐ Saucer	4.00	5.00

BELLEVUE MAROON
☐ No recent listings.

BELLEVUE SEA GREEN

☐ Bread and butter plate	15.00	20.00
☐ Cup and saucer	40.00	47.00
☐ Dinner plate	23.00	28.00
☐ Platter, *small oval*	47.00	55.00
☐ Salad, dessert plate	17.00	22.00
☐ Sugar and creamer	80.00	95.00
☐ Vegetable bowl, *large oval*	47.00	55.00

BELMONT

☐ Dinner plate	16.00	21.00
☐ Salad, dessert plate	9.00	13.00

Bellevue Sea Green, *creamer*

	Price Range	
BELTANE		
☐ **Cream soup cup and underplate,** *green with white*	23.00	28.00
☐ **Dinner plate,** *pale peach with white*	27.00	32.00
☐ **Fruit saucer,** *blue with white*	15.00	20.00
☐ **Soup plate,** *yellow with white*	18.00	23.00
BELVIDERE		
☐ **Bread and butter plate**	13.00	16.00
☐ **Cup and saucer**	37.00	43.00
☐ **Gravy boat**	68.00	78.00
☐ **Platter,** *large oval*	80.00	95.00
☐ **Platter,** *small oval*	55.00	63.00
☐ **Salad, dessert plate**	14.00	18.00
☐ **Soup plate**	18.00	23.00
☐ **Sugar and creamer**	80.00	95.00

Belvidere, *sugar and creamer*

BERKELEY
☐ No recent listings.

BLUE BELL
☐ No recent listings.

BLUE RIDGE

	Price Range	
☐ Bread and butter plate	13.00	16.00
☐ Cup and saucer	37.00	43.00
☐ Dinner plate	18.00	23.00
☐ Salad, dessert plate	14.00	18.00

BLUE TREE

☐ Cookie plate, *square*	47.00	55.00

BRADFORD

☐ Creamer	40.00	47.00
☐ Cup and saucer	23.00	28.00
☐ Salad, dessert plate	13.00	16.00
☐ Sugar bowl and lid	47.00	55.00

BROOKDALE
☐ Current pattern.

BROOKLINE

☐ Cup and saucer	40.00	47.00
☐ Dinner plate	27.00	32.00
☐ Salad, dessert plate, *8¼", diameter*	17.00	22.00

BROOKSIDE
☐ No recent listings.

CAMBRIDGE

☐ Bread and butter plate	17.50	22.50
☐ Cup and saucer	47.50	55.00
☐ Salad, dessert plate	23.00	28.00
☐ Service for 6, *50 pieces*	500.00	600.00

CAPRI

☐ Bread and butter plate	9.00	13.00
☐ Cream soup cup *with underplate*	23.00	28.00
☐ Cup and saucer	37.00	43.00
☐ Dinner plate	19.00	24.00
☐ Salad, dessert plate	15.00	20.00
☐ Vegetable bowl, *large oval*	47.00	55.00

CAPRICE

☐ Footed compote, *9" diameter*	33.00	38.00

CARIBBEE

☐ Service for 12, *total of 80 pieces*	1350.00	1550.00
☐ Dinner plate	19.00	24.00

CARLYLE
☐ No recent listings.

CAROLINA
☐ No recent listings.

Price Range

CASCADE
- ☐ Dinner plate 33.00   28.00
- ☐ Salad, dessert plate 13.00   16.00

CASINO
- ☐ Cup and saucer 30.00   35.00
- ☐ Dinner plate 23.00   28.00

CASTLE GARDEN
- ☐ Current pattern.

CATTAILS
- ☐ Bread and butter plate 13.00   16.00
- ☐ Cup and saucer 30.00   35.00
- ☐ Dinner plate 19.00   24.00
- ☐ Fruit saucer 15.00   20.00
- ☐ Salad, dessert plate 15.00   20.00
- ☐ Teapot 47.00   55.00

CECILE
- ☐ No recent listings.

CELESTE
- ☐ Bread and butter plate 9.00   13.00
- ☐ Cup and saucer 33.00   38.00
- ☐ Dinner plate 23.00   28.00
- ☐ Salad, dessert plate 10.00   14.00

CHALET
- ☐ Bread and butter plate 13.00   16.00
- ☐ Dinner plate 23.00   28.00
- ☐ Salad, dessert plate 14.00   18.00
- ☐ Sugar and creamer 78.00   88.00
- ☐ Teapot 60.00   70.00
- ☐ Vegetable bowl, *large oval* 47.00   55.00

CHANSON
- ☐ Bread and butter plate 8.00   11.00
- ☐ Cup and saucer 33.00   38.00
- ☐ Dinner plate 17.50   22.50
- ☐ Salad, dessert plate 13.00   16.00
- ☐ Small platter 45.00   52.00

CHANTILLY
- ☐ Dinner plate 19.00   24.00
- ☐ Teapot 60.00   70.00
- ☐ Vegetable bowl, *large oval* 33.00   38.00

CHARMAINE
- ☐ Bread and butter plate 13.00   16.00
- ☐ Cup and saucer 33.00   38.00
- ☐ Dinner plate 17.50   22.50
- ☐ Gravy boat 60.00   70.00
- ☐ Platter, *small oval* 47.00   55.00
- ☐ Vegetable bowl, *covered* 85.00   100.00
- ☐ Vegetable bowl, *large oval* 40.00   47.50

Chanson, *bread and butter plate*

	Price Range	

CHELSEA

☐ Gravy boat	55.00	63.00
☐ Platter, *large oval, gold worn*	23.00	28.00
☐ Platter, *round buffet, gold worn*	18.50	23.50
☐ Vegetable bowl, *large oval, tiny fleck under rim and gold worn* .	13.00	16.00

CHESTERFIELD

☐ **No recent listings.**

CHIPPENDALE

☐ Demitasse cup, *no saucer*	13.00	16.00
☐ Dinner plate, *badly scratched and worn*	6.75	7.75
☐ Salad, dessert plate	9.00	13.00

CINDERELLA

☐ Sugar bowl and lid	40.00	47.00
☐ Vegetable bowl, *large oval*	55.00	63.00
☐ Vegetable bowl, *covered*	105.00	120.00

CLAREMONT

☐ **No recent listings.**

CLARION

☐ Bread and butter plate	13.00	16.00
☐ Cup and saucer	40.00	47.50
☐ Dinner plate	19.00	24.00
☐ Platter, *large oval*	68.00	78.00
☐ Salad, *dessert plate*	16.50	21.50
☐ Soup, *salad bowl*	23.00	28.00
☐ Vegetable bowl, *large*	40.00	47.50

CLASSIC

Classic is very similar to the Temple shape, but the fluting does not extend as far on Classic as it does on Temple. The Temple serving pieces were used with Classic.

	Price Range	
☐ Cup and saucer	17.50	22.50
☐ Dinner plate	17.50	22.50
☐ Salad, dessert plate	9.00	11.00

CLASSIC ROSE
☐ No recent listings.

COLONIAL

☐ Bread and butter plate	13.00	16.00
☐ Cream soup cup, *with underplate*	18.50	23.50
☐ Dinner plate	17.50	22.50
☐ Service for 12, *120 pieces, badly worn, several chips*	400.00	470.00

COLONNADE GOLD

☐ Bread and butter plate	10.00	14.00
☐ Cup and saucer	33.00	38.00
☐ Dinner plate	18.50	23.50
☐ Salad, dessert plate	15.00	20.00
☐ Soup plate	16.50	21.50
☐ Vegetable bowl	40.00	47.00

COLONNADE PLATINUM

☐ Bread and butter plate	13.00	16.00
☐ Cup and saucer	30.00	35.00
☐ Dinner plate	16.50	21.50
☐ Salad, dessert plate	14.00	18.00

COQUETTE

☐ Bread and butter plate	9.00	11.00
☐ Cup and saucer	30.00	35.00
☐ Dinner plate	17.50	22.50
☐ Fruit saucer	15.00	20.00
☐ Platter, *large oval*	60.00	70.00
☐ Platter, *small oval*	47.00	55.00
☐ Salad, dessert plate	13.00	16.00
☐ Soup bowl	15.00	20.00

CORALTON

☐ Dinner plate	19.00	24.00
☐ Teapot	90.00	110.00

CORINNE

☐ Coffeepot	68.00	78.00
☐ Sugar and creamer	68.00	78.00

CORINTHIAN
☐ No recent listings.

CORONADO

☐ Cup and saucer, *after dinner*	27.50	32.50
☐ Dinner plate	30.00	35.00

	Price Range	
☐ **Fruit saucer**	23.00	28.00
☐ **Serving bowl,** *9" diameter, round*	68.00	78.00

COUNTRY GARDEN

☐ **Bread and butter plate**	13.00	16.00
☐ **Cup and saucer**	30.00	35.00
☐ **Salad, dessert plate**	15.00	20.00

COUPE (PLAIN)

☐ **Bread and butter plate**	9.00	13.00
☐ **Cup and saucer**	27.50	32.50
☐ **Dinner plate**	16.50	21.50
☐ **Salad, dessert plate**	13.00	16.00
☐ **Salad serving bowl**	47.50	55.00

COVINGTON

☐ **Service for 12,** *8 piece place settings with several serving pieces, total of 110 pieces*	900.00	1100.00

CRETAN

☐ **Bouillon cup and saucer,** *current pattern*	18.50	23.50

CRINOLINE

☐ **Cup after dinner,** *mismatched saucer of unknown origin*	15.00	20.00
☐ **Bread and butter plate**	9.00	13.00

CYNTHIA

☐ **Cup and saucer**	17.50	22.50
☐ **Dinner plate**	37.00	43.00
☐ **Vegetable bowl**	40.00	47.50

DAYBREAK

☐ **Bread and butter plate**	12.00	15.00
☐ **Cup and saucer**	33.00	38.00
☐ **Dinner plate**	19.00	24.00
☐ **Salad, dessert plate**	13.00	16.00

DIANA

☐ **No recent listings.**

DUBARRY GRAY

☐ **Cup and saucer,** *after dinner*	19.00	24.00
☐ **Bread and butter plate**	13.00	16.00
☐ **Cup and saucer**	37.00	43.00
☐ **Dinner plate**	18.50	23.50
☐ **Salad, dessert plate**	18.50	23.50

ECLIPSE

☐ **Current pattern.**

EMPRESS

☐ **Dinner plate**	19.00	24.00
☐ **Gravy boat**	60.00	70.00

ESSEX BLUE

☐ **Soup plate,** *scalloped rim*	17.50	22.50

Price Range

ESSEX GREEN
☐ No recent listings.

ESSEX MAROON
☐ Cup and saucer	47.50	55.00
☐ Dinner plate	19.00	24.00
☐ Sugar and creamer	80.00	95.00
☐ Vegetable bowl, *large oval*	60.00	70.00

ETERNAL
☐ Current pattern.

ETNA
☐ Cup and saucer	23.00	28.00
☐ Dinner plate	16.50	21.50

ETRUSCAN
☐ Gravy boat	68.00	78.00
☐ Platter	60.00	70.00

EVANSTON
☐ Bouillon cup and saucer	16.50	21.00
☐ Ramekin	13.00	16.00

FAIRFIELD
☐ No recent listings.

FAIR LADY
☐ Current pattern.

FAIRMOUNT
☐ Cup and saucer, *after dinner*	19.00	24.00
☐ Bread and butter plate	13.00	16.00
☐ Cup and saucer	33.00	38.00
☐ Dinner plate	23.00	28.00
☐ Salad, dessert plate	15.00	20.00
☐ Tete-a-tete *cup with 8¼" plate*	18.50	23.50

FANTASY
☐ Bread and butter plate	13.00	16.00
☐ Cup and saucer	30.00	35.00
☐ Dinner plate	17.50	22.50
☐ Salad, dessert plate	15.00	22.00
☐ Soup, salad bowl	18.50	23.50

FESTIVAL
☐ Bread and butter plate	15.00	20.00
☐ Candlesticks, *8", tall*	68.00	78.00
☐ Cup and saucer	40.00	47.00
☐ Dinner plate	27.50	32.50
☐ Salad, dessert plate	18.50	23.50
☐ Vegetable bowl, *large oval*	55.00	63.00

FIRESONG
☐ Cup and saucer	30.00	35.00
☐ Dinner plate	17.50	22.50

	Price Range	
☐ Gravy boat	68.00	78.00
☐ Salad, dessert plate	15.00	20.00
☐ Soup, salad bowl	18.50	23.50

FLORALIA *(GREEN)*

☐ Soup plate	15.00	20.00
☐ Vegetable bowl, *large oval*	30.00	35.00

FLORALIA *(PINK)*

☐ Cup and saucer, *after dinner*	18.50	23.50
☐ Cereal bowl	9.00	13.00
☐ Soup plate	13.00	16.00

FLORIDA

☐ Bread and butter plate	18.50	23.50
☐ Cup and saucer	42.00	48.00
☐ Dinner plate	33.00	38.00
☐ Platter, *round, 16" diameter, worn*	33.00	38.00
☐ Sugar and creamer	80.00	95.00
☐ Teapot	80.00	95.00
☐ Teapot, *individual size, tiny fleck on spout*	33.00	38.00

Florida, *teapot*

FLOURISH

☐ Bread and butter plate	13.00	16.00
☐ Cup and saucer	37.00	43.00
☐ Dinner plate	19.00	24.00
☐ Salad, dessert plate	15.00	20.00
☐ Vegetable bowl	55.00	63.00

FONTAINE

☐ No recent listings.

	Price Range	

FOUNTAIN

☐ Bread and butter plate	16.50	21.50
☐ Cup and saucer	42.00	48.00
☐ Dinner plate	27.50	32.50
☐ Salad, dessert plate	18.50	23.50
☐ Teapot, coffeepot, sugar and creamer	260.00	320.00

FOUNTAINBLEU

☐ No recent listings.

FRONTENAC

☐ No recent listings.

FUTURA

☐ Bread and butter plate	10.00	14.00
☐ Cup and saucer	27.50	32.50
☐ Dinner plate	17.50	22.50
☐ Gravy boat	68.00	78.00
☐ Salad, dessert plate	14.00	18.00
☐ Vegetable bowl, *oval*	47.50	65.00

GADROON

☐ Cup and saucer, *after dinner*	15.00	20.00
☐ Bread and butter plate	9.00	11.00
☐ Cup and saucer	27.50	32.50
☐ Dinner plate	17.50	22.50
☐ Platter, *round, 13" diameter*	55.00	63.00

GADROON ROSE

☐ Bread and butter plate	13.00	16.00
☐ Dinner plate	27.50	32.50
☐ Salad, dessert plate	16.50	21.50
☐ Vegetable bowl	55.00	63.00

GAYLORD

☐ Bread and butter plate	13.00	16.00
☐ Coffeepot	40.00	47.50
☐ Cup and saucer	30.00	35.00
☐ Dinner plate	17.50	22.50
☐ Salad, dessert plate	15.00	20.00
☐ Soup bowl	17.50	22.50

GENEVIEVE

☐ Dinner plate	18.50	23.50
☐ Saucer, *no cup*	2.50	3.50

GEORGIAN

☐ No recent listings.

GLENDALE

☐ Bread and butter plate	13.00	16.00
☐ Cup and saucer	37.00	43.00
☐ Dinner plate	23.00	28.00
☐ Salad, dessert plate	15.00	20.00
☐ Sugar and creamer	90.00	110.00

Glendale, *creamer*

	Price Range	

GLENTHORNE
☐ Bread and butter plate	13.00	16.00
☐ Dinner plate	23.00	28.00
☐ Soup plate	17.50	22.50
☐ Vegetable bowl, *oval large*	47.50	55.00
☐ Vegetable bowl, *oval small*	42.00	48.00
☐ Vegetable bowl, *round, covered*	80.00	95.00

GOLD CASINO
☐ No recent listings.		

GOLDEN BLOSSOM
☐ Cup and saucer	40.00	47.50
☐ Dinner plate	27.50	32.50
☐ Salad plate, *square*	18.00	23.50

GOLDEN GATE
☐ Cup and saucer, *after dinner*	23.00	28.00
☐ Bread and butter plate	15.00	20.00
☐ Cup and saucer	40.00	47.50
☐ Dinner plate	27.50	32.50
☐ Fruit saucer	17.50	22.50
☐ Platter, *oval, 16"*	68.00	78.00
☐ Salad, dessert plate	18.50	23.50
☐ Sugar and creamer	90.00	110.00

GOLDEN MOOD
☐ Bread and butter plate	9.00	13.00
☐ Cup and saucer	33.00	38.00
☐ Dinner plate	18.50	23.50
☐ Salad, dessert plate	13.00	16.00

	Price Range	
☐ Sugar and creamer	68.00	78.00
☐ Teapot	60.00	70.00
☐ Vegetable bowl, *large round*	55.00	63.00

GOLDEN WREATH

☐ Bread and butter plate	10.00	14.00
☐ Cup and saucer	30.00	35.00
☐ Dinner plate	19.00	24.00
☐ Fruit saucer	15.00	20.00
☐ Salad, dessert plate	15.00	20.00
☐ Sugar and creamer	68.00	78.00

GREENFIELD

☐ Bread and butter plate	8.00	10.00
☐ Cup and saucer	33.00	38.00
☐ Dinner plate	18.50	23.50
☐ Fruit saucer	17.50	22.50
☐ Soup plate	17.50	22.50

GREENWICH
☐ No recent listings.

GRENOBLE

☐ Dinner plate	18.50	23.50
☐ Soup plate	17.50	22.50

GRENOBLE IVORY
☐ No recent listings.

HARVEST

☐ Bread and butter plate	9.00	13.00
☐ Cup and saucer	27.00	32.00
☐ Dinner plate	15.00	20.00
☐ Gravy boat	68.00	78.00
☐ Salad, dessert plate	13.00	16.00
☐ Soup plate	15.00	20.00
☐ Vegetable bowl, *large oval*	40.00	47.50
☐ Vegetable bowl, *round, covered*	120.00	140.00

HARWOOD
☐ No recent listings.

HATHAWAY
☐ No recent listings.

HAWTHORN

Items in the Hawthorn pattern were among the earliest pieces made by Lenox, and Item #1 in C.A.C. catalogues was a Hawthorn cup and saucer. In the 1960's, the pattern was briefly brought back to life as a limited edition, both in plain white and with gold trim. Earlier versions were produced in a variety of colors.

☐ Bread and butter plate, *coral and white*	9.00	13.00
☐ Cup and saucer, *bouillon, blue and white*	17.50	22.50
☐ Cup and saucer, *covered, two-handled, white*	23.00	28.00
☐ Cup and saucer, *cream soup, coral and white*	40.00	47.50

	Price Range	
☐ **Cup and saucer,** *full size, white, very thin*	68.00	78.00
☐ **Cup and saucer,** *full size, white, gold trim*	33.00	38.00
☐ **Cup and saucer,** *full size, blue and white*	33.00	38.00
☐ **Cup and saucer,** *small size, white, C.A.C., thin*	60.00	70.00
☐ **Cup and saucer,** *small size, white with gold trim*	28.00	33.00
☐ **Dinner plate,** *white*	40.00	47.50
☐ **Luncheon plate,** *coral and white*	13.00	16.00
☐ **Luncheon plate,** *white*	10.00	14.00
☐ **Salad plate,** *white*	13.00	16.00
☐ **Salad plate,** *coral and white*	15.00	20.00
☐ **Salad plate,** *white, thin*	23.00	28.00
☐ **Salad plate,** *blue and white*	13.00	16.00
☐ **Sugar and creamer,** *white, C.A.C., very thin*	195.00	235.00
☐ **Teapot, sugar and creamer,** *coral and white*	165.00	195.00
☐ **Teapot, sugar and creamer,** *blue and white*	165.00	195.00
☐ **Waste bowl,** *plain white*	40.00	47.50

Note: See the Limited Edition section for prices on the reproduction Hawthorn items.

HUDSON
☐ **No recent listings.**

IMPERIAL
☐ **Bread and butter plate**	9.00	13.00
☐ **Cup and saucer**	27.50	32.50
☐ **Dinner plate**	18.50	23.50
☐ **Gravy boat**	68.00	78.00
☐ **Platter,** *large oval*	80.00	95.00
☐ **Salad, dessert plate**	13.00	16.00
☐ **Sugar and creamer**	68.00	78.00
☐ **Teapot**	105.00	120.00
☐ **Vegetable bowl,** *large oval*	40.00	47.50

INTERLUDE
☐ **No recent listings.**

JEWEL
☐ **Cup and saucer,** *after dinner*	18.50	23.50
☐ **Bread and butter plate**	13.00	16.00
☐ **Coffeepot**	60.00	70.00
☐ **Cup and saucer**	33.00	38.00
☐ **Dinner plate**	18.50	23.50
☐ **Gravy boat**	60.00	70.00
☐ **Platter,** *large oval*	68.00	78.00
☐ **Platter,** *medium oval*	55.00	63.00
☐ **Platter,** *small oval*	40.00	47.50
☐ **Salad, dessert plate**	15.00	20.00
☐ **Soup plate**	18.50	23.50
☐ **Teapot**	60.00	70.00

JOAN
☐ **No recent listings.**

JOSEPHINE
☐ **No recent listings.**

KENMORE
☐ No recent listings.

KINGSLEY

	Price	Range
☐ Cup and saucer, *after dinner*	23.00	28.00
☐ Bread and butter plate	13.00	16.00
☐ Cup and saucer	40.00	47.50
☐ Dinner plate	23.00	28.00
☐ Footed bowl, *small triangular shape*	17.50	22.50
☐ Salad, dessert plate	16.50	21.50
☐ Soup plate	19.00	24.00
☐ Sugar bowl and lid	33.00	38.00

LAFAYETTE

☐ Cup and saucer	30.00	35.00
☐ Dinner plate	19.00	24.00
☐ Salad, dessert plate	13.00	16.00
☐ Teapot	40.00	47.50

LAUREL
☐ No recent listings.

LAURENT
☐ Current pattern.

LENORE
☐ No recent listings.

LENOX ROSE

First introduced in 1934, this pattern enjoyed tremendous popularity and until last year was still available on a custom order basis.

Lenox Rose is perhaps the only pattern that can come close to Ming in collectibility, since both patterns were made in a huge assortment of items with a wide distribution over the years. In general, we find Lenox Rose to be superior to the Ming in that it does not show wear as quickly as the Ming does.

The Lenox Company made many variations on the basic Lenox Rose idea (e.g., Pavlova and Aurora), and most of the variations were also successful patterns.

On the used china market, Lenox Rose brings almost as much as the new. In the collecting market, giftware items with this design on them are avidly sought.

☐ Bouillon cup and saucer	18.50	23.50
☐ Bread and butter plate	13.00	16.00
☐ Cream soup cup and saucer	27.50	32.50
☐ Cup and saucer	33.00	38.00
☐ Cup and saucer, *after dinner*	18.50	23.50
☐ Dinner plate	23.00	28.00
☐ Egg cup, *large*	27.50	32.50
☐ Fruit saucer	15.00	20.00
☐ Gravy boat	68.00	78.00
☐ Mayonnaise bowl	27.50	32.50
☐ Milk pitcher	68.00	78.00
☐ Platter, *medium oval*	90.00	110.00
☐ Platter, *small oval*	80.00	95.00

	Price Range	
☐ **Platter,** *round*	55.00	63.00
☐ **Salad, dessert plate**	16.50	21.50
☐ **Salt and pepper,** *3" high*	33.00	38.00
☐ **Sugar and creamer**	80.00	95.00
☐ **Teapot**	68.00	78.00
☐ **Vegetable bowl,** *large oval*	55.00	63.00
☐ **Vegetable bowl,** *small oval*	40.00	47.50
☐ **Vegetable bowl,** *round, covered*	165.00	195.00

LEXINGTON
☐ **No recent listings.**

LINCOLN
☐ **No recent listings.**

LOMBARDY
☐ **No recent listings.**

LONSDALE
☐ **No recent listings.**

LOWELL
☐ **Cup and saucer**	23.00	28.00
☐ **Compote,** *8" diameter*	55.00	63.00
☐ **Teapot,** *individual size*	40.00	47.50

LUXORIA
☐ **No recent listings.**

LYRIC
☐ **No recent listings.**

MADISON
☐ **Dinner plate**	33.00	38.00
☐ **Mustard pot** *with underplate*	55.00	63.00
☐ **Salad, dessert plate**	17.50	22.50

MAJESTIC
☐ **Bread and butter plate**	13.00	16.00
☐ **Cup and saucer**	30.00	35.00
☐ **Dinner plate**	17.50	22.50
☐ **Fruit saucer**	16.50	21.50
☐ **Gravy boat**	55.00	63.00
☐ **Salad, dessert plate**	15.00	20.00
☐ **Vegetable bowl,** *large oval*	40.00	47.50
☐ **Vegetable bowl,** *covered*	80.00	95.00

MALMAISON
☐ **Cup and saucer, after dinner**	19.00	24.00
☐ **Bread and butter plate**	13.00	16.00
☐ **Creamer**	40.00	47.50
☐ **Cream soup cup** *with underplate*	18.50	23.50
☐ **Cup and saucer**	30.00	35.00
☐ **Dinner plate**	23.00	28.00
☐ **Salad, dessert plate**	15.00	20.00
☐ **Vegetable bowl,** *large oval*	47.50	55.00

Price Range

MANDARIN

☐ Cup and saucer, *after dinner*	25.00	32.50
☐ Bread and butter plate	16.00	21.50
☐ Coffeepot	85.00	100.00
☐ Cream soup cup *with underplate*	18.50	23.50
☐ Cup and saucer, *full size*	40.00	47.50
☐ Dinner plate	27.50	32.50
☐ Gravy boat	85.00	100.00
☐ Platter, *large oval*	80.00	95.00
☐ Platter, *small oval*	68.00	78.00
☐ Salad, dessert plate	18.50	23.50
☐ Sugar and creamer	90.00	110.00
☐ Tazza, *considerable gold wear*	17.50	22.50
☐ Teapot	85.00	100.00
☐ Vegetable bowl, *large oval*	80.00	95.00
☐ Vegetable bowl, *round, covered*	165.00	195.00

Mandarin, *sugar and creamer*

MANSFIELD

Current pattern. Many of the old, numbered gold-banded patterns which are not listed in this price guide can be compared against current Mansfield prices.

MARLBORO

☐ No recent listings.

MARYLAND

☐ Bread and butter plate	10.00	14.00
☐ Dinner plate	18.50	23.50
☐ Platter, *round*	90.00	110.00
☐ Salad, dessert plate	14.00	18.00

MAYFAIR

☐ No recent listings.

MAYWOOD

☐ No recent listings.

Price Range

MEADOWBROOK

☐ Compote, *gold worn*	18.50	23.50
☐ Cookie plate, *square with handles*	33.00	38.00
☐ Cup and saucer	40.00	47.50
☐ Dinner plate	27.50	32.50
☐ Salad, dessert plate	15.00	20.00
☐ Tete-a-tete set *cup 8" and 8¼" plate*	18.50	23.50

MELISSA

☐ Bread and butter plate	9.00	13.00
☐ Cup and saucer	33.00	38.00
☐ Dinner plate	19.00	24.00
☐ Salad, dessert plate	13.00	16.00

MELODY

☐ Salad, dessert plate	14.00	18.00
☐ Saucer *no cup*	4.00	5.00

MEMOIR

☐ Bread and butter plate	13.00	16.00
☐ Coffeepot	68.00	78.00
☐ Cup and saucer	40.00	47.50
☐ Dinner plate	18.50	23.50
☐ Platter, *small oval*	47.50	55.00
☐ Salad, dessert plate	16.50	21.50
☐ Soup bowl	18.50	23.50

MEREDITH

☐ Cup and saucer	40.00	47.50
☐ Dinner plate	19.00	24.00
☐ Salad, dessert plate, *badly worn*	5.00	7.00
☐ Sugar and creamer	68.00	78.00
☐ Teapot	80.00	95.00
☐ Vegetable bowl, *large oval*	55.00	63.00

MERRIVALE

☐ Cup and saucer	30.00	35.00
☐ Dinner plate	17.50	22.50
☐ Gravy boat	68.00	78.00
☐ Luncheon plate, *9" diameter*	9.00	13.00
☐ Salad, dessert plate	15.00	20.00

MINERVA

☐ No recent listings.

MING

Ming was introduced in 1917, and was the first Lenox pattern to be copyrighted. It enjoyed immense popular appeal through the years, and has become the "in" pattern for people to collect, which has resulted in very inflated prices for the pattern.

Ming coloration can vary greatly from one piece to another, due both to minor variations in the original dyes and to fading from excessive or careless use. In many cases, the blue borders are faded almost completely to gray, leading many people to believe Ming was made in more than one color. Since the pattern was made for so many years, flat pieces such as dinner plates will vary somewhat in shape.

The pattern does have a certain charm, however, and the wide variety of items available in the pattern can make life very interesting for the Ming collector.

Ming was originally produced on the standard shape dinnerware, and was later also produced on coupe and temple shape items as well. We have no current listings for Ming Coupe or Ming Temple.

Ming, *covered muffin dish*

		Price Range	
☐ Cup and saucer *after dinner, footed*	33.00	38.00
☐ Cup and saucer, *after dinner, rounded shape*	23.00	28.00
☐ Biscuit jar, *covered*	165.00	195.00
☐ Bouillon cup and saucer	27.50	32.50
☐ Bread and butter plate, *5¾"*	13.00	16.00
☐ Bread and butter plate, *6½"*	13.00	16.00
☐ Butter tub	68.00	78.00
☐ Cake plate, *footed, 12" diameter*	115.00	130.00
☐ Candlesticks, *pair, small*	85.00	100.00
☐ Cereal bowl, *6" diameter*	15.00	20.00
☐ Cheese and cracker dish, *2 pieces*	105.00	120.00
☐ Chocolate pot	165.00	195.00
☐ Coffeepot, *full size*	135.00	155.00
☐ Coffeepot, *individual size*	80.00	95.00
☐ Covered muffin dish	90.00	110.00
☐ Cup and saucer, *footed type cup*	40.00	47.50
☐ Cup and saucer, *rounded bottom*	30.00	35.00
☐ Cup and saucer, *cream soup*	27.50	32.50
☐ Decanter	135.00	155.00
☐ Dinner plate, *10"*	27.50	32.50
☐ Dinner plate, *10½"*	33.00	38.00

Price Range

☐ **Egg cup,** *large*	33.00	38.00
☐ **Egg cup,** *small*	33.00	38.00
☐ **Fruit saucer,** *5½" diameter*	15.00	20.00
☐ **Gravy boat,** *attached underplate*	80.00	95.00
☐ **Gravy boat,** *separate underplate*	80.00	95.00
☐ **Luncheon plate,** *9"*	13.00	16.00
☐ **Marmalade jar,** *covered, 6½" high*	68.00	78.00
☐ **Mayonnaise compote** *with underplate*	80.00	95.00
☐ **Milk pitcher**	105.00	120.00
☐ **Olive dish,** *3-footed*	55.00	63.00
☐ **Pitcher, lemonade**	125.00	145.00
☐ **Platter,** *16" oval*	110.00	125.00
☐ **Platter,** *13" round*	68.00	78.00
☐ **Platter,** *12" oval*	105.00	120.00
☐ **Ramekin**	18.50	23.50
☐ **Salad plate,** *7½"*	17.50	22.50
☐ **Salad plate,** *8¼"*	17.50	22.50
☐ **Salt and pepper shaker,** *3" high*	40.00	47.50
☐ **Soup plate,** *8¼" diameter*	18.50	23.50
☐ **Sugar and creamer,** *full size*	105.00	120.00
☐ **Sugar bowl,** *individual size*	33.00	38.00
☐ **Tea tile**	105.00	120.00
☐ **Teapot**	135.00	155.00
☐ **Tumbler**	40.00	47.50
☐ **Vegetable bowl,** *oval, open, 9½" long*	55.00	63.00

MODERN PROFILE

☐ **Bread and butter plate**	8.00	10.00
☐ **Cup and saucer**	27.50	32.50
☐ **Dinner plate**	17.50	22.50
☐ **Fruit saucer**	15.00	20.00
☐ **Sugar, creamer, and coffeepot**	135.00	155.00

Modern Profile, *creamer*

Price Range

MONTCLAIR
☐ Current pattern.

MONTEREY
☐ Cup and saucer	33.00	38.00
☐ Dinner plate	27.50	32.50
☐ Sugar and creamer	68.00	78.00
☐ Teapot	47.50	55.00

Monterey, *sugar bowl*

MONTICELLO
☐ Complete service for 12, *120 pieces, badly worn*	900.00	1100.00
☐ Dinner plate	18.50	23.50
☐ Salad, dessert plate	13.00	16.00

MOONLIGHT
☐ Bread and butter plate	9.00	13.00
☐ Cup and saucer	23.00	28.00
☐ Dinner plate	17.50	22.50
☐ Salad, dessert plate	13.50	16.00

MOONLIGHT MOOD
☐ Current pattern.

MOONSPUN
☐ Current pattern.

MORNING BLOSSOM
☐ Current pattern.

MOUNT VERNON
This pattern is sometimes referred to as "poor man's Virginian, since it is so very similar yet not quite so opulent.

	Price Range	
□ Bread and butter plate	23.00	28.00
□ Cup, *no saucer, small footed*	33.00	38.00
□ Salad, dessert plate	23.00	28.00
□ Sugar, creamer, teapot	165.00	195.00

MUSETTE

□ Bread and butter plate	13.00	16.00
□ Cup and saucer	30.00	35.00
□ Dinner plate	18.00	23.50
□ Salad, dessert plate	15.00	20.00
□ Vegetable bowl, *small oval*	33.00	38.00

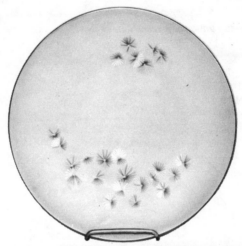

Moonlight, *bread and butter plate*

MYSTIC

□ Bread and butter plate	9.00	13.00
□ Cup and saucer	33.00	38.00
□ Dinner plate	18.50	23.50
□ Mustard pot *with underplate*	47.50	55.00
□ Ramekin with underplate	18.50	23.50
□ Salad, dessert plate	15.00	20.00

MYSTIQUE

□ Cup and saucer	30.00	35.00
□ Gravy boat	60.00	70.00
□ Platter, *small oval*	60.00	70.00
□ Salad, dessert plate	15.00	20.00

NATOMA

□ Cup and saucer	33.00	38.00
□ Salad, dessert plate	13.00	16.00

NAUTILUS
☐ No recent listings.

NEWPORT
☐ No recent listings.

NOBLESSE
☐ Current pattern.

NOCTURNE
☐ No recent listings.

NORMAND
☐ No recent listings.

NYDIA

	Price Range	
☐ Cream soup cup *with underplate*	27.50	32.50
☐ Cup and saucer	33.00	38.00
☐ Dinner plate	18.00	23.50

OAKLEAF BLUE
☐ No recent listings.

OAKLEAF GREEN

☐ Bread and butter plate	13.00	16.00
☐ Dinner plate	18.50	23.50

OAKLEAF RED

☐ Dinner plate	18.50	23.50

OLYMPIA GOLD
☐ Current pattern.

ORCHARD

☐ Coffeepot	55.00	63.00
☐ Creamer	33.00	38.00
☐ Cup and saucer	33.00	38.00
☐ Dinner plate	23.00	28.00
☐ Relish tray, *9" oval*	18.50	23.50
☐ Sugar bowl *with lid*	40.00	47.00

ORLEANS

☐ Bread and butter plate	13.00	16.00
☐ Cup and saucer	30.00	35.00
☐ Dinner plate	18.50	23.50
☐ Gravy boat	55.00	63.00
☐ Salad, dessert plate	15.00	20.00
☐ Salad serving bowl	68.00	78.00
☐ Soup bowl	17.50	22.50
☐ Vegetable bowl, *large oval*	40.00	47.50

OSLO

☐ Bread and butter plate	10.00	14.00
☐ Dinner plate	15.00	20.00
☐ Salad, dessert plate	13.00	16.00
☐ Saucer *no cup*	5.00	7.00

Orchard, *coffeepot*

	Price Range	

PAGODA

☐ **Bread and butter plate,** *white* 9.00 13.00
☐ **Cream soup cup** *with underplate, white* 18.50 23.50
☐ **Fruit saucer,** *blue and white* 13.00 16.00
☐ **Luncheon plate,** *white* 13.00 16.00
☐ **Salad, dessert plate,** *white* 13.00 16.00

PALISADES

☐ **No recent listings.**

Orleans, *bread and butter plate*

Price Range

PASADENA
☐ **No recent listings.**

PAVLOVA
☐ Bread and butter plate	13.00	16.00
☐ Centerpiece or serving bowl, *12" long, footed, small chip on base*	40.00	47.50
☐ Cup and saucer	33.00	38.00
☐ Dinner plate	17.50	22.50
☐ Fruit saucer	13.00	16.00
☐ Salad, dessert plate	15.00	20.00
☐ Soup plate	15.00	20.00

PEACHTREE
☐ Bread and butter plate	13.00	16.00
☐ Cup and saucer	30.00	35.00
☐ Dinner plate	17.50	22.50
☐ Salad, dessert plate	15.00	20.00
☐ Salad serving bowl	60.00	70.00

PEKING
☐ Bread and butter plate	10.00	14.00
☐ Cup and saucer, *two-handled*	13.00	16.00
☐ Dinner plate	17.50	22.50
☐ Salad, dessert plate	15.00	20.00

Peking, *dinner plate*

PEMBROOK
☐ Cup and saucer	40.00	47.50
☐ Dinner plate	23.00	28.00

PINE
☐ Bread and butter plate	10.00	14.00

	Price Range	
☐ Cup and saucer	33.00	38.00
☐ Dinner plate	18.50	23.50
☐ Gravy boat	68.00	78.00
☐ Luncheon plate	9.00	13.00
☐ Platter, *small oval*	47.00	55.00
☐ Salad, dessert plate	15.00	20.00
☐ Soup plate	17.50	22.50
☐ Teapot	68.00	78.00
☐ Vegetable bowl, *large oval*	47.50	55.00
☐ Vegetable bowl, *round, covered*	80.00	95.00

Pine, *bread and butter plate*

PINEHURST BLUE

☐ Bread and butter plate	15.00	20.00
☐ Cream soup cup *with underplate*	27.50	32.50
☐ Cup and saucer	37.00	43.00
☐ Dinner plate	18.50	23.50
☐ Luncheon plate	13.00	16.00
☐ Salad, dessert plate	17.50	22.50
☐ Vegetable bowl, *large oval*	55.00	63.00

PINEHURST RED

☐ Cup, no saucer	13.00	16.00

PLATINA
☐ No recent listings.

PLUM BLOSSOM
☐ Current pattern.

PLYMOUTH

☐ Bread and butter plate	7.00	9.00
☐ Cream soup cup *with underplate*	9.00	13.00

	Price Range	
☐ Cup, no saucer	13.00	16.00
☐ Dinner plate	15.00	20.00
☐ Salad, dessert plate	9.00	13.00

Pinehurst Blue, *dinner plate*

PRINCESS

☐ Bread and butter plate	9.00	13.00
☐ Cup and saucer	30.00	35.00
☐ Dinner plate	17.50	22.50
☐ Luncheon plate	4.00	5.00
☐ Platter, *medium oval*	68.00	78.00
☐ Platter, *small oval*	40.00	47.50
☐ Salad, dessert bowl	15.00	20.00
☐ Salad, dessert plate	13.00	16.00
☐ Sugar and creamer	68.00	78.00

PRINCETON

☐ No recent listings.

PRISCILLA

☐ Cup and saucer	33.00	38.00
☐ Dinner plate, *repaired*	3.00	4.00

PROJECTION

☐ Bread and butter plate	9.00	13.00
☐ Cup and saucer	27.50	32.50
☐ Dinner plate	15.00	20.00
☐ Salad, dessert plate	13.00	16.00
☐ Saucer, *no cup*	6.75	7.75

PROMISE

☐ Current pattern.

Princess, *sugar bowl*

RADIANCE
☐ Current pattern.

RAPTURE

	Price Range	
☐ Bread and butter plate	6.75	7.75
☐ Cup and saucer	18.50	23.50
☐ Dinner plate	15.00	20.00
☐ Salad, dessert plate	9.00	13.00

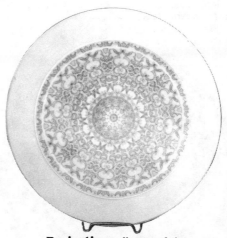

Projection, *dinner plate*

Price Range

RENAISSANCE
☐ Bread and butter plate 15.00   20.00
☐ Cream soup cup *with underplate*......................... 27.50   32.50
☐ Dinner plate 23.00   28.00
☐ Salad, dessert plate 15.00   20.00

REPERTOIRE
☐ Current pattern.

REVERE
☐ No recent listings.

REVERIE
☐ Current pattern.

RHAPSODY
☐ No recent listings.

RHODORA
☐ Current pattern.

RHYTHM
☐ Cup and saucer 27.50   32.50
☐ Dinner plate 15.00   20.00
☐ Luncheon plate 17.50   22.50

RIVOLI
☐ No recent listings.

ROCK GARDEN
☐ Bread and butter plate 15.00   20.00
☐ Cream soup cup *with underplate*....................... 27.50   32.50
☐ Cup and saucer 40.00   47.50

Rock Garden, *bread and butter plate*

	Price Range	
☐ Dinner plate	23.00	28.00
☐ Luncheon plate	18.50	23.50
☐ Salad, dessert plate	18.50	23.50

ROMANCE

☐ Bread and butter plate	13.00	16.00
☐ Cup and saucer	33.00	38.00
☐ Dinner plate	19.00	24.00
☐ Platter, *medium oval*	68.00	78.00
☐ Salad, dessert plate	16.50	21.50

RONDELLE

☐ Bread and butter plate	10.00	14.00
☐ Cup and saucer	27.50	32.50
☐ Dinner plate	16.50	21.50
☐ Salad, dessert plate	13.00	16.00

ROSEDALE

☐ Bread and butter plate	13.00	16.00
☐ Cup and saucer	30.00	35.00
☐ Fruit saucer	15.00	20.00
☐ Salad, dessert plate	14.00	18.00
☐ Soup bowl	17.50	22.50

ROSELYN

☐ Bread and butter plate	9.00	13.00
☐ Cup and saucer	30.00	35.00
☐ Dinner plate	16.50	21.50
☐ Salad, dessert plate	13.00	16.00
☐ Sugar and creamer	68.00	78.00

ROSEMONT

☐ Bread and butter plate	13.00	16.00
☐ Dinner plate	17.50	22.50
☐ Soup bowl	15.00	20.00

ROYAL

☐ No recent listings.

ROYAL OAK

☐ Bread and butter plate	15.00	20.00
☐ Dinner plate	30.00	35.00

RUTLEDGE

☐ Current pattern.

SARATOGA

☐ No recent listings.

SAVOY MAROON

☐ Cup and saucer	40.00	47.50

SCULPTURE PLAIN

☐ Bread and butter plate	9.00	13.00
☐ Cup and saucer	27.50	32.50
☐ Dinner plate	17.50	22.50
☐ Salad, dessert plate	13.00	16.00

Price Range

SHALIMAR
☐ Bread and butter plate	9.00	13.00
☐ Cup and saucer	33.00	38.00
☐ Dinner plate	16.50	21.50
☐ Luncheon plate	8.00	10.00
☐ Salad, dessert plate	15.00	20.00
☐ Vegetable bowl, *large oval*	47.50	55.00

SHEFFIELD
☐ Bread and butter plate	8.00	12.00
☐ Cup and saucer	18.50	23.50
☐ Dinner plate	15.00	20.00
☐ Salad, dessert plate	9.00	13.00

SHENANDOAH
☐ **No recent listings.**

SHERATON
☐ Cup and saucer	22.00	28.00

SHERATON IVORY
☐ **No recent listings.**

SNOW LILY
☐ **Current pattern.**

SOLITAIRE
☐ **Current pattern.**

SOMERSET
☐ Dinner plate	27.50	32.50
☐ Luncheon plate	8.00	10.00
☐ Salad, dessert plate	14.00	18.00

SONATA
☐ Cup and saucer	38.00	43.00

SONNET
☐ Bread and butter plate	15.00	20.00
☐ Cup and saucer	42.00	48.00
☐ Dinner plate	23.00	28.00
☐ Salad, dessert plate	16.50	21.50
☐ Sugar and creamer	80.00	95.00

SOUTHERN GARDEN
☐ Cup and saucer	47.50	55.00
☐ Dinner plate	27.50	32.50

SPRINGDALE *(NEW)*
☐ **Current pattern.**

SPRINGDALE *(OLD)*
☐ **No recent listings.**

SPRINGFIELD
☐ **No recent listings.**

Price Range

SPRINGTIME

☐ Cream soup underplate	13.00	16.00
☐ Dinner plate	18.50	23.50
☐ Salad, dessert plate	15.00	20.00

STANDARD PLAIN

☐ Bread and butter plate	6.75	7.75
☐ Cup and saucer	18.50	23.50
☐ Dinner plate	13.00	16.00
☐ Luncheon plate	8.00	10.00
☐ Salad, dessert plate	9.00	13.00

STANFORD

☐ Bread and butter plate	15.00	20.00
☐ Cup and saucer	40.00	47.50
☐ Dinner plate	23.00	28.00
☐ Salad, dessert plate	18.50	23.50
☐ Teapot	80.00	95.00
☐ Vegetable bowl, *large oval*	55.00	63.00

STARFIRE

☐ Current pattern.

STARLIGHT

☐ Bread and butter plate, *worn*	3.00	4.00
☐ Cup and saucer	30.00	35.00
☐ Dinner plate	16.50	21.50
☐ Salad, dessert plate	13.00	16.00
☐ Teapot	47.50	55.00

STRADIVARIUS

☐ Cup and saucer, *after dinner*	15.00	20.00

STRATFORD

☐ No recent listings.

SUMMER BREEZE

☐ Bread and butter plate	10.00	14.00
☐ Cup and saucer	30.00	35.00
☐ Dinner plate	15.00	20.00
☐ Salad, dessert plate	13.00	16.00
☐ Salad serving bowl	47.50	55.00

SYMPHONY

☐ Cup and saucer	30.00	35.00
☐ Dinner plate	17.50	22.50
☐ Luncheon plate	9.00	13.00
☐ Salad, dessert plate	13.00	16.00

TABLEAU

☐ No recent listings.

TEMPLE PLAIN

☐ Bread and butter plate	8.00	10.00
☐ Cup and saucer	23.00	28.00
☐ Dinner plate	17.50	22.50

	Price Range	
☐ Gravy boat	40.00	47.50
☐ Salad, dessert plate	9.00	13.00
☐ Serving bowl, *round, 9" diameter*	40.00	47.50
☐ Sugar and creamer	68.00	78.00

TEMPO

☐ Bread and butter plate	13.00	16.00
☐ Cup and saucer	40.00	47.50
☐ Dinner plate	23.00	28.00
☐ Platter, *large oval*	80.00	95.00
☐ Platter, *small oval*	68.00	78.00
☐ Salad, dessert plate	16.50	21.50
☐ Vegetable bowl, *large oval*	55.00	63.00

TERESA

☐ No recent listings.

TERRACE

☐ Luncheon plate, *badly scratched*	4.00	5.00
☐ Salad, dessert plate	8.00	10.00

THREE-STEP

☐ No recent listings.

TRANSITIONAL

☐ Bread and butter plate	9.00	13.00
☐ Cup and saucer	30.00	35.00
☐ Dinner plate	17.50	22.50
☐ Salad, dessert plate	13.00	16.00
☐ Vegetable bowl, *round*	47.50	55.00

TRELLIS

☐ Gravy boat	55.00	63.00
☐ Soup plate	13.00	16.00
☐ Vegetable, *large oval*	40.00	47.50
☐ Vegetable, *round, covered*	68.00	78.00

TRELLIS IVORY

☐ Bread and butter plate	7.00	10.00
☐ Soup plate	9.00	13.00

TREMONT THE

☐ Cup and saucer, *after dinner*	19.00	24.00
☐ Bread and butter plate	13.00	16.00
☐ Cup and saucer	23.00	28.00
☐ Dinner plate	18.50	23.50
☐ Luncheon plate	13.00	16.00
☐ Salad, dessert plate	13.00	16.00

TRENT

☐ Bouillon cup and saucer	18.50	23.50
☐ Bread and butter plate	13.00	16.00
☐ Dinner plate	27.50	32.50
☐ Luncheon plate	13.00	16.00
☐ Salad, dessert plate	15.00	20.00
☐ Sugar and creamer	80.00	95.00

	Price Range	
☐ **Vegetable bowl,** *large oval*	47.50	55.00
☐ **Vegetable bowl,** *small oval*	40.00	47.50

TRIANON
☐ No recent listings.

TRIO

☐ **Bread and butter plate**	10.00	14.00
☐ **Cup and saucer**	30.00	35.00
☐ **Dinner plate**	16.50	21.50
☐ **Gravy boat**	55.00	63.00
☐ **Luncheon plate**	9.00	13.00
☐ **Salad, dessert plate**	13.00	16.00

TRIUMPH
☐ No recent listings.

TROY
☐ No recent listings.

TUDOR
☐ Current pattern.

TUSCANY
☐ Current pattern.

TUXEDO

☐ **Bouillon cup, no saucer**	13.00	16.00
☐ **Coffeepot,** *individual size*	40.00	47.00
☐ **Compote,** *footed, 9" diameter*	47.50	55.00
☐ **Egg cup,** *large size*	18.50	23.50
☐ **Coffeepot,** *individual size*	40.00	47.50
☐ **Compote,** *footed, 9" diameter*	47.50	55.00
☐ **Egg cup,** *large size*	18.50	23.50
☐ **Sugar and creamer,** *individual size*	33.00	38.00
☐ **Teapot,** *individual size*	40.00	47.50

VALERA

☐ **Bread and butter plate**	13.00	16.00
☐ **Cup and saucer**	33.00	38.00
☐ **Dinner plate**	17.00	22.50
☐ **Gravy boat**	68.00	78.00
☐ **Platter,** *medium oval*	68.00	78.00
☐ **Cup and saucer**	33.00	38.00
☐ **Dinner plate**	17.50	22.50
☐ **Gravy boat**	68.00	78.00
☐ **Platter,** *medium oval*	68.00	78.00
☐ **Salad, dessert plate**	15.00	20.00
☐ **Soup bowl**	17.50	22.50

VASSAR
☐ No recent listings.

VENDOME
☐ No recent listings.

VENTURE
☐ **Current pattern.**

VERNON
☐ **No recent listings.**

VICTORIA

	Price	Range
☐ **Cup,** *after dinner, no saucer*	9.00	13.00
☐ **Cup and saucer**	37.00	43.00
☐ **Dinner plate**	18.50	23.50
☐ **Platter,** *large oval*	60.00	70.00

VILLA
☐ **No recent listings.**

VIRGINIAN

☐ **Cup and saucer,** *after dinner*	47.50	55.00
☐ **Bread and butter plate**	27.50	32.50
☐ **Coffeepot**	135.00	155.00
☐ **Compote,** *9" high, scalloped rim*	165.00	195.00
☐ **Dinner plate**	55.00	63.00
☐ **Tea caddy**	135.00	155.00
☐ **Teapot**	135.00	155.00

Virginian, *bread and butter plate*

WASHINGTON

☐ **Bread and butter plate**	13.00	16.00
☐ **Dinner plate**	23.00	28.00
☐ **Salad, dessert plate**	16.50	21.50

WASHINGTON/WAKEFIELD

Washington/Wakefield is a reproduction of the English salt-glazed stoneware that was found during the excavation of George Washington's boyhood home at Wakefield, Westmoreland County, Virginia. This homestead burned to the ground on Christmas Day, 1780. Excavation of the site began in 1925. Shards of pottery that were found there were taken to the Lenox Company to be reproduced, and the result was the Washington/Wakefield pattern. Advertising literature of the day indicates that a portion of each sale of this pattern was donated by Lenox to help restore the Wakefield home. Sharpness of the pattern can vary greatly, which can create patterns when trying to complete a set.

Washington / Wakefield, *sugar, creamer and teapot*

	Price Range	
☐ **Bowl, cereal,** *7⅞″*	16.50	21.50
☐ **Bowl, dessert,** *6¼″*	16.50	21.50
☐ **Bowl, soup,** *9⅛″*	17.50	22.50
☐ **Bowl, soup,** *8¼″*	16.50	21.50
☐ **Bowl, vegetable,** *oval covered*	165.00	195.00
☐ **Bowl, vegetable,** *oval, open*	60.00	70.00
☐ **Coffeepot**	105.00	120.00
☐ **Cup and saucer,** *after dinner*	27.50	32.50
☐ **Cup and saucer,** *full size*	40.00	47.50
☐ **Cup and saucer,** *two-handled, bouillon*	18.50	23.50
☐ **Cup and saucer,** *twh-handled, cream soup*	27.50	32.50
☐ **Plate, dessert,** *7¼″*	17.50	22.50
☐ **Plate, dinner,** *10¼″*	30.00	35.00
☐ **Plate, luncheon,** *9″*	13.00	16.00
☐ **Plate, salad,** *8¼″*	15.00	20.00
☐ **Plate, salad,** *square, 8¼″*	18.50	23.00
☐ **Plate,** *square, two-handled (for cookies)*	68.00	78.00
☐ **Platter,** *14″ oval*	60.00	70.00
☐ **Platter,** *large round*	135.00	155.00
☐ **Platter,** *small round*	68.00	78.00
☐ **Sauce boat,** *attached underplate*	85.00	100.00
☐ **Sugar and creamer,** *small, open*	105.00	120.00
☐ **Teapot**	105.00	120.00

WEATHERLY
☐ **Current pattern.**

Price Range

WESTBURY

☐ Cup and saucer	40.00	47.50

WESTCHESTER (M-139)

☐ Bouillon cup and saucer................................	27.50	32.50
☐ Compote, *5" diameter*....................................	33.00	38.00
☐ Fruit bowl, *doubled handled, 9" without handles*	80.00	95.00
☐ Mustard pot *with lid and underplate*	55.00	63.00
☐ Relish tray, *9"x 6" oval*	40.00	47.50
☐ Teapot, *individual size*	40.00	47.50

WESTCHESTER (S40C)

☐ Bread and butter plate	13.00	16.00
☐ Cup and saucer	27.50	32.50
☐ Dinner plate	18.50	23.50

Westchester, *cup and saucer*

WESTFIELD

☐ Bread and butter plate	9.00	13.00
☐ Cream soup cup *with underplate*........................	18.50	23.50
☐ Cup and saucer	30.00	35.00
☐ Dinner plate	17.50	22.50
☐ Salad, dessert plate	13.00	16.00

WESTPORT

☐ Bread and butter plate	23.00	28.00
☐ Coffeepot	155.00	185.00
☐ Cup and saucer	55.00	63.00
☐ Dinner plate	40.00	47.50
☐ Luncheon plate	23.00	28.00
☐ Salad, dessert plate	27.50	32.50
☐ Teapot	155.00	185.00

Price Range

WEST WIND

☐ Bread and butter plate	9.00	13.00
☐ Cup and saucer, *cream soup*	27.50	32.50
☐ Cup and saucer, *regular*	30.00	35.00
☐ Dinner plate	18.50	23.50
☐ Gravy boat	55.00	63.00
☐ Platter, *small oval*	40.00	47.50
☐ Salad, dessert plate	13.00	16.00
☐ Sugar and creamer	60.00	70.00
☐ Vegetable bowl, *small oval*	40.00	47.50

WHEAT

☐ Current pattern.

WINDSONG

☐ Current pattern.

WINDSOR

☐ Bread and butter plate	15.00	20.00
☐ Cup and saucer	40.00	47.50
☐ Dinner plate	23.00	28.00
☐ Platter, *large oval*	68.00	78.00
☐ Salad, dessert plate	17.50	22.50
☐ Soup plate	18.50	23.50
☐ Sugar and creamer	80.00	95.00
☐ Vegetable bowl, *large oval*	55.00	63.00
☐ Vegetable bowl, *round, covered*	105.00	120.00

WYNDCREST

☐ Bread and butter plate	10.00	14.00
☐ Cream soup cup and underplate	19.00	24.00
☐ Cup and saucer	27.50	32.50
☐ Dinner plate	17.50	22.50
☐ Gravy boat	55.00	63.00
☐ Platter, *large oval*	60.00	70.00
☐ Salad, dessert plate	13.00	16.00
☐ Soup bowl	15.00	20.00
☐ Vegetable bowl, *small oval*	40.00	47.50

A-319

☐ Service plate	23.00	28.00

A-375

☐ Service plate	33.00	38.00

A-386FQ

☐ Service plate	40.00	47.00

A-393G

☐ Large oval platter	135.00	155.00

C-318

☐ Service plate	27.50	32.50

C-416

☐ Service plate	18.50	23.50

A-386 FQ, *service plate*

	Price Range	
D-366X11-1		
☐ Service plate	40.00	47.50
E-88		
☐ Compote	55.00	63.00
F-40		
☐ Dinner plate	18.00	23.00
☐ Cup and saucer	33.00	38.00
F-308B		
☐ Dinner plate	18.50	23.50
F-372		
☐ Bread and butter plate	6.75	7.75
☐ Cereal bowl	9.00	13.00
☐ Cup and saucer	17.50	22.50
☐ Salad, dessert plate	8.00	10.00
☐ Sugar and creamer, *individual size*	33.00	38.00
☐ Teapot, *individual size*	33.00	38.00
G-31		
☐ Luncheon plate	27.50	32.50
G-44B		
☐ Service plate	125.00	145.00
H-30B		
☐ Dinner plate	23.00	28.00
☐ Soup plate	15.00	20.00
J-34		
☐ Bread and butter plate	9.00	12.00
☐ Coffeepot	40.00	47.50

	Price Range	
☐ **Cup and saucer**	18.50	23.50
☐ **Dinner plate**	15.00	20.00
☐ **Fruit saucer**	13.00	16.00
☐ **Gravy boat,** *separate underplate*	40.00	47.50
☐ **Platter,** *large oval*	68.00	78.00
☐ **Platter,** *medium oval*	55.00	63.00
☐ **Platter,** *small oval*	40.00	47.50
☐ **Platter,** *round*	40.00	47.50
☐ **Salad, dessert plate**	9.00	13.00
☐ **Soup bowl**	15.00	20.00
☐ **Soup plate**	13.00	16.00
☐ **Sugar and creamer**	68.00	78.00
☐ **Teapot**	40.00	47.50
☐ **Tray, relish,** *6"x9" oval*	18.50	23.50
☐ **Vegetable bowl,** *oval, open*	27.50	32.50
☐ **Vegetable bowl,** *round, covered*	68.00	78.00

J-319

☐ **Salad plate**	10.00	14.00

J-332

☐ **Luncheon plate**	13.00	16.00

J-417A

☐ **Dinner plate**	19.00	24.00

K-1

☐ **Creamer**	40.00	47.50

K-344B, *cup and saucer*

Price Range

K-344B

☐ Bread and butter plate	15.00	20.00
☐ Cup and saucer	40.00	47.50
☐ Dinner plate	27.50	32.50
☐ Fruit saucer	17.50	22.50
☐ Salad, dessert plate	18.50	23.50
☐ Soup plate	18.50	23.50

M-16

☐ Cup	13.00	16.00

M-391

☐ Cup and saucer	40.00	47.50

M-391-X-15-1

☐ Service plate	17.50	22.50

O-46F

☐ Dinner plate	17.50	22.50
☐ Sugar and creamer	80.00	95.00
☐ Teapot	68.00	78.00

O-46G

☐ Sugar and creamer	80.00	95.00
☐ Teapot	60.00	70.00

P-72

☐ Demitasse cup and saucer	37.00	43.00

P-73

☐ Service plate	47.50	55.00

P-73, *service plate*

	Price Range	
P-380		
☐ Service plate	40.00	47.50
P-525W		
☐ Bread and butter plate	9.00	13.00
R-407-247		
☐ Salad, dessert plate	13.00	16.00
S-32		
☐ Salad, dessert plate	23.00	28.00
S-62		
☐ Dessert plate, ½″	13.00	16.00
☐ Salad plate, 8¼″	15.00	20.00
☐ Sugar and creamer, *small, open*	55.00	63.00

S-62, *sugar and creamer*

	Price Range	
T-372-X-196		
☐ Luncheon plate	16.50	21.50
W-5C		
☐ Service plate	18.50	23.50
W-335R		
☐ Dinner plate	15.00	20.00
X-54		
☐ Service plate	18.50	23.50
X-95		
☐ Service plate	27.50	32.50
Y-69G		
☐ Service plate	27.50	32.50
Z-32A		
☐ Service plate	33.00	38.00
Z-33		
☐ Service plate	47.50	55.00
Z-81-X-9-1		
☐ Service plate	47.50	55.00

#70, blue dot creamer

#70 *(BLUE DOT)*

	Price Range	
☐ **Creamer**	40.00	47.50
☐ **Muffin dish,** *covered*	23.00	28.00
☐ **Salt dip**	15.00	20.00
☐ **Teapot,** *infuser type*	90.00	110.00

#82

Pattern #82 is perhaps the most prevalent of the early hand-painted patterns. It is found with C.A.C. marks as well as the first Lenox wreath mark and is frequently seen with a store name as well. For whatever reason, it is often the case that the saucers are marked but not the cups. This is particularly true of those items with C.A.C. marks.

There is a large pink rose with green leaves on the front of the cups, a small rosebud on the back, and occasionally an additional rosebud on the inside of the cups. Earlier pieces are much more likely to have the extra rosebud. Saucers have one large rose and two rosebuds, and other flat pieces are similarly decorated.

Variations occur in the color of the artwork as well as in the placement. Although the roses are a fairly standardized shade of pink, the green leaves vary considerably from one piece to the next. Rosebuds can face left or right, apparently depending on the whim of the artist. These variations should not be considered flaws, and one should not go out of one's way to obtain pieces that match exactly.

All of the pieces of this pattern that we have seen to date have been decorated with gold trim on handles and rims.

We have never seen any dinner plates, and it would appear that the pattern was used mainly on luncheon and tea sets.

It should be noted that the roses on this pattern are quite similar to those done by Morley on vases and other items, and perhaps were indeed done by him when he was not working on more important pieces. Many collectors and dealers have taken to calling this pattern "Morley Rose," and the decision to place this pattern in the dinnerware section was made with a great deal of hesitation.

#82, *cup and saucer, transition mark*

	Price Range	
☐ Bouillon cup and saucer, item #175, *C.A.C. transition mark* ...	47.50	55.00
☐ Chocolate cup, *double handled, transition mark*	80.00	95.00
☐ Coffeepot, *transition mark*	165.00	195.00
☐ Cup and saucer, item #309, *transition mark on saucers, cups unmarked*	60.00	70.00
☐ Cup and saucer, item #309, *Lenox wreath mark, both items marked*	47.50	55.00
☐ Salad, dessert plate, *Lenox green wreath mark*	33.00	38.00
☐ Sugar and creamer, items #372 and 373, *transition mark*	165.00	195.00

#83

Pattern #83 has small hand-painted roses and forget-me-nots and is always seen with early marks, both C.A.C. and Lenox.

☐ Salt and pepper shaker	40.00	47.50

#86

Pattern #86 is perhaps most familiar as the pattern that was used on many of the Lenox liners for silver holders. It was also available in dinnerware, however, and was also used on a variety of other useful and decorative items.

☐ Bread and butter plate	9.00	12.50
☐ Cup and saucer, *demitasse*	18.50	23.50
☐ Cup and saucer, *full size*	23.00	28.00

	Price Range	
☐ **Dinner plate**	18.50	23.50
☐ **Nut dish,** *footed, 3" diameter*	23.00	28.00
☐ **Platter,** *oval, 14" diameter*	40.00	47.50
☐ **Platter,** *round, 12"*	47.50	55.00
☐ **Salad plate**	9.00	12.00
☐ **Sugar and creamer,** *breakfast size*	40.00	47.50
☐ **Teapot**	68.00	78.00

#86-1/2

Pattern #86-1/2 is a fairly common dinnerware pattern, and was also used extensively on giftware items and on liners for silver holders.

#86-1/2 sugar bowl and lid

☐ **Bread and butter plate**	6.75	7.75
☐ **Candlesticks,** *9" tall, pair*	47.50	55.00
☐ **Compote,** *miniature*	23.00	28.00
☐ **Dinner plate**	18.50	23.50
☐ **Fruit bowl,** *two-handled, 9" diameter not including handles* . . .	55.00	63.00
☐ **Sugar bowl and lid**	33.00	38.00
☐ **Teapot**	55.00	63.00
☐ **Tete-a-tete set**	23.00	28.00

SPECIAL ORDER CHINA

From its earliest beginnings, the Lenox company welcomed special orders, and there is a wide assortment of such items still available today at reasonable prices. Colleges, businesses, sports groups, fraternal organizations and others all ordered Lenox with their insignias on it. In the eyes of most Lenox collectors, these markings diminish a piece and they would prefer the same items without the emblems. They bring the highest prices among members of those clubs or among collectors of, say, Masonic or Elks items. On the average, they can be valued at about the same as comparable items without the emblems.

Governments also ordered Lenox china with their State seals and the like decorating it. Here again, these items are not yet of primary interest to most Lenox collectors and this is reflected in the relatively low prices for such items. A State of New York plate sold recently for $20, which is rather typical. As a rule, they can be rated at the replacement cost of the plate plus perhaps a 10 percent premium for having an interesting history.

Many of the more interesting hand-painted plates were special orders, but they were put in the Artware section with the other plates. Other similar special orders were put there also, since we tried to put things where beginners would look first.

PRESIDENTIAL CHINA

Three sets of Lenox china have been made for the White House, and with the exception of a Wedgwood tea service ordered during Woodrow Wilson's time, all of the china purchased for the President's use during the last sixty years has been American-made. Lyndon B. Johnson ordered a set of Castleton during his administration, but all of the other sets were mady by the Lenox Company.

Woodrow Wilson was the first American president to order Lenox, through the Washington, D.C., firm of Dulin and Martin. Tiffay and Company had submitted designs which were deemed not satisfactory, and there apparently was some unhappiness with the way in which the whole order was handled. The final design was by frank G. Holmes of the Lenox factory and the order finally placed in 1918, at a cost of $11,251,60. It was comprised of the following items:

120 Dinner plates (10½ ")	36 Bouillon cups and saucers
120 Soup plates (8")	120 After dinner cups and saucers
120 Fish plates (8")	24 Cream soups and saucers
120 Entree plates (8")	96 Cocktails cups
120 Dessert plates (6")	24 Ramekings and underplates
120 Salad plates (")	24 Oatmeals
84 Bread and butter plates (5")	6 Chop plates (14")
96 Oyster plates (9½")	96 Service plates (11")
96 Tea cups and saucers	

Extra gold crests were ordered at the time of the original order. Delivery of the set began in August and was completed in November. The service plates have the Presidential seal in the center, with the eagle's head turned toward the bundle of arrows since it was wartime. On the well there is a narrow, acid-etched border with starts and stripes. The rim is a deep blue, and the outer edge is done in the Westchester M-139 acid-etched border. Other piecesbto the set are done with the stars and stripes acid-etched border on the outer edge, with an acid-etched border. Other pieces to the set are done with the stars and stripes acid-etches border on the outer edge, with an ivory-colored border, and another narrow etched border on the well. The backs of the items are marked with the Lenox backstamp and "The White House, 1918."

This set continued in use through the administration of Hardin, Coolidge and Hoover, and replacements were ordered from time to time. Franklin D.

Roosevelt ordered the next set of White House Lenox in 1934, at a cost of $9,301.20. These were Depression years, and the expenditure caused some criticism at that time. Mrs. Roosevelt claimed that it was cheaper to replace the entire set than to purchase individual replacements and that the order of a new set would give work to an American company. The set, ordered through William H. Plummer of New York City, was delivered finally in January, 1935, and included the below-listed items:

120 Dinner plates (10½ ")	96 Bouillon cups and saucers
120 Soup plate (8")	120 After dinner cups and saucers.
120 Fish plates (8")	24 Cream soup cups and saucers
120 Entree plates (8")	96 Cocktail cups
120 Dessert plates (6")	24 Ramekins and underplates
120 Salad plates (7")	24 Oatmeals bowls
84 Bread and butter plates (5")	6 Chop plates
96 Oyster plates (9½ ")	120 Service plates
96 Teacups and saucers	

The Roosevelt china has a narrow outer gold band with a cobalt inside it. The cobalt band has 48 gold stars in it.

A rose and plume design in gold and the Presidential seal in color and gold complete the rim design, and there is a narrow pencil-line of gold on the well.

An additional set of china, part American-made Haviland and part Lenox, was donated to the White House in 1940 after the close of the New York World's Fair where it had been in use at the Federal Building.

The Truman Lenox, ordered through B. Altman and Company of New York City, was delivered in October 1951, and included the following items.

120 Dinner plates	120 Teacups and saucers
120 Soup plates	120 Bouillon cups and saucers
240 Entree plates	120 After dinner cups and saucers
120 Tea plates	120 Cream soups cups and underplates
120 Salad plates	12 Chop plates
120 Bread and butter plates	120 Service plates
120 Oyster plates	

The new set of china cost $28,271.40, and was done in celadon green and ivory to match the newly-decorated State dining room.

The Eisenhowers ordered some gold-banded Castleton service plates, and the Kennedys ordered no china at all. The Johnsons ordered a set of Castleton china through Tiffany and Company in 1966, at a cost of $80,000 which was raised through private donation. A set of Lenox for the Nixon administration was in the works at the time of the Watergate scandal, but was cancelled shortly before Nixon's resignation. The funds for the Nixon set were also to have been supplied by private donation. All three sets of Lenox china are put to use by the current Carter administration.

To the best of our knowledge, no Lenox White House china has come on the market, so no prices can be listed here. It is our understanding that china and silver are counted after each use to prevent the pieces being taken as souvenirs, no doubt a wise precaution on the part of the White House staff. If there is any Presidential Lenox being sold, it is certainly being done very quietly, since it is unlikely that the owner of such items would care to advertise them publicly. We would suggest paying the asking price without quibbling should a piece come your way.

LENOX AND METAL ITEMS

This section concerns itself with a category of Lenox unfamiliar to many collectors — those items which have been combined in various ways with an assortment of metals. These items share some or all of the following characteristics:

(1) They require special care. (This is especially true of those items combined with silver.)

(2) The Lenox collector faces stiff competition from those in other fields (e.g., silver or stein collectors.)

(3) Many of the items were finished away from the Lenox factory, and were, therefore, not necessarily subjected to the same rigorous standards as those items completed at the factory.

(4) Many of these items are pre-World War I, and they possibly represent the efforts of the then-young company to stay afloat until it had made a name for itself.

(5) For a long time they were considered to be "illegitimate" Lenox, somehow unworthy of more than a passing glance. This has changed dramatically in the past few years with the emergence of a whole new group of collectors fro whom Lenox has no interest unless it is wrapped in silver.

(6) They are still priced far below comparable current retail prices. If a sterling silver spoon costs around $40 on today's market, surely a sterling silver demitasse cup and saucer with Lenox liner has to be a bargain at $25 or $30.

This section is divided as follows: (1) Lenox liners for sterling holders; (2) silver overlay on Lenox items, and (3) miscellaneous items.

LENOX LINERS FOR SILVER HOLDERS

Although examples of European china liners or those by other American manufacturers do turn up now and then, the overwhelming majority of these items seen today were made by Lenox. Liners were among the earliest items made at Lenox: A ramekin appears as item #151 in C.A.C. catalogues, and a demitasse liner is item #290.

Gorham and/or Mauser were probably the first silver companies to order Lenox liners for their sterling holders, with other silver manufacturers soon following suit until most major United States silver companies were producing sets. To date, no examples of foreign silver holders with Lenox liners have been seen. (The reverse is not true, however — one does see American holders with European liners.)

As a rule, the silver companies initiated the order by specifying a certain size and shape of liner, although in rare cases this procedure might have been reversed, with Lenox ordering a silver holder to fit a particular liner. The retailing of the sets was done by the silver company through jewelry stores.

These items were popular wedding gifts for many years, and usually came in velvet or satin-lined presentation cases. Few of the cases have survived to the present day, perhaps due to inexpensive construction. Most of the cases had spots for either six or eight items, and the so-called sets of twelve, so popular with today's collector, were the exception at the time they were manufactured. Gorham was the only silver company that made sets of twelve on a regular basis.

Around the time of World War II, production of liners by Lenox had just about come to an end, due to wartime production problems at Lenox and the silver companies, and also perhaps to changing life styles. The Lenox Company did make an attempt to have the silver manufacturers decide on a standard shape and size for liners, but the silver companies each wanted their own model to be the standard one. Production of liners on a special order basis must have continued for at least awhile after the war, however, since gold mark samples are seen.

The numbering system for Lenox liners seems to have been a retroactive one for the most part. For example, although bouillon liners are frequently seen with C.A.C. marks, no shape number appears on them until much later, when they were assigned #1201. Many of the items in the 1200 series of Lenox numbers were meant to be in silver holders, and it would appear that this was an attempt on the part of Lenox to make some rhyme and reason out of the rather chaotic liner situation.

Lenox collectors have ignored this aspect of Lenox for some reason, although no collection should be considered complete without a sample. From the collector's point of view, the most desirable pieces are those that have C.A.C. hand-decorated liners. These are generally found in Gorham or Mauser holders, although other marks are occasionally seen. The early Gorham and Mauser ones are quite charming and original in that the decoration on the liner quite often carries out the design on the silver. Later versions used a more or less standard pattern on the liner regardless of what the holder looked like.

Lenox collectors should bear in mind that this category is one where they will have to battle it out with another group of collectors. Since the manufacturing of these items covered a span of some fifty years, many of this country's most collectible silver patterns are included in this period. Tiffany "Chrysanthemum", Kirk "Repousse", Unger Brothers patterns in Art Nouveau designs, and others are highly prized by silver collectors. We suggest that the would-be collector of sterling and Lenox items concentrate on the quality of the liner first and the silver second, since this will tend to eliminate a lot of the competition.

There are also many unmarked holders available, and the obvious reason for this (that the manufacturer was not especially proud of the product) appears to be wrong at least part of the time. Many of the unmarked holders are of a good quality silver, and are obviously the work of a fine company. So long as the word "sterling" appears on them, we see no particular reason to ignore them simply because the maker's mark is missing.

Roughly 99 percent of the liners made by Lenox can be found in sterling holders, but we do occasionally see them in silver-plated holders, and also in brass or other metals. Judging from the Lenox marks, those items in silver-plated holders came much later and are probably not of much interest to collectors. It is possible they were made during World War II when precious metals were hard to obtain. Some of the shapes are interesting, but other than this there is little to recommend them. They are invariably priced close to the sterling models, and for the price difference we suggest buying the sterling ones.

The overwhelming majority of liners are in pattern #86 (a narrow gold band at the top, with a pencil line of gold beneath it both inside and out.) Others are considerably more elaborate, with hand-painted flowers, ribbons, raised gold paste work, cobalt and gold combinations, blue-dot enamel work, etc. The liners were also available in some dinnerware patterns such as Tuxedo, Lowell, Mandarin, and others. As a rule, the nicer liners were made for the better holders, although exceptions have been seen.

Altogether, at least a couple of hundred different decorations have been noted, some of which are worthy of special mention. The lovely liners for Tiffany "Chrysanthemum" holders are marked as pattern #E-45, and are done in two different shades of raised gold paste. The Mauser company specialized in the use of liners with a bright, apple-green exterior with garlands of flowers on the inside. This was known as pattern #338, although this number usually does not appear on the pieces. The same garlands of flowers, without the colored exterior, were used on a variety of liners for other companies, but we have no pattern numbers for most of these variations.

Blue-dot pattern #70 occurs on liners, and #69-B (blue-dot flowers with hand-painted, tiny gold leaves and borders) also shows up now and then. Many variations on these basic themes have been noted, but most are not numbered. Other patterns used combinations of blue-dot work with hand-painted floral designs.

Many of the designs used on liners were not used on any other Lenox items, making it difficult (if not impossible) to match them with a set of dinnerware. One exception to this would be the blue-dot liners, particularly #70, which is also found on dinnerware. For those patterns which did not have matching dinnerware, we suggest using them with one of the current Lenox gold-banded patterns.

One of the problems facing the collector is deciding if the liner and holder have been "married" — an empty holder filled with any liner that happens to fit. The following hints should help.

(1) Liners marked "Made for Tiffany and Co." **always** belong in a Tiffany holder (although the reverse is not necessarily true.)

(2) Some silver companies, particularly Gorham, helpfully date-marked their items. Liners and holders should, therefore, match somewhat in their markings. A Gorham holder date-marked for 1926 but filled with a C.A.C. liner is probably a marriage, although a Gorham holder date-marked for 1908 and with a C.A.C. liner probably is not (items frequently sat on warehouse shelves waiting for mates.)

(3) Other discrepancies can sometimes be seen with silver and Lenox marks, such as a particular silver company going out of business in 1910, yet the liner is marked "Made in U.S.A."

(4) Liners which do not fit well are not necessarily married. China can shrink approximately 15 percent in the firing process, and this accounts for many of the misfits. In addition, the silver holders made of a thin gauge of silver can easily be bent out of shape ever so slightly, preventing the liner from fitting properly. Not all liners have to go to the bottom to be considered "right." Sometimes the silver companies used a liner from one type of holder to go in a different one, rather than special ordering a new liner from Lenox, and they are not always good fits.

(5) Both liners and holders followed the fashions of the day, and liner and holder should be in keeping with each other.

For the most part, the easy days of collecting these items are gone, and collectors should be prepared to pay handsomely for prime specimens. They are still an excellent investment in our opinion, since so many liners get broken and the then-empty holders melted for scrap value.

See the table on page 85 at the end of this section for a listing of silver company marks.

BUTTER DISHES

Small, round dishes originally meant to hold butter show up now and then, but never seem to be of exceptionally good quality. They are about 1" to 1-1/2" high, and about 4" in diameter. Some have metal holders and others have metal lids. They occasionally have small tab handles, either in the china or in the silver. We have only three listings for these dishes, all of which are pictured.

Butter dishes

	Price Range	
☐ **International holder,** *shape* #1364, pattern #86, *openwork design, Lenox wreath mark liner*	40.00	47.50
☐ **Watson holder** *pattern* #4487, shape #1364, pattern #86, *openwork design, Lenox wreath mark liner*	40.00	47.50
☐ **Silver lid,** *shape* #1366, pattern #86, *mark rubbed, possibly International or Woodside, Lenox base, Lenox wreath mark, gold worn on handles*	40.00	47.50

DEMITASSE, CHOCOLATE, AND OTHER CUPS

Demitasses, consisting of a Lenox liner, a silver holder with handle, and (usually, but not always) a silver saucer, are undoubtedly the most common of the silver and Lenox items. All of the major silver companies made them, and many of the lesser manufacturers produced them as well. Unlike bouillon liners, which came in only a few shapes and sizes, demis were put out in a large array, the most common of which were item #1203 and #1208, both bell-shaped. There were at least ten or fifteen other bell-shaped liners, four or five barrel shaped, hexagons and octagons, and in all must have been available in at least a hundred different sizes and shapes.

Decorations on demitasse liners vary from the simple pattern #86 all the way to elaborate hand-painted specimens, and the backstamps range from the earliest C.A.C. marks right up to gold-mark samples. As it is with all of the items in the liner category, the emphasis is on early C.A.C. marks.

It is interesting to observe that although the silver makers obviously expended a great deal of time and effort in designing unique holders, in many cases, they would use the same saucer with all or most of their demis. In other instances, however, the saucers show the same degree of workmanship as the holders. In rare cases, the demitasse cups came without saucers.

Chocolate cups are exceedlingly rare, and only a few shapes and sizes have been noted. Full-size coffee or teacups are either very rare or possibly non-existent, but a 3/4 size, somewhere between a demi and a full, was made. The punch cup that is pictured is of a size and shape to be used as a teacup if desired.

Demitasse can vary in silver weight from a little over a troy ounce for holder and saucer all the way to five troy ounces. Three ounces would be considered a healthy weight. Those with shape #1203 liners are somewhat more popular than those with the #1208 liners, due to the larger size of the #1203.

The most expensive demitasse we have seen was a single one at an antique show in Washington, D. C. It was priced at $125. The average demi, however, will be priced somewhere around the scrap value of the silver plus an appropriate fee for the liner.

Note: An original box adds $5 to $25 to price depending on its condition.

Chocolate cup, *Wallace holder*

	Price Range	
CHOCOLATE AND OTHER CUPS		
☐ **Chocolate cup,** *Wallace holder, Lenox liner in pattern #86*	33.00	38.00
☐ **Chocolate cup,** *liner only, patter #338, C.A.C. mark*	80.00	95.00
☐ **Punch cup,** *Mauser, 3½ troy ounces, ornate floral and open-work design, fancy gargoyle type handle, never had saucer, patter #338 liner in Lenox wreath mark, set of six*	415.00	485.00
DEMITASSE CUPS		
☐ **Alvin holder and saucer,** *total weight 1-1/2 troy ounces, Lenox liner in pattern #86*	18.50	23.50
☐ **Alvin holder and saucer,** *total weight 1-1/2 troy ounces, open work on silver, Lenox liner in pattern #86*	23.00	28.00

Punch cup, *Mauser holder*

Price Range

☐ **Bailey, Banks, and Biddle holder and saucer,** *no maker's mark, solid plain silver with rolled rims, hollow handle, 2-1/2 troy ounces, Lenox liners in pattern #86, set of six* 235.00 285.00

☐ **Barbour Silver Company holder and saucer,** *filigree openwork design, rolled rims, total weight 2-1/2 troy ounces, Lenox liner shape #1208, rainbow set with each liner a different color (purple, pink, yellow, brown, sky blue, and tan) all with narrow gold band at rim, set of six* 260.00 320.00

Demitasse cup, *Charter Company holder*

Demitasse cup, *Dominick & Haff, plain design*

Price Range

☐ **Charter Company holder and saucer,** *weighing over 4 troy ounces, hollow handle, ornate with raised work and applied bands, Charter #SP60, possibly a special order. Lenox liner shape #1203 in pattern #P66, embossed gold band with filigree type garlands underneath, set of six* 400.00 470.00

☐ **Dominick & Haff holder and saucer,** *3 troy ounces, hollow handles in an inverted "S" pattern, ornate design with raised roses, Lenox #1203 liners in pattern #86, set of 12* 525.00 625.00

☐ **Dominick & Haff holder and saucer,** *plain design with hollow handle, rolled rim, 3 troy ounces, Lenox liners in shape #1203, pattern #86, set of six* 260.00 320.00

☐ **Dominick & Haff holder and saucer,** *geometric openwork design, hollow handle, 2-1/2 troy ounces, Lenox liners shape #86, set of eight* 260.00 320.00

☐ **Durgin holder and saucer,** *2 troy ounces, openwork design, Lenox liner #1208, pattern #86* 27.50 32.50

☐ **Durgin holder and saucer,** *2 troy ounces, hammered finish to silver, strap handle, Lenox #1208 liner, pattern #86, set of six* .. 195.00 235.00

☐ **Gorham holder,** Gorham *#A1224 on holder, also marked for Shreve, Crump and Low, total weight of 2 troy ounces deceiving because so much of holder is left open, actually a good gauge of silver, Lenox liner shape number and pattern number unknown, small, hand-painted garlands of roses with gold trim, transition mark* 68.00 78.00

Note: This same holder has been seen with a variety of lovely liners, including blue dot designs, and all have been C.A.C. marks. This holder has turned up on occasion with china saucers as is also the case with many of the early Gorham demis.

Demitasse cup, *Gorham holder*

Price Range

☐ **Gorham holder and saucer,** *2 troy ounces, openwork design with strap handle, Lenox #1208 liner, pattern #86, set of 12 in original case* 400.00 470.00

☐ **Gorham holder and saucer,** *solid design with hollow handles, 2-1/2 troy ounces, Lenox #1203 liners, pattern #86, set of 12* ... 400.00 470.00

☐ **Gorham holder and saucer,** *openwork design, strap handles, weight 2-1/2 troy ounces, pink Lenox liners in shape #1208, set of six* 235.00 285.00

Demitasse cup, *Gorham holder, openwork design*

Price Range

☐ **Hickok-Matthews holder and saucer,** *3 troy ounces, hollow inverted "S" handles, raised floral design with piercing near rim, Lenox #1203 liners, pattern J33 (Tuxedo), set of 12* 460.00 550.00

☐ **Hickok-Matthews holder and saucer,** *2-1/2 troy ounces, hollow handles, plain design, Lenox #1203 liners, pattern #86, set of six* 195.00 235.00

☐ **International holder and saucer,** *2 troy ounces, openwork design with hollow handles, Lenox #1208 liner, pattern #86, set of 12* 330.00 395.00

☐ **International holders,** *4 troy ounces, very similar to the Charter ones shown, Lenox liners shape #1203, pattern J30 (etched gold design), set of 12, one liner missing* 460.00 550.00

☐ **Kirk holder and saucer,** *"Repousse" pattern, silver weight unknown, Lenox liners #1203, pattern #86, 12 holders and saucers, 10 liners* 1050.00 1200.00

☐ **Kirk holder and saucer,** *hollow handles, silver weight unknown, plain design, Lenox #1203 liners, pattern #86, set of eight* 425.00 500.00

☐ **Lunt holder and saucer,** *2 troy ounces, hammered effect, strap handles, Lenox #1208 liners in pattern #86B, set of 12* 260.00 320.00

☐ **Mauser holder, no saucer, stock** #5711, *openwork, hollow handle very ornate, beading on top and bottom, Lenox liner shape number unknown, pattern #338 (green exterior with garlands of flowers on the inside, gold trim), transition mark* .. 105.00 120.00

Note: This demi never had a saucer. Also, although the silver weight is under 2 troy ounces, this type of demi is considered highly desirable.

Demitasse cup, *Mauser holder*

Demitasse cup, *Redlich & Co. holder*

Price Range

☐ **Redlich & Co. holder and saucer,** *5 troy ounces, exceptional silver work, special order for Bailey, Banks and Biddle, item #6661 (not clear whether this is Redlich's number or BB&B's), applied ornate rim, ornate hollow handle with roses and engraving, main body has lots of hand engraving and raised roses. Saucers are dated 1913 on bottom, saucer and holder both monogrammed "HMS CCC" with crown above. Probably a one-of-a-kind set. The liners are #1203, pattern E81E, cobalt exterior, etched gold rims, natural Lenox interiors* 775.00   975.00

☐ **Reed & Barton holder and saucer,** *2½ ounces, openwork design, hollow handle, Lenox #1208 liner with pattern #86, set of eight* 210.00   255.00

☐ **Reed & Barton holder and saucer,** *2½ ounces, plain silver with rolled rims, strap handle, Lenox #1203 liner with pattern P-1 (Mandarin), pair* 105.00   120.00

☐ **Rogers holder and saucer,** *2½ troy ounces, openwork design with hollow handles, Lenox #1208 liner with pattern #86* 27.50   32.50

☐ **Schofield holder and saucer,** *3½ troy ounces, plain design with hollow handles, Lenox #1208 liner with pattern #86* 33.00   38.00

☐ **Tiffany holder and saucer,** *Chrysanthemum pattern, weight unknown but not exceptionally heavy, original liners with gold paste flowers, set of six* 600.00   700.00

Note: These also came with gold plating over the silver, and this type commands a much higher price.

☐ **Tiffany holder and saucer,** *in Chrysanthemum pattern, replacement liners with pattern #86 trim, set of six* 400.00   470.00

☐ **Tiffany holder and saucer,** *ornate pattern with a 1920's look to it, 4 troy ounces, Lenox liner shaped like egg cup in pattern #E88* 80.00   95.00

☐ **Towel holder and saucer,** *openwork holder with hollow handle, Lenox #1208 liner with pattern #86B, set of six* 195.00   235.00

Price Range

☐ **Unger Brothers holder only (saucers missing),** *Art Nouveau flowers, Lenox #1208 liners in pattern #86, set of six* 235.00   285.00

☐ **Wallace holder and saucer,** *openwork design with strap handles, Lenox #1203 liners in pattern #86B, set of 12 in original box* 400.00   470.00

☐ **Whiting holder and saucer,** *plain with strap handles, Lenox #1208 liners in pattern #86, set of six* 195.00   235.00

JARS

A nice assortment of jars and pots, usually covered, is available, although the quality of the silver is in many cases not particularly overwhelming. Note that some items have been included here which are not liners per se, but rather bases with silver tops.

Honey pot

☐ **Honey pot, Lenox shape** #894, pattern #86, *shaped like beehive with applied bees decorated in gold, silver marker's mark unreadable, bee finial, perfect* 105.00   120.00

☐ **Honey pot,** *same as above but with a few minor flecks on wings of china bees* 85.00   100.00

☐ **Honey pot,** *same as above but lid has pinecone shaped finial instead of bee* 85.00   100.00

☐ **Jam jar,** *Lenox wreath mark, hand-painted strawberries, no shape or pattern number, Watson openwork holder with handle and silver lid* 125.00   145.00

☐ **Jam jar,** *Lenox wreath mark, hand-painted insects which are probably supposed to be bees but which actually resemble dragonflies, Tiffany holder and lid, no shape or pattern numbers available* 135.00   155.00

☐ **Relish pot,** *no shape number known, pattern #86, silver lid by Reed & Barton* 47.50   55.00

Relish pot

	Price Range	
☐ **Relish pot,** *Lenox shape #1288,* pattern #86, *silver-plated holder by unknown maker*	40.00	47.50

PLATES AND PLATTERS

Plates and platters with sterling rims are relatively scarce, but current prices do not seem to reflect this. Dinner and luncheon plates and one large chop plate have been seen, but no oval platters have turned up.

☐ **Dinner plate,** *Lenox Rose pattern, 3/4" sterling band, maker of silver unknown*	60.00	70.00
☐ **Dinner plate,** *Beltane pattern, 3/4" sterling band, maker unknown*	68.00	78.00
☐ **Dinner plate,** *Ballad pattern, 3/4" sterling band, maker unknown, underpriced at*	33.00	38.00
☐ **Luncheon plate,** *Lenox Rose pattern, 3/4" sterling band, maker unknown*	60.00	70.00
☐ **Platter,** *round, Lenox Rose pattern, 1" ornate silver band, maker unknown*	320.00	380.00

RAMEKINS

Although ramekins are not rare, they are certainly less common than soups or demitasses. As with all of the other silver and Lenox items, there is quite a difference between the best and the worst, but this is not as pronounced with ramekins as it is with, say, demitasses.

☐ **Ramekins,** *very thin china with gold filigree work on rim and inside, garlands of hand-painted flowers also inside, some with transition mark and some with C.A.C. palette mark. Holders are by Gorham, weighing almost 6 troy ounces each, ornate silver with permanently attached underplate, set of six*	600.00	700.00

Ramekin, *Gorham holder*

Price Range

☐ **Ramekins,** *same as above except gold work less elaborate on rim and outsides of ramekins are decorated in color (two green, two raspberry, two yellow). Since the monograms on this set are identical to those on the first listing, it is assumed they were originally part of the same set. Set of six* 800.00   925.00

☐ **Ramekins,** *Lenox liners with pattern #86 trim, International sterling holders with teaspoon type handles, holders weigh approximately 2½ troy ounces, set of 12* 500.00   600.00

☐ **Ramekin,** *Lenox liner with pattern #86 liner, Tiffany holder weighing 2 troy ounces, no handle* 40.00   47.50

☐ **Ramekins,** *Lenox liners in pattern #86, International silver holders with applied piecrust rim and small ring handles, each holder about 2½ troy ounces, set of eight* 320.00   380.00

☐ **Ramekins,** *covered, Lenox wreath mark, pattern #86, Gorham openwork holders weighing 2½ troy ounces each, teaspoon handles, set of six* 260.00   320.00

Note: The teaspoon handles mentioned above were apparently available in a variety of patterns to match flatware patterns.

SALT AND PEPPER HOLDERS

This category seems to have been somewhat neglected by the silver companies since so few types have appeared on the market. Salt and pepper shakers with silver fittings have been found in only two different designs. The first type has cruet-shaped shakers with handles, sterling caps, and snap-on sterling bases. The second type has a salt and pepper with silver caps on a small silver tray (or on a Lenox tray in rare cases.)

There are two types of liners for open salt dips, varying only slightly in size and shape. All of the salt liners we have seen were done in pattern #86.

☐ **Salt and pepper shakers,** *cruet type, maker unknown, silver caps and snap-on bottoms, pair* 60.00   70.00

☐ **Salt and pepper shakers,** *sterling lids and tray, maker unknown* 75.00   85.00

	Price Range	
☐ **Salt and pepper shakers,** *sterling lids, Lenox tray, maker unknown*	60.00	70.00
☐ **Salt dip,** *International openwork holder, pattern #86 liner*	18.50	23.50
☐ **Salt dip,** *Wallace openwork holder, pattern #86 liner*	18.50	23.50
☐ **Salt dip,** *Watson openwork holder #716, pattern #86 liner, also marked Wm. Wise & Son (retailer)*	18.50	23.50
☐ **Salt dip,** *liner only, pattern #86*	15.00	20.00

SHERBERTS

Identifying Lenox sherberts can be something of a problem, since they were rarely marked. (The stems are too narrow to bear a mark, and if they were marked on the body it might show through the openwork on the holder.) All sherbert liners seen thus far have been done in pattern #86.

☐ **Liner and holder,** *openwork International holder liner has straight rim in pattern #86*	40.00	47.50
☐ **Liner and holder,** *maker unknown, Shreve & Co. name appears as retailer, scalloped rim liner with pattern #86, holder in Art Nouveau design*	68.00	78.00
☐ **Liner only,** *straight rim type, pattern #86*	30.00	35.00

SOUP CUPS

Two-handled cups for soup are the second most common of the silver items with Lenox liners. They consist of a china liner and a two-handled silver holder, and in 99.9% of the cases have no underplate. We have only seen one sample that had what was obviously an original underplate. This particular set was by the Frank M. Whiting Company, and the manufacturer's item number was the same on both silver pieces. Other bouillons that might appear to have underplates have actually been matched up with a silver bread and butter plate. None of the early presentation cases we have seen have had spots for saucers, and we conclude that the Frank M. Whiting item is a rarity.

Bouillons, although they appear to be small, hold about six ounces, roughly the same as the current Lenox rimmed soups. In addition to using them for soup, they are also a convenient size to use for desserts or as small serving pieces.

Almost all of the bouillons are item #1201, and this number can be found written or impressed on later samples. Although earlier bouillon liners are the exact same size and shape as the #1201 ones, no number appears on most of them.

Another type of bouillon, similar in size to the #1201, had a scalloped rim. All liners in this shape seen by us so far have been beautifully decorated and had C.A.C. marks on them. They had rainbow effects on the outside, with hand-painted flowers and gold on the inside. We have been unable to find an item number for this shape.

There was also a third type of bouillon, slightly larger than the #1201 but the same shape, which the silver companies also used as the liner for an assortment of small serving pieces.

Cream soups are extremely scarce, and the last set we saw was too long ago to be included in the price guide. They were rather ugly, with heavy, unimaginative holders, with liners done in pattern #86B. They held approximately eight ounces. Since the silver weight was considerable (it had to cover a large liner), we would estimate their current retail value to be about $40 each, despite their unappealing appearance. The liners for cream soups resemble cereal bowls.

Bouillons should weigh at least two troy ounces to be considered respectable, and most of the better ones are better than three ounces. There are exceptions to this, of course. The Gorham A21 holder pictured in this section barely weighs in at two ounces, yet its design is unique enough to have it be considered in the top grouping.

As is the case with all items of this type, there is usually a premium price tag on sets of six, eight and twelve.

Price Range

☐ **Alvin holder,** *1 troy ounce, pattern #86 liner, openwork design on silver* 18.50   23.50

☐ **Alvin holder,** *2 troy ounces, plain silver with strap handles, pattern #86 liner, gold worn* 15.00   20.00

☐ **Barbour holders,** *2 troy ounces each, openwork silver, hollow handles, pattern #86B liners, set of six* 120.00   140.00

☐ **Dominick & Haff holders,** *2½ troy ounces each, openwork with raised rose design on rim, pattern #86 liners, set of eight* 260.00   320.00

☐ **Dominick & Haff holder,** *2½ troy ounces, embossed gold rim on liner* 30.00   35.00

☐ **Dominick & Haff holders,** *2 troy ounces, openwork design on silver, ornate reverse "C" handles, set of 12* 400.00   470.00

☐ **Durgin holders,** *2 troy ounces each, plain silver, strap handles, pattern #86 liners, set of 12* 400.00   470.00

☐ **Durgin holder,** *2 troy ounces, openwork silver, strap handles, pattern #86B liner* 23.00   28.00

☐ **Gorham holders** *#A21, hollow handles, raised on four feet, vertical openwork, beading around rim, liners are transition mark, with hand-painted green and gold ribbons on inside, and gold work on rim and outside. Set of six* 475.00   575.00

Note: That the bottom of the liner is allowed to show through, and that there is gold trim on the bottom. This is a unique feature among Gorham items with Lenox liners.

Soup cup, *Gorham holder #A21*

Soup cup, *Gorham holder #A2559*

Price Range

☐ **Gorham holder** #A2559, *date mark for 1902, bent twig handles, raised on four feet, openwork design of flowers and leaves, over 3 troy ounces, liner is hand-done with a geometric gold design inside and outside, and has the transition mark. Although it does not show in photograph, the bottom of the liner shows through in this model as it did with the A21 model above, and it is also banded with gold on the bottom* 80.00   95.00
☐ **Gorham holders,** *2½ troy ounces each, strap handles, pattern #86 liners, set of six* 235.00 285.00
☐ **Gorham holders,** *2½ troy ounces each, hollow handles, openwork design resembling hearts, pattern #86 liners, set of four* . 135.00 155.00
☐ **Gorham holder,** *silver pattern #A31, strap handles, raised on four feet, openwork silver with applied ornate rim, pattern #86 liner* 55.00   63.00

Soup cup, *Gorham holder #A31*

Price Range

- ☐ **International holder,** *1½ troy ounces, openwork design, strap handles, pattern #86B liner* 23.00   28.00
- ☐ **International holder,** *2 troy ounces, plain, hollow handles, pattern #86 liner* 27.50   32.50
- ☐ **Matthews holders,** *2 troy ounces each, squared-off hollow handles, pattern #86 liners, set of eight* 250.00   300.00
- ☐ **Matthews holders,** *2 troy ounces each, inverted "S" hollow handles, bright-cut work, pattern #86 liners, set of six* 235.00   285.00
- ☐ **Mauser holders,** *2½ troy ounces each, openwork design with ornate handles, C.A.C. liners in pattern #338 (green on outside, garlands of flowers inside), set of six* 600.00   700.00
- ☐ **Reed & Barton holders,** *2 troy ounces each, inverted "S" handles and openwork design, pattern #86B liners, set of 12* .. 400.00   470.00
- ☐ **Reed & Barton holders,** *2 troy ounces each, plain, squared-off hollow handles, pattern #86 liners, set of eight* 210.00   255.00
- ☐ **Reed & Barton holders,** *2½ troy ounces each, openwork silver with band of flowers at top, set of six* 235.00   285.00
- ☐ **Towle holders,** *2 troy ounces each, plain silver, rolled rim at top, hollow handles, pattern #86 liners, set of 12* 400.00   470.00
- ☐ **Towle holders,** *1¼ troy ounces each, openwork design with hollow handles, pattern #86B liners, pair* 55.00   63.00
- ☐ **Unger Brothers holders,** *floral Art Nouveau design, free-form hollow handles, estimated at 3 troy ounces each, pattern #86 liners, set of four* 195.00   235.00
- ☐ **Wallace holders,** *1½ troy ounces, openwork design, inverted "S" handles, pattern #86½ liners, set of eight* 210.00   255.00
- ☐ **Wallace holders,** *2 troy ounces, openwork design, strap handles, pattern #86 liners, set of 10* 330.00   395.00
- ☐ **Wallace holders,** *2 troy ounces, plain silver, strap handles, pattern #86 liners, set of 12* 330.00   395.00
- ☐ **Watson holders,** *2 troy ounces each, vertical openwork design, pattern #86 liners, set of six* 235.00   285.00
- ☐ **Watson holders,** *2 troy ounces each, vertical openwork design, unknown pattern of flowers, set of six* 400.00   470.00

Soup cup, *Whiting holder, engraved*

Price Range

☐ **Whiting (Frank M.) holder,** *ordinary openwork with strap
handles, blue dot liner, possibly a married piece* 85.00   100.00

☐ **Whiting (Frank M.) holder,** *2 troy ounces, plain silver, strap
handles, pattern #86 liners, set of six* 160.00   190.00

☐ **Whiting (Frank M.) holder,** *matching underplate, total weight 5
troy ounces, nice engraved work on silver and hollow handles,
pattern #E88 liner. (Note that this is the only bouillon we have
seen with a true matching underplate.)* 68.00   78.00

☐ **Whiting Mfg. Co. holders,** *2 troy ounces, "Adam" silver pattern
(could be matched with flatware of same name), pattern #86
liners, set of six* 235.00   285.00

☐ **Woodside holders,** *2¼ troy ounces each, openwork design,
beading on rim, ornate hollow handles, liners have transition
mark, and are decorated inside and out with hand-painted
pink, lavender and blue flowers with raised gold paste work.
The holder hides much of the design on the outside, which is
not uncommon in early pieces and does not mean they did not
go with each other. Set of eight* 635.00   745.00

Soup cup, *Woodside holder*

MISCELLANEOUS

The items listed below, mainly serving pieces, represent a sampling of the
large assortment of items that were available with Lenox liners. We have
sewen or heard of many more than these, but space allows us only this brief
listings. We cannot account for why so many of these miscellaneous items
were by the Watson Company.

☐ **Durgin bowl,** *openwork holder, 5" diameter, Lenox wreath
mark liner in sky blue with gold rim* 68.00   78.00

☐ **Gorham epergne,** *center vase and four small hanging baskets
on spokes coming out from center vase, Lenox wreath mark
basket and vase liners. It is interesting to note that the liners
for the baskets are the same small pieces that were used by
Lenox as the sauce holders for their oyster plates* 460.00   550.00

Durgin bowl

	Price Range	
☐ **Kirk bowl,** *Revere style, plain, heavy silver, 6" diameter, Lenox liner shape #1234, patter #86*	135.00	155.00
☐ **Reed & Barton egg cup,** *4" high, R&B shape #1145, Lenox wreath mark liner, shape number unknown, decorated in pattern #86*	68.00	78.00

Egg cup, *Reed & Barton*

Watson bowl, *shape #15*

Watson bowl, *shape #4043*

Watson bowl, *shape #311*

Watson candy dish

Watson mayonnaise

Price Range

☐ **Watson bowl,** *shape #315, two handled, 6½" diameter handle to handle, openwork, Lenox liner #1234, pattern #378 (hand-painted roses,) transition mark* 135.00 155.00

☐ **Watson bowl,** *shape #4043, two-handled, same size as above, openwork silver, Lenox wreath mark liner shape #1234, no pattern number, garlands of hand-painted flowers* 135.00 155.00

☐ **Watson bowl,** *shape #311, footed with two handles, 8¼" across top of liner, openwork design, transition mark liner, shape and pattern numbers unknown, hand-painted flowers* . . 165.00 195.00

☐ **Watson candy dish,** *shape #3391, 6" diameter, openwork design, raised on four ball feet, transition mark liner, shape number and pattern number unknown, hand-painted flowers* . . 110.00 125.00

Watson covered casserole

	Price Range	
☐ **Watson mayonnaise,** *silver shape number unreadable, open-work design, 5½" handle to handle, footed, transition mark liner with garlands of hand-painted flowers, no shape or pattern number for liner*	115.00	130.00
☐ **Watson covered casserole,** *shape #58, openwork design, raised on four elaborate feet, 11", handle to handle, transition mark liner with cover, shape number and pattern number unknown, hand-painted flowers, crack in bottom part*	165.00	195.00

LINERS ONLY

☐ **Pattern 69B,** *transition mark (blue dot)*	80.00	95.00
☐ **Pattern 70,** *transition mark (blue dot)*	80.00	95.00
☐ **Pattern 86,** *(plain gold)*	18.50	23.50
☐ **Pattern 86½,** *(wide gold)*	23.00	28.00
☐ **Pattern 86B,** *(plain gold)*	18.50	23.50
☐ **Pattern J30,** *(etched gold)*	27.50	32.50
☐ **Pattern J33,** *(Tuxedo pattern)*	27.50	32.50
☐ **Pattern 338,** *(hand-painted floral garlands)*	80.00	95.00
☐ **Pattern unknown,** *(gold filigree, transition mark)*	55.00	63.00
☐ **All pink**	23.00	28.00
☐ **All yellow**	27.50	32.50

The above prices apply to Lenox liners without holders and equally to demis and soups. By adding these figures to the scrap value of the silver, it is possible to estimate the value of your items. (For example, a two ounce holder with a pink liner would be valued at $30.) Silver is currently priced at around $6 per troy ounce, but prices can change quickly.

SILVER OVERLAY

For a period of about 40 years, Lenox supplied blanks for a number of silver companies to decorate with sterling silver overlay. This overlay was applied by an electrolytic method in designs usually chosen by the silver companies, and the marketing was also done by the silver companies so far as we can determine. As was also the case with Lenox liners in sterling holders, this procedure may have been reversed occasionally, with the Lenox Company special-ordering a piece for a particular silver design.

Lenox china decorated with silver overlay is not as easy to categorize as the hand-painted items. Unlike the painted wares, which can be roughly grouped into good artwork and bad artwork, the overlay is divided into STYLE of decoration rather than QUALITY of decoration. This is not to say that the quality of the silver work doesn't enter into the matter, for it does, but rather that more people seem to find Art Nouveau florals more appealing than Art Deco geometrics.

Some of the silver overlay patterns are encountered over and over again, and although we do not know their official names, they have been given nicknames by collectors and dealers. The most common of these are:

(1) Cherry blossom — sprays of flowers with branches and leaves.

(2) Chinese pattern — groupings of human figures with pagodas or other Oriental motifs.

(3) Floral — any arrangement of flowers, branches and leaves which is not cherry blossom.

(4) Flying geese — scenic overlay with geese flying over a marsh. Occasionally this pattern will have hand-tinted colors in the sky and water, which adds to its value.

(5) Geometric — refers to a number of patterns with more or less straight lines or banding, usually in the Art Deco style.

(6) Ornate — an assortment of patterns with elaborate designs which cover a large part of the china.

Although a variety of marks appear on overlay items, the ones most commonly seen are the Lenox wreath and palette marks. Overlay is one area where palette mark items should not be considered inferior to wreath mark ones. They bear the palette mark because they were being sent away from the Lenox factory for the silver work, not because the final item was in some way inferior. The C.A.C. marks are still considered more valuable, particularly C.A.C. wreath marks, but this is because of their age and styling rather than because of the mark itself.

Several silver companies were actively engaged with Lenox silver overlay, including Gorham, Mauser, Reed & Barton, Wallace, Rockwell, Depasse and others. The Gorham and Mauser marks tend to increase the value of an item by their mere presence. Some of the silver companies entirely covered the bottom of the items with silver, obscuring the Lenox marks completely.

As a rule, the silver overlay items which are marked with the silver company's name as well as the Lenox mark are more desirable than those without the silver mark. There is a definite correlation between those items which are marked and the type of silver work done. "Name" silver companies tended to be more generous both with the gauge of silver used and the amount of territory it covered, and they also seemed to finish off the items with nice engraving work on the overlay.

The blanks supplied by Lenox to the silver manufacturers were both the regular, creamy Lenox and the early bone china. In fact, it is in the overlay category that a great deal of this bone china makes its appearance.

The variety of shapes used for silver overlay is not as large as it was for hand-painting, and for the most part the shapes are very simple. Items with lots of curves and corners made overlay work difficult, if not impossible.

The infuser teapot, shape #522, turns up quite frequently with overlay on it.

The infuser is a china piece with pinpoint holes in it which fits down inside the teapot. The main idea was to put the tea in the infuser and then run the hot water through it. The infuser could be removed when the tea was strong enough. Many times the infusers to these sets are missing, and the lids to the teapots will not fit properly without them. This round-bodied teaset was perfectly suited to a variety of overlay patterns, which probably accounts for the large number of them seen today.

In general, vases and teasets were made in such abundance that they must be unusual in one fashion or another in order to attract a great deal of attention.

The color of the Lenox is very important. The most common color is, of course, the basic Lenox color. Following this would be cobalt blue, brown, and antique ivory, all three of which seem to occur with the same degree of frequency. Green, light blue, and pink also occur, but only rarely. Some items are done in more than one color, starting out with one color and then subtly changing to another. The most common shaded colors are green, brown and orange in combination with each other.

There are some items which appear to be black, but it is hard to tell if they are indeed black or merely a very dark cobalt. A lot of these "black" items have been decorated with a great deal of overlay which tends to obscure the color. If an item is truly black and not a dark blue, it would be in the very rare class. A few pieces of turquoise have shown up, including a beautifully overlaid tea tile. There is another blue, somewhere between the turquoise and the cobalt, which turns up occasionally. In any case, there is always a premium on rarer colors. Plain white seems to go begging, unless it is extravagently decorated or an unusual shape.

Some of the earlier items combined overlay with hand-painting. It appears that all of the painting was done at the Lenox factory, and then the item shipped out to the silver company for the overlay work.

The hand-painting can vary from simple, small pink roses to the finest samples of Lenox artwork. DeLan painted on items ear-marked for overlay, and Heidrich apparently made a specialty of it since his name primarily appears on overlay items. Other names crop up now and then, and many fine items are not artist signed at all.

Taking care of silver overlay can be something of a problem since the silver can be worn thin by over-zealous polishing. Many collectors allow the overlay on white or light-colored items to darken (it will become almost black with time,) but this approach looks dreadful with cobalt or other dark colors. Careless handling can sometimes cause the overlay to be lifted off the china if the bond between the two materials is not perfect.

Copper and gold overlay are also seen in rare instances, usually on white but also on cobalt in at least one case. No prices for copper or gold overlay have been included here because none have been seen recently enough. In general, copper overlay items are worth about the same as comparable items with silver on them, and the gold would be worth more.

Simple or common overlay is still underpriced in our estimation, and even the top items still probably have some room left yet. The prices on all overlay should rise sharply in the near future as the hand-painted items become harder to find and as people realize that overlay is collectible in its own right.

In the price section, items are listed alphabetically by type of ware. Within these categories, they are in numerical order by shape number. Those items with no shape number will be found at the end of their proper grouping. Please note that the word "white" is used interchangeably to mean either natural Lenox color or the bone china color.

	Price Range	
☐ **Beehive honey jar,** *shape number unknown, bees covered with silver and band of silver on base, Rockwell silver mark and Lenox wreath mark, tiny fleck on wing of one bee*	68.00	78.00
☐ **Bowl,** *shape #512, filigree effect on antique ivory body, Lenox palette mark, no silver mark*	125.00	145.00
☐ **Bowl,** *shape #527, ornate overlay on white body, green Lenox palette mark, no silver mark*	165.00	195.00
☐ **Bowl,** *shape #527, geometric bands on white body, Lenox palette mark, no silver mark*	105.00	120.00
☐ **Bowl,** *shape #586, 10"x3", geometric design on white body, handles covered in silver, Reed & Barton silver mark, Lenox green wreath mark*	135.00	155.00
☐ **Bowl,** *shape #586, 10"x3", cherry blossom design on white body, handles covered, no silver mark, Lenox palette mark* ...	150.00	175.00
☐ **Bowl, mayo,** *shape #644, mediocre overlay on white body, hand-painted small pink roses, tiny chip under rim, Lenox wreath mark*	55.00	63.00
☐ **Bowl,** *shape #793, 7" diameter, cherry blossom design on white body, Lenox palette mark, no silver mark*	80.00	95.00
☐ **Bowl,** *shape #793, geometric design on pale blue body, Lenox wreath mark*	135.00	155.00
☐ **Bowl,** *shape #896, 5½" diameter, strips of silver on white body, green wreath mark, Reed & Barton silver mark*	47.50	55.00
☐ **Bowl,** *shape #896, 5½" diameter, geometric pattern resembling musical symbols, Lenox palette mark, no silver mark* ...	68.00	78.00
☐ **Bowl,** *shape #922, 10¾" diameter, cherry blossom pattern on white, green wreath mark*	150.00	175.00
☐ **Bowl,** *shape #922, 10¾" diameter, geometric design on brown, Depasse silver mark, Lenox wreath mark*	135.00	155.00
☐ **Bowl,** *shape #922, 10¾" diameter, floral design on antique ivory, no silver mark, Lenox palette mark*	120.00	140.00
☐ **Bowl,** *shape #1723, strip outlining and wreath in silver on white ground, Lenox wreath mark, no silver mark*	90.00	110.00
☐ **Bowl,** *shape #1723, geometric bands on antique ivory body, Lenox palette mark, no silver mark*	90.00	110.00
☐ **Bowl,** *shape #1723, ornate overlay on white ground, Gorham silver mark, Lenox palette mark*	135.00	155.00
☐ **Candlesticks,** *shape #930, 8¼" high, outlining in silver with hand-painted flowers, slight damage to silver work, Lenox wreath mark, pair*	110.00	125.00
☐ **Candy dish,** *shape #10, 5"x7¼", narrow silver bands, green wreath mark*	40.00	47.50
☐ **Candy dish,** *shape #10, 5"x7¼", narrow silver bands on coral body, Lenox wreath mark*	90.00	110.00
☐ **Candy dish,** *shape #133, 3¼"x3¾", vertical stripes on white body, Lenox palette mark*	47.50	55.00
☐ **Candy dish,** *shape #510, geometric design on white, Lenox palette mark*	33.00	38.00

Price Range

☐ **Candy dish,** *shape #510, geometric design on antique ivory, Lenox palette mark* 37.00   43.00

☐ **Candy dish,** *shape #514, covered, 8"x3¾", geometric bandings on white, Lenox palette mark* 135.00   155.00

☐ **Candy dish,** *shape #514, covered, 8"x3¾", ornate design covering most of lid, silver bands on base, C.A.C. transition mark, Mauser silver mark, white body* 175.00   200.00

☐ **Candy dish,** *shape #1018, footed boat shape with handles, Art Deco silver work, green palette mark* 68.00   78.00

☐ **Chocolate pot,** *shape #842, ornate overlay on cobalt, transition mark and Mauser silver mark* 195.00   235.00

☐ **Chocolate pot,** *shape #842, ornate overlay on white, Lenox wreath mark and Reed & Barton mark* 135.00   155.00

Coaster

☐ **Coaster, no shape number,** *ornate overlay on brown, Lenox wreath mark* 47.50   55.00

☐ **Coffeepot, sugar and creamer,** *shapes #371, #372 and #373, square pedestal base, geometric overlay on white body, Lenox palette mark* 225.00   275.00

☐ **Coffeepot, sugar and creamer,** *shapes #371, #372 and #373, floral overlay on cobalt body, transition mark* 365.00   435.00

☐ **Coffeepot, teapot, sugar and creamer,** *shapes #521, #522, #523, and #524, ornate overlay on cobalt, Lenox green wreath and Depasse marks, slight damage on inside lip of sugar bowl* 525.00   625.00

☐ **Coffeepot, sugar and creamer,** *shapes #521, #523, and #524, geometric bands on brown body, Lenox wreath mark and Reed & Barton mark* 250.00   300.00

☐ **Coffeepot, sugar and creamer,** *shapes #597, #598, and #599, floral overlay on cobalt, Lenox wreath mark* 250.00   300.00

☐ **Coffeepot, sugar and creamer,** *shapes #692, #694, and #695, geometric bands on white, Lenox palette mark* 195.00   235.00

Price Range

☐ **Coffeepot, sugar and creamer, demitasse size,** *shapes #787, #788, and #789, Chinese pattern on white body, Lenox wreath mark* 300.00   360.00

☐ **Coffeepot, sugar and creamer, all demitasse sizes,** *shapes #787, #788, #789, simple banding of overlay on ivory color, Lenox palette mark* 210.00   255.00

☐ **Coffeepot, sugar and creamer, individual size,** *shapes #933, #935, and #936, geometrical vertical bands on white body, Lenox palette mark* 105.00   120.00

☐ **Coffeepot, sugar and creamer,** *shapes #1013, #1015, and #1016, ornate overlay on cobalt ground, Lenox palette mark* .. 225.00   275.00

☐ **Coffeepot, individual size,** *shape #1353, 5¾" high, filigree overlay work on white, Lenox wreath mark* 55.00   63.00

☐ **Coffeepot, individual size,** *shape #1353, 5¾" high, ornate overlay on cobalt, transition mark* 135.00   155.00

☐ **Coffeepot, sugar (open) and creamer,** *shapes #1544, #1546, and #1547, geometric design on white, Lenox palette mark* ... 195.00   235.00

☐ **Coffeepot, sugar (open) and creamer,** *shapes #1544, #1546, and #1547, ornate overlay on ivory color, Lenox wreath mark, Gorham silver mark* 225.00   275.00

☐ **Coffeepot, sugar and creamer on tray,** *shapes #1654, #1656, #1657, no number for tray, cherry blossom design on white body, Lenox palette mark* 500.00   600.00

☐ **Coffeepot, sugar and creamer,** *shapes #1654, #1656, and #1657, wreath and outlines in silver on cobalt body, Lenox wreath mark and Reed & Barton silver mark* 300.00   360.00

☐ **Coffeepot, sugar and creamer,** *shapes #1654, #1656, and #1657, geometric pattern, Lenox palette mark, white body* 195.00   235.00

☐ **Coffeepot, sugar and creamer on tray,** *six matching cups and saucers, flying geese pattern with hand-painting, Lenox palette mark, all items perfect* 665.00   785.00

☐ **Compote,** *shape #825, ornate overlay on white, Lenox palette mark* 135.00   155.00

☐ **Compote,** *shape #825, ornate overlay on cobalt, transition mark and Gorham mark* 195.00   235.00

☐ **Cracker jar,** *shape number unknown, 6" high, ornate overlay on brown, Lenox palette mark* 195.00   235.00

Creamer and sugar, *geometric latticework overlay*

Price Range

☐ **Creamer and sugar (open),** shapes #1063, and #1062, geometric lattice work overlay on white body, Lenox wreath mark and Reed & Barton mark, spider crack in bottom of sugar   47.50   55.00

☐ **Creamer and sugar,** no shape number, Art Nouveau floral overlay on brown background, Lenox palette mark 85.00   100.00

☐ **Creamer and sugar,** no shape number, lattice work overlay on cobalt body, Lenox wreath mark 125.00   145.00

☐ **Creamer and sugar,** no shape number, square pedestal bases, geometric overlay on white body, Lenox palette mark 80.00   95.00

☐ **Creamer and sugar,** no shape number, fat-bodied, ornate overlay on cobalt, transition mark and Mauser silver mark 150.00   175.00

☐ **Cup and saucer,** shape #448, square handles done in silver, silver banding on rims, Lenox palette mark 33.00   38.00

☐ **Cup and saucer,** shape #448, square handles in silver, ornate overlay on cobalt, Lenox wreath mark 68.00   78.00

☐ **Cup and saucer,** shape #1094, double outlining in silver, Lenox palette mark 40.00   47.50

☐ **Humidor, covered,** no shape number, cobalt blue with ornate overlay, Lenox wreath mark 195.00   235.00

☐ **Inkwell,** shape #313, 4", cobalt background, silver maker's mark blurred, transition mark 195.00   235.00

Inkwell, shape #313

☐ **Jam pot and underplate,** no shape number, straps of overlay on white body, Lenox palette mark 68.00   78.00

☐ **Jam pot,** no shape number, thin strap overlay with hand-painted strawberries, Lenox palette mark 90.00   110.00

☐ **Jug,** shape #217, 8" high, ornate silver on brown, transition mark 195.00   235.00

Jug, *shape #381*

Price Range

☐ **Jug,** *shape #381, with stopper, oval portrait on one side of Victorian lady dressed in pink gown toasting with a glass of wine. Rest of jug is a vibrant deep rose color covered with ornate Art Nouveau silver in the form of grape clusters and leaves. Gorham silver mark, dated 1896 and signed A. H. (Antonie Heidrich), minor crack in base of piece, transition mark* 600.00 700.00

☐ **Jug,** *shape #534, small size, 4" high, ornate floral design on brown body, transition mark* 135.00 155.00

☐ **Jug,** *same as above except marked with the word "Whisky", Lenox wreath mark, Depasse silver mark* 150.00 175.00

☐ **Mug,** *shape #251, 5" high, tankard shape, thick strap overlay on cobalt, transition mark* 125.00 145.00

Mug, *shape #251*

Mug, *shape #256*

Price Range

☐ **Mug,** *shape number unknown, 4" high, tankard shape, silver banding top and bottom, silver handle, seated monk toasting with a glass of wine, monochromatic brown colors, transition mark* 195.00   235.00

☐ **Mug,** *shape #256, 5¾" high, dog holding dead bird in its mouth on air-brushed yellow and brown background, overlay in form of leaves, rim bands and handle cover, artwork signed E. A. DeLan, transition mark* 600.00   700.00

☐ **Mustard pot and underplate,** *no shape number, footed, artwork signed E. A. DeLan, transition mark, see photo* 600.00   700.00

☐ **Mustard pot and underplate,** *no shape number, footed pot, Art Deco overlay on white body* 55.00   63.00

☐ **Mustard pot,** *shape number unknown, Reed & Barton silver mark, strap overlay on cobalt, Lenox wreath mark* 105.00   120.00

☐ **Nut dish,** *shape #51, 3" high, footed shell shape, outside covered entirely in silver, green palette mark, no silver mark* . . 47.50   55.00

☐ **Pitcher, covered,** *shape #270, 12" high, floral design on white, green Lenox wreath mark* 135.00   155.00

☐ **Pitcher,** *shape #526, 6" high, geometric design on white, Lenox palette mark* 68.00   78.00

☐ **Pitcher,** *shape #567, 7½" high, ornate overlay on white, mark obscured by silvHr on bottom* 90.00   110.00

☐ **Pitcher,** *shape #567, 7½" high, ornate overlay on white, Lenox wreath mark* 105.00   120.00

☐ **Pitcher,** *shape #666, sparse but nicely done silver banding, hand-painted roses, Lenox wreath mark* 105.00   120.00

☐ **Plate,** *8", flying geese pattern, Lenox palette mark* 85.00   100.00

☐ **Plate,** *8", hand-painted roses with strap type overlay work, Lenox wreath mark* 90.00   110.00

☐ **Plate,** *9", flying geese pattern, tinted backgrounds, Lenox palette mark* 110.00   125.00

Price Range

☐ **Plate,** 9", plain bands of silver on rim, white, Lenox palette mark 27.50   32.50

☐ **Powder box,** shape #152, ½"x2⅞", ornate silver on cobalt, transition mark 165.00   195.00

☐ **Salt dip,** shape #103, 1¾", outside all silver, Lenox palette mark 13.00   16.00

☐ **Shaving mug,** shape #201, 4" high, ornate silver on brown, transition mark 225.00   275.00

☐ **Shaving mug,** shape #201, 4" high, strap banding on white, Lenox palette mark 195.00   235.00

☐ **Swan,** shape #59, 1¾", covered all over with silver, Lenox palette mark 50.00   60.00

☐ **Teapot, sugar and creamer,** shapes #522, #523, and #524, infuser type, ornate overlay on white, Lenox green wreath mark 225.00   275.00

☐ **Teapot, sugar and creamer,** shapes #522, #523, and #524, infuser type, ornate overlay on cobalt, transition mark and Mauser mark 310.00   370.00

☐ **Teapot, sugar and creamer,** shapes #522, #523, and #524, infuser type, ornate overlay on cobalt, transition mark and Mauser mark 310.00   370.00

☐ **Teapot, sugar and creamer,** shapes #522, #523, and #524, infuser type, infuser missing, sugar bowl damaged, teapot and creamer perfect, geometric overlay on brown, Lenox wreath mark and Reed & Barton silver mark 105.00   120.00

☐ **Teapot, sugar and creamer,** shapes #522, #523, and #524, infuser type, all items perfect, geometric overlay on brown, Lenox wreath mark 255.00   315.00

☐ **Teapot, sugar and creamer,** shapes #542, #543, and #544, geometric overlay on white ground, Lenox palette mark 195.00   235.00

☐ **Teapot, sugar and creamer,** shapes #1061, #1062, #1063, floral over-lay on brown, Lenox wreathbmark, Reed & Barton silver mark 250.00   300.00

☐ **Teapot, sugar and creamer,** shapes #1061, #1062, and #1063, ornate overlay on cobalt, Lenox wreath mark and Gorham silver mark 365.00   435.00

☐ **Teapot, sugar and creamer,** shapes #1084, #1085, and #1086, geometric overlay on brown ground, Wallace silver mark, green Lenox wreath mark 275.00   335.00

☐ **Teapot, sugar and creamer,** shapes #1182, #1183, and #1184, ornate overlay on cobalt, Lenox wreath mark and Depasse silver mark 260.00   320.00

☐ **Teapot, sugar and creamer,** shapes #1182, #1183, and #1184, ornate overlay on white, Lenox wreath mark, no silver mark ... 195.00   235.00

☐ **Teapot, sugar and creamer,** shape #1610, stackable variety, overlay in ornate pattern on white, lid not the original one and teapot has minor damage to inside lip, Lenox wreath mark ... 68.00   78.00

☐ **Vase,** shape #297, 8½" high, filigree design on white body, Lenox palette mark 135.00   155.00

☐ **Vase,** shape #297, 8¼" high, ornate design on cobalt, transition mark and Mauser mark 175.00   225.00

☐ **Vase,** shape #297, 8¼" high, strap banding on white, Lenox palette mark, no silver mark 80.00   95.00

Price Range

☐ **Vase,** *shape #314, 8" high, cherry blossom pattern on white body, green palette mark* 135.00   155.00

☐ **Vase,** *shape #314, 8" high, geometric design on brown, Lenox wreath mark, Reed & Barton silver mark* 150.00   175.00

☐ **Vase,** *shape #315, 5¾" high, ornate floral overlay on background which appears to be black but is possibly dark cobalt, transition mark and Gorham mark* 210.00   255.00

☐ **Vase,** *shape #315, 5¾" high, geometric overlay on white, Lenox palette mark* 80.00   95.00

☐ **Vase,** *shape #318, geometric design on white body, Lenox wreath mark* 105.00   120.00

☐ **Vase,** *shape #318, floral design on white body, Lenox wreath mark* 115.00   130.00

☐ **Vase,** *shape #320, 10¼" high, cherry blossom design on white, Lenox palette mark* 225.00   275.00

☐ **Vase,** *shape #320, 10¼" high, geometric design on antique ivory, Lenox palette mark* 135.00   155.00

☐ **Vase,** *shape #412, 9" high, bulbous, floral design, on white body, green wreath mark* 135.00   155.00

☐ **Vase,** *shape #416, 5¾" high, geometric design on white, green palette mark* 68.00   78.00

☐ **Vase,** *shape #416, 5¾" high, floral design on antique ivory, Lenox wreath mark* 105.00   120.00

☐ **Vase,** *shape #470, 18½" high, flying geese pattern with no background tinting, the Lenox shape number is impressed on bottom but there is no Lenox mark* 210.00   255.00

☐ **Vase,** *shape #574, ornate overlay on cobalt, Lenox wreath mark and Depasse silver mark* 115.00   130.00

Vase, *no shape number*

	Price Range	
☐ **Vase,** *shape #574, ornate overlay on cobalt, no Lenox mark or silver mark*	55.00	63.00
☐ **Vase,** *shape #877, 12½" high, geometric design on cobalt, Lenox palette mark*	150.00	175.00
☐ **Vase,** *shape #877, 12½" high, ornate lattice design, Reed & Barton silver mark, Lenox wreath mark*	160.00	190.00
☐ **Vase,** *shape #879, 7" high, ornate overlay on green, Lenox wreath mark and Mauser mark*	210.00	255.00
☐ **Vase,** *shape #880, 7⅞" high, geometric on white body, Reed & Barton and Lenox wreath marks*	68.00	78.00
☐ **Vase,** *shape #880, 7⅞" high, floral design on antique ivory, Lenox palette mark*	68.00	78.00
☐ **Vase,** *shape #897, 12¼" high, ornate overlay on white, Lenox wreath mark and Depasse marks*	200.00	240.00
☐ **Vase,** *shape #1185, 10" high, vertical lines on antique ivory, Lenox palette mark*	68.00	78.00
☐ **Vase,** *shape #1312, 8¾" high, ornate overlay on cobalt, Lenox wreath and Reed & Barton marks*	150.00	175.00
☐ **Vase,** *no shape number, 214" high, overall decoration with hand-painted flowering begonias. Ornate overlay in strap banding with rim and foot also banded in silver, no artist signature, transition mark*	525.00	625.00

SILVER COMPANY MARKS

In an effort to assist the Lenox collector in identifying the markers of silver items used with Lenox, following is a list of companies and a description of their marks. Most of the companies listed here used a variety of marks on their items, but we have only included those marks likely to appear on holders or overlay.

Alvin Corporation
(Providence, RI, 1886 to present)
Few items have been seen, but all were marked in one way or another with the word "Alvin."

Bailey, Banks, and Biddle
(Philadelphia, PA, 1832 to present)
The name will either be spelled out in full or abbreviated BB&B. So far as we can tell, BB&B did not actually manufacture any of the holders, and their name appears on them as the retail store that sold them rather than as the maker. Sometimes the maker's mark will appear on the item as well.

Barbour Silver Co.
(Hartford, CT)
The company's initials, B.S.C., is seen on most items.

Caldwell, J. E. & Co.
(Philadelphia, PA)
Caldwell is a retailer rather than manufacturer. The name can be spelled out in full or sometimes seen as J.E.C. & Co.

Charter Company
(See Barbour)
Marks include: (1) oak leaf in a rectangle; (2) acorn in a rectangle; (3)the initial "C" in a rectangle flanked by oak leaves.

Depasse Mfg. Co.
(New York City, NY)
The Depasse mark was the letter "D" inside a jug shape. The name was later changed to Depasse, Pearsall Silver Co., and the mark then became "DP" inside a jug.

Dominick & Haff
(Newark, NJ, and New York, NY)
The usual mark was a rectangle, circle and diamond close together in a row. Occasionally the initials "D&H" also appear.

Durgin
(Concord, NH and Providence, RI)
Durgin's mark was the letter "D" in an oval.

Electrolytic Art Metal Company
(Trenton, NJ)
Their name was sometimes spelled out, but more often appears as EAMCO in a rectangle with coffin corners.

Elgin Silversmith Co., Inc.
(New York City, NY)
Their mark was EL–SIL–CO in a diamond shape.

Gorham Corporation (Division of Textron)
(Providence, RI)
All marks appearing on holders thus far have had some variation of a lion, an anchor, and the letter "G" in a row. Sometimes these marks appear inside blocks and other times not. Many of the turn-of-the-century items are date-marked as well.

Hickok–Matthews Company
(Newark, NJ)
The mark was the letter "M" imposed over a scimitar.

International Silver Co.,
(Meriden, CT)
The following marks have been noted: (1) some version of the word "International;" (2) the letter "W" with a quarter moon around it; (3) I.S.CO.

Kirk, Samuel and Son
(Baltimore, MD, 1815 to present)
The Kirk Company has used a number of different marks, but all using the Kirk name. Since some of the marks were used for only a short period of time, they can be used to pinpoint fairly precise dates.

Lunt Silversmiths
(Greenfield, MA)
Only a few items have been seen that were made by this company. All had the word "Lunt" somewhere on them.

Mauser Manufacturing Company
(New York City, NY, founded 1887)
The Mauser mark was a unicorn emerging from a horn of plenty.

Redlich & Co.
(New York City, NY)
The Redlich mark was a mythical creature with the head of a lion and the body of a serpent.

Reed and Barton
(Tauton, MA)
This company's mark is an eagle, the letter "R," and a standing lion. The letter "R" is sometimes enclosed in a shield.

Rockwell Silver Co.
(Meriden, CT, founded 1907)
Rockwell's mark consisted of a shield with the word Rockwell in it, or sometimes just the company's initials.

Roger
There were several companies by this name, and we feel that the marks are too confusing to be listed here.

Schofield Co., Inc.
(Baltimore, MD)
The Schofield mark consisted of the letter "H" in a diamond, a lion in a circle, and then the letter "S" in a diamond, all in a row.

Shreve & Co.
(San Francisco, CA)
Their name usually appears as the retailer rather than maker, and is usually spelled out in full on the item.

Shreve, Crump & Low Co., Inc.
(Boston, MA)
This is a retail store, not a manufacturer. The name is usually spelled out in full.

Tiffany & Co.
(New York City, NY)
All of the Tiffany holders were marked in one way or the other with the name spelled out in full. Many items are also marked with an initial which refers to the company president's last name, which is handy for dating purposes.

Towle Silversmiths
(Newburyport, MA)
The Towle mark most frequently seen is a script letter "T" with a lion climbing up it.

Unger Brothers)
(Newark, RI)
The most frequently seen mark are the letters "UB" intertwined inside of a circle. Sometimes just the letter "U" was used by itself.

Wallace, R. & Sons Mfg. Co.
(Wallingford, CT)
They used many marks, the most common being the initial "RW&S" with a stag's head.

Watson Company
(Attleboro, MA)
Watson used a wreath (similar to the Lenox one) with a sword going up through the middle.

Whiting, Frank M. Co.
(North Attleboro, MA)
This company, frequently confused with the Whiting Mfg. Co., used the initial "W" inside a circle. Three lines branch out from each side of the circle.

Whiting Manufacturing Co.
(Providence, RI)
Their mark is mythical creature with its paw on a circle with the letter "W" inside it. Some items were date-marked.

Woodside Sterling Co.
(New York City, NY)
Woodside used the letter "W" inside a circle. It is very close to the mark used by International and should not be confused with it.

Note: Marks are hard to find on some items. They can be on the inside or outside of items, and in some instances can be found on the undersides of handles. On overlay items, the mark can either be somewhere on the silver or on the bottom of the item next to the Lenox marck. When the mark is found on the china itself, it would seem obvious that Lenox put the silver company's mark on the same time they put on their own, thus saving an additional firing at a later time. We occasionally see items, usually plain brown or cobalt, with the Lenox and silver company marks on bottom but having no silver on them. These are items which were ear-marked for silver overlay work but which somehow never made it to the silver company.

FIGURINES

Lenox figurines of all types have long been popular collectibles. They probably account for less than one or two percent of total Lenox production, and this coupled with the public's fondness for them raises prices to a level which in many cases cannot be justified by size or workmanship.

The fully-detailed figurines are the ones which are probably still underpriced considering the amount of work which went into each one. Considering the lace work, applied flowers, unbelievably thin fingers, and the hand-painted outfits, they are by a far stretch still below current replacement value. Items such as the llama are on dangerous ground for they could be manufactured today for less than what people are paying for older ones.

Production problems plagued many of the figurines, and it would seem that the very qualities that make Lenox into such fine dinnerware prevent its effective use in the manufacture of figurines. Mold cracks and firing cracks are very common in the figurine line, due to the fact that a variation of more than 1/1000th of an inch in the thickness of the glaze will cause such cracks. Since it is harder to apply glaze evenly to a figure with folds and crevices than to dinnerware, this probably accounts for most of the firing cracks.

This may have been one of the reasons why so many of the figures were left in the bisque state, and is certainly the reason for the many unmarked figurines encountered today.

The lack of a backstamp on a verifiable shape does not totally kill the value as it might on other types of items, partly because in many cases, the shapes can be positively identified as Lenox and partly because the public demand for the figurines is so great that they will accept unmarked items.

Minor damage is also acceptable on many of the figurines and is almost expected on the fully-detailed ones. Just how much the value is affected depends on the extent of the damage and the rarity of the figurine.

Collectors tend to refer only to the Pat Eakin items as figurines, and all others are called figurals, a rather off choice considering that figural is an adjective and not a noun. They are in fact all figurines, and we would suggest referring to the fully-detailed figurines as Eakin type and the Deco type either by that name or as DeVegh type after the man who designed many of them. Animals can, of course, be called animals.

ANGELS

There were two pairs of Lenox angels made, and, the smaller pair, which bend toward each other, is purely decorative. The larger pair, one with candle on the right and the other holding the candle on the left, is obviously both decorative and useful. Both angel pairs were available in plain white or with gold trim.

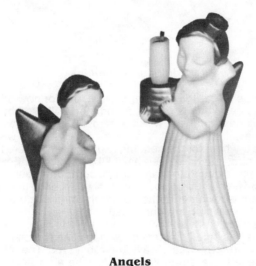

Angels

	Price Range	
☐ **Angel,** *shape #2764, 2"x 2¼"x4⅛", white, Lenox wreath mark* .	120.00	140.00
☐ **Angel,** *shape #2764, 2"x2¼"x4½", white with gold trim, Lenox wreath mark*	135.00	155.00
Note: The mate to angel #2764 is #2765. Both have the same dimensions and are priced the same.		
☐ **Angel,** *shape #2981, 2¼""x 2¾"x6", candlestick type, undecorated, Lenox wreath mark*	165.00	195.00

Price Range

☐ **Angel,** *shape #2981, 2¼"x 2¾"x6", candlestick type, gold trim, Lenox wreath mark* 170.00   200.00
   Note: Angel #2982 is the mate for #2981. Both have the same dimensions and are priced the same.

BIRDS

There are two types of Lenox birds, crested and not crested. They are usually called jay and robin. The three sizes are referred to as tiny, small and large. A further distinction is made between those with tail up and those with tail down with tail up being more desirable.

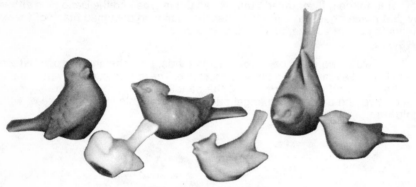

Birds, *jays and robins*

Color and shape affect the price somewhat, but for now all of them are in the under $75 range. White is the most common, followed by pink and blue, green is perhaps next and yellow is the rarest. The tail-down small jay and robin were also available as salt and pepper shakers, and will frequently be unmarked since the hole for the cork takes up the spot where the mark would usually go. The birds we have seen have all been glazed. For the most part, the birds were never decorated, and any decoration should be viewed with some suspicion. The mark is almost invariably the Lenox green wreath/U.S.A. to the point where we will not bother to list the marks in the pricing section, except to note those which are unmarked.

The large size birds came sometimes with a circle cut out of their backs so they could be used as small planters or perhaps candy dishes. The large bird, if we remember correctly, was always the robin type. The robin can also be found on a base with several holes in it for use as a flower "frog", and a Trenton collector has one of thesobin can also be found on a base with several holes in it for use as a flower "frog", and a Trenton collector has one of these in a cocoa brown.

Currently in production is a pair of partridge salt and pepper shakers, in a shape and size very similar if not identical to a much older pair we have seen.

Jay Shapes

☐ **Dimensions** *for the small tail-down jay are 1⅜"x3⅝"x1¾", and item numbers are #1790 for the regular and #2252 for the salt and pepper version. It comes in the full range of colors and is usually priced at $10 or $12 for the white up to $25 for the various colors.*

☐ **Dimensions** *for the tiny tail-up jay are not available, and item number also not available. As a rule, priced at perhaps $15 for the white up to $30 for rarer colors.*

Robin Shapes

☐ **Dimensions** *for tail-down one in the small size are 1½"x3"x2⅞", item numbers are #1788 for the regular and #2251 for the salt and pepper, colors include coral, yellow, blue, green and white. Prices vary from $10 for white to $30 for rarer colors.*

☐ **Dimensions** *for the tail-up robin in the small size are 1½"x2⅝"x3⅛", item number is #1789, available in full range of colors. Prices range from $15 for white to $35 for rarer colors.*

☐ **Dimensions** *and item number for the tail-up tiny robin are not available, but the full range of colors was available. Typically they bring as much (if not more) than the larger ones, i.e., at least $15 for white to $35 for rarer colors.*

☐ **Dimensions** *for the tail-up large robin are 2"x6½"x5", and the item number is #1822. It was available in five colors, and prices range from $25 for white to $40 for hard-to-find colors.*

Covered bonbon

Other Bird Items

Price Range

☐ **Covered bonbon,** *with bird finial, item #2363, 6¼" diameter x 5" to top of bird's tail, white with pink bottom, other colors available, Lenox wreath mark* 105.00 120.00

☐ **Covered bon bon,** *same description as above but bird damaged* . 60.00 70.00

☐ **Covered cigarette box,** *with bird finial, item #3165, 3½"x4⅞"x3½", white bird with pale blue box, Lenox wreath mark (other colors were also available)* 68.00 78.00

☐ **Flower frog bird,** *item number unknown, no recent sales but owner of brown one estimates value at no less than $50.*

☐ **Tree flower holder with bird,** *crested jay type, shape #2438, 2¾"x2¾"x3"x5¼", all white, Lenox wreath mark* 68.00 78.00

☐ **Tree flower holder with bird,** *as above but with color, add $10 to $15 depending on color combination.*

☐ **Tree flower holder with bird,** *robin type, item #2434, 4"x6½"x9", white tree with coral bird, Lenox wreath mark on nudes* 105.00 120.00
Note: The above tree worth about $10 less in all-white, other colors worth about the same as the pink or a little more.

☐ **Tree flower holder with bird,** *robin type, item #2436, 2⅝"x2¼"x7¼", all white, Lenox wreath mark* 68.00 78.00
Note: Add $10 to $15 for color.

BOOKENDS

The so-called Trojan horse bookends, measuring 3½"x5"x7½", were available in white only and apparently in glazed only. The usual mark is the Lenox wreath mark. Among Lenox collectors, a pair typically sells for $200 to $275; however, we have heard that among Art Deco collectors the price can go as high as $400.

Women's head bookends

The woman's head bookends, are 10″ high and have the Lenox green wreath mark. One story we have heard about them is that they were done in honor of Amelia Earhart's flight around the world, and whether this is true or not, they are sometimes given her name. They usually sell in the $200 to $275 a pair range.

Another pair of bookends seen recently was unmarked but quite possibly Lenox, and they were shaped like books with gold trim on the pages. A signed set would be in the $200 range. Another pair of possibly Lenox bookends was shaped like a pile of stones. Very square looking plain ones, also unmarked, have been noted.

BULLDOG

The bulldog, shape #1832-½, measuring 4″x8″x5″, was available in both glazed and bisque finishes, and will sometimes sport a royal blue collar. The mark can be either impressed or green wreath. The detailing is quite good, which perhaps accounts for the bulldog's popularity with collectors.

There is a hole on the bottom of his collar through which (presumably) a medallion could be suspended, although we have never seen one done in this fashion. Since it would be rather silly for the company to go to all that trouble for no particular reason, we are making the assumption that perhaps the first bulldogs were special orders for a team or organization and that each member received a bulldog with an engraved medallion.

A bulldog, glazed or unglazed, should be an easy $200 sale, more in some parts of the country. Although it is strictly conjecture on our part, a bulldog with the blue collar and the original medallion might bring $65 more.

Bulldog

DOLLS

During World War I, German bisque doll heads were unobtainable so Lenox began producing the heads for the Effenbee doll company. The Lenox heads are perhaps more prized for their rarity than for their beauty, and are avidly sought by both doll collectors and Lenox collectors. The dolls had stuffed bodies and composition hands, and we assume that the one shown above has her original clothes and wig. On the back of the head under the hairline is an impressed Lenox mark and also the Effenbee mark. The face is, of course, hand-painted, and the eyes are the non-movable type. This particular doll was purchased in 1978 for $750, and the present owner has turned down higher offers.

A 1939 *Fortune* article on Lenox china showed a picture of a pincushion doll, which once again is unexceptional in appearance but which would be a nice addition to a Lenox collection. To the best of our knowledge, the item exists only as a prototype and was not put into general production. A marked sample would probably sell for $400 or more.

Any Lenox doll should be considered a rarity and will probably be priced accordingly. The Lenox Company perhaps came on the scene a little too late to have been actively involved with dolls. Among the unanswered questions is who modeled the head.

Doll, *hand-painted*

ELEPHANTS

For the most part, elephants are middle-period Lenox items, usually with the green wreath/U.S.A. mark (if any.) They were made in several shapes and sizes, at least four different colors, and were available both in glazed and bisque. Considering the variety of elephants produced, there are remarkably few to be found, which is reflected in their prices. Interestingly, there are no known donkeys made by Lenox.

Elephant, *shape #3072-1/2*

The Coxon family has in its possession what is possibly a much earlier elephant. It is very light in weight, and the detailing is exceptionally good. Although it is unmarked, it is possibly Lenox. To find such an elephant with, say, a C.A.C. mark would be exciting to say the least, since C.A.C. figurines of any sort are virtually unknown.

Of the four colors we have seen, white is by far the most common followed by gray, black and cobalt. Although most of the elephants were available both in bisque and glazed, the larger elephants usually seem to be glazed while the smaller ones are usually unglazed.

	Price Range	
☐ **Elephant,** *shape #2119, 7⅞"x4¼"x6⅝", glazed, white, Lenox wreath mark*	225.00	275.00
☐ **Elephant,** *shape #2120, 9½"x4¼"x6⅛", white bisque, unmarked*	135.00	155.00
☐ **Elephant,** *shape #2120, 9½"x4¼"x6⅛", white, glazed, Lenox wreath mark*	195.00	235.00
☐ **Elephant,** *shape #2120, 9½"x4¼"x6⅛", white, bisque, Lenox wreath mark*	195.00	235.00
☐ **Elephant,** *shape #2120¼, 3"x6¾"x4⅜", white, bisque, Lenox wreath mark, good sized chip on left front foot*	165.00	195.00
☐ **Elephant,** *shape #2120½, 3½"x7¾"x5", glazed, black unmarked*	225.00	275.00
☐ **Elephant,** *shape #3072, 2¾"x7"x4½", white, bisque, Lenox wreath mark*	170.00	200.00
☐ **Elephant,** *shape #3072, 2¾"x7"x4½", white, glazed, Lenox wreath mark*	195.00	235.00
☐ **Elephant,** *shape #3072½, 2½"x6"x3½", white, glazed, Lenox wreath mark*	195.00	235.00
☐ **Elephant,** *shape #3072¼, 2⅛"x5"x3", white, bisque, Lenox wreath mark*	165.00	195.00

	Price Range	
☐ **Elephant,** *shape #3074, 4"x8½"x6½", white, glazed, crack in trunk and several chips (small) on front feet, Lenox wreath mark*	180.00	220.00
☐ **Elephant,** *shape #3074, 4"x8½"x6½", white, bisque, Lenox wreath mark*	200.00	250.00
☐ **Elephant,** *shape #3074, 4"x8½"x6½", cobalt with white tusks, unmarked*	300.00	360.00
☐ **Elephant,** *shape #3222, 1¼"x3"x1¼", bisque, gray, both tusks broken off, Lenox wreath mark*	68.00	78.00
☐ **Elephant,** *shape #3222, 1¼"x3"x1¾", bisque, gray, Lenox wreath mark*	160.00	190.00
☐ **Elephant,** *shape #3222, 1¼"x3"x1¾", glazed, white, unmarked*	68.00	78.00
☐ **Elephant,** *shape #3299, 1⅝"x4⅞"x2⅜", gray, bisque, (small elephant on white stand, dimensions include stand), Lenox wreath mark*	170.00	200.00
☐ **Elephant,** *shape #3299, 1⅝"x4⅞"x2⅜", white, glazed, one tusk broken off halfway, Lenox wreath mark*	150.00	175.00
☐ **Elephant,** *shape #3301, 2¼"x4¼"x2¼", bisque, gray, (two small elephants on stand), Lenox wreath mark*	210.00	255.00
☐ **Elephant,** *shape #3301, 2¼"x4¼"x2¼", bisque, white, Lenox wreath mark, (two small elephants on a stand)*	175.00	225.00

Note: All of the elephants except #2119 are referred to as "trunk up" elephants. Obviously, #2119 is called the "trunk down" one.

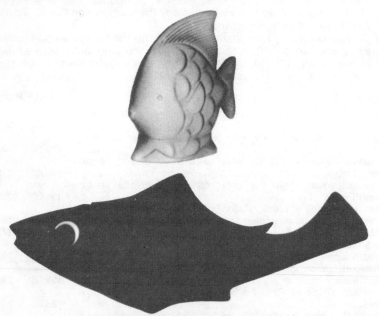

Fish, *shape #2912 and #3483*

Price Range

FISH

☐ **Fish,** *shape #2912, 1⅞"x3¾"x4¼", apple green, Lenox green wreath mark* 110.00   125.00
☐ **Fish,** *shape #2912, 1⅞"x3¾"x4½", white, Lenox green wreath mark* 55.00   63.00
☐ **Fish,** *shape #3483, 12" long x 4½" high, black with gold trim, Lenox wreath mark* 225.00   275.00

FULLY–DETAILED FIGURINES

The delightful Lenox figurines are perhaps the most keenly sought Lenox collectibles of all. They are a product of the 1940's and 1950's, and were primarily the work of Patricia Jean Eakin, who later also worked for Boehm and Cybis.

Miss Eakin, who had been a ceramics engineer with the Tennessee Valley Authority, came to Trenton where she resided on Stokeley Avenue. There is at least some evidence to suggest that she originally designed the figurines long before coming to work at Lenox, but that they were the only American company capable of producing them at that time. She died only recently, in 1976, and instead of the customary funeral parlor services her family and friends gathered at a Trenton hotel for cocktails and canapes.

She made some of the original molds for the production of the Lenox figurines, and the figurines from her molds have the impressed initials PJE on the bottom (sometimes hard to read.) Although it is not yet the case, we feel that in years to come the figurines with her mark will have a higher value than those which don't. Her Lenox figurines were intended to be an American costume series.

A few of the figurines were designed after Eakin left Lenox, so they will never have her initials on them. The small, hand-written initials on most of the figurines are those of the artist who decorated the figurines. The Lenox backstamp can be either green or gold. A list and description of the figurines follows:

  (1) Ballerina (6")
      (a) White dress with flowered skirt
      (b) Light blue dress with flowered skirt
      (c) Pink dress with flowered skirt

  (2) **Colonial Lady (7-1/4")**
      (a) Turquoise dress, green and blue garlands on underskirt
      (b) Fawn dress, green and blue garlands on underskirt
      (c) Maroon and green dimity print, ruffled underskirt

  (3) **Crinoline Miss (Name in doubt, 6")**
      Holding muff, tiny ruffle on back of bonnet

  (4) **The Dandy (10-3/4")**
      Gray suit and hat, checked vest and blue cravat. He is rumored to be a likeness of Walter Lenox

  (5) **Floradora (9-1/4")**
      (a) Pink blouse, black-plumed hat, lavender and pink skirt
      (b) Fawn jacket, green scallops on skirt, plumed hat

Lady Diana

(6) **Lady Diana (10")**
White horse with rider, dressed in gray riding skirt, brown jacket and black hat

(7) **Madonna (11")**
Blonde hair, gold trim on robe

Madonna

(8) **Mistress Mary (6")**
    (a) White dress, floral motifs, blue-trimmed ruffles
    (b) Yellow dress, blue daisy motifs, black-trimmed ruffles
(9) **Natchez Belle (7-1/2")**
    (a) Green bodice, green-trimmed skirt, white ruffles
    (b) Pink bodice, aqua-striped skirt, trimmed ruffles
(10) **Prima Donna (8-1/4")**
    (a) Floral hat, white coat and dress and bustle
    (b) Floral hat, black coat and bustle
    (c) Floral hat, pale orchid coat and bustle
(11) **The Reader (5-1/2")**
    (a) Red-flowered skirt
    (y) Yellow skirt

The Reader

(12) **Southern Belle (6-1/2'oat and bustle**
(11) **The Reader (5-1/2")**
    (a) Red-flowered skirt
    (b) Yellow skirt
(12) **Southern Belle (6-1/2")**
    (a) Blue-flowered bonnet and coat, blue dress, blue-flowered underskirt
    (b) Pastel-flowered bonnet and dress, pink coat, blue underskirt

Sportswoman

(13) **Sportswoman (6-1/2")**
Celadon green riding skirt and coat, black hat and red vest
(14) **The Twins (3-1/2")**
(a) Girls had either a blue dress, pink dress, green dress, blue polka-dot apron, or pink polka-dotted apron.
(b) The boy is usually done in brown and black.
Note: That the original twins were two girls. One of the same girls was used later with the boy, and there was never a second boy.

The Twins

Sizes vary somewhat from those listed, and two Floradoras seen recently were 3/4" different. The differences in size are due both to original assembly of the figurines and to variation in the size of platform used. Trim color can also vary considerably, probably due to the whim of the artist on a particular day.

Damage is very common, and does not affect the value all that much if limited to minor lace damage or a missing finger. In general, damage is less forgivable on the more common figurines such as the twins or Mistress Mary.

Prices have not moved very much on the figurines in five or ten years, and they are overdue for a huge jump in value. Many dealers are justifiably unwilling to ship the figurines, creating a situation where if the collector wants a figurine and sees one locally, it might be best to pay the asking price.

In addition to the above figurines, there are several others known or thought to be products of Lenox. Jonathan Coxon's family has a figure of a woman sitting on a toilet, unmarked but quite likely a Lenox item. A private collector in New York has a large figure of a sitting Indian with beautiful detailing, which we gather is an authentic likeness of a Plains Indian. It is marked with the Lenox wreath, and additionally has the name Tollen (or possibly Toller) impressed on the side. The Lenox museum has a set of figurines modeled after famous opera characters. All of these are probably one-of-a-kind items and should be considered treasures.

Since some of the figurines have never been sold on the open market, we will alter our usual pricing scheme somewhat to include several estimates, either ours or the owners.

	Price Range	
☐ **Ballerina,** *perfect, continue style*	525.00	625.00
☐ **Ballerina,** *badly damaged, most of crinoline skirt missing on one side, continue style*	260.00	320.00
☐ **Colonial Lady,** *most of front ruffle missing, continue style*	300.00	360.00
☐ **Colonial Lady,** *moderate overall damage, continue style*	260.00	320.00
☐ **Colonial Lady,** *slight damage (average price from three sales)* .	525.00	625.00
☐ **Crinoline Lady,** *perfect, continue style*	460.00	550.00
☐ **Floradora,** *perfect, continue style*	525.00	625.00
☐ **Floradora,** *plumes missing from hat, rare decoration of green dress with embossed white design, continue style*	460.00	550.00
☐ **Floradora,** *hand professionally repaired, continue style*	500.00	600.00
☐ **Floradora,** *minor damage to hand, continue style*	460.00	550.00
☐ **Indian,** *owner values figure at $7,000*		
☐ **Lady Diana,** *two currently on the market, both with asking price of $1,000, no other known sales*		
☐ **Lady on toilet,** *unmarked, authors' estimate of $200, a marked one probably in the area of $500*		
☐ **Madonna,** *perfect, owner's estimate is $500*		
☐ **Mistress Mary,** *perfect, continue style*	460.00	550.00
☐ **Mistress Mary,** *slight damage to ruffles, continue style*	435.00	505.00
☐ **Mistress Mary,** *tips of fingers missing, continue style*	435.00	505.00
☐ **Mistress Mary,** *heavy damage, continue style*	300.00	360.00
☐ **Natchez Belle,** *perfect, continue style*	500.00	600.00
☐ **Natchez Belle,** *minor damage, continue style*	475.00	575.00
☐ **Natchez Belle,** *bottom ruffle entirely gone, damage to hand, continue style*	300.00	360.00

Price Range

- ☐ **Opera figures,** *no known sales, authors' estimate of no less than $500 each*
- ☐ **Prima Donna,** *perfect, continue style* 500.00 600.00
- ☐ **Prima Donna,** *slight damage in several spots, continue style* .. 435.00 505.00
- ☐ **Southern Belle,** *perfect, usually priced in the $350 to $400 range, but one recently sold for $500*
- ☐ **Sportswoman,** *perfect (owner's estimate $350)*
- ☐ **The Dandy,** *perfect, continue style* 800.00 950.00
- ☐ **The Reader,** *perfect, yellow dress, continue style* 435.00 505.00
- ☐ **The Reader,** *perfect, flowered dress, continue style* 435.00 505.00
- ☐ **The Reader,** *damaged neck ruffle, continue style* 435.00 505.00
- ☐ **The Reader,** *damaged on side with firing crack, undecorated, "back door" item, continue style* 435.00 505.00

  Note: The Reader is the perfect example of an item which has become stuck at a certain price and just refused to budge.
- ☐ **Twin boy,** *perfect (owner's estimate of $175)*
- ☐ **Twin boy,** *undecorated, continue style* 180.00 220.00
- ☐ **Twin girl,** *perfect, continue style* 165.00 195.00
- ☐ **Twin girl,** *part of braid missing and damage to skirt, continue style* 135.00 155.00

FULL-LENGTH FIGURES

The full-length figures, mainly nudes, were available in a large variety of shapes and sizes.

Two Vases, *woman's shape and robin's shape*

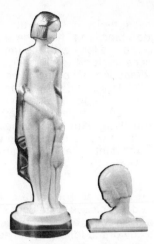

Woman with greyhound, Woman's head, *shape #2138*

	Price Range	
☐ **Woman,** *shape #1850, nude, sitting with one hand behind her and the other on her head, white, glazed, Lenox wreath mark* ..	175.00	225.00
☐ **Woman,** *shape #1851, nude, reclining, unmarked but matches picture in old catalogues*	68.00	78.00
☐ **Woman,** *shape #1852, nude, sitting, hands behind her on the ground, Lenox wreath mark, white, glazed*	165.00	195.00
☐ **Woman, nude,** *shape #2551, sitting on top of tree vase, one arm raised to her hair, white, glazed, 2⅝"x3½"x6¾", Lenox wreath mark*	115.00	130.00
☐ **Woman, nude,** *shape #2552, sitting on top of tree vase, both arms down, 3¼"x4"x8¼", white, glazed, Lenox wreath mark* .	135.00	155.00
☐ **Woman and man,** *shapes #2682 and #2681, 12" high, glazed, white, dressed holding sheaves of wheat, Lenox wreath mark, pair*	500.00	600.00
☐ **Woman,** *shape #3152, wide skirt and fan, vase behind her, 3⅝"x5⅛"x8½", bisque finish, impressed Lenox mark, called "Crinoline vase"*	180.00	220.00
☐ **Woman,** *shape #3153, standing nude, 3¼"x4" 12½", vase behind her, glazed, Lenox wreath mark, called the "Spring vase"*	225.00	275.00
☐ **Woman,** *shape #3154, Leda and the swan, 4"x5½"x10", vase behind her, bisque finish, impressed mark, called the "Leda vase"*	195.00	235.00
☐ **Woman,** *shape #3156, kneeling nude, 3"x3¾"x10⅞", vase behind her, glazed, Lenox wreath mark, called the "Evening vase"*	215.00	265.00
☐ **Woman with greyhound,** *13" high, gold trim, Lenox wreath mark*	240.00	290.00

Similar items, without vases, typically sell in the $200 and up range. They include the "knee-up" nude which is 14″ high, the standing nude which is 13″ high, Leda and the swan, and the lady with the fan. The lady with fan is the exception in the pricing scheme, for it rarely brings more than $125 or $150. In addition, she causes a great deal of confusion because she is called "Crinoline Lady" in the books, "Colonial Lady" by some collectors, and probably other names we haven't heard. The terms Crinoline Lady and Colonial Lady result in confusion over the fully-detailed figurines with similar names. We suggest the use of the term "Lady with Fan" to clear up the matter. Most of the Deco figures were available with a metal base which held a light which went inside the figure, making it into a lamp. The lamp base does not seem to increase or decrease the value.

GERMAN SHEPHERD

The German Shepherd was available in three different sizes of the same shape, and came both glazed and bisque. Catalogues indicate that it was available both in white and in a fawn color, but all of those we have seen have been white. Add at least $50 to any of the following prices for a fawn-colored one.

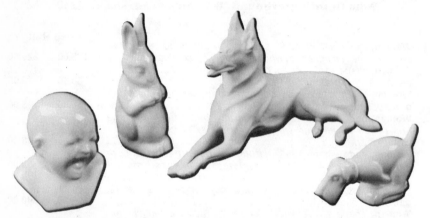

Baby's head, Rabbit, German Shepherd, Schnauzer

	Price Range	
☐ **German Shepherd,** *shape #3166½, 4″x9″x5″, white glazed,* Lenox wreath mark	195.00	235.00
☐ **German Shepherd,** *shape #3166½, 4″x9″x5″, white, glazed* unmarked	135.00	155.00
☐ **German Shepherd,** *shape #3166½, 4″x9″x5″, white, bisque,* marked	180.00	220.00
☐ **German Shepherd,** *3166½, 3½″x7¾″x4¼″, white, glazed,* marked	165.00	195.00
☐ **German Shepherd,** *3166¼, 3½″x7¾″x4¾″, white, bisque,* marked, damage to front paw	115.00	130.00
☐ **German Shepherd,** *shape #3166, 5″x10½″x5⅝″, white, glazed,* marked	210.00	255.00

Price Range

☐ **German Shepherd,** *shape #3166, 5"x10½"x5⅝", white, bisque, marked* 195.00   235.00
☐ **German Shepherd,** *shape #3166, 5"x10½"x5⅝", white, bisque, unmarked* 135.00   155.00

HANDS AND ARMS

The hand ashtray, shape #2759, 2½"x7"x1⅜", was available in white, coral and green, and usually sells in the $40 to $50 range. An upright arm and hand which is unmarked is sometimes sold as Lenox. The arm, as the story goes, was used to test rubber gloves for holes.

HEADS AND BUSTS

Perhaps the most spectacular Lenox bust is the one shown in the color section of the young man with a gold turban. According to Lenox catalogues it was available in three different sizes, but the one shown, owned by a collector in California, is the only one we know of. There are no known sales for this item, but the owner of the one pictured states he would not sell his for less than $2,000.

There are two different types of baby heads: one type stands by itself and the other is resting on a pair of hands (or according to some accounts a pair of angel's wings.) The standing type was available both in smiling and crying versions, and is frequently called a doll's head, which is unlikely since there are not the usual pinholes which would be used to attach the head to the body. Regardless of this, the name persists and we see no harm in its use since it helps to differentiate it from the other type of baby.

Young man with turban

Price Range

☐ **Baby's head,** *shape number unknown, smiling baby, white, glazed, Lenox wreath mark* 165.00   195.00

☐ **Baby's head,** *shape number unknown, crying baby, white, bisque finish, no mark* 120.00   140.00

☐ **Baby's head,** *resting on hands, shape #2968¼, 3⅝" diameter x 3" high, Lenox wreath mark, glazed* 165.00   195.00

☐ **Baby's head,** *resting on hands, shape #2668½, 4¼" diameter x 3⅝" high, bisque finish, Lenox wreath mark* 165.00   195.00

☐ **Baby's head,** *resting on hands, shape #2968, 4¾" diameter x 4¼" high, glazed, white, Lenox wreath mark* 195.00   235.00

Note: Adult heads are usually of the Art Deco type, and can be either flat-back or fully fashioned. They are very popular which accounts for their prices.

☐ **Woman's head,** *shape #2138, 1½"x3¾"x3⅞", light green, Lenox wreath mark* 165.00   195.00

☐ **Woman's head,** *shape #2138, 1½" x3¾"x3⅞", white, Lenox wreath mark* 110.00   125.00

☐ **Woman's head,** *shape #2673 and man's head shape #2672, both 9½" high, all coral, Lenox wreath mark, man has shock fracture on back of head, pair* 400.00   470.00

☐ **Woman's head,** *shape #2857, 1½"x2¼"x4", bisque, finish, Lenox wreath mark* 105.00   120.00

☐ **Woman's head,** *shape #2857, 1½"x2¼"x4", glazed, finish, Lenox wreath mark* 110.00   125.00

LLAMAS

The Lenox Llama is item #3042, and its measurements are 2"x6"x9". It will usually be white, although gray and yellow have been seen and other colors will no doubt turn up. All of the ones we have seen have been glazed and a bisque one should be considered possibly incomplete.

Although it is really nothing more than a blob of Lenox with a long neck, it remains immensely popular both with Lenox collectors and with Art Deco collectors, and $175 should be considered as a minimum price for a white one. They are almost always perfect and backstamped, so a damaged or un marked one should not be worth anywhere near that price.

NIPPER

The little dog with his head cocked to one side which has long been the emblem of the R.C.A. organization was twice done in Lenox china. One version, apparently done for the opening of Rockefeller Center in New York City, was a pair of little Nippers made into salt and pepper shakers. The Lenox mark is impressed along the bottom rim. A second version of Nipper, done for some anniversary of R.C.A., is about 12" high and has a bisque finish. The bigger figure is extremely scarce, and one account has no more than a dozen of them being made. It is fully marked on the bottom.

Both versions have a decorated collar, ears, and facial features, and the larger version has "His Master's Voice" painted in as well. This one little dog manages to, at the same time, be the most common and the rarest of the Lenox canines.

The salt and pepper shakers typically sell in the $30 to $40 range (for the pair.) There were no known sales for the large one within the past year, but the owner of the one shown in the photograph values it at $485, which seems fair considering how scarce it is.

Nipper

PENGUINS

Penguins are not readily available as the swans or other birds, but are still obtainable. The #1827 penguin was available only in white, while the #2678 series came in both coral and white. The white ones are occasionally decorated. Broken beaks are fairly common since the beak hits first if the penguin is knocked over.

Penquins

	Price Range	
☐ **Penguin,** *shape #1827, 1⅞"x2¼"x4⅛", white, Lenox wreath mark*	47.50	55.00
☐ **Penguin,** *shape #2678, 3⅛"x3⅝"x6⅛", coral, Lenox wreath mark*	85.00	100.00
☐ **Penguin,** *shape #2678, dimensions as above, white, Lenox wreath mark*	80.00	95.00
☐ **Penguin,** *shape #2678¼, 2⅜"x2½"x4½", white, Lenox wreath mark*	47.50	55.00
☐ **Penguin,** *shape #2678¼, dimensions as above, white, broken beak, Lenox wreath mark*	18.50	23.50
☐ **Penguin,** *shape #2678¼, dimensions as above, coral, Lenox wreath mark*	60.00	70.00
☐ **Penguin,** *shape #2678¼, dimensions as above, decorated, Lenox wreath mark*	80.00	95.00
☐ **Penguin,** *shape #2678½, 2⅝"x2⅞"x5⅜", white, Lenox wreath mark*	60.00	70.00
☐ **Penguin,** *shape #2678½, dimensions as above, coral, Lenox wreath mark*	68.00	78.00

RABBITS

The little Lenox rabbit shown in the photo with the Schnauzer is item #2911, and measures 1¾"x2½"x5⅜". It is usually glazed and will have the Lenox wreath mark, and so far as we can determine was usually white, although other colors are seen on rare occasions.

The same rabbit was used as the lid for one of the Lenox atomizers, and the atomizer rabbit will be open across the bottom while the purely decorative one will be closed.

The rabbit will usually be in the $70 to $110 range, although a rare color would certainly bring more.

SCHNAUZERS

The Schnauzers were available in two styles, a sitting one and a running one, and in at least two colors, white and blue. The sitting model is considered scarcer than the running one and, of course, blue is more desirable than white. Unlike so many of the animals and other figurines, the Schnauzer is usually perfect. The 1939 catalogue indicates they were available glazed only, so perhaps a bisque one should be considered incomplete. The mark is usually the standard Lenox green wreath one. The name Schnauzer is given to the figure by collectors, since the catalogue refers to it only as "running dog" and "sitting dog".

☐ **Schnauzer,** *shape #2877, 1⅜"x3⅛"x3", sitting, white, Lenox wreath mark*	80.00	95.00
☐ **Schnauzer,** *shape #2877, 1⅜"x3⅛"x3", sitting, blue, Lenox wreath mark*	85.00	100.00
☐ **Schnauzer,** *shape #2878, 1½"x4½"x2", running, white, Lenox wreath mark*	60.00	70.00
☐ **Schnauzer,** *shape #2878, 1½"x4½"x2", running, blue, Lenox wreath mark*	75.00	85.00

SCOTTIES

A small Scottie is shown in the 1939 catalogue, and the price list accompanying it tells us it was available both in white and in black. No one we know, however, has this little dog, and we have a feeling that since they were inexpensive at the time they were made that most of them ended up being played with by children and being broken.

Another small Scottie, unmarked but belonging to a Lenox workman who says it is Lenox is up on its hind legs as if begging for food. It is perfectly adorable and is in yellow Lenox.

Since we have never seen the one in the first paragraph, our prices are estimates.

	Price Range	
☐ **Scottie,** *shape #2661, 3/4"x1⅞"x1¼", white, Lenox mark*	105.00	120.00
☐ **Scottie,** *shape #2661, dimensions as above, black, Lenox mark*	135.00	155.00
☐ **Scottie,** *no shape number, perhaps 1¾" high, base no more than ½" across, yellow, unmarked*	33.00	38.00

SEALS

Seals were made in two shapes, one shape #2727, the other unknown. Both types are very much in the "blob" category but are rare enough to bring respectable prices.

☐ **Seal,** *shape number unknown, white, Lenox wreath mark*	85.00	100.00
☐ **Seals,** *shape #2727, white, Lenox wreath mark*	90.00	110.00

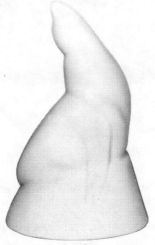

Seal

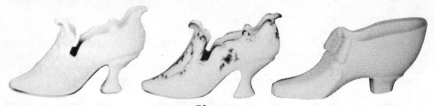

Shoes

SHOES

Lenox shoes are rather scarce, and the marks can range all the way from C.A.C. ones right up to gold wreath. Those with decoration are naturally more desirable, and a decorated one with a C.A.C. mark would probably bring an easy $200. The others with later marks bring from $75 to $140 depending on type and trim.

It is not clear at this point whether the earlier ones were meant to be pincushion holders or not, and the pincushion would probably neither add nor subtract value.

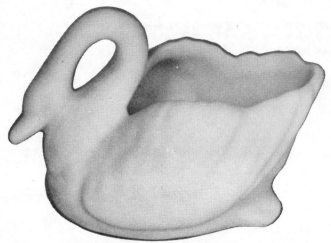

Small swan, *shape #59*

SWANS

Lenox produced their first swan in 1890, and the swan continued to be a popular item to the present day although the shape has changed. In an informal poll taken by us to determine which single Lenox item was most readily identified with Lenox better, than 60 percent of those polled named the swan.

The smallest Lenox swans, shape #59, were intended to be used both as a salt dip (a small pepper shaker and a ceramic salt spoon were available with them), and as individual creamers with the #93 individual sugar.

The medium swans are also identified as sugars and creamers in Lenox catalogues, and in at least one case they are listed as flower holders. The two medium swans are of the same era, and the #68 (generally called "wings up") is not earlier as sometimes claimed. The #68 swan is 4¼" high and was meant to be the sugar bowl. The #100 swan (called "wings back") is 3" high and intended to be a creamer. In addition to being somewhat impractical to use, the notion of pouring cream from the tail end of a swan seems something less than appetizing, and the overwhelming majority of these swans was used as candy dishes or decorative accessories.

The large swans, shapes #3252 and #3252½, are in the "wings up" position, and are primarily used as centerpiece items. The large swans are the rarest, perhaps because of fewer sales due to the higher cost and to a higher attrition rate through the years.

Swans are still being produced, and are available in 8", 6", and 4" is the swan pictured above on the left.

Medium swans, *shape #68 and current shape*

Price Range

☐ **Swan,** *shape #59, 1¾"x2¾"x1¾ coral, Lenox wreath mark* . . . 23.00 28.00
☐ **Swan,** *shape #59, dimensions as above, white, Lenox wreath mark* 13.00 16.00
☐ **Swan,** *shape #59, dimensions as above, white with gold trim, Lenox wreath mark* 15.00 20.00
☐ **Swan,** *shape #59, dimensions as above, white outside, lavender lustre trim inside, gold trim on feathers, gold eyes and beak, C.A.C. green palette mark* 40.00 47.50
☐ **Swan,** *shape #59, dimensions as above, light green with gold trim, Lenox wreath mark* 23.00 28.00
☐ **Swan,** *shape #68, 3¾"x5"x4¼" plain white, Lenox wreath mark* 30.00 35.00
☐ **Swan,** *shape #68, dimensions as above, white with gold trim, Lenox wreath mark* 40.00 47.00
☐ **Swan,** *shape #68, dimensions as above, exceptionally thin, unmarked but definitely Lenox, firing crack probably accounts for lack of backstamp* 40.00 47.50
☐ **Swan,** *shape #68, dimensions as above, coral, Lenox wreath mark* 40.00 47.00
☐ **Swan,** *shape #68, dimensions as above, green, Lenox wreath mark* 42.00 48.00
☐ **Swan,** *shape #68, dimensions as above, white with Lenox Rose design and gold trim, Lenox wreath mark* 60.00 70.00
☐ **Swan,** *shape #68, dimensions as above, all gold exterior, Lenox palette mark, not as garish as it sounds* 55.00 63.00
☐ **Swan,** *shape #100, 2⅝"x3⅞"x3" plain white, Lenox wreath mark* 18.00 23.00
☐ **Swan,** *shape #100, dimensions as above, coral, Lenox wreath mark* 27.50 32.50
☐ **Swan,** *shape #100, dimensions as above, dark green, Lenox wreath mark* 37.00 43.00
☐ **Swan,** *shape #100, dimensions as above, white with gold trim, Lenox wreath mark* 30.00 35.00
☐ **Swan,** *shape #100, dimensions as above, white with Lenox Rose pattern and gold trim, Lenox wreath mark* 47.50 55.00
☐ **Swan,** *shape #100, dimensions as above, eggshell thin, C.A.C. brown palette mark* 68.00 78.00
☐ **Swan,** *shape #100, dimensions as above, baby pink, Lenox wreath mark* 28.00 33.00
☐ **Swan,** *shape #3252, 6¾"x9¼"x8", white, Lenox wreath mark* . 115.00 130.00
☐ **Swan,** *shape #3252½, 5¾"x7¾"x6¾", white with gold trim, Lenox wreath mark* 105.00 120.00

TOBY MUGS

The Teddy Roosevelt toby is almost always decorated, and was made for the Toby Potteries, New York. They were designed by Edward Penfield and are marked with the Lenox wreath mark and with the letter P in a shield (for Penfield.)

The 7" high William Penn toby, frequently mistaken for Ben Franklin, was produced in larger numbers, and both decorated and undecorated versions are available today. The decorated William Penn is usually found with the Lenox mark and the Bailey, Banks and Biddle store mark as well. BB&B apparently ordered several plain mugs from Lenox and had them painted by outside decorators. The undecorated William Penns are found in several color combinations (white with coral handle, all blue, etc.) The white ones are often taken and decorated, so any decorated William Penn without the BB&B mark should be compared against a BB&B marked authentic one to be sure the decoration is original with the item.

Toby mug, *William Penn*

A similar situation exists with the George Washington tobies. To the best of our knowledge, the Lenox factory did not decorate their Washington, and sold them only in the white. The decorated Washingtons are never marked with the Lenox backstamp, and any decorated mug bearing a Lenox backstamp should be viewed with some suspicion. For whatever reason, the unmarked items were sold as a group to a decorating company who did the painting. Since they have no markings at all, it is uncertain who did the artwork, although a possibility would be the Toby Potteries mentioned in the first paragraph.

There are vague stories that Isaac Broome designed the Lenox tobies, and it is known that he did indeed once model a George Washington toby. What is not certain is if the one he did is the one put out by Lenox, since he supposedly did his in the 1890's, yet the Lenox models have the Lenox wreath marks and not the C.A.C. marks. Since he definitely did bring some of his earlier molds with him when he came to Lenox, it remains a possibility that the George Washington was his.

The William Penn toby has an impressed initial "B" on the back beneath the left hand (hard to see on some models.) Broome signed some of his earlier works (particularly his tiles) in just such a manner, so there appears to be some likelihood that this might be his work. Once again, however, employment dates and production dates don't match up, so our identification of

Broome as the modeler will remain a tentative one. The William Penn is the most available of all the tobies, and if it is indeed a Broome it would be perhaps a not too expensive way to acquire Broome's work.

	Price Range	
☐ **Toby,** *George Washington, large, undecorated, Lenox wreath mark*	525.00	625.00
☐ **Toby,** *George Washington, large, decorated, no mark*	665.00	785.00
☐ **Toby,** *George Washington, small, undecorated, Lenox wreath mark*	400.00	475.00
☐ **Toby,** *George Washington, small, decorated, no mark*	525.00	625.00
☐ **Toby,** *Teddy Roosevelt, decorated, Lenox wreath mark and Penfield mark*	525.00	625.00
☐ **Toby,** *William Penn, decorated, Lenox wreath and BB&B mark*	330.00	395.00
☐ **Toby,** *William Penn, decorated, Lenox wreath mark, no BB&B mark but well-decorated*	225.00	275.00
☐ **Toby,** *William Penn, undecorated, all white, Lenox wreath mark*	135.00	155.00
☐ **Toby,** *William Penn, undecorated, white with coral handle, Lenox wreath mark*	195.00	235.00
☐ **Toby,** *William Penn, undecorated, white with blue handle, no mark*	68.00	78.00
☐ **Toby,** *William Penn, gold trim on white, probably gilded recently, Lenox wreath mark*	135.00	155.00
☐ **Toby,** *William Penn, undecorated, white, crack, in handle, Lenox wreath mark*	47.50	55.00

Note: That the decorated but unmarked George Washington is apparently more desirable than the undecorated but marked version. Since the item is readily identifiable as Lenox, the lack of a backstamp seems to have no effect on the value.

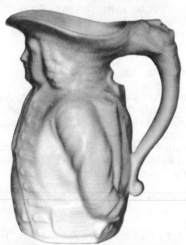

Toby mug, *William Penn, undecorated*

LIMITED AND SPECIAL EDITIONS

AMERICAN EXPRESS CHRISTMAS PLATES

Beginning in 1976, Lenox has issued a Christmas plate through the American Express organization. The plates issued so far have been the Douglas Fir in 1976, the Scotch Pine in 1977, the Blue Spruce in 1978, and the Balsam Fir for 1979. Production has been in the area of 15,000 for each year, and the price of the current plate is $60. We have not seen any of these plates sold on the secondary market, so cannot give prices for any of the others.

Christmas plate

ARCHITECTS' TEA SET

This tea set is perhaps the best known of all the early Lenox limited editions. It is a reproduction of a shape from colonial days, and is decorated with sepia scenes of famous buildings and has copper lustre trim on handles, rims and lids. The set includes:

	Price Range	
☐ **Creamer,** *Mount Vernon, Virginia*	47.50	55.00
☐ **Cups and saucers,** *each*	33.00	38.00
☐ **Same as above,** *Bull Pringle House, Charleston*	33.00	38.00
☐ **Same as above,** *Faneuil Hall, Boston*	33.00	38.00
☐ **Same as above,** *Library of the University of Virginia*	33.00	38.00
☐ **Same as above,** *Monticello, Charlottesville*	33.00	38.00
☐ **Same as above,** *Santa Barbara Mission, California*	33.00	38.00
☐ **Same as above,** *Westover, Virginia*	33.00	38.00
☐ **Jug, hot water,** *Old North Church, Hartford*	85.00	100.00
☐ **Sugar bowl,** *Independence Hall, Philadelphia*	55.00	63.00
☐ **Tea plates,** *same scenes as on cups*	18.50	23.50

Tea Set creamer and sugar

	Price Range	
☐ **Teapot,** *Federal Hall, New York*	105.00	120.00
☐ **Waste bowl,** *first coat of arms of U.S.A.*	55.00	63.00

Note: The tea plates, hot water jug, and waste bowl were available only as extras to the sets, and those sets without them should not be considered incomplete.

BICENTENNIAL AND SESQUICENTENNIAL ITEMS

The Lenox offering for the nation's 150th birthday in 1926 was a peacock blue cup and saucer with "1776-1926" in simple gold lettering on the front of the cup. Few are around today, and they should bring in the area of $75. Bicentennial items included the Patriots' Bowl and the Patriots' Pitcher, neither of which is being sold currently for more than issue price.

BOEHM BIRD SERIES

☐ **1970, Wood Thrush,** *24 Kt gold decorative border, 10½"*	265.00	335.00
☐ **1971, Goldfinch,** *24 KT gold decorative border, 10½"*	85.00	95.00
☐ **1972, Mountain Bluebird,** *24 KT gold decorative border, 10½"* ..	65.00	75.00
☐ **1973, Meadowlark,** *24 KT gold decorative border, 10½"*	62.00	70.00
☐ **1974, Rufous Hummingbird,** *24 KT gold decorative border, 10½"*	62.00	70.00
☐ **1975, American Redstart,** *24 KT gold decorative border, 10½"* .	52.00	58.00
☐ **1976, Cardinals,** *24 KT gold decorative border, 10½"*	52.00	58.00
☐ **1977, Robins,** *24 KT gold decorative border, 10½"*	47.00	53.00
☐ **1978, Mockingbirds,** *24 KT gold decorative border, 10½"*	56.00	63.00
☐ **1979, Golden Crowned Kinglets,** *24 KT gold decorative border, 10½"*	56.00	63.00
☐ **1980, Black-Throated Blue Warbler,** *24 KT gold decorative border*	75.00	85.00
☐ **1981, Eastern Phoebes,** *24 KT gold decorative border, 10½"* ...	85.00	95.00

BOEHM BIRDS, YOUNG AMERICA SERIES

☐ **1972, Bird of Peace**	265.00	335.00
☐ **1973, Eaglet**	200.00	250.00

Price Range

BOEHM WILDLIFE SERIES

☐ **1973, Raccoons,** *24 KT gold decorative border, 10½″*	**85.00**	**95.00**
☐ **1974, Red Fox,** *24 KT gold decorative border, 10½″*	**47.00**	**53.00**
☐ **1975, Rabbits,** *24 KT gold decorative border, 10½″*	**62.00**	**70.00**
☐ **1976, Chipmunks,** *24 KT gold decorative border, 10½″*	**56.00**	**63.00**
☐ **1977, Beaver,** *24 KT gold decorative border, 10½″*	**56.00**	**63.00**
☐ **1978, White-Tailed Deer,** *24 KT gold decorative border, 10½″* ..	**56.00**	**63.00**
☐ **1979, Squirrels,** *24 KT gold decorative border, 10½″*	**65.00**	**75.00**
☐ **1980, Bobcats,** *24 KT gold decorative border, 10½″*	**85.00**	**100.00**
☐ **1981, Marten,** *24 KT gold decorative border, 10½″*	**90.00**	**110.00**

THE CONFEDERACY COLLECTION

☐ **1972, States of The Confederacy,** *set*	**850.00**	**1000.00**

THE GOLD OF TUTANKHUMUN

The mask is approximately 6″ tall, and is limited to 15,000 unnumbered pieces with an issue price of $200. It is not yet being sold on the secondary market. One word of caution — do not immerse the mask, for the water seeps up inside and is impossible to get out.

HAWTHORN TEA SET

☐ **Cup and saucer,** *gold trim*	**33.00**	**38.00**
☐ **Cup and saucer,** *no gold*	**33.00**	**38.00**
☐ **Sugar and creamer,** *sugar lid missing*	**125.00**	**145.00**
☐ **Teapot,** *gold trim*	**135.00**	**155.00**
☐ **Teapot,** *no gold*	**135.00**	**155.00**

MINGA POPE PATCHIN ITEMS

These items are primarily products of the 1930's, and for the most part are sepla-tone scenics with gold trim. Series by her include the Old New York group and a set of plates done for the Colonial Dames of America which have scenes of colonia homes.

The 10½″ plates are the most common, but mugs, cups and saucers, and bowls are not unknown. Most of the items are in the $30 range, but the large bowl recently brought $75 at auction.

LEWIS BROTHERS CERAMICS, INC.,

This company is located on the corner of Mulberry & Breuning Avenues.

Marks: *Not known*
Prices: $6.50 minimum for any sample.

LINCOLN POTTERY

See International Pottery.

MADDOCK POTTERY COMPANY

Beginning in 1893, Maddock Pottery produced decorated and undecorated semi-porcelain in a pottery known as the Lamberton Works, which was apparently also occupied during this time by John Maddock & Sons, and which had previously been occupied by Trenton China Co. The owners of the Maddock Pottery Company included Moses Collear, C. A. May, Thomas P. Donoher, and the Thomas Maddock & Sons Company.

Marks: Backstamps include the one shown and at least two others, both of which incorporate the Maddock and Lamberton names.

	Price Range	
☐ **Bowl, punch,** *14" diameter, overall transfer cobalt decoration on outside, scattered large flowers in cobalt on inside, gold trim on rim, very attractive for a lower level type of item, gold trim on rim in worn*	235.00	285.00

Note: Other items can be compared to similar items appearing elsewhere throughout this book.

MAYER PORCELAIN MANUFACTURING COMPANY

See Arsenal Pottery.

MELLOR & COMPANY

See Cook Company.

MERCER POTTERY COMPANY

Mercer was founded in 1868 by James Moses. They made white granite, ironstone and other such wares. Under James Moses and W. B. Allen the company made sanitary wares from 1893 to 1904.

Marks: Several backstamps are known, including those shown.
Prices: The following prices are estimates.

	Price Range	
☐ **Bowls,** *serving*	25.00	40.00
☐ **Bowls,** *soup or desert*	10.00	15.00
☐ **Cups and saucers**	13.00	15.00
☐ **Dinner plates**	13.00	15.00
☐ **Mugs**	15.00	40.00
☐ **Platters,** *depending on size*	35.00	50.00
☐ **Smaller plates**	5.00	7.00

Note: For Mercer products made after the turn of the century, cut the above in half.

MILLINGTON & ASTBURY

See Millington, Astbury & Poulson

MILLINGTON, ASTBURY & POULSON

M.A.P. was started in 1853 on Carroll Street by Richard Millington and John Astbury. Poulson entered the firm in 1859. The company made white wares, and their most famous item was a Civil War pitcher modeled by Josiah Jones. The pitcher was sold both decorated and undecorated, and the decorated ones were done by noted New York ceramics artist Edward Lycett.

Marks: As shown.
Prices: The Civil War pitcher mentioned above turns up now and then. Prices have been as follows:

☐ **Undecorated and unmarked,** *minor damage*	235.00	285.00
☐ **Undecorated,** *marked, minor damage*	500.00	600.00
☐ **Estimate of value for marked, decorated sample**	875.00	1075.00

Note: Other M.A.P. products seem to have a much higher value than comparable Trenton items. Andy of their will probably have a minimum price tag of $25.

MONUMENT POTTERY COMPANY

Monument began manufacturing sanitary wares in 1896. Company officers included L. Wolff, John Clifford, J. M. Wolff, and J. M. Hoelscher.

Marks: *Not known*
Prices: A three-piece miniature bathroom set should be valued around $50. Any other items they might have made can be compared to similar Trenton items listed elsewhere.

MORRIS & WILLMORE

See Columbian Art Pottery.

NATIONAL CERAMICS

National was founded in 1906. The company is located on Southard Street and manufactures electrical porcelain.

Marks: *Not known*
Prices: $6.50 minimum for a sample.

NEWCOMB COLLEGE POTTERY

The late 19th century renewed a great interest in arts and crafts. Many American schools added art courses to their curriculum, and in a few of these — all too few, as far as the collector is concerned — students were instructed in the art of pottery painting. Pottery making and decorating became the chief specialty at the art department of Newcomb College in New Orleans. Its efforts in the field were launched in 1896. As all the work was performed under expert guidance and at a pace much slower and more conducive to artistic achievement than that of a commercial factory, some very noteworthy results were obtained. Most of the Newcomb pottery is brilliant. Its level of quality is consistently high and the decorating reflects imagination and spirit. Since its works were never produced in large quantities, they ranked as collectors' items almost from the beginning. Lovers of fine art pottery have been seeking out Newcomb products for at least 80 years.

Though one must be something of a connoisseur to fully appreciate the Newcomb pottery, the collecting potential it offers is broad. Nearly every piece carries an artist's marking, and the names of all artists (having been registered students) are recorded. Some hobbyists collect them by the artist, buying the works of their special favorites. Others try to accumulate pieces by as many different Newcomb artists as possible. This is a challenging task because there are many artists involved.

The Newcomb Pottery operations were headed by Dr. Ellsworth Woodward and Mary G. Sheerer. They did not manufacture or decorate any wares themselves but served only as instructors. Newcomb wares carry underglaze designs, picturing subjects from nature. Local subject-matter predominates, as the objective was to have students paint "from life" rather than from pictures in books (which was usually the case in commercial potteries). Thus the designs present an intriguing panorama of the flowers, leaf types, birds, etc. of Louisiana.

Marks: The collector of Newcomb pottery has a bit of a task in learning to read the marks before he does any serious buying. There are normally *five marks* on any given piece. First is the general mark of Newcomb, which will appear either as a white-on-black vase with the initials *N.C.*, or consist merely of those initials without symbolization (the N resting within the C). Another variety of the mark has *NEWCOMB COLLEGE* spelled out. Additionally, the piece will (or should) carry a potter's mark, an artist's or decorator's mark, a recipe mark, and finally a registration mark. The purpose of using potters' marks was to identify which works were produced by the students. The artists' marks were more elaborate than those of the potters, consisting usually of boldly drawn initial letters within geometrical frames. Obviously, the students took some inspiration in signing their names from the practices of artists at commercial art pottery factories. The *recipe mark* is a single capital letter, which relates to a book of clay mixtures used by the class. By using these various marks, it was possible to determine, even at a much later date, exactly how any particular object had been made and by whom.

NEW JERSEY PORCELAIN COMPANY

The company is located on Plum Street.

Marks: *Not known*
Prices: $6.50 minimum for a sample.

NEW JERSEY POTTERY COMPANY

This company was incorporated in 1869, and in 1883 the name was changed to Union Pottery Company. They went out of business in 1889. Union made some tiles and plates for the 1880 Presidential campaign. There was no connection between this company and the Union Porcelain Works of New York.

Marks: A circular mark inside a wreath, lettering "N. J. Pottery Co."
Prices: We have never seen any samples of this company's products sold on the open market. A minimum price for one of their Presidential campaign tiles or plates would be in the area of $35.

NILOAK PTTTERY COMPANY

The products of this 20th century art pottery are highly creative. Prior to closing in 1946, Niloak sold decorative wares with very simple shapes, whose textures resembled marble. All the shapes and styles were inspired by so-called primitive work, by the ancient Greeks and Romans and especially by the American Indians. The Niloak pottery is essentially old classic redware, the same type you find in museums, but with the drastic difference of a marbelized texture. To achieve an even more natural, striking appearance, the company decided to stop using exterior glazes. Thus, most of the Niloak pottery has a glaze on the inside only. This interior glaze was considered necessary from a utilitarian point of view, in the event any owner wanted to keep liquids in them. It is highly doubtful, though, if anyone did more with Niloak creations than to display them as decorative objects of art. They were dazzlers, especially in a setting with subdued lighting.

Today, Niloak has become a favorite art pottery with collectors. It never fails to intrigue the general public, too, though there are many who instinctively believe it to have an Indian origin.

Niloak products were developed in an old family pottery business in 1909 in Benton, Arkansas, when the company was being run by Charles D. Hyten. Charles was the son of J.H. Hyten, who had come to Arkansas from Iowa many years earlier to establish a pottery works. Niloak was nothing more than an experiment at the factory when it was initially produced. The word "niloak" is kaolin spelled backwards, kaolin being the special clay which serves as chief ingredient in porcelain. Since Niloak pottery was about as opposite to porcelain as any ware could be, the use of this name was appropriate. Clays of various colors all from the neighborhood around Benton went into Niloak. They were blended on the wheel so that one streaked into another and always left traces of unblended color — thereby creating the styrated or marbelized effect.

Hyten made arrangements with a jewelry shop in Benton to show some of his strange new creations on consignment. They aroused interest and very soon the Hyten Pottery became the Niloak Pottery Company. Distribution was made to the leading market areas of the country, but Niloak never expanded to the point of actually mass producing its wares. The firm's most successful decade was the 1920's. Like other art potteries it was hit hard by the depression and never regained momentum, though it managed to survive into the 1940's.

Marks: Niloak pottery will either have an impressed mark or a circular paper label, reading simply *NILOAK POTTERY*. The mark is contained in a collar and is printed in plain block letters. Paper labels became standard with Niloak in its later years. As with other pottery bearing paper labels, the labels sometimes came loose, leaving the item without any indication of its origin. A more elaborate form of the mark reads *FROM THE NILOAK POTTERIES AT BENTON, ARKANSAS*. Some pieces carry model numbers and some do not. It is incorrect to refer to these as MOLD numbers, since the Niloak ware was always thrown on the wheel, not pressed from molds.

OLIPHANT AND COMPANY

See Delaware Pottery.

OTT & BREWER

The company which was later to be known as Ott & Brewer was founded in May 1863, by Bloor, Ott and Booth. Bloor had the necessary technical know-how and his two partners supplied the financial backing. The building they erected was called the Etruria Pottery Works, perhaps in imitation of the Wedgwood establishment in England. During that period, however, the name Etrurian (or Etruscan) was commonly applied to wares which were copied from ancient specimens, so perhaps the founders had something like this in mind.

Booth left the business in 1864, and his part of the company was bought by Garret S. Burroughs. Burroughs also lasted only one year, due to illness. It was at this point that John Hart Brewer entered the firm, and items which are marked "O.B.B." could mean Bloor, Ott & **Booth,** Bloor, Ott & **Burroughs,** or Bloor, Ott & **Brewer.**

The young company produced a variety of everyday wares, primarily decorated granite ware. Herman Rolege was the only decorator in Trenton at that time, and he decorated for B.O.B. as well as all the other companies. Since undecorated granite ware has not been seen, we can draw the conclusion that either the company decorated all their items or else their undecorated wares were not marked with their name.

Although Isaac Broome is generally given credit for establising O&B's parian line for the 1876 Centennial, the company did make at least two parian busts before that time. Two busts, one of Ulysses S. Grant ant the other of Abraham Lincoln, are marked with the "B.O.B." mark, and since Bloor left the company in 1873 we can be relatively certain that these two parian items came before that time. It would be interesting to find out who developed the parian body and/or sculpted the figures.

Broome came to Ott & Brewer in 1875 or 1876 and greatly expanded the parian line there. Many of his items were shown at the Philadelphia exposition in 1876. Broome/O&B parian items include: Busts of Apollo, Abraham Lincoln (presumably not the same one the company did earlier), Rutherford B. Hayes, Benjamin Franklin, George Washington (two sizes), Cleopatra (a Mrs. Thompson of Trenton was the model), Ulysses S. Grant (again, presumably not the same one discussed above), Pope Pius IX (originally designed by Broome in 1858 and cast by the O&B company in 1876), William Shakespeare, and eight "races of the world" miniature heads; two vases — the famous baseball vase (two subsections of the baseball vase, the pitcher and the batter, were additionally done separately), and a pastoral vase (two sizes); a plaque of Robert Fulton; and the George and Martha Washington tea set.

Beginning around 1876 the company made a ware known as ivory porcelain. Although in color, styling and type of decoration it resembles Irish Belleek, it is not the same composition and not quite as fine. True Belleek experimentation by John H. Brewer and William Bromley, Jr., began in 1882 and was aided a year later by the arrival of John and William Bromley, Sr.

Ott & Brewer used the full range of decorating methods on their wares,

Mark A

Mark B

Mark C

Mark D

O.&B.

Mark E

Mark F

Mark G

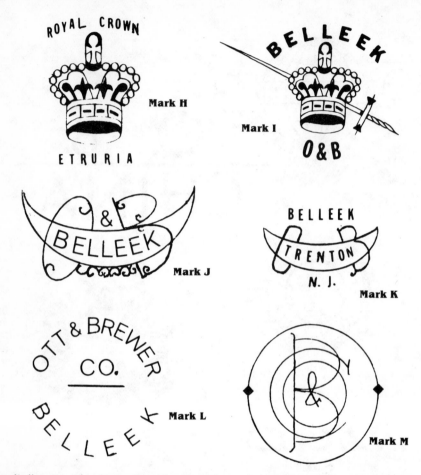

Mark H

Mark I

Mark J

Mark K

Mark L

Mark M

including transfer decoration of various types (primarily on their non-porcelain wares), hand-painting, gold paste, Royal Worcester "cloisonne" style artwork, and Irish Belleek type pearlized glazes. Pate-sur-pate work was done there, primarily by a man named Saunders. (Where is all that pate-sur-pate now?)

Many of the better-known Trenton ceramics people got their training at O&B, including Jonathan Coxon and Walter Lenox. The company experimented with a great variety of things down through the years, and if imitation is indeed the greatest form of flattery then Ott & Brewer must have been practically flattered to death by the other Trenton Companies. O&B is generally considered to be the finest china ever made in the Unites State, and is certainly the most expensive of the Trenton chinas. The company folded in 1893 (or 1892) due to prolonged labor problems and the depression of the 1890's Cook Pottery later took over the Etruria Pottery, although it is not certain whether they merely bought the building or if they also bought the O&B molds.

Marks: Mark A is usually impressed and was used on nonporcelain items. It will frequently appear along with another mark, usually mark C. Marks B, C, and D are usually printed and are also found on non-porcelain items. Mark C is usually printed in brown, and on the rare occasions when it is found in its green version it is usually on a non-factory decorated item. In addition to these marks, the company used at least two different British coat of arms marks for their semi-vitreous wares. Mark A is commonly called the globe mark and mark C is known as the rising sun mark.

Marks E and F were used primarily on ivory porcelain, usually in conjunction with one of the other marks. Marks G through J were also used on ivory porcelain, with the crown marks probably pre-dating the crescent mark. They are printed marks and will usually be reddish-brown in color. Variations of the marks are seen and include a crown with a squared-off look instead of the rounded shape shown here.

With the development of a true Belleek product, mark J was altered slightly to give us mark K. Mark K is also a printed mark, usually reddish-brown, and once again is sometimes seen along with one of the other marks. Retail store names show up now and then with Mark K, and from this we can gather that at the very least O&B had contracts with Shreve, Crump and Gow of Boston, Tiffany and Company of New York, and John McDonald & Sons Company.

Pieces exhibited at the Southern Art Union in New Orleans in 1884 are marked with that information in a circle along with mark K. A cup and saucer seen recently, however, has the New Orleans mark with mark J. The use for marks L and M is uncertain.

Item numbers appear on some of the later pieces, and apparently went up at least as high as 1200. It is not certain whether this system applied to porcelain and non-porcelain items or whether different types of china had different numbering systems. O&B items are rarely if ever artist signed, however initials occasionally are seen on the bottoms of later pieces which could very well be decorators' marks.

The Ott & Brewer marking system is not nearly as precise as the above information would lead one to believe, and although we do not have samples at hand to prove our point we are sure we have seen ivory porcelain items with mark K and Belleek items with mark J, etc.

Prices: Ott & Brewer Belleek has never been cheap, and recent rises in price have pretty much eliminated the middle class collector. It is still possible to occasionally come across a piece of O&B at a flea market or yard sale, but for the most part now antiques dealers know what they have. Most collectors do not distinguish between the ivory porcelain and the true Belleek, although most are aware that items with the crown marks can be a little heavier than those with the crescent marks, and there is little or no diff³rence in pricing between the two types. (Remember that although the se with the crescent marks, and there is little or no difference in pricing between the two types. (Remember that although the true Belleek is thinner, the ivory porcelain is older.)

Non-porcelain items still are to be found at popular prices, although this situation may not last long. As more and more O&B Belleek becomes unreachable, the granite wares and cream-colored wares will become more interesting to collectors and this is almost always followed by a rise in price.

Parian items and pieces signed by Broome are the most expensive of all. The only known sale of a Broome item during the past year was the egg shown in the color section, which was sold for $1,200. It is marked with a variation of mark F, and has the date 1877 and the Broome signature. Expect to pay a minimum of $1,500 for a marked parian bust.

NOT-PORCELAIN WARES   Price Range

☐ **Cracker jar,** *granite ware, oxblood color, hand-done sponged gold clouds covering jar and lid, gold trim on finial and handles somewhat worn, marks A and C* 120.00   140.00

☐ **Cracker jar, same as above,** *except green background and not marked* 80.00   95.00

☐ **Plates,** *9-1/2" diameter, hand-painted game birds, colored rims with sponged gold finish, one rim copper color and the other gray, pencilline gold banding on outer rim and on shoulder, crazing on surface, otherwise perfect, marks A and C on one plate, mark A only on the other, see photo of one plate, pair* 120.00   140.00

☐ **Vase,** *9" high, slightly rounded shape, hand-painted red and pink flowers on green background, marks A and C in green,* 115.00   130.00

Note: Expect to pay a minimum of $65 for any decorated piece of Ott & Brewer opaque ware. Earlier samples of this type of item are
usually crazed, and this is not held against them where value is concerned.

Plate, *game bird*

PORCELAIN ITEMS

No attempt will be made to differentiate between ivory porcelain and true Belleek.

Price Range

☐ **Basket,** 6" high, rustic handle, raised gold paste trim in thistle
pattern on beige matte finish, mark I, see photo in color section   600.00   700.00

☐ **Chocolate pot,** 12" high, green bottom section, top section has
raised gold paste trim in several shades of gold, gold trim on
dragon handle andbspout and en bottom section, top section
has raised gold paste trim in several shades of gold, gold trim on
dragon handle and spout and on finial and rims, Mark I 700.00   820.00

☐ **Cup and saucer,** after dinner size, gold paste trim, mark K and
Tiffany & Co. mark, saucer only marked, gold is not the same
color on the cup as on the saucer for some reason, but it is obvi-
ous the pieces belong together 115.00   130.00

☐ **Cup and saucer,** after dinner size, plain shape, spray of raised
enamel flowers across front of cup, smaller spray on back, two
sprays on saucer, pearlized pink interior, gold trim on rims and
handle, mark J with New Orleans inscription, saucer broken in
half and glued back together 135.00   155.00

☐ **Cup and saucer,** Tridacna pattern, teacup size, pearlized yellow
interior, gold trim on handle and rims, mark K 150.00   175.00

☐ **Cup and saucer,** Tridacna pattern, bouillon, pearlized pink
interior, gold trim on handle and rims, mark K, small fleck on
underside of saucer 140.00   170.00

☐ **Cup and saucer,** cactus pattern, teacup size, pearlized white
finish, gold trim on handle and rim, crack in handle 120.00   140.00

☐ **Cup and saucer,** after dinner size, enamel ribbon design, gold
trim, mark I 180.00   220.00

☐ **Ewer,** double spouted, rustic handle, top section covered with
gold, bottom section has hand-painted coral colored water lilies,
two small chips on top section, mark I 750.00   850.00

☐ **Ewer,** raised gold paste cattail pattern, two turtle figurines
applied to side of piece, turtles and coral handle decorated in
green and gold, small fleck on one of the turtles, mark I 800.00   1000.00

☐ **Ewer,** bulbous shape, raised gold paste in thistle pattern on
beige matte finish, gold trim on handle and rims, 8" high, mark I   650.00   750.00

☐ **Ewer,** similar in size and shape to the one with turtles listed
above, hand-painted water lilies outlined in gold, handle is
formed like
stem to buds and leaves which are applied near the rim, piece
has been totally devastated in the back and is held together with
glue, damage does not show very much in front, handle badly
cracked so piece has to be picked up by the body, mark I 210.00   255.00

☐ **Ewer,** 7" high, shaped like a vinegar cruet, raised gold paste trim
in chrysanthemum design on beige matte finish, mark K 385.00   455.00

☐ **Ewer,** melon-ribbed, 8" high, white glazed background with gold
paste trim in oak leaf pattern, mark I, spider crack in bottom of
piece 170.00   200.00

☐ **Shell,** raised on coral and seashell base, pearlized pink interior
to shell, gold trim on rim and on base, one of the small shells
that form the base has been broken off, mark I 400.00   470.00

☐ **Shell,** 1-1/2" high, 3-1/4" (handle included) wide, very delicate
and thin, forked handle and two small shell feet decorated in
gold, gold trim on rim, little shell are misplaced so the item wob-
bles ever so slightly, mark I 90.00   110.00

☐ **Shell,** similar to one above but with no handle, pearlized blue
interior, mark J 90.00   110.00

Price Range

☐ **Shoe,** 5" long, hand-painted small flowers in scatter pattern,
gold trim, marks I and J 400.00   470.00

☐ **Sugar and creamer,** cactus pattern, pearlized finish, gold trim
on rim, bronze trim on handles, mint condition, mark I 385.00   455.00

☐ **Sugar and creamer,** Tridacna pattern, pearlized pink inside,
gold trim on handles and rims, mark J 260.00   320.00

Sugar and creamer, *cactus pattern*

Sugar bowl, *Tridacna pattern*

☐ **Sugar and creamer,** ruffled top sugar, creamer fits inside of
sugar, raised gold paste trim in oak leaf pattern on beige matte
finish, mark K 300.00   400.00

☐ **Sugar and creamer,** same shape as above, transfer print with
raised enamel work, gold trim on rims, mark I 260.00   320.00

*Note: Sugars and creamers are frequently found without their
mates, and in this event a creamer is probably worth a hint
more than a sugar bowl alone. The little creamer shown by*

itself in the photo is probably worth $10 to $15 more than a matching sugar bowl alone. The creamer sold recently for $125.

Creamer

	Price Range	
☐ **Teapot,** *dented sides, covered with grotesque coral trim, raised gold paste work on bottom half, gold trim on coral branches, spout has been repaired and there is a small crack coming down from the rim, mark I*	260.00	320.00
☐ **Vase,** *7" high, beautiful hand-painted orchid, raised gold paste work, openwork handles, raised on small openwork feet one of which is damaged, probably had a lid at one time which is no longer present, mark K*	400.00	470.00
☐ **Vase,** *7" high, calla lily shape on rustinc base, applied leaf on side helps support the lily, pearlized ivory interior, leaf pale lavender, gold trim on rim and on base section, a few small rough spots, mark I*	675.00	875.00
☐ **Vase,** *bulbous bottom with long neck, 10" high, hand-painted yellow and brown flowers, raised gold trim, mark I*	525.00	625.00
☐ **Vase,** *12" high, bulbous bottom with long narrow square neck, green background with raised gold paste trim done in at least five different shades ranging all the way from a silver color to a bronze, mark I*	875.00	1075.00
☐ **Vase,** *12" high, bulbous bottom with long neck, hand-painted roses outlined in gold on high-glaze white finish, small repaired spot on top, mark H*	600.00	700.00
☐ **Vase,** *10" high, double-handled, raised gold paste in three shades of gold, mark J*	525.00	625.00
☐ **Watering can,** *7-1/2" high, raised gold paste trim on beige matte finish, damage to spout, mark I*	375.00	475.00

PERLEE BELLEEK

Perlee was made in Trenton in the late 1920's, and possibly went under during the Depression. Their dinnerware resembles that of Lenox made during the same time.

Marks: All marks include the word Perlee in one fashion or another.
Prices: Rate against comparable Lenox items. Although Perlee is rare, there is too little demand for it at this time for prices to be very high.

	Price Range	
☐ **Cup and saucer,** *enamel trim*	37.00	43.00
☐ **Cup and saucer,** *gold trim*	30.00	35.00
☐ **Dinner plate,** *floral pattern*	23.00	28.00
☐ **Dinner plate,** *gold trim*	18.00	23.00
☐ **Dinner plate,** *Oriental pattern*	23.00	28.00
☐ **Salad plate,** *8-1/4" diameter, gold trim*	10.00	15.00
☐ **Tea set,** *three pieces, overall decoration with teardrop shaped multi colored enamel work*	210.00	255.00
☐ **Tray,** *olive, oval, gold trim*	30.00	35.00
☐ **Vase,** *unmarked but has the same enamel work as the above listed tea set*	30.00	35.00

PFALTZGRAFF

This well-known producer of dinnerware originated back in the early 19th century. For most of its long history (the firm is still in operation today) it was a maker of stoneware, as well as clay pipes, tobacco humidors, and miscellaneous pottery articles of all kinds. Its entry into the dinnerware field did not come until 1940, when the firm was already well over 100 years old and had gained a standing with collectors. Though its fine dinnerware from the 1940's and 1950's is the best-known of Pfaltzgraff "collectibles" on the current market, there are many other — and much scarcer — Pfaltzgraff pieces available for the enthusiast.

The Pfaltzgraffs (the P is silent) were immigrants to western Pennsylvania from the Rhineland area of Germany. They arrived along with tens of thousands of their countrymen to settle into the region known incorrectly as "Pennsylvania *Dutch*." With reasonably good local clays available, pottery business were attempted, and some proved fairly successful. The Pfaltzgraff Pottery was built in York County, Pennsylvania. Throughout the early and mid 19th century, it mainly served the local residents. After the Civil War, its products were increasingly retailed in Philadelphia to the "town folk" and thereafter on a much larger scale. Nearly all of this was stoneware attractively but modestly painted. At various times, Pfaltzgraff also made feeding and watering troughs for barnyard animals. Its line gradually diversified and business expanded with the best growth decade being the 1920's. The decision to go into the chinaware table service market, in 1940, was undoubtedly prompted by the belief that hostilities in Europe would bring an end to foreign imports. The postwar years saw the rise of the four familiar Pfaltzgraff lines of dinnerware, Yorktowne, Heritage, Village and Gourmet.

Marks: The standard mark for Pfaltzgraff is a stylish, tall letter P superimposed on a badge, reading YORK. Another mark reads PFALTZGRAFF, YORK, PA. Various other marks will also be found, relating to the different trade names under which its products were distributed.

POOLE AND STOCKTON

The name of this Trenton decorating company will sometimes appear along with that of the manufacturer.

Prices: The Poole and Stockton mark on a piece of china would probably be worth $6.50 beyond the basic price of the item.

POPE AND LEE

Pope and Lee was a Trenton decorating establishment whose name will occasionally be found on wares decorated by them.

Prices: This decorating company's mark would probably raise the value of a given item by $6.50.

PROSPECT HILL POTTERY

Prospect Hill was founded in 1880 by Dale and Davis. Products included semi-porcelain, white granite, and opaque porcelain. Isaac Davis ran a company prior to the partnership with Dale but it isn't certain whether or not it was called Prospect Hill Pottery at that time.

Marks: Prospect Hill marks include several using the British coat of arms. All their marks include the name I. Davis or the names of the partners, Dale and Davis. The Dale and Davis is sometimes abbreviated as D-D or D&D.
Prices: The following prices are estimates.

	Price Range	
☐ **Bowls,** *dessert or soup*	7.00	10.00
☐ **Bowls,** *serving*	20.00	30.00
☐ **Cups and saucers**	10.00	15.00
☐ **Dinner plates**	10.00	20.00
☐ **Mugs**	15.00	40.00
☐ **Platters,** *depending on size*	30.00	50.00
☐ **Smaller plates**	5.00	10.00

PROVIDENTIAL TILE WORKS

Mr. James H. Robinson and Mr. C. Louis Whitehead founded the Providential Tile Works in 1885, although their first items were not produced until 1886. Isaac Broome was their first modeller and designer, and Scott Callowhill was the designer after Broome left. Although the company is best known for its embossed tiles, they alsŏ engaged in both underglaze and overglaze decorated ones, including some which were gilded and painted in a cloisone effect.

Marks: The marks used by Providential are uncertain, but many possibly include a star. Tiles signed by Broome are sometimes marked with this star, and since none of the other companies where he worked used this mark, they are generally considered to be Providential by default. There was a Star Encaustic Tile Company in Pittsburgh, but this company used the initials S.E.T. rather than a star as a backstamp.

Prices: (All prices listed are for tiles which are 6" x 6" or smaller in size, and for tiles which are in mint or near-mint condition. The prices are estimates rather than actual selling prices, since the Providential mark is in doubt and this makes positive identification difficult.)
Embossed tiles — $50 and under for those which are not artist-signed. $100 for a signed Broome.
Decorated tiles — $50 and under for run-of-the-mill decorated tiles, either underglaze. Special or unique designs such as the cloisonne-type ones described have no established prices but they would possibly be in the $100 range.

REDWING

The fine art pottery of Red Wing is its best-known and most avidly collected ceramic ware in the United States. However, this long-established manufacturer, which was in business nearly a century, closed down in 1967. Red Wing produced many other types of pottery as well. Those who wish to collect its artware will find it in the stocks of many dealers. It is not rare by any means, but the increasing interest and competition have worked together to drive up prices far beyond levels of the mid 1970's.

This is certainly one of the more versatile and original firms, and therefore carries a special collecting intrigue. Its medium-priced lines for the mass market never failed to show pleasing creativity, either in the shapes or (more often) types of decoration which could be standard patterns in unusual colors of those which bordered on "optical art." Originally, this was a stoneware firm and its primary product was stoneware for the first 50 or more years of its operations. Its stoneware is fine, thick-walled, and attractively finished; the decorative painting is generally blue and may consist of flowers, vines, leaves, birds, fruits or insects. The novelty ware produced in later years, much of which ended up at carvinals as prize-pieces, was sometimes in bright solid colors or in combinations of rich solid colors. Even its traditional items such as teapots were often very brightly decorated. There are always surprises for the collector of Red Wing because the company's creative brains never ran in the same direction twice.

Red Wing Stoneware Company was founded in 1878 in Red Wing, Minnesota. It was one of the earliest midwestern potteries outside of Ohio. Pottery factories straying from the eastern Ohio region were usually doomed to an early failure, but Red Wing showed remarkable staying power. As the population of the area increased, its production increased, and the business thrived. The concept of expanding its line beyond stoneware was first explored in the early 1920's when the market for pottery in general broadened out as never before. The first new item put into production at that time was a line of flowerpots. This marked the entry of Red Wing into the art pottery area. Its flowepots were followed in later years by artware cookie jars, jugs, trays, candleholders and vases. Also, a general line of dinnerware was added to the factory's schedule in the depression years to take up slack from the loss of artware sales. The best years for Red Wing art pottery were from the middle 1920's to the early 1930's.

Marks: Red Wing manufactured under its own name and also as Rumrill, sometimes spelled RumRill. When the Rumrill mark is used, it will generally be with the second R capitalized. The Red Wing house-marks changed through the years. If one includes the early stoneware markings a long list would be necessary to record them all. In the era of its art pottery, there were at least three distinctive marks. One consisted of the wording *RED WING ART POTTERY* arranged in a circle with *ART* at the center and no other symbols or decoration. An impressed mark from the 1930's states simply *RED WING* followed by the mold or model number. The most elaborate mark is a badge, with the company name in bold script lettering in Art Deco style.

	Price Range	
☐ **Ashtray,** *no item number, cedar brown, semi gloss, of roughly circular form in the shape of a horse's head and neck, with a shellwork design at the lower portion, marked RED WING U.S.A.*	14.00	18.00
☐ **Ashtray,** *no item number, red, semi gloss, of bird's-wing form with textured molding, special anniversary product, marked 1879-1953*	20.00	25.00
☐ **Ashtray,** *item #738, salmon, matt glaze, oval, flattened, no lip, marked RED WING U.S.A.*	5.00	7.00
☐ **Ashtray,** *no item number, salmon tinged with lavender, semi gloss, of roughly circular form in the shape of a horse's head and neck, with a shellwork design at the lower portion, marked RED WING U.S.A.*	14.00	18.00
☐ **Ashtray,** *item #695, shocking pink, high gloss, of shaped oval form with a widely flaring exaggerated lip, the lip decorated with molded fluting to resemble a seashell, marked RED WING U.S.A.*	10.00	14.00
☐ **Bowl,** *item #219, ivory white, matt glaze, oval form with overlapping rim, decorated at the bowl with bas-relief moldings of a flower and leaves, highlighted with touches of burgundy coloring, marked RED WING U.S.A.*	24.00	28.00
☐ **Bowl,** *item #M-1493, black, matt glaze, oval with square handles, marked RED WING U.S.A.*	7.00	10.00
☐ **Bowl,** *no item number, black, matt glaze, oval with rising lip, marked RED WING U.S.A.*	7.00	10.00

Price Range

☐ **Bowl,** *item #M-5006, salmon, semi gloss, flattened oval (boat form), resting on a classical-style pedestal base, marked RED WING U.S.A.* 8.00   10.00

☐ **Bowl, console,** *item #B-2014, red, semi-gloss, of freeform shape, low-slung, with bird's-wing molding at the sides, marked RED WING U.S.A.* 10.00   13.00

☐ **Candleholder,** *item #B-1411, blue, high gloss, of roughly rectangular form with shaped sides, giving the appearance of an ashtray, marked RED WING U.S.A.* 3.00   4.00

☐ **Candleholder,** *item #847, blue, matt glaze, in the form of a classical urn with fluted sides and vaulted scrolling terminals at the rim, resting on a flat base, marked RED WING U.S.A.* 7.00   10.00

☐ **Candleholder,** *item #B-2111, blue, semi gloss, Aladdin's lamp design with texturing consisting of narrow alternating bands of blue and pastel blue, twin handles, marked RED WING U.S.A.* 8.00   10.00

☐ **Candleholder,** *item #M-4003, blue, semi gloss, in the form of a water fountain with tall columned body, decorated with geometrical fluting at the body and bowl, marked RED WING U.S.A.* 8.00   11.00

☐ **Candleholder,** *no item number, bright blue, matt glaze, of spherical shape with molded leaves at the base, marked RED WING U.S.A.* 3.00   4.00

☐ **Candleholder,** *item #B-2111, caramel brown, semi gloss, of Aladdin's lamp design with texturing consisting of narrow alternating bands of caramel and very pale brown, twin handles, marked RED WING U.S.A.* 8.00   10.00

☐ **Candleholder,** *item #B-1412A, cedar brown, high gloss, of freeform oval design pinched at one end, marked RED WING U.S.A.* 7.00   10.00

☐ **Candleholder,** *item #847, cedar brown, matt glaze, in the form of a classical urn with fluted sides and vaulted scrolling terminals at the rim, resting on a flat base, marked RED WING U.S.A.* 7.00   10.00

☐ **Candleholder,** *item #B-1409, chestnut, matt glaze, teardrop shape, the interior is a slightly lighter shade than the exterior, marked RED WING U.S.A.* 3.00   5.00

☐ **Candleholder,** *item #M-4003/8, dark gray, semi gloss, in the form of a water fountain with tall columned body, decorated with geometrical fluting at the body and bowl, marked RED WING U.S.A.* 8.00   11.00

☐ **Candleholder,** *item #408A, elephant gray with red interior, high gloss, of impressionistic triangular form, marked RED WING U.S.A.* 3.00   4.00

☐ **Candleholder,** *item #B-1412A, green, high gloss, of freeform oval design pinched at one end, marked RED WING U.S.A.* 7.00   10.00

☐ **Candleholder,** *item #B-1411, green, high gloss, of roughly rectangular form with shaped sides, giving the appearance of an ashtray, marked RED WING U.S.A.* 3.00   4.00

☐ **Candleholder,** *no item number, green, matt glaze, of spherical shape with molded leaves at the base, marked RED WING U.S.A.* 3.00   4.00

Price Range

☐ **Candleholder,** *item #M-4003, green, semi gloss, in the form of a water fountain with tall columned body, decorated with geometrical fluting at the body and bowl, marked RED WING U.S.A.* 8.00   11.00

☐ **Candleholder,** *no item number, gray, matt glaze, of spherical shape with molded leaves at the base, marked RED WING U.S.A.* 3.00   4.00

☐ **Candleholder,** *item #847, grayish ivory, matt glaze, in the form of a classical urn with fluted sides and vaulted scrolling terminals at the rim, resting on a flat base, marked RED WING U.S.A.* 7.00   10.00

☐ **Candleholder,** *item #B-1411, ivory white, high gloss, of roughly rectangular form with shaped sides, giving the appearance of an ashtray, marked RED WING U.S.A.* 3.00   4.00

☐ **Candleholder,** *item #622, ivory white, matt glaze, of dome form decorated with grape and leaf molding and highlighted with burgundy coloring, marked RED WING U.S.A.* 12.00   15.00

☐ **Candleholder,** *item #408A, marble white, matt glaze, of rectangular block form (impressionistic), undecorated, marked RED WING U.S.A.* 7.00   10.00

☐ **Candleholder,** *no item number, marble white with jungle green and pink, semi gloss, in the form of a socket placed on a scrolled stand, accompanied by floral and leafwork ornament, marked with an applied paper label* 8.00   10.00

☐ **Candleholder,** *item #B-1412A, pastel blue, high gloss, of freeform oval design pinched at one end, marked RED WING U.S.A.* 7.00   10.00

☐ **Candleholder,** *item #408A, pastel blue, matt glaze, of rectangular block form (impressionistic) undecorated, marked RED WING U.S.A.* 7.00   10.00

☐ **Candleholder,** *item #408A, pink, matt glaze, of rectangular block form (impressionistic), undecorated, marked RED WING U.S.A.* 7.00   10.00

☐ **Candleholder,** *item #B-1411, red, high gloss, of roughly rectangular form with shaped sides, giving the appearance of an ashtray, marked RED WING U.S.A.* 3.00   4.00

☐ **Candleholder,** *item #B-1412A, red, high gloss, of freeform oval design pinched at one end, marked RED WING U.S.A.* 7.00   10.00

☐ **Candleholder,** *item #B-2111, rose, semi gloss, of Aladdin's lamp design with texturing consisting of narrow alternating bands of rose and very pale pink, twin handles, marked RED WING U.S.A.* 8.00   10.00

☐ **Candlestick,** *item #1558, dark salmon, semi gloss, of shaped cylindrical form, flared at the top, composed of a set of four oval pillars joined together in freeform composition, marked RED WING U.S.A.* 8.00   10.00

☐ **Candlestick,** *item #1558, green, semi gloss, of shaped cylindrical form, flared at the top, composed of a set of four oval pillars joined together in freeform composition, marked RED WING U.S.A.* 8.00   10.00

☐ **Candlestick,** *item #1558, gray, semi gloss, of shaped cylindrical form, flared at the top, composed of a set of four oval pillars joined together in freeform composition, marked RED WING U.S.A.* 8.00   10.00

Price Range

☐ **Candlesticks (two-in-one),** *item #397, light blue, matt glaze, a pair of cornucopia-shaped holders together on a domed base, marked RED WING U.S.A.* 12.00   15.00

☐ **Cookie jar, rooster,** *item #249, pale sea green with various tonal effects, semi gloss, in the form of a realistically modeled rooster, seated, upper portion serves as the jar lid, the dividing line occurring just above the wings, tail is the lid handle, marked RED WING U.S.A.* 23.00   28.00

☐ **Dish, candy,** *item #801, mud brown, semi gloss, of shaped triangular form, consisting of three bowls in one, each formed by a hexagon of diagonal wedges, marked RED WING U.S.A.* 10.00   13.00

☐ **Ewer,** *item #1219, ivory white, matt glaze, of cruet form with bulbous bowl and tall narrow cylindrical neck, with vertical handle rising from the bowl and connecting with the lip. Decorated at the bowl with molded leafwork, highlighted with pale burgundy coloring, marked RED WING U.S.A.* 26.00   32.00

☐ **Figurine, Chinaman,** *item #1309, ivory white, matt glaze, a priest dressed in long flowing robes, hands clasped, wearing a ceremonial headpiece, marked RED WING U.S.A.* 15.00   19.00

☐ **Figurine, Donkey,** *item #376, ivory white with touches of blue and burgundy, in the form of a seated donkey with head upturned and mouth open wide, marked RED WING* 11.00   14.00

☐ **Figurine, Oriental female,** *item #1308, ivory white, matt glaze, a standing figure with hands clasped, possibly representing a goddess, marked RED WING U.S.A.* 15.00   19.00

☐ **Jug,** *item #33, dark blue, matt glaze, egg shape with pouring spout at one end, the handle reaching from back of bowl to neck, decorated with a molded wreath, marked RED WING U.S.A.* 19.00   24.00

☐ **Jug (or Pitcher),** *no item number, pastel beige, matt glaze, of spherical form with mouth and pouring spout positioned to one side, C-shape handle, marked RUM RILL* 20.00   25.00

Note: Red Wing produced a considerable amount of work for the Rum Rill Pottery Co. It is collected both by Red Wing enthusiasts and those who specialize in the Rum Rill products.

☐ **Pitcher,** *item #M-1565, deep sea green, matt glaze, of elongated form with bulbous base and tall neck, loop handle, marked RED WING U.S.A.* 18.00   23.00

☐ **Plate,** *item #621, ivory white, matt glaze, circular, decorated with three molded grape bunches highlighted with burgundy coloring, and additionally with burgundy colored slits along the rim, marked RED WING U.S.A.* 21.00   26.00

☐ **Pitcher,** *item #766, marble white, matt glaze, pot form with twin spouts (one at either side), connected by a modified C-shape handle, decorated at the sides with a molded wreath, marked RED WING* 24.00   29.00

☐ **Pitcher,** *no item number, yellow, semi gloss, of trophy form with flatted sides, loop handle, marked RED WING* 9.00   12.00

☐ **Planter,** *item #M-1467, black, matt glaze, in the form of a stylized dove with Art Deco overtones (though of later design than the Art Deco era), the back hollowed out to form the planter, marked RED WING U.S.A.* 14.00   18.00

Price Range

☐ **Planter,** *item #M-1484, black, semi gloss, in the form of a stringed guitar, the body consisting of a pocket which forms the planter, with four turning keys, marked RED WING U.S.A. .* 13.00 16.00

☐ **Planter,** *item #526, black and bone white, the bowl of inverted hat shape with exaggerated shaped lip, a pedestal rising out of the bowl surmounted by a black sculptured figure of an antelope, marked RED WING U.S.A.* 25.00 31.00

☐ **Planter,** *item #1210, blue, high gloss speckled finish, of pot form with flared shoulders, the body composed of vertical lobes, fitted with a pair of ring-type copper handles painted in gold gilt, marked RED WING U.S.A.* 9.00 12.00

☐ **Planter,** *item #869, blue, matt glaze, of shaped pot form with flattened sides, resting on feet, marked RED WING U.S.A.* 7.00 9.00

☐ **Planter,** *item #5018, blue, matt glaze, of rectangular form with sloping sides, marked RED WING U.S.A.* 7.00 10.00

☐ **Planter,** *item #835, blue, matt glaze, of oval form, low-slung, decorated at the sides with loopwork, marked RED WING U.S.A.* 7.00 10.00

☐ **Planter,** *item #815, blue, matt glaze, rectangular, of tub form with shaped sides resting upon squat feet, marked RED WING U.S.A.* 7.00 10.00

☐ **Planter,** *item #M-1467, in the form of a stylized dove with Art Deco overtones (though of later design than the Art Deco era), the back hollowed out to form the planter, marked RED WING U.S.A.* 14.00 18.00

☐ **Planter,** *item #1264, blue, semi gloss, of lampshade form with shaped fluted sides, marked RED WING U.S.A.* 7.00 10.00

☐ **Planter,** *item #M-1612, blue, semi gloss, oval with partial fluting at the sides interrupted by a plaque carrying a molded decoration of gold-gilt leaves, marked RED WING U.S.A.* 10.00 14.00

☐ **Planter,** *item #M-1491, blue, semi-gloss, of roughly oval free-form shape with turned in lip, resting on three spike feet, marked RED WING U.S.A.* 7.00 10.00

☐ **Planter,** *item #1342, blue, semi-gloss, in the form of a dachsund dog reclining, its tail looped, the back hollowed out to form the planter, marked RED WING U.S.A.* 11.00 14.00

☐ **Planter,** *item #1265, blue, speckled, high gloss, of rectangular form with shaped sides, pinched into flattened columns to form a scalloped effect along the rim, marked RED WING U.S.A.* 7.00 10.00

☐ **Planter,** *item #637, bone white, matt glaze, of square shape with caved-in sides, decorated along the lower portion with a sawtooth design, marked RED WING U.S.A.* 8.00 10.00

☐ **Planter,** *item #1546, bone white, matt glaze, circular with fluted verrical ribbing encircling the body, marked RED WING U.S.A.* 6.00 8.00

☐ **Planter,** *item #1251, bone white interior with green exterior, of roughly oval form with two lobed sides, decorated in the bowl with a molded design of a floral stem with branches, marked RED WING U.S.A.* 8.00 11.00

☐ **Planter,** *item #665, burnt orange, high gloss, of flattened ovoid form with vaulting sides, resting on a pedestal base. Decorated at the sides with molded ribbing, marked RED WING U.S.A.* 8.00 10.00

Price Range

☐ **Planter,** *item #1342, caramel brown, semi-gloss, in the form of a dachsund dog reclining, its tail looped, the back hollowed out to form the planter, marked RED WING U.S.A.* 11.00   14.00

☐ **Planter,** *item #M-1446, caramel brown, semi gloss, of roughly oval form with shaped sides, the lip turned over toward the center, marked RED WING U.S.A.* 7.00   10.00

☐ **Planter,** *item #M-1525, cedar brown, semi-gloss, in the form of a grand piano, the interior hollow to form the planter, marked RED WING U.S.A.* 16.00   19.00

☐ **Planter,** *item #1304, dark blue, high gloss, of freeform shape in imitation of a natural volcanic lava formation, marked RED WING U.S.A.* 7.00   10.00

☐ **Planter,** *item #1463, dark green, high gloss, shaped oval form with sculptured rim to give the appearance of carved rockstone, marked RED WING U.S.A.* 10.00   13.00

☐ **Planter,** *item #M-1477, dark pink, speckled, semi-gloss, of pot form with deep vertical fluting encircling the entire bowl, marked RED WING U.S.A.* 7.00   10.00

☐ **Planter,** *item #M-1612, dark salmon, semi-gloss, oval with partial fluting at the sides interrupted by a plaque carrying a molded decoration of gold-gilt leaves, marked RED WING U.S.A.* 10.00   14.00

☐ **Planter,** *item #M-1572, dark yellow, high gloss, in the form an Aladdin's lamp with oval handle at one hand, arched above the bowl, marked RED WING U.S.A.* 8.00   10.00

☐ **Planter,** *item #5018, dusky green, matt glaze, of rectangular form with sloping sides, marked RED WING U.S.A.* 7.00   10.00

☐ **Planter,** *item #1348, egg yolk interior with dark blue and gray two-tone exterior, high gloss, square with lip turned over and curved, marked RED WING U.S.A.* 9.00   12.00

☐ **Planter,** *item #1348, elephant gray interior with red exterior, semi-gloss, of rectangular shape with a rising lip on two sides, shaped to resemble the jaws of an abalone shell, marked RED WING U.S.A.* 9.00   12.00

☐ **Planter,** *item #B-1405, elephant gray interior with green exterior, semi-gloss, shaped square form with lobed sides, marked RED WING U.S.A.* 7.00   10.00

☐ **Planter,** *item #B-2110, elephant gray interior with reddish brown exterior, high gloss, of basically oval form with curved freeform shaping to sluggest a curled fragment of treebark, marked RED WING U.S.A.* 9.00   12.00

☐ **Planter,** *item #B-2202, greenish blue, semi-gloss, oval with flaring shaped sides and a cut-away pedestal base, marked RED WING U.S.A.* 7.00   10.00

☐ **Planter,** *item #1265, gray, speckled, high gloss, of rectangular form with shaped sides, pinched into flattened columns to form a scalloped effect along the rim, marked RED WING U.S.A.* 7.00   10.00

☐ **Planter,** *item #B-1402, grayish lavender exterior with dark rose interior, semi-gloss, of oval form with fluted sides and molded leafwork decoration along the lower portion of the bowl, marked RED WING U.S.A.* 7.00   9.00

Price Range

☐ **Planter**, *item #735, ivory white, matt glaze, in the form of a canoe with painting at the sides to suggest stitching and texturing, red·interior, marked RED WING U.S.A.* 26.00   32.00

☐ **Planter**, *item #815, ivory white, matt glaze, rectangular, of tub form with shaped sides resting upon squat feet, marked RED WING U.S.A.* 7.00   10.00

☐ **Planter**, *item #M-1467, ivory white, matt glaze, in the form of a stylized dove with Art Deco overtones (though of later design than the Art Deco era), the back hollowed out to form the planter, marked RED WING U.S.A.* 14.00   18.00

☐ **Planter**, *item #5018, ivory white, matt glaze, of rectangular form with sloping sides, marked RED WING U.S.A.* 7.00   10.00

☐ **Planter**, *item #B-1407, jade green interior with tan exterior, matt glaze, of freeform shape with bulging and pinched sides, marked RED WING U.S.A.* 7.00   10.00

☐ **Planter**, *item #1342, jade green, semi-gloss, in the form of a dachsund dog reclining, its tail looped, the back hallowed out to form the planter, marked RED WING U.S.A.* 11.00   14.00

☐ **Planter**, *item #B-1396, lavender and gray interior with red exterior, semi-gloss, of square shape with mildly sloping sides and pinched corners, marked RED WING U.S.A.* 7.00   9.00

☐ **Planter**, *item #M-1446, light blue, semi-gloss, of roughly oval form with shaped sides, the lip turned over toward the center, marked RED WING U.S.A.* 7.00   10.00

☐ **Planter**, *item #1240, marble white, matt glaze, of freeform design resembling the cut section of a tree, marked RED WING U.S.A.* 7.00   10.00

☐ **Planter**, *item #M-1484, moss green, semi-gloss, in the form of a stringed guitar, the body consisting of a pocket which forms the planter, with four turning keys, marked RED WING U.S.A.* . 13.00   16.00

☐ **Planter**, *item #1387, pale and deep gray, matt glaze, of leaf shape, marked RED WING U.S.A.* 10.00   13.00
Note: This shape was marketed in other colors, too. Values are about the same.

☐ **Planter**, *no item number, pale ivory green, matt glaze, pot form decorated with an impressed design of a tree, marked RED WING U.S.A.* 6.00   8.00

☐ **Planter**, *item #B-2016, pale lavender, semi-gloss, of squared pot form resting on a pedestal base, marked RED WING U.S.A.* 7.00   10.00

☐ **Planter**, *item #869, pale moss green, matt glaze, of shaped pot form with flattened sides, resting on feet, marked RED WING U.S.A.* 7.00   9.00

☐ **Planter**, *item #1251, pale sea green interior with bone white exterior, matt glaze, of roughly oval form with two lobed sides, decorated in the bowl with a molded design of a floral stem with branches, marked RED WING U.S.A.* 7.00   10.00

☐ **Planter**, *item #1264, pastel green, semi-gloss, of lampshade form with shaped fluted sides, marked RED WING U.S.A.* 7.00   10.00

☐ **Planter**, *item #835, pink, matt glaze, of oval form, low-slung, decorated at the sides with loopwork, marked RED WING U.S.A.* 7.00   10.00

Price Range

☐ **Planter,** *item #1265, pink, speckled, high gloss, of rectangular form with shaped sides, pinched into flattened columns to form a scalloped effect along the rim, marked RED WING U.S.A.* 7.00   10.00

☐ **Planter,** *item #M-1445, robin's-egg blue, speckled, semi-gloss, of oval leaf shape, scooped at the center and with a network of darker blue bands to suggest leaf veins, marked RED WING U.S.A.* 8.00   10.00

☐ **Planter,** *item #1037, rose interior with bluish lavender bowl, semi-gloss, of square shape with sides collapsing inward, marked RED WING U.S.A.* 8.00   10.00

☐ **Planter,** *item #M-1485, salmon, high gloss, square with ruffled lip on two sides and scalloped lip on the other two, decorated with seashell-like vaulting along two sides of the body, marked RED WING U.S.A.* 7.00   10.00

☐ **Planter,** *item #888, salmon, matt glaze, of budding flower form with molded ornament at the sides, pedestal base, marked RED WING.* 9.00   12.00

☐ **Planter,** *item #M-5032, salmon, matt glaze, shaped oval with rising sides (boat form), scooped center, resting on a classical-style pedestal base, marked RED WING U.S.A.* 9.00   12.00

☐ **Planter,** *item #1264, salmon, semi-gloss, of lampshape form with shaped fluted sides, marked RED WING U.S.A.* 7.00   10.00

☐ **Planter,** *item #835, sea green, matt glaze, of oval form, low-slung, decorated at the sides with loopwork, marked RED WING U.S.A.* 7.00   10.00

☐ **Planter,** *item #M-1446, sea green, semi-green, of roughly oval form with shaped sides, the lip turned over toward the center, marked RED WING U.S.A.* 7.00   10.00

☐ **Planter,** *no item number, tan with sea green interior, semi-gloss, of pot form with shaped sides, molded into fluted arches of various widths, marked RED WING U.S.A.* 7.00   10.00

☐ **Planter,** *item #M-1447, various shades of pink, semi-gloss, of roughly oval freeform shape with bulging sides, marked RED WING U.S.A.* 8.00   10.00

☐ **Planter,** *item #431, violet, semi-gloss, narrow rectangular box form, marked RED WING U.S.A.* 8.00   10.00

☐ **Planter,** *item #428, yellow, matt glaze, of elongated leaf shape, marked RED WING U.S.A.* 9.00   12.00

☐ **Planter,** *item #B-2011, yellow, semi-gloss, of inverted hat form with exaggerated lip, the lip decorated on the upper surface with floral molding, marked RED WING U.S.A.* 10.00   13.00

☐ **Planter,** *item #B-1396, yellow and tan exterior, with salmon interior, semi-gloss, with two compartments, each in semi-rectangular shape and decorated on the sides with vertical fluted molding, marked RED WING U.S.A.* 9.00   12.00

☐ **Sign, "True China By Red Wing,"** *no item number, bone white, matt glaze, rectangular with raised lettering. Show window sign for dealers selling the Red Wing Line. (Not offered for public sale.)* 50.00   65.00

	Price Range	
☐ **Sugar and creamer,** *items #262 and #263, ivory white, matt glaze, decorated with molded figures of grape bunches highlighted with touches of burgundy coloring, marked RED WING U.S.A.*	25.00	32.00
☐ **Tray,** *item #1037, sea green interior with brown exterior, matt glaze, square, shallow, marked RED WING U.S.A.*	7.00	9.00
☐ **Vase,** *item #887, aqua blue, matte glaze, of cylindrical form widening out at the top, the body crimped to resemble a budding flower, marked RED WING U.S.A.*	9.00	12.00
☐ **Vase,** *item #951, blue, high gloss, of pot form with squared sides, the lip edges scrolled, decorated with molded scrolling at the body, marked RED WING U.S.A.*	7.00	9.00
☐ **Vase,** *item #899, blue, matt glaze, of bulb form with widely flaring shaped lip, with fluted designs at the body, marked RED WING U.S.A.*	7.00	10.00
☐ **Vase,** *item #1197, blue, matt glaze, bulbous bowl with wide shaped neck, no lip, the neck fluted to form a corrugated design, the bowl decorated with small molded stars, marked RED WING U.S.A.*	10.00	13.00
☐ **Vase,** *item #1556, black, matt glaze, of freeform shape with bulging sides, flaring out toward the top into an exaggerated lip, marked RED WING U.S.A.*	7.00	9.00
☐ **Vase,** *item #1105, blue, semi-gloss, of squared shape slightly flaring at the top and bowed out toward the lower body, decorated with molded leafwork along the corners of two sides, marked RED WING U.S.A.*	9.00	12.00
☐ **Vase,** *item #1161, blue, semi-gloss, of cylindrical form with flattened bulbous bowl, the bowl decorated with vertical fluting, the neck with impressed floral designs. With an Oriental-inspired shaped lip, scrolling outward at the sides, marked RED WING U.S.A.*	11.00	15.00
☐ **Vase,** *item #B-2000, bone white, high gloss, of pot form with shaped sides, decorated with molded floral ornament within emblems at the body, marked RED WING U.S.A.*	9.00	12.00
☐ **Vase,** *item #M-1570, bone white, matt glaze, of squared form with bulging sides, decorated with molded starbursts, marked RED WING U.S.A.*	13.00	16.00
☐ **Vase,** *item #1354, bone white, semi-gloss, of classical urn form with bulbous bowl, flaring neck, the neck crimped and set between a pair of branchwork handles, fluted bowl, marked RED WING U.S.A.*	8.00	10.00
☐ **Vase,** *item #M-1456, bone white semi-gloss, of flattened rectangular form without neck, decorated with impressed designs of geese in flight against a ribbed background, marked RED WING U.S.A.*	10.00	13.00
☐ **Vase,** *item #1203, bone white with pastel gray, semi gloss, bulbous form, decorated with an impressed line pattern along the base and lower sides, colored in red to contrast with the bodycolor, marked RED WING U.S.A.*	10.00	13.00
☐ **Vase,** *item #1174, bone white with suggestions of pastel green, mug form with handles and a molded leafwork pattern, marked RED WING U.S.A.*	7.00	10.00
☐ **Vase,** *item #886, dark blue, matt glaze, of flattened shell form with small thumb-type handles., marked RED WING U.S.A.*	9.00	12.00

Price Range

☐ **Vase,** *item #730, deep jungle green, semi-gloss, pineapple form with molded ridges running vertically and horizontally, marked RED WING U.S.A.* 13.00 16.00

☐ **Vase,** *item #1160, dusky gray, semi-gloss, of pot form with molded veritcal ribs extending the entire height of the body, decorated with molded bas-relief leafwork painted in bright red, yellow interior, marked RED WING U.S.A.* 9.00 12.00

☐ **Vase,** *item #404, elephant gray, semi-gloss, of flattened tubular form with tripled molded banding and a flattened vertical panel rising the entire height of the body, red interior, marked RED WING U.S.A.* 9.00 12.00

☐ **Vase,** *item #1357, elephant gray, semi-gloss, fluted panels, scrolled handles at either side, with molded leafwork at the base, marked RED WING U.S.A.* 9.00 12.00

☐ **Vase,** *no item number, forest green, matt glaze, of bucket form with C-shape handles, marked RED WING U.S.A.* 8.00 10.00

☐ **Vase,** *item #946, green matt glaze, bulging sides with vertical depressions between (lobed design), modified C-shape handles at sides, marked RED WING U.S.A.* 7.00 9.00

☐ **Vase,** *item #656, grayish green semi-gloss, of shaped cylindrical form pinched vertically to form a series of half-columns around the body, marked RED WING U.S.A.* 8.00 10.00

☐ **Vase,** *item #732, ivory white, matt glaze, in the form of a tree stump, with bark texturing and knotholes suggested by maroon painting, marked RED WING U.S.A.* 19.00 24.00
Note: These sometimes turn up as lamp bases. They were not sold that way but converted by previous owners.

☐ **Vase,** *item #975, ivory white, matt glaze, of spherical form with a wide molded grape bunches highlighted with pale burgundy coloring, marked RED WING U.S.A.* 13.00 16.00

☐ **Vase,** *item #1165, ivory white, matt glaze, of ovoid form with pinched neck, twin loop handles one atop another, decorated with an overall design of molded leafwork against a burgundy ground, marked RED WING U.S.A.* 19.00 24.00

☐ **Vase,** *item #1190, ivory white, matt glaze, of cylindrical form with a flattened bulbous bowl, decorated with floral molding along the bowl, resting on a classical-style base, marked RED WING U.S.A.* 18.00 23.00

☐ **Vase,** *item #1208, ivory white, matt glaze, of sectioned form with a wide cylindrical bowl supporting a narrower cylindrical neck, crimped handle, decorated along the shoulder with a series of bosses (hobnails), and with horizontal banding around the neck, marked RED WING U.S.A.* 8.00 10.00

☐ **Vase,** *item #1320, ivory white, matt glaze, of rising pot form with squared sides, decorated with molding of leaves and stems, marked RED WING U.S.A.* 18.00 23.00

☐ **Vase,** *no item number, ivory white, matt glaze, of tubular form decorated with bas-relief molding of a bird perched on a treebranch with flowers and berries, marked RED WING U.S.A.* 14.00 17.00

☐ **Vase,** *item #1351, ivory white with pastel gray admixture, semi-gloss, of cylindrival form with rounded base, slightly pinched neck, with ornamental scrolled handles, marked RED WING U.S.A.* 6.00 8.00

Price Range

☐ **Vase,** *no item number, lavender high gloss, of bulb form with large C-shaped handles rising form the bowl and connecting to the flared lip, resting on sectioned pedestal base, marked RED WING U.S.A.* 9.00   12.00

☐ **Vase,** *item #926, marble white high gloss, the bowl of squat bulbous form with a tall funnel-shaped neck and wide mouth, sloping handles at either side, and with molded decoration along the lower portion of the neck, marked RED WING U.S.A.* 10.00   13.00

☐ **Vase,** *item #1360, marble white with pastel gray admixture, high gloss, of cylindrical form pinched at the sides, with a crimped handle reising on each side from the base to the shoulder, decorated with a molded pattern of flowers, leaves and berries, marked RED WING U.S.A.* 8.00   10.00

☐ **Vase,** *no item number, olive green high gloss, milk bottle shape with squared shoulders, vertical handles rising out of shoulder to meet lip, marked RED WING ART POTTERY* 13.00   16.00

☐ **Vase,** *item #412, orange semi-gloss, of cylindrical form with pressed octagonal sides, marked RED WING U.S.A.* 8.00   11.00

☐ **Vase,** *item #1359, red high gloss, of novelty form in the shape of a number of teacups stacked together, with the uppermost cup turned upside-down on the rest, marked RED WING U.S.A.* 9.00   12.00

☐ **Vase,** *no item number, reddish maroon, matt glaze, of bulb form with serpentine molding covering the entire body, including the base, with two flattened handles rising up from the lower body and extending over the lip, marked with gold and red factory label.* 11.00   14.00

☐ **Vase,** *item #999, pale pink, matt glaze, of budding flower form with slightly pressed sides, widely flaring and vaulting lip, marked RED WING U.S.A.* 6.00   8.00

☐ **Vase,** *item #1155, pastel blue semi-gloss, of shaped cylindrical form with pinched sides, flared lip, decorated with a series of vertical leafy vines rising the entire height of the body, marked RED WING U.S.A.* 9.00   11.00

☐ **Vase,** *item #999, pastel green and white, matt glaze, of egg form with widely flaring, shaped lip. Decorated with a detailed floral painting in various sharp, bright colors, marked RED WING U.S.A.* 9.00   11.00

☐ **Vase,** *item #886, pastel green with hints of beige, matt glaze, of budding flower form with scrolling supports at the sides, fluting at the central body, resting on a stepped pedestal base, marked RED WING U.S.A.* 9.00   12.00

☐ **Vase,** *item #M-1460, salmon semi-high gloss, of tubular form decorated with a molded pattern of loopwork, marked RED WING U.S.A.* 10.00   13.00

☐ **Vase,** *item #211, sea green, high gloss, spherical bowl with tall semi-cylindrical neck, vertical handles rising out of the bowl and ending in a scroll shape at the lip, decorated with impressed banding at the bowl, and floral work at the neck, marked RED WING ART POTTERY* 7.00   9.00

☐ **Vase,** *item #930, various shades of violet, high gloss, of bulbous form with budding-flower neck, loop handles, decorated along the lower portion by a series of molded leaves, rising vertically from the base, marked RED WING.* ... 7.00   10.00

		Price Range	
☐ **Vase,** item #B-2003, yellow high gloss, of pressed mug form decorated with a recessed panel containing molded leafwork, marked RED WING U.S.A.		9.00	12.00
☐ **Vase,** item #871, olive green high gloss, of classical urn shape with upturned handles at either side of the flattened bowl, resting on pedestaled base, marked RED WING U.S.A.		10.00	13.00
☐ **Wall pocket,** #1831, ivory white, matt glaze, triangular with a pinched base, decorated with floral molding and highlighted by pale burgundy coloration, marked RED WING U.S.A.		23.00	28.00

Note: So-called "wall pockets" (for want of a better name) were, in effect, vases that hung on a wall and could be used for the display of artificial flowers.

RESOLUTE POTTERY COMPANY

Resolute was founded in 1903 by William H. Bradbury and manufactured sanitary specialties.

Marks: *Not known*
Prices: A three-piece miniature bathroom set would be in the $50 range.

RHODES AND YATES

See City Pottery.

RITTENHOUSE AND EVANS

See American Art China Works.

ROOKWOOD

In terms of its length of operation, number of pieces manufactured, and collector interest, Rookwood reigns as king of the art pottery makers. For nearly 60 years, this firm was either the absolute leader for American art-ware, or very close to the top. It had many competitors, some of whom wanted to almost identically copy the Rookwood styles and patterns. In fact, it was the success of Rookwood in making and selling artware that brought so many other companies into the field, and even led to courses in pottery making at some of the major universities. Rookwood — more than any other company in the United States — made pottery into an art form. Its designers and artists showed the potential that pottery had for true art. Even more importantly, the public demonstrated in its zest for Rookwood that fine art pottery would be recognized and prized, even if it was made domestically. The pottery makers of 1860 or even 1880 would not have believed this just a few years before Rookwood achieved its huge nationwide sales volume. It had long been felt in the trade that imported European wares had a firm lock on the market for decorative ceramics — that it was not even worth trying to buck tradition. This is largely why the earlier makers contented themselves with serviceable stoneware. Rookwood proved that the public would "buy American," if the quality was fully comparable to that of foreign goods — and even if the price was a little higher. Though the original selling prices look like giveways by today's standards, Rookwood was always one of the most expensive wares on the market. On the collector market, values for Rookwood did not advance measurably beyond the original list sums until the late 1940's. This was the era of Rookwood rediscovery, and the company was still operating at the time. Within less than ten years therafter, prices had tripled or quadrupled on most of the early pieces, and the 1960's witnessed an even sharper increase. Even this does not compare to the activities of the later 1970's, when the combination of increased collector interest and investor buying sent Rookwood values to even greater heights. Since then, the Rookwood market has stabilized somewhat, and value levels attained over the past two years have tended to remain firm and reliable.

Collecting Rookwood is an adventure. You cannot learn ALL about this fabled company, its pottery, and its artists even in several months of active collecting. The information presented here is a summary of basic facts. Anyone who wants to seriously study Rookwood should begin with a visit to the local public library and to art museums in the area. Then, trips to the better antique shops and antique fairs will bring you into direct contact with the market, where the prices are created. By all means, fully investigate what is available in your area before doing any buying. There may possibly be a Rookwood collector club nearby, too.

Rookwood was founded in 1879 in Cincinnati. Many pottery companies were already active in Ohio at the time, but the majority were still making stoneware or other wares which did not qualify as art pottery. There was also a huge trade in such incidental wares as plumbing fixtures, druggists' paraphernalia, ceramic floor and wall tiles. William M. Taylor, Rookwood's director, envisioned a type of pottery which would rise well above the level of its rivals, supplying artistic wares to the public and maintaining a consistent quality in all its products. While this seemed a rather ambitious goal, it was soon brought to reality. By the early 1880's Rookwood was already beginning to take on a reputation for quality art pottery. Not only did the company's reputation increase steadily over the decades, but its size as well — mushrooming from a small organization to one of Cincinnati's major industrial employers. In the 1890's, its standing as the leading U.S. art pottery was already secure. Some might claim that Grueby surpassed it briefly in the early years of the next century, but Grueby was fast absorbed by Tiffany and there were really no other serious challengers. Roseville sought to corner a share of Rookwood's market by making wares similar in style and offering them at lower prices. The Roseville products sold very well, but the audience for them was quite different and Rookwood's sales did not suffer. Rookwood was clearly acknowledged as the most fashionable ware to be bought — that is, aside from the secondhand market (the term "antiques" was not used.) It gained such a high standing that collectors of the late 1800's to the early 1900's bought it just as avidly as the public, proudly displaying it alongside 18th century Dresden and Chelsea. And in most cases, the prices were just as high as for 18th century Dresden and Chelsea!

Much of Rookwood's success was derived from its use of large, bold underglaze painting which gave its wares the appearance of oil paintings captured in porcelain rather on canvas. The familiar Indian head was only one of many subjects. There were also birds and flowers, animals and country scenes, windmills and waterfalls, and a vast variety of other subjects. Though the artists were not "names" in the conventional sense, Rookwood succeeded in assembling remarkable talent under its roof. Its operation was similar to an Old Master's studio of 200 or 300 years earlier in which each artist had his specialty: some were skilled at birds, others at human figures and so on. The difference was that at Rookwood, each artist completed a whole object, whereas the Old Masters' assistants worked in teams on the same canvases. Rookwood's artists signed their productions with initials. Since all of the names have been recorded, there is no problem assigning any given piece to the artist who created it. Mainly, this was local talent from the Cincinnati area, but some artists from other parts of the country worked at Rookwood as well — and even from as far away as Japan.

By all odds the most famous, most talked-of, and most awe-inspiring of all the factory's merchandise was its vases. Rookwood's popularity was founded more upon its vases than anything else in the line. Long after the company had diversified into many additional products, it continued to satisfy the vase demand. The most familiar Rookwood vases are those with bulbous bodies, very dark rich coloring with varied tonal effects, and of course underglaze painting. To say that they became a "fad" would be understating the case. Those who bought one or two nearly always came back for more. Some late Victorian and Edwardian homes soon had great elaborate collections, thanks to the owner's fascination with Rookwood vases. There was almost no danger of getting two alike or even nearly alike. Therefore every collection was original and became the focal point of its setting. Instead of being measured by tens and twenties, values of Rookwood vases are now measured by hundreds and thousands. These are the supreme products of their class. They were, to pottery, what Tiffany lamps were to glass.

Success led to more success for Rookwood. Orders for artware and other items came from public buildings, hotels, and even from the New York Subway System, which wanted to line the walls of its stations with Rookwood tiles. In 1899, the factory was expanded, but even this did not prove sufficient to handle the growing workload. Whenever a major fair or exposition was held, Rookwood exhibited choice samples from its lines, and an innundation of orders followed. It received more press coverage, not only nationally but internationally, than any other pottery. It was seen in the best places and seen repeatedly. One could hardly walk in a building lobby, salon, or doctor's waiting room without finding Rookwood. It advertised itself. There was never any doubt about where to buy Rookwood. The collector needed only to visit the most exclusive decorating shop in town and it was certain to be there.

In 1915, Rookwood introduced its "Soft Porcelain," which was sometimes made with a crackle glaze. This was followed by its "Jewel Porcelain" and by lines of dinnerware. While the wares turned out by Rookwood during the 1920's were not perhaps as exquisite as those of the 1890's, this was nevertheless a very rewarding decade for the firm. Its dinnerware and other new products were well received, and more and more of its competitors were giving up trying to compete. But the 1930's proved almost as devastating to Rookwood as the 1920's had been successful. A sharp reversal within a handful of years was brought about by the national financial collapse. When the depression hit, Rookwood riskily continued turning out its art pottery, hoping the bleak economic picture would be temporary. It wasn't, and the market for art pottery dwindled. Rookwood could no longer maintain its staff of decorators, so the artware line was phased out. The last piece was made in 1937. Believing it could exist on its other lines until artware came back into demand, Rookwood kept stoking its furnaces. However, the firm had simply gotten too big with too many creditors and too much payroll to ride out that kind of financial burden. The company filed for bankruptcy in 1941. Walter Schott, a Cincinnati car dealer, bought most of the company's stock when it was offered for liquidation. It passed through several more hands before the close of World War II with negligible production. Production was resumed following the war with the intent of selling moderately-prices lines of artware for general distribution. Long-standing fans of Rookwood were not satisfied with the quality; those new to Rookwood approached it as just another name, and it was faced with reestablishing its market virtually from scratch. By around 1960, it hit on the plan of reproducing some of its stellar creations from earlier years and possibly kindling a renaissance of interest in art pottery. While these reproductions brought some rare items within range of the average collector, they were not really a satisfactory substitute for the real thing. Finally, Rookwood shut down in 1967. The problems and doubtful quality of Rookwood's wares over the last three decades of its operations (1937-67) should not tarnish its place among the immortals of American pottery. It topped the industry for more than half a century.

Marks: Traditionally, the Rookwood products bore a factory mark and artist mark, as mentioned earlier. In addition, most pieces also carry other markings, which are invariably confusing to a beginner. They include the clay mark which denotes the basic color of the slip or fabrique, the size mark used on pieces produced in more than a single size, and the process mark (usually found on experimental or trial pieces only), which relate to the step-by-step manufacturing process. Any item with a process mark is automatically worth a premium. The process mark is either a symbol, such as a diamond or lozenge, or a number — which can be enclosed in a square, in brackets, or placed between letters. While the purpose of the process mark is known, the actual processes to which these marks relate are now a matter of speculation. The factory was understandably cautious with its methods for fear of its secrets landing in the hands of competitors. Details of the manufacturing processes were kept secret even from the employees themselves, except those whose actual tasks involved them. Thus we are porbably correct in imagining that the master book in which the processes were recorded was kept under safeguard and was available for examination to only a trusted few. No one ever learned the Rookwood secrets, and unfortunately, today's collectors and researchers are having no more luck in that regard, than did the company's competitors.

Price Range

☐ **Bookends,** *item #2695, 5-1/2", green, in the form of sailing ships, with an impressed factory mark and the initials of artist William P. McDonald, dated 1936.* 150.00   180.00

Price Range

☐ **Bowl,** *item #1375V, 8-1/2", blue and pink, decorated with a painting of cherries by Edward T. Hurley (signed with initials), bearing an impressed factory mark and the date 1920.* 425.00 500.00

☐ **Bowl,** *item #1069, 5-1/2", cream white matt glaze, decorated with a ribbon of pale rose-colored flowers by Cecil Duell (signed with initials), impressed factory mark.* 115.00 135.00

☐ **Bowl,** *item #2268B, 13-1/2", cream white and charcoal gray, decorated with a floral painting and a frog, bearing an impressed factory mark and the date 1927* 400.00 500.00

☐ **Box,** *item #6286, 5-1/4", brown aventurine glaze, lidded, of dome form, decorated by Louise Abel (signed with full signature), bearing an impressed factory mark and the date 1930.* . . 1800.00 2300.00

☐ **Dish,** *item #603/W, 7-1/2", orange and cream white, boat form, decorated with a painting of daisies (unnamed artist), impressed factory mark and the date 1891* 215.00 250.00

☐ **Ewer,** *item #495/B, 9-1/2", dark brown standard factory glaze, decorated with a painting of leaf arrangements by Mary Nourse (signed with initials), bearing an impressed factory mark* 280.00 330.00

☐ **Ewer,** *item #626/W, 5-1/4", dark brown standard factory glaze with silver overlay, modified tankard form, decorated with a slip-painting of flowers and foliage by Anna M. Valentien (signed with initials), bearing an impressed factory mark and the date 1892* 775.00 950.00

☐ **Ewer,** *item #725/B, 8-1/4", dark brown standard factory glaze, decorated with a painting of yellow flowers by Josephine Zettel (signed with initials), bearing an impressed factory mark and the date 1896* 400.00 500.00

☐ **Ewer,** *item #785B, 12-1/2", dark brown standard factory glaze, decorated with a painting of chestnuts by Sallie Coyne (signed with initials), bearing an impressed factory mark* 220.00 265.00

☐ **Ewer,** *no item number, 7", dark brown standard factory glaze, bulbous form with narrow neck, decorated with a slip-painting of apple blossoms and foliage, bearing an impressed factory mark and the date 1889* 380.00 460.00

☐ **Jar,** *9", yellow-brown, lidded, pot form with shaped shoulder, hat-type lid, decorated with a painting of red flowers by Laura Fry (signed with initials), marked ROOKWOOD 1885* 950.00 1125.00

☐ **Jardiniere,** *item #484B/W, 11-7/8" in diameter, dark brown, standard factory glaze, decorated with floral blossoms by Matthew Daly (signed with initials), bearing an impressed factory mark and the date 1891* 520.00 610.00

☐ **Jug,** *item #12A-S, 8-1/2", dark brown, standard factory glaze, ovoid form, decorated with a painting of an Oriental-style dragon by Kataro Shirayamadani (signed with full signature), bearing an impressed factory mark and the date 1889* 2600.00 3100.00

☐ **Jug,** *item #676/W, 7-1/4", dark brown, standard factory glaze with silver overlay, decorated with stalks of wheat painted by Olga G. Reed (signed with initials), with a silver stopper marked by the Gorham Co., bearing an impressed factory mark and the date 1892* 1200.00 1475.00

☐ **Same as above,** *but without stopper* 1100.00 1350.00

Price Range

☐ **Jug,** item #818, 7-1/2", dark brown, standard factory glaze, decorated with a floral painting by Catherine Hickman (signed with initials), bearing an impressed favtory mark and the date 1898 .... 415.00 495.00

☐ **Jug,** item #512/C, 7", dark brown, standard factory glaze, of squat form with narrow neck and mosque-type lid, decorated with a painting of an ear of corn by Josephine Zettel (signed with initials), bearing an impressed factory mark and the date 1899 .... 725.00 850.00

☐ **Jug,** commemorative, no item number, 6-1/2", dark brown standard factory glaze, bearing the molded seal of Cincinnati, Ohio on one side and the molded seal of the state of Ohio on the other, with an impressed factory mark and the date 1888 .. 700.00 875.00

☐ **Mug,** item #587B, 5-1/2", dark brown, standard factory glaze, decorated with a portrait of the Sioux Indian chief Peter Ironshell by Edith Felten (signed with initials), bearing an impressed factory mark and the date 1900 .... 5000.00 6500.00

☐ **Mug,** item #587/C, 4-1/2", dark brown, standard factory glaze, tankard form, decorated with a painting of an ear of corn by Lenore Asbury (signed with initials), bearing an impressed factory mark and the date 1902 .... 200.00 265.00

Note: Item #587/C obviously remained in production a long time, as Ora King was decorating these same mugs in 1946 — 44 years later. This is not, however, a proof that the shape was still being fired in 1946, merely that specimens were being painted and distributed to the trade. Quite possibly they had been fired at some previous time (before World War II) and kept in the company's stockpile to be painted and released later.

☐ **Mug,** item #587C, 5", dark brown, standard factory glaze, of tankard form, decorated with a painting of a spaniel-type dog by Ora King (signed with monogram), impressed factory mark, and the date 1946 .... 1700.00 2100.00

☐ **Mug,** item #587C, 5", dark brown, standard factory glaze, of tankard form, decorated with a painting of a terrier-type dog by Ora King (signed with monogram), impressed factory mark and the date 1946 .... 1700.00 2100.00

☐ **Mug,** item #587/W, 5", dark brown, standard factory glaze, decorated with a slip-painting of a fox riding a horse by Artus Van Briggle (signed with initials), bearing an impressed factory mark and the date 1891 .... 2700.00 3400.00

☐ **Mug,** item #587/W, 5", dark brown, standard factory glaze, decorated with a slip-painting of a huntsman blowing a horn by William McDonald (signed with initials), impressed factory mark and the date 1891 .... 3300.00 3875.00

☐ **Mug,** item #711, 5", dark brown, standard factory glaze, decorated with a portrait of a black youth by an unidentified artist, bearing an impressed factory mark and the date 1897 .... 5500.00 6700.00

☐ **Mug,** item #711/V, 5", dark brown, standard factory glaze, so called Puzzle-mug (because of an arrangement of holes at the collar and rim), tankard form with thick handle, decorated with a portrait of a lion by Edward Hurley (signed with initials), bearing an impressed factory mark, and the date 1897 .... 4300.00 5100.00

Price Range

☐ **Mug,** item #837, 5", dark brown, standard factory glaze, decorated with a painting of the Indian chief Cheyenne by Matthew Daly (signed with initials), bearing an impressed factory mark and the date 1898 .... 2100.00 2600.00

☐ **Mug,** item #837, 5", dark brown, standard factory glaze, decorated with a portrait of an Indian warrior or chief by Matthew A. Daly (signed with initials), bearing an impressed factory mark plus the words "Upper Yukon," presumably the tribal territory of the Indian, and the date 1898 .... 1900.00 2400.00

☐ **Mug,** item #837, 5", dark brown, standard factory glaze, decorated with a portrait of the Sioux Indian chief Two-Strike by William McDonald (signed with initials), bearing an impressed factory mark and the date 1897 .... 1900.00 2400.00

☐ **Mug,** item #837, 5", dark brown, standard factory glaze, decorated with a portrait of the Sioux Indian chief Gall by William McDonald (signed with initials), bearing an impressed factory mark and the date 1897 .... 2100.00 2600.00

☐ **Mug,** item #837, 5", dark brown, standard factory glaze, decorated with a portrait of the Arapaho Indian chief Yellow Horse by Matthew Daly (signed with initials), bearing an impressed factory mark and the date 1898 .... 2100.00 2600.00

☐ **Mug,** item #837, 5", dark brown, standard factory glaze, a portrait mug depicting the American Indian chief Lone Wolf of the Sioux, by William P. McDonald, bearing an impressed factory mark and the date 1897 .... 450.00 600.00

☐ **Mug,** item #837, 5", dark brown, standard factory glaze, a portrait mug depicting the American Indian chief Red Cloud of the Sioux, by William P. McDonald, bearing an impressed factory mark and the date 1897 .... 450.00 600.00

☐ **Mug,** no item number, 5-3/4", dark brown, standard factory glaze, marked on the side by F.Z. Burley, bearing an impressed factory mark and coded date (1889), along with a date of March 21, 1890 on the side 425.00 525.00

☐ **Mural, faience,** no item number, 40" x 38" (3'4" x 3'2"), chiefly in blue and greenish yellow, decorated with a wooded landscape in Art Nouveau style, no indication of artist, bearing an impressed factory mark but no date, believed to have been manufactured c. 1912 .... 3300.00 4000.00

Note: These wall murals were designed for the homes of the wealthy, who would sometimes buy a dozen or more duplicate specimens to line a whole wall.

☐ **Pitcher,** item #259B, 8-1/2", dark brown, standard factory glaze, decorated with a painting of ears of corn by Lenore Asbury (signed with initials), bearing an impressed factory mark and the date 1900 .... 330.00 390.00

☐ **Pitcher,** 8", gray, Limoges style, of bulbous form with C-shape handle, decorated with a painting of orange and cream-white flowers by Albert Valentien (signed with initials), marked ROOKWOOD 1882 .... 1600.00 1900.00

☐ **Pitcher, Indian portrait,** item #837, 10-1/4", dark brown, standard factory glaze, decorated with a portrait of the Sioux Indian chief Sitting Bull, by William McDonald (signed with full name), bearing an impressed factory mark and the date 1897 .... 6800.00 8100.00

Note: Sitting Bull engineered the Sioux massacre of Custer and his troops at the Little Bighorn. This is the most sought-after and valuable of all the Indian portraits used by Rookwood. It's interesting that Sitting Bull was considered a salable commodity in 1897, when many of the relatives of the slain were still alive.

Price Range

☐ **Plaque, faience,** *no item number, 18" x 12", pastel blue, decorated with a bas-relief molding of a cherub, with additional moldings of flowers, marked ROOKWOOD FAIENCE, undated, c. 1910* 450.00   525.00

☐ **Plaque,** *no item number, 13-1/2" x 9-1/2", sea green, decorated with a painting of chrysanthemums by an unidentified artist, bearing an impressed factory mark and the date 1896, unframed* **4700.00   5800.00**
Note: This painting of high quality has been tentatively attributed to Albert Valentien.

☐ **Plaque,** *no item number, 10" x 12", vellum glaze, decorated with a lakeside landscape at nightfall, mountains in the distance by Edward T. Hurley (signed with initials), bearing an impressed factory mark and the date 1946* 3800.00   4750.00

☐ **Plaque,** *no item number, 10" x 12", vellum glaze, decorated with a lakeside scene of tall trees dotting the lakebank by Edward T. Hurley (signed with initials), bearing an impressed factory mark and the date 1948, enclosed in a wooden frame for wall hanging. (The frame is not included in the above measurements.)* 3600.00   4800.00

☐ **Plaque,** *no item number, 7-1/4" x 9-1/2", vellum glaze, decorated with a winter landscape of barren trees and snow-laden ground, by Elizabeth F. McDermott (signed with full name on the front), bearing an impressed factory mark and the date 1917* 1600.00   1900.00
Note: World War I brought about a market for artwork with melancholy themes.

☐ **Plaque,** *no item number, 15" x 9", vellum glaze, decorated with a lakeside landscape scene by Lenore Asbury (signed with initials), bearing an impressed factory mark and the date 1918* ... 3600.00   4900.00

☐ **Plaque,** *no item number, 5" x 9", vellum glaze, painted with a seascape during a snowfall by Lenore Asbury (signed with full name), bearing an impressed factory mark and the date 1919, mounted in a wooden frame for wall hanging. (The frame is not included in the above measurements.)* 700.00   875.00

☐ **Plaque,** *no item number, 12-1/2" x 14-1/4", vellum glaze, painted with a lake scene and a mountain in the background by Edward T. Hurley (signed with initials), bearing an impressed factory mark and the date 1945* 5300.00   6500.00

☐ **Plaque,** *no item number, 8" x 10", vellum glaze, Approaching Dusk (so named by the factory), decorated with a distant view of a peasant village amid a rolling landscape, by Frederick Rothenbusch (signed with initials on the face), bearing an impressed factory mark and the date 1935. (Contained in the original plain wooden factory frame, whose dimensions are not included in the above measurement.)* 1000.00   1275.00

Price Range

☐ **Vase,** *item #614C, 13", blue and purple with medium and intense tones, decorated with floral painting by Harriet Wilcox (signed with initials), bearing an impressed factory mark and the date 1923* 725.00   875.00

☐ **Vase,** *item #950D, 9-1/4", blue and rose matt glaze, decorated with a floral painting by Edward Diers (signed with initials), bearing an impressed factory mark* 650.00   775.00

☐ **Vase,** *no item number, 9-1/4", blue matt glaze, decorated with a floral painting by Kataro Shirayamadani (signed with full name), bearing an impressed factory mark and the date 1940* . 530.00   615.00

☐ **Vase,** *item #S1702A, 14-1/2", brownish gray, decorated with a painting of flowers and leaves by Matthew Daly (signed with full name), bearing an impressed factory mark and the date 1901* 4300.00   5200.00

☐ **Vase,** *no item number, 10", cream white, cone shape with tall neck decorated with geometrical motifs in blue by Fannie Auckland (signed with initials), bearing an impressed factory mark and the date 1882* 1000.00   1300.00

☐ **Vase,** *item #907DD, 9-1/4", cream-white and gray, cylindrical form with pinched neck, decorated with a painting of an iris by Sara Sax (signed with initials), bearing an impressed factory mark and the date 1906* 1000.00   1300.00

☐ **Vase,** *item #30C/R, 6", dark brown, standard factory glaze, decorated with a painting of a lily and leafwork by Matthew A. Daly (signed with initials), bearing an impressed factory mark and the date 1887* 520.00   615.00

☐ **Vase,** *item #431, 9-1/2", dark brown, standard factory glaze, with a slip-painting of clover blossoms and foliage in cedar brown and green, with an impressed factory mark* 430.00   510.00

☐ **Vase,** *item #578D, 10", dark brown, standard factory glaze, decorated with a painting of red flowers by Sallie E. Coyne (signed with initials), bearing an impressed factory mark and the date 1901* 400.00   500.00

☐ **Vase,** *item #614, 6-1/2", dark brown, standard factory glaze, decorated with a painting of a grape vine by Katherine Van Horne (signed with initials), bearing an impressed factory mark and the date 1908* 400.00   500.00

☐ **Vase,** *item #786D, 8-1/4", dark brown, standard factory glaze, decorated with a chiefly white floral painting by Olga G. Reed (signed with initials), bearing an impressed factory mark and the date 1897* 450.00   525.00

☐ **Vase,** *item #787C, 11", dark brown, standard factory glaze, decorated with a painting of birds in flight by Kataro Shirayamadani (signed with initial, in Japanese), bearing an impressed factory mark and the date 1898* 5300.00   6200.00

☐ **Vase,** *item #807, 13", dark brown, standard factory glaze, bulbous base with cylindrical body, decorated with a painting of daffodils, stems and leaves by Amelia Sprague (signed with initials), bearing an impressed factory mark and the date 1902* 700.00   875.00

☐ **Vase,** *item #925B, 13", dark brown, standard factory glaze, decorated with a floral painting by Matthew Daly (signed with initials), bearing an impressed factory mark and the date 1902* .. 2100.00   2600.00

Price Range

☐ **Vase,** *item #2347, 8", dark brown, standard factory glaze, decorated with a foliage painting by Arthur Conant (signed with monogram), bearing an impressed factory mark and the date 1917* 170.00   200.00

☐ **Vase,** *no item number, 8-1/2", dark grey and violet, modified cylindrical form, decorated with a painting of cactus branches and small flowers by Lenore Asbury (signed with initials), bearing an impressed factory mark and the date 1907* 650.00   800.00

☐ **Vase,** *item #1665, 12", deep blue matt glaze, bulbous upper section with cylindrical support, painted by Sara Sax (signed with initials), bearing an impressed factory mark and the date 1909* 115.00   135.00

☐ **Vase,** *item #2783, 9-3/4", gray, with handles, decorated with a painting of a flower by Kay Ley (signed with full name), impressed factory mark and the date 1946* 180.00   220.00

☐ **Vase,** *item #861/G, 6-1/2", green, decorated with a painting of butterflies by Sara Sax (signed with initials), bearing an impressed factory mark and the date 1900* 1900.00   2375.00

☐ **Vase,** *item #C905/251, 9-1/2" green, decorated with a painting of fish by Edward Hurley (signed with initials), bearing an impressed factory mark and the date 1904* 3000.00   3600.00

☐ **Vase,** *item #T1244, 9-1/4", green with electro-deposit overlay, of modified flask form with bottle-type neck and mouth, decorated with molded and painted foliage, bearing a blurred artist's initials, impressed factory mark and the date 1900* 1100.00   1325.00
Note: If you found one with readable initials and could identify the artist, the value should be slightly higher.

☐ **Vase,** *no item number, 26", green with matt glaze, bulbous base with tubular body, flaring lip, decorated with carved floral arrangements and painted by Charles S. Todd (signed with initials), bearing an impressed factory mark along with the initials of the carver C.S.T. on the side (not the base), dated 1913* 1400.00   1700.00

☐ **Vase,** *item #614B, 14-1/2", green, blue and brown with various tonal shadings of each, decorated with a large-scale wooded landscape scene by Margaret H. McDonald (signed with monogram), bearing an impressed factory mark and the date 1940* .. 510.00   630.00

☐ **Vase,** *#218B, 10-1/4", grayish blue and green, decorated with a painting of foliage in various colors by Charles Schmidt (signed with initials), bearing a factory mark and the date 1903* 650.00   800.00

☐ **Vase,** *no item number, 10", iris glaze, cylindrical form, decorated with a floral painting by Lenore Asbury (signed with initials), bearing an impressed factory mark but lacking a date, believed to have been executed prior to World War I* 140.00   170.00

☐ **Vase,** *no item number, 17", iris glaze, decorated with a floral painting in various colors by Albert Valentien (signed with full name), bearing an impressed factory mark and the date 1902* . 4200.00   4900.00
Note: In this case, the lack of an item number can probably be taken to indicate that the piece was made in limited quantities, not as part of the regular factory stockpile. It might have been a special order by a retailer, and was almost certainly expensive even when new.

Price Range

☐ **Vase,** item #130, 7'', pale green matt glase, ovoid form decorated with a painting of blue, cream yellow and red flowers by Elizabeth McDermott (signed with initials), bearing an impressed factory mark and the date 1925 .... 120.00 145.00

☐ **Vase,** no item number, 19'', reddish brown, cylindrical with flaring shoulder, wide mouth, decorated with a floral painting by Albert R. Valentian (signed with initials), bearing an impressed factory mark and the date 1887 .... 1300.00 1600.00

☐ **Vase,** item #11266, 10-1/2'', salmon-colored matt glaze, cylindrical form widening out toward shoulder, decorated with floral paintings by Sara Sax (signed with initials), bearing an impressed factory mark 550.00 675.00

☐ **Vase,** item #482/R, 9-1/2'', tiger's-eye glaze, decorated with slip painting in various tonal shades, by Harriet Wilcox (signed with initials), bearing an impressed factory mark and the date 1894 .... 6000.00 7500.00

☐ **Vase,** item #165E/V, 8-1/4'', vellum glaze, decorated with a floral painting in ivory white and greenish gray by Katherine Van Horn (signed with monogram), bearing an impressed factory mark and the date 1913 .... 310.00 380.00

☐ **Vase,** item #614D, 11'', vellum glaze, decorated with a sea and landscape painting by Edward Hurley (signed with initials), bearing an impressed factory mark and the date 1939 .... 1000.00 1275.00

☐ **Vase,** item #829/V, 9-1/2'', vellum glaze, shaped cylindrical form, decorated with a landscape painting by Frederick Rothenbusch (signed with initials), bearing an impressed factory mark and the date 1921 .... 750.00 900.00

☐ **Vase,** item #838E/V, 7'', vellum glaze, decorated with a painting by Sallie E. Coyne (signed with initials), bearing an impressed factory mark and the date 1913 .... 260.00 300.00

☐ **Vase,** item #907D, 12'', vellum glaze, shaped cylindrical form, decorated with a sombre landscape painting of tall, nearly barren trees by Sallie E. Coyne (signed with initials), bearing an impressed factory mark and the date 1914 .... 725.00 875.00

☐ **Vase,** item #925/D/V, 9'', vellum glaze, modified cylindrical form, decorated with a landscape painting by Frederick Rothenbusch (signed with monogram), bearing an impressed factory mark and the date 1921 .... 1700.00 2100.00

☐ **Vase,** item #1658F/V, 7'', vellum glaze, bullet shape, with an overall landscape painting in shades of green and blue by Sallie Coyne (signed with initials), bearing an impressed factory mark and the date 1920 .... 1200.00 1475.00

☐ **Vase,** item #1660B/V, 13-1/2'', vellum glaze, decorated with a painting of three Indians in canoes on a lake by Edward Hurley (signed with initials), bearing an impressed factory mark and the date 1910 .... 5200.00 6300.00

☐ **Vase,** item #1663, 11-1/2'', vellum glaze, tapering cylindrical form, decorated with a landscape painting by Lenore Asbury (signed with initials), bearing an impressed factory mark and the date 1914 .... 1000.00 1300.00

☐ **Vase,** item #1778/V, 8'', vellum glaze, decorated with a landscape painting by Lenore Asbury (signed with initials), bearing an impressed factory mark and the date 1913 .... 1000.00 1300.00

Price Range

☐ **Vase,** *item #2441, 14-1/2", vellum glaze, the glaze in tones of pin cream white and grayish green, decorated with a painting of magnolias and leaves by Lorina Eppley (signed with initials), bearing an impressed factory mark* 360.00   415.00

☐ **Vase, commemorative,** *no item number, 9-1/2", blue and green with various tonal effects, of bulbous form decorated with elaborate floral plainting, issued to commemorate the company's 50th anniversary, bearing an incised factory mark and the date 1930* 310.00   380.00

☐ **Vase, Indian portrait,** *item #614E, 8", dark brown, standard factory glaze, decorated with a portrait of the Sioux Indian chief Horn Dog by Matthew Daly (signed with full name), bearing an impressed factory mark and the date 1899* 8000.00 9750.00

☐ **Vase, pillow,** *(so-called because of the shape), item #836/W, 5-1/4", dark brown, standard factory glaze, decorated with a painting of a pair of storks by Sadie Markland (signed with initials), impressed factory mark and the date 1894* 1800.00 2175.00

☐ **Vase, portrait,** *item #80B, 6-3/4" dark brown, standard factory glaze, decorated with a slip painting in the Dutch 17th century manner of a gentleman in period costume by Sturgis Laurence (signed with initials), impressed factory mark and the date 1898* 4200.00 4900.00

☐ **Vase, portrait,** *item #659/B, 8", brown, three-handled, decorated with a portrait of a Dutch cavalier in the manner of a 17th century Old Master by Matthew Daly (signed with initials), bearing an impressed factory mark and the date 1896* 6000.00 7500.00

ROSEVILLE

Roseville is the most abundant of all art potteries. It is also the most widely collected in terms of the number of active buyers. But if you weigh the total amount of money taken in on the antique market for Roseville sales, they are probably equaled or surpassed by Rookwood's sales volume. More Roseville is sold, but the average price-per-piece is lower than that of Rookwood. And this is a fair reflection of the situation which prevailed, when these two companies were in head-to-head competition. Rookwood was acknowledged to be the leader in quality; but Roseville, with its somewhat lower prices and greater mass distribution, had at least as many customers or even more.

Actually, Roseville considered Weller to be its chief rival, more than Rookwood. Both Roseville and Weller were manufacturing wares of an almost identical type, and striving for sales to the same market. They were imitators of Rookwood but not direct competitors of that company, because of the differences in quantity-per-piece that were manufactured and the retail prices. Just about all the U.S. potters — with the exception of Grueby — considered it useless to make an all-out challenge to Rookwood. Instead, they fought amongst themselves to capture the markets that Rookwood ignored.

Many people bought Roseville because they could not afford Rookwood and that is precisely what happens on the antique market of today. For every Rookwood enthusiast who can afford it, there are at least a dozen hobbyists with Rookwood tastes and Roseville budgets. Some buy the works of other potters including Weller, but quite a few have a greater interest in Roseville.

Then, there are others to whom Roseville appeals more than Rookwood, and who would buy it regardless of the price advantages or disadvantages. But even many of those who start collecting Roseville because of the price and availability, find that it makes no less worthy a collectible than Rookwood or any other ware. Like Rookwood, the Roseville wares are signed by their artists in some cases. The number of unidentified artists is somewhat higher with Roseville, but the great majority are known to us. They include the much-heralded Gazo Fujiyama, called Fudji for short, who painted Japanese-style decorations on Roseville vases. Though no pottery artist ever became a celebrity through his work in that medium, Fudji was undoubtedly the best known. The buyers of Roseville's Oriental wares oook for his mark. Even at Rookwood, which also had native Japanese artists for its specialty work, there was nobody with quite the standing of Fudji. The name has been spelled many different ways, and in old publications is apt to turn up as Fujiyama, Fujigama, Fudjijama, and so forth. It is all one and the same individual. The problem was simply that Japanese names do not conform very well to American ways of spelling.

The Roseville factory started up in 1885 in Roseville, Ohio. It was operated by George Young, C.F. Allison and other partners, and got off to a modest beginning as a maker of general stoneware lines. Cuspidors were among its early products. In 1902, the factory bought out an old stoneware plant in Zanesville, and soon thereafter began making art pottery at Zanesville. This phase of its operations overshadowed the stoneware business at Roseville, so in 1910 the Roseville arm of the company was closed down. After this, all manufacturing was at Zanesville, but the name Roseville Pottery Co. was retained. A controversy has long raged over whether the factory ever produced artware at Roseville. Though it operated in the town for 25 years, there is no clear evidence that anything beyond stoneware was made.

Roseville called its artware Rozane, a coined name made from ROseville and ZANEsville. At first all the products were in deep brown, similar to those being produced by Rookwood. Soon the shades were lightened up a bit, and eventually a good deal of variety was worked in. Various lines were introduced, including "Egypto," "Mongol," "Woodland," "Mara," and "Royal." There were vases, water pitchers, jugs, lamp bases, ashtrays, and a full array of other decorative products — but mainly vases. The vase was naturally the most ideal object for painting, and since it was purely decorative there were no restraints on its size or shape. Many collectors of Roseville restrict themselves to vases. In terms of price, many Roseville vases are still available for less than $100. Because it had already built up a number of lines of moderately-priced ware, Roseville was not hurt quite so much by the financial depression of the 1930's as was Rookwood. It did, nevertheless, feel the pinch; sales declined and never again reached their peaks of the 1920's and earlier years. In 1954, Roseville went out of business.

Marks: Most of the art pottery is marked Rozane or Rozane Ware, in conjunction with an artist's mark. There is likely to also be another mark indicating the line from which the piece has come. Apparently one of the earliest marks used at Zanesville was a three-line block-letter arrangement reading *ROSE-VILLE POTTERY CO., ZANESVILLE, O.* On much of the earlier ware, the name *ROZANE WARE* is enclosed in a circular border, with a banner beneath giving the line name (*MONGOL, ROYAL,* etc.). A figure of a rose appears within the circle. This mark was heavily outlined and always impressed into the ware.

Sometimes the marking was done by circular paper labels, which had decorative borders. These labels carried printing in red ink, which is often blurry and poorly centered.

ANTIQUE GREEN MATT *(Introduced 1910-1915)*

Olive green colored glaze with somewhat of a rusty appearance; variations: light olive overglaze, red flecks in creases of the designs.

Price Range

☐ **Vase,** *9-1/2", simple shape, no trim, mottled look, rusty color at rim, no mark* 75.00   85.00
☐ **Wall pocket,** *10", triangular in shape, no trim, no mark* 115.00   140.00

APPLE BLOSSOM *(Introduced 1948)*

Realistic white blossoms embossed on pastel backgrounds, with green leaves and twigs used as handles; variations: pink, blue or green backgrounds.

☐ **Basket,** *shape #309, 8", blue, handle makes complete circle, marked Roseville in relief* 55.00   67.50
☐ **Basket,** *shape #310, 10", green, horizontal, with the handle curving under one side, marked Roseville in relief* 55.00   67.50
☐ **Basket,** *shape #311, 12", blue, stylistic "V" shape, with handle curving under one side, marked Roseville in relief* 85.00   95.00
☐ **Bowl,** *shape #326, 2-1/2" x 6-1/2", blue, round, with small handles, marked Roseville in relief* 35.00   40.00
☐ **Bud vase,** *shape #379, 7", pink, handles attached at the base, marked Roseville in relief* 28.00   35.00
☐ **Cornucopia,** *shape #381, 6", green, with mouth upright, standing on a base with the handles as support, marked Roseville in relief* 28.00   35.00
☐ **Ewer,** *shape #316, 8", pink, oval body, with tall spout, marked Roseville in relief* 50.00   55.00
☐ **Ewer,** *shape #318, blue, oval body, very extended neck and spout, with handle, marked Roseville in relief* 115.00   140.00
☐ **Jardiniere,** *shape #342, 6", pink, sphere shape, with two small dips in the rim, marked Roseville in relief* 50.00   55.00

AUTUMN *(Introduced 1910-1915)*

Landscape scenes of autumn trees in various soft shades of colors; variations: blending background colors of yellow and brown to pink and green.

☐ **Pitcher,** *8-1/2", orange, with light brown design, bulbous shape with handle, no mark* 625.00   725.00
☐ **Pitcher with basin,** *12-1/2", orange, with light brown design, bulbous shape with handles on both pitcher and basin, no mark* 1400.00   1575.00
☐ **Shaving mug,** *4", orange, with light brown design, bulbous shape with handle, no mark* 395.00   450.00
☐ **Wash bowl,** *14-1/2", orange, with light brown design, bulbous shape with finger handles, no mark* 500.00   565.00

AZTEC *(Introduced 1910-1915)*

Earthy tone backgrounds with raised designs in contrasting colors. Designs are made from squeezing long strings of clay through a small opening; variations: azure blue, beige, brown, gray, olive and teal backgrounds.

	Price Range	
☐ **Lamp base,** *11", gray, with white and blue geometric designs, narrow long pedestal widening at the top, no mark*	**285.00**	**310.00**
☐ **Pitcher,** *5", blue, with white designs, wide base, narrows at neck, no mark*	**255.00**	**285.00**
☐ **Vase,** *8", gray, with white, blue and gold design, widens from base to rim, slight flair at the base, no mark*	**225.00**	**255.00**
☐ **Vase,** *11", beige, with blue and yellow trim shaping arrowheads, pear shaped, the rim extends wider than the body, ink stamped stylized R*	**310.00**	**340.00**
☐ **Vase,** *11-1/2", blue, yellow arrowheads circle the base and neck, column-shaped with the rim extending wider than the body, no mark*	**285.00**	**340.00**

AZUREAN *(Introduced 1902)*

Azure blue and white underglazed designs on a blue background with many different designs; variations: floral, landscape and seascape designs.

☐ **Mug,** *4-1/2", floral leaves and flowers, with dark blue classic handle, simple shape, the base is slightly wider than the body, impressed mark RPCo*	**450.00**	**500.00**
☐ **Vase,** *4-1/2", very light leafy design, two handles coming out from the sides which join at the rim, the holes formed from this are egg-shaped, impressed mark RPCo, signed VA*	**340.00**	**395.00**
☐ **Vase,** *7-1/2", floral design, classic Greek shape, with long, slender neck, impressed mark RPCo*	**450.00**	**500.00**
☐ **Vase,** *9", landscape scene which covers most of the vase, egg-shaped, narrowing at the neck, no mark*	**1700.00**	**1800.00**

AZURINE, ORCHID, TURQUOISE *(Introduced 1920)*

Shiny glazes of azure blue, pastel rose and light turquoise on simple shapes with very little or no trim.

☐ **Double bud vase,** *5" x 8", high gloss blue, no trim, two cylindrical columns which are separated by a bridge draping between the two with four cutout circles, no mark*	**50.00**	**55.00**
☐ **Vase,** *8", high gloss turquoise, classic Greek shape, no trim, no mark*	**50.00**	**55.00**
☐ **Vase,** *10", rose high gloss, urn shape, with pointed handles, no mark*	**85.00**	**95.00**

BANEDA *(Introduced 1933)*

Green leaves, orange pumpkins and yellow flowers create a vine-like design on a blue background. The blue is a horizontal band on the item's background of red or green.

Price Range

☐ **Bowl,** *3" x 10", with slender handles, band of design covers almost all surface area, no mark* 50.00 55.00

☐ **Urn,** *5", small finger handles, classic shape on small pedestal, marked with paper label, silver* 45.00 50.00

☐ **Vase,** *9", design between the top and bottom of the handle, with a slight impression where the band of design begins and ends, bulbous shape, with handles that extend from the body to the rim, marked with paper label, silver* 85.00 100.00

☐ **Wall pocket,** *8", design extends across the pocket just below the opening, fan-shaped, with two cut-outs at the edges flush with the wall, marked with paper label, silver* 140.00 170.00

BITTERSWEET *(Introduced 1945-1950)*

Orange embossed flowers and green leaves made a single sprig across various colored backgrounds. Handles are made to look like branches; variations: green, gray, yellow or rose background colors.

☐ **Basket,** *shape #808, 6", rose, asymmetrical base of a darker rose, rippled rim, looks like a cracked egg shell, marked Roseville in relief* 34.00 40.00

☐ **Cornucopia,** *shape #882, 8", yellow shape on a rose base, with a branch handle for support, vertical with the mouth facing upwards, marked Roseville in relief* 45.00 50.00

☐ **Ewer,** *shape #816, 8", yellow, classic shape, with bulbous base, long slender neck and extended spout, marked Roseville in relief* 50.00 55.00

☐ **Planter,** *shape #868, 8", green, with two handles, rectangular, on base, marked Roseville in relief* 40.00 45.00

☐ **Vase,** *shape #874, 7", yellow, two semi-circle handles, rectangular base, on two prong pedestal, rim shaped like a tulip, marked Roseville in relief* 45.00 50.00

BLACKBERRY *(Introduced 1933)*

Blackberries and vines form a band of design on a textured background of green.

☐ **Console bowl,** *13" wide, the design covers complete surface area, oblong, two small brown handles, marked with paper label, black* 140.00 170.00

☐ **Jardiniere,** *6", spherical shape with two small handles, marked with paper label, black* 140.00 170.00

☐ **Jardiniere,** *7", spherical shape with two small handles, marked with paper label, black* 140.00 170.00

☐ **Urn,** *6", spherical shape with two small handles, marked with paper label, black* 115.00 140.00

☐ **Vase,** *8", hourglass shape, with two handles that connect above and below the narrow area, marked with paper label, black* 140.00 170.00

☐ **Wall pocket,** *8-1/2", fan shape, with three loop hanger, no mark* 175.00 200.00

BLEEDING HEART (Introduced 1938-1940)

A string of pink drooping flowers extends from a cluster of leaves on shaded backgrounds; variations: green, blue or pink backgrounds.

	Price Range	
☐ **Basket,** shape #360, 10", pink, V shaped with the handle making a complete circle, connecting at the base and the sides, marked Roseville in relief	55.00	67.50
☐ **Bowl,** shape #377, 4", blue, with two small handles, spherical with six-pointed rim, marked Roseville in relief	35.00	40.00
☐ **Ewer,** shape #972, 10", pink, with small cut-outs on each side of the neck, bulbous shape on a pedestal, one handle and a long extended spout, marked Roseville in relief	75.00	85.00
☐ **Vase,** shape #976, 15", blue, with two semi-circular handles, bulbous shape with a six-pointed rim, marked Roseville in relief	90.00	100.00
☐ **Wall pocket,** shape #1287, 8", blue, tulip shape with two handles and a rippled rim, marked Roseville in relief	50.00	60.00

BUSHBERRY (Introduced 1948)

A cluster of berries hangs from green leaves on a textured horizontal background. Handles are made to look like branches; variations: background colors may be green, blue or rusty orange.

☐ **Bowl,** shape #657, 3", blue, solid contoured handles, spherical shape, marked Roseville in relief	28.00	34.00
☐ **Cornucopia,** shape #3, 5", green and tan, on a dark green base with a branch handle for support, mouth opens upwards, marked Roseville in relief	45.00	50.00
☐ **Double bud vase,** shape #158, orange, the design is seen between the two vases in ornate scrollwork, marked Roseville in relief	40.00	45.00
☐ **Planter,** shape #383, 6-1/2", orange, rectangular, marked Roseville in relief	28.00	34.00
☐ **Urn,** shape #411, 6", blue, with two ear-shaped handles, that are not perpendicular with the body, spherical, with rippled rim, marked Roseville in relief	50.00	55.00

CAMEO (Introduced 1920)

Embossed designs of dancing figures underneath trees in a circular band or an embossed peacock on a vertical panel. Colors are usually ivory design on green background; variations: ivory design on ivory background.

☐ **Jardiniere, with pedestal,** shape #439, 34", ivory with light design at rim of the jardiniere, geometric designs on the pedestal, spherical, with jardinere standing on four feet, pedestal stands on three feet, no mark	625.00	750.00

CARNELIAN I (Introduced 1910-1915)

Two color glaze with a light shade as the base and a darker shade dripped over it. Many pieces have handles which are very elaborate; variations: aqua on light aqua, blue on pink, blue on beige; some have a textured finish.

Price Range

☐ **Bowl**, *3", dark blue over light blue, two ear-shaped handles, dish shape with the mouth being the widest, Rv marked in ink* . 28.00 34.00
☐ **Candleholder**, *3", blue on blue, handles connect at the base and just below the rim, wide pedestal base, Rv marked in ink* . . 28.00 34.00
☐ **Ewer**, *15", dark blue on pink, very ornate handle, light bulb shape on a pedestal base, the handle is as tall as the neck and spout, Rv marked in ink* 85.00 100.00
☐ **Urn**, *9-1/2", dark aqua on aqua, two handles which connect on the body and the rim, classic urn shape, Rv marked in ink* 67.50 80.00
☐ **Vase**, *10", dark tan on tan, ornate handles, urn shape with long cylindrical neck, Rv marked in ink* 55.00 67.50

CARNELIAN II *(Introduced 1915)*

Mottled colors thickly cover decorative pieces; variations: color combinations are rose, green and purple, green, blue and lilac, and many other combinations.

☐ **Basket**, *10" wide, rose, blue and lilac, with handle, six-sided on six-sided base, Rv marked in ink, paper label, black* 50.00 55.00
☐ **Bowl**, *4", purple, brown and gold, circular, with the mouth widest, on a base, with two evenly spaced ripples, Rv marked in ink* 70.00 80.00
☐ **Planter**, *3", pink, tan and lilac, rippled body on a base, marked with paper label, black* 28.00 34.00
☐ **Vase**, *8", lilac drizzling over pink, simple shape, with slight rim and base, no mark* 40.00 45.00
☐ **Vase**, *9", mottled rose, simple shape with slight rim and base, no mark* 45.00 50.00

CERAMIC DESIGN *(Introduced 1910-1915)*

Ivory colored ware with many different sytles of design. Some are embossed simplistic designs with black outlines, other colors are green, yellow, blue. Some may have a more realistic design with softer colors.

☐ **Wall pocket**, *10", two small cut-outs, V shape, no mark* 140.00 170.00
☐ **Wall pocket**, *11", two small cut-outs, V shape, no mark* 200.00 225.00
☐ **Wall pocket**, *17", three small cut-outs, oval shape, no mark* . . . 285.00 340.00

CHERRY BLOSSOM *(Introduced 1932)*

Clusters of white cherry blossoms on branches extend usually from the top of the item across ivory color fluted bands which appear like a trellis for the branches; variations: pink bands on blue background, yellow on brown.

☐ **Bowl**, *5", brown, with two finger handles, spherical, the rim flairs slightly outward, paper label, silver* 85.00 95.00
☐ **Candleholder**, *4", brown, two small finger handles, wide, square pedestal base, paper label, silver* 55.00 75.00
☐ **Jardiniere**, *10", brown, two small finger handles, spherical, the rim flairs slightly outward, paper label, silver* 200.00 225.00
☐ **Jug**, *7", blue, with two small finger handles, cylindrical, narrowing at the neck, paper label, gold* 115.00 140.00

Price Range

☐ **Jug,** *7", brown, with two small finger handles, cylindrical, narrowing at the neck, paper label, gold* 115.00 140.00

☐ **Vase,** *7-1/2", blue, with two small finger handles, cylindrical, smaller base, paper label, silver* 85.00 95.00

☐ **Vase,** *8", large semi-circle handles which connect within the trellis design, cylindrical shape that flairs at the base, paper label, silver* 108.00 125.00

CHLORON *(Introduced 1907)*

Green thin matte glaze with an unusual style of items which imitates old Greek pottery; variations: some pieces have sections of the design in ivory.

☐ **Vase,** *6-1/2", textured design, cone shape, no trim, no mark* ... 200.00 225.00

☐ **Vase,** *7", textured design, with handles, spherical with a rippled rim, Chloron marked in ink, TRPCo marked* 225.00 285.00

☐ **Vase,** *12", smooth, with a three footed base, slender, widens at the rim, flat extended rim, no mark* 225.00 285.00

CLEMANA *(Introduced 1934)*

Clusters of flowers with drooping leaves create a simplistic design on mostly pastel backgrounds; embossed designs appear on azure blue and light green backgrounds.

☐ **Bowl,** *shape #281, 4-1/2", blue, with the design covering almost all surface area, cylindrical, flairs at the mouth, impressed mark Roseville* 60.00 75.00

☐ **Candleholder,** *4-1/2", green, wide pedestal base, cylindrical, no mark* 85.00 100.00

☐ **Urn,** *shape #754, 8-1/2", blue, pointed handles, spherical, impressed mark Roseville* 100.00 125.00

☐ **Vase,** *shape #756, 9-1/2", green, pinch handles, spherical shape with long cylindrical neck, impressed mark Roseville* .. 115.00 140.00

☐ **Vase,** *shape #758, 12-1/2", blue, two pointed handles, bulbous shape base, narrows at the neck, then flairs at the rim, impressed mark Roseville* 115.00 140.00

CLEMATIS *(Introduced 1944)*

Large relief clematis blossoms on a slightly mottled matte background; variations: ivory blossoms on aqua background, pink on green, and ivory with orange tint on golden background.

☐ **Basket,** *shape #387, 7", orange, one circular handle which connects each side in two places, cylindrical, narrows at the center, marked Roseville in relief* 45.00 50.00

☐ **Cookie jar,** *shape #3, 10", aqua, with lid and two pointed handles, spherical, narrows at the neck, marked Roseville in relief* 85.00 95.00

☐ **Double bud vase,** *shape #194, 5", the two vases are connected by one large ivory flower, cylindrical on pedestal bases, marked Roseville in relief* 45.00 50.00

Price Range

☐ **Ewer,** *shape #18, 15", orange, pointed handle, small cut-outs on either side of the neck, bulbous base on base, with long neck and spout, marked Roseville in relief* 105.00   130.00

☐ **Wall pocket,** *shape #1295, 8", orange, two pointed "ear" handles, acorn shape, marked Roseville in relief* 40.00   45.00

COLONIAL *(Introduced 1900)*

Victorian styled spongeware with embossed designs and many with handles; variations: blue or green.

☐ **Pitcher,** *7-1/2", mottled blue and beige, with handle, bulbous base, narrows at the neck, no mark* 85.00   100.00

☐ **Pitcher with basin,** *11", mottled blues, with ornate handle, bulbous base, cylindrical neck, basin has a rippled rim, no mark* 340.00   450.00

☐ **Soap dish,** *4", with lid, mottled green, spherical shape, the lid has a small handle, no mark* 95.00   105.00

COLUMBINE *(Introduced 1940)*

Embossed flowers, leaves and vines extend across blended backgrounds of a matte glaze; variations: pink flowers on rose and green, blue flowers on orange and green, and yellow on blue and green.

☐ **Bowl,** *shape #401, 2-1/2", blue, two small pointed handles, dish shape, wide mouth, no base or rim, marked Roseville in relief* .   35.00   40.00

☐ **Ewer,** *shape #18, 7", ornage with green base, one pointed handle, severe cone shape, narrow neck, marked Roseville in relief*   50.00   55.00

☐ **Hanging basket,** *shape #17, 8-1/2", rose, with three pierced holes for hanging, spherical, with rim turned up, marked Roseville in relief* 60.00   75.00

☐ **Vase,** *shape #151, 8", blue, pointed handles at the bottom of the body, cylindrical shape, wider where the handle connects, on a tall pedestal base, marked Roseville in relief* 45.00   50.00

COMMERCIAL LINE *(Introduced 1940)*

Blue, green or tan glaze coats twisted and rippled pieces with flaired rims. The inside of each piece is tan.

☐ **Vase,** *shape #80, 6", green, shaped like a celery stalk, marked R. USA in relief* 35.00   40.00

☐ **Vase,** *shape #81, 7", tan, rippled sides, no uniformity in shape, marked R. USA in relief* 40.00   45.00

CORINTHIAN *(Introduced 1923)*

Ivory vertical fluted bands on green with a band of twisting vines and grapes on green. Decorative trim in ivory and green usually appears above the vine design.

☐ **Compote,** *4-1/2", embossed design at rim, semi-circular on pedestal base, RV stamped in ink* 50.00   55.00

Price Range

☐ **Double bud vase,** *7", two vases joined by rectangular wall with cut-outs, vases are column shapes, RV stamped in ink* 35.00 40.00
☐ **Vase,** *6", narrow base widens to band of design, RV stamped in ink* 35.00 40.00
☐ **Vase,** *8", cylindrical shape, flairs at rim, base is wider than body, RV stamped in ink* 28.00 34.00

CORNELIAN *(Introduced around 1900)*

High gloss glaze of different colors appear on spongeware with embossed designs. Metalic gold is found on handles, spouts, rims or just randomly on each piece; variations: colors include ivory, brown, yellow, green and blue.

☐ **Jardiniere,** *7", mottled brown and beige, simple shape, no trim, no mark* 75.00 85.00
☐ **Pitcher,** *5", mottled ivory and tan, with handle, simple cylindrical shape, no mark* 50.00 55.00
☐ **Pticher,** *5", mottled blue and brown, with embossed corn motif, simple shape, semi-circle handle, no mark* 70.00 85.00
☐ **Pitcher,** *5-1/2", mottled blue, brown and ivory, with brown handle, classic shape, bulbous base, curved neck and spout, no mark* 55.00 67.50

COSMOS *(Introduced 1940)*

Orchid and white flowers form a horizontal design on a textured background of green, blue or tan; variations: some pieces have fragile cut-top decorations.

☐ **Console bowl,** *shape #374, 15-1/2", four cut-outs at the rim, two handles on the underside of the bowl, on a base with a rippled rim, impressed Roseville* 75.00 85.00
☐ **Ewer,** *shape #951, 15", blue, semi-oval handle, bulbous base, with long neck and spout, marked Roseville in relief* 95.00 110.00
☐ **Vase,** *shape #945, 5", egg-shaped holes in the handles, cutouts in the rim, marked Roseville in relief* 28.00 34.00

CREMONA *(Introduced 1927)*

The lightly textured background can be found in many pastel colors. The design of simplistic flowers in very low relief; variations: pink mottled background with bluish flowers, light green mottled with bluish flowers.

☐ **Bowl,** *9" across, rose, impressed base, eight-sided with a rippled rim, paper label, black* 45.00 50.00
☐ **Vase,** *10", light green, with pointed handles, egg shape with flaired rim, paper label, black* 65.00 80.00
☐ **Vase,** *10-1/2, pink, classic shape with flaired rim, paper label, black* 55.00 65.00

CRYSTALIS ROZANE *(Introduced 1906)*

Tan and some other colors form a textured and almost mottled effect on many uniquely styled pieces.

Price Range

☐ **Candleholder,** *9", green, tall pedestal base, flat rim, marked with ROZANE WARE circle seal* 1000.00 1125.00
☐ **Ewer,** *7-1/2", mottled tan and orange, with one handle, unusual shape, with no uniformity at the base or spout, marked with ROZANE WARE circle seal* 1350.00 1450.00
☐ **Vase,** *11", mottled olive green with blue spots, flairing outward from the base, then narrowing at the neck, marked with ROZANE WARE circle seal* 2250.00 2850.00

DAHLROSE *(Introduced 1924)*

Embossed ivory flowers and green leaves form a band on a textured and mottled tan, brown and green background.

☐ **Bowl,** *4-1/2", with two pointed handles, oval shape, narrowing at the rim and base, marked with paper label, black* 50.00 55.00
☐ **Hanging basket,** *7", three holes pierced in the rim, semi-sphere shape, narrowing at rim, no mark* 85.00 95.00
☐ **Jardiniere,** *6", two small finger handles, spherical shape, with base and rim, no mark* 50.00 55.00
☐ **Vase,** *8", two handles which square off the rounded sides, spherical shape, narrows at the top and bottom of the band of design, marked with paper label, black* 45.00 50.00
☐ **Vase,** *10", square, flairs at the band of design, marked with paper label, black* 45.00 50.00

DAWN *(Introduced 1937)*

Simple shapes carry a simple design of long, thin petaled flowers of bluish-lilac or bluish-green; variations: backgrounds are found in blue, pink or yellow.

☐ **Bowl,** *shape #318, 16" wide, yellow, with two pinch handles, oval with rippled rim, impressed mark Roseville* 45.00 55.00
☐ **Ewer,** *shape #834, 16", pink, semi-oval handle, body is shaped like a shield, on a base, impressed mark Roseville* 115.00 140.00
☐ **Vase,** *shape #827, 6", yellow, square pinch handles, bulbous shape, no pronounced rim, impressed mark Roseville* 40.00 45.00
☐ **Vase,** *shape #826, 6", pink, square pinch handles, cylindrical shape, with square base, impressed mark Roseville* 40.00 45.00

DECORATED *(Introduced 1900)*

Creamware with decals or designs of fruits and berries with some leaves or vining; variations: some pieces have gold trim on edges and handles, a well known use for the decorated line was a mug and tankard set.

☐ **Pitcher,** *7", one orange stripe on the body, black pin-striping around rim, simple shape, RV stamped in ink* 35.00 40.00
☐ **Pitcher,** *7", embossed with four designs of slender leaves and berries, simple shape, narrows just above base, RV stamped in ink* 45.00 50.00
☐ **Pitcher,** *6", one green stripe on the body, black pin-striping around rim, simple shape, RV stamped in ink* 40.00 45.00

Price Range

☐ **Basket,** *15", tall handle that connects on both sides and forms a point, spherical shape, no mark* 200.00   225.00

☐ **Bowl,** *shape #238, 3-1/2", rounded bottom on a cylindrical shape, the mouth slightly flairs, marked RV stamped in ink* ... 75.00   85.00

☐ **Double bud vase,** *one vase is 5" tall, the other is 3" tall, two column vases joined by a panel of embossed design, cylindrical shape, no mark* 35.00   40.00

☐ **Pitcher,** *6-1/2", ivory handle, bulbous shape, marked RV stamped in ink* 175.00   200.00

☐ **Wall pocket,** *10", one pierced hole for hanging, oval shape, no mark* 55.00   65.00

DUTCH *(Introduced 1910-1915)*

Decals of Dutch people, often children, are added to creamware along with one blue stripe for trim. This line was used to make many household items.

☐ **Creamer,** *3", small child decal, simple shape, with handle and spout at right angle, no mark* 55.00   67.50

☐ **Mug,** *5", decal of three playing children, simple shape with handle, no mark* 50.00   55.00

☐ **Plate,** *11", decal of four playing children, round with pronounced rim, no mark* 90.00   100.00

☐ **Pitcher,** *7-1/2", decal of a man and woman, unique handle that joins as part of the rim, bulbous shape, no mark* 125.00   140.00

☐ **Tankard,** *11-1/2", decal of a boy and girl fishing, squared off handle, simple shape, narrows at the rim, no mark* 115.00   140.00

☐ **Tumbler,** *4", decal of a girl with a doll, cylindrical shape, no mark* 100.00   125.00

EARLAM *(Introduced 1930)*

Green matte glaze mottled with specks of blue, peach and yellow form a smooth surface on each piece. The inside lining of vases and other items is a peach-tan color.

☐ **Candleholder,** *4", holder on a dish with one loop handle, column shape, marked with paper label, black* 95.00   105.00

☐ **Planter,** *5-1/2", two small handles, rectangular shape with a rise in the rim, no mark* 50.00   55.00

☐ **Urn,** *6", with two small handles, simple shape, no mark* 55.00   67.50

☐ **Vase,** *9", simple shape, no pronounced rim or base, no mark* .. 75.00   85.00

EGYPTO *(Introduced 1905)*

A brilliant green forms a matte glaze over many pieces that imitate the ancient Egyptian style of pottery. (Also called Rozane Egypto)

☐ **Compote,** *9", designed to look like a tree, wide base, pedestal and bowl on top, marked with EGYPTO seal* 310.00   340.00

☐ **Pitcher,** *7", swirling design, classic shape with handle, marked with EGYPTO seal* 200.00   225.00

☐ **Vase,** *11", embossed geometric design, classic shape, narrowing just above the base and just below the neck, marked with EGYPTO seal* 285.00   310.00

DELLA ROBBIA *(Introduced 1906)*

A wide variety of designs in many different colors. All designs are produced by etching out clay from around an incised motif. (Also known as Rozane Della Robbia)

	Price Range	
☐ **Bowl,** *9-1/2", Oriental motif with dragons heads, blue, tan and ivory color design, round, with small opening, marked HS ....*	1450.00	1600.00
☐ **Jar,** *8", ivory with blue, pink and brown designs of spades and flowers, urn shape, marked G ....*	1350.00	1450.00
☐ **Mug,** *4", dark brown with a band of blue design, with a handle, slightly flaired at the base, marked KD ....*	500.00	565.00
☐ **Vase,** *8-1/2", tan and dark brown designs of flowers and vines, urn shape, small opening, marked with ROZANE WARE circle seal ....*	1450.00	1600.00
☐ **Vase,** *14", ivory, tan and gray, flowers, and lily pads in a pond, simple shape, no base or rim, marked with ROZANE WARE circle seal, H Smith marking ....*	2850.00	3000.00

DOGWOOD *(Introduced 1918)*

Embossed dogwood blossoms, leaves and branches circle each piece on a textured background. The colors are green to olive green background, light green and white blossoms, and brown traces in the branches.

☐ **Bowl,** *4", spherical shape, with rim, marked RV stamped in ink*	45.00	50.00
☐ **Hanging basket,** *7", three pierced holes in the rim, round, narrows at the rim, marked RV stamped in ink ....*	95.00	110.00
☐ **Jardiniere,** *8", spherical on short base, marked RV stamped in ink ....*	95.00	115.00
☐ **Vase,** *6", urn shape, short neck, marked RV stamped in ink ...*	50.00	55.00
☐ **Wall pocket,** *8", V shape with rounded corners, marked RV stamped in ink ....*	55.00	65.00

DOGWOOD II *(Introduced 1928)*

Embossed dogwood blossoms and branches extend vertically and horizontally across pieces with dark olive green smooth backgrounds. Blossoms are white, branches are black and many times form the oddly shaped edges.

☐ **Basket,** *6", with semi-circle handle, cylindrical shape, rim is not parallel with base, no mark ....*	40.00	45.00
☐ **Bud vase,** *9", shape is not uniform, base is wider than the rest of the body, no mark ....*	35.00	40.00
☐ **Jardiniere,** *8", spherical shape, no pronounced rim or base, no mark ....*	65.00	80.00
☐ **Vase,** *9", cylindrical shape, no pronounced rim or base, no mark ....*	35.00	40.00
☐ **Vase,** *14-1/2", slender vase, narrows at the neck, the rim is rippled, no mark ....*	170.00	190.00

DONATELLO *(Introduced 1915)*

An elaborate frieze pictures cherubs and trees horizontally on a band that crosses vertical fluted bands; variations: colors range from all white to ivory and green with a brown frieze.

Price Range

☐ **Vase,** *12-1/2", small embossed heads at the rim on each side, four-sided, marked with EGYPT seal* 285.00 310.00

FALLINE *(Introduced 1933)*

Quarter moon designs that look like pea pods circle each item. The backgrounds are a satin matte of various blending colors; variations: backgrounds may be green or blue base blending to tan-brown, or just tan-brown.

☐ **Bowl,** *11" wide, tan-brown, two handles, round, no mark* 140.00 170.00
☐ **Urn,** *6", green and tan, two handles, urn shape, narrowing at neck and base, marked with paper label, silver* 175.00 200.00
☐ **Urn,** *8", tan-brown, two circular handles, more narrow at the base, and narrows at the neck, marked with paper label, silver* 140.00 170.00
☐ **Vase,** *6", blue-green, two large handles that extend beyond the rim, cylindrical shape, with a small pedestal base, no mark* ... 115.00 140.00
☐ **Vase,** *9", tan-brown, two large handles, with horizontal fluting below the handles, cylindrical with a bulbous base, no mark* .. 175.00 200.00

FERRELLA *(Introduced 1931)*

A brown to rose mottled glaze covers ornate pieces with impressed shell designs around base and rim. Decorative cut-outs add detail to the piece with a slight greenish tint at the base and rim.

☐ **Bowl,** *5", with flower frog, cut-outs circle the rim and base, round, flairing at the rim and base, no mark* 175.00 200.00
☐ **Bowl,** *12", mottled rose, aqua rim and base, with small cut-outs at rim and base, round, flairing at the rim, on a small pedestal base, no mark* 175.00 200.00
☐ **Vase,** *4", small pointed handles, spherical shape, with flaired rim and base, no mark* ....:..................... 90.00 105.00
☐ **Vase,** *8", spherical shape, with flairing rim and base, no mark .* 175.00 200.00

FLORANE *(Introduced 1920)*

Very simplistic shapes with no trim or elaborate designs are covered with a matte glaze of tan-brown which smoothly blend into a dark brown or dark olive green.

☐ **Bowl,** *2-1/2" x 8", three foot base, round, marked RV stamped in ink* 28.00 34.00
☐ **Bowl,** *5", two small pointed handles, urn shape, with a slight narrowing at the neck, marked RV stamped in ink* 45.00 55.00
☐ **Bud vase,** *8", one continuous piece, slender cylinder with flairing at the base and rim, marked RV stamped in ink* 28.00 34.00
☐ **Vase, double bud,** *5", joined by ornate design, one horizontal line, three vertical lines and a curving line, slightly bulbous shape with a flairing rim and on a pedestal base, marked RV stamped in ink* 45.00 50.00

FLORENTINE *(Introduced 1924)*

Alternating panels of textured sections and clusters of leaves and berries extending vertically carry earth colors of tan, beige, green and brown. (Similar to the Panel line)

Price Range

☐ **Bowl,** *7", two squared-off handles, round on a small base, no mark*	40.00	45.00
☐ **Bowl,** *9" wide, disc shape, curving inward at the rim, marked RV stamped in ink*	35.00	40.00
☐ **Jardiniere,** *5", two squared-off handles, spherical shape on a small base, narrows just below the rim, marked RV stamped in ink*	45.00	50.00
☐ **Wall pocket,** *9-1/4", one small pieced hole for hanging, shield shape, marked RV stamped in ink*	45.00	50.00
☐ **Window box,** *11-1/2", rectangular, no pronounced rim or base, marked RV stamped in ink*	115.00	140.00

FOXGLOVE *(Introduced 1942)*

Embossed tall reeds of pink and white flower buds that stand out against blending backgrounds; variations: colors of backgrounds may be one color or a blending of two, green, rose and blue.

☐ **Cornucopia,** *shape #164, 8", green, on a round base, with a supporting arm, with the mouth opening upwards, marked Roseville in relief*	35.00	40.00
☐ **Ewer,** *shape #5, 10", green and blue, with one ornate handle, bulbous base, on a pedestal, narrowing at the neck, marked Roseville in relief*	55.00	65.00
☐ **Flower frog,** *shape #46, 4", blue, cornucopia shape, marked Roseville in relief*	35.00	40.00
☐ **Tray,** *8-1/2", green, with one small handle, shaped like a leaf, marked Roseville in relief*	35.00	40.00
☐ **Vase,** *shape #659, 3", blue, with two small handles, cylindrical on a base, marked Roseville in relief*	22.50	27.50

FREESIA *(Introduced 1945)*

Clusters of six or seven flowers from a fan-like design which when joined by vines circle each item. The flowers are usually white or yellow on blue-green, blue or tan-brown backgrounds. The background also has a textured pattern incised into it.

☐ **Basket,** *shape #391, 8", tan-brown, one semi-circular handle, that connects on the sides below the rim, uneven rim, on a small pedestal base, marked Roseville in relief*	45.00	50.00
☐ **Bowl,** *shape #669, 4", tan-brown, two small finger handles, spherical, marked Roseville in relief*	35.00	40.00'
☐ **Cornucopia,** *shape #198, 8", green, on an asymmetrical base, with the mouth opening upwards, marked Roseville in relief* . .	28.00	34.00
☐ **Console,** *shape #469, 3-1/2" x 16-1/2", green, with two handles, oval with uneven rim, marked Roseville in relief*	55.00	65.00
☐ **Flower pot,** *shape #670, 5-1/2", tan-brown, with saucer, bell shape with flair at the neck, marked Roseville in relief*	40.00	45.00

Price Range

☐ **Urn,** shape #196, 8", tan-brown, with two handles, classic urn shape on a pedestal base, narrowing at the neck, marked Roseville in relief 50.00   55.00

FUCHSIA (Introduced 1939)

Embossed designs of pink fushsia blossoms and leaves stand out against a blending and slightly textured background. Parts of the background are smooth and in one color. As the textured areas become visible, the color also changes; variations: color combinations are green and tan, blue and yellow, or brown and gold.

☐ **Bowl,** shape #645, 3", blue, with two finger handles, eliptical shape with base and rim, impressed marked Roseville 35.00   40.00
☐ **Console,** shape #351, 3-1/2" x 12-1/2", two handles, oval on a pedestal base, with a rippled rim, impressed marked Roseville 50.00   55.00
☐ **Pitcher,** shape #1322, 8", green, with one handle, spherical with the spout coming out to the side, impressed marked Roseville 60.00   75.00
☐ **Vase,** shape #903, 12", blue, with two large handles which connect just above and below the base and rim, cylindrical with a slight flair at the neck and base, impressed marked Roseville . 75.00   85.00

FUJIYAMA (Introduced 1906)

White or ivory bisque backgrounds lend great contrast to the glossy floral designs with incised outlines. Designs are imitative of Oriental designs. (Similar to the Woodland line.)

☐ **Vase,** 9", yellow flowers and stems, lined in yellow, lighthouse shape, marked Fujiyama stamped in ink 800.00   900.00
☐ **Vase,** 11", yellow flowers, green leaves and vines, lined in yellow, lighthouse shape, marked Fujiyama stamped in ink 900.00   1000.00

FUTURA (Introduced 1928)

This line includes pieces with many different styles and colors. Some are simplistic geometric designs, some with a hint of Art Deco, others have a floral design. More than eighty styles have been found.

☐ **Candleholder,** 4", yellow with green accents at the base, box holder on a pedestal base, marked with paper label, black 22.50   27.50
☐ **Jardiniere,** 6", tan with yellow, blue and green geometric shapes in the design, with two pointed handles, from the base the body flairs out to a point, then narrows to the neck and rim, no mark 75.00   85.00
☐ **Planter,** 7" wide, yellow with green accents, a yellow swirling vine and green leaves, rectangular with a slight narrowing at the base, and a flairing at the neck, marked with paper label, black 45.00   50.00
☐ **Vase,** 8-1/2", tan with dark green leaves, bee hive shape, no mark 100.00   115.00
☐ **Vase,** 10", tan and aqua, with a design of long lines forming seagulls and trees, cylindrical shape with a pronounced base, marked with paper label, black 75.00   85.00

GARDENIA *(Introduced 1945-1950)*

One large gardenia bloom is the center feature with detailed leaves extending from around it. The flower is embossed over a horizontal band of a different color than the rest of the background; variations: background colors are a soft green, tan or blue-gray, the band has tints of golds.

	Price Range	
☐ **Bowl,** *shape #641, 5", pink, with two finger handles, spherical shape with the rim uneven, marked Roseville in relief*	35.00	40.00
☐ **Cornucopia,** *shape #621, 6", tan, on a circular base, with the mouth opening upwards, marked Roseville in relief*	35.00	40.00
☐ **Ewer,** *shape #617, 10", pink, with one handle, bulbous base, with slender neck, marked Roseville in relief*	55.00	65.00
☐ **Vase,** *shape #658, 10", green, two handles that connect above the base and in the middle of the body, small pedestal base, the rim has the shape of a flower blossom, marked Roseville in relief*	45.00	50.00
☐ **Vase,** *shape #687, 12", pink, two handles that connect above the base and in the middle of the body, small pedestal base, the rim has the shape of a flower blossom, marked Roseville in relief*	60.00	75.00

HOLLAND *(Introduced 1910-1915)*

Embossed figurines of Dutch people, often children, in low relief on a basic ivory background. The figures are painted in blues, grays and roses. The top of each piece has a shade of rose and the bottom has a shade of green.

☐ **Mug,** *4", white and gray, with an embossed figure, simple shape, no mark*	40.00	45.00
☐ **Pitcher,** *6-1/2", tan, with two embossed figures, simple shape, no mark*	125.00	150.00

HOLLY *(Introduced 1910-1915)*

Green striping follows along rims and handles on ivory colored creamware. The design is painted green leaves and red holly berries.

☐ **Creamer,** *3", one handle, simple shape, no mark*	115.00	140.00
☐ **Teapot,** *4-1/2", with lid, handle, and spout which connects at the base, simple shape, no mark*	225.00	275.00

IMPERIAL I *(Introduced 1916)*

A stylized cluster of grapes, leaves and pretzel-shaped vines is the motif on a very textured background of green, black or a blend of green, beige and brown.

☐ **Basket,** *6", thick circular handle, round, no mark*	45.00	50.00
☐ **Bud vase,** *12", one continuous piece, with two small pinch handles, cylindrical, with flaired base, no mark*	50.00	55.00
☐ **Vase,** *8", with two pointed handles, urn shape, narrowing at the rim, no mark*	65.00	80.00

Price Range

☐ **Vase, 10",** *with two handles, urn shape, narrowing at the rim,*
no mark 80.00   90.00

IMPERIAL II *(Introduced 1924)*

This is a line with many different colors. The style of items, particularly the shape, is very simplistic. Most items have bright colored glazes with a contrasting color dripping over the main color, giving it a drizzling effect.

☐ **Bowl,** *4-1/2", lilac and yellow, spherical shape, no mark* 140.00   170.00
☐ **Bowl,** *5-1/2", blue and yellow, exaggerated bell shape, no mark* 200.00   225.00
☐ **Vase,** *5-1/2", aqua, thimble shape, no mark* 85.00   100.00
☐ **Vase,** *5-1/2", yellow, bee hive shape, no mark* 85.00   100.00
☐ **Vase,** *7", aqua and white, urn shape, no mark* 175.00   200.00

IRIS *(Introduced 1938)*

White iris blossoms with green stem and leaves are embossed on blended background colors; variations: background colors are rose and green, two-tone blue and gold into green or brown.

☐ **Basket,** *shape #354, 8", rose, with one handle that connects on*
each side, round on a small base, impressed mark Roseville 60.00   75.00
☐ **Ewer,** *shape #926, 10", rose, with one decorative handle, bul-*
bous base, narrow at the neck, impressed mark Roseville 60.00   75.00
☐ **Urn,** *shape #358, 6-1/2", blue, with handles that connect under-*
neath at the base, spherical on a small base, impressed mark
Roseville 45.00   50.00
☐ **Vase,** *shape #924, 10", tan, two small handles, cylindrical, nar-*
rowing at the base and rim, impressed mark Roseville 55.00   65.00

IVORY *(Introduced 1937)*

All white version of other lines, many of which are decorative pieces. Some figurines were also done in ivory; variations: the lines duplicated in white are Dawn, Donatello, Florentine, Foxglove, Luffa, Orian, Russco, Savona, Topeo and Velmoss.

☐ **Candlestick,** *2-1/2", spherical shape on a flat disc base,*
impressed mark Roseville 17.50   22.50
☐ **Cornucopia,** *5-1/2", on a base, with the mouth opening upwards,*
mark Roseville in relief 35.00   40.00
☐ **Urn,** *shape #271, 6-1/2", urn shape on a base, without a neck or*
rim, impressed mark Roseville 45.00   50.00

IXIA *(Introduced 1930)*

A sprig of flowers and branches are delicately embossed on a smooth background. The flowers are sometimes white, on other pieces they may be pink. Handles are unique with cut-off edges, no finger holes; variations: background colors are green, yellow and pink blends.

☐ **Bowl,** *shape #326, 4", pink and aqua, with two pinch handles,*
round with no rim or base, impressed mark Roseville 28.00   34.00

Price Range

☐ **Bowl,** *shape #387, 6", yellow and pink, with two pinch handles, spherical, with no rim or base, impressed mark Roseville* 40.00 45.00

☐ **Vase,** *shape #857, 8-1/2", yellow and pink, with two pinch handles, urn shape with an extended neck, impressed mark Roseville* 40.00 45.00

☐ **Vase,** *shape #862, 10-1/2", pink and aqua, with two pinch handles, urn shape with an extended body, impressed mark Roseville* 40.00 45.00

JONQUIL *(Introduced 1931)*

Heavily mottled brown backgrounds with embossed clusters of flowers and long slender reeds of grass. The brown background blends at the top of many items into green.

☐ **Bowl,** *4", two small handles, slightly bell-shaped narrowing at the base, no mark* 50.00 55.00

☐ **Candlestick,** *4", cylinder holder on a wide disc base, no mark* . 45.00 50.00

☐ **Vase,** *8", with two handles that connect above the base and below the rim, pear shape, no mark* 50.00 55.00

☐ **Vase,** *8", with two ear handles, urn shape, narrowing below the rim, no mark* 50.00 55.00

JUVENILE *(Introduced 1910-1915)*

Ivory colored, smooth creamware with hand-painted transfer designs for children; variations: many different patterns were used, included are rabbits, chicks, cats, dogs, Santa Claus and Sunbonnet girls.

☐ **Cup and saucer,** *2", Santa motif, simple shape, one handle, marked RV stamped in ink* 140.00 170.00

☐ **Egg cup,** *4", rabbit motif, simple shape, marked RV stamped in ink* 95.00 105.00

☐ **Mug,** *3", chicks motif, simple shape, one handle, marked RV stamped in ink* 40.00 45.00

☐ **Plate,** *8", duck motif, rolled edges, marked RV stamped in ink* . 40.00 45.00

☐ **Plate,** *8", Sunbonnet girl motif, marked RV stamped in ink* 45.00 50.00

LA ROSE *(Introduced 1924)*

Four pink flowers with blue criss-crossing bands are the centered feature on a green garland that drapes across the ivory slightly textured background. The rim has a beaded trim that matches in style to its classic rolled handles.

☐ **Bowl,** *6", green bead trim just below the rim, shallow bowl, RV stamped in ink* 35.00 40.00

☐ **Double bud vase,** *5", two column vases joined by a gate, column shape, with wide base and flaired rim, RV stamped in ink* . 35.00 40.00

☐ **Jardiniere,** *6-1/2", green bead trim just below the rim, spherical, RV stamped in ink* 55.00 65.00

☐ **Vase,** *4", two rolled handles, urn shape with a flaired rim, RV stamped in ink* 40.00 45.00

☐ **Wall pocket,** *9", decorative hanging handle, shield shape, no mark* 50.00 55.00

LAUREL (Introduced 1934)

Slightly textured and mottled backgrounds of orange, gold or green carry an embossed design of a laurel branch. The branch and leaves are lightly colored. Three deep vertical grooves are spaced evenly between the laurel branches.

	Price Range	
☐ **Bowl,** 3-1/2", gold, short shallow, with a rippled rim, no mark ..	40.00	45.00
☐ **Urn,** 6-1/2", orange, two squared pinch handles, slightly bulbous shape with three horizontal grooves at the rim, no mark .	40.00	50.00
☐ **Vase,** 6-1/2", green with two pinch handles, chalice shape with the handles at the narrow neck at the bottom, paper label, silver	35.00	40.00
☐ **Vase,** 7", orange, with two rounded pinch handles, jar shape, paper label, silver	45.00	50.00

LOTUS (Introduced 1952)

Tall symmetrical leaves of green surround pieces which are often square or rectangular in shape. Contrasting backgrounds trim the rim and base; variations: color combinations are green leaves on blue, maroon or brown, beige on turquoise or brown.

☐ **Bowl,** shape #L6, 3", brown, short, shallow, marked Roseville in relief	55.00	85.00
☐ **Candleholder,** shape #L5, 2-1/2", white on blue, cylindrical shape on a small pedestal base, marked Roseville in relief ...	30.00	35.00
☐ **Vase,** shape #L4, 10-1/2", green on aqua, rectangular with a slight flair just above the base, marked Roseville in relief	85.00	115.00

LUFFA (Introduced 1934)

Large vining leaves and small flowers circle each item. Shapes are usually simplistic with a wavy pattern of horizontal lines in the otherwise smooth and glossy texture; variations: colors found are green and brown, aqua is rare.

☐ **Bowl,** 4", green, with two pinch handles, semi-spherical, paper label, silver	40.00	45.00
☐ **Candlestick,** 5", brown, with two small decorative handles, bell holder, with a circular pedestal base, no mark	45.00	50.00
☐ **Lamp,** 9-1/2", green, with two small pointed handles, oblong, with a narrow rim and base, no mark	175.00	225.00
☐ **Vase,** 6", green, with two pointed handles, oblong, paper label, silver	50.00	55.00
☐ **Vase,** 7", brown, with two pointed handles, oblong, paper label, silver	55.00	65.00

LUSTRE (Introduced 1921)

Most notable is the simple shapes with no trim and very high gloss luster; color variations: orange, purple, rose, silver and yellow.

☐ **Basket,** 6", pink, with one piece handle shaped like a spade, classic shape with circular pedestal base and flaired rim, no mark	140.00	170.00

	Price Range	

☐ **Candleholder,** *8", silver, one piece, flaired rim and base, paper label, black* 25.00   30.00

☐ **Vase,** *10", pink, cylindrical, no trim, paper label, black* 45.00   55.00

☐ **Vase,** *12", pink, tall urn shape, narrowing below the rim, paper label, black* 50.00   60.00

MAGNOLIA *(Introduced 1943)*

Big white magnolia blossoms are embossed on a textured background. Black twigs extend from the blossom; variations: colors of backgrounds are blended tan and green or shades of blue with pink accents.

☐ **Bowl,** *shape #665, 3", green, with two pointed handles, spherical with lightly pronounced rim, marked Roseville in relief* 22.50   27.50

☐ **Cookie jar,** *shape #2, 10", blue, with two handles and a lid, urn shape with the widest area where the handles join, marked Roseville in relief* 85.00   100.00

☐ **Cornucopia,** *shape #184, 6", tan, on an asymmetrical base, with the mouth opening upwards, marked Roseville in relief* .. 28.00   34.00

☐ **Ewer,** *shape #15, 15", tan, with one handle and two small cutouts in the neck, bulbous base, long neck, marked Roseville in relief* 115.00   140.00

☐ **Planter,** *shape #389, 3", blue, with two pointed handles, rectangular, slightly curved at the base, marked Roseville in relief* 28.00   34.00

☐ **Vase,** *shape #88, 6", tan, with two pointed handles connecting low on the base, chalice shape, marked Roseville in relief* 28.00   34.00

MATT GREEN *(Introduced 1910-1915)*

Medium green glaze on many different styles of items; variations: some items are without any kind of trim, some are embossed with leaves and cherub faces.

☐ **Hanging basket** *9", four pierced holes for hanging, rippled body, no uniformity, no mark* 65.00   80.00

☐ **Jardiniere,** *shape #456, 5-1/2", four small handles, simple with large rolled rim, paper label* 45.00   50.00

☐ **Planter,** *4", on four footed base, embossed eagle on the panels, rectangular, rim is smaller than base, no mark* 140.00   170.00

MAYFAIR *(Introduced around 1950)*

Contemporary shapes with little or no detail or trim, new high gloss colors and combinations of gray and beige, brown and pink, green and chartreuse.

☐ **Bowl,** *shape #1119, 7", beige, one scroll handle, shell shape, impressed with Roseville* 25.00   30.00

☐ **Bowl,** *shape #1119, 10", beige, one scroll handle, shell shape, impressed with Roseville* 40.00   45.00

☐ **Pitcher,** *shape #1105, 8", beige, one decorative handle, classic shape with a textured swirling pattern below the neck, marked Roseville in relief* 45.00   50.00

☐ **Planter,** *shape #1113, 8", brown with beige lining, oval with a rippled rim, marked Roseville in relief* 28.00   34.00

Price Range

☐ **Vase,** shape #1106, 12-1/2", brown, with evenly spaced rows of
impressed circles, cylindrical, marked Roseville in relief 60.00 75.00

MING TREE (Introduced 1949)

Shapes are stylized with the Oriental accent as well as the design. Twisted brown branches with the cotton ball greenery topping each branch are embossed over a slightly textured background of a high gloss glaze; twisted branches also form handles; variations: color combinations are pink leaves on green background, green on white, and white on light blue.

☐ **Bowl,** shape #526, 4-1/2", blue, two uneven branches, rectangular with uneven rim, marked Roseville in relief 45.00 50.00
☐ **Basket,** shape #508, 8", white, one handle, circular with uneven rim, marked Roseville in relief 60.00 75.00
☐ **Ewer,** shape #516, 10", blue, with one pointed handle, slender but uneven, marked Roseville in relief 75.00 85.00
☐ **Planter,** shape #568, 4", white, rectangular with uneven rim, marked Roseville in relief 40.00 45.00
☐ **Vase,** shape #581, 6", green with two uneven handles, cylindrical, marked Roseville in relief 35.00 40.00

MOCK ORANGE (Introduced 1950)

Small clusters of white or pink flowers with green leaves are embossed on a satin matte backgrounds of pastel colors. This line was more asymmetrical in shapes than most Roseville lines; variations: backgrounds are pastel blue, green, rose or yellow.

☐ **Basket,** shape #908, 6", green and blue, with semi-circular handle, bell shape with uneven rim, marked Roseville U.S.A. Mock Orange in relief 45.00 50.00
☐ **Bowl,** shape #900, 4", yellow, with two small pinch handles, spherical, marked Roseville U.S.A. Mock Orange in relief 22.50 27.50
☐ **Planter,** shape #931, 3-1/2", yellow, on a three footed base, oval with a rippled rim, marked Roseville U.S.A. Mock Orange in relief 35.00 40.00
☐ **Vase,** shape #930, 7", rose, on a three footed base, shaped like a flower bud, marked Roseville U.S.A. Mock Orange in relief . . 45.00 50.00

MODERNE (Introduced 1930's)

Embossed vertical lines and stylish swirls are the designs on matte smooth backgrounds; variations: color combinations are white trim and highlight on blue, tan on white, gold on turquoise.

☐ **Comport,** shape #295, 5", white, shallow bowl on a pedestal base which is encircled by a coil, impressed with Roseville . . . 50.00 60.00
☐ **Urn,** shape #299, 6-1/2", tan, spherical on a circular base, impressed with Roseville 45.00 50.00
☐ **Vase,** shape #789, 6", white, with two handles, urn shape with tall neck, on a pedestal base, impressed with Roseville 28.00 34.00

Price Range

☐ **Vase,** *shape #796, 8-1/2", tan, with two supporting pieces at the base that look like nails, cylindrical with a rounded bottom above a small pedestal base, impressed with Roseville* **45.00**   **50.00**

MORNING GLORY *(Introduced 1935)*

Lightly embossed designs of morning glory flowers and vines cover almost all surface areas on these pieces. The flowers are yellow and pink or lilac, with mint green leaves and brown tints to the vines.

☐ **Basket,** *10-1/2", ivory background, with one oval handle, spherical shape with a flaired rim and small circular base, paper label, silver* **225.00**   **285.00**
☐ **Bowl,** *4", ivory background, with two small handles, bulbous body, with a short neck, paper label, gold* **115.00**   **140.00**
☐ **Console,** *4-1/2", aqua background, with two small handles, spherical shape with rim curved inward, and on a small base, no mark* **140.00**   **170.00**
☐ **Pot,** *5", aqua background, with two small handles, bell shape, with a flair at the rim, no mark* **115.00**   **140.00**
☐ **Vase,** *8", ivory background, with two handles, urn shape, paper label, gold* **140.00**   **170.00**

MOSS *(Introduced 1930's)*

Hanging moss droops over branches and leaves on monotone backgrounds of various colors: variations: natural green moss and leaves on tan-green, green and yellow on tan, pink and green on turquoise, green, yellow and blue on a pink shading to blue background.

☐ **Candlestick,** *shape #1104, 2", ball holder on a flat circular base, impressed with Roseville* **17.50**   **22.50**
☐ **Console,** *3" x 13", with two handles, oblong, with a rippled rim, impressed with Roseville* **55.00**   **65.00**
☐ **Urn,** *shape #290, 6", with two small handles, spherical on a small base, impressed with Roseville* **55.00**   **65.00**

MOSTIQUE *(Introduced 1915)*

Indian-like incised designs appear on simple shapes with roughly textured backgrounds. The designs and the linings of pieces are glossy. Some rare pieces are glossy all over; variations: colors range from white, tan, green, yellow, to royal blue and turquoise.

☐ **Bowl,** *2-1/2", blue, white, red and green design, with solid blue lining, shallow bowl, with the rim curved inward, no mark* **25.00**   **30.00**
☐ **Bowl,** *3-1/2" x 9", brown horizontal bands, with white and blue accents, with two handles, shallow bowl, cylindrical from the base, no mark* .... **50.00**   **65.00** •
☐ **Jardiniere,** *8", tan and brown lines and stylized flowers, uniform widening from the base to the rim, with the rim curved inward, no mark* **75.00**   **85.00**

Price Range

☐ **Jardiniere**, *10", mottled colors of yellow, red and blue making geometric designs, with two pinch handles, urn shape, with a flaired rim, no mark* 85.00   100.00

☐ **Vase**, *10", yellow, green and blue arrow designs, with solid green lining, cylindrical, with a flaired base and rim, no mark* . 28.00   34.00

OLD IVORY *(Introduced 1910-1915)*

Detailed designs sculptured into bands on all white or ivory items. Many times, these were just white duplicates of designs produced in green matte glaze. (Also called Ivory Frieze)

☐ **Humidor**, *6", light blue tint, with a lid, spherical shape on a small base, no mark* 140.00   170.00

☐ **Double bud vase**, *5-1/2", detailed design of a gateway, with double doors and brick columns with two bells, rectangular vases, no mark* 85.00   95.00

☐ **Jardiniere**, *9", embossed panorama of Greek figures, with detailed design above and below the scene, cylindrical, no mark* 280.00   340.00

☐ **Tankard**, *13-1/2", pink tint, detailed scroll work one handle, cylindrical, with slight narrowing at the rim, no mark* 280.00   340.00

ORIAN *(Introduced 1935)*

Many different shapes are finished in high gloss glaze, often two-tone, with very little trim. Handles are generally slender and blending into the base; variations: color combinations are turquoise and orange, yellow and green, tan and turquoise.

☐ **Bowl**, *6", blue with yellow lining, with two handles, spherical shape, on small pedestal base, paper label, gold* 70.00   80.00

☐ **Candleholder**, *4-1/2", turquoise, with two handles, cylindrical shape, rounding at the bottom above a small flat circular base, no mark* 55.00   65.00

☐ **Vase**, *8", turquoise with yellow lining, with two handles, blubous base, narrowing to a cylindrical neck, paper label* 60.00   75.00

☐ **Vase**, *12-1/2", rose, with blue accents, with two handles, bulbous body on a small pedestal base, with long neck, no mark* . 140.00   170.00

PANEL *(Introduced 1920)*

Decorative embossed designs are displayed on sections of panels. Designs show influence of Art Nouveau and Art Deco styles. Round specimens have four panels, items with flat sides have two, wall pockets have one: variations: colors are dark green or brown with a lighter shade to highlight the design.

☐ **Vase**, *6", orange, with nude design, flat bell shape, on a round pedestal base, RV stamped in ink* 115.00   140.00

☐ **Vase**, *6", orange, with flower design, with two small handles, flat round shape, RV stamped in ink* 50.00   55.00

☐ **Vase**, *8", green, with two pinch handles, widening from base to rim, also flairs at the base, RV stamped in ink* 45.00   55.00

Price Range

☐ **Vase,** *8", green, with nude design, flat fan shape, on a tall pedestal base, RV stamped in ink* 115.00   140.00

PASADENA PLANTER *(Introduced 1952)*

High gloss trim of white drizzling glaze over a matte glaze of various colors. The drizzling glaze creates an effect like oil and water; variations: colors for backgrounds may be black, blue, green and rose.

☐ **Bowl,** *3", rose, round with flaired rim, marked Roseville, Pasadena Planter in relief* 35.00   40.00
☐ **Flower pot,** *shape #L36, 4", rose, square, with rounded corners and base, marked Roseville, Pasadena Planter in relief* 35.00   40.00
☐ **Planter,** *shape #L17, 3-1/2", blue, rectangular, marked Roseville Pasadena Planter in releif* 40.00   45.00

PAULEO *(Introduced 1914)*

Two types of glazes were used to finish these pieces, a continuous luster tone and a marbelized finish with cracks and veins. Both finishes were produced in over two hundred colors and in eighteen shapes.

☐ **Vase,** *9", brown, egg shape with a small mouth, no mark* 500.00   565.00
☐ **Vase,** *14", rose, with painted flower, egg shape, no mark* 900.00   1000.00
☐ **Vase,** *16-1/2", mottled rose shades, tall bulbous shape, no mark* 625.00   675.00
☐ **Vase,** *17", blue with a stylized flower, outlined in black, urn shape, narrowing at the neck and flairing at the rim, no mark* . .   1250.00   1350.00
☐ **Vase,** *18-1/2", rose, bulbous shape, narrowing slightly at the rim, Pauleo seal* 1250.00   1350.00
☐ **Vase,** *19", purple base blending into ivory, with a stylized flower design, bulbous shape, narrowing slightly at the neck, no mark* 1250.00   1350.00

PEONY *(Introduced 1942)*

Large peony flowers are embossed on swirling textured backgrounds; variations: colored combinations possible are yellow blossoms on gold, beige and rose, ivory-tan on pink and blue or turquoise.

☐ **Basket,** *shape #378, 10", gold, with one handle, bell shape, with exaggerated flair and uneven rim, marked Roseville in relief* 55.00   65.00
☐ **Bookend,** *shape #11, 5-1/2", turquoise, L shape, marked Roseville in relief* 25.00   30.00
☐ **Ewer,** *shape #8, 10", pink and turquoise, with one handle, bulbous base with narrow neck and spout, marked Roseville in relief* 75.00   85.00
☐ **Planter,** *shape #387, 10", rose and blue, rectangular with uneven rim, marked Roseville in relief* 28.00   34.00
☐ **Vase,** *shape #169, 8", gold, with two handles, urn shape on small pedestal base, marked Roseville in relief* 45.00   50.00

PERSIAN (Introduced 1916)

Creamware with stylized flowers and leaves or geometric shapes. The designs are in bright colors, such as green, red, blue, yellow, and outlined in black. Simple shapes with simple trim.

	Price Range	
☐ **Bowl,** 3-1/2", with three finger handles, shallow, with the rim curved inward, no mark	75.00	85.00
☐ **Jardiniere,** 5", cylindrical with pronounced rim and base, marked with Roseville Pottery, Zanesville, O" in ink	170.00	200.00
☐ **Sugar bowl,** 4", with lid and two handles, four-sided, no mark .	40.00	45.00

PINE CONE (Introduced 1931)

Embossed pine cones and slender needles extend from branches which form handles on matte finish backgrounds of earth tones; variations: colors of backgrounds are green, blue with orange lining, golden brown with green lining.

☐ **Bowl,** shape #320, 4-1/2", golden brown, with two handles, plain shape, impressed with Roseville	35.00	40.00
☐ **Cornucopia,** shape #126, 6", blue, on asymmetrical base, with a branch as support, impressed with Roseville	40.00	45.00
☐ **Mug,** shape #960, 4", golden brown, with one handle, simple shape, marked Roseville in relief	50.00	55.00
☐ **Urn,** shape #745, 7", blue, with two handles, simple shape on a square base, impressed with Roseville	55.00	65.00
☐ **Vase,** shape #747, 10-1/2", green, with two handles and two decorative supports, bell shape on a round pedestal base, impressed with Roseville	55.00	65.00

POPPY (Introduced 1930)

A bright pink poppy blossom with a large green leaf is embossed into a textured background of vertical swirling grooves. The line is noted for cut-outs in the rims which are also rippled, themselves, like the outline of a flower; variations: colors of background include pink and blue.

☐ **Basket,** shape #347, 10", with one circular handle with rolled ends where they connect, on a round base, impessed with Roseville	60.00	70.00
☐ **Ewer,** shape #880, 18-1/2", one handle with rolled ends, bulbous body on a round pedestal base, impressed with Roseville	175.00	200.00
☐ **Jardiniere,** shape #335, 6-1/2", with two small circular handles, spherical, impressed with Roseville	50.00	60.00
☐ **Vase,** shape #872, 9", with two small handles, bulbous body, narrowing at the neck, impressed with Roseville	55.00	65.00

RAYMOR (Introduced 1952)

Utility items and dinnerware in futuristic designs and bright colors. Plates and platters are oval with finger pinches on two edges, bowls, cups and pitchers are rounded; variations: colors include tan, gray, green, ivory, orange, black, and brown.

Price Range

☐ **Casserole,** *shape #183, 11" wide, with lid, black, marked Raymor by Roseville, U.S.A. in relief* 28.00   34.00

☐ **Cup and saucer,** *shape #151, brown cup and white saucer, marked Raymor by Roseville, U.S.A. in relief* 12.00   18.00

☐ **Gravy boat,** *shape #190, 9-1/2", brown, marked Raymor by Roseville, U.S.A. in relief* 12.00   18.00

☐ **Plate, salad,** *shape #154, brown, marked Raymor by Roseville, U.S.A. in relief* 6.50   10.00

☐ **Plate, dinner,** *shape #152, white, marked Raymor by Roseville, U.S.A. in relief* 10.00   12.00

ROSECRAFT *(Introduced 1916)*

Classic and usually untrimmed shapes produced in many bright colors; variations: green, orange, yellow and blue.

☐ **Bowl,** *5", blue, with two small handles, round with pronounced rim and base, RV stamped in ink* 50.00   55.00

☐ **Bud vase,** *8", yellow, cylindrical, slender on a small round pedestal base, RV stamped in ink* 50.00   55.00

☐ **Vase,** *13-1/2", blue, with two small pointed handles, urn shape, marked with paper label* 140.00   170.00

ROSECRAFT BLACK *(Introduced 1916)*

Classic in shape and usually untrimmed, this line was produced in a high gloss glaze making the complete object black. It is one of only two lines that was made in black and it is very rare.

☐ **Bowl,** *3", shallow, curving at the rim, no mark* 55.00   65.00

☐ **Jar,** *8", with lid, urn shape, classic, marked with paper label* . .   175.00   225.00

☐ **Vase,** *10", with decorative handles, urn shape with long neck and flaired rim, no mark* 115.00   140.00

☐ **Vase,** *13-1/2", classic vase shape with narrow mouth, marked with paper label* 140.00   170.00

ROSECRAFT HEXAGON *(Introduced 1924)*

Hexagonal, or six-sided, shaped in different color combinations with other Rosecraft characteristics of basic design untrimmed; variations: colors include brown with orange lining, green with yellow lining and blue, some pieces have a circular motif on one panel in the same color as the lining.

☐ **Bowl,** *4", brown, orange, urn shape, RV stamped in ink* 55.00   65.00

☐ **Vase,** *5", blue, urn shape, RV stamped in ink* 115.00   140.00

☐ **Vase,** *5", brown, orange, urn shape, RV stamped in ink* 70.00   85.00

☐ **Vase,** *6", brown, orange, with two squared off handles, cylindrical, with a slight flair at the lower half, RV stamped in ink* . .   50.00   55.00

ROSECRAFT VINTAGE *(Introduced 1924)*

Classic shapes with a band of design that circles each piece. The band is formed out of twining vines, leaves and berries which are a lighter color than the background; variations: backgrounds are usually dark brown, but others have been found with dark purple and charcoal, almost black.

Price Range

- [ ] **Bowl,** *3", simple shape, with pronounced rim, RV stamped in ink* 35.00 45.00
- [ ] **Bowl,** *3-1/2", shallow, with pronounced rim, RV stamped in ink* 28.00 34.00
- [ ] **Jardiniere,** *9", spherical, RV stamped in ink* 90.00 115.00
- [ ] **Urn,** *10", egg shape, narrowing to a small mouth, RV stamped in ink* 70.00 80.00
- [ ] **Vase,** *4", with two small finger handles, egg shape, narrowing at the neck, RV stamped in ink* 40.00 50.00
- [ ] **Vase,** *6", egg shape, narrowing into a small mouth, RV stamped in ink* 55.00 65.00

ROZANE *(Introduced 1900)*

High gloss finish with underglaze decoration of many different kinds; florals, animals, leaves, landscapes. The backgrounds are usually dark brown or burnt orange. When the general characteristics were changed, the name of the line was changed; variations of Rozane exist under other line names.

- [ ] **Bowl,** *shape #927, 2-1/2", leaf design, marked ROZANE RPC...* 115.00 140.00
- [ ] **Candlestick,** *9", floral design, tall pedestal base with a flat rim, with ROZANE WARE seal* 175.00 200.00
- [ ] **Bud vase,** *shape #915, 6-1/2", floral design, bulbous base with a long slender neck, marked ROZANE RPCo* 175.00 200.00
- [ ] **Mug,** *shape #856, 4-1/2", design of nursery rhyme Three Men in a Tub, cylindrical, with a flaired base, stamped ROZANE RPCo* 200.00 225.00
- [ ] **Tankard,** *14", with handle and spout, cylindrical, with a flaired base, with ROZANE WARE seal* 285.00 310.00
- [ ] **Vase,** *shape #821, 9-1/2", floral design, egg shape with narrow neck and turned out rim, marked ROZANE RPCo* 175.00 200.00
- [ ] **Vase,** *shape #891, 14", Indian head design, egg shape with a narrowed neck, stamped ROZANE RPCo* 3000.00 3500.00
- [ ] **Vase,** *15", cluster of grapes and leaves, urn shape, with very narrow and longer neck, with ROZANE WARE seal, initialled L.M.* 350.00 400.00

ROZANE MARA *(Introduced 1904)*

Simple designed shapes with little trim, noted for its metallic iridescent luster. Some pieces may have a design of detailed squiggling lines within its shiny surface, but backgrounds are blendings of colors, mainly deep maroon or magenta, some rare pieces may be gray or opal.

- [ ] **Vase,** *5-1/2", with two handles, urn shape, narrowing below the rim at the neck, no mark* 3000.00 2500.00
- [ ] **Vase,** *5-1/2", with two small circular handles, pear shape, with small mouth, no mark* 2750.00 3000.00
- [ ] **Vase,** *13", cylindrical, flairing slightly below the rim, no mark* . 1450.00 1750.00

ROZANE MONGOL *(Introduced 1904)*

Oriental shapes those which are smooth and have no trim are glazed with a very high gloss bright red. These specimens sometimes have delicate silver overlay to add to its design.

Price Range

☐ **Vase, 5",** *bulbous body on a small round base, narrows at the neck and then flairs at the rim, marked with Rozane Mongol seal* 600.00   700.00

☐ **Vase, 7",** *bulbous shape, narrowing at the neck then flairing just below the rim, marked with Rozane Ware seal* 900.00   1000.00

☐ **Vase, 10-1/2",** *cylindrical, with a slight narrowing at the rim and base, no mark* 900.00   1000.00

ROZANE OLYMPIC *(Introduced 1905)*

Greek figures of ivory, outlined in black are the design on a red background. A band of ivory and black design circles the rim and base. Handles are usually black.

☐ **Pitcher, 7",** *design of Pandora being brought to Earth, spherical shape, marked ROZANE POTTERY stamped in ink* 2250.00   2500.00

☐ **Vase, 14-1/2",** *three large thick feet, design of Persia and Ionia Yoked to the Chariot of Xesxes, urn shape, with a cylindrical neck, marked ROZANE POTTERY stamped in ink* 4500.00   5000.00

ROZANE ROYAL *(Introduced 1904)*

Underglaze decoration on high gloss finishes. The name was changed to Rozane Royal when lighter shade backgrounds were added to the Rozane line. Many colors and designs were used, but most were flowers and clusters of fruit on backgrounds which blend from a light shade to a darker shade of a color, or from ivory to another color.

☐ **Bowl, 5",** *large leaf design, spherical, on a small base, with the rim curved inward, no mark* 175.00   200.00

☐ **Jardiniere, 5",** *floral design, spherical, on a three footed base, no mark* 140.00   170.00

☐ **Mug, 5",** *floral design, with one handle, cylindrical, with a slight flair at the base, marked M.T.* 255.00   285.00

☐ **Sugar bowl, 4-1/2",** *small white floral design, with lid and two handles, cylindrical, no mark* 225.00   250.00

☐ **Tankard, 11",** *grapes, leaves and vines design, with one handle, cylindrical, flairing at the base, marked with Rozanne Royal seal* 450.00   500.00

☐ **Vase, 6-1/2",** *leaf and holly berry design, pear shape, marked with Rozane Royal seal* 285.00   310.00

☐ **Vase, 11",** *lilac floral design, lighthouse shape, marked with Rozane Royal seal* 285.00   310.00

RUSSCO *(Introduced 1920's)*

Narrow vertical shapes with a pedestal base. Many have octagonal shapes. The simple design on each is several vertical embossed lines which also extend the length of the piece (vertically); variations: colors include many combinations of gold and green, ivory and gold, orange and gold, or one color of turquoise, green or yellow.

☐ **Bud vase, 8",** *yellow, with two small handles, tall tulip shape on a round pedestal base, marked with paper label, gold* 55.00   65.00

Price Range

☐ **Vase,** *12-1/2", yellow and green, bulbous shape, on a round pedestal base, marked with paper label, gold* 85.00   100.00

SILHOUETTE *(Introduced 1952)*

Art Deco shapes, many of which are rectangular which form flat sides or panels. On these panels are silhouettes of flowers, leaves or nude figures with the area behind the figure recessed and textured. Details are only lightly impressed into the figures; variations: colors include maroon, mint green, tan, blue, turquoise and white figures on turquoise which is very rare.

☐ **Basket,** *shape #708, 6", turquoise, with a spade shaped handle, with a floral design, bell shape on a small pedestal base, marked Roseville in relief* 35.00   40.00
☐ **Cornucopia,** *shape #721, 8", white, with a leaf design, mouth opens upwards, marked Roseville in relief* 28.00   34.00
☐ **Ewer,** *shape #717, 10", tan, with floral panels, evenly narrows towards the neck, marked Roseville in relief* 50.00   55.00
☐ **Vase,** *shape #783, 7", turquoise, with a nude design, fan shape, with a rippled rim, on a tall decorative pedestal base, marked Roseville in relief* 95.00   110.00

SNOWBERRY *(Introduced 1946)*

White clusters of berries with scattered leaves are embossed on satin matte finish backgrounds. The shapes are somewhat stylized with many pieces having geometric or pointed handles. A simple semi-circular pattern is incised behind the design; variations: colors include blue with pink accents, green with tan accents, and deep pink with light pink accents.

☐ **Bowl,** *shape #1RB, 5", green, with two pointed handles, spherical with a rippled rim, marked Roseville in relief* 35.00   40.00
☐ **Cornucopia,** *shape #1CC, 6", blue, on an asymmetrical base, mouth opens upwards, marked Roseville in relief* 28.00   34.00
☐ **Ewer,** *shape #1TK, 16", green, with one handle, cylindrical with rounded ends on a pedestal base, marked Roseville in relief* . .   85.00   100.00
☐ **Tray,** *shape #1BL, 14", pink, with one handle, leaf shape, very shallow, marked Roseville in relief* 45.00   55.00
☐ **Vase,** *shape #1UR, 8-1/2", blue, with two pointed handles, chalice shape, on a pedestal base, marked Roseville in relief* .   45.00   50.00

SUNFLOWER *(Introduced 1930)*

Long-stemmed sunflowers circle in a vertical pattern on simply shaped pieces. The flowers are embossed and colored yellow with green leaves and stems on a mottled and blending green to brown matte background.

☐ **Urn,** *4", with two small handles, spherical, no mark* 45.00   50.00
☐ **Urn,** *7", spherical, no mark* 75.00   85.00
☐ **Vase,** *6", with two pointed handles, cylindrical, marked with paper label* 50.00   55.00
☐ **Vase,** *8", with two small handles, egg shape with flaired rim, marked with paper label* 70.00   80.00

Price Range

☐ **Window box,** *3-1/2" x 11", with two handles, rectangular, no mark* 85.00   100.00

TEASEL *(Introduced 1936)*

Lightly embossed long stems of a teasel weed are the design on this line. The shapes are traditional with little trim other than the design; variations: the matte finish background comes with a variety of colors, such as blue, green, deep rose, ivory, turquoise and combinations of each.

☐ **Vase,** *5", blue, with two handles, urn shape, impressed mark Roseville* 28.00   34.00
☐ **Vase,** *shape #882, 6", orange, with two pinch handles and small cut-outs in the rim, cylindrical on a round base, impressed mark Roseville* 28.00   34.00
☐ **Vase,** *shape #888, 12", rose, with two small pinch handles and cut-outs circle the rim, bell shape on a pedestal base, impressed mark Roseville* 75.00   85.00

THORN APPLE *(Introduced 1930's)*

On one side of the matte background is an embossed design of a white cone-shaped blossom and leaves, on the other a green prickly pod; variations: background colors include blending of orange and tan, pink and green, and turquoise and blue.

☐ **Cornucopia,** *6", pink and green, mouth opens upwards, impressed mark Roseville* 28.00   34.00
☐ **Planter,** *5", orange and tan, with two small handles, cylindrical on a round base, impressed mark Roseville* 45.00   50.00
☐ **Vase,** *shape #308, 4", orange, with two small pointed handles, inkwell shape, impressed mark Roseville* 35.00   40.00
☐ **Vase,** *shape #820, orange and tan, with two pointed handles, egg shape, impressed mark Roseville* 55.00   65.00

TOPEO *(Introduced 1937)*

Four evenly spaced high relief cones of trim extends downward. The trim is made up of rounded balls which decrease in size until it forms a point at the bottom of each cone; variations: color combinations include mottled blue and light green with pink highlights and bright red or mahogany in a very high gloss.

☐ **Bowl,** *2-1/2", red, shallow bowl, marked with paper label* 85.00   100.00
☐ **Bowl,** *4" high, 13" wide, red, rippled sides, and uneven rim, marked with paper label* 150.00   175.00
☐ **Urn,** *6", blue, simple shape, marked with paper label* 85.00   100.00
☐ **Urn,** *6", red, simple shape, marked with paper label* 150.00   175.00
☐ **Vase,** *9-1/2", red, elongated urn shape, marked with paper label* 150.00   175.00
☐ **Vase,** *15", red, cylindrical, with pronounced rim, marked with paper label* 285.00   340.00

TOURMALINE *(Introduced 1933)*

Simple shapes with little or no trim are covered in mottled shades or a blending of two colors. The finishes vary with some pieces having a satin matte finish and others with high gloss finish or just spots of high gloss finish; variations: colors include blue and gold, rose and gray, tan and yellow, turquoise and brown.

	Price Range	
☐ **Bowl,** *8" wide, pink and blue, shallow, with flaired rim, on a small base, marked with paper label, silver*	50.00	60.00
☐ **Vase,** *5-1/2", tan, with two handles, urn shape, narrowing at the neck, marked with paper label, sliver*	55.00	65.00
☐ **Vase,** *7-1/2", turquoise, with small band of decorative embossing at the rim, square sides, flairing evenly to the rim, marked with paper label, silver*	50.00	55.00
☐ **Vase,** *8", blue, with embossed design, with two pinch handles, cylindrical, marked with paper label, silver*	50.00	55.00
☐ **Vase,** *10", turquoise, with embossed circle design, six-sided, marked with paper label, silver*	60.00	75.00

TUSCANY *(Introduced 1927)*

Mottled colors in a matte glaze on simple shapes with little trim. Slight outlines of leaves and some kind of berry fruit can be found at the base of rounded handles; variations: background colors include mottled pink, mint green and gray.

☐ **Candleholder,** *4", gray, with two handles that connect on the base, simple holder on a round small pedestal base, no mark* .	35.00	40.00
☐ **Console,** *11" wide, pink, two square sides, two round sides, shallow, no mark*	40.00	45.00
☐ **Vase,** *6", pink, with two circular handles, egg shape, no mark* .	35.00	40.00
☐ **Vase,** *8", pink, with blue accents on two handles, urn shape, narrowing at the neck, no mark*	40.00	45.00

VELMOSS *(Introduced 1935)*

Green slender leaves extend over the rim of traditional shapes with very little trim. Around the neck of each item appears three rippled lines in the otherwise smooth satin matte finish; variations: background colors include blue, red, rose, green, turquoise and tan.

☐ **Vase,** *6", blue, with two pointed handles, cylindrical with slight flair at the neck, marked with paper label, gold*	45.00	50.00
☐ **Vase,** *8", turquoise, with two pointed handles, cylindrical, narrowing at the base and rim, marked with paper label, gold*	50.00	55.00
☐ **Vase,** *9", green, with two pointed handles, bulbous base, with narrowing at the neck, marked with paper label, gold*	65.00	75.00

VELMOSS SCHROLL *(Introduced 1916)*

Incised stylized designs of roses, leaves and stems on creamware. Colors are added to the incised designs, but only in the etched out areas. Roses are red, leaves are green, and the stems are brown.

Price Range

☐ **Bowl,** *2-1/2", 9" wide, disc shape, narrowing at the neck, with a pronounced rim and base, no mark* 40.00   45.00
☐ **Vase,** *6", cylindrical, on a small base, no mark* 45.00   50.00
☐ **Vase,** *8", urn shape, with narrowing at the neck, no mark* 55.00   65.00
☐ **Vase,** *12", bulbous shape, no mark* 100.00   115.00

VICTORIAN ART POTTERY *(Introduced 1924)*

Matte or semi-gloss finish is characteristic of this line of very simple shapes with little or no trim or design.

☐ **Jar,** *8", blue, with leaves and berries design, egg shape, marked RV stamped in ink* 200.00   225.00
☐ **Urn,** *4", brown and orange, with flowers and leaves design, urn shape, with narrowing at the neck, no mark* 85.00   100.00
☐ **Urn,** *10", brown and orange, with flowers and leaves design, urn shape, with narrowing at the neck, marked RV stamped in ink* 175.00   200.00
☐ **Vase,** *6", blue, with leaves and berries design, urn shape, with narrowing at the neck, no mark* 90.00   100.00

VOLPATO *(Introduced 1918)*

Some pieces are characterized by vertical ribbing, with drooping garlands of greenery draped around each piece. Elaborate lids with ribbing and pedestal bases also are characteristics of this line. Some pieces, though, do not follow the line, either they don't have the greenery or the ribbing. Colors are ivory or light green.

☐ **Console,** *4", two handles that connect on the underneath side of the bowl, exaggerated bell shape on a small round pedestal base, no mark* 140.00   170.00
☐ **Window box,** *9" wide, rectangular with pronounced rim, no mark* 85.00   100.00

WATER LILY *(Introduced 1916)*

A large embossed water lily rests on a huge green lily pad. The embossed design forms a contrast against a rippled textured background; variations: color combinations include yellow lilies on golden brown, pink on rose and green, and white blossoms on blue.

☐ **Bowl,** *shape #663, 3", brown, with two handles, spherical, narrowing slightly at the neck, marked Roseville in relief* 25.00   30.00
☐ **Cornucopia,** *shape #178, 8", pink and blue, mouth opens upwards, marked Roseville in relief* 40.00   45.00
☐ **Ewer,** *shape #12, 15", brown and orange, with one handle and small cut-outs in the neck, bulbous base on a round pedestal base, narrows at the neck, marked Roseville in relief* 110.00   125.00
☐ **Vase,** *shape #72, 6", blue, with two large handles, cylindrical, flairing at the rim, marked Roseville in relief* 28.00   34.00
☐ **Vase,** *shape #75, 7", green and tan, with two pointed handles, cylindrical, with a flaired base, marked Roseville in relief* 35.00   40.00

WHITE ROSE *(Introduced 1940's)*

One white rose on a sprig of green leaves is embossed on a satin matte finish with a slight textured pattern; variations: background colors include a mixture of green and pink, green and brown, and various shades of blue.

Price Range

☐ **Basket,** *shape #362, 7-1/2", brown, with spade shaped handle, disc shape bowl, marked Roseville in relief* 55.00   65.00
☐ **Bowl,** *shape #387, 4", green and rose, with two handles, spherical, marked Roseville in relief* 30.00   35.00
☐ **Ewer,** *shape #993, blue, with one handle and small cut-outs in the neck, bulbous base, with slender neck, marked Roseville in relief* 85.00   100.00
☐ **Urn,** *shape #147, 8", brown and green, with two handles, urn shape on a small pedestal base, marked Roseville in relief* . . . 50.00   55.00
☐ **Vase,** *shape #991, 12-1/2", blue, with two handles and small cut-outs in the rim, urn shape, marked Roseville in relief* 85.00   100.00
☐ **Vase,** *shape #992, 15-1/2", blue, with two handles and small cut-outs in the rim, bulbous base, narrowing at the neck slightly, marked Roseville in relief* 85.00   100.00

WINCRAFT *(Introduced 1948)*

Many different designs are used on the Wincraft lines in many different colors. The name describes the shapes which are Art Deco basically with floral or other figures embossed designs; variations: the high gloss glaze includes colors such as bright yellows, green, turquoise and orange.

☐ **Basket,** *shape #208, 8", yellow, with asymmetrical handle, cracked egg shape, marked Roseville in relief* 40.00   45.00
☐ **Candleholder,** *shape #2CS, 2", blue, round holder on a square base, marked Roseville in relief* 14.00   17.00
☐ **Cornucopia,** *shape #222, 8", yellow on a brown base, mouth opens upwards, marked Roseville in relief* 30.00   35.00
☐ **Mug,** *4-1/2", turquoise, with one handle, simple shape, marked Roseville in relief* 45.00   50.00
☐ **Vase,** *shape #282, 8", turquoise, on a small asymmetrical base, shaped like a flower blossom, marked Roseville in relief* 40.00   45.00
☐ **Vase,** *shape #290, 10", turquoise, with two pinch handles, cylindrical, with slight narrowing at the neck, marked Roseville in relief* 150.00   175.00

WINDSOR *(Introduced 1931)*

Impressionistic ferns, floral patterns or geometric designs are slightly impressed into a mottled blue or beige-brown background. The designs are lightly colored and appear faint next to the satin matte finish on each piece.

☐ **Bowl,** *3-1/2", orange, with two pointed handles, exaggerated bell shape, no mark* 85.00   100.00
☐ **Console,** *16" wide, orange, with two pointed handles, oblong, marked with paper label, silver* 140.00   170.00
☐ **Vase,** *5", blue, with fern pattern, with two handles, urn shape, narrowing at the neck, marked with paper label, silver* 55.00   65.00

Price Range

☐ **Vase**, *7", orange, with two circular handles, urn shape, narrowing at the neck, marked with paper label, silver* 200.00   225.00

WISTERIA *(Introduced 1933)*

Drooping clusters of wisteria blossoms and leaves drape across the tops of each item. Backgrounds are textured tan with drizzled colors that deepen in hue at the base; variations: drizzling colors may be blue, brown, green and yellow and combinations of these.

☐ **Urn**, *7-1/2", blue, with two small finger handles, spherical, marked with paper label, silver* 75.00   85.00
☐ **Vase**, *6", yellow, with two handles, pear shape, marked with paper label, silver* 60.00   75.00
☐ **Vase**, *8", blue, with two pointed handles, gradually narrows from the base to the rim, marked with paper label, silver* 95.00   110.00
☐ **Vase**, *10", yellow, with two pointed handles, cylindrical, slightly narrowing at the rim, marked with paper label, silver* 95.00   110.00

WOODLAND *(Introduced 1905)*

Non-gloss finish bisque backgrounds with high gloss enamel colors on flowers. The realistic design of the flowers have incised outlines. Colors and kinds of flowers vary.

☐ **Vase**, *6-1/2", large floral design, cylindrical shape, flairing at the neck, then narrowing to a small opening, marked with ROZANE WARE seal* 450.00   500.00
☐ **Vase**, *7", floral design, bulbous shape, narrowing to a very small opening, marked with ROZANE WARE Woodland seal* . .   450.00   500.00
☐ **Vase**, *9", detailed geometric design, bulbous base, narrowing uniformly to the rim, marked with ROZANE WARE Woodland seal* 625.00   675.00
☐ **Vase**, *15", floral design with long thin leaves, urn shape, marked with ROZANE WARE Woodland seal* 900.00   1000.00
☐ **Vase**, *19", large floral design, elongated urn shape, marked with ROZANE WARE Woodland seal* 1400.00   1700.00

ZEPHYR LILY *(Introduced 1946)*

One or two lilies are embossed in high relief on various shades of blended backgrounds. The backgrounds are textured with incised circular patterns, as long slender leaves accent the length or width of each item; variations: color combinations include tan and green, ivory and green or turquoise, various shades of blue.

☐ **Basket**, *shape #393, 7", blue, with one thick handle, spherical on small pedestal base, marked Roseville in relief* 45.00   50.00
☐ **Bowl**, *shape #671, 4", orange, with two handles, spherical, marked Roseville in relief* 28.00   34.00
☐ **Ewer**, *shape #24, 15", green, with one handle, bulbous shape on small base, narrow neck, marked Roseville in relief* 95.00   105.00
☐ **Hanging basket**, *7-1/2", with two handles, three pierced holes for hanging, acorn shape, marked Roseville in relief* 50.00   60.00

	Price Range	
☐ **Tray**, 14-1/2", blue, shaped like a leaf, marked Roseville in relief	45.00	50.00
☐ **Vase**, shape #137, 10", blue, with two handles, bulbous base, narrowing at the neck, and flairing at the rim, marked Roseville in relief	50.00	55.00

ROUSE PARIAN

No information is available about this recent Trenton company except that it is basically a one-man operation. Rouse made small ornamental items of parian, including a popular figurine of John-John Kennedy.

Marks: The word Rouse
Prices: Under $50 for most items.

SALEM CHINA COMPANY

Salem China Company was one of the more prolific manufacturers of dinnerware, beginning around 1920. The firm originated earlier, but its pioneer years saw slow growth and little recognition. Once it became firmly established in the dinnerware trade, Salem concentrated on the middle-income market and frequently introduced new lines to maintain public interest. It sold whiteware, creamware, and solid-color patterns, as well as a great variety of shapes. Most of the color-decorated patterns featured floral sprays or arrangements. Some merely had borders of lacy vines or patterns formed by berries and nuts. Brightly colored birds were occasionally used placed delicately on the rims of dishes. Even less frequently, you may find pictures of figures attired in colonial or early post-colonial costumes. The colonial theme was a natural for this company. Salem, Ohio (its headquarters) had been named for Salem, Massachusetts — one of the puritan colonies in the 1600's. In fact, the likeness of a woman wearing a colonial-style bonnet was incorporated into one of the company's trademarks.

The Salem China Company started up in 1898, a three-way partnership between Daniel Cronin, Biddam Smith and John McNichol. All had previously been employed by the Standard Pottery Company of East Liverpool, Ohio. With so many potteries crowding into East Liverpool, they felt that the future of Ohio's pottery industry lay elsewhere and saw Salem as a potential boom town. Things did not quite turn out that way, but the Salem China Company proved successful. It had some tough times in the years around World War I, but business improved in the 1920's. Salem made effective use of advertising and succeeded in having its wares distributed by the giant mail-order houses and also for use as promotional giveaways. The innovativeness of this company is probably most evident in its square plates and even more so in its "Tricorne" wares — plates and saucers with three sides.

Marks: As already mentioned, the head of a colonial maiden wearing a bonnet was sometimes incorporated into the Salem mark. It was usually accompanied by a banner and the wording SALEM CHINA CO., SALEM, OHIO, MADE IN U.S.A. Another mark, for the "Symphony" line of dinnerware, featured a musical note and several bars, along with the notation WARRANTED

23 KARAT GOLD. This referred to the gold gilding around the rims of plates and saucers. A similar mark reads WARRANTED PLATINUM GOLD ALLOY, MADE IN AMERICA, accompanied by a medal like design bearing the company's name and address.

SANITARY EARTHENWARE SPECIALTY COMPANY

Sanitary was founded in 1897 by Thomas Swetman and Arthur Plantier for the production of sanitary items.

Marks: Not known
Prices: A three-piece miniature bathroom set can be figured at around $50.

SCAMMELL

Scammell came along considerably later than many of the other companies listed here, but they did produce at least a few items which are of interest to collectors. DeVegh designed many of their Art Deco figurines, as he was also to do for Lenox, and the Scammell ones are quite a bit rarer than the Lenox ones. The company also made a great number of commemorative items, particularly plates. The overwhelming majority of their pieces, however, are lower level dinnerware items.

Marks: Most of their marks incorporated the word Scammell in one way or another. Marks can be either printed or impressed.

	Price Range	
☐ **Figurine,** seated woman, marked and signed DeVegh, looks for all the world like Lenox china	150.00	175.00
Note: This price is three years old, and we have not seen a Scammell figurine sold since then. It is our feeling that the Scammell ones should probably keep pace with the comparable Lenox items.		
☐ **Horn-of-plenty centerpiece,** undecorated, marked Scammell and signed DeVegh	80.00	95.00
☐ **Plate,** commemoration of George Washington's 200th birthday, cobalt transfer decoration, 10-1/2" diameter	60.00	70.00

Lower-level wares are typically sold in the 50¢ to $1.00 range in the Trenton area. They are just too new common yet to bring much more than that.

SHAWNEE POTTERY COMPANY

Many beginning colletors are introduced to art pottery through the works of Shawnee. The Shawnee crerations, made in large quantities in the 1940's and 1950's, were a kind of inexpensive substitute for art pottery for those who could not afford the real thing. It is understandably abundant in today's collector shops and the current enthusiasm for it belies its humble origins. While the Shawnee products may not be equal in quality to their more prestigious contemporaries, the passage of time has given them a certain magic. Many of these pieces have a definite "art deco" flavor. They include figureware and novelties of various kinds. Shawnee Pottery Company sold its wares through the major department and variety stores throughout the country from the 1940's up into the 1950's. They were also used at carnivals and as advertising premiums.

The Shawnee Pottery Company was founded in 1937 in Zanesville, Ohio. Its first president was Addis Hull Jr. of the Hull pottery family, which had been one of the leading factories in neighboring Crooksville. Discovering by chance an Indian arrow on the grounds when the factory was being readied for opening led to the company being called Shawnee. Shawnee played up the Indian theme at various times in its history, notably with its line of corn-pattern dinnerware. This famous set in yellow and green was textured on every piece (including the teapot and salt and pepper shakers) to resemble an ear of corn. It was officially known as Corn King, then as Corn Queen beginning in the mid 1950's.

The final year of the Shawnee operations was 1961.

Marks: The trademarks used by Shawnee usually carry the letters *U.S.A.,* together with the factory name and a mold number. A low mold number is not necessarily an indication of early production. Most pieces of Shawnee figureware and such novelties as toy banks, ashtrays, etc., can be easily dated (approximately) on the basis of style. The vases are a little more difficult to accurately date, but a collector who makes educated guesses will probably score hits than misses.

SOUTHERN POTTERIES

Blue Ridge wares were manufactured by Southern Potteries of Erwin, Tennessee — the name of course referring to the Blue Ridge Mountains. For many years, it was the largest business operation in Erwin, employing at one time over 1,000 people. The Blue Ridge wares which were mainly dinnerware, were retailed throughout the country in variety and department stores. They were also sold extensively by mail-order houses. For the contemporary buyer, it was an inexpensive ware whose eye-appeal surpassed most of the competitors' products: painting was applied under the glaze and, as the company's ads repeatedly proclaimed, "would not wash off or wear off." Today, for the hobbyist, Blue Ridge dinnerware represents one of the more intriguing and collectible dinnerwares of the 20th century. It is abundantly available and the prices are very reasonable.

Southern Potteries was launched into operation during World War I. It was the first pottery works in the area. Labor was recruited from the neighborhood but a number of experienced workmen were imported from East Liverpool, Ohio. At first, the company's product was termed Clinchfield Pottery, after the Carolina Clinchfield railroad which ran close to the town. The earliest lines were far from noteworthy, consisting mainly of decal wares. Southern Potteries enjoyed a period of impressive growth in the 1920's and in that decade introduced its painted-under-the-glaze lines. Teams of artists painted the wares with sponges and brushes before it passed to the glazing kilns. This type of ware remained in production many years at Southern, and the age of any given piece can usually be determined (when other evidence is lacking) by the quality of execution. Owing to lack of experience on the part of decorators, the earliest pieces tend to be a bit more crude than those of later date. The finest work was done in the late 1930's and throughout the 1940's.

Blue Ridge ware, like other dinnerware of the time, profited from the conditions brought about by World War II. Importing goods from Japan and elsewhere came to a virtual halt, opening up much greater potential for the domestic manufacturers. So the mid to late forties witnessed the growth in Southern Potteries' history. Just the reverse of this situation prevailed in the following decade, however, when competition, both domestic and foreign, increased. The firm found itself unable to weather the storm and closed down in 1957. Its wares continued turning up in the stocks of retail merchants for several years thereafter, and in the 1970's began attracting the attention of collectors.

The majority of Blue Ridge products have floral patterns in bright colors, complimented by a rich glaze. There were many variations from the floral theme, however, including plates with paintings of barnyard animals, farm houses, country scenes and various other topics. Among the specialty items produced by this factory were a number of finely modeled toby jugs, which belong to the late production period of the 1950's. These average about six and one quarter inches in height and portray American subjects, but the style is unmistakably inspired by English toby jugs of the preceding century. These pieces apparently had a limited production, though they were not aimed at collectors in the modern sense of "limited editions."

Marked: A wide variety of markings, incorporating various trade names, are found on Blue Ridge. The collector should be cautioned, however, that this company was notorious for letting items slip through its production line unmarked. Absence of a mark is not an indication that a piece is not genuine Blue Ridge. Nor is there (as yet) any difference in valuation between marked and unmarked specimens, though it would seem that marked specimens should be the more desirable.

The earliest mark of Southern Potteries was strongly British in design. It consisted of the words *CLINCHFIELD CHINAWARE* arranged in a circular frame, at the center of which was the initials S.P.I. (Southern Potteries Incorporated). The frame was surmounted by a five-pointed crown. A variation of this mark lacks the crown, and the lettering reads *SOUTHERN HAND PAINTED CLINCHFIELD WARE.* At the center appears the wording *MADE ERWIN, TENN U.S.A.* Any mark with the name Clinchfield can be assumed to represent an early piece.

When the period of underglaze painting began, many different marks came into use, some of which must have been used simultaneously. A simple version states merely *UNDERGLAZE HAND PAINTED S.P. INC. ERWIN, TENN.,* without border or ornament. In some variants of this mark, the expression *MADE IN U.S.A.* without border or ornament. In some variants of this mark, the expression *MADE IN U.S.A.* was added; and often the mark is found contained in a lozenge-shaped border, with *S.P.I.* at the center. For a rather long period of time, the lettering in most of the Blue Ridge marks was in script, excepting that "Made in U.S.A.," when appended, was invariably in block letters. In later years the marks became decorative. The best-known of these has an illustration of the *BLUE RIDGE* in large script letters. The words *DETERGENT PROOF* and *OVEN SAFE* were later added to this mark as a sales vehicle. The terms *OVEN PROOF* and *FADE PROOF* are also sometimes found incorporated into the marks of Blue Ridge.

Southern Potteries wares were hand decorated with over 400 patterns. They were generally very colorful, with wide brush stroke flowers. Each pattern was fairly simple, not usually covering the entire item. The blanks before decoration, which are nearly always white, are produced in eight basic shapes or lines.

ASTOR

This line was distinguished by its defined cupped rim, which is formed by the center of an object being recessed. The smooth rim both outside and inside the defined ring has no ripples or any other decorative border.

CANDLEWICK

The rims and edges of items in this line are characterized by a decorative border of connected round beads. Shapes are simple other than the edges, and any objects such as cups or pitchers have the beaded rows also for the handles.

COLONIAL

The Colonial line is very simple shapes, but with light fluting on the flat objects. Flaired rims are common and the fluting curves inward and to the left. The fluting is not noticeable at the center of the specimens.

CLINCHFIELD

This line is the first that was produced and is fairly scarce in the market today. It is recognized by a wide flat rim and usually is outlined by a band of paint that corresponds with the decoration. This shape was no longer used when the company began to decorate the dinnerware that was painted by hand.

PIECRUST

This line is appropriately named because the edges of the wares are crimped like the crust of a pie. Other than the crimping, the line has no decorative aspects. The shapes are simple, with some pieces having flaired rims.

SKYLINE

Skyline was noted for a streamline shape, with no decorative handles, rims or edges. The surface of these wares were completely smooth, containing no fluting, ribbing or embossing. The items, such as cups, creamers, and pitchers also carried the same streamline shape.

TRAILWAY

One of the last lines introduced was the Trailway line. It is noted for the flat painted textured border. This is more appropriately called a line treatment rather than a shape. Many of the blanks before being grooved were Skyline blanks.

WOODCREST

This was also a late line treatment rather than a shape. These wares were called "Burlap" because of the coarse textured finish. The Skyline blanks were also used in producing these wares.

	Price Range	
☐ Ashtray	1.50	3.50
☐ Bon-bon, 9", divided into four sections, clover leaf shape, handle at the center	5.00	9.00
☐ Bowl, cereal, 6", astor shape, shallow, with cupped rim	2.00	4.00
☐ Bowl, mixing, 8-1/2", leaf pattern	3.00	6.00
☐ Bowl, salad, 10-1/4"	8.00	12.00
☐ Bowl, sauce, 5-1/4"	2.00	3.00
☐ Bowl, soup, 8"	2.00	4.00
☐ Bowl, vegetable, covered, shallow, with notched lid and two handles	10.00	13.00
☐ Bowl, vegetable, divided	7.50	10.00
☐ Bowl, vegetable, 9", open, Colonial shape, fluting at edges, shallow	5.00	9.00
☐ Bowl, vegetable, oval, Colonial shape, fluting at edges, shallow	5.00	9.00
☐ Box, cigarette, 4-1/4", pink daisy, square, with lid	5.00	7.00
☐ Box, round, 6", covered, flower shaped with handle on lid	13.00	16.00
☐ Box, sculptured, 4-1/4" x 5-1/2", rose step, rippled sides, notched lid	13.00	16.00
☐ Butter dish, with notched cover, two small pinch handles	8.00	12.00
☐ Carafe, with lid	8.00	12.00
☐ Chocolate pot, tulip shape, on pedestal base, with slender decorative handle and spout, notched lid	28.00	32.00
☐ Coffee pot	10.00	15.00
☐ Creamer, demi, inverted dome shape, no handles	5.00	7.00
☐ Creamer	3.00	6.00
☐ Creamer, with pedestal	7.50	10.00
☐ Cup, cylindrical, flaired rim	4.00	6.00
☐ Dish, baking, 8" x 13"	7.50	10.00
☐ Dish, casserole	5.00	7.50
☐ Egg cup, double, back to back semi-circles, base carries the design	4.00	6.00
☐ Gravy boat, candlewick shape, beaded handle, inverted dome shape	6.00	9.00
☐ Gravy boat tray	2.50	5.00
☐ Jugs, character	50.00	60.00
☐ Jug, covered	5.00	7.50
☐ Pitcher, 6-1/2", bulbous shape, with vertical fluting, no fluting on handle or rim and spout	20.00	30.00
☐ Plate, cake, 10-1/2"	6.00	10.00
☐ Plate, dinner, 9-1/2"	3.00	6.00
☐ Plate, dinner, 10"	3.00	6.00
☐ Plate, pie, 7"	2.00	4.00
☐ Plate, salad, 6"	1.50	3.00
☐ Plate, salad, 8-1/2"	2.00	4.00
☐ Plate, serving, 12"	5.00	10.00
☐ Plate, square, 6-1/2"	2.00	4.00
☐ Plate, square, 7-1/2"	2.00	4.00

	Price Range	
☐ **Plate,** compartment	7.50	10.00
☐ **Platter,** 17-1/2", artist signed	50.00	60.00
☐ **Platter,** 11", oval	5.00	7.50
☐ **Platter,** 13", oval	5.00	10.00
☐ **Platter,** 15", oval	7.50	12.00
☐ **Ramekin,** 5", with lid and decorative handle	5.00	7.50
☐ **Ramekin,** 7-1/2", with lid	5.00	7.50
☐ **Saucer,** demi	2.50	3.50
☐ **Saucer,** 4-1/4", recessed circle for cup	1.50	3.00
☐ **Shakers,** yellow and green, bud top, pair, bulbous, flaired base	9.00	12.00
☐ **Shakers,** yellow, rose and green, blossom top, pair, inverted teardrop, with flaired base	9.00	12.00
☐ **Shakers,** yellow, brown, rose and green, chickens, pair, rooster 4-3/4", hen 4"	6.00	10.00
☐ **Shakers,** brown, green and yellow, mallards pair, male 4", female 3-1/2"	6.00	10.00
☐ **Sugar,** demi, bulbous with simple handle and spout	4.00	7.00
☐ **Sugar,** covered, two decorative handles, on a small pedestal base	5.00	10.00
☐ **Sugar,** no handles, flaired rim	5.00	7.00
☐ **Teapot,** Colonial shape, with decorative handle and notched lid	12.00	16.00
☐ **Tea tile,** 6", round	3.00	7.00
☐ **Tea tile,** 6", square	3.00	7.00
☐ **Tidbit,** 10-1/2", 7-1/2", 5-1/2" levels, three tier, with ring metal handle	9.00	12.00
☐ **Tidbit,** two tier	6.00	10.00
☐ **Toast,** dish, square, with notched cover, cupped rim	20.00	25.00
☐ **Tray,** shell shape	7.00	10.00
☐ **Tray, relish,** 6-1/4" x 10-1/2", leaf shape, with handle	8.00	12.00
☐ **Tray, relish,** 10", leaf shape, with handle	8.00	12.00
☐ **Vase,** 8", boot shape	12.00	16.00
☐ **Vase,** 7-3/4", urn shape, with narrowed neck, pedestal base, decorative ring handles	10.00	15.00
☐ **Vase,** 5-1/2", spherical base, flaired rim, small pedestal base .	10.00	15.00
☐ **Vase,** 9-1/4", narrow, widens at the base, ruffled rim	15.00	20.00

SPEELER AND SONS

See International.

SPEELER POTTERY COMPANY

See International.

STANDARD SANITARY POTTERY COMPANY

Standard manufactured sanitary items, and was founded in 1901. Company officials included P.H. Moohan, Richard T. Potts, Owen Healey, and John Kelly.

Prices: Three-piece miniature bathroom sets typically sell in the area of $50.

STANGL POTTERY

The Stangl Pottery Company was one of the later producers of fine artware and also dinnerware. Among its best-known works are the famous "Stangl birds," a series of statuettes released during the early part of World War II. These charming pieces ended up being produced in very limited numbers, probably because of the war, and are now valuable "finds" wherever they turn up. Stangl was also well known for its fine vases with rich colors and satiny glazes, similar to the wares turned out by Grueby (and then by Tiffany, which acquired Grueby) some 30 or 40 years earlier. A good representative collection of Stangl is still possible to build under current market conditions. The pieces are available; but how much longer this will hold true is difficult to say. Prices for the best Stangl artware are high, but this is nothing new. Most pieces carried rather high pricetags when first released to the retail market. It was never a mass-produced product.

This company was an outgrowth of the Fulper Pottery Company of Flemington, New Jersey. In 1910, J.M. Stangl assumed the post of ceramic engineer at Fulper and was directly responsible for much of its creative work during the next two decades. During the 1920's, Fulper with its business rapidly expanding bought out the old Anchor Pottery Company factory in Trenton. When the main Fulper plant was destroyed in a fire in 1929, the firm was reorganized as Stangl Pottery and Trenton became its headquarters. J.M. Stangl was one of the hard-driving, innovative geniuses of the American pottery industry. He constantly strove for eye-catching patterns and similarly eye-catching descriptive names for his mellow color shades. One shade of gray was ambitiously referred to by Stangl as "elephant's breath gray." The Stangl Pottery Company was taken over by Wheaton Industries in 1972.

Marks: It appears as though the first mark used by the Stangl Pottery Company was *STANGL USA*, without periods between the initial letters. This was followed by a series of others, including an oval mark in which the trade name of the line appears at the center, with *MADE IN TRENTON, U.S.A.* beneath. A more elaborate version has the name *STANGL, TRENTON, N.J.* within an oval, accompanied by such wording as *HAND PAINTED, OVEN PROOF, COUNTRY GARDEN* or *HAND PAINTED, GRANADA GOLD*, denoting different lines of ware.

	Price Range	
BELLA ROSA		
☐ **Server,** *handle at center*	13.00	16.00

Price Range

BLUEBERRY

☐ **Butter dish,** *lidded, holds 1/4 pound stick of butter*	8.00	11.00
☐ **Cup and saucer**	5.00	6.50
☐ **Plate,** *6"*	1.50	2.25
☐ **Plate,** *9"*	3.25	4.50
☐ **Plate,** *10-1/2"*	4.50	6.00
☐ **Saucer**	1.50	2.25

BLUE DAISY

☐ **Cup and saucer**	3.25	4.50
☐ **Plate, dinner**	4.25	5.50

COLONIAL ROSE

☐ **Bowl, soup,** *5", green*	5.00	6.50
☐ **Creamer,** *item #1388*	3.00	4.50
☐ **Dish, vegetable,** *9", blue, oval*	4.00	5.50

COUNTRY GARDEN

Double outer border of solid band accompanied by scalloped band; with printed pictures of various flowers, stems and leaves

☐ **Bowl, cereal**	3.00	4.25
☐ **Bowl, fruit**	3.00	4.00
☐ **Coffeepot**	13.00	16.00
☐ **Plate, dinner**	3.00	4.00
☐ **Country life plate,** *vegetable, 9-1/4", circular*	21.00	26.00
☐ **Dahlia plate,** *hanging, 6"*	3.00	4.00
☐ **Festival** *mug*	3.00	4.00

FRUIT

Narrow solid outer border, enclosing a scalloped border; with (on plates) a brightly colored inner border and printed pictures of grapes, cherries, etc.

☐ **Bowl, sugar,** *lidded*	6.00	8.00
lacking lid	4.00	5.50
☐ **Pot, bean,** *lidded*	22.00	27.00
☐ **Salt and pepper**	8.00	11.00

FRUIT AND FLOWERS

Twin scalloped border (one superimposed on the other), enclosing multi-colored printed pictures of various fruits and flowers.

☐ **Bowl, cereal**	3.00	3.75
☐ **Golden grape plate,** *dinner*	3.00	3.75
☐ **Golden harvest plate,** *dinner, 9-1/2"*	8.00	11.00

MAGNOLIA

A borderless ware, very brightly colored, with printed pictures of magnolia blossoms, stems, leaves and buds.

☐ **Plate, dinner,** *8-1/4"*	4.00	5.50
☐ **Saucer**	1.50	2.00

ORCHARD SONG

A borderless ware, decorated with printed pictures of various fruits, brightly colored.

	Price Range	
☐ **Tray, relish**	4.50	6.00
☐ **Pink cosmos** *plate, dinner*	3.00	4.00
☐ **Starflower** *plate, dinner, 10-1/4"*	4.00	5.75
☐ **Terra rose** *pitcher, 5-3/4", white and beige*	10.00	13.00

THISTLE

A borderless ware, with bright colored printed pictures of stems, leaves and thistles.

☐ **Bowl, berry**	4.00	5.25
☐ **Bowl, salad,** *11-3/4"*	27.00	33.00
☐ **Bowl, soup**	6.00	8.50
☐ **Creamer,** *4-1/4"*	8.00	10.75
☐ **Dish, vegetable,** *10-1/2"*	10.00	13.00
☐ **Plate, dinner,** *10-1/4"*	7.00	9.75
☐ **Plate, pie,** *6"*	2.50	3.25
☐ **Sugar and creamer,** *lidded*	11.00	14.00
☐ **Town and country,** *bowl, 8", circular*	8.00	10.00
☐ **Butter dish,** *green, lidded*	15.00	19.00
☐ **Pitcher,** *10"*	36.00	43.00
☐ **Plate, dinner,** *10-1/4"*	8.00	11.00
☐ **Pot, bean,** *greenish*	22.00	27.00
☐ **Saucer,** *6", green*	2.25	3.00
☐ **Yellow tulip** *pitcher, 5-3/4"*	4.00	6.00
☐ **Plate, dinner,** *10"*	4.00	5.25
☐ **Bowl, berry,** *6"*	2.00	3.00
☐ **Bowl, sugar,** *lidded*	5.50	8.00

MISCELLANEOUS

☐ **Ashtray,** *item #3914, white*	15.00	19.00
☐ **Ashtray, clamshell,** *5-1/2", blue and green*	4.50	6.00
☐ **Basket,** *item #3252, green*	40.00	52.00
☐ **Candleholder, callalily,** *3-1/2" x 4-1/4"*	14.00	17.00
☐ **Carafe,** *8", blue and yellow, with stopper, wooden handle*	11.00	14.00

BIRD FIGURINES

The following is a selective listing of the items in Stangl's "Audubon's Birds of America" series. Each represents a bird species that had originally been depicted in the great Audubon "double elephant folios," a set of four giant books that measured 37 inches tall. The poses and colorations closely followed those from the book's aquatint plates. Though most of these specimens are quite scarce, prices are higer than might normally be expected, because a double market exists: Stangl collectors plus Audubon collectors, thereby creating much greater competition.

☐ **Bird of paradise,** *item #2040*	70.00	85.00
☐ **Bird of paradise,** *item #3408*	75.00	90.00

	Price Range	
☐ Black throated warbler, *item #3814*	50.00	65.00
☐ Bluebird, *item #3276*	70.00	87.00
☐ Bluebirds, *item #32760, 5", pair (resting on a single base)*	125.00	145.00
☐ Blueheaded vireo, *item #3448*	42.00	55.00
☐ Brewer's blackbird, *item #3591*	25.00	32.00
☐ Cardinal, *item #3444, matt finish*	75.00	90.00
☐ Carolina wren, *item #33590*	45.00	57.00
☐ Cerulean warbler, *item #3456, 4-1/4"*	40.00	49.00
☐ Chat, *item #3590*	41.00	52.00
☐ Chestnut-backed chickadee, *item #3811*	70.00	85.00
☐ Chestnut-sided warbler, *item #3812, 5"*	41.00	52.00
☐ Chickadee grouping, *item #3581*	100.00	115.00
☐ Cockatoo, *item #3405, 6"*	40.00	52.00
☐ Cockatoo, pair, *item #3405D, (resting on a single base)*	105.00	125.00
☐ Duck, *item #3250B*	190.00	230.00
☐ Duck in flight, *item #3443, 8-3/4"*	210.00	240.00
☐ Duck, preening, *item #3250, 2-3/4"*	33.00	41.00
☐ Evening grosbeak, *5"*	65.00	80.00
☐ Gold crowned kinglet, *5-1/4" x 5". grouping*	80.00	100.00
☐ Golden crowned kinglet, *item #3848, 4-1/4"*	40.00	50.00
☐ Goldfinch, *item #3635, grouping (four birds resting on a single base)*	120.00	140.00
☐ Gray cardinal, *item #3596, 4-1/2"*	48.00	62.00
☐ Gray cardinal, *item #3596, 5-1/2" (larger version of the above)* .	57.00	70.00
☐ Hummingbird, *item #3585*	27.00	32.00
☐ Hummingbird, *item #3634*	40.00	52.00
☐ Indigo bunting, *item #3589, 3-1/4"*	37.00	45.00
☐ Kentucky warbler, *item #3598, 3"*	40.00	48.00
☐ Kingfisher, *item #3406, 3-1/2"*	40.00	52.00
☐ Lovebird, *item #3400, 4"*	38.00	45.00
☐ Lovebird, pair, *(resting on a single base)*	90.00	110.00
☐ Nuthatch, *item #3593, 2-1/2"*	32.00	38.00
☐ Oriole, *item #3402, 3-1/2"*	36.00	43.00
☐ Oriole, pair, *item #3402D, (resting on a single base)*	70.00	90.00
☐ Painted bunting, *item #3452*	50.00	62.00
☐ Parkeet, pair, *item #3582D, green, (resting on a single base)* ...	135.00	155.00
☐ Parula warbler, *item #3583, 4-1/2"*	50.00	62.00
☐ Red-faced warbler, *item #3594, 3"*	33.00	40.00
☐ Rieffer's hummingbird, *item #3628, 4-1/2"*	60.00	75.00
☐ Rooster, *item #3445, 9"*	100.00	125.00
☐ Rufous hummingbird, *item #3585, 3"*	50.00	65.00
☐ Wren, *item #3401, 4"*	50.00	62.00

STAR PORCELAIN COMPANY

The Star Porcelain Company, located on Muirhead Avenue, was founded in 1899 by Herbert Sinclair, Dr. Charles Britton (a drugstore owner) and Dr. Thomas H. MacKenzie (a doctor). The company manufactures electrical specialties as it has done since its founding. In 1919, Star built a plant in

Frenchtown NJ, for the manufacture of spark plug insulators. The French-town Porcelain Company was later sold when the automotive industry began manufacturing their own spark plugs. Star acquired the Bay Ridge Company in 1969.

Marks: As shown
Prices: To someone trying to fill out a one-from-each-company collection, one of Star's products would probably we worth at least a couple of dollars.

STEPHEN, TAMS & COMPANY

See Greenwood Pottery.

TAYLOR & COMPANY

Founded in 1865, this partnership was succeeded in 1879 by Taylor & Goodwin. See Trenton Pottery Company.

TAYLOR & GOODWIN

In 1870, Taylor & Goodwin replaced Taylor & Company. See Trenton Pottery Company.

TAYLOR & HOUDAYER

This company manufactured sanitary wares and was founded in 1883 by Taylor & Houdayer.

Marks: *Not known*
Prices: See comparable listings.

TAYLOR & SPEELER

Taylor & Speeler was the first Trenton company to manufacture pottery on a full-scale commercial basis, and their success was responsible for the huge pottery industry in Trenton that followed. They made Rockingham and yellow wares beginning in 1953, and continued in business for about 20 years. In 1858 Bloor entered the organization and provided financial backing, and the company began producing white granite ware. The Fell & Thropp Company took over the pottery at a later date.

Marks: *Not known*
Prices: We have no definite selling prices during the past year for Taylor & Speeler products. We would estimate as follows:

	Price Range	
☐ **Rockingham wares,** *a minimum of*	60.00	70.00
☐ **White granite wares,** *a minimum of*	30.00	35.00
☐ **Yellow wares,** *a minimum of*	30.00	35.00

Since their wares are scarce and since so few have survived in absolutely mint condition, expect to pay much more than this for anything of unusual size or shape or in particularly good condition.

TAYLOR, GOODWIN & COMPANY

Same as Taylor & Goodwin.

TAYLOR, SPEELER & BLOOR

See Taylor & Speeler.

THOMAS MADDOCK & SONS

Thomas Maddock & Sons was founded as an outgrowth of Millington, Astbury & Poulson. After Poulson died in 1861, Mr. Coughley bought his interest in M.A.P., and after Coughley died in 1869, Thomas Maddock bought Coughley's share in M.A.P. and Millington's share as well. By about 1876 the firm was known as Astbury & Maddock. At some point Maddock took sole ownership of the company and brought his sons into the business.

The company had a huge pottery on Carroll Street, and their wares included sanitary items and all-purpose stoneware. Dinnerware was included in their output, and vases and other decorative items were also made. The once great Carroll Street pottery is now occupied by the Rescue Mission.

Marks: Backstamps include the one shown, which was primarily used on sanitary wares, and a circular mark with a crown on top which was used on dinnerware. All marks included the initals T.M.&S.

Prices: Maddock wares are rather common in the Trenton area, and this is reflected in prices for them. Some of their designs and decorations are quite attractive and we would expect to see an increase in prices shortly. For run-of-the-mill items, the following figures apply.

	Price Range	
☐ **Bowls,** *dessert or soup*	5.00	10.00
☐ **Bowls,** *serving*	12.00	25.00
☐ **Cups and saucers**	7.00	14.00
☐ **Dinner plates**	5.00	10.00
☐ **Mugs**	7.00	20.00
☐ **Platters,** *depending on size*	15.00	30.00
☐ **Smaller plates**	2.00	7.00
☐ **Three-piece miniature bathroom sets**	40.00	60.00

TRENT TILE COMPANY

Trent was founded in 1882 as the Harris Manufacturing Company. Although it is not certain at what point the name changed to Trent, it was probably Harris only a short while. Chief designers and modellers were Isaac Broome (beginning in 1883) and William Wood Gallimore (beginning in 1886). The company is best known for its embossed tiles, although other types were made. At one point over 20 kilns were in operation.

Marks: Several backstamps were used, all incorporating the name Trent. The marks are usually impressed and rarely printed in ink.

☐ **Embossed tile,** *6" x 6", wine color, floral design, framed in wood to make a tea tile*	23.00	28.00
☐ **Embossed tile,** *6" x 6", gold and brown, boy in lace collar, signed Broome*	120.00	140.00
☐ **Embossed tile,** *4" x 4", golds and browns, Benjamin Franklin* .	90.00	110.00
☐ **Embossed tiles,** *6" x 6", peacock blue, two, girl and boy each with a bird, not artist signed but attributed to Gallimore due to a picture of identical tiles by him which appear in a book on ceramics, pair*	150.00	175.00

Note: Except for the first tile listed, all the tiles have been framed. Prices are for the tile only and a professional framing would add to the value.

All other tiles can be rated as follows:
Artist signed, around $100 for a human figure or face, less for other subjects.
Non-artist signed, around $75 for human subjects, down to a minimum of $10 for other subjects.

TRENTON CHINA COMPANY

This company operated from 1859 to 1891, producing both decorated and undecorated wares.

Marks: The one shown, which is impressed in the china, is the only known mark.
Prices: For a company which supposedly operated for so many years, there are remarkably few samples of their wares. The following prices are estimates:

TRENTON CHINA CO.

TRENTON, N.J.

	Price Range	
☐ **Bowls,** *serving*	20.00	30.00
☐ **Bowls,** *soup or dessert*	7.00	10.00
☐ **Cups and saucers**	10.00	20.00
☐ **Dinner plates**	10.00	20.00
☐ **Mugs**	15.00	40.00
☐ **Platters,** *depending on size*	25.00	45.00
☐ **Smaller plates**	5.00	10.00

TRENTON FIRE CLAY & PORCELAIN COMPANY

T.F.C.&P. Company was founded in 1893 by O.O. Bowman, R.K. Bowman, and W.J.J. Bowman. They were primarily producers of sanitary wares.

Marks: *Not known*
Prices: A three-piece miniature bathroom set would be in the $50 price range.

TRENTON POTTERIES COMPANY

In 1892, David K. Bayne and William S. Hancock were able to consolidate five Trenton potteries into the Trenton Potteries Company. The five were:

Crescent, Delaware, Empire, Enterpirse, Equitable. At a later date another pottery, the ideal, was built and brought into the organization. Chief products were sanitary items and hotel-type china.

Marks: A star with the initials "T.P.Co." was the primary mark of Trenton potteries. A number within the star indicated the plant where the item was made. Number 1 was Crescent, number 2 Delaware, number 3 Empire, number 4 Enterprise, number 5 Equitable. Number 6 would have been Ideal, but for the most part the 6 was not used and the word "Ideal" is inside the star instead. The star without a circle around it was typically used on sanitary wares, while the star within a circle was used on dinnerware.

Prices: Products from Trenton Potteries are still abundant and usually sell in the under $5 range. If anything interesting was produced after the consolidation, figure it at about the same as a comparable Lenox item. (Also see individual listings for each of the constituent companies.) T.P.C. made a particularly cute three-piece minature bathroom set which sells (as most of these sets do) in the $50 range. One of their miniature sets was designed for the toilet to hold cigarettes, the wash basin to hold matches, and the bathtub to be used as an ashtray. We haven-t seen one of these sold in some time, but expect it would bring a little more than the average set of this type.

Mark A

TRENTON POTTERIES CO

TRENTON, NEW JERSEY

U S A

Mark B

Mark C

Mark D

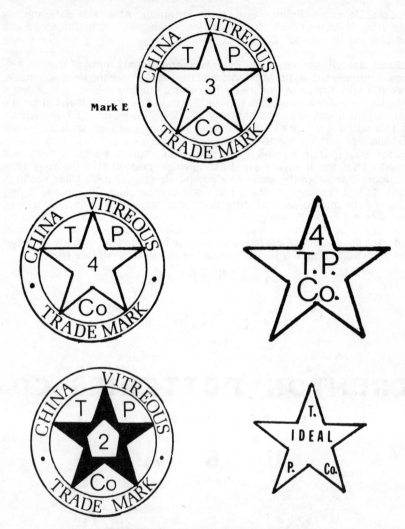

Mark E

TRENTON POTTERIES WORKS

T.P.W. was founded in 1883 for the production of both sanitary wares and white granite dinnerware.

Marks: Backstamps include the New Jersey coat of arms with the word "Royal" above it, and a shield with crossed swords and the words "Porcelain Opaque" above and "French, TPW" below.
Prices: See comparable items listed elsewhere.

TRENTON POTTERY COMPANY

Trenton Pottery Company was incorporated in 1865, and was later known as Taylor, Goodwin & Company. Fell & Thropp operated the pottery at a later date. Since Trenton Potteries Company used the same mark as Trenton Pottery Company, it is assumed there was a connection between the two.

Marks: The mark shown, usually printed in black, is the only one known.
Prices: The following prices are estimates.

T. P. Co.

CHINA

	Price	Range
☐ **Bowls,** *dessert or soup*	7.00	10.00
☐ **Bowls,** *serving*	15.00	25.00
☐ **Cups and saucers**	7.00	15.00
☐ **Dinner plates**	7.00	15.00
☐ **Mugs**	7.00	30.00
☐ **Platters,** *depending on size*	15.00	40.00
☐ **Smaller plates**	2.00	7.00
☐ **Three-piece miniature bathroom set**	40.00	60.00

TRENTON TERRA-COTTA COMPANY

Trenton Terra-Cotta officers included Joseph McPherson and O.O. Bowman. Their most interesting products were garden vases and ornaments, although they also made pipes, chimney parts, and other such products.

Marks: *Not known*
Prices: Although we have not seen any sold recently on the open market, a garden vase or ornament would probably be a minimum of $100. Other itmes would have a base value of $5.

UNION ELECTRICAL PORCELAIN COMPANY

Union is located on Muirhead Avenue, and they manufacture electrical porcelains.

Marks: *Not known*
Prices: Electrical porcelains are usually not considered to be exciting collectibles, but once again these products might be of interest to someone trying to finish out a Trenton collection. As such, any item is probably worth at least a few dollars.

UNION POTTERY COMPANY

See New Jersey Pottery Company.

VAN BRIGGLE

Van Briggle was one of the earliest art potteries in the west and one of the most successful. Located in Colorado Springs, it acquired a grasp on the western market — from Denver to San Francisco — which nearly equaled the hold that Rookwood had on the east. Van Briggle's wares perfectly reflected the western taste. They weren't frilly or delicate like the Old World porcelains. Instead, they had a rugged charm, their creative shapes suggesting the gnarled limbs of old trees, driftwood, cactus, and other products of nature. They proved to be quite an influence on the potters of the east who adapted some of Van Briggle's innovative ideas into their own wares. In terms of its importance to the art pottery movement, Van Briggle stands very high.

Artus Van Briggle, descended from an old Flemish family, worked as a decorator at Rookwood. He was born in 1869 and attended the Cincinnati Academy of Art, then studied art in France for several years. In terms of artistic background, few potters had better credentials. But credentials without cash do not start a business, so Van Briggle contented himself with his position at Rookwood until the opportunity arose. In 1899, he settled in Colorado, mainly for health reasons — he had survived an attack of tuberculosis as a youth but remained weak. The drier air of the west was thought to be beneficial. By 1901, he had set up a small pottery and did most of the work himself. Though far from the media centers, it received some attention. The mere fact that an art pottery was operating in cattle country made news in itself. Within three years, it had grown impressively in size, to the point of employing 14 laborers and craftsmen. Artus Van Briggle's lifelong struggle with ill-health ended with his death at 35 in 1904, whereupon his widow continued to operate the Van Briggle Pottery Company. Designs that Artus had developed were kept in production, and new ones devised. Further growth followed, but the company later suffered decreases in growth and went into bankruptcy in 1913. After reorganization, it prospered once more and continues in operation to the present day.

Marks: The first and most famous mark used by this firm consisted of the letters *AA,* the initials of the first names of Van Briggle and his wife, Anne. It was used in conjunction with an incised mark reading *VAN BRIGGLE,* scratched into the ware itself by hand. The date of production usually accompanied these markings, and often (especially at a later period) a stock number. Sometimes, the word *ORIGINAL* appears along with the mark. This apparently refers to the fact that the piece was hand-thrown on a wheel, rather than pressed from a mold. This is, however, confusing, because it suggests that other manufacturers were bringing out imitations of Van Briggles. *HAND CARVED* is likewise found, occasionally, along with the factory mark on pieces with raised decoration. Pottery is not really carved in the conventional sense, but this meant that the relief decoration was worked up from the body rather than applied with loose bits of clay. "Sculptured" might have been a clearer term.

WARREN KIMBLE POTTERY

No information available.

W.C. HENDRICKSON

Trenton decorating company.
Prices: Add $5 to the basic price of any item if it has the name of the W.C. Hendrickson decorating company on the bottom.

W. CORY

Cory operated in Trenton during the 1860's primarily making yellow wares. Wares by this company are exceptionally rare, and although rather clumsy in appearance, they should be considered desirable additions to any Trenton collection.

WELLER

To say the Weller Pottery grew from small beginnings is an understatement. Sam Weller started out making flowerposts and tried to sell them door-to-door in Zanesville, Ohio. When they failed to sell, he put plants in them and went out to knock on doors again. This was in 1873. Less than ten years later, Weller Pottery was one of the leading manufacturers of the area.

Weller pottery has long been one of the collector's favorites. It combines imaginative shapes and designs with skilled artwork, and the variety is just about endless. The pieces are hand-decorated and represent the efforts of numerous artists, each of whom had his or her individual style. They include full lines of decorative ware, with vases, lamp bases, book ends, ashtrays, paperweights, bowls, pitchers, and many other products. Weller always had a reputation of producing the most colorful of all the potteries, even if it was not as bold or classic as Rookwood or Grueby. Buyers came from all ranks of society, and all parts of the nation. And this is basically the case today with its following by collectors.

In 1893, Sam Weller visited the Columbian Exposition in Chicago and saw samples of Lonhuda ware. He offered a position in his firm to William Long of Lonhuda, a Steubenville pottery, and soon Weller was making his own version of Lonhuda. Afterwards, he changed the name to "Louwelsa," but the basic character of the ware was maintained. This was followed by numerous other art pottery wares with domestic and foreign touches. Oriental-style wares were added to the line, too. The first decade of the 20th century was hectic for Weller. It was rapidly climbing to the top of the pottery industry and tussling with one rival after another along the way. The most obstinate of these proved to be Roseville (also of Zanesville), which tried to copy nearly everything that Weller brought out.

As the market for art pottery declined during the depression, so did Weller's business. It survived into the 1940's but was closed in 1948.

Collectors who specialize in Weller generally confine themselves to one of three basic periods in the factory's development: the early years (from which it is not easy to find a great deal of specimens on the market), the Lonhuda years, and the years following 1900, when more and more diversity was introduced into Weller's lines.

Marks: The factory mark is used in combination with the pattern or style name, such as *AURELIAN WELLER, DICKENSWARE WELLER, TURADA WELLER, SICARDO WELLER,* etc. In the earliest period of Weller's venture into art pottery, the name of the line was in script letters, written horizontally above the company name (which was in block letters). This format was then dropped in favor of block lettering for the mark as a whole, but with the innovation of a curved shape for the pattern or style name. The artist's mark appears in conjunciton. There are numerous artists' marks and variations of them.

AURELIAN *(Introduced before 1900)*

Almost identical to Louwelsa, but with the glaze brushed on to purposely create streakiness. Samuel Weller "inherited" the Louwelsa line when his company merged with the Lonhuda Pottery Co. in 1895. In an effort to further capitalize on its enormous sales appeal, he brought out Aurelian, thus creating two versions of the basic Louwelsa ware. The streakiness of Aurelian did not really give more lustre, but the *appearance* was of more lustre, since the streaks of glaze reflected light from a variety of angles. Some people liked it — some didn't. Aurelian was never manufactured in nearly the quantity of Louwelsa.

	Price Range	
☐ **Ewer, 6'',** cedar brown, dark brown and black, squat cruet shape, loop handle turning outward at the bowl, decorated with floral painting in green, cream yellow and red. Bearing the Weller Aurelian double circular mark, and the artist's initials M.P.	130.00	150.00
☐ **Vase, 7'',** black with dark brown and olive toning, bulbous form with narrow neck, decorated with paintings of speckled leaves. With a hand-inked factory mark, and bearing the artist's initials E.A. .... *Note: Darker than usual for Aurelian — but this didn't hurt the glaze.*	180.00	210.00
☐ **Vase, 9'',** mahogany shading to purple and balck-brown, tubular shape rounded at shoulder and base, decorated with a painting of a large flower with orange petals and a dark brown center. Unmarked, either by the factory or the artist. .... *Note: The absence of a mark holds down the value of this specimen somewhat. If one with a mark (factory or artist, or, preferably, both) turned up, it would be worth more than the range shown.*	150.00	170.00
☐ **Vase, 12-1/2'',** mahogany shading to purple and balck-brown, ovoid form with narrow neck, decorated with bold floral paintings in a variety of colors, large flowers near neck of vase. Circular factory mark, and bearing the artist's initials R.A.	380.00	440.00

AURORO (Also known as AUROSO; introduced before 1900)

A high-gloss ware with a basically white body, to which pastel shades of various colors were added, often to give an effect of streakiness, and with underglaze paintings. The paintings are mainly simple and decorative, not the large-scale or thought-inspiring works found on some pieces of Louwelsa.

Price Range

☐ **Vase, 9",** *cream white with pastel blue and yellow, of egg shape with narrow neck and mouth, decorated with paintings of swimming goldfish by Hattie MITCHELL. Factory mark AURORO, WELLER inked by hand.* 1325.00   1500.00

BLUE LOUWELSA (Date of introduction undetermined, probably shortly after 1900.)

If the standard Weller Louwelsa (see below) could be such a big hit with the same basic scheme repeated over and over, why not try a color variation? It sounded like a good idea to Sam Weller, who suppliemeted his "basic brown" Louwelsa with "Blue Louwelsa." It was the same highly glazed ware in the same shapes, with underglaze paintings — except that the color was blue instead of dark brown. Apparently it did not prove too popular as few pieces were made. Collectors of the regular Louwelsa sometimes add a specimen or two of "Blue Louwelsa" to their shelves, just for comparison.

☐ **Vase, 3",** *light and dark lavender blue, flattened bulbous form with Asiatic influence, handle rising out of bowl and joining neck, very narrow mouth, decorated with paintings of lillies. With the LOUWELSA, WELLER semi-circular mark.* 320.00   355.00

DICKENS WARE (Introduced c. 1887)

This began as a line (chiefly vases) decorated with paintings of characters and scenes from the novels of Charles Dickens. It was later widened out to include many novelty products and many paintings which did not relate in any way to Dickens. Doulton Pottery of England (now known as Royal Doulton) had pioneered in transforming the characters of Dickens into porcelain, notably with its famous Toby Jugs. They sold well in America and it was inevitable that a domestic maker would try to seize a share of the market. By coincidence, the name "Sam Weller" — owner of Weller Pottery Company — had been used by Dickens for a fictitious character in "The Pickwick Papers." Toby Weller, also in the book, became the model for the first *Toby* jugs.

☐ **Plate, advertising,** *12-1/2", dark brown (Louwelsa finish), with a scene from the novel The Pickwick Papers, reading in molded and painted letters on the front DICKENS POTTERY, S.A. WELLER, in smaller letters Pickwick Papers. Not marked on the back.* 1800.00   2100.00
Note: This advertising plate is extremely rare. It was not originally offered for public sale, but was given to dealers (for window display) who handled the Dickens Ware line. It is probably the earliest American advertising plate, so far as shop-window advertising is concerned. The precise date is not known but it undoubtedly falls into the pre-World War I era.

	Price Range	

☐ **Vase,** *15", dark and pale lavender with beige, shaped cylin-drical form, decorated with a painting of an elderly shepherd and flock of sheep, marked DICKENS WARE.* 1450.00   1675.00

☐ **Vase,** *10-1/2", lavender, cylindrical, with a painted scene from the novel Dombey & Son of a gentleman and a youth seated on chairs, marked DICKENS WARE.* 800.00   950.00

EOCEAN *(Introduced 1898)*

In its shapes Eocean was similar to Louwelsa, and also in the fact that it carried underglaze paintings. However in Eocean ware the body colors were pastel or muted, and the paintings usually executed in rather bright colors, which made them distinct from the backgrounds. There was no main body color for Eocene, though greys and blues were used quite frequently. The line remained in production for many years and was popular, but never reached the sales volume of Louwelsa. Apparantly the name was derived from *eocene,* an era in geological time when dinosaurs roamed the earth — but what connection that could have with pottery is hard to fathom. Quite possibly Sam Weller just liked the sound of the word.

☐ **Basket,** *6-1/2", white with dusky brown, violet and black, of half-circle form with a pedestal base and handle, decorated with a painting of light and dark red cherries. Unmarked.* 120.00   140.00

☐ **Candlestick,** *9", ivory white, of cruet form with a wide flattened bowl, widely flaring lip, decorated with a painting (in grey) of leaves. With a hand-inked mark reading EOCEAN, WELLER, and the artist's initials L.J.B.* 260.00   295.00

☐ **Same shape as above,** *with medium grey to dark grey body, painting of leaves and berries.* 295.00   330.00

☐ **Vase,** *12", cream white and pastel beige, ovoid form, decorated with a very pale painting of flowers growing in a field, bearing the artist's signature of RAUCHFUSS.* 300.00   350.00

Note: The painting is noticable at close range only; from any distance it appears to be nothing more than tonal highlighting.

☐ **Vase,** *13-1/4", grey and grey-brown, ovoid form, decorated with a painting of white flowers, white and purple berries, and stems with leaves. With a hand-inked mark reading EOCENE, WELLER, and the artist's initials L.J.B.* 350.00   390.00

☐ **Vase,** *16", greyish brown shading to intense dark brown, cylin-drical form with a series of six tiny C-shape handles along the top, decorated with a painting of cherries growing on a leafy vine. With a hand-inked mark reading WELLER, no further markings.* 340.00   385.00

Note: If you find one with an artist's mark, figure a minimum of $375 and possibly as much as $425.

☐ **Vase,** *8-1/2", lavender with hints of pink, of modified pot form decorated with large paintings of pink and white flowers against a dark green background, unmarked.* 145.00   170.00

Note: A marked specimen might bring a little more.

☐ **Vase,** *7", marble white with olive green, of shaped cylindrical form, decorated with a painting of longstemmed violets with deep red centers. With a hand-inked mark reading EOCEAN, WELLER.* 140.00   165.00

Price Range

☐ **Vase,** 6-1/4", *pale lavender and green, of cylindrical form swelling outward toward the base, decorated with a painted floral arrangement against a deep green background. Unmarked. . .*   90.00   110.00

☐ **Vase,** 10-1/2", *pink and lavender, bulb form, decorated with a painted floral arrangement against a deep green background. No factory mark but bearing the artist's initials M.T. . . . .*   170.00   200.00

☐ **Vase,** 13-1/2", *rich lavender with pink, cylincrical form with slight shaping, pinched in at neck, narrow mouth, decorated with a painting of red roses on thorny stems. With the artist's mark A.H. . . . .*   240.00   275.00
Note: In the pottery world this color is sometimes called "Easter egg purple."

HUDSON-PERFECTO *(Introduced between 1898 and 1900)*

Also called Louwelsa "matt finish," but it bore very little resemblance to Louwelsa (see below). There was not just a difference in the glaze, but in the coloration; and also in the fact that Hudson-Perfecto paintings were executed more as canvas paintings, to be entirely distinct from the background. However, the shapes were usually the same from Hudson-Perfecto to Louwelsa (both lines were sold at the same time, though Louwelsa outlived Hudson-Perfecto by many years). Many collectors simply object to the name "perfecto" as it suggests a cigar. Some of the paintings found on this ware are of extraordinarily high quality. On the whole it would seem to deserve more attention than it has received. This might be an area for investors to probe.

☐ **Vase,** 12-7/8", *pinkish brown, ovoid form decorated with a superbly executed painting of a mounted Arab holding a rifle. With a die-stamped WELLER mark. . . . .*   2800.00   3300.00

L'ART NOUVEAU *(Introduced c. 1906)*

A decorative ware which usually impresses the beginning collector. The bas-relief patterns, which are a feature of this line, give it an aspect of appeal which even Louwelsa and Lonhuda lack. However, as art objects the L'Art Nouveau crerations rank well behind Louwelsa and most of the other Weller art pottery. The bas-relief designs were not hand-molded but pressed in molds, therby creating numerous duplicate specimens. The coloring was added by hand, but the artists were required to follow prescribed approaches in the coloring. Thus the work was given to newcomers rather than top factory talent. In favor of L'Art Nouveau it can be said that it represents an important school of design, one in which there is considerable collecting interest.

☐ **Bank, ear of corn,** 8", *purple and yellow, in the shape of an ear of corn with coin-slot on the side. Textured to represent kernels. Unmarked. . . . .*   95.00   115.00
Note: Interest from still-bank collectors has brought up the value in recent years. This was rather an oddity for the Weller people.

Price Range

☐ **Ewer, 15",** slate grey with gold, cylindrical form with squared sides, widened base, scalloped lip, C-shape handle. Decorated with molded and painted foliage ornament, marked ART NOUVEAU, WELLER. 190.00 225.00

☐ **Mug, 5",** salmon with yellow and blue, of drinking-cup shape with modified C-shape handle, decorated with molded and partially painted floral ornament. With a die-stamped WELLER mark. 140.00 165.00

☐ **Vase, 16-1/4",** blue base with tan body, of table-leg shape with low squared bowl, decorated with a molded and painted figure of a maiden with blonde hair dressed in a flowing gown, holding a large rose. Unmarked. 380.00 430.00

☐ **Vase, 7-3/4",** bluish-grey with cream white, shell shape with footed pedestal base, decorated with the molded and colored portrait of a classical goddess with flowing hair. With a die-stamped WELLER mark. 120.00 150.00

☐ **Vase, 12-1/4",** bone white with slate grey, cylindrical with squared sides, paneled, decorated with molded and painted foliage at the lip, with a die-stamped WELLER mark. 115.00 135.00

Note: This type of vase is sometimes called a "column vase," as it resembles an architectural column or pillar.

☐ **Vase, 8",** grey, cylindrical with bulbous bowl, molded and painted design of brown flowers, with a die-stamped WELLER mark. 70.00 90.00

☐ **Vase, 12-7/8",** greyish green, of tall pot form with pinched neck, decorated with a molded and painted scene of a reclining woman being fanned by an Egyptian slave. Marked ART NOUVEAU, WELLER. 975.00 1100.00

Note: Certainly one of the best L'Art Nouveau vases.

☐ **Vase, ear of corn,** 4-3/4", greenish purple and pale yellow, ovoid form in the shape of an ear of corn, textured to represent kernels. With ART NOUVEAU, WELLER mark in double circle. . 85.00 110.00

LONHUDA (First made by Weller in 1895, but previously made by Lonhuda Pottery Company of Stubenville, Ohio.)

When Weller merged with Lonhuda, the Lohhuda ware continued to be made. Not long thereafter, the name of this line was changed to Louwelsa. Its basic characteristics are the same as Louwelsa's, however Louwelsa tended to develop a deeper and somewhat higher-gloss glaze with each passing production year. Much of the old Lonhuda ware has paler tones than Louwelsa, and the glaze is not as mirrorlike. Yet many of the shapes are identical, and so is (of course) the method of decroation, in underglaze painting.

☐ **Vase, pillow (so-called becuase of its shape),** shape #275, 11-1/2", dusky olive green, decorated with a scene of cattle grazing at twilight, Lonhuda shield mark, not signed by the artist. 2450.00 2875.00

LOUWELSA

This was a continuation of the earlier Lonhuda ware under a different name. The change of name occurred around 1896, though for a while both names may have been used simultaneously — Louwelsa for new pieces,

Lonhuda for those already being produced. The name Louwelsa was constructed from the first three letters of Samuel Weller's surname, sandwiched between the first three letters of his daughter's name, Louise, and his initials, S.A., thus LOU(ise)WEL(ler)S.A. Weller's fame and success were founded in large measure upon this line. Louwelsa is a high grade of art pottery, with rich deep brown shimmering glaze and hand-painted decorations. Though the decorations were attractive, Louwelsa's glazes made them many times more striking.

Price Range

☐ **Clock (shelf type),** *10-1/2" tall by 12-1/2" wide, dark amber brown with black tonal effects, extra-glossy glaze. In a free-form shape roughly as a horizontal oval with short stumpy legs, the design intended to suggest a natural formation of nature. Decorated with small strategically placed paintings of orange flowers. Marked LOUWESLA, WELLER in semi-circular mark.* 475.00   535.00

☐ *Non-operating but intact* 325.00   360.00

☐ **Ewer,** *6-3/4", dark magenta brown shading to lighter brown at the base, touches of purple intermingled. Of cruet shape with bulbous bowl and tall narrow neck, sloping handle which rises from bowl to lip. Decorated with floral paintings in shades of burnt orange, orange, and cream yellow. Marked LOUWELSA, WELLER in semi-circular mark, and bearing the initials J.B. (artist's mark).* 130.00   155.00

☐ **Ewer,** *10", dark magenta brown with purple. Of modified cruet form with bulbous bowl, tall neck, loop handle. Decorated with paintings of yellow flowers and green leaves. Double-circle factory mark. Not marked by the artist.* 220.00   245.00

☐ **Ewer,** *12", magenta brown shading to a deep brown at base and lip. Of tankard form with flattened C-shape handle, vaulting spout, slightly irregualr (wavy) lip. Decorated with a painting of a smiling white-haired man wearing a skullcap and green toga-like garment, possibly intended to represent a member of the ancient Roman senate. Marked LOUWELSA, WELLER in circular mark (circle at the center, but no outer border), and bearing an artist's mark of BURGESS.* 1700.00   2000.00

☐ **Jug vase,** *6", dark magenta brown with purple. Of bulbous form with a pouring nozzle and C-shaped handle, the handle resting almost at the top. Decorated with paintings of grape bunches, mainly in pale orange, with green leaves. Marked LOUWELSA, WELLER in semi-circular mark, and bearing the artist's initial D.* 135.00   155.00

☐ **Mug,** *6-1/4", chocolate brown with brown-black. Of tankard form with C-shape thick handle. Decorated with large paintings of flowers in tones of orange, red and pale green. Marked LOUWELSA, WELLER in semi-circular mark and bearing the artist's initials E.A.* 260.00   300.00

☐ **Mug,** *6-1/2", dark magenta brown with highlights of lighter brown and green. Of tankard form with a twin pedestaled base, C-shape thick handle. Decorated with a painting of an elderly man in 19th century costuming, perhaps intended as a sea captain, wearing cap, high-collared white shirt, pale reddish necktie. He has white hair showing from beneath the cap and a*

Price Range

ruddy complexion. Marked LOUWELSA, WELLER in semi-circular mark, and bearing an artist's mark of FERRELL. 1175.00 1325.00

☐ **Pitcher,** 5-1/4", dark magenta brown with hints of purple and deep intense brown. Of stylized bulbous form (sometimes called "kettle form"), with a large vaulting ring-type handle and three squat feet. Decorated with subdued floral paintings (which are visible only at close range). Marked LOUWELSA, WELLER in semi-circular mark, and bearing the initials M.T. (artist's mark). 135.00 160.00

☐ **Vase,** 25", cedar brown at the central body with deep brown toning at the shoulder and neck. Of ovoid form with a tall neck and sloping shoulder, flaring into a wide horizontal lip. Decorated with a painting of grape bunches, vines and leaves, chiefly in purple, red and green. Marked LOUWELSA, WELLER in semi-circular mark, and bearing an artist's mark of DIBOWSKY. 950.00 1100.00

☐ **Vase,** 14", cedar brown shading to intense black-brown. Of narrow ovoid form, with cornered shoulder and tapering neck. Modestly flaring lip. Decorated with a painting of fish swimming about in a pool. With a hand-lettered mark of LOUWELSA, WELLER, and an aritst's mark of PILLSBURY. 1300.00 1550.00

☐ **Vase,** 5-1/2", chocolate brown with purple. In freeform bulbous shape, with shoulders rising into loop handles, which turn inward and meet rim of mouth., Short neck, no lip. Resting upon three stylized animal feet. Decorated with floral painting, chiefly in tones of yellow. Marked LOUWELSA, WELLER in semi-circular mark, and bearing the artist's initials M.H. 170.00 200.00

Note: Reminiscent of pre-Columbian Indian pottery in its shape (not in the color or glaze!)

☐ **Vase,** 10", dark chocolate brown and black-brown. Of pure cylindrical shape, with a narrower cylindrical neck flaring out into an extremely wide lip (wider than the body of the vase). With vertical handles rising up from either side of the shoulder to meet the underside of the lip. Decorated with a painting of a lilly in white and yellow. Die-stamped mark. Not signed by the artist. 160.00 190.00

☐ **Vase,** 10-1/4", dark magenta brown with some choclate and cedar shading. Of heart shape, the sides sloping into a narrow base. With a pair of very narrow, fragile-looking handles rising out of the shoulder, to connect with the rim. Decorated with paintings of flowers and leaves, mainly in white, cream yellow and moss green. Marked LOUWELSA, WELLER in semi-circular mark, and bearing the artist's mark of ADAMS. 190.00 220.00

☐ **Vase,** 6", dark magenta brown with black-brown, some tonal highlighting. Pear shape with swelled lower body, tiny neck. Decorated with floral painting, primarily in hues of yellow. Marked LOUWELSA, WELLER in semi-circular mark, and bearing the artist's initials V.A. 160.00 190.00

☐ **Vase,** 10-1/4", dark olive green and dark brown. Of ovoid form with narrow flattened neck, moderately flaring lip. Decorated with paintings of large leaves in white, cream yellow, auburn, and other colors. Marked LOUWELSA, WELLER in semi-circular mark. Not signed by the artist. 215.00 240.00

Price Range

☐ **Vase,** 5-1/2", dusky olive green with chocolate brown and other shades of brown. Of bulbous form with very narrow neck and narrow mouth, roughly following a traditional shape of Persian and Turkish ware. Decorated with a network of autumn and summer leaves, in shades of burnt orange, brown, and pastel green. Marked LOUWELSA, WELLER in semi-circular mark, and bearing the artist's mark E.A. 150.00 175.00

☐ **Vase,** 11", dusky olive green with shades of brown. Of cylindrical shape with pinched neck, moderately flared at the top, and with a pair of narrow handles rising out of the shoulder to meet the rim of the mouth. The handles are of T-square form. Decorated with paintings of small yellow-white flowers growing on thorned stems. Marked LOUWELSA, WELLER in semi-circular mark, and bearing the artist's initials M.M. 220.00 250.00

☐ **Vase,** 3", magenta brown shading to intense brown with some purple. Of pitcher form in squat bulbous shape, with a loop handle and pouring spout, sometimes referred to (incorrectly) as "oil lamp design." Decorated with floral paintings, chiefly in tones of yhellow, along the upper portion of the bowl. Marked LOUWELSA, WELLER in semi-circular mark, and bearing the initials A.C. (artist's mark). 115.00 135.00

Note: These unusual vases are appealing and cannot be too common, to judge from the infrequency of reported sales. However they have not, for some reason, made a hit with collectors.

☐ **Vase,** 7", greyish mud-green shading to intense black-brown, with various tonal highlights. Of squat bulbous form with pinched collar and widely flaring lip, small pedestal base. Decorated with a painting of a hound dog, in shades of brown with white snout and white under chest and neck, retreiving a bird. Marked LOUWELSA, WELLER in semi-circular mark, and bearing an artist's mark of BLAKE. 640.00 715.00

☐ **Vase,** 16", magenta brown with mahogany and intense dark brown. In V-form with squared shoulder, narrow neck, no lip. Natural base. Decorated with a painting after the 17th century Dutch school, showing a gentleman wearing a broad-brimmed rakish hat. The portrait is in three-quarter, his eyes turned toward the viewer's left. He has a moustache and VanDyke beard, and grey-brown woolly hair. Probably copied from an Old Master. Marked LOUWELSA, WELLER in semi-circular mark, and bearing an artist's mark of BURGESS. 2900.00 3400.00

☐ **Vase,** 3-3/4", magenta and deep choclate browns. Of flattened bulbous form, double-tiered with "bowl upon bowl" effect, roughly following a traditional shape of Persian and Turkish vases. Decorated with casual floral painting, mostly in yellow. Marked LOUWELSA, WELLER in semi-circular mark. No artist's mark. 120.00 140.00

☐ **Vase,** 11", olive green and black with touches of brown. Of ovoid form, no neck, very narrow mouth. Decorated with a half-length, full-face portrait of an Indian chief wearing ceremonial headdress. Marked LOUWELSA, WELLER in full circle mark (no outer border), and signed by the artist BURGESS. 2250.00 2600.00

☐ **Vase,** 11", reddish magenta with tones of purple, shading to various intensities of black-brown. Of bulbous flask form,

Price Range

deeply pinched neck, narrow lip, narrow mouth. Natural base. Decorated with a painting of a gentleman's head in profile, with thick wavy reddish hair. Though this may be a purely random portrait, there is a facial resemblance to Lord Byron, the Scottish poet. Marked LOUWELSA, WELLER in semi-circular mark, and bearing the initials R.G.T. (artist's mark) 975.00 1125.00

☐ **Vase,** 10-1/2", rust and magenta brown shading to intense balck-brown. Of ovoid form with wide shoulder, pinched in severely at the neck, flattened neck, narrow mouth. Natural base. Decorated with a painting of the head and neck of a doberman-type dog, white with some black splotches, chiefly on the ears. The dog's mouth is open and tongue extended. He wears a narrow collar. Marked LOUWELSA, WELLER in circular mark (circle at the center, but no outer border), and bearing an artist's mark of WILSON. 1450.00 1685.00

☐ **Vase,** 6", very dark black-brown with minimal highlighting. In free form bulbous shape, with tall handles rising out of the bowl and turning downward to meet the neck, forming inverted "V" shapes. Resting on three squat feet. Decorated with a painting of yellow, orange and red flowers, cleverly arranged in such a way that they could be mistaken for a human skull. Marked LOUWELSA, WELLER in semi-circular mark. Not signed by the artist. 140.00 165.00

Note: Just for its originality, this type of vase ought to be bringing higher prices. But apparently the Louwelsa collectors include many staunch traditionalists, to whom any deviations from the normal styles are not appealing.

☐ **Vase,** 5", very dark brown with purple overtones. Of modified cylindrical form, widening out at the shoulder. Flattened neck, narrow mouth. Decorated with casual paintings of orange flowers along the shoulder. Marked LOUWELSA, WELLER in semi-circular mark. No artist's mark. 100.00 120.00

Note: Small vases like this, with a minimum of hand painting, were a standard factory item for the Louwelsa line for a number of years. Their ratio on the antiques market, versus the larger painted vases, is 10-1 or perhaps as great as 20-1, which accounts in part for the correspondingly lower value.

☐ **Vase,** handled, 23", dark green and rust brown at the base, shading into a dusky lime green and then to intense earth-brown. Of semi-cylindrical Grecian form, with a pair of handles rising out of the body and turning inward to meet the neck. Modestly flared lip, narrow mouth. Decorated with a painting of reddish flowers with velvety petals and tall stems. Marked LOUWELSA, WELLER in semi-circular mark, and bearing an artist's mark of HAUBRICH. 630.00 690.00

☐ **Vase, pillow (so-called for its shape),** 4-1/4", orange-brown with hints of purple and green, minimal highlighting. With lip sloping inward toward the center, decorated by a pair of molded bands; four squat feet. Decorated with a painting of a flower in burnt orange, red and reddish-yellow. No factory mark, but bearing the initial M. (artist's mark). 120.00 145.00

SICARD *(also called SICARDO; introduced 1901 or 1902)*

A high quality art line, very distinctive. It was the work of Jacques Sicard, a French potter, who was employed by Weller beginning in 1901. The pieces were all hand-thrown on the wheel. While pre-determined patterns were followed, the hand shaping injected an element of uniqueness in each specimen, as no two were quite identical. Sicard ware was finished with highly lustrous metallic glazes, which gave the appearance of old silver with irridescent toning. Tones of purple, blue, green, red and other colors are often found on the same item; and if it were possible to count the number of tonal shadings on a piece, they would probably total up into the hundreds. Sicard has its avid collectors, but the prices on today's market still look like bargains.

Price Range

☐ **Mug,** *3-1/2", metallic violet and blue, cylindrical, with painted floral designs, unmarked.* 500.00   550.00

☐ **Vase,** *4-1/2", metallic red, egg shape (modified), decorated with silvery paintings of fans, unmarked.* 390.00   435.00

☐ **Vase,** *5-1/2", metallic red with hints of violet, tankard shape with bloated shaped lip, decorated with a fine network of small silvery speckles, marked SICARD.* 240.00   280.00

TURADA *(Introduced before 1900)*

Highly glazed dark brown bodies, *or* two-toned with dark brown and caramel brown. Unpainted, but decorated with applied molding of various colors (sometimes uncolored). This is worked into delicate, intricate designs, using extremely thin lengths of slip. The duration of Turada's manufacture is a matter of dispute among the experts. It was traditionally believed that Weller phased out the line quite early — not long after 1900 or possibly right at 1900. In comparing the appearance of different specimens, however, it now seems likely that some continued to be made until a much later date, perhaps into the 1920's or even as late as 1930. This question will not be satisfactorily answered until some positive record is found.

☐ **Jar, tobacco,** *5-1/2", dark brown blended with puirple (solid overall color), pot form, lidded, decorated with a band of applied cream-yellow emblems around the shoulder. With the Turada semi-circular mark.* 270.00   310.00
Note: In dealers' and auctioneers' catalogues this often appears as a humidor. When the lid is lacking, figure $210.00 to $240.00.

☐ **Jardiniere,** *8-1/2", two-tone black-brown with caramel brown, of pot form pinched in slightly at the center, decorated with a band of applied ornament in the form of cream-yellow lozenges and purple flowers set against cream-yellow squares. Not marked.* 320.00   370.00

☐ **Lamp base (kerosene lamp),** *8", dark brown, of flattened bulbous form, with brass head, bulb holder and fuel cap. Resting on four squat legs. Decorated with blue and salmon applied ornament, encircling the shoulder, in a classical pattern of interlacing vines. Unmarked.* 875.00   975.00
Note: These were presumably made before 1900, probably in 1896 or 1897. Some specimens have been converted to electricity. This reduces the value by nearly 1/2.

Price Range

☐ **Mug,** *shape #562/7, 6", very dark brown, modified cylindrical shape, C-style handle, decorated with cream white applied molding encircling the girth, in a classical pattern of interlacing vines. With the Turada semi-circular mark.* 265.00   300.00

WENCZEL TILE

Current Trenton tile company.

WILLETS MANUFACTURING COMPANY

Willets was founded in 1879 by the Willets brothers, Jospeh, Daniel and Edmund. The company was located in what had previously been the William Young & Sons pottery. Although they are best known for their Belleek-type wares, they also made opaque china, white granite ware, electrical porcelain majolica, and sanitary wares.

The Thomas Maddock book indicates that Willets started manufacturing sanitary items in 1909, and that Joseph and Daniel Willets were the owners of the company. It is possible that Edmund had died by that time, or else that his brothers bought out his interest in the company.

The exact date when the company went out of business is not known, but 1912 seems to be the date most people accept. The year 1909, also occasionally mentioned as the closing year, was probably the year when they stopped making Belleek in favor of making sanitary wares.

The Willets Company is something of the exception in that its founders had no other known connections in the Trenton ceramics industry. We do not know where they gained their experience in making china, or what happened to them after the company closed.

Many of the better-known Trenton people worked at Willets at one time or another. William Bromley, Jr., was art director there for awhile (possibly beginning in 1886,) and he was followed by Walter Lenox. There probably was no real art director there before Bromley, and we do not know who followed Lenox in that position.

A photo in the possession of George Houghton's family shows the Willets art department with four artists seated at their work spaces and one man standing, presumably the art director. He is a rather dapper man of about 35, and it is not Walter Lenox. George Houghton can be identified as one of the artists, but the names of the others remain a mystery. Since Houghton worked at Willets virtually the entire time they made decorated artware, his presence cannot be used to date the photo or to aid in the identification of the others.

Another view of the Willets art department shows Oliver Houghton at work, and the same man standing. A woman is also in the picture, which raises the possibility that Willets had a female artist at one time. Once again, the photo is undated and without names except for Oliver Houghton's. (Put down this book right now and go date all your photographs!)

Willets has only recently come into its own, and for the most part people have stopped calling it "early Lenox." As of this year, the earliest items produced there can legally be termed antiques, and there has been a great deal of activity with Willets during the past year.

Marks: The original house mark for Willets stoneware was the British lion and unicorn, used by nearly all makers of British-style softpaste ware. This was accompanied by the initials of the firm and (as usual) no address, as the purchaser was supposed to imagine he was buying an import. Later, the term *OPAQUE PORCELAIN* was used, along with an intricate monogram. For its Belleek, Willets used a serpent (snake) marking, sometimes with the word *BELLEEK* and sometimes merely with the factory name.

Mark A **Mark B**

Other marks used by the company include a globe mark with the initials "W. M. Co.," usually appearing with a dinnerware pattern name, and intertwined "W Co" with the wording "Opaque Porcelain." These marks usually appear on lower-level items which are of lesser importance to collectors. Another mark is sometimes called the chewing gum mark — a small pad of porcelain applied to the bottom of items such as the basket with applied flowers shown in the color section. The Willets mark is impressed into the pad. Marks of this type were generally used on items which were difficult to mark in the ordinary fashion, and the so-called spaghetti strand baskets are in this category.

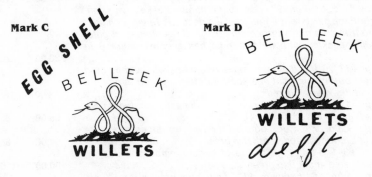

Mark C **Mark D**

WILLETS
Mark E

CHINA

Willets shape numbers will be found on many of their items, and will look like pencil-written numbers on the bottom. These numbers correspond to catalogue item numbers, and can be a great aid in positive identification of a given item. Maybe 50 percent of the items will be so marked, including both factory and nonfactory decorated pieces.

Prices: Although Willets prices can fluctuate quite a bit from one part of the country to another, as a general rule they will be somewhere between those for early Lenox and those for Ott & Brewer. This is probably about where they belong, both from an availability and an age point of view.

One of the things keeping back prices on Willets items is the inability to easily distinguish factory and nonfactory-decorated items via mail or telephone. Unlike Lenox items of the same period which are virtually 100 percent factory-decorated if they bear the wreath mark, Willets items with mark B in brown really have to be examined close up. Even then there is sometimes room for doubt since Willets did not apply quality control standards that strictly.

In the following price section, item numbers are used to positively identify the items, and the terminology from the old catalogues is also used. Although we find some of their classifications questionable, we suppose the company that made the items has the right to name them.

BASKETS

Price Range

☐ Shape #121, 5-1/2" high, small ribbed basket, twig handle, undecorated, mark B in green 90.00 110.00

☐ Shape #173, 8" high, 9" wide, rustic handle basket, twig handle, outside glazed with gold trim, inside matte finish with gold paste trim on a chrysanthemum design, three shades of gold, handle speckled with gold, handle has a crack, mark B in brown 220.00 270.00

☐ Shape #174, 3-1/2" diameter, small round basket, hand-painted flowers outlined in gold in a scatter pattern, gold trim on handle and rim, mark B in red 115.00 130.00

☐ Shape #174, 3-1/2" diameter, small round basket, undecorated, mark B in green 55.00 63.00

☐ Shape #205, 7" wide, pointed arches on sides opposite handles, undecorated, mark B in green 50.00 58.00

☐ Shape #341, 5-1/4" high to top of handle, embossed design, undecorated, mark B in green 90.00 110.00

☐ Shape number unknown, 11" long, spaghetti strand type, applied flowers in pastel colors, chewing gum mark, some rough spots on petals, see photo in color section 550.00 650.00

Basket, *shape #173*

Price Range

BON BONS

☐ *Shape #0, 6-1/2" diameter, 1-1/4" deep, curled handles, ruffled rim, undecorated, mark B in green* 50.00 58.00

☐ *Shape #0, dimensions as above, hand-painted flowers, gold trim on handles and rim, artist signed and dated, mark B in green* ... 65.00 75.00

☐ *Shape #0, dimensions as above, pearlized pin interior, sponged gold trim on exterior, mark B in red* 75.00 85.00

Bonbon, *shape #190*

☐ *Shape #1, 6-1/4" diameter, 1-1/4" deep, undecorated, mark B in green* 23.00 28.00

☐ *Shape #1, dimensions as above, single large pink rose in center, outside totally covered in gold, artist's initials on bottom, mark B in green* 40.00 47.50

☐ *Shape #1-1/2, 5-1/2" diameter, 1" deep, hand-painted small pink roses outlined in gold in scatter pattern, small fleck on rim, mark B in red* 80.00 95.00

Price Range

☐ Shape #8, 6-1/2" long, 5-1/2" wide, 1-1/4" deep, veined design in china, undecorated, exceptionally thin, mark B in green 75.00   85.00

☐ Shape #190, 6" diameter, covered, two rustic handles and rustic finial, pearlized white finish with bronze colored handles and finial, mark A in red 150.00   180.00

☐ Shape #242, 6-1/2" long, heart-shaped, covered undecorated, mark B in green 80.00   95.00

☐ Shape #244, 7-1/4" long, heart-shaped with ruffled rim, small hand-painted wildflowers with gold outlining, gold trim on rim, several tiny flecks on rim, mark B in red 80.00   95.00

BOTTLES

☐ Shape #148, 7-1/2" high, rustic handled water bottle, fluted, matte finish with gold paste trim, mark B in brown 180.00   220.00

☐ Shape #148, size as above, undecorated, mark B in green 125.00   145.00

☐ Shape #228, 5" high, Pilgrim bottle, glazed finish, single coral-colored orchid outlined in gold, gold trim on feet and handles, crack in one handle, mark B in red 225.00   275.00

BOUQUET HOLDERS

Bouquet Holder,
shape #97

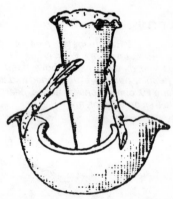

Bouquet Holder, shape #229

☐ Shape #97, 3-1/4" high, pyramid type comprised of five tiny jugs piled on top of each other, undecorated, handle of one jug broken, mark B in brown 75.00   85.00

☐ Shape #229, 4" high, small fluted-top trumpet shape vase inside a curled-edge bowl, vase part supported by three twigs connected to side of bowl, vase is pearlized pink on the outside, white on inside, trim reversed on bowl, sponged gold trim on branches, gold trim on rims, mark B in red 150.00   175.00

BOWLS

☐ Shape #4, 7" square, 3-1/2" deep, square salad, undecorated, mark B in green 50.00   58.00

Price Range

☐ Shape #4, square salad, dimensions as above, gold paste in oak leaf pattern inside of bowl, speckled gold on outside, mark B in red 170.00   200.00

☐ Shape #5, 9-1/2" diameter, 3-1/2" deep, crimped salad, chains of daisies hand-painted on outside, gold trim on trim, artist signed, mark B in green 75.00   85.00

☐ Shape #5, dimensions as above, crimped salad, undecorated, mark B in green 65.00   75.00

☐ Shape #11, 10-1/2" diameter, 3-1/4" deep, plain salad, hand-painted water lilies on inside, solid green exterior, gold banding on rim and base, although obviously home-done it is nonetheless a very attractive item, mark B in green 160.00   190.00

☐ Shape #11, dimensions as above, plain salad, undecorated, mark B in green 60.00   70.00

☐ Shape #75, 6" diameter, 2-3/4" deep, handled bowl, ruffled rim, gold trim on handles and rim, mark B in green 55.00   63.00

☐ Shape #165, low crimped diamond shape, 3-1/2" high, 9-1/2" wide, pearlized yellow interior, sponged gold on outside, mark B in red 140.00   170.00

☐ Shape #201, 3-1/2" diameter, small footed bowl, fishnet finish on outside, speckled gold trim on feet and gold pencil line on rim, mark B in red 120.00   140.00

☐ Shape #201-1/2, as above but with no fishnet, undecorated, mark B in green 65.00   75.00

☐ Shape #206, 9-1/2" diameter, ice bowl, ruffled rim, missing its tray, hand-painted daffodils with gold trim, artist signed, mark B in green 105.00   120.00

☐ Shape #240, 7" diameter, twisted ribbing, scalloped rim, undecorated, mark B in green 90.00   110.00

Bowl, shape #320

☐ Shape #320, 4-1/8" high, 7" diameter, dragon-handled, pale green exterior, gold trim on rim and dragons, very nicely done, mark B in green 115.00   130.00

☐ Shape number unknown, 7" handle to handle, ruffled rim, hand-painted monochromatic blue scene, mark D in blue 180.00   220.00

BREAD AND MILK SETS
Price Range

☐ *Shape #74, pitcher 6" high, bowl 6" diameter, ruffled rim on bowl, curly handle on pitcher, hand-painted small red roses, gold trim, mark B in brown* 140.00   170.00

BUTTER TUBS

☐ *Shape #31, 5-1/2" diameter, drainer damaged and glued together, gold trim on lid finial, gold pencil line around mid-section, mark B in green* 60.00   70.00

CANDLESTICKS

☐ *Shape #314, 1-5/8" candlestick on trivet shaped base, undecorated, mark B in green* 55.00   63.00

CHOCOLATE POTS

Chocolate pot,
shape #39

☐ *Shape #39, 10" high, veining in china, bud finial, delicate pink tinting with brushed gold over it, gold trim on handle and finial, absolutely divine, mark B in red* 320.00   380.00
☐ *Shape #210-1/4, 10" high, gold paste on matte finish, mark B in red, see photo in color section* 320.00   380.00
☐ *Shape #210-1/2, 10" high, undecorated, lid cracked, mark B in green* 120.00   140.00

CLOCKS

☐ *Shape, number unknown, 7" high, embossed design on china and hand-painted roses, gold trim, replacement clock work, mark B in red, see photo* 300.00   250.00

Clock, *shape number unknown*

COFFEEPOTS

☐ *Shape #672, 6-1/4" high, gold trim, gold handle and finial, nicely done, probably the work of one of the decorating establishments, gold too brassy looking to have been done at factory, mark B in green, see photo* . . . .

Price Range

120.00   140.00

Coffeepot, *shape #672*

Price Range

☐ *Shape #725, 7-1/2" high, hand-painted peacocks and garlands of flowers, artist's initials E.C. (probably Edward Chalinor), mark B in brown, handle clumsily repaired and a crack in the body, see photo* 60.00   70.00

(Note: For whatever reason, the Willets company referred to most of their pots as teapots regardless of their shape or size. For additional listings on coffeepots, see the teapot section.)

Coffeepot, *shape #725*

COMPORTS

☐ *Shape #16, 2" high, shell raised on three twig feet, pearlized blue interior, speckled gold trim on outside and on feet, mark A in red* 140.00   170.00

☐ *Shape #16, 2" high, shell raised on three twig feet, undecorated, small fleck on rim, mark B in green* 55.00   63.00

☐ *Shape #40, 10" diameter, shell raised on coral and seashell pedestal base, pearlized finish, base done in different shades of gold, speckled gold trim on rest of the item, mark B in red* ..   250.00   300.00

☐ *Shape #41, 9" diameter, ruffled rim top section resting on six-footed geometric design twig base, undecorated, several flecks on rim, large hairline crack across top, mark B in green* .   40.00   47.50

CRACKER JARS

☐ *Shape #38, 6" high, 5" diameter, bamboo pattern, shaded pale green colors with gold highlights, lid does not fit particularly well although it is probably the original one, mark B in brown* .   160.00   190.00

CROCUS POTS

☐ *Shape number unknown, two twigs form the handle, hand-painted flowers outlined in gold in scatter pattern, gold trim on rims and handle, mark B in red, see photo* 115.00   130.00

Crocus pot, *shape number unknown*

CUPS AND SAUCERS
Price Range

☐ *Shape #22, Piedmont tea, plain shape, undecorated mark B in green* 17.00 22.00

☐ *Shape #22, Piedmont tea, hand-painted lily of the valley on green background, gold trim on handle and rims, mark B in green* 37.00 43.00

☐ *Shape #23, shell tea, pearlized lavender interior, sponged gold on exterior, filigree gold on handle, mark B in red* 50.00 58.00

☐ *Shape #23, shell tea, undecorated, mark B in green* 30.00 35.00

☐ *Shape #23, shell tea, exceptionally thin and fine, gold trim, mark B in red* 60.00 70.00

☐ *Shape #24, ribbed tea, undecorated, mark B in green* 15.00 20.00

☐ *Shape #25 (Piedmont after dinner coffee), #26 (Three-footed tea), #27 (shell after dinner coffee), and #30 (ribbed after dinner coffee) are all shown in the catalogues without saucers. Since they are often erroneously sold as being incomplete, the prices are much lower than they should be. They are frequently priced around* 15.00 20.00

☐ *Shape #47, 7-1/2" diameter, 5 o'clock cup and tray, veined design on tray, cup has narrow fluting and forked handle, shade coral coloring with sponged gold trim over it, mark B in red, small fleck on rim* 160.00 190.00

☐ *Shape #96, leaf after dinner coffee, footed, pale green with embossed veining traced over in a darker green, mark B in green* 50.00 58.00

☐ *Shape #96, leaf after dinner coffee, footed, undecorated, mark B in green* 37.00 43.00

☐ *Shape #99, scalloped edge tea, undecorated, mark B in green* . 20.00 25.00

☐ *Shape #99, scalloped edge tea, small hand-painted blue forget-me-nots, gold trim, mark B in green* 30.00 35.00

☐ *Shape #102, flutted bottom after dinner coffee, beige and gray with gold paste trim, mark B in red* 90.00 110.00

Price Range

☐ Shape #102, fluted bottom after dinner coffee, salmon colored flowers outlined in gold, gold trim on handles and rims, mark B in red 80.00 95.00

☐ Shape #103, oval panel and footed after dinner coffee, undecorated, mark B in green 27.00 32.00

☐ Shape #104, square panel, square handle after dinner coffee, gold trim on handle and outlining panels, mark B in brown 37.00 43.00

☐ Shape #105, plain top, twisted, fluted bottom after dinner coffee, pale pink with darker pink flowers, gold trim on handle and rim, mark B in green 50.00 58.00

☐ Shape #115, bowl 3-3/4" diameter, saucer 5-3/4" diameter, doubled flowered bouillon cup and saucer, undecorated, mark B in brown 37.00 43.00

☐ Shape #126, 5 o'clock after dinner coffee, embossed lily petals, forked handle, lemon yellow exterior with gold trim, mark B in red 80.00 95.00

☐ Shape #126, 5 o'clock after dinner coffee, embossed lily petals, forked handle, undecorated, mark B in green 37.00 43.00

☐ Shape #162, bowl 4" diameter, saucer 5-1/4" diameter, flower handled bouillon with lid, undecorated, unmarked 15.00 20.00

Bouillon cup, *gold trim, shape #163*

☐ Shape #163, shell bouillon, gold trim, mark D in red, no saucer, see photo 37.00 43.00

☐ Shape #163, shell bouillon, pearlized yellow interior, gold trim on handles and rims, mark B in red 60.00 70.00

☐ Shape #164, cactus pattern covered bouillon, undecorated and unmarked 23.00 28.00

☐ Shape #164, cactus pattern covered bouillon, gold trim, mark B in green 37.00 43.00

☐ Shape #164-1/2, cactus pattern bouillon, outside painted in green with brown highlights, brown handles, mark B in green . 65.00 75.00

☐ Shape #164-3/4, cactus tea, undecorated, mark B in green, two small flecks on saucer 40.00 47.50

Bouillon cup, *yellow flowers, shape #251*

Price Range

☐ *Shape #164-3/4, cactus tea, pearlized pink interior, gold trim, mark B in red* 80.00 95.00

☐ *Shape #182, saucer 6" diameter, covered plain bouillon, hand-painted small poppies, gold trim on handles, rims and finial, mark B in green* 37.00 43.00

☐ *Shape #183, bouillon, bowl 3-3/4" diameter, saucer 5-1/2" diameter, hand-painted yellow flowers with brown centers, green leaves, handles painted green with gold highlights, mark B in brown, see photo* 80.00 95.00

☐ *Shape #211, footed shell tea, pearlized blue interior, gold trim, several small flecks, set of 6, mark B in red* 320.00 380.00

☐ *Shape #211, footed shell tea, undecorated, mark B in green* ... 60.00 70.00

☐ *Shape #212, footed shell after dinner coffee, exceptionally thin, gold trim, mark B in red* 90.00 110.00

☐ *Shape #246, 2-1/2", fluted after dinner coffee with dragon handle, gold trim, mark B in green* 60.00 70.00

☐ *Shape #247, 3" fluted chocolate, no saucer, unmarked* 15.00 20.00

☐ *Shape #247-1/2, fluted tea, set of 4, each one decorated with a different flower, gold trim on rims and on dragons, artist signed and dated, mark B in green* 135.00 155.00

☐ *Shape #249-1/2, 2-1/2" after dinner coffee with dolphin handle, undecorated, mark B in green* 50.00 58.00

☐ *Shape #260, after dinner coffee, twisted, sacalloped, with dolphin handle, gold banding between scallops, gold trim on handle and rim, crack in handle, mark B in brown* 30.00 35.00

☐ *Shape #261, chocolate cup, twisted, scalloped, with dolphin handle, pale pink exterior with small, hand-painted gold roses, exceptionally attractive for a home-done piece, mark B in green* 60.00 70.00

☐ *Shape #274, heart-shaped after dinner coffee, forked handle, saucer missing, St. Valentine's greeting down inside, gold trim on handle and feet, mark B in green* 55.00 63.00

☐ *Shape #282, shell tea, speckled gold trim on handle and body, mark B in brown* 75.00 85.00

Price Range

☐ Shape #308, embossed and scalloped after dinner coffee, single large pink rose on one side of cup and three buds on saucer, gold trim, nicely done, mark B in green 55.00   63.00

☐ Shape #309, embossed and scalloped chocolate cup, very thin, gold trim, no mark 15.00   20.00

☐ Shape #310, embossed and scalloped tea, hand-painted lily of the valley, gold trim, mark B in green 30.00   35.00

☐ Shape #312, embossed teacup, hand-painted bouquet of flowers, gold trim, mark B in green 37.00   43.00

☐ Shape #313, embossed after dinner coffee, pearlized white, gold trim, mark B in red 65.00   75.00

☐ Shape #313-1/2, embossed bouillon, undecorated, small chip on rim of saucer, mark B in green 20.00   25.00

DISHES

☐ Shape #29, ice cream dish, pencil line gold around top rim, mark B in brown, set of 6 . . . .   115.00   130.00

☐ Shape #325, strawberry dish, 8" diameter, 2" high, ruffled top, small, hand-painted gold flowers, sponged gold near rim, mark B in red 80.00   95.00

☐ Shape #326, strawberry dish, 7" diameter, 1-3/4" high, ruffled rim, undecorated, unmarked 15.00   20.00

EGG CUPS

☐ Shape #42, 3" high, lily egg cup, undecorated, several flecks on rim, mark B in green 23.00   28.00

☐ Shape #42, 3" high, lily egg cup, pink shading on ouside, two flecks on inside of rim, mark B in red 65.00   75.00

Egg cup, shape #42, pink shading

Price Range

☐ Shape #42, lily egg cup, gold trim, mark B in red, see photo ... 120.00 140.00
☐ Shape #42, lily egg cup, coral shading with sponged gold over it, mark B in red 175.00 225.00

EWERS

☐ Shape #43, 10-1/2" high, stick handle rustic ewer, matte beige finish with gold paste trim in chrysanthemum pattern, gold trim, on handles and rims, mark B in red 300.00 350.00
☐ Shape #44, 10" high, branch handle rustic ewer, single water lily on front outliner in gold, gold trim on handle and rim, crack in handle and 1/2" chip out of spout, mark B in red 150.00 175.00
☐ Shape #45, 10-1/2" high, straight handle rustic ewer, undecorated and unmarked 90.00 110.00
☐ Shape #45, 10-1/2" high, straight handle rustic ewer, shaded from lavender at bottom to pea green at top, gold paste trim, gold trim on handles and rims, mark B in red 320.00 380.00
☐ Shape #46, 10" high, claret ewer, beige matte finish, gold paste flowers, gold trim on handle and rims, spider crack in bottom, mark B in red 160.00 190.00
☐ Shape #81-1/2, Worcester ewer, piercing on handle and neck, unmarked and piercing damaged in several places 60.00 70.00
☐ Shape #166, 8" high, small, rustic handled ewer, hand-painted bluebird on one side, branch with pink blossom on other, gold handle, gold trim on rims, artist signed and dated, mark B in brown 175.00 225.00
☐ Shape #179, 10" high, oval, crimped top, rustic handled French ewer, undecorated, mark B in green 135.00 155.00
☐ Shape #199, 9-1/2" high, rustic ewer, beige matte finish, gold paste Queen Anne's lace, gold trim on handle, mark B in red .. 175.00 225.00
☐ Shape #202, 11-1/2" high, handled ewer, hand-painted portrait of a little girl in bonnet, raised blue dot enamel work, about three times more gold trim than the item needs, very sloppy looking, artist signed and dated, small hairline on rim, mark B in green 150.00 175.00
☐ Shape #208, 7-1/2" high, rustic handled ewer, undecorated, mark B in green 60.00 70.00
☐ Shape #208, 7-1/2" high, rustic handled ewer, hand-painted red rose, gold trim, artist signed, mark B in green 90.00 110.00
☐ Shape #210, 9" high, dragon handle claret ewer, pearlized pink with speckled gold trim, mark B in red 210.00 255.00
☐ Shape #210, 9" high, dragon handle claret ewer, sloppy gold trim, mark B in green 120.00 140.00
☐ Shape #231, 6" high, globe ewer, undecorated, mark B in green 95.00 115.00
☐ Shape #231, 6" high, globe ewer, gold trim, mark B in green ... 120.00 140.00
☐ Shape #287, 9-1/2" high to top of spout, embossed ewer, hand-painted cocker spaniel, gold trim, absolutely icredible, mark B in green 120.00 140.00
☐ Shape #323, 8-1/4" high, beige matte finish, bottle ewer, gold paste in oak leaf pattern, gold trim on handle and top, mark A in brown 210.00 255.00

Ewers

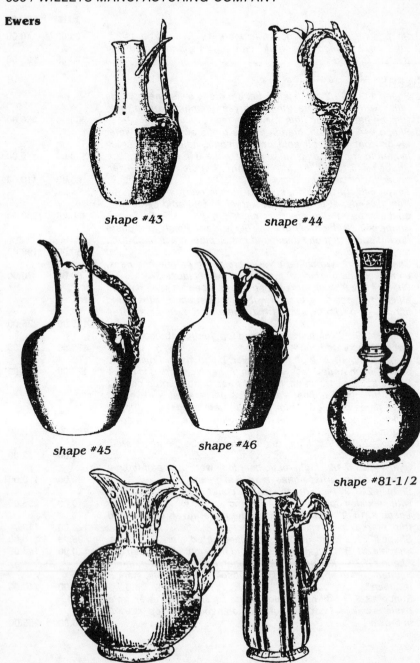

shape #43

shape #44

shape #45

shape #46

shape #81-1/2

shape #231

shape #210

FLOWER HOLDERS

Price Range

☐ Shape #176, 5-1/2" high, crimped edge flower holder, oval cut center, undecorated, mark B in green 85.00   100.00

☐ Shape #224, 6" high, double handled flower holder, cut top, hand-painted trailing vines, gold trim on handles and rim, mark B in green 115.00   130.00

☐ Shape #264, shell globe flower holder, coral handles, ruffled top, gold paste floral decoration on beige matte background, inside glazed in pearlized yellow, mark B in red 175.00   225.00

☐ Shape #315, 5-1/4" long, low shell flower holder, undecorated, mark B in brown 40.00   47.50

☐ Shape #316, 4-1/4" long, low shell flower holder, hand-painted small pink roses outlined in gold, gold trim on rims, mark B in red 105.00   120.00

FLOWER POTS

☐ Shape #334, 4-1/2" wide, 6" high, beige matte finish, cactus flower pot, gold trim on flower, leaves, and other high points, mark B in brown, one foot repaired 160.00   190.00

Flower pot, *shape #334*

GLOBES

☐ Shape #149, 6-3/4", rustic footed globe, hand-painted red and pink, cabbage roses all around, gold trim on rim and base, artist signed and dated, mark B in green 120.00   140.00

☐ Shape #324, 5-1/2" diameter, embossed and footed globe, gold trim on embossing, feet and rim, mark B in green 105.00   120.00

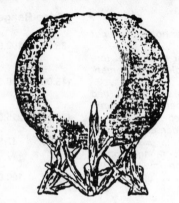

Globe, *shape #149*

Globe, *shape #324*

JARDINIERES

Price Range

☐ *Shape #268, 7-1/2" high, 8-1/2" wide, tall, footed jardiniere, cut and folded top, gold paste chrysanthemums in three shades of gold, beige matte finish, sponged gold on feet and rim, mark B in brown* 250.00 350.00

Jardiniere, *shape #268*

Jardiniere, *shape #333*

☐ *Shape #333, 6-1/2" wide, 5-3/4" high, embossed jardiniere, hand-painted mixed flowers on both sides, gold highlighting on embossing and rims, home-done but very nice, artist signed and dated, mark B in green* 160.00 190.00

☐ *Shape #333, 6-1/2" wide, 5-3/4" high, embossed jardiniere, undecorated and unmarked* 30.00 35.00

☐ *Shape #333-1/4, 7" wide, garden scene, gold trim, artist signed, mark B in green* 160.00 190.00

☐ *Shape #333-1/2, 8" high, gold initials, gold trim on embossing and rim, mark B in green* 90.00 110.00

JARS
Price Range

☐ *Shape #6, 7-1/4" high, small covered jar, hand-painted white and pink roses, ornate blue dot and gold work, signed M. J. Parker, mark B in brown, see photo in color section* 375.00   425.00

☐ *Shape #6, 7-1/4" high, hand-painted garlands of pink roses, gold trim, mark B in green* 115.00   130.00

☐ *Shape #6, 7-1/4" high, undecorated and unmarked* 40.00   47.50

☐ *Shape #50, 8-1/2" high, Oriental jar, undecorated, mark B in green* 80.00   95.00

☐ *Shape #50, 8-1/2" high, Oriental jar, hand-painted pink and maroon cabbage roses all around, gold trim, artist signed, mark B in green* 120.00   140.00

☐ *Shape #50, 8-1/2" high, Oriental jar, hand-painted water lilies and gold trim, artist signed and dated, mark B in green* 160.00   190.00

☐ *Shape #51, 11-3/4" high, rose jar, pierced top, gold filigree effect and gold trim on lid, lid badly damaged, mark B in green*   90.00   110.00

☐ *Shape #230, 6" high, cracker jar, hand-painted ivy with gold trim, mark B in green* 105.00   120.00

☐ *Shape #241, 7" high, twisted cracker jar, undecorated, mark B in green* 135.00   155.00

Jars

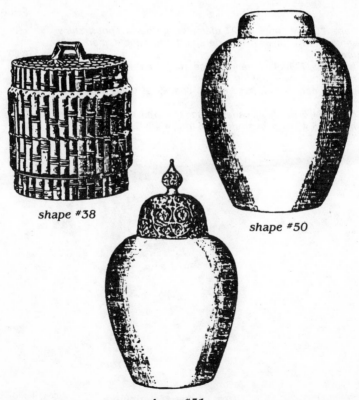

shape #38

shape #50

shape #51

shape #230

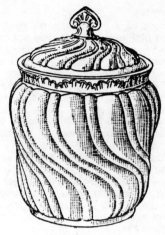

shape #241

JUGS

Price Range

☐ Shape #52, 7" high, 6-1/2" diameter, gargoyle spout, shiny Chinese red with gold trim on spout and handle, mark B in green 170.00 200.00

☐ Shape #53, 7" high, cane jug, decorated in natural looking colors of light brown highlighted with a darker brown, green leaf on side, dark brown handle with specks of gold, mark B in brown 135.00 155.00

☐ Shape #54, 5-1/2" high, cane jug, undecorated, mark B in green 80.00 90.00

☐ Shape #55, 4" high, cane jug, gold trim, mark B in green 60.00 70.00

Jug, shape #56, bamboo

Price Range

☐ Shape #56, 6-1/2" high, bamboo jug, beige matte background, gold paste in trailing design, green bamboo leaves around handle, pinkish-beige handle, sponged gold highlights, gold trim on rim, 1-1/2" hairline on spout, mark B in red, see photo 110.00   125.00

☐ Shape #57, 5-1/2" high, bamboo jug, glazed finish, coral-colored flowers outlined in gold, gold trim on handle and rims, mark B in red 150.00   175.00

☐ Shape #58, 3" high, bamboo jug, undecorated and unmarked . 18.00   23.00

☐ Shape #62, 7-1/2" high, shell jug, coral handle, unmarked and undecorated, see photo in color section 375.00   425.00

☐ Shape #101, 5" high, small rustic jug, hand-painted blue forget-me-nots, gold trim on handle and rim, mark B in green 90.00   110.00

☐ Shape #101, 5" high, small rustic jug, gold trim on handle, mark B in green 65.00   75.00

☐ Shape #108, 7-1/2" high, rustic-handled ewer, hand-painted orchid, gold trim, artist signed, mark B in green 150.00   175.00

☐ Shape #145, 5-1/2" high, globe jug, undecorated, mark B in green 65.00   75.00

☐ Shape #145, 5-1/2" high, globe jug, hand-painted pansies with very pretty gold work on spout and handle, exceptionally nice for home decoration, artist signed, mark B in green 120.00   140.00

☐ Shape #177, 5-1/2" high, oval, broad bottom, crimped top, rustic handled jug, gold paste trim in oak leaf pattern, mark B in red 120.00   140.00

☐ Shape #177, description as above, hand-painted white and yellow roses in shaded brown background, gold trim on handle and rims, small chip on handle, artist signed and dated, mark B in green 70.00   80.00

☐ Shape #210-3/4, 11-1/2" high, jug, dragon handle, monochromatic blue floral design, mark B in green 175.00   225.00

☐ Shape #218, 6" high, embossed jog, undecorated and unmarked 40.00   47.50

☐ Shape #235, 6-3/4" high jug, dolphin handle, vertical rainbow shading, pink top and handle with speckled gold trim, crack in handle, mark B in brown 135.00   155.00

☐ Shape #235, 6-3/4" high jug, dolphin handle, gold trim on handle and spout, mark B in green 120.00   140.00

☐ Shape #236, 5-1/2" high jug, dolphin handle, banding of small yellow flowers around top section, gold trim on handle, rims and spout, mark B in green 105.00   120.00

☐ Shape #311, 9-1/2" high, embossed and scalloped jug, hand-painted pink and red flowers on shaded green and yellow background, silver overlay work on embossed sections and on handle, mark B in brown, see photo in color section 450.00   550.00

KETTLES

☐ Shape #48, 4" high, gypsy kettle, round, hand-painted small pink roses outlined in gold, gold trim on handles and rim, mark B in red 175.00   225.00

☐ Shape #48, 4" high, gypsy kettle, round, undecorated, mark B in green 55.00   63.00

☐ Shape #49, 4-1/4" long, 2-1/2" wide, gypsy kettle, oval, undecorated and unmarked, small chip on handle 18.00   23.00

LOVING CUPS

Price Range

☐ *Shape #456, three-handled loving cup, raised blue enamel flowers with gold paste trim, mark B in red, see photo in color section* 200.00 250.00

☐ *Shape #456, three-handled loving cup, hand-painted small roses and gold trim on handles and rims, marked on front "New England Sanitary Club" and on back with date and name of hotel where a meeting was apparently held, in addition to usual Willets mark also has the mark of the Trenton Potteries Company, see photo* 85.00 100.00

Loving cup, *shape #456*

☐ *Shape #488, 9", three-handled footed loving cup, portrait of woman, pale blue banding at top and on pedestal covered with gold filigree work, raised gold paste trim around portrait, gold trim on handles, signed Mary J. Coulter and dated 1906, mark B in brown, see photo in color section* 500.00 600.00

MATCH BOXES

☐ *Shape #19, 3" long, shaped like treasure chest with acorn finial, undecorated and unmarked* 40.00 50.00

MUGS AND STEINS

Shape numbers for mugs are not known, partly because catalogue pictures are too indistinct to allow us to differentiate between them.

☐ **Mug,** *5" high, hand-painted ears of corn on shaded brown background, mark B in green* 90.00 110.00

☐ **Mug,** *5" high, hand-painted berries on shaded green background, very nicely done, artist signed and dated, mark B in green* 135.00 155.00

☐ **Mug,** *5" high, hand-painted monk scene in monochromatic browns, mark B in green* 120.00 140.00

Stein, *grapes and leaves*

	Price Range	

- ☐ **Mug,** 5" high, hand-painted grapes and leaves on pale green background, artist signed and dated, mark B in green 90.00   110.00
- ☐ **Mug,** 5-1/2" high, monochromatic brown tavern scene, part hand-painted and part transfer, mark b in brown 110.00   125.00
- ☐ **Mug,** 5-1/2" high, hand-painted red berries on shaded brown background, gold handle and rim, artist's initials and date, mark B in green 110.00   125.00
- ☐ **Mug,** 5-1/2" high, hand-painted red berries on shaded brown backgrtound, gold handle and rim, artist's initials and date, mark B in green 90.00   110.00
- ☐ **Mug,** 5-1/2" high, hand-painted small white dog on brown, green and orange shaded background, signed G. Houghton and dated, mark B in brown 400.00   500.00
- ☐ **Mug,** 5-1/2" high, transfer decoration of carriage scene, gold trim on handle and rim, very sloppy, mark B in green . . .·. 60.00   70.00
- ☐ **Mug,** 5-3/4" high, covered with drippy enamel, resembles a Chianti bottle that has been used to hold candles, artist signed and dated, mark B in green 120.00   140.00
- ☐ **Mug,** 6" high, hand-painted portrait of cavalier, shaded purple background, horrible, mark B in green 90.00   110.00
- ☐ **Mug,** 6" high, hand-painted flowers on shaded green and yellow background, very pretty, gold trim on handle and rims, artist signed and dated, mark B in green 115.00   130.00
- ☐ **Mug,** 6" high, transfer-decorated with Masonic emblem, mark B in green 120.00   140.00
- ☐ **Mug,** 6" high, geometric enamel designs, gold trim on handle and rim, mark B in green 60.00   70.00
- ☐ **Stein,** hand-painted purple grapes and green leaves on shaded green background, porcelain insert in lid with hand-painted monogram, silver manufacturer unknown, mark B in green, see photo 300.00   350.00

PLATES

Price Range

☐ Shape #7, 9-1/2" diameter, crimped edge plate, pearlized yellow exterior, gold past trim inside, three small flecks on rim, mark B in red 90.00   110.00

☐ Shape #7, 9-1/2" diameter, crimped edge plate, hand-painted buttercups and leaves on shaded brown background, artist signed and dated, mark B in green 75.00   85.00

☐ Shape #7-1/2, 9-1/2" diameter, 3-1/4" high, footed crimped edge plate, sponged gold trim on rim, gold feet, mark B in brown . . .   105.00   120.00

☐ Shape #65, 8-1/2" diameter, scalloped rim plate, brown lustre finish, square section on bottom part of plate with portrait of a woman, cocoa-colored enamel work around the square, raised gold paste trim over rest of plate, artist signed, mark B in brown 175.00   225.00

☐ Shape #65, 8-1/2" diameter, scalloped rim plate, undecorated, set of 6, mark B in green 60.00   70.00

☐ Shape #65-1/4, scalloped rim plate, banding of small blue flowers near rim, gold trim on rim, mark B in green, pair 40.00   50.00

☐ Shape #65-3/4, 5-1/2" diameter, scalloped rim plate, gold initials in center, gold trim on rim, mark B in green, pair 7.50   10.00

☐ Shape #127-1/2, 6-1/4" diameter, scalloped and fluted rim plate, single large pink rose in center, gold trim on rim, mark B in green 37.00   43.00

☐ Shape #221, 6" across, square plate with ruffled rim and turned-down corners, hand-painted butterflies and flowers, gold trim on rim, mark B in green 55.00   63.00

☐ Shape #221, square plate with ruffled rim and turned-down corners, gold paste trim in chrysanthemum design, gold trim on rim, 1/8" fleck on one corner, mark B in red 85.00   100.00

☐ Shape #221-1/2, 6" long, 4" wide, rectangular plate with ruffled rim and turned-down corners, hand-painted small pink roses in scattered design, gold trim on rim, mark B in red 115.00   130.00

☐ Shape #222, square plate with ruffled rim and turned-down trim on rim, nicely done, artist signed and dated, a few small rough spots on rims, mark B in green 105.00   120.00

☐ Shape #222, 5" wide, square plate with ruffled rim and turned-down corners, undecorated, mark B in green 30.00   35.00

☐ Shape #278, 8-1/2" diameter, embossed plate, hand-painted small pink roses on pale green background, gold trim on rim on embossed sections, very nicely done but artwork much newer than the plate since the decoration fills in old scratch mark, set of 4, mark B in green 30.00   35.00

☐ Shape #278, 8-1/2" diameter, embossed plate, hand-painted single iris in center, gold trim on rim, artist signed and dated, mark B in green 30.00   35.00

PUFF BOXES

☐ Shape #69, 2-3/4" high, 3" diameter, embossed design, undecorated, mark B in green 75.00   85.00

☐ Shape #284, 4" wide, 3" high, hand-painted small flowers around outside, gold trim on rims and finial, mark B in green . .   90.00   110.00

☐ Shape #284, 4" wide, 3" high, undecorated, mark B in green . .   60.00   70.00

☐ Shape #291, 3-1/2" wide, 3" high, undecorated, mark B in green   65.00   75.00

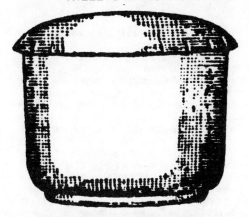

Puff box, *shape #291*

	Price Range	

☐ *Shape #291, 3-1/2" wide, 3" high, hand-painted pink and white roses on shaded yellow background, gold trim on rims, artist signed and dated, mark B in green* 110.00 125.00

☐ *Shape #291, 3-1/2" wide, 3" high, hand-painted cherubs holding up garlands of roses on pale blue background, artist's initials and date, mark B in green* 150.00 175.00

SALT AND PEPPER HOLDERS

☐ *Shape #14, 3-1/4" high, demijohn pepper, no handle, undecorated, mark B in green* 40.00 47.50

☐ *Shape #14-1/2, demijohn pepper, same as #14 but with handle, gold trim, mark B in brown* 60.00 70.00

☐ *Shape #15, 3-1/4" high, champagne bottle pepper, small hand-painted flowers, gold trim, mark B in red* 80.00 95.00

☐ *Shape #18, 3-1/2" long, 1/2" high, basket-shaped salt dip, oval, undecorated and unmarked* 20.00 25.00

☐ *Shape #21, 2-1/2" long, basket salt, rectangular, gold exterior, artist's initials and date, small fleck on rim, mark B in green* .. 40.00 47.50

☐ *Shape #68, pomogranate-shaped pepper with leaf base, shaded coral background covered with sponged gold, small chip on one leaf, mark B in red* 60.00 70.00

☐ *Shape #68, pomogranate-shaped pepper with leaf base, undecorated, pair, mark B in green* 90.00 110.00

☐ *Shape #277, 1-3/4" wide, individual salt dip, heart-shaped, wide, hand-painted flowers and gold trim, artist's initials, mark B in green* 20.00 25.00

☐ *Shape #277, 1-3/4" wide, individual salt dip, heart-shaped, undecorated, mark B in green* 12.00 18.00

☐ *Shape #277, 1-3/4" wide, individual salt dip, heart-shaped, gold trim, mark B in green* 15.00 20.00

☐ *Shape #277-1/2, 1-3/4" wide, individual salt dip, heart-shaped with ruffled rim, gold trim, fleck on one ruffle, mark B in brown* 15.00 20.00

☐ *Shape #277-1/2, individual salt dip, heart-shaped with ruffled rim, small pink roses outlined in gold, gold trim on ruffles, mark B in red* 23.00 28.00

Price Range

☐ Shape #277-1/2, individual salt dip, heart-shaped with ruffled rim, undecorated and unmarked 8.00 12.00

☐ Shape #286, 2" round, individual salt dip, ruffled rim, round, small scattered flowers, gold trim on rim, unmarked 20.00 25.00

☐ Shape #286, 2" diameter, individual salt dip, ruffled rim, round, hand-painted banding of pink roses on green background, pearlized green interior, artist signed and dated, mark B in green 15.00 20.00

☐ Shape #286, 2" diameter, individual salt dip, ruffle rim, round, gold exterior, artist's initials, mark B in green 10.00 15.00

☐ Shape number unknown, pedestal-type individual salt dip, all gold exterior and interior, mark B in brown 12.00 18.00

☐ Shape number unknown, master salt on three ball feet, gold trim on rim and on feet, mark B in brown 23.00 28.00

☐ Shape number unknown, individual salt dip on three ball feet, gold trim on rim and feet, set of 6, mark B in brown 90.00 110.00

☐ Shape number unknown, individual salt dip, three ball feet, undecorated, mark B in green 12.00 18.00

☐ Shape number unknown, individual salt dip, scalloped rim, gold band on rim, mark B in green 10.00 15.00

SHELLS

☐ Shape #70, 2-1/2" high, small coral foot shell, pearlized white finish with gold trim, mark B in green 160.00 190.00

☐ Shape #70, 2-1/2" high, small coral foot shell, undecorated and unmarked 55.00 63.00

☐ Shape #71, 4-1/12" long, loaf sugar shell, undecorated, mark B in green 40.00 50.00

SMOKING COMBINATION

☐ Shape #318, 3-1/2" high smoking combination, includes basket for matches, tree trunk for cigarettes or cigars, and ruffled-rim boat-shaped ashtray, all on rustic base, undecorated, mark B in brown, see photo in color section 150.00 175.00

☐ Shape #318, as above except that handle of basket is gone, mark B in brown 60.00 70.00

SUGARS AND CREAMERS

☐ Shape #13, 4" high, footed creamer, hand-painted portrait of woman, blue enamel work and gold trim, not bad, artist signed and dated, mark B in green 120.00 140.00

☐ Shape #13, 4" high, footed creamer, hand-painted poppies on shaded green background, mark B in green 65.00 75.00

☐ Shape #35, cane creamer, beige matte finish with raised gold paste work, gold trim on handle, mark B in red 10.00 15.00

☐ Shape #36, 3" high, medallion cream, hand-painted dragon on shaded brown background, gold trim, small chip on spout, mark B in green 120.00 140.00

☐ Shape #37, 3" high, basket cream, undecorated, mark B in green 40.00 50.00

☐ Shape #72, 3" high, cane sugar, mate to #35 creamer with gold paste trim, mark B in red 120.00 140.00

Sugars and Creamers

shape #13

shape #35

shape #36

shape #72

shape #151

shape #155

shape #216

Shell, *shape #70*

Price Range

☐ *Shape #73, 3-1/2" diameter sugar, 4" high creamer, individual sugar and creamer, crimped rim, raised enamel flowers outlined in gold, gold trim on handle and rims, small fleck on rim of sugar, mark B in green* 160.00 190.00

☐ *Shape #73, 3-1/2" diameter sugar, 4" high creamer, individual sugar and creamer, crimped rim, hand-painted daisies on pale blue shaded background, gold trim on handles and rim, artist signed and dated, mark B in green* 120.00 140.00

☐ *Shape #73, 3-1/2" diameter sugar, 4" high creamer, individual sugar and creamer, crimped rim, raised gold paste in oak leaf design, gold trim on handle and rims, beige matte finish, mark B in red* 175.00 225.00

☐ *Shape #95, 3" diameter, 2-1/2" high, basket sugar, open, undecorated, mate to creamer #37, mark B in green* 40.00 50.00

☐ *Shape #118, 5" high, small, crooked neck Tuscan creamer, hand-painted flowers outlined in gold, beige matte background, sponged gold trim, mark B in red* 135.00 155.00

☐ *Shape #118, 5" high, small, crooked neck Tuscan creamer, undecorated, mark B in green* 40.00 47.50

☐ *Shape #151, 3-1/2" high, doubled handled, footed sugar, hand-painted single large yellow rose on front, small yellow rosebud on back, gold trim on handles, rims and finial, artist signed and dated, mark B in green* 90.00 110.00

☐ *Shape #155, sugar and creamer, rope handles, crimped rims on both pieces, undecorated and unmarked* 50.00 60.00

☐ *Shape #155, sugar and creamer, rope handles, crimped rims on both pieces, beige matte finish with raised gold paste leaf design, gold trim on handles and rims, mark B in red* 150.00 200.00

☐ *Shape #170 and #171, oval sugar 4-1/2" high, oval creamer 2-1/2" high, hand-painted bunches of violets, part of a four-piece set which includes tray and teapot, mark B in brown, see those sections for prices on rest of set* 120.00 140.00

☐ *Shape #170 and #171, oval sugar 4-1/2" high, oval creamer 2-1/2" high, undecorated and unmarked* 55.00 63.00

Price Range

☐ *Shape #210-1/2, creamer 6-1/2" high, dragon handle, gold trim, mark B in green* **80.00   95.00**

☐ *Shape #216 and #217, sugar 4" high, creamer 3" high, shell sugar and creamer, raised gold paste cattail design, gold trim on rims and on coral-shaped handles, part of a three piece set, see teapot section for matching pot, see photo in color section*   **235.00   285.00**

☐ *Shape #216, creamer 3" high, shell design with coral handle, decorated in a burnt orange color with gold trim, artist signed and dated, mark B in green* **55.00   63.00**

☐ *Shape #233, and #234, sugar 3-3/4" high, creamer 3-1/2" high, twisted sugar and creamer, gold trim, mark B in green, see teapot section for matching pot* **90.00   110.00**

☐ *Shape #239, 4-1/2" high fluted creamer, dragon handle and mask spout, pearlized pink interior, speckled gold trim on handle and spout, mark B in red* **150.00   175.00**

☐ *Shape #306 and #307, sugar 4-1/2" high, creamer 4-1/2" high, embossed and scalloped sugar and creamer, hand-painted red and pink cabbage roses on shaded green background, gold trim on handles, rims and finial, artist signed and dated, mark B in green* **150.00   175.00**

SWANS

Swan, *shape #252*

☐ *Shape #252, 2" high, swan salt, undecorated, few rough spots on wings, mark B in green, see photo on front cover* **35.00   45.00**

☐ *Shape #253, 4" high, swan cream, undecorated, few rough spots on wings, mark B in green, see photo* **60.00   70.00**

TANKARDS

Price Range

☐ Shape #453-1/4, 14" high, monochromatic monk scene, no artist signature, mark B in brown, see photo in color section .. 275.00 325.00

☐ Shape #453-1/4, 14" high, hand-painted bunches of grapes in green and purple on shaded green background, artist signed and dated, mark B in green 235.00 285.00

☐ Shape #453-1/4, 14" high, hand-painted red berries on shaded brown background, very nicely done, artist signed and dated, mark B in brown 300.00 350.00

☐ Shape #453-1/4, 14" high, transfer decoration of horses on shaded brown background, gold trim on handle and rims, mark B in green 200.00 250.00

☐ Shape #572, 15-1/8" high, dragon handle, nude stepping into water, in colors of sepia, orange and green, gold band inside rim, signed George Houghton and dated, mark B in brown, see photo on front cover 525.00 625.00

☐ Shape #572, 15-1/8" high, dragon handle, black and white St. Bernard on shaded background, signed George Houghton, dated, mark B in brown 700.00 820.00

Note: The price difference between the two Houghton tankards is due to marketing variables, and the two should be priced closer together. Houghton was virtually unknown before this year and his popularity with collectors is zooming.

☐ Shape #572, 15-1/8" high, dragon handle, undecorated, mark B in green 80.00 95.00

TEAPOTS

Teapot, shape #76, 77

☐ Shape #76, 5" high, cane teapot, beige matte finish with raised gold paste work, gold trim on handle, small fleck on spout, matches sugar and creamer listed earlier, mark B in red 175.00 225.00

☐ Shape #169, 5" high, oval teapot, hand-painted bunches of violets, gold trim, part of a set, see tray section and sugar and creamer section for prices on rest of set, mark B in brown 120.00 140.00

☐ Shape #169, 5" high, oval teapot, gold trim on handle and finial, mark B in green 75.00 85.00

Teapot, *shape #215*

Price Range

☐ *Shape #215, 5" high, shell teapot, raised gold paste cattail design, gold trim on rims and on coral-shaped handle, part of a three-piece set, see sugar and creamer section for other items, see photo in color section, damaged spout on teapot, mark B in red* 200.00 250.00

☐ *Shape #215, 5" high, shell teapot, undecorated and unmarked, several spots of minor damage* 40.00 50.00

☐ *Shape #232, 4-3/4" high, twisted teapot, dolphin handle, gold trim, see sugar and creamer section for matching items, mark B in green* 90.00 110.00

☐ *Shape number unknown, hand-painted roses in garlands held up by Cupids, gold trim on handle, rims, spout and finial, artist signed and dated, crack in handle, mark B in green* 150.00 200.00

TRAYS

Tray, *shape #17, small flowers*

Price Range

☐ Shape #17, 4-1/2" long, olive tray, ruffled rim, undecorated, mark B in green 50.00 58.00

☐ Shape #17-1/2, 3-1/2" long, olive tray, gold exterior, mark B in green 55.00 63.00

☐ Shape #100, 5" long, 4-1/4" wide, diamond olive tray, hand-painted yellow buttercups with green leaves, gold trim on rim, mark B in green 60.00 70.00

☐ Shape #100, 5" long, 4-1/4" wide, diamond olive tray, gold trim on rim, mark B in green 40.00 50.00

☐ Shape #157, 4-1/2" long, 3-1/2" wide, 1-1/2" deep, oval crimped olive tray, rustic handles, undecorated, mark B in green 80.00 95.00

☐ Shape #158, 5-1/2" wide, triangular olive tray, rustic handle, small scattered pink roses, gold trim on handle and rim, mark B in red 120.00 140.00

☐ Shape #159, 7" wide, 4" high, five-sided crimped tray with handle, undecorated and unmarked 60.00 70.00

☐ Shape #159-1/2, same as shape #159 but with no handle, single large red rose in center, sponged gold trim on rim, not bad for home artwork, artist signed and dated, mark B in green 140.00 160.00

☐ Shape #213, 4-1/4" long, 4" wide, shell tray, pearlized pink interior, outside has gold trim, mark B in red 120.00 140.00

☐ Shape #213-1/2, 3" long, 2-7/8" wide, shell tray, gold paste trim, mark B in red 115.00 130.00

☐ Shape #214, 1-1/2" high, 4" diameter, round tray, several flecks on rim, hand-painted small scattered flowers, gold trim, mark B in red 90.00 110.00

☐ Shape #250, 4-1/2" long, cactus olive tray, gold trim, mark B in red 115.00 130.00

☐ Shape #250-1/2, cactus olive tray with two handles, undecorated, several small flecks, mark B in green 40.00 50.00

☐ Shape #254, 6-1/4" long, heart tray, ruffled rim, small scattered pink roses outlined in gold, gold trim on rim, mark B in red 120.00 140.00

☐ Shape #254, heart tray, undecorated in Valentine fashion with hearts, blue ribbon, and appropriate gold inscription, gold trim on rim, very pretty, artist's initials and date, mark B in green .. 150.00 175.00

☐ Shape #263, 7-1/2" long, pickelette tray, undecorated, mark B in green 37.00 43.00

☐ Shape #285, 5" wide, pin tray, five-sided, monogram in gold in center, gold trim on rim, mark B in green 47.00 53.00

☐ Shape #285, 5" wide, pin tray, five-sided, small hand-painted forget-me-nots and the inscription "forget-me-not" in gold, gold trim on rim, mark B in green 110.00 125.00

☐ Shape #295, 9-1/4" long, 2-3/4" wide, pin tray, Delft-type monochrome blue decoration, mark D 140.00 160.00

☐ Shape #296, 6" long, 2-3/4" wide, pin tray, tiny red roses, gold trim on rim, couple of flecks on ruffled rim, mark B in green ... 80.00 95.00

☐ Shape #297, 5" long, 3" wide, pin tray, undecorated, mark B in green 15.00 20.00

☐ Shape #301, 6" wide, brush and comb tray, raised gold paste trim in chrysanthemum design, gold work done in five different shades ranging from an almost silver to a deep bronze color, exceptional work, more gold trim on ruffled rim, mark B in red . 225.00 275.00

☐ Shape #303, 11-1/2" long, celery tray, crimped edge, gold trim, artist's initials and date, mark B in green 80.00 95.00

Price Range

☐ Shape #327, 4-3/4" long, 2-1/2" wide, embossed tray, undecorated, mark B in green 25.00 30.00

☐ Shape #328, 6-1/2" long, 2-1/4" wide, embossed tray, transfer decorated with pins and needles and spools of thread, gold trim, mark B in green 80.00 95.00

☐ Shape #329, 6-1/4" long, 4-3/4" wide, harp tray, gold trim on rim, mark B in green 40.00 50.00

☐ Shape #330, 7-1/2" long, 4" wide, embossed tray, hand-painted picture of kitten, shaded blue background, gold trim, mark B in green 105.00 120.00

TUBS

☐ Shape #340, 3-1/4" wide, embossed design, undecorated, mark B in green 75.00 85.00

VASES

☐ Shape #3, 8" high, small, crimped top vase, gold paste floral decoration, beige matte finish, gold trim on rim and base, mark B in red 175.00 225.00

☐ Shape #3, 8" high, small, crimped top vase, hand-painted shasta daisies on garlands around vase, gold trim on rim, very nice for home artwork, mark B in green 150.00 175.00

☐ Shape #3, 8" high, small, crimped top vase, hand-painted single large pink rose, gold trim on rim, artist signed, mark B in green 120.00 140.00

☐ Shape #9, 10-1/2" high, water bottle vase, undecorated, mark B in green 90.00 110.00

☐ Shape #9, 10-1/2" high, water bottle vase, raised gold paste work in oak leaf pattern, beige high glaze finish, gold trim on rim, mark B in red 235.00 285.00

☐ Shape #9, 10-1/2" high, water bottle vase, hand-painted little girls romping in field, artist signed and dated, so-so art work, mark B in green 175.00 225.00

☐ Shape #9, 10-1/2" high, water bottle vase, hand-painted picture of cocker spaniel on shaded green background, artist signed and dated, mark B in green 170.00 210.00

☐ Shape #12, 10-1/2" high, long neck plain vase, hand-painted single orchid on bulbous bottom section of vase, sponged gold trim, mark B in green but good enough to be factory decorated 220.00 270.00

☐ Shape #12, 10-1/2' high, long neck plain vase, geometric gold work on bottom section, pencil line gold on rim, mark B in green 150.00 175.00

☐ Shape #28, 11" high, French flat vase, hand-painted red and pink cabbage roses on shaded green background, artist signed and dated, mark B in green 150.00 175.00

☐ Shape #28, 11" high, French flat vase, undecorated and unmarked 40.00 50.00

☐ Shape #87, 7-1/4" high, small water bottle vase, hand-painted portrait of woman, gold trim on rim, mark B in green 135.00 155.00

☐ Shape #87, 7-1/4" high, small water bottle vase, raised gold paste in cattail design, high glaze white finish, mark B in red .. 175.00 225.00

Vases

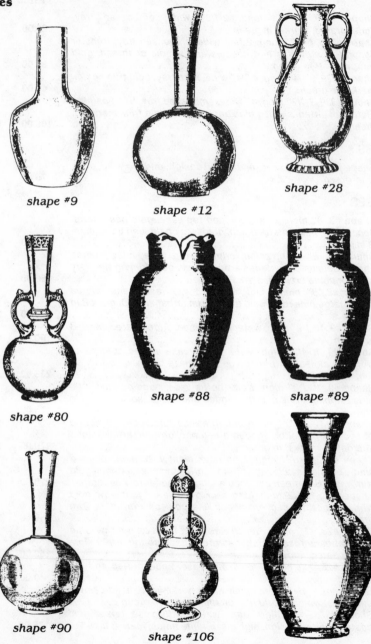

shape #9

shape #12

shape #28

shape #80

shape #88

shape #89

shape #90

shape #106

shape #131

Price Range

☐ *Shape #87, 7-1/4" high, small water bottle vase, hand-painted monochromatic blue Delft type scene, artist signed and dated, mark B in green* 175.00   225.00

☐ *Shape #88, 5" high, small cut top vase, hand-painted blue and purple violets on shaded green background, gold trim on rim, nice, mark B in green* . . . . : 150.00   175.00

☐ *Shape #88, 5" high, small cut top vase, undecorated, mark B in green* 50.00   58.00

☐ *Shape #88, 5" high, small cut top vase, transfer decoration of dog, gold trim on rim, mark B in green* 105.00   120.00

☐ *Shape #89, 5" high, small plain top vase, transfer-decorated with horse and carriage, gold trim on rim, mark B in green* 90.00   110.00

☐ *Shape #89, 5" high, small plain top vase, hand-painted bouquet of wildflowers, gold trim on rim, mark B in green* 90.00   110.00

☐ *Shape #89, 5" high, small plain top vase, raised gold paste floral design, beige matte finish, mark B in red* 175.00   225.00

☐ *Shape #90, 10-1/2" high, long neck, crimped top, dented vase, shaded from lavender at bottom to green at top with raised gold paste decoration, mark B in red* 235.00   285.00

☐ *Shape #90, 10-1/2" high, long neck, crimped top, dented vase, undecorated, mark B in green* 110.00   125.00

☐ *Shape #106, 14" high, Mosque vase, handles damaged and lid missing, gold trim, mark B in green* 90.00   110.00

☐ *Shape #131, 8" high, Vienna vase, panels of flowers, filigree gold work between panels, gold trim on rims, artist signed and dated, not bad, mark B in green* 175.00   200.00

☐ *Shape #131, 8" high, Vienna vase, hand-painted and enameled parrot, gold trim, mark B in green* 160.00   190.00

☐ *Shape #131, 8" high, Vienna vase, undecorated, mark B in green* 90.00   110.00

☐ *Shape #132, 8" high, globe water bottle vase, hand-painted pansies in shaded green background, artist signed and dated, pretty, mark B in green* 150.00   175.00

☐ *Shape #132, 8" high, globe water bottle vase, transfer decoration of gypsy, gold trim, mark B in green* 90.00   110.00

☐ *Shape #132-1/2, 8" high, globe water bottle vase, dented sides gold trim, mark B in green* 120.00   140.00

☐ *Shape #138-1/2, 6" high, miniature water bottle vase with handles, hand-painted morning glories on tan background, gold trim on handles and rim, artist signed and dated, mark B in green* 120.00   140.00

☐ *Shape #140, 7-1/2" high, beaded top water bottle vase, gold trim on rims, gold banding around top section, artist's initials and date, hairline crack in base, mark B in green* 55.00   63.00

☐ *Shape #191, 6" high, double handled crimped top vase, gold trim on handles, mark B in green* 90.00   110.00

☐ *Shape #191-1/2, 4-1/2" high, double handled crimped top vase, hand-painted pink roses, raised gold and blue dot enamel work, gold trim on handles and rims, signed and dated, mark B in brown, see photo in color section* 300.00   350.00

☐ *Shape #203, handled vase, pierced neck, heavily damaged in several spots, undecorated and unmarked* 15.00   20.00

Price Range

☐ Shape #204, 12" high, double handled vase, gold paste trim in beige matte finish, mark B in red 235.00   285.00

☐ Shape #204, 12" high, double handled vase, hand-painted chrysanthemums on shaded yellow and brown background, gold trim, artist signed and dated, mark B in green 175.00   200.00

☐ Shape #227, 8" high, fluted Vienna vase, raised gold paste trim on beige matte finish, repair to top, mark B in red 120.00   140.00

☐ Shape #227, 8" high, fluted Vienna vase, hand-painted poppies on green background, gold trim, mark B in green 175.00   200.00

☐ Shape #269, 6-1/2" high, cactus handled vase, small scattered flowers outlined in gold, pink pearlized interior, gold trim, mark B in red 175.00   225.00

☐ Shape #269, 6-1/2" high, cactus handled vase, hand-painted daffodils, sponged gold trim, beautifully done, mark B in green 150.00   175.00

☐ Shape #270, 9-1/4" high, medallion vase, gold trim on face and on rims, mark B in green 200.00   250.00

☐ Shape #290, 4" high, 2-3/4" wide, can vase, hand-painted garlands of little roses around vase, gold trim on rim, small fleck on rim, artist signed and dated, mark B in green 120.00   140.00

☐ Shape #290, 4" high, 2-3/4" wide, can vase, hand-painted birds and butterflies, gold trim on rim, artist signed and dated, mark B in green 120.00   140.00

☐ Shape #290, 4" high, 2-3/4" wide, can vase, transfer decoration of horses, gold trim on rim, small hairline coming down from rim, mark B in green 60.00   70.00

☐ Shape #319, 10" high, foot vase, hand-painted cabbage roses on shaded blue background, gold trim, artist signed, mark B in green 170.00   200.00

☐ Shape #319, 10" high, foot vase, gold trim on rim and feet, mark B in green 135.00   155.00

☐ Shape #337, 7" high, double-handled, hand-painted water lilies on shaded green background, gold trim on handles and rim, especially nice for home work and very well suited to the vase, artist signed and dated, crack in one handle, mark B in green . 175.00   200.00

☐ Shape #337, 7" vase, undecorated and unmarked 120.00   140.00

☐ Shape #481, (or possibly 487), 12" high, beautiful portrait of woman, elaborate raised gold work, unfortunately no artist signature, mark B in brown, see photo in color section 700.00   820.00

☐ Shape #550, (or possibly 556), 15-1/4" rounded vase, shaded blue background with gold wheat, butterflies and clouds, mark B in brown, see cover photo 235.00   285.00

☐ Shape number unknown, two-handled 6" vase, gold paste on beige matte finish, gold wear on handles, mark B in red, see photo in color section 200.00   250.00

MISCELLANEOUS

Liners in sterling holders — rate against comparable Lenox items. If Willets made anything exciting in this category, we have not seen it.

Figurines — extremely rare, so double the comparable Lenox price.

Porcelain dinnerware decorated at the factory in more or less standard patterns — rate against comparable Lenox item.

Opaque dinnerware — see Table X.

Opaque decorative ware — rate against Burroughs & Mountford or Greenwood Pottery, or else use Table X.

WILLIAM YOUNG & SONS

William Young, Sr., began manufacturing earthenware in the Hattersley Pottery in 1853. The pottery was located on Perry Street east of the Delaware and Raritan Canal.

After they outgrew the Hattersley Pottery, Young & Sons built a new pottery in a different location. This new building, the Excelsior Pottery Works, was operated by the family until 1879 at which time it was taken over by Willets.

Marks: The first mark was an eagle, which was used until 1858. The next mark was the British coat of arms with the initials WYS underneath.

Prices: Since Wm. Young & Sons was such an early Trenton company their wares are of more than average interest. Expect to pay a minimum of $25 to $50 for their earlier items, and if something is particularly large or unusual it can go much, much higher. Some of their later very commericial products can be rated against similar items listed elsewhere in this book.

WOOD & BARLOW

See Empire Pottery.

WOODBRIDGE POTTERY COMPANY

This current company is located on Frazier Street and manufactures lamp bases.

Marks: *Not known*

Prices: To the Trentoniana collector, a sample lamp base would probably be worth a minimum of $5.

W.S. GEORGE

W.S. George was primarily a manufacturer of dinnerware. The company made extensive lines of low and medium priced wares which were heavily advertised and enjoyed a strong sale for many years. In recent years, the W.S. George products have been coming into greater collector popularity, especially the firm's creamwares and its lines of colored china known as "Petalware" and "Rainbow." Many sets are still in the hands of the original purchasers, but quite a few are filtering down into the market. Since prices are still well within the reasonable range, this might be an excellent collecting target for the beginner or low-budgeted hobbyist.

W.S. George started out an executive with the Sebring brothers in the Ohio China Company around 1895. Ohio China was just getting into business at the time, born out of an effort by local residents to pump some economic life into the town of East Palestine, Ohio. A public fund was set up and $25,000 raised to get the operation under way in hopes the business would grow and provide employment for many of the local residents. In 1904, W.S. George acquired the East Palestine Pottery Company, a neighbor of Ohio China Company and its chief competitor. He then began opening up other factories to accommodate the overflow of business, one of them as far away as Kittanig, Pennsylvania. By around 1910, W.S. George had become one of the titans of the midwestern pottery trade. In the history of pottery making, he stands out as one of the legendary characters. In his earlier days, he had been a prize-fighter but always had a flair for salesmanship. Often he would try his luck at selling his factories' products himself direct to consumers — as if he were a salesman rather than the director of a business empire. Stories have been told about W.S. George packing up suitcases with various china samples, then boarding a railroad train and selling them to the passengers! This seems to have given him more satisfaction than running his company from a plush office.

The W.S. George Company (it was seldom referred to as "Pottery Company") continued its success after the founder died. It was particularly successful during the Depression years of the 1930's, because its wide selection of inexpensive kitchenwares suited the strapped budgets of that time. The W.S George wares were sold by the leading mail-order houses and by F.W. Woolworth along with other retailers. Saturation advertising campaigns were begun in the 1930's and continued up to the 1950's in all the womens' and family-oriented magazines.

Though the W.S. George wares are not overly creative in shape, the finishing work is attractive. In quality, its products were certainly the equal of anything on the market at a comparable price.

Marks: Numerous marks were used by this organization to denote its various lines. The most colorful and instantly recognizable of these is the "Hopalong Cassidy," a late mark dating from the beginning of the era of TV. It consists of a western-style boot with the name in script lettering across it and the wording *BY W.S. GEORGE* beneath. The company also had a white-on-black stamp in which the name W.S. George is contained in an oval; beneath this is a banner reading *FINE DINNERWARE*. The earlier marks are much plainer and sometimes are accompanied by mold numbers. Lettering in plain block letters is usually the indication of an early mark but this is not always the case.

YATES, BENNETT & ALLAN

See City Pottery.

YATES & TITUS

See City Pottery.

MISCELLANEOUS

Every time we think we have finally listed all of the Trenton pottery and porcelain companies, somebody calls us with another one. Following is a general guide which can be used for either companies which are not listed or various types of items which are not listed individually under previously-mentioned companies.

BELLEEK-TYPE AND OTHER PORCELAIN ITEMS

Depending on its age, fineness and rarity, rate any item in this category against comparable items listed in the Lenox, Willets or Ott & Brewer sections.

IRONSTONE AND SIMILAR PRODUCTS

Compare against listed prices or use the following guide:

	Price Range	
☐ **Bowls**, *dessert or soup size, decorated*	5.00	8.00
☐ **Bowls**, *dessert or soup size, undecorated*	4.00	7.00
☐ **Bowls**, *serving, decorated*	15.00	30.00
☐ **Bowls**, *serving, undecorated*	15.00	30.00
☐ **Cups and saucers**, *decorated*	7.00	15.00
☐ **Cups and saucers**, *undecorated*	5.00	15.00
☐ **Dinner plates**, *decorated*	8.00	15.00
☐ **Dinner plates**, *undecorated*	7.00	15.00
☐ **Mugs**, *decorated*	15.00	30.00
☐ **Mugs**, *undecorated*	15.00	20.00
☐ **Platters**, *decorated, depending on size*	20.00	40.00
☐ **Platters**, *undecorated, depending on size*	15.00	30.00
☐ **Smaller plates**, *decorated*	3.00	6.00
☐ **Smaller plates**, *undecorated*	2.00	4.00

FIGURINES

Consider any Trenton figurine to be worth a hint less than the comparable Lenox item if they are about the same age, or to be worth more than the comparable Lenox item if from before the turn of the century.

LAMP BASES

As a sample of a particular company's work, any lamp base should be worth a minimum of $6.50.

ITEMS WITH SILVER HOLDERS

Figure items in this category to be worth a minimum of $10 for a small liner plus the scrap value of the silver. Add to the price for a highly-collectible silver company or pattern (see the Lenox section for further information about this) and add for a liner which is by a top company or which is particularly early.

POLITICAL ITEMS

Since you are a collector of Trenton ceramics and not of political campaign items, we would suggest not paying a premium for these items.

RAILROAD, STEAMSHIP, AND HOTEL CHINA, ETC.

The above comments about political collectibles apply to this category as well. Since all of these items have their own devoted followers already, there is no particular reason to slug it out with them over these items when a less collectible item by the same company will serve the purpose. As a general rule, you can double or triple many of the prices listed if the item is in these categories.

BIBLIOGRAPHY

Sanitary Pottery in the United States, Thomas Maddock, introductory pages missing so no date or publisher available (probably 1909).

The Dictionary of World Pottery and Porcelain, Louise Ade Boger, Charles Scribner's Sons, New York, 1971.

Encyclopedia of British Pottery and Porcelain Marks, Geoffrey A. Godden, Bonanza Books, New York, 1964.

Modern Porcelain, Alberta C. Trimble, Harper & Brothers Publishers, New York, 1962.

Encyclopedia of American Silver Manufacturers, Dorothy T. Rainwater, Crown Publishers, Inc., New York, 1975.

White House China, Marian Klamkin, Charles Scribner's Sons, New York, 1972.

The Pottery and Porcelain of the United States & Marks of American Potters, Edwin A. Barber, originally published in 1909 and reprinted in 1976 by Feingold and Lewis.

Lenox China, The Story of Walter Scott Lenox, Lenox, Inc., 1924.

The Antique Trader, "American Belleek", Nettie Goldblum, March 30, 1976.

The Antique Trader, "Collectible Lenox China", Nori and Mark Mohr, December 30, 1975.

Trenton Times and Daily State Gazette, as quoted in text.

1891 C.A.C. white ware catalogue

Undated C.A.C. white-ware catalogue

1939 Lenox, Inc., "Anniversary" catalogue

1921 white-ware catalogue

Lenox Annual Report 1977

Undated Lenox, Inc., press releases

Willets Belleek white-ware catalogue, 1893

How did your plates do?

Reco's "Little Boy Blue" by John McClelland

UP 214% in 1 Year

Some limited edition plates gained more in the same year, some less, and some not at all ... But Plate Collector readers were able to follow the price changes, step by step, in Plate Price Trends, a copyrighted feature appearing in each issue of the magazine.

Because The Plate Collector is your best source guide ... has more on limited editions than all other publications combined ... and gives you insight into every facet of your collecting ... you too will rate it

> Your No. 1. Investment
> In Limited Editions.

In 1972, Plate Collector was the first to feature limited editions only. It's expanded, adding figurines, bells and prints, earning reader raves like you see below.

To bring you the latest, most valuable information, our editors crisscross the continent. Sometimes stories lead them to the smaller Hawaiian Islands, or to the porcelain manufactories of Europe.

Their personal contact with artisans, hobby leaders, collectors, artists and dealers lets you share an intimate view of limited editions.

Each fat, colorful issue brings you new insight, helps you enjoy collecting more.

You'll find Plate Collector a complete source guide. Consider new issue information and new issue announcements, often in full color. Use the ratings of new releases and wide array of dealer ads to help you pick and choose the best.

Read regular columns, including one on Hummels, and check current market values in Plate Price Trends to add to your storehouse of knowledge.

You'll profit from tips on insurance, decorating, taxes ... just a sample of recurring feature subjects.

Read Plate Collector magazine to become a true limited edition art insider. Order now. See new and old plates in sparkling color. Enjoy 2 issues every month, delivered to your home at savings up to 37% from newsstand price.

12 issues (6 months) $17.50
24 issues (year) $30
The PLATE COLLECTOR
P.O. Box 1041-HC   Kermit, TX 79745

To use VISA and MasterCard, include all raised information on your card.

Here is Plate Collector, as viewed by our readers in unsolicited quotes ...

"Objective and Impartial," has *"great research,"* yet is warm and personal ... *"I am delighted in 'our' magazine."* A New York couple says flatly, *"It is the best collector magazine on the market."*

"Quality printing is valuable to me because there are no stores near me where I can view and decide," says an Arizona reader. It is *"a major guide to the plates I buy,"* says a Massachusetts reader, while *"It is the best investment in a magazine I ever made,"* comes from Illinois.

"I enjoy your articles on artists," *"The full-color pictures are great,"* *"Your staff was most helpful,"* *"I depend on Plate Collector,"* and *"I look forward to receiving it twice a month,"* are other reader reactions.

A California reader said simply, *"I am glad there is a Plate Collector."*

There is only one ...
THE OFFICIAL®
PRICE GUIDE

THE <u>MULTI-PURPOSE</u> REFERENCE GUIDE!!

THE OFFICIAL PRICE GUIDES SERIES has gained the reputation as the <u>standard barometer of values</u> on collectors' items. When you need to check the market price of a collectible, turn first to the OFFICIAL PRICE GUIDES ... for impartial, unbiased, current information that is presented in an easy-to-follow format.

• **CURRENT VALUES FOR BUYING AND SELLING.** ACTUAL SALES that have occurred in all parts of the country are CAREFULLY EVALUATED and COMPUTERIZED to arrive at the most ACCURATE PRICES AVAILABLE.

• **CONCISE REFERENCES.** Each OFFICIAL PRICE GUIDE is designed primarily as a *guide to current market values.* They also include a useful summary of the information most readers are seeking: a history of the item; how it's manufactured; how to begin and maintain a collection; how and where to sell; addresses of periodicals and clubs.

• **INDEXED FORMAT.** The novice as well as the seasoned collector will appreciate the unique alphabetically *indexed format* that provides *fast retrieval* of information and prices.

• **FULLY ILLUSTRATED.** All the OFFICIAL PRICE GUIDES are richly illustrated. Many feature COLOR SECTIONS as well as black-and-white photos.

Over 20 years of experience has made
THE HOUSE OF COLLECTIBLES
the most respected price guide authority!

PRICE GUIDE SERIES

Collector Plates
Destined to become the ''PLATE COLLECTORS' BIBLE.'' This unique price guide offers the most comprehensive listing of collector plate values — *in Print! Special information includes: company histories; artist backgrounds; and helpful tips on buying, selling and storing a collection.* ILLUSTRATED.
$9.95-1st Edition, 640 pgs., 5⅜″ x 8″, paperback, Order #: 349-X

Collector Prints
Over *14,750 detailed listings* representing over 400 of the most famous collector print artists from Audubon and Currier & Ives, to modern day artists. *Special feature includes gallery/artist reference chart.* ILLUSTRATED.
$9.95-4th Edition, 544 pgs., 5⅜″ x 8″, paperback, Order #: 189-6

Comic & Science Fiction Books
Over *30,000 listings with current values* for comic and science fiction publications *from 1903-to-date. Special sections on Tarzan, Big Little Books, Science Fiction publications and paperbacks.* ILLUSTRATED.
$9.95-5th Edition, 512 pgs., 5⅜″ x 8″, paperback, Order #: 183-7

Hummel Figurines & Plates
The most complete guide ever published on every type of Hummel — including the most recent trademarks and size variations, with *4,500 up-to-date prices. Plus tips on buying, selling and investing.* ILLUSTRATED.
$9.95-3rd Edition, 448 pgs., 5⅜″ x 8″, paperback, Order #: 325-X

Military Collectibles
This detailed historical reference price guide covers the largest accumulation of military objects — 15th century-to-date — listing over *12,000 accurate prices. Special expanded Samuri sword and headdress sections.* ILLUSTRATED.
$9.95-2nd Edition, 544 pgs., 5⅜″ x 8″, paperback, Order #: 191-8

For your convenience use the handy order form.

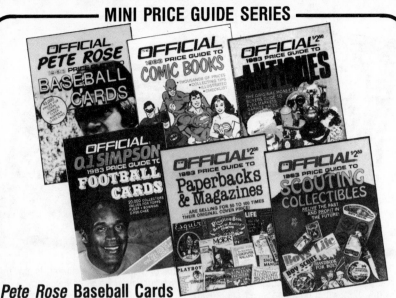

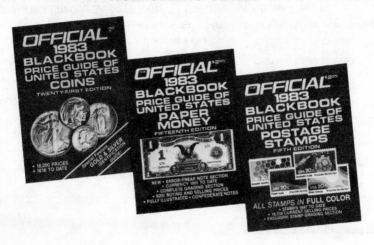

SEND ORDERS TO: **THE HOUSE OF COLLECTIBLES,** *ORLANDO CENTRAL PARK*
1900 PREMIER ROW, ORLANDO, FL 32809 PHONE (305) 857-9095

☐ *Please send the following price guides — (don't forget to add postage & handling):*

___ 188-8 @ $9.95 + (1.50)	___ 183-7 @ $9.95 + (1.50)	___ 315-5 @ $2.50 + (.75)
___ 184-5 @ $9.95 + (1.50)	___ 325-X @ $9.95 + (1.50)	___ 314-7 @ $2.50 + (.75)
___ 190-X @ $9.95 + (1.50)	___ 191-8 @ $9.95 + (1.50)	___ 342-2 @ $2.50 + (.75)
___ 172-1 @ $9.95 + (1.50)	___ 351-1 @ $9.95 + (1.50)	___ 343-0 @ $2.50 + (.75)
___ 354-6 @ $9.95 + (1.50)	___ 186-1 @ $9.95 + (1.50)	___ 344-9 @ $2.50 + (.75)
___ 350-3 @ $9.95 + (1.50)	___ 159-4 @ $9.95 + (1.50)	___ 173-X @ $2.50 + (.75)
___ 180-2 @ $9.95 + (1.50)	___ 348-1 @ $9.95 + (1.50)	___ 171-3 @ $6.95 + (1.00)
___ 181-0 @ $9.95 + (1.50)	___ 322-8 @ $2.50 + (.75)	___ 300-7 @ $6.95 + (1.00)
___ 324-4 @ $9.95 + (1.50)	___ 345-7 @ $2.50 + (.75)	___ 301-5 @ $6.95 + (1.00)
___ 349-X @ $9.95 + (1.50)	___ 323-6 @ $2.50 + (.75)	___ 302-3 @ $6.95 + (1.00)
___ 189-6 @ $9.95 + (1.50)	___ 308-2 @ $2.50 + (.75)	

☐ Check or money order enclosed $_____

(include postage and handling)

☐ Please charge $_____ to my: ☐ MASTER CHARGE ☐ VISA

My account number is:_____ (all digits)

Expiration date _____

NAME (please print)_____

ADDRESS_____ APT. #_____

CITY _____ STATE_____

ZIP_____ PHONE _____

SIGNATURE_____

SEND ORDERS TO: **THE HOUSE OF COLLECTIBLES,** *ORLANDO CENTRAL PARK*
1900 PREMIER ROW, ORLANDO, FL 32809 PHONE (305) 857-9095

☐ *Please send the following price guides — (don't forget to add postage & handling):*

___ 188-8 @ $9.95 + (1.50)	___ 183-7 @ $9.95 + (1.50)	___ 315-5 @ $2.50 + (.75)
___ 184-5 @ $9.95 + (1.50)	___ 325-X @ $9.95 + (1.50)	___ 314-7 @ $2.50 + (.75)
___ 190-X @ $9.95 + (1.50)	___ 191-8 @ $9.95 + (1.50)	___ 342-2 @ $2.50 + (.75)
___ 172-1 @ $9.95 + (1.50)	___ 351-1 @ $9.95 + (1.50)	___ 343-0 @ $2.50 + (.75)
___ 354-6 @ $9.95 + (1.50)	___ 186-1 @ $9.95 + (1.50)	___ 344-9 @ $2.50 + (.75)
___ 350-3 @ $9.95 + (1.50)	___ 159-4 @ $9.95 + (1.50)	___ 173-X @ $2.50 + (.75)
___ 180-2 @ $9.95 + (1.50)	___ 348-1 @ $9.95 + (1.50)	___ 171-3 @ $6.95 + (1.00)
___ 181-0 @ $9.95 + (1.50)	___ 322-8 @ $2.50 + (.75)	___ 300-7 @ $6.95 + (1.00)
___ 324-4 @ $9.95 + (1.50)	___ 345-7 @ $2.50 + (.75)	___ 301-5 @ $6.95 + (1.00)
___ 349-X @ $9.95 + (1.50)	___ 323-6 @ $2.50 + (.75)	___ 302-3 @ $6.95 + (1.00)
___ 189-6 @ $9.95 + (1.50)	___ 308-2 @ $2.50 + (.75)	

☐ Check or money order enclosed $_____

(include postage and handling)

☐ Please charge $_____ to my: ☐ MASTER CHARGE ☐ VISA

My account number is:_____ (all digits)

Expiration date _____

NAME (please print)_____

ADDRESS_____ APT. #_____

CITY _____ STATE_____

ZIP_____ PHONE _____

SIGNATURE_____